January, 1986

To Sue:

"Thanks" for being
a "real friend"!
Hope you enjoy this
book!

Dorothy Dauphinais

PICTURESQUE EXPRESSIONS:
A Thematic Dictionary

PICTURESQUE EXPRESSIONS:
A Thematic Dictionary

Laurence Urdang
Editorial Director

Nancy LaRoche
Editor in Chief

Gale Research Company • Book Tower • Detroit, Michigan 48226

Editorial Director: Laurence Urdang

Editor in Chief: Nancy LaRoche

Assistant Editor: Catherine A. Eckert

Editors: Faye C. Allen, Anthony J. Castagno,
Joseph M. Castagno

Library of Congress Cataloging in Publication Data

Main entry under title:

Picturesque expressions.

    Includes index.
    1. English language--Terms and phrases.
2. Figures of speech. 3. English language--Ety-
mology. I. Urdang, Laurence. II. LaRoche,
Nancy.
PE1689.P5   428.3   80-22705
ISBN 0-8103-1122-4

Introduction

Our language is rife with figurative expressions whose familiarity has obscured their peculiarity. Seldom do we pause to wonder about the origins or to note the often bizarre literal implications of phrases we hear and use daily. A contest may be won **hands down** and **with flying colors,** or it may be **nip and tuck** all the way, with the outcome determined **by a nose.** Some speakers always **beat around the bush** or **go round Robin Hood's barn,** while others **pull no punches** and **call a spade a spade.** Experts **know the ropes; greenhorns** are **wet behind the ears. Red-letter days** may find us **on cloud nine** and **in fine fettle;** but a **bad break** can put us **out of sorts** or **under the weather.**

Many such expressions have only recently made their way into our dictionaries, where they are defined but rarely explained. Others have yet to acquire lexicographical legitimacy. *Picturesque Expressions: A Thematic Dictionary* includes more than 3000 examples of such phrases. Entries are defined, their origins explained, and the approximate date of their appearance in the written language cited whenever possible. In some cases, the editors have acknowledged the difficulty of pinpointing the origin of a phrase with any degree of accuracy. In such instances, probable theories have been offered, or oft-repeated etymological apocrypha have again been recounted—but with plausibility questioned or authenticity disproved. Where appropriate, entries include comments on connotations or usage, as well as illustrative quotations.

Phrases found in *Picturesque Expressions* have entered the general language from a variety of specialized fields: sports, politics, games, finance, the world of entertainment, the events of history, and the customs of long ago have all contributed a wealth of words and sayings. As might be expected, the Bible and other major literary works are the source of a significant number of expressions. In dealing with this plethora of material, our principles of selection were simple in nature and two in number: variety and interest. *Picturesque Expressions* includes both newly coined and vintage phrases. The slang and the literary, the commonplace and the esoteric have been placed side by side, as have the crude and the overly nice. In selection and treatment, the editors have

Introduction

tried to avoid both obscurity and obviousness. Despite a few self-evident expressions whose ubiquity or colorfulness demanded their admission, most words and phrases found on the following pages required some degree of explanation, offered particularly interesting origins, or simply surprised us by their longevity in the language.

The editors have tried to make *Picturesque Expressions: A Thematic Dictionary* a reference work that is both useful and enjoyable. We hope it **cuts the mustard.**

Nancy LaRoche

Essex, Connecticut
August 1980

How to Use This Book

Picturesque Expressions: A Thematic Dictionary is designed to serve as a browsing book for word fanciers, as a reference book for language students, and as a resource book for writers. This unique third purpose required a unique arrangement of entries. Expressions have been grouped according to thematic categories, a system which makes the book similar in function to a thesaurus.

To use *Picturesque Expressions* as a browsing book, browse.

To use *Picturesque Expressions* as a reference book, go first to the Index to find whether the phrase about which you seek information has been included in the book. The Index will provide the thematic category where the expression can be found.

To use *Picturesque Expressions* as a thesaurus, determine the likely thematic category for the concept you want to express (e.g., **BRAVERY, INNOCENCE**) and look to see if it has been included. The book is arranged alphabetically by thematic category.

All entries, whether single words, phrases, or sentences, follow strict letter-by-letter alphabetization, both in the Index and in the thematic categories; the only exceptions are an initial article and an initial bracketed "[*one's*]." In all cases, the editors have sought to enter an expression in the form in which it is most frequently heard. (Thus, phrases usually used negatively may begin with *not* or *neither,* e.g., **not worth a continental;** those usually used with *have* or *got* may begin with *have,* e.g., **have a screw loose.**) Variants are listed in italics in the Index.

Cross references have been kept to a minimum. Thematic categories are cross-referred to others containing similar entries (e.g., **EXPLOITA-TION,** See also **VICTIMIZATION**); or synonyms are given which send the user to the appropriate thematic category (e.g., **REVELATION,** See **EXPO-SURE**). Entries that properly belong to more than one thematic category are treated in full only once, but are cross-referred from other appropriate categories. For example, **catch-as-catch-can** appears under **UNRE-STRAINT,** but the expression itself is listed with cross references, under the thematic categories of **DISORDER** and **EXPEDIENCE** as well; in the latter instances, the user is sent to **UNRESTRAINT.**

A

ABANDONMENT (See also **REJEC-TION**.)

dead as Chelsea Useless; no longer of value. Chelsea, England, was the location of a military hospital for severely injured soldiers. Since many of these soldiers had lost limbs or were otherwise disabled, they were of no further value to the military effort. According to one source, this expression was first used during the Battle of Fontenoy (1745) by a soldier whose leg had been shot off by a cannonball.

left high and dry Left in the lurch, abandoned, forsaken, rejected, deserted, stranded. The allusion is to a vessel in dry dock or grounded on the shore.

> Meanwhile, Dr. Flood's successor had been appointed, and Dr. Flood was left high and dry without preferment owing to an undoubted breach of faith on the part of Duckworth. (E. W. Hamilton, *Diary*, 1881)

Both literal and figurative uses of this expression date from the nineteenth century.

left in the lurch To be deserted while in difficulty; to be left in a dangerous predicament without assistance. *Lurch* is derived from the French *lourche* 'discomfited,' implying that someone left in the lurch is likely to find himself in the uncomfortable position of facing a threatening or perilous situation alone.

> The Volscians seeing themselves abandoned and left in the lurch by them, . . . quit the camp and field. (Philemon Holland, *Livy's Roman History*, 1600)

In medieval times, a *lurch* was a lurking place where poachers would hide as they placed illegal animal traps. If a he was "left in the lurch." *Lurch* was also the name of an ancient, backgammon-like game in which the objective was to leave the other players as far behind as possible. *Left in the lurch* also describes the predicament of a cribbage player whose opponent wins before the player has even "turned the corner," i.e., moved his pieces halfway around the board.

ABEYANCE

hanging fire Undecided, up in the air; delayed, postponed. In munitions the term describes a delay in the explosion or charge of a firearm. The phrase was used in its figurative sense by Sir Walter Scott in 1801.

in a holding pattern Waiting; in a state of suspension. The phrase is aeronautical in origin, referring to "a specified flight track . . . which an aircraft may be required to maintain about a holding point" (*Chambers's Technical Dictionary*, 1958) before being instructed by air traffic control to land. The term has been assimilated into everyday speech to describe a condition characterized by delay or systematic dilatory tactics.

in cold storage Temporarily put aside; on a back burner; in a state of readiness. Cold storage is literally the storing of provisions in refrigerated compartments for protection and preservation. Figuratively this expression applies to ideas, plans, etc., which are temporarily shelved.

> When may a truth go into cold storage in the encyclopedia? and when shall it come out for battle? (William James, *Pragmatism*, 1907)

in limbo In abeyance; in a suspended or uncertain state, usually one between two alternatives or extremes; in a relegated; in prison or other place of confinement. According to early Christian theological writings, the souls of the righteous who died before the time of Christ, as well as the souls of unbaptized infants who died since, were sent to Limbo (from the Latin *limbus* 'edge'), a place on the border of hell. These souls are due to be reunited with those already in heaven during the second coming of Christ.

> Into a limbo large and broad, since called
> The Paradise of Fools, to a few unknown.
> (John Milton, *Paradise Lost III,* 1667)

> The piece . . . ran for 11 nights before descending into the limbo of oblivion. (J. Knight, *Garrick,* 1894)

on a back burner In a position of lesser priority; set aside for later consideration; in reserve. The reference is to the burners on a stove. A cook naturally places on the front burners those pots requiring constant attention. Those that demand less careful watching are moved to the rear burners. Thus the expression *on a back burner* is figuratively used for issues or items of business of less than pressing concern.

on ice Set aside temporarily, postponed, held in abeyance; also, assured, certain, in the bag. Ice is a common food preservative. A longer phrase, *to put on ice* 'to assure or guarantee the certainty of a given outcome,' probably stems from the same sense of ice as a preservative. *On ice* may be related conceptually to *in the bag* in that bagged game or caught fish were often placed on ice until dressed. Both meanings of *on ice* gained currency in the late 19th and early 20th centuries.

on the shelf In a state of inactivity or uselessness; set beyond immediate reach, postponed. A shelf is generally used to store concrete items not being used at the moment, such as canned goods or books. By extension, abstractions such as ideas or political issues not currently being acted upon are said to be "on the shelf." The term is also often applied to people who because of age or infirmity are thought to be useless and unproductive to society; in such a context the phrase carries the implicit criticism that persons are being treated as objects. The figurative use of the phrase appeared as early as 1575 in *The Princely Pleasures at the Court at Kenelworth* by George Gascoigne.

rain check A promised but usually indefinite repeat invitation, so-called from the ticket stub or separate check issued for later use when events are interrupted or postponed due to inclement weather. The literal term *rain check* may have been coined by the Detroit Base Ball Association in 1890. The current figurative meaning must have already been in wide use when the following was written:

> The idea . . . was for an actual raincheck, to be handed to those jaunty types who say they will take a raincheck when declining an invitation. (*The New Yorker,* June, 1945)

treading water Waiting; marking time; in suspension. A tired swimmer rests by treading water, an action which requires a minimal amount of effort since it involves merely keeping the head above water.

ABILITY

all is fish that comes to his net A proverbial phrase describing the luck of one for whom nothing ever goes awry because of a seemingly innate ability to turn everything to profit. Most fishermen expect to discover undesirable animals or debris in their nets, but the fortuitous fisherman's net overflows with valuable fish only. The expression is used of one with an extraordinary capacity to develop invariably successful schemes and make consistently lucrative financial investments.

green thumb An above-average ability to grow plants; the knack of successfully cultivating and propagating plants. This phrase and its variant *green fingers* date from the early 1900s. A "green thumb" is like a magic touch which encourages rapid growth. Although the phrase is usually heard in the context of gardening, it can apply to any innate ability to make things grow and prosper.

> "Success with money is often accidental," she sighed. "One needs 'green fingers' to make it grow." (*Daily Telegraph*, April 26, 1969)

keep one's hand in To keep in practice, to dabble in, to maintain one's proficiency in a certain activity. The expression usually implies sporadic or intermittent interest and activity.

know one's beans See KNOWLEDGE.

the Midas touch An uncanny ability to make money; entrepreneurial expertise. Midas, legendary king of Phrygia, was divinely granted the power to transform anything he touched to gold. The gods relieved Midas of his power when the king realized that everything he touched, including food and his daughter, changed to gold. Still in general use, this expression often describes the moneymaking abilities of an entrepreneur.

> Picasso, with his Midas touch, has at first try made the lino-cut a more dignified medium. (*Times*, July, 1960)

play a straight bat To know what you are doing, to know your business. This Briticism comes from the game of cricket.

to the manner born See STATUS.

ABSENCE

eighty-six Nothing left, no more, no, nix; from American restaurant argot for being sold out of a certain dish. The term was apparently chosen because it rhymes with *nix*, slang for nothing or no. Although this expression is still most commonly heard among restaurant workers, it has recently gained popularity in general slang.

missing link The absent or unknown integral step in a progression; the lacking, unifying component of a series. This expression probably originated as an allusion to a chain that is minus a vital part. The phrase is most often applied to the unknown connection in the anthropological progression of man's theoretical evolution from the lower primates.

> Albertus [Magnus] made the first attempt to bridge the gap between man and the rest of the animal world by means of a kind of "missing link" in the shape of the pygmy and the ape. (R. and D. Morris, *Men and Apes,* 1966)

neither hide nor hair Nothing at all, not a trace. *Hide* here of course means 'skin.' The expression *in hide and hair,* in the language since the 14th century but now rarely heard, has an opposite meaning—'wholly, entirely.' The oldest citation for *neither hide nor hair* shows that more than a century ago it was used much the same as it most frequently is today: in a negative construction following *see.* However, contemporary usage usually limits its application to humans or animals—literal possessors of hide and hair.

> I haven't seen hide nor hair of the piece ever since. (Josiah G. Holland, *The Bay-path,* 1857)

scarce as hen's teeth Very scarce, nonexistent; rarely occurring. This Americanism dating from the mid-1800s is a superlative of 'scarce,' since a hen has no teeth.

> North of Mason and Dixon's line, colored county officials are scarce as hen's teeth. (*Congressional Record,* October 2, 1893)

This expression and the variant *rare as hen's teeth* are still in use.

> Stoppages are as rare as hen's teeth. (*Times*, June 12, 1969)

sweet Fanny Adams Nothing; usually used in reference to the failure of a potentially promising enterprise or occasion. Fanny Adams was a woman who was brutally murdered in 1810. Her hacked and mutilated body was thrown into a river. Because of the gruesomeness of the crime and the dour humor of the British Navy, Fanny Adams became the nickname for canned mutton served to the sailors. The implication is clear. Over the years, *Fanny Adams* became *sweet Fanny Adams,* or *Sweet F. A.*, with the abbreviated form serving as a popular euphemism for an obvious obscenity.

ABSTINENCE (See TEMPERANCE.)

ABUNDANCE

hand over fist See PACE.

happy hunting ground See PARADISE.

land of milk and honey See PARADISE.

loaves and fishes See MONEY.

my cup runneth over Any state of abundance, profusion, or excess; a run of luck or good fortune. This phrase from the well-known Twenty-third Psalm ("The Lord is my shepherd") is now commonly used in a secular sense, though in its original context it referred to the plentitude of God's goodness and spiritual gifts.

> Thou preparest a table before me in the presence of mine enemies:
> Thou hast anointed my head with oil;
> My cup runneth over.
> Surely goodness and mercy shall follow me all the days of my life;
> And I shall dwell in the house of the Lord for ever. (Psalms 23:5-6)

spring up like mushrooms To proliferate; to appear in great quantity all at once. Mushrooms, a type of fungus, grow rapidly and abundantly following the slightest rainfall.

ACCOMPLISHMENT

feather in [one's] cap A distinction or honor, a noteworthy achievement. In the 14th century, a soldier added a feather to his cap for each enemy soldier he had killed. A similar practice existed among the American Indians who added feathers to their headdress. Among hunters, it was a common practice (and still is in Scotland and Wales) to pluck a feather from the first kill of the season and display it proudly in one's hunting cap. By the mid-1600s, the feather had lost much of its "killing" significance while retaining its symbolic value as a sign of bravery and honor. At that time, many British noblemen considered themselves to be men of distinction by virtue of their birthright and frequently wore feathers as a somewhat garish addition to their attire. Since men, regardless of virility or pugilistic prowess, no longer wear feathers as badges of accomplishment, in contemporary usage the expression is exclusively figurative.

> He wore a feather in his cap, and wagg'd it too often. (Thomas Fuller, *The Church History of Belgium*, 1655)

hat trick A triple accomplishment; a streak of three successful undertakings. This British expression originated as cricket slang for the taking of three wickets, a feat for which the triumphant player was awarded a tall hat. The term's current figurative meaning is extended to include any triple achievements or victories.

> British aircraft constructors are hoping that an official attempt will shortly be made on the world's height record, and the "hat trick" accomplished by the annexation of all three of the records which really matter in aviation. (*Statesman*, December, 1931)

ACCURACY   (See **CORRECTNESS, PRECISION.**)

ADAPTATION

cut the coat according to the cloth To live within one's means; to adapt oneself to a situation. The implication is that given only enough cloth to make a waistcoat or vest, one cannot make a full-length coat. Thus, someone with limited funds should be prudent about expenses and not attempt to live beyond his means. Though first cited in the 16th century, the expression was already in common use at the time.

> I shall cut my coat after the cloth. (John Heywood, *Dialogue Containing Proverbs and Epigrams,* 1562)

stretch one's legs according to the coverlet To live within one's means; to adjust to a situation, especially a financial one. This uncommon expression alludes to the way in which one must conform to an undersized bed, being sure not to extend himself beyond the bounds of his coverlet, or bedspread. Figuratively, the expression implies that one must be certain not to overextend himself beyond his resources.

trim one's sails To reshape or alter one's opinion, position, or policy to fit the situation; to adapt oneself to the circumstances or the times. *To trim the sails* was originally a nautical expression meaning to adjust the sails of a ship according to the direction of the wind and the course of the vessel in order to gain the greatest possible advantage.

ADULTERY   (See **INFIDELITY.**)

ADVANCEMENT

a new wrinkle An innovation, a new development; an improved technique or method, or a hint or suggestion regarding one; sometimes, a new development that acts as a hindrance, snag, or further complexity. Precisely how *wrinkle* took on the colloquial meaning of *clever trick* some time in the 1800s remains unclear, but it is this usage from which the above current meanings derive. *Webster's Third* cites P. J. C. Friedlander's use of the term:

> . . . a new wrinkle whereby the exhaust gases are used to spin small turbines geared direct to the propeller shaft.

quantum leap A sudden enormous step forward; an unexpected discovery or breakthrough. This expression is a physics term for the jumping of an electron from one energy state to another. As used figuratively, *quantum leap* denotes a great and sudden change in a positive direction, often with far-reaching consequences.

> The ability of marine technology to take "quantum" leaps in innovation means that a laissez-faire approach to the ocean mineral resources can no longer be tolerated. (Tony Loftas, *New Scientist,* December, 1970)

ADVANTAGE

ace in the hole A trump card; something advantageous held in reserve until needed, and especially until needed to turn apparent failure into actual success. In stud poker a hole card is the card dealt face down in the first round. Since an ace is the highest and most valuable card, the player who receives an ace as his hole card has a decided advantage.

beat to the punch To get the drop on, to beat to the draw, to be a step ahead; to gain the advantage through quickness and alertness; to steal someone's thunder; to win at oneupmanship. *Webster's Third* cites W. J. Reilly's use of this boxing metaphor:

> . . . beats you to the conversational punch by having his say before you have a chance to open your mouth.

catch a weasel asleep To gain an advantage over something due to its inattentiveness. A sleeping animal is an easy target. This expression is an older equivalent of the current *to catch someone napping.*

catch napping To acquire an advantage over someone through his inattentiveness. A sleeping person or animal is easily taken off guard by another person or predator. As used in the phrase, however, *napping* does not carry its literal meaning of 'sleeping.' It means simply 'unawares, off guard, inattentive.'

get the drop on To have the advantage over someone; to be in a superior, controlling position, such that one cannot be taken unawares. Most sources cite the following quotation from Alexander K. McClure's *Three Thousand Miles through the Rocky Mountains* (1869) as the first use of this colloquial American expression.

So expert is he with his faithful pistol that the most scientific of rogues have repeatedly attempted in vain to "get the drop" on him.

This original use referring exclusively to a fast draw may be related to *at the drop of a hat.* (See **INSTANTANEOUSNESS**.) The idea of covering a person with a gun before he can draw his own soon gave rise to the current figurative use.

At any rate, we will not let Arcturus get the drop on the reading public. (*Texas Siftings,* August, 1888)

get the weather gage of To obtain the advantage over; to get the better of. In the sea battles of bygone days, a ship on the weather gage, or windward, side of an adversary's vessel would have the advantage of being better able to maneuver into a strategic position. The expression's principal use still usually concerns war and fighting, although not necessarily of a maritime nature.

He had got the weather gage of them, and for us to run down to them would be to run ourselves into the lion's mouth.

(John Mackey Wilson, *Tales of the Borders,* 1835–40)

go in with good cards To have reason to expect success; to anticipate triumph. This expression is derived from a card player's foreknowledge of victory upon being dealt an exemplary hand. The phrase maintains limited use in the United States and Great Britain.

They went in upon far better Cards to overthrow King Henry, than King Henry had to overthrow King Richard. (Francis Bacon, *Henry VII,* 1622)

have the ball at one's feet To be in a strategically advantageous position; to be in the driver's seat. In the British game of football (American soccer), whoever has the ball at his feet has the power to call the shots. This expression can be used in regard to politics, personal relations, or any area in which there are plays for power as one person or group attempts to gain control.

We have the ball at our feet, and if the Government will allow us . . . the rebellion will be crushed. (W. E. Auckland, *Journal and Correspondence,* 1788–98)

inside track An advantageous position granting one an edge over others; a favorable status; influence, or the power to secure favors. In racing, the *inside track* 'inner side of a curved track' is the shortest route. By the mid-19th century, this Americanism was used figuratively to refer to any position of advantage.

When a woman knows where she stands, and has the inside track, . . . the man has no show whatever. (Atherton, *Perch of Devil,* 1914)

in the catbird seat In an advantageous position or condition; ahead of the game; also *sitting in the catbird seat.* This U.S. slang expression, dating at least from 1942, was popularized by baseball announcer "Red" Barber during his 1945–55 radio broadcasts of the Brooklyn Dodgers baseball games.

keep one jump ahead To advance or increase before someone or something else and thus maintain an advantageous position or superior status. The exact origin of this 20th-century expression is unknown; it may come from the game of checkers in which one player *jumps* 'takes possession of' another player's checkers—literally advancing one checker in front of another one—in order to win the game.

> That would allow the Government to permit wage rises to keep one jump ahead of prices. (*Sun,* January 6, 1973)

sitting pretty In a favorable situation or condition; at an advantage; successful; well-to-do; well-off, set. This expression has been in use since 1926.

steal a march on To gain an advantage over, to get the jump on, to be a step ahead of. This expression originally had to do with the stealthy movement of troops without the enemy's knowledge. It still retains connotations of furtiveness or secrecy.

> Happening to awake earlier than usual, he stole a march on his nurses, and . . . walked out and tottered into the jail. (Charles Reade, *It Is Never Too Late To Mend,* 1856)

ADVERSITY

the black ox has trod on [someone's] foot Said of a person who has been the victim of misfortune or adversity. This proverb, in use since 1546, is rarely heard today.

blood, sweat and tears See EXERTION.

cross to bear See BURDEN.

crown of thorns Any excruciatingly painful hardship, tribulation, trial, suffering, etc.; a grievous and enduring wound. This expression refers to the crown which soldiers mockingly placed on Jesus' head before his crucifixion.

> And they platted a crown of thorns and put it upon his head, and a reed in his right hand; and they kneeled down before him, and mocked him, saying, Hail, King of the Jews! (Matthew 27:29)

get one's lumps To be harshly treated or abused; to be punished, chastised, or criticized; to be physically beaten or harassed. In this expression a lump is literally a swelling on the body caused by physical violence.

> Their greatest fun is to see a cop getting his lumps. (H. Lee in *Pageant,* April, 1951)

This 20th-century American slang expression is frequently used to describe nonphysical abuse and punishment or unpleasant, painful experiences.

> Now I take my lumps, he thought. Maybe for not satisfying Mary. (Bernard Malamud, *Tenants,* 1971)

lead a dog's life To live a miserable, servile life; to lead a wretched, harassed existence. This expression, which dates from the 16th century, apparently refers to the abuses heaped on the less fortunate of man's best friends.

> She . . . domineers like the devil: O Lord, I lead the life of a dog. (Samuel Foote, *The Mayor of Garret,* 1764)

the most unkindest cut of all The cruelest of cruel treatment; the last and most painful of a series of hurts; used especially in reference to betrayal by a friend. The *cut* of the original expression referred to one of the rents in Julius Caesar's mantle, specifically that made by his dearest friend Brutus. The line is from Marc Antony's famous oration over the dead Caesar's body.

> This was the most unkindest cut of all,
> For when the noble Caesar saw him stab,
> Ingratitude, more strong than traitors' arms,
> Quite vanquished him.
> (Shakespeare, *Julius Caesar,* III,ii)

Today the phrase is most often found in contexts where *cut* means 'slight, snub, insult,' though the idea that the hurt involves a friend's rejection is usually retained. Other uses play on other meanings of *cut*, such as deletions from a manuscript or bowdlerization of a text.

run the gauntlet To be subjected to attack from all sides; to be made to endure abusive treatment or severe criticism. Running the gauntlet was a form of military punishment in which the offender was compelled to run between two rows of men armed with whips or scourges, each of whom struck him a painful blow. The *gauntlet* (or *gantlet*) of the expression bears no relationship to *gauntlet* 'mailed glove' but is a corruption of *gantlope,* from the Swedish *gatlopp* 'a running lane.' The literal expression came into English during the Thirty Years' War (1618–1648) and the phrase was used figuratively shortly thereafter.

> To print, is to run the gantlet, and to expose ones self to the tongues strapado. (Joseph Glanvill, "Preface" *The Vanity of Dogmatizing,* 1661)

slings and arrows See CRITICISM.

through the mill Through much suffering, through many hardships and difficulties, through an ordeal or trial. The allusion is to the way a mill grinds whole grains of wheat into fine flour.

> His hardships were never excessive; they did not affect his health or touch his spirits; probably he is in every way a better man for having . . . "gone through the mill." (G. Gissing, *The Private Papers of H. Ryecroft,* 1903)

Use of the expression dates from the 19th century.

through the wringer Through an emotionally or physically exhausting experience.

> Workers, who have already undergone two loyalty or security in-

> vestigations . . . must go through the wringer a third time. (Elmer Davis, as quoted in *Webster's Third*)

A wringer is an apparatus for squeezing out excess water or liquid, as from clothes after washing.

ADVICE

don't let anyone sell you a wooden nutmeg This bit of advice to the unwary to be on the lookout for fraudulent sales schemes derives from the 19th-century practice of selling imitation nutmegs made of wood.

> A Yankee mixes a certain number of wooden nutmegs, which cost him 1–4 cents apiece, with a quantity of real nutmegs, worth 4 cents apiece, and sells the whole assortment for $44; and gains $3.75 by the fraud. (Hill, *Elements of Algebra,* 1859)

This practice was supposedly prevalent in Connecticut, "The Nutmeg State," although whether the sellers were itinerant peddlers or natives of Connecticut is debatable.

don't take any wooden nickels According to Wentworth and Flexner *(Dictionary of American Slang),* an Americanism equivalent to "Good-bye, take care, protect yourself from trouble." A wooden nickel is a wooden disc or souvenir which costs a nickel but has no legal value. The exhortation may have originated as a reminder not to be duped into buying such a worthless thing. Popular in the early 1900s, *don't take any wooden nickels* is less frequently heard today.

> In the mean wile [*sic*]—until we meet again—don't take no wood nickels and don't get impatient and be a good girlie and save up your loving for me. (Ring W. Lardner, *The Real Dope,* 1919)

keep your breath to cool your porridge This Briticism is an oblique admonition to "mind your own business" or "practise what you preach."

kitchen cabinet A group of unofficial, personal advisers to an elected official. The original *kitchen cabinet* consisted of three friends of President Andrew Jackson who met with him frequently for private political discussions. They reportedly entered by the back door (perhaps through the kitchen) so as to avoid observation and were believed to have had more influence than Jackson's official Cabinet. Use of the expression dates from at least 1832.

> One of the most important members of Gov. Stevenson's kitchen cabinet will be the new head of the State Department of Labor. (*The Chicago Daily News,* December, 1948)

reck one's own rede To follow one's own advice; to "practice what you preach." *Reck* 'heed, regard' appears only in negative constructions. *Rede* 'advice, counsel' is now archaic and limited to poetical or dialectal use. This expression is found in Shakespeare's *Hamlet.*

> Do not, as some ungracious pastors do,
> Show me the steep and thorny way to heaven,
> Whilst, like a puffed and reckless libertine,
> Himself the primrose path of dalliance treads,
> And recks not his own rede. (I,iii)

Today *reck one's own rede* is met only in literary contexts.

the tune the old cow died of Advice instead of aid, words in lieu of alms. This expression alludes to the following old ballad:

> There was an old man, and he had an old cow,
> But he had no fodder to give her,
> So he took up his fiddle and played her the tune;
> "Consider, good cow, consider,
> This isn't the time for the grass to grow,
> Consider, good cow, consider."

Needless to say, the old cow died of hunger. Occasionally *the tune the old cow died of* is used to describe unmelodious or poorly played music.

> The tune the old cow died of throughout, grunts and groans of instruments. (Countess Harriet Granville, *Letters,* 1836)

AFFECTATION

camp or **campy** Flagrantly and flauntingly effeminate or homosexual; affected, artificial; theatrical, exaggerated, ostentatious. Although the exact origin of this slang term is obscure, the second and third senses seem to be outgrowths of the first. *Campy* did not come into use until 1959, although the adjective *camp* dates from 1909. The verb *to camp,* in use since 1931, means to flaunt one's homosexuality; to ham it up; to overact or exaggerate; often *camp up* or *camp it up.*

> Boys and men with painted faces and dyed hair flaunt themselves camping and whooping for hours each night. (*New Broadway Brevities* (N.Y.), 1931)

The noun *camp* refers to an "ironic or amusing quality present in an extravagant gesture, style, or form, especially when inappropriate or out of proportion to the content that is expressed" *(Random House Dict.).* When such a relationship is consciously used it is known as *high camp,* whereas when it is unwittingly or inadequately used it is called *low camp.*

> High Camp is the whole emotional basis of the Ballet . . . and of course of Baroque art. (Christopher Isherwood, *World in Evening,* 1954)

kewpie doll A woman who affects infantile behavior and mannerisms. This expression is derived from the cherubic doll designed by R. C. O'Neill, and named after the mythological god Cupid. The phrase is usually applied disparagingly to women who act overly cute and coquettish, assume baby talk, and dress younger than their years.

> She'd be like some kewpie doll, all sheen and varnish and eyes that

really roll. (N. Cohn. *A WopBopa-LooBop,* 1969)

la-di-da Exhibiting affectations in appearance, mannerisms, speech, style, or status; pretentious; foppish. This expression is an onomatopoeic and derisive imitation of the speech patterns of those with affected gentility. A variation is *lardy-dardy.*

> I may tell you we are all homely girls. We don't want any la-di-da members. (*The Westminster Gazette,* January 31, 1895)

La-di-da is sometimes used as a noun referring to a person who fits the above definition, or as an interjection, particularly when one intends derision or ridicule of those who put on the airs of high society. The latter usage received renewed popularity as a result of its repeated use in Woody Allen's movie, "Annie Hall" (1977).

macaroni See STYLISHNESS.

make dainty To be scrupulous, overly sensitive, or unnecessarily wary; to have great respect or awe for something and exercise restraint in all matters relating to it. Although no longer current, this expression was popular in the 16th century and appears in Shakespeare's *Romeo and Juliet:*

> Ah ha, my mistresses! which of you all
> Will now deny to dance? She that makes dainty,
> She, I'll swear, hath corns. (I,v)

As in the above citation, *make dainty* often connotes pretense and affectation.

niminy-piminy Affected, mincing, namby-pamby; artificially nice or refined; effeminate; childishly cute. This once popular British colloquialism, combining two rhyming nonsense words, was first used in *The Heiress* in an attempt to teach one of the characters, Miss Alscrip, to speak in a refined manner:

> The way to acquire the correct Paphian mimp is to stand before the glass and pronounce repeatedly "niminy piminy." The lips cannot fail to take the right ply. (John Burgoyne, *The Heiress,* 1786)

prunes and prisms Affectedly proper speech or behavior, mincing mannerisms. This expression, once used to ridicule a saccharine manner of speaking or writing, derives from Charles Dickens' *Little Dorrit* (1855), in which Amy Dorrit is urged to develop a more refined manner of speech:

> Father is rather vulgar, my dear.
> . . . Papa . . . gives a pretty form to the lips. Papa, potatoes, poultry, prunes, and prism, are all very good words for the lips; especially prunes and prism.

put on the dog To affect sophistication and urbanity; to adopt pretentious mannerisms. This expression, of dubious American origin, has seen an upsurge in usage during the 20th century.

> An editor's unexampled opportunities for putting on the dog and throwing his weight about. (P. G. Wodehouse, *Eggs, Beans, and Crumpets,* 1940)

AFFIRMATION

Bob's your uncle A British informal expression like *there you are, there you have it,* often used at the end of a list of instructions; a phrase used in place of something unstated but obvious.

> Three curves and a twiddle, label it "object," and bob's your uncle. (N. Blake, *Head of Traveller,* 1949)

One conjecture says the phrase derives from Robert Peel's campaign slogan for a seat in Parliament: "Vote for Bob—Bob's your uncle." Robert Peel founded the Metropolitan Police Force in 1829, hence the label *bobby* for a police officer. Supposedly, *Bob* alluded to his stance on law and order and *uncle* implied benevolence. This theory is unlikely, however, considering that the earliest citation in the *OED* is from 1937, almost a century after the slogan would have been spoken.

O.K. All right, fine, correct, satisfactory; also, *okay, okey-dokey.* The origin of this saying has been the subject of much controversy among etymologists. One explanation traces it to a group of witty Bostonian writers who reveled in abbreviating ludicrously misspelled words. Their only abbreviation of any lasting consequence was *O.K.,* which stood for *oll korrect* 'all correct.' The accepted etymology today is the following: A group of Democrats, in support of Martin Van Buren's 1840 presidential bid, founded an organization entitled the Democratic O.K. Club, in which O.K. stood for Old Kinderhook, Kinderhook being the New York birthplace of Van Buren. *O.K.* soon became Van Buren's campaign slogan. By late 1840, *O.K.* was firmly established in American English and appeared in songs and literature of the day.

> I'm O.K.—off for the calaboose, and so is you. (*New Orleans Picayune,* January, 1841)

The expression has also developed the related meaning of a stamp of approval.

> The High Official added his O.K. to the others. (S. E. White, *Rules of the Game,* 1909)

Even though its usage has now spread to other English speaking nations, *O.K.* is perhaps the most typical American colloquialism.

that's the ticket That's the proper or correct thing; that's the right procedure or attitude, that fills the bill. This expression, dating from the early 1800s, probably derives from the 19th century practice among charities of offering to the needy tickets exchangeable for necessities such as food or clothing.

> This [idealizing of portraits] is all wrong. Truth is the ticket. (Edward FitzGerald, *Letters and Literary Remains,* 1847)

AFFLUENCE   (See also **PROSPERING.**)

beggar on horseback An upstart, nouveau riche, or parvenu; one who goes from rags to riches overnight. Various expressions incorporating this phrase have been cited as its source. The earliest is attributed to Robert Greene, a contemporary of Shakespeare's. In Richard Burton's *Anatomy of Melancholy* (1621) appears the line

> Set a beggar on horseback and he will ride a gallop.

Cited in *Bartlett* is Bohn: *Foreign Proverbs (German):*

> Set a beggar on horseback and he'll outride the Devil.

And, finally, there is the folk proverb, "If wishes were horses, beggars would ride." All seemed to have influenced the meanings of this expression.

eat high off the hog To be in a prosperous, luxurious situation, able to eat the best food and to indulge one's extravagant tastes; to live a life of material comfort. This U.S. expression is said to derive from the fact that choice cuts of meat come from high up on a hog's side. *Eat* or *live high off the hog* dates from the early 1900s.

> I have to do my shopping in the black market because we can't eat as high off the hog as Roosevelt and Ickes and Joe Davis and all those millionaire friends of the common man. (*Call-Bulletin,* May 27, 1946)

fat cat See **PERSONAGE.**

full-bagged Rich, wealthy, affluent. The allusion is to the full moneybags of a rich man. The term, now obsolete, appeared in John Taylor's *Works* (1630):

> No full bag'd man would ever durst have entered.

in clover Enjoying success and living in luxury; in luck; prosperous; well-off. Used figuratively as early as 1710, *in clover* alludes to the best pasturage known for cattle—fields of clover.

the Midas touch See **ABILITY.**

moneybags A rich person; a nabob. This popular expression of obvious origin is used throughout the English-speaking world.

Though squarsons and squires, landlords and moneybags leagued together against me, I was returned by a majority of 34. (Joseph Arch, *Story of His Life*, 1898)

money to burn Excessive wealth; money to spare; more than sufficient financial assets. This expression implies a large fortune which, if partially destroyed, would still be extraordinary. The phrase is frequently heard in the United States and Great Britain.

People in the States have "money to burn." (*Sunday Express*, May, 1928)

on Easy Street Living a life of financial independence; enjoying a comfortable, prosperous life style. This expression first appeared in George V. Hobart's *It's Up to You* (1902) which tells of a young man "who could walk up and down Easy Street."

piss on ice To live luxuriously; to live high off the hog; to be wealthy, successful, or lucky. It was once the custom in posh restaurants to place a cake of ice in the urinals of men's rooms. Thus, this expression implies that the only men who urinated on ice were those wealthy enough to patronize these exclusive and expensive dining establishments.

ride the gravy train To become prosperous, to have much success or luck in acquiring wealth; to partake of the good life, to live high off the hog. Dating from the turn of the century, *gravy* refers to money or profits easily and sometimes illegally acquired. A *gravy train* or *boat* is a situation or position which offers the advantages necessary for putting prosperity and fortune within easy reach. *To board* or *ride the gravy train* is to take advantage of such a situation, to go for a free ride. This U.S. slang expression dates from the 1920s.

They is on the gravy train and don't know it, but they is headed straight for 'struction and perdition. (Botkin, *My Burden*, 1945)

sugar daddy A wealthy man, usually middle-aged or elderly, who spends freely on a young woman, providing material luxuries in exchange for companionship and sex. *Sugar* is a slang term for money. The expression was popular in the middle of the 20th century, especially in the jazz world. *Candy man* is another label for a similar type of man. The material luxury he provides is "candy," a slang term for cocaine.

well-heeled Wealthy, affluent, monied. Though it might appear that this term evolved as the opposite of *down-at-the-heel*, such is not the case. Of American origin, *well-heeled* derives from the sport of cockfighting, and was first used in reference to the metal spurs put on fighting cocks. It later came to mean 'armed, equipped, furnished' with any kind of weapon, usually a revolver. This latter usage was common in the 19th century, toward the close of which is found the term's first application to being 'furnished with money.' This last is the only meaning retained.

Though the million and a quarter left by his grandfather has been spread among a large family he is still well-heeled enough. (*The Daily Telegraph* [Color Supplement], January, 1968)

AGE (See also **OBSOLESCENCE, YOUTH**.)

before one had nails on one's toes See **TIME**.

brand-new Entirely or completely new; unused; absolutely or perfectly new; also *bran-new*. This term, in use since 1570, is said to have come from the Anglo-Saxon word *brand* 'torch' and formerly denoted metals or metal articles fresh from the fire or furnace. A synonym is *fire-new* used by Shakespeare in *Richard III*:

Your fire-new stamp of Honor is scarce current. (I,iii)

knee-high to a grasshopper See **PHYSICAL STATURE**.

long in the tooth   Old; showing signs of old age. Although currently used of people, this expression originally applied exclusively to horses. It refers to the seemingly longer length of an older horse's teeth, due to gum recession.

> To be honest I am getting quite long in the tooth and this is a method of bringing children into my Christmas. (*Sunday Express*, December 24, 1972)

over the hill   Past the time of greatest efficiency or power, past the prime of life, too old, aging; also, past the crisis, over the hurdles. The expression's latter meanings may be derived from a traveler's achievement of crossing a hill, after which the going is easier. The phrase's more common meanings, however, allude to a hill as being the high point, or apex, of one's effectiveness and authority, after which the only course is downhill. In contemporary usage, the phrase most often describes a person of advancing age.

> As they say about boxers who are getting on in years, she is over the hill. (I. Cross, *God Boy*, 1957)

salad days   Youth; the time of juvenile inexperience and naivete; the springtime of one's life. This expression may have derived as an analogy between *green* 'inexperienced, immature' and the predominant color of salad ingredients. This comparison was made in Shakespeare's *Antony and Cleopatra* (I,v):

> My salad days,
> when I was green in judgment.

Today, in addition to the phrase's youthful sense, *salad days* also refers to any period in a person's life or career characterized by callowness and unsophistication.

> In directing "The Pride and the Passion" Stanley Kramer created a picture as vast, heavily populated, and downright foolish as anything the Master [Cecil B. DeMille] confected in his salad days. (*New Yorker*, July, 1957)

AGREEMENT

Lamourette's kiss   A short-lived reconciliation, particularly one that is made insincerely; an ephemeral rapprochement; subterfuge; shrewd or cunning deceit. The *Lamourette* in this expression was Abbé Lamourette, a French politician who, on July 7, 1792, convinced the many discordant factions of the Legislative Assembly of France to lay aside their differences and work together for the common good. After much demonstration and protestation of peace-making, the legislators soon lapsed into their former hostilities, but with even more animosity and rancor than before. Since that time, the expression has been used figuratively, usually in reference to transitory or disingenuous political agreements.

make no bones about   See CANDIDNESS.

package deal   An agreement or settlement in which all of the conditions must be either accepted or rejected; an all-or-nothing arrangement or plan which involves the acceptance of one or more negative elements as a requisite to achieving a generally favorable goal. Originally, a package deal was a group of goods which were wrapped in one package and sold at a bargain price, one lower than the combined cost of purchasing each item separately. Although this connotation is still retained, *package deal* usually refers to a political or industrial pact which contains several related or unrelated provisions, all of which must be accepted or rejected as a unit. *Package deal* has also enjoyed some jocular use, often in reference to a person's spouse or family.

strike a bargain   To conclude a bargain or other deal; to settle or arrange the terms of a transaction; to agree on a compromise or other settlement. This expression alludes to the ancient Greek and Roman custom of sealing a business contract by striking (i.e., killing) an animal and offering it as a sacrifice to their deities. Although this tradition is long since gone, the expression persists.

> As soon as the bargain is struck, the property of the goods is transferred to the vendee. (Sir William Blackstone, *Commentary on the Laws of England,* 1766)

With the demise of sacrificial offerings, it became customary in many societies to seal an agreement by shaking or striking hands, thus the related and synonymous *strike hands.*

ALERTNESS (See also SHREWDNESS.)

Argus-eyed Vigilant, watchful; keen-eyed, alert. Argus was a mythical 100-eyed giant set by Juno to keep watch over the heifer Io. Only two of his eyes slept at a time. Mercury, however, was able to charm him to sleep, and slew him, whereupon Juno set Argus' many eyes upon the peacock's tail. Language ignores his failure and preserves his vigilance with *Argus-eyed.*

beat to the punch See ADVANTAGE.

keep one's ear to the ground To be alert to what's going on, to be abreast of rumors and hearsay, to be aware of the prevailing trends of public opinion. The expression is said to derive from a practice of plainsmen in the Old West. They reputedly believed that a neckerchief on the ground would amplify otherwise inaudible sounds, such as the beating of horses' hooves. Consequently, they would often put an ear to a neckerchief so placed in order to discern another's approach. This expression and its variants *hold* or *have one's ear to the ground* date from the early part of this century, and still enjoy widespread currency.

> What's the gossip of the market, Tom? You fellows certainly do keep your ears to the ground. (Graham Greene, *The Quiet American,* 1955)

keep one's eyes peeled To be on the qui vive; to be alert and watchful; to keep a sharp lookout. Although this version of the expression is currently popular, it appears to be a variant of *keep one's eyes skinned,* which appeared in print presumably for the first time in *The Political Examiner* in 1833. The eyelid is the "skin" which must be "peeled" to permit one to see.

> I kept my eyes peeled, but I didn't see her in the afternoon crowd. (*Munsey's Magazine* XXIV, 1901)

keep one's weather eye open To be vigilant, watchful, or alert; to observe closely. This expression's nautical origin refers to the diligent attentiveness of a sailor assigned to weather observation duty. The expression still carries its implication of astute observation.

> Job returned in a great state of nervousness, and keeping his weather eye fixed upon every woman who came near him. (Rider Haggard, *She: A History of Adventure,* 1887)

no flies on [someone] Said of a person who is alert, astute, shrewd, or active, one not likely to be caught napping. The apparent allusion is to cattle which constantly move their tails in an attempt to discourage flying pests from settling and inflicting painful bites. Thus, the presence of flies implies stagnation or inactivity, while their absence implies the opposite.

> There are no flies on Benaud. . . . No one will have to draw his attention to it. (*Observer,* April 23, 1961)

The expression is also used in reference to a business, project, or other matter which is thriving, reputable, and above reproach.

on one's toes Alert, on the ball, ready to take advantage of an opportunity. A runner who starts a race "on his toes" has a decided edge over one who starts from a flatfooted position. Thus the phrase's figurative sense of preparedness and alertness. *Webster's Third* cites W. L. Gresham's use of the expression:

> In working for real money you've got to be on your toes.

on the ball Alert, keen, quick, sharp; intelligent, bright, perspicacious. The now common truncated phrase and its earlier, longer antecedents derive from sport, though which sport it is difficult to determine. *Keep your eye on the ball* probably came from a game such as tennis or baseball, where timing and concentration on the rapidly moving object are crucial. *Have something on the ball* is still used literally of pitchers with extraordinary control over the ball's speed and direction. Being "on the ball" thus results from "having something on the ball" or "keeping one's eyes on the ball" and is equivalent to them. A person on the ball is on top of things, in control, ready for all emergencies and contingencies. The phrase connotes the coordinated, nearly simultaneous anticipation and action of the accomplished athlete.

on the qui vive On the lookout, on the alert; watchful, aware, awake. *"Qui vive?"* was the French equivalent to the English "Who goes there?" a sentinel's challenge to passers-by to identify themselves as friend or foe. *"Qui vive?"* called for a response of allegiance such as *"Vive le roi"* 'long live the king' or *"Vive la France"* 'long live France.' Use of the expression *on the qui vive* dates from at least 1726.

> "What now?" cried Burtis, all on the qui vive. (Edward P. Roe in *Harper's Magazine*, December, 1883)

quick on the draw Alert; quick-thinking; vigilant. This expression originated in the Old West, where a gunfighter's survival depended upon the celerity with which he handled his weapon. The phrase is commonly used today to describe a keen-witted, sharp-minded person.

rough-and-ready See VITALITY.

take the ball before the bound To anticipate an opportunity, to be one step ahead of the game; to be overhasty or impetuous. Figurative use of this expression derives from a game such as cricket, tennis, or football. Whether such a move is advantageous or foolish depends on the situation. In the following citation, taking the ball before the bound has negative connotations.

> It concerns you not to be over-hasty herein, not to take the ball before the bound. (James Howell, *Epistolae Ho-Elianae*, 1645)

up to snuff See COMPETENCE.

ALLOCATION

earmarked Set aside for a particular purpose; allocated for use in specified ways; marked so as to be recognized. This expression, dating from the 1500s, alludes to the practice of marking the ears of cattle and sheep to show ownership. An even older example of "earmarking" comes from Exodus 21:6:

> . . . his master shall bore his ear through with an awl; and he shall serve him for ever.

Figuratively, *earmarked* is often used in regard to monetary allocations although it is heard in other contexts as well.

> I need only earmark sufficient time in the summer for certain people whose hospitality I've accepted. (S. McKenna, *Happy Ending*, 1929)

lion's share The largest portion; a disproportionately large share; all or most. This expression is derived from Aesop's fable in which three animals joined forces with a lion for a hunt. When dividing their quarry, the lion claimed three fourths as his: one fourth as his just share, one fourth because of his great courage, and one fourth for his lioness and cubs. The lion offered the remaining fourth to any of the fellow-hunters who was able to defeat him in a fight. The intimidated animals declined the challenge, however, and left empty-handed.

> The art of finding a rich friend to make a tour with you in autumn, and of leaving him to bear the lion's share of the expenses. (*Punch*, June 22, 1872)

a piece of the action See INVOLVE-MENT.

a piece of the pie A share in the profits; a portion of whatever is being divvied up and parceled out—usually money, but also applicable to intangibles such as attention, affection, time, etc. This expression probably has its origin in the graphic representation of budget allotments in circular, pie-shaped form, with various sized wedges or pieces indicating the relative size of allocations to different agencies, departments, etc. *Webster's Third* cites A. H. Rashkin:

> Industry is getting its share of the prosperity pie.

AMALGAMATION (See also MIX-TURE.)

curate's egg Any amalgam of good and bad features; any combination of assets and liabilities, strengths and weaknesses, pros and cons, etc. This British term dates from an 1895 *Punch* cartoon in which a deferential, diplomatic curate, unwilling to acknowledge before his bishop that he had been served a bad egg, insisted that "Parts of it are excellent!" The expression *curate's egg* came into vogue almost immediately, and still enjoys considerable popularity.

> All the same it is a curate's egg of a book. While the whole may be somewhat stale and addled, it would be unfair not to acknowledge the merits of some of its parts. (*Oxford Magazine*, November 22, 1962)

melting pot A place where the assimilation of racial groups and ethnic cultures occurs; the amalgamation of qualities or concepts, resulting in an improved or unprecedented end-product. This expression alludes to a large cauldron where dissimilar ingredients are blended to form a distinctive mixture. In the United States, the phrase often refers to the ongoing assimilation of vastly different immigrants into the mainstream of American society. Nonetheless, *melting pot* often carries its meaning of a medley of heterogeneous elements combined into a single work or idea; this concept is illustrated in the *American Guide Series: Connecticut*, as cited by *Webster's Third:*

> The architectural melting pot is seen in the tall Romanesque columns, the Gothic hammer-vault roofing. . . .

portmanteau word See LANGUAGE.

AMOROUSNESS (See LOVE, LUST.)

ANECDOTE

chestnut An old, stale joke; a trite, oft-repeated tale or story. Although the exact origin of this term is unknown, one plausible explanation is that it comes from an old melodrama, *The Broken Sword,* by William Dillon. In the play, Captain Zavier is retelling, for the umpteenth time, a story having to do with a cork tree. His listener Pablo breaks in suddenly, correcting cork tree to chestnut tree, saying "I should know as well as you having heard you tell the tale these twenty-seven times." The popularization of the term is attributed to the comedian William Warren, who had played the role of Pablo many times, and who is said to have repeated Pablo's line about the chestnut in response to an unoriginal story told at a dinner party. The expression has been in use since 1883.

cock and bull story See NONSENSE.

fish story See EXAGGERATION.

Joe Miller A stale joke; a chestnut. In 1739 a man by the name of John Mottley put together a book of jests and called it *Joe Miller's Jest-Book,* after the name of an illiterate comedian who lived 1684–1738. Current use of this name to describe an overused joke or saying implies that Mottley's compilation was not very funny, and perhaps included jokes which were old even at that time.

Many of the anecdotes are mere Joe Millers. (*Reminiscences of Scottish Life and Character,* 1870)

megillah A long, detailed explanation or account; a lengthy, often exaggerated story; frequently in the phrase *the whole megillah. Megillah* is Hebrew for 'roll, scroll' and commonly refers to any or all of a certain five books of the Old Testament to be read on specified feast days. The extraordinary length and tediousness of these readings gave rise to the slang sense of the term as it is popularly used outside of Judaism today.

Feeding all the megillah to the papers about his family of Irish Polacks who came over with the Pilgrim Fathers. (*Punch,* May, 1968)

old wives' tale See SUPERSTITION.

shaggy dog story An involved, often seemingly interminable story that derives its humor from its unexpected, absurd, or punning ending; any joke or story involving a talking animal, especially a dog. This expression describes the wryly humorous stories which feature a shaggy dog as the main character or as the speaker of a surprise punch line. Though most popular in the 1940s, shaggy dog stories are still recounted in certain contemporary circles.

song and dance See EXAGGERATION.

ANGRINESS (See also FURY, ILL TEMPER, IRRITATION, VEXATION.)

bent out of shape Vexed, irritated, annoyed. This phrase, of recent vintage, has yet to find its way into our lexicons. The implicit analogy between an object's physical shape and an individual's mental state suggests that the latter condition has a specific cause, a temporary nature, and contrasts with one's "usual self."

cross as two sticks Angry, vexed, out of humor; irritated; in high dudgeon. This British pun alludes to the image of crossed sticks in the shape of an "X."

The image of two sticks "passing or lying athwart each other" *(OED)* gives rise to associations of contrariness, opposition, and adversity.

He has been as cross as two sticks at not having been asked to dinner at Court. (R. M. Milnes Houghton in *Life, Letters, and Friendships,* 1855)

fit to be tied Incensed, enraged, livid, irate, very angry. This expression probably comes from the hospital practice of restraining patients who pose a danger to themselves or others. In its contemporary hyperbolic usage, *fit to be tied* refers to anyone (not just a patient) who is extremely angry or who is acting irrationally, implying that if this person were in a hospital, he would be tied down for his own protection as well as for the protection of others.

It threw the place into a tizzy. . . . The boss is fit to be tied. When he gets hold of you. . . . (C. Simak, *Strangers in the Universe,* 1956)

hot under the collar Angry, mad, infuriated; hot and bothered, distraught, upset, agitated. The allusion is to the red or "hot" color of an enraged person's neck and face due to the rush of blood to those areas.

After years of this sort of puling imbecility one gets hot under the collar and is perhaps carried to an extreme. (Ezra Pound, *Letters,* 1918)

The expression dates from at least 1895.

in a snit In a tiff, peeved; agitated, in a fuss or stew, all worked-up. *Webster's Third* cites the following usage from *Information Please Almanac:*

Wall Street brokers were in a snit because nobody bought stocks.

In an obsolete, literal sense *snit* was 'the glowing part of the wick of a candle when blown out,' perhaps the source of the figurative meaning of the word today.

a little pot is soon hot A small person is quickly provoked; a little person is easily roused to anger. A small pot, which naturally contains less water than a larger one, comes to a boil more quickly. *Little* in this expression apparently means both small in size and small in mind. Shakespeare alludes to the proverb in *The Taming of the Shrew* (IV,i):

Now, were not I a little pot and soon hot, . . .

Use of the expression dates from at least 1546.

mad as a hatter See IRRATIONALITY.

mad as a wet hen Very angry, furious, enraged. Chicken farmers maintain that this popular simile has no basis in fact, since hens do not get particularly excited when wet. These female fowl are, however, known for their angry clucking and pecking when provoked.

The chicken farmers of Quebec . . . are mad as, well, a wet hen. (*The Wall Street Journal,* July, 1971)

mad as hops Extremely angry; livid, infuriated, incensed; enraged, furious. This expression is probably a twist on *hopping mad,* implying that a person has become so angry that he hops about in a frenzied rage.

Such a grin! It made me mad as hops! (*Harper's Magazine,* October, 1884)

out of countenance Visibly abashed, ashamed, confounded, or disconcerted; upset, annoyed, perturbed. When a person is flustered or upset, the feeling is usually registered on his face. The phrase dates from the 16th century.

ANNOYANCE (See **IRRITATION, VEXATION.**)

ANXIETY (See also **FEAR.**)

butterflies A queasy feeling in the stomach caused by anxiety, nervousness, fear, or excitement; the jitters, the willies, the heebie-jeebies; usually in the phrase *to have butterflies in one's stomach.* The term, in use since 1908, provides an apt description of the flut-

tering sensation felt in the pit of the stomach during times of extreme anxiety or nervous tension.

cliff-hanger Any event or situation in which the outcome is suspensefully uncertain up until the very last moment. The term was originally applied to a serial film in which each episode ended with the hero or heroine left in a perilous plight, such as hanging from a cliff, so that the viewers anxiously awaited the next installment. The extended figurative sense of the term, and the only one commonly heard today, has been in use since at least 1948.

fussy as a hen with one chick Overprotective, overanxious, overparticular and fussy. A hen with one chick, as any mother with only one child, tends to be more possessive and protective than a parent with many offspring. This tendency usually manifests itself in finicky, fretful behavior.

get the wind up To be nervous; to be distressed or anxious. This British expression is similar to the American slang *jumpy* 'tense, edgy.' An analogous British colloquialism, *put the wind up,* carries a somewhat stronger sense of dread or fright.

I tell you you've absolutely put the wind up Uncle Bob and Peter! They're scared to death of your finding them up. (C. Alington, *Strained Relations,* 1922)

high-strung Nervous, tense, edgy; thin-skinned, sensitive, spirited. This expression, dating from the late 14th century, literally means 'strung to a high tension or pitch.' The allusion is probably to stringed musical instruments: the tighter the string, the higher the pitch. Taut strings are also more brittle and thus more likely to break.

Writers often tend to be high-strung creatures. (M. Lowry, *Letters,* 1946)

keyed up Excited, high-strung; nervous, tense; intensified, stimulated; psyched up (for), full of nervous energy and anticipation. The verb *key* refers literally to tuning a musical instrument —that is, raising or lowering the pitch. Since the 17th century this term has been applied figuratively to a person's thoughts and feelings that affect the overall color or tone of his mood. Thus "key up" is to heighten, intensify, or stimulate feelings.

Although he was emotionally keyed up, Sherman yawned. (Carson McCullers, *Clock Without Hands,* 1961)

like a cat in a strange garret Uneasy, nervous; fearful, afraid. This expression is an allusion to the behavior of a cat in strange surroundings. The March 16, 1824 edition of the *Woodstock* [Vermont] *Observer* contains the phrase:

"What was King Caucus like?" said an old gentleman. "Why, like a cat in a strange garret, frightened at every step it took."

like a cat on a hot tin roof Very uncomfortable, uneasy, nervous. This self-evident expression is a more current variant of *like a cat on hot bricks.* The latter dates from 1862 and has the additional meanings 'swiftly, nimbly.' *Cat on a Hot Tin Roof* was the title of a 1955 play by Tennessee Williams.

on pins and needles Apprehensive, anxious; in a state of nervous or uneasy anticipation; on tenterhooks. *Pins and needles* refers to the tingly, prickly sensation felt in the arms and legs when they are recovering from having been numbed or "asleep." Although a person who is "on pins and needles" might not be experiencing the attendant physical sensations, the expression implies that he is.

He was plainly on pins and needles, did not know whether to take or to refuse a cigar. (*Pall Mall Magazine,* August, 1897)

on tenterhooks Taut with anxiety; in a state of painful suspense of expectation; tense, uneasy, on edge. Tenterhooks are literally the hooks of a tenter, i.e.,

the frame on which cloth is stretched to shape it. The word was used figuratively as early as the late 17th century; *The Winthrop Papers* records a 1692 usage of "the tenterhooks of expectation" by G. Saltonstall. In *Roderick Random* (1748) Tobias Smollett writes:

I left him upon the tenter-hooks of impatient uncertainty.

Eventually such explanatory phrases became elliptically understood, leaving us with the now common *on tenterhooks.*

on the anxious seat In a state of apprehension or suspense; in a state of difficulty or doubt. The figurative expression derives from the literal anxious seat or bench, or mourners' bench, of American revivalist camp meetings, on which penitents desirous of forgiveness and seeking conversion were wont to sit while anxiously awaiting the call or sign of salvation. The term was used in its still current figurative sense early in this century:

The entire diplomatic corps at Havana is . . . on the "anxious bench." (*New York Evening Post,* November 1, 1906)

on the rack Under great pressure or strain; in painful suspense or acute psychological torment; on tenterhooks; tense, anxious, nervous. The rack, a former instrument of torture, consisted of a frame with rollers at either end to which the victim's ankles and wrists were attached in order to stretch his joints. The expression *on the rack* was used figuratively for psychological suffering as early as the 16th century.

. . . Let me choose,
For as I am, I live upon the rack.
(Shakespeare, *The Merchant of Venice* III,ii)

the screaming meemies Excessive fretfulness or uneasiness; the jitters, the heebie-jeebies; fear-induced delirium. In World War II, American soldiers originated this phrase as a nickname for the German rocket shells. The terrifying noise and devastating effect of these weapons caused anyone within earshot to be petrified with fear. While the expression is still used today for dread and horror, it is occasionally applied jocularly to the extremes of other emotional states, such as frightful boredom.

> Madison [Wisconsin] is a town that would give the ordinary thrill seeker the screaming meemies in one quiet weekend. (G. S. Penny, in *Saturday Evening Post,* January 1945)

sit tight   See PATIENCE.

sit upon hot cockles   See IMPATIENCE.

sweat blood   To worry or agonize; to be apprehensive or anxious; to be heavy-hearted; to be under a great strain. This expression and its variant, *a bloody sweat,* allude to Christ's agony in the Garden of Gethsemane:

> And being in agony he prayed more earnestly; and his sweat became like great drops of blood falling down upon the ground. (Luke 22:44)

These expressions have been used figuratively in various contexts, most of which refer to suffering occasioned by awaiting a likely, if not inevitable, fate.

> War . . . which yet, to sack us, toils in bloody sweat to enlarge the bounds of conquering Thessalie. (Thomas Kyd, *Cornelia,* 1594)

APATHY   (See INDIFFERENCE.)

APPEARANCE   (See PHYSICAL APPEARANCE, PRETENSE.)

APPEASEMENT   (See PLACATION.)

APPROVAL

amen corner   A coterie of fervent believers or ardent followers, so-called from the place in a church, usually near the pulpit, occupied by those who lead the responsive "amens." A person in the amen corner is, figuratively speaking, a disciple or devotee; often a yes-man or sycophantic toady. The expression is now thoroughly American, but it may well derive from the Amen Corner of London's Paternoster Row, the supposed point at which the Corpus Christi procession reached the "Amen" of the "Pater Noster."

get the nod   To receive approval or affirmation; to be selected. In this expression, *nod* 'a slight, quick inclination of the head as in assent or command' is used figuratively more often than literally. A variation is *give the nod.*

> Paul L. Troast got the G.O.P. nod, beating his nearest rival . . . by more than 53,000 votes. (*The Wall Street Journal,* April 23, 1953)

O.K.   See AFFIRMATION.

rubber stamp   To approve as a matter of course; to authorize without the proper examination or review. This phrase is derived from the rubber stamps used in lieu of a signature on documents, bank checks, etc. The expression is often applied adjectivally to describe persons or groups without a will or mind of their own, whose decisions and judgments are totally determined by others.

> He has been more of a rubber stamp voter than most so-called "machine" officeholders. (*Chicago Sun Times,* April, 1948)

thumbs up   Approval, approbation, affirmation. This expression stems from the days when gladiators fought in the Roman Colosseum and other large amphitheaters for the entertainment of the spectators. When one of the combatants was clearly vanquished, the victor would look to the crowd before making his next move—thumbs up (thumb close to or inside a closed fist) indicated that the throng approved of the effort expended by the loser, and his life was spared. Thumbs down (thumb extended downward from a closed fist) signified disapproval, and gave the winner the license to slay his opponent. Eventually, *thumbs up* was demonstrated by making a fist, extending the thumb, and pointing it upward. This gesture assumed a cultish popularity in the 1950s as evidenced by its frequent use in the ABC television series *Happy Days*, a situation comedy that started in 1974. See also **thumbs down, REFUSAL**.

ARGUMENTATION

chop logic See **NIT-PICKING**.

devil's advocate One who argues an opposing cause or who takes the negative side of a case, primarily for the sake of argument. This expression derives from the custom in the Roman Catholic Church of appointing an *advocatus diaboli*, more properly known as *promotor fidei* 'protector of the faith,' whose task it is to argue the case against persons proposed for canonization.

wrangle for an ass's shadow See **NIT-PICKING**.

ARRANGEMENT

Indian file Single file, one after the other. The expression supposedly derives from the American Indian practice of moving stealthily through the woods in this fashion—each walker stepping into the footprints of the preceding, with the final man obliterating the single set of tracks thus leaving no trace of their course. *Webster's Third* cites a *Newsweek* article:

Along this road the inhabitants slowly moved in Indian file.

ASSISTANCE (See also COOPERA-TION.)

candle-holder An abettor; an assistant or attendant. The reference is to the Catholic practice of having someone hold a candle for the reader during a religious service. In everyday language, the expression applies to anyone who helps out in some small way, but who is not a real participant in the action or undertaking. Shakespeare used the term in *Romeo and Juliet*:

I'll be a candle-holder and look on. (I,iv)

give a leg up To lend a helping hand; to give someone assistance through a difficult or trying time. This expression, originally meaning to help someone mount a horse, now carries the figurative sense of assisting another over life's obstacles or helping someone advance through the ranks.

She was now devoting all her energies to give them a leg up. (William E. Norris, *Misadventure*, 1890)

good Samaritan A compassionate person who selflessly helps those in need; a friend in need; also simply a *Samaritan*. The allusion is to the Biblical parable (Luke 10:30–37) which tells of a man who had been beaten by thieves. He lay half-dead by the roadside while his neighbors, a priest and a Levite, passed him by. It was a Samaritan, his supposed enemy, who finally showed compassion for the man and took care of him. This expression dates from at least 1644.

I wish some good Samaritan of a Conservative with sufficient authority could heal the feuds among our friends. (Lord Ashburton, *Croker Papers*, 1846)

go to bat for To support actively, to stick up for or defend; to intercede for, to go to the assistance of. This American slang expression owes its origin to baseball—specifically the role of the pinch hitter. In the mid-1800s, *go to the bat* was used; by the turn of the century *go* or *come to bat for* gained currency. Now *go to bat for* is heard almost exclusively.

The daughter of old man Brewster who owns the *Evening Tab*, my meal ticket, came to bat when my show was ready to close. (J. P. McEvoy, *Show Girl*, 1928)

ka me, ka thee See **RECIPROCITY**.

pinch-hit To substitute for a regular worker, player, speaker, or performer, especially in an emergency; to take another person's place. In this expression, *pinch* refers to an emergency, a time of stress, and *hit* refers to a successful, or hopefully successful, attempt. A person called upon in such a predicament is called a *pinch-hitter*. Though it originated and is most commonly used in baseball to describe the substitution of a batter for the regularly scheduled one, usually at a crucial point in the game, *pinch-hit* has been expanded to include many other situations and contexts.

> In his absence, he has called upon three good friends, also authors of daily columns, to pinch-hit for him and give his readers a "change of pace." (*Lubbock* [Texas] *Morning Avalanche,* February, 1949)

ASTONISHMENT (See **SURPRISE.**)

ASTUTENESS (See **PERCEPTIVENESS, SHREWDNESS.**)

ATTIRE (See **CLOTHING.**)

ATTRIBUTION

chalk it up To ascribe, credit, or attribute. In the 16th century, it became common practice in British pubs and alehouses to keep track of a customer's bill by making chalk marks on a slate. In this way, the barkeep had an accurate count of all drinks ordered on credit.

> All my debts stande chaukt upon the poste for liquor. (*The Returne From Parnassus,* 1597)

In current usage, the expression is employed figuratively.

> What [16-year-old Tracy Austin] has that the others don't is an uncluttered spirit—a clean slate, if you will, on which plenty of victories will be recorded and losses chalked up to experience. (AP wire story, March 25, 1979)

AUGMENTATION (See also **EXACERBATION.**)

beef up To strengthen, reinforce; to augment, increase. Prior to slaughter, cows, steer, and bulls raised for their meat are fattened in order to increase their body weight and thus the profits derived from their sale. An early figurative usage appeared in 1941 in A. O. Pollard's *Bombers over Reich:*

> When the Fortresses reach Britain from the United States certain alterations are made; the larger guns are . . . "beefed up" so as to give them a rate of fire of 900 rounds a minute.

blow the coals To increase, augment, or heighten; to exacerbate or aggravate. Like *fan the fires* or *add fuel to the fire,* the meaning and origin of this phrase are obvious, referring to the action of bellows on coals.

fatten the kitty To increase the stakes, usually in reference to gambling; to add money or chips to a common pot to be awarded to the winner. In many forms of gambling, particularly in card games such as poker, all the players bet by putting money into a pot or pool called a *kitty*. "To fatten the kitty" is to add more to it, to increase its size. According to several sources, however, *kitty* can also refer to a percentage of the pot set aside for some special purpose such as buying refreshments or paying the house share. Similar expressions include *sweeten the kitty,* and *fatten* or *sweeten the pot.*

gear up To accelerate or speed up; to increase or boost. Figurative use of *gear up* derives from the literal mechanical meaning 'to go into a higher gear so that the driven part goes faster than the driving part'—in other words, to shift into a higher gear in order to go faster. This expression is frequently heard in economic contexts, as in "to gear up production."

up the ante To raise the stakes, to increase the risk. In poker the ante is the sum that each player pays into the pot in advance; by extension, in other monetary contexts it refers to the share invested in a business venture. The variant *raise the ante* is usually limited to these more literal uses. *Up the ante*, however, frequently appears in a nonfinancial sense, with respect to the increased personal or emotional cost entailed by a given decision, relationship, or course of action.

AUTHENTICITY   (See GENUINENESS.)

AUTHORITATIVENESS

chapter and verse An authority that gives credence and validity to one's opinions or beliefs; a definitive source that can be specifically cited. The phrase derives from the Scriptures which are arranged in chapters and verses, thus facilitating easy reference to particular lines. In non-Biblical contexts, *chapter and verse* is frequently a challenge to produce incontrovertible, detailed evidence for one's opinions. Figurative use dates from the early 17th century.

> She can give chapter and verse for her belief. (William Makepeace Thackeray, *The Adventures of Philip on His Way Through the World*, 1862)

ex cathedra Authoritatively, dogmatically, officially; Latin for 'from the chair.' *Cathedra* itself refers to the chair or seat of a bishop in his church. Most specifically, it refers to that of the Bishop of Rome, the Pope, who according to church doctrine is infallible when speaking ex cathedra since he is not speaking for himself but as the successor and agent of Saint Peter. More generally *cathedra* means any seat of office or professorial chair. Anyone speaking from such a seat of power or knowledge would naturally speak with great authority. The phrase dates from at least 1635.

from the horse's mouth On good authority, from a reliable source, directly from someone in the know; often in the phrase *straight from the horse's mouth*. The allusion is to the practice of looking at a horse's teeth to determine its age and condition, rather than relying on the word of a horse trader.

> The prospect of getting the true facts—straight, as it were, from the horse's mouth—held him . . . fascinated. (P. G. Wodehouse in *Strand Magazine*, August, 1928)

in black and white In writing or in print—black referring to the ink, white to the paper; certain, verifiable. Written opinion or assertion is assumed to carry more weight than a verbal one. The phrase has been in use since the time of Shakespeare.

> Moreover sir, which indeed is not under white and black, this plaintiff here . . . did call me ass. (Shakespeare, *Much Ado About Nothing* V,i)

AUTOMOBILES   (See VEHICLES.)

AVARICE   (See DESIRE.)

AVOIDANCE   (See EVASIVENESS.)

AWKWARDNESS

all thumbs Awkward, inept; clumsy, butterfingered. A forerunner of the current expression appeared in John Heywood's *Proverbs* in 1546:

> When he should get ought, each finger is a thumb.

The phrase as we know it was in use by 1870:

> Your uneducated man is all thumbs, as the phrase runs; and what education does for him is to supply him with clever fingers. (*The Echo*, November 16, 1870)

flub the dub See RUINATION.

have two left feet To be unusually clumsy; uncoordinated, maladroit. The expression does not constitute an image of deformity, but an emphasis on the negative concepts of *left* as 'gauche, awkward, clumsy.'

> Mr. Dawson . . . gave it as his opinion that one of the lady dancers had two left feet. (P. G. Wodehouse, *Psmith Journalist*, 1915)

B

BARGAIN   (See **AGREEMENT**.)

BASICS   (See **FUNDAMENTALS**.)

BEGINNINGS   (See also **INITIATION**, **STARTING**.)

at first blush   At first sight; apparently, at first appearances; on the first impression. The *blush* of this expression is from the Middle English *blusche* 'glance, glimpse.' Thus, given a brief exposure to something, one might qualify an evaluation by using this expression.

> At the first blush, it would seem that little difficulties could be experienced. (Benjamin Disraeli, *Coningsby; or the New Generation*, 1844)

back to the drawing board   See **FAILURE**.

a clean slate   *Tabula rasa*, a blank record; a fresh start, a new beginning; often in the phrase *to wipe the slate clean*, meaning to forget the past and make a fresh start.

> I can conceive nothing more desirable in the interests of these embarrassed tenants than that they should have a clean slate. (*The Pall Mall Gazette*, September, 1888)

Literally a slab of slate rock for writing, *slate* is used figuratively to represent the record or history of a person's life. A clean slate, then, is one from which the past has been erased and which is ready to be written on again. The equivalent Latin term, now a part of the English language, means 'scraped tablet.'

a foot in the door   An in, a start, an opportunity or chance; usually in the phrase *to get one's foot in the door*. Although the exact origin of this expression is unknown, it may be an expansion of the phrase *to get one's foot in*, dating from the early 19th century. Putting one's foot in a doorway prevents it from being closed completely. In this expression *foot* is synecdochic for the body as a whole, the point being that once one's foot is inside the door, the rest of the body will follow.

from scratch   From the very beginning; without building on a pre-existing product or structure; without using prepared ingredients. *Scratch* is a line or mark indicating the starting point in a race. Figurative use of *from scratch* stresses the idea of a true beginning which allows for no head start or short cuts, as implied in William DuBois' reference to "the task of organizing a major institution of learning almost from scratch" cited in *Webster's Third*. The expression is frequently heard in regard to cooking without using a "mix" or other ready-made ingredients.

get off on the right foot   To begin propitiously, to have an auspicious start. The phrase's origin probably lies in the now less frequently heard *right foot foremost*, an expression related to the Roman superstition that one should always enter and leave a room or dwelling right foot first. Thus the current *right* 'correct' figurative meaning was originally *right* 'right side' contrasted with *left* 'left side' and its attendant sinister, evil connotations. See also **get up on the wrong side of the bed**, **ILL TEMPER**.

get to first base   To complete the initial step of a task; to finish the preliminaries of a project or undertaking. This expression originated in baseball, where a batter's initial task is to reach first base. The phrase's figurative meaning of making a preliminary breakthrough is commonly heard, though most often in a context of failure to do so.

> I thought I'd read Italian to read Dante and didn't get to first base. (F. Scott Fitzgerald, *Letters*, 1938)

The expression is frequently used by men to describe a minor victory in the seduction of a woman.

> She gives you the feeling that you'll never get to first base with her.
> (P. G. Wodehouse, *Service with a Smile*, 1962)

hang out one's shingle To advertise one's professional status; to open an office; to begin one's career. This colloquial Americanism derives from the practice of displaying a shingle, or sign, to advertise the names and services of professionals. Today the expression is used in referring to the beginning of a practice or career, regardless of whether an actual sign is involved.

> Jobless, Metcalf put out his shingle as a food consultant. (*Newsweek*, August 22, 1949)

pick up the pieces To rebuild one's shattered life; to put the past behind one and make a fresh start. Though this common expression is most often heard in a context of personal, emotional crisis, it is also possible to "pick up the pieces" of any project or undertaking that has been left in shambles and carry it forward to fruition.

pick up the threads To resume an undertaking after a period of absence or inactivity; to pick up where one left off. The allusion is to weaving.

stick one's spoon in the wall To move into new quarters; to establish residence. In former times, one of the first things a person did upon acquiring a new domicile was to hang a leather pouch on a wall by the fireplace for the placement of spoons, scissors, and other sundry items. The expression is rarely heard nowadays.

BELLIGERENCE

all horns and rattles Belligerent; angry; enraged. The allusion is to the horns of cattle, used to butt or gore when these animals are angered; and to the rattles of rattlesnakes—horny, loosely connected rings at the end of the tail which are shaken vigorously in warning when this reptile is provoked to attack. The expression was originally used in reference to American cowboys, who because of their work would be closely associated with both cattle and snakes.

at daggers drawn or **drawing** About to quarrel; on the verge of open hostilities; at swords' points. In the 16th century, gentlemen often carried daggers. When affronted by either look or gesture, these men would defend their honor by using the dagger.

> They . . . among themselves are wont to be at daggers drawing.
> (Nicholas Grimaldi, *Cicero's Offices*, 1553)

a chip on one's shoulder A quarrelsome or antagonistic disposition; the attitude of one spoiling for a fight; an unforgiven grievance; usually in the phrase *to have a chip on one's shoulder.* The following explanation of this American expression appeared in the May 1830 *Long Island Telegraph* (Hempstead, N.Y.):

> When two churlish boys were determined to fight, a chip would be placed on the shoulder of one, and the other demanded to knock it off at his peril.

hawk An exponent of war; an adamant proponent of warlike policy. This term, clearly derived from the aggressive bird of prey, was first used figuratively by Thomas Jefferson in 1798, prior to the War of 1812. The expression was revived during President John F. Kennedy's handling of the Cuban missile crisis in 1962. During the controversial Vietnam War, *hawk* became an American household word for any person in favor of the war, as opposed to *dove* 'peace advocate.'

> The committee seems to have become immersed immediately in a struggle between doves and hawks.
> (D. Boulton, *Objection Overruled*, 1967)

horn-mad Belligerent, infuriated; mad enough to butt or gore with the horns, as cattle. This term, which dates from at least 1721, appeared in *The American Museum:*

> He is horn mad, and runs bellowing like a bull. (1787)

on the warpath Antagonistic, hostile, deliberately looking for a fight. The warpath was the route taken by the North American Indians on warlike expeditions. By extension, this American-ism came to refer to any individual or group preparing for war or behaving in a hostile, contentious manner.

> She was on the war-path all the evening. (Mark Twain, *Tramps Abroad,* 1880)

speak daggers To speak in such a way as to offend someone, hurt someone's feelings, or convey open hostility; to use words as weapons of attack; also *look daggers.*

> I will speak daggers to her, but use none. (Shakespeare, *Hamlet* III,ii)

> And do thine eyes shoot daggers at that man that brings thee health? (Philip Massinger and Thomas Dekker, *The Virgin Martyr, A Tragedy,* 1622)

trail one's coat To spoil for a fight, to try to pick a fight, to look for trouble. This expression reputedly refers to an Old Irish custom whereby a person spoiling for a fight would drag his coat on the ground as provocation for another to step on it.

BENEFICENCE (See CHARITABLE-NESS.)

BETRAYAL

fifth columnist A traitor, quisling; a subversive or an enemy sympathizer. This term's origin dates from the Span-ish Civil War (1936–39) when the Loy-alist government in Madrid had been infiltrated by many Franco sympathiz-ers. In a radio broadcast to the Loyalists, General Gonzalo Queipo de Llano y Sierro, a Fascist revolutionary, stated, "We have four columns on the bat-tlefield against you, and a fifth column inside your ranks."

Fifth Column is also the title of a play (1938) by Ernest Hemingway. During World War II, these expressions re-ceived widespread use, usually refer-ring to revolutionary sympathizers who had secured positions of influence in matters of security and policy decision. These insurgents spread rumors and practised espionage and sabotage, ex-ploiting the fears of the people and often inciting panic.

> Parliament has given us the powers to put down the fifth column activ-ities with a strong hand. (Winston Churchill, *Into Battle,* 1941)

Judas kiss A sign of betrayal, duplicity, or insincerity. The reference is to the kiss Judas Iscariot gave Jesus in betray-ing him to the authorities:

> And he that betrayed him had given them a token, saying, Whomsoever I shall kiss, that same is he. (Mark 14:44)

The term dates from as early as 1400.

> Candour shone from his eyes, as insincere as a Judas kiss. (R. Lewis, *Blood Money,* 1973)

the most unkindest cut of all See AD-VERSITY.

rat To inform or squeal; to desert and turn renegade, to bolt and join the op-position. The noun *rat* has been an op-probrious epithet since Elizabethan times. During the 18th century it took on, in political slang, the more specific denotation of traitor or turncoat. By the 19th century the corresponding verb usage appeared. It is generally believed that these slang meanings came by way of comparison with the apostate rats of the proverbial sinking ship, though the older more general 'scoundrel' mean-ing would suffice—rodents having long been objects of aversion and loathing to man.

scab A worker who resists union membership; a union member who refuses to strike. This disparaging expression likens the blue collar maverick to a pus-filled lesion. The epithet is often applied to an employee who crosses picket lines or more specifically, to a person who takes over the job of a striker for the duration of the work halt.

sell down the river To abandon or desert; to turn one's back on another; to delude or take advantage of. This expression originated in the Old South, where uncooperative slaves were often punished by being shipped downstream to the harsh, sweltering plantations of the lower Mississippi. The phrase maintains regular usage today.

> I think we are, as a people, a little inclined to sell our state down the river in our thinking. (*Daily Ardmoreite* [Ardmore, Oklahoma], December, 1949)

stool pigeon or **stoolie** A person who acts as a decoy; an informer, particularly one associated with the police. This expression is derived from the former practice of fastening a pigeon to a stool to attract other pigeons. Today the phrase usually refers to an informer who is betraying his cohorts.

> In New York City he is also called a Stool-pigeon. The "profession" generally speaks of him as a Squealer. (Willard Flynt, *World of Graft*, 1901)

turncoat One who abandons his convictions or affiliations; an apostate or renegade. This expression purportedly originated with a ploy of Emanuel, an early duke of Savoy, whose strategic territory was precariously situated between France and Italy. According to legend, in order to maintain peace with his powerful neighbors, Emanuel had a reversible coat made which was white on one side and blue on the other. He wore the white side when dealing with the French and the blue side when dealing with the Italians. The duke was

subsequently called Emanuel Turncoat, and the epithet attained its now familiar meaning of renegade or tergiversator.

> The Tory who voted for those motions would run a great risk of being pointed at as a turncoat by the . . . Cavaliers. (Thomas Macaulay, *History of England*, 1855)

BIAS (See **PREFERENCE, PREJUDICE.**)

BLACKMAIL (See **EXTORTION.**)

BOASTING

blow one's own trumpet To brag or boast; to call attention to one's own accomplishments, usually with the implication that no one else is likely to do so; also, *to toot one's own horn.* Though specific customs have been cited as giving rise to the phrase, the widespread and longstanding use of trumpets as attention-getting instruments seems explanation enough. Important personages and proclamations have long been heralded by a flourish of trumpets. In the New Testament, Jesus tells his followers not to blow their own horns, so to speak:

> When therefore thou doest alms, sound not a trumpet before thee, as the hypocrites do in the synagogues and in the streets, that they may have glory of men. Verily I say unto you, They have received their reward. (Matthew 6:2)

crow over To exult over a victory or accomplishment; to boast or vaunt. The allusion is to a gamecock's exultant crowing after defeating an opponent. This expression dates from 1588.

Dutch courage See **BRAVERY.**

geneva courage See **BRAVERY.**

BOISTEROUSNESS

hell on wheels Rowdy, riotous, wild, boisterous. The expression is said to have been commonly applied to towns that sprang up along the Union Pacific Railroad line during the 1860s because of the gunmen, gamblers, and prostitutes who inhabited them in such large numbers. The phrase has been in use since at least 1843.

> He's hell on wheels on Monday mornings. (J. Pearl, *The Crucifixion of P. McCabe*, 1966)

joy ride A reckless, high-speed excursion, often made in a borrowed or stolen car; a pleasant jaunt in an automobile or aircraft. This expression conjures up an image of exhilarated teenagers screeching through city intersections in high-powered hot rods. Modern use of the phrase, however, usually carries an implication of illegality.

> A man who drove away two cars for a "joy ride" was fined 75 pounds. (*Scottish Sunday Express*, August, 1973)

raise Cain To behave in a boisterous and rowdy manner, to create a disturbance, to raise a ruckus; also to protest vigorously, to raise a hue and cry, to make a fuss. Most sources relate the expression to the Biblical fratricide, Cain, but make no attempt to explain his transition from agent to object. It may be that his name became associated with evil incarnate and thus came euphemistically to replace *devil*, once considered profane, so that *raise the devil* gave way to *raise Cain* which found favor because of its greater brevity and musicality. Since the first recorded American usage involves a pun, it is safe to assume that the expression was commonplace by that time.

> Why have we every reason to believe that Adam and Eve were both rowdies? Because . . . they both raised Cain. (*St. Louis Pennant*, May, 1840)

BOREDOM

cut and dried See SIMPLIFICATION.

dry-as-dust Boring, extremely dull or dry; prosaic, unimaginative; concerned with petty, uninteresting details. Dr. Dryasdust is the name of a fictitious character created by Sir Walter Scott in the early 19th century. The Doctor, a learned antiquary, wrote the introductory material or was mentioned in the prefaces to Scott's novels. Currently, adjectival use of the term is most common.

> She considered political economy as a dry-as-dust something outside the circle of her life. (Mary E. Braddon, *Just as I am*, 1880)

a month of Sundays See DURATION.

the screaming meemies See ANXIETY.

BRAVERY

as bold as Beauchamp Brave, courageous, daring. Some say this now little-heard phrase derives from the celebrated feat of Thomas Beauchamp, who in 1346 defeated 100 Normans with one squire and six archers. Almost 300 years later a play entitled *The Three Bold Beauchamps* was written, which is cited as another possible source for *as bold as Beauchamp* or *bold Beauchamp*.

derring-do Daring deeds, brave feats, acts of heroism. The term owes its existence to a series of repeated printing and copying errors which converted the original verb phrase *daring to do* to the now common noun *derring-do*.

Dutch courage A false sense of courage or bravery induced by alcohol; pot-valor or pot-valiancy. This colloquial expression, in use since at least 1826, is an allusion to the heavy drinking for which the Dutch people were known. The term appeared in Herbert Spencer's *The Study of Sociology* (1873):

> A dose of brandy, by stimulating the circulation, produces "Dutch courage."

fear no colors To be audacious; to be unflinching in the face of hostility or danger. In this expression, *colors* carries its early military meaning of 'flag.' In Shakespeare's *Twelfth Night*, Malvolio ascribes this military origin to the phrase. The term was more figuratively used by Jonathan Swift in *Tale of a Tub* (1704):

He was a person that feared no colours, but mortally hated all.

geneva courage Courage produced by alcohol intoxication; foolhardy boasting triggered by drunkenness. The *geneva* of this expression has no connection with the Swiss city, but refers rather to a Dutch gin called Hollands or *geneva*. *Geneva courage* is thus virtually synonymous with *Dutch courage* or *pot-valor*.

heart of oak A valiant, stalwart spirit; a man of great courage and endurance; a man of superior quality. The heart or core of a tree is literally 'the solid central part without sap or albumen.' The expression has been in figurative use since at least 1609.

Heart of oak are our ships, heart of oak are our men. (*New Song* in *Universal Magazine*, March, 1760)

BRIBERY (See also **EXTORTION, GRAFT, PLACATION.**)

blood money The price on someone's head, the money paid as reward for incriminating evidence or betrayal, especially such as will result in another's death. The term *blood money* also refers to the Anglo-Saxon *wergild* or compensation paid to the kin of a murder victim to prevent continued retaliatory feuding.

cross [someone's] palm To give money to someone, especially as a bribe; to grease someone's palm or hand. *Cross [someone's] palm* is not as common, nor as old, as *grease [someone's] palm*, and its connotations not so strongly sinister. *Cross* probably refers to the action of placing bills across a person's hand as a bribe is transacted. In another sense, it was customary to pay fortune tellers, especially gypsies, by crossing their palms (with silver), perhaps in a ritualized making of the sign of the cross to ward off prognostications of evil or merely for a lucky reading.

glove money Bribe money; so-called from the gratuity or tip given to servants for the purpose of buying a pair of gloves; also *glove-silver.* Thomas F. Thiselton-Dyer offers this slightly different explanation of the expression in his book on folklore:

The gift of a pair of gloves was at one time the ordinary perquisite of those who performed some small service; and in process of time, to make the reward of greater value, the glove was "lined" with money; hence the term "glove-money."

The term, no longer in current use, dates from the early 18th century.

grease [someone's] palm To bribe someone; to use money illegally for unauthorized services; sometimes *grease the hand* or *fist.* This slang phrase dates from the early 16th century.

With gold and grotes they grease my hand. (John Skelton, *Magnificence,* 1526)

Grease used figuratively means 'to facilitate or smooth the way.' In the case of bribery, one smooths the way by placing money in someone else's hands. A variant of the full expression is the truncated *grease.* Current since the turn of the century is another variant *oil [someone's] palm.*

grease the wheels To take action to make things run smoothly; to use money as an expedient. In use since the 19th century, this expression does not necessarily connote financial deceit, although it clearly does so in the following citation:

The party I mean is a glutton for money, but I will do my best with him. I think a hundred pounds . . . would grease his wheels. (Sir A. H. Elton, *Below the Surface,* 1857)

have an ox on the tongue To be paid to remain silent; to be bribed to secrecy. This obsolete expression originated in ancient times, when cattle was considered an important commodity for barter; moreover, early metallic coins often bore the visage of an ox. Thus to *have an ox on the tongue* came to mean 'made mute by money.'

oil of angels Money or gold, particularly when used as a gift or bribe. Angel in this expression refers to the 15th century English coin which bore the visage of Michael the Archangel. Figuratively, the phrase implies that money provides soothing, oil-like relief to greedy hands.

> The palms of their hands so hot that they cannot be cooled unless they be rubbed with the oil of angels. (Robert Greene, *A Quip from an Upstart Courtier*, 1592)

a sop to Cerberus A token intended to pacify another; a gift or tribute to appease an adversary; a bribe, hush-money. This expression is derived from the ancient Greek and Roman custom of placing a *sop* cake in the hands of a cadaver. The sop was intended to placate Cerberus, the three-headed dog that guarded the gates of Hades, who, after receiving the offering allowed the dead to pass.

> I will throw down a napoleon, as a sop to Cerberus. (Horatio Smith, *Gaities and Gravities*, 1825)

BURDEN

albatross around the neck Burden, weight; any inhibiting encumbrance. In Samuel Taylor Coleridge's *The Rime of the Ancient Mariner* (1798), the slayer of the albatross—a bird of good omen to sailors—was punished by having the dead bird hung about his neck. Though within the context of the poem the dead albatross symbolizes guilt and punishment for sin, its contemporary use rarely carries this connotation. Often an albatross around one's neck is no more than a burdensome annoyance, a "drag" that inhibits one's freedom or lessens one's pleasure.

ball and chain A wife; one's girl friend or mistress; any person perceived as a burden or hindrance. This figurative meaning of *ball and chain* is derived from the iron ball which is secured by a chain to the leg of a prisoner in order to prevent escape. Insofar as having a wife inhibits one's freedom, this slang expression is apt.

> He deliberately attempted to commit suicide by askin' me "How's the ball and chain?" meanin' my wife. (*Collier's*, June 25, 1921)

cross to bear A painful burden or affliction; an oppressive encumbrance. The expression derives from the heavy cross which Jesus was forced to carry up Mount Calvary, and upon which he was subsequently crucified. Though the phrase most often applies to serious illness, pain, or handicaps, it is frequently extended to include any bothersome annoyance, any unpleasant person or circumstance that must be endured.

a millstone around the neck A heavy burden, an onus, a cross. A millstone is either of a pair of round, weighty stones between which grain and other like materials are ground in a mill.

> The mill-stone intended for the necks of those vermin . . . the dealers in corn, was found to fall upon the heads of the consumers. (Jeremy Bentham, *Defence of Usury*, 1787)

The metaphor is said to have been suggested by the Biblical passage (Matthew 18:6) in which Jesus warns those who would corrupt the pure and humble nature of children:

> But whoso shall offend one of these little ones which believe in me, it were better for him that a millstone were hanged about his neck, and that he were drowned in the depth of the sea.

a monkey on one's back A depressing, often controlling burden; a cross to bear; an addiction or dependence. This phrase may be a variation of the obsolete *a turkey on one's back*, but the implication remains the same: an addict carries an extra burden, one demanding a large, if not total, commitment of time, effort, and money to support.

> Having a monkey on your back . . . always worked out logically to be the first purpose in a junkie's life. (E. R. Johnson, *God Keepers*, 1970)

white elephant An unwanted or useless possession that is difficult to dispose of; a possession that costs more to keep and maintain than it is worth. This expression probably alludes to the albino elephants which were once considered sacred in Siam (now Thailand). Since an elephant of any color is inconvenient and expensive to own, it was purportedly a custom for a king to bestow one of these unique white elephants as a gift upon a courtier or other person whom he wished to subject to financial ruin. In the United States, tag sales, garage sales, and rummage sales are often appropriately nicknamed *white elephant sales*.

BURIAL

Davy Jones's locker A watery grave; the bottom of the ocean, especially as the grave of those who die at sea. In nautical slang, Davy Jones is the spirit of the sea, the sailor's devil. Of the many conjectures as to the derivation of this expression, the most plausible include theories such as: *Jones* is a corruption of Jonah; *Davy* is derived from *duppy* a ghost or spirit among West Indian

Negroes; and *locker* is a seaman's chest. While the phrase *Davy Jones's locker* has been in use only since 1803, the term *Davy Jones* dates from 1751.

God's acre A churchyard, a cemetery. Although Longfellow called this phrase "an ancient Saxon phrase," others claim that it is a more modern borrowing from the German *Gottesacker*.

> The Greeks call their Church-yards dormitories, sleeping-places. The Germans call them Godsacre. (John Trapp, *Annotations upon the Old and New Testament*, 1646)

According to *OED* citations, the phrase has been in print since the early 17th century.

hic jacet A tombstone or gravemarker; specifically, the inscription on such a tablet, from the Latin *hic jacet* 'here lies,' a common introduction to a gravestone epitaph.

> Among the knightly brasses of the graves,
> And by the cold Hic Jacets of the dead.
> (Alfred, Lord Tennyson, *Merlin and Vivien*, 1859)

marble orchard A graveyard or necropolis; also, *bone orchard*. This American slang expression is clearly derived from the multitudinous stone tablets in cemeteries.

> A couple more punches and it would have been the marble orchard for him. (B. Broadfoot, *Ten Lost Years*, 1973)

put to bed with a shovel See DRUNKENNESS.

C

CALLOUSNESS

key-cold Completely lacking in personal warmth and compassion; emotionally frigid; apathetic. This expression is derived from a key's metallic coldness, a property which was once thought to remedy nosebleeds. This obsolete phrase saw its heyday during the 1500s.

> The consideration of his incomparable kindness could not . . .
> fail to inflame our key-cold hearts.
> (Sir Thomas More, *Comfort Against Tribulation,* 1534)

weep millstones Said sarcastically of a callous, hard-hearted person, implying that he is not likely to weep at all. This expression is probably derived from *The Tale of Beryn* (1400):

> Tears . . . as great as any millstone.

Since a millstone is a large stone that grinds grain in a mill, its use here is, of course, hyperbolic. This expression was used several times by Shakespeare; for example, in *Richard III,* Gloucester states:

> Your eyes drop millstones, when fool's eyes drop tears. (I,iii)

CANDIDNESS

above-board In full view, in open sight; honestly, unsurreptitiously. The most widely held theory claims the phrase for card playing; gamblers were wont to engage in chicanery when their hands were out of sight and under the table (or board). Another source also attributes the term to the practice of gamesters, but to those who controlled wheels of fortune by means of a treadle hidden beneath a counter.

call a spade a spade To speak plainly or bluntly; to be straightforward and candid, sometimes to the point of rudeness; to call something by its real name. The ultimate source of this expression is Erasmus' translation of Plutarch's *Apophthegmata.* According to the *OED,* the phrase in question was mistranslated from the original Greek. The expression has been popular in English since Nicholas Udall's 1542 translation of the Erasmus version. An early example is in Humfrey Gifford's *A Posie of Gilloflowers* (1580):

> I cannot say the crow is white,
> But needs must call a spade a spade.

flat-footed Direct, to the point; firmly resolved, uncompromising; often heard in the phrase *come out flat-footed* 'to make a direct and firm statement of one's opinion or preference.' This American colloquial expression most likely derives from body language—a firm stance with legs slightly apart and both feet flat on the ground as a sign of determination and will. Both *flat-footed* and *come out flat-footed* have been in use since the mid-19th century.

> Mr. Pickens . . . has come out flat-footed for the Administration, a real red-hot Democrat, dyed in the wool. (*New York Herald,* June 30, 1846)

lay it on the line See RISK.

let one's hair down To relax; to act or speak informally; to speak candidly or intimately; to behave in an uninhibited, unrestrained manner, particularly in a situation requiring dignity and reserve. This figurative expression alludes to the fact that until fairly recently, a woman was expected to maintain a very staid and formal public image, and as a result, often wore her hair pinned up on the top of her head. In the privacy and relative comfort of her own home, however, such a woman usually felt free to relax and would let her hair down. It was in these informal moments that her true personality would be revealed.

You can let your hair down in front of me. (Jerome Weidman, *I Can Get It For You Wholesale!*, 1937)

A related expression is *hairdown* 'an intimate conversation.' In recent years, *let one's hair down* has largely been replaced by, and may in fact have given rise to, expressions such as *hang loose, loosen up,* and *let it all hang out.*

make no bones about To be outspoken, to deal with someone directly and openly; to go along with, to acquiesce without raising any objections. Variants of this expression appeared in print as early as the 15th century. A number of theories have been suggested to explain its origin, the most plausible being that it grew out of the literal *find bones in,* referring to the bones in soup which are an obstacle to its being safely swallowed. Thus *find bones in* became *make bones about,* meaning 'to scruple, to raise objections, or to offer opposition.'

Do you think that the Government or the Opposition would make any bones about accepting the seat if he offered it to them? (William Makepeace Thackeray, *The History of Pendennis*, 1850)

Currently the expression is heard almost exclusively in the negative.

On the other hand, Dr. Libby makes no bones about the catastrophe of a nuclear war. (*Bulletin Atomic Science*, September, 1955)

naked truth Plain, unadorned truth; unvarnished truth. According to an ancient fable, two goddesses, Truth and Falsehood, were bathing. Falsehood came out of the water first and adorned herself in Truth's clothes. Truth, not wishing to wear the trappings of Falsehood, decided to go naked. Thus the expression.

point blank Direct, straightforward, explicit; blunt, frank, unmincing. In ballistics, a weapon fired point-blank is one whose sights are aimed directly at a nearby target so that the projectile travels in a flat trajectory to its destination. By extension, then, a point-blank comment, question, accusation, etc., is one which is direct and to the point, one which does not mince words.

This is point-blank treason against my sovereign authority. (Samuel Foote, *The Lame Lover*, 1770)

skin the bear at once To come straight to the point, to waste no time getting down to brass tacks.

But now, to skin the *bar* at once, can you give me and five other gentlemen employment? (*The New Orleans Picayune*, September, 1844)

This U.S. colloquialism, the opposite of *to beat around the bush,* refers to the skinning of an animal immediately after it is slain because the hide is more easily removed then.

speak by the card To express oneself in a clear and concise manner; to carefully select one's words; to speak honestly. This expression appears in Shakespeare's *Hamlet:*

We must speak by the card, or equivocation will undo us. (V,i)

This phrase refers to a compass card, on which every point has its own precise and unambiguous designation.

I speak by the card in order to avoid entanglement of words. (Benjamin Jowett, *Plato*, 1875)

straight from the shoulder Frankly; candidly; truthfully; directly. This expression originated as a boxing term for the delivering of a direct, full-force punch. Today, the phrase retains its figurative meaning of the voicing of a forthright, unembellished comment.

A man that talks old-fashioned American Democracy straight from the shoulder. (R. D. Saunders, *Colonel Todhunter*, 1911)

talk turkey To speak frankly or plainly, to talk seriously and straightforwardly, to get to the point.

> Let's talk turkey about this threat to your welfare. (*Florida Grower*, February, 1950)

Legend has it that an American Indian and a white man out hunting together bagged a turkey and a crow. When the time came to split the catch, the white man said, "You may have your choice, you take the crow and I'll take the turkey, or if you'd rather, I'll take the turkey and you take the crow"; whereupon the Indian replied "Ugh! you no talk turkey to me a bit." Although this bit of etymological folklore should be taken with a massive dose of salt, it does serve to point out the importance of the turkey as food and therefore as serious business, a fact which may have given rise to the expression as it is used today.

warts and all With no attempt to conceal blemishes, weaknesses, failings, vices, foibles, etc. Portrait painters, particularly those commissioned by the powerful and prideful, were wont to depict their subjects in a favorable and flattering light. In doing so, they frequently completed canvases bearing but slight resemblance to the original, their artist's scalpel having excised warts, moles, scars, and other such blemishes; they also smoothed wrinkles, straightened bones, and otherwise played the plastic surgeon. The phrase *warts and all* has come to describe a visual or verbal portrait which aims at a realistic picture of its subject by presenting his "ugly" as well as his commendable side. According to William Safire's *Political Dictionary* (1978), the British statesman Oliver Cromwell (1599–1658) is reputed to have directed his portraitist:

> Use all your skill to paint my picture truly like me, and not to flatter me . . . remark all those roughnesses, pimples, warts, and

everything as you see me; otherwise I will never pay one farthing for it.

Occasionally the phrase is extended to intangibles such as plans, intentions, etc., when liabilities as well as assets are clearly communicated.

CAPABILITY (See ABILITY, COMPETENCE.)

CAREFULNESS (See CAUTIOUSNESS.)

CARELESSNESS

asleep at the switch Off one's guard; negligent; having slow reflexes. This expression derives from early American railroad terminology. To switch a train is to transfer it from one track to another, and an unaware or negligent worker who was "asleep at the switch" could cause a serious accident. The expression is no longer restricted to railroad usage and can apply to any irresponsible lack of attention which could have adverse consequences.

give short shrift To pay little attention or give insufficient time or consideration to a person or matter; to treat in a cursory or perfunctory manner. *Shrift* is an archaic word for confession or absolution (from the verb *shrive*). *Short shrift* originally referred to the brief period prior to an execution during which a prisoner could make a confession to a priest.

> Short trial, shorter shrift, had been given to the chief criminals. (William Hepworth Dixon, *Royal Windsor*, 1879)

The phrase eventually came into more general use referring to any brief respite or short period of time. Thus "to give short shrift" means to treat summarily or brusquely, giving little of one's time or energy.

> Every argument . . . tells with still greater force against the present measure, and it is hoped that the House of Commons will give it

short shrift tonight. (*Times,* February 15, 1887)

a lick and a promise A hasty and perfunctory way of doing something; a half-hearted or nominal compliance with a request or command. In this expression, *lick* is used in the colloquial sense of 'a slight and hasty wash,' implying a lackadaisical or superficial performance of a task. *Promise* implies an assurance that a more complete and thorough job will be done at some unspecified time in the future.

> The lassie gi'es a lick and a promise when I tell her to sweep! (E. F. Heddle, *Marget at Manse,* 1899)

slap-bang Hastily, often without consideration of possible consequences; hurriedly; haphazardly. This expression was originally used to describe sleazy eateries and "greasy spoons" where one received fast service by "slapping" his money down to pay for food that was indelicately "banged" onto the table.

> They lived in the same street, walked to town every morning at the same hour, dined at the same slap-bang every day, and revelled in each other's company every night. (Charles Dickens, *Sketches by Boz,* 1837)

Thus, by extension, *slap-bang* came to refer to anything done in a quick, careless, and unceremonious manner.

> After fooling a man like a child in leading-strings for half a year, to let him go slap-bang, as I call it, in a minute, is an infernal shame. (Theodore Hook, *The Parson's Daughter,* 1833)

slapdash Carelessly; in a hasty though thoughtless manner; hurriedly; haphazardly. Originally, *slapdash* was a technique of painting a wall to give it the appearance of wallpaper by "slapping" on a coat of paint and then "dashing" or splashing on spots or blotches of a contrasting color. Although *slapdash* is frequently applied as a criticism to a writer's or an artist's style, it is also applied in other contexts to denote careless haste.

> I cannot plunge, slapdash, into the middle of events and characters. (Sir George Trevelyan, *The Life and Letters of Lord Macaulay,* 1838)

CAUTIOUSNESS

butter one's bread on both sides See IMPROVIDENCE.

cover all bases To protect oneself against possible loss by anticipating and preparing for all possible alternatives in a given situation; to hedge one's bets. This American slang expression derives from baseball. An infielder is stationed near or at a base at which a play is anticipated; the base is then said to be "covered."

cover one's tracks See CONCEALMENT.

handle with kid gloves To handle very gingerly and tactfully, to treat very gently and with the utmost caution and care; to pamper or mollycoddle. Leather made from the skin of a kid, or young goat, is especially soft. Perhaps this expression, which dates from at least 1864, is in some way connected with the opposing phrase *to handle without gloves* or *with gloves off* 'to deal with harshly or with exceptional plainness or frankness,' in use as early as 1827. In James Bryce's *The American Commonwealth* (1888) he refers to

> . . . the Americans who think that European politics are worked, to use the common phrase, "with kid gloves."

have two strings to one's bow To have an alternative plan of action should an unexpected emergency occur; to have something to fall back on; not to put all one's eggs in one basket; to have more than one means of supporting oneself. In print since the 16th century, this expression alludes to the custom of archers carrying a spare bowstring in case the original one should break. In current use, such precaution can take the form of financial savvy, practicality in affairs of the heart (as in the following quotation), or any expedient employed to prevent one from being left in the lurch.

> Miss Bertram . . . might be said to have two strings to her bow. (Jane Austen, *Mansfield Park,* 1812)

hedge one's bets To protect against possible loss by cross-betting; to wager against a previous bet or other speculation in order to lessen possible losses; to equivocate or shift, to beat around the bush; also simply *hedge.* This expression, which dates from 1672, appears in Macaulay's *History of England:*

> He (Godolphin) began to think . . . that he had betted too deep on the Revolution and that it was time to hedge.

look to one's laurels To be aware of the ephemeral nature of one's preeminence; to continually strive to protect one's status as the lead in any field. The opposite of *rest on one's laurels,* this expression appeared in print by the middle of the 19th century.

> The fair widow would be wise to look to her laurels. (Mrs. J. H. Riddell, *Prince of Wale's Garden-Party,* 1882)

the mouse that has but one hole is quickly taken An old proverb expressing the necessity of alternate plans, somewhat similar to the currently popular *don't put all your eggs in one basket.* The original Latin was *mus non uni fidit antro* 'the mouse does not trust to one hole.' A variant of the expression appears in Chaucer's "Prologue" to *The Wife of Bath's Tale* (1386).

play close to one's vest To take no unnecessary risks, to act cautiously or carefully. Originally a gambling phrase, this expression referred to a player who kept his cards close to his vest to hide them from the sight of others. By extension, the expression came to mean a skillful, cautious player who does not reveal his strengths or weaknesses, one

who does not *tip his hand.* It subsequently came to be applied to a person who exercises extreme caution in any venture.

walk a tightrope To maintain a precarious balance between opposing forces; to manage to please, or at best not to offend opposing factions; to straddle the fence, to play both ends against the middle. Obviously drawn from the acrobat's act, the figure finds appropriate application in many political contexts. In *Gulliver's Travels* Swift describes the rope dancers at the court of Lilliput, conceptual if not verbal forebears of today's tightrope walkers.

> Those persons who are candidates for great employments, and high favour, at court . . . petition the Emperor to entertain his Majesty and the court with a dance on the rope, and whoever jumps the highest without falling, succeeds in the office.

The expression is not limited to political contexts, however, and can be applied to anyone trying to reconcile or mediate seemingly antithetical entities or enemies—labor and big business, for example, or as in the following recent usage, artistic value and financial profit.

> Mayer . . . is dedicated to the idea of books as works of the spirit and not just products for cost accounting. Those who are drawn to the spectacle of tightrope walking can look forward to more of Peter Mayer's inventive and exciting balancing acts. (Walter Arnold, in *Saturday Review,* February, 1979)

walk on eggs To act cautiously and carefully because of the delicacy of a situation, to skate on thin ice; also to *tread on eggs.* This expression dates from the early 18th century.

CENSURE (See **REPRIMAND**.)

CERTAINTY

bet one's boots To be absolutely sure or certain of something. The reference is to a gambler (perhaps a cowboy, whose boots are among his most important possessions) so sure of winning that he will bet everything he owns, including his boots. The phrase appeared in 1856 in *Spirit of Times.* Similar expressions are *bet one's life* and *bet one's bottom dollar.*

dead to rights Indisputably, unquestionably; positively, assuredly; usually in the phrases *have someone dead to rights* or *caught dead to rights,* in which it is equivalent to 'in the act, redhanded.' Attempts to explain the origin of this American colloquial expression are frustrating and futile. *Dead* appears to be used in its meaning of 'absolutely, utterly'; but the equivalent British expression *bang to rights* suggests something closer to 'directly, precisely.' The context of wrongdoing in which the phrase always appears in early citations indicates that *to rights* may relate to the rights of the guilty party, but the theory does not withstand careful analysis. The *OED* suggests a connection between the *to rights* of the phrase and the obsolete *to rights* 'in a proper manner,' but no citations contain analogous syntactic constructions. Despite its refusal to yield an elucidating explanation, *dead to rights* has been a commonly used expression since the mid-1800s.

dollars to doughnuts A sure thing, a certainty; usually in the phrase *bet you dollars to doughnuts,* in use since 1890. Although the precise origin of this expression is unknown, it obviously plays on the value of a dollar contrasted with the relative small worth of a doughnut, which once cost 5¢. Anyone willing to wager dollars to doughnuts is confident of winning his bet. One use of the expression apparently referred to the declining value of the dollar:

> Dollars to doughnuts is a pretty even bet today. (*Redbook*, 1947)

eat one's hat To admit willingness to "eat one's hat" is to express certainty and confidence, and to be ready to

abase oneself should things not turn out as one had anticipated. Should such cocksureness prove ill-founded, "eating one's hat" would be analogous to "eating crow" or "eating one's words." The first use of this expression is attributed to Charles Dickens in *The Pickwick Papers* (1837).

> If I knew as little of life as that, I'd eat my hat and swallow the buckle whole.

Of British origin, *eat one's hat* is currently popular in the United States as well.

eggs is eggs Surely, definitely, absolutely, without a doubt. Usually used as an interjection or in the phrase *sure as eggs is eggs,* this British colloquialism is probably a humorous twist or an ignorant mispronunciation of "X" in the familiar algebraic equation, "X is X."

> [After examining me] the doctor shook his head and said, "Eggs is eggs." (Johnny Carson, on *The Tonight Show,* NBC Television, 1978)

far and away Absolutely, incomparably, easily, undoubtedly; by far. Used to increase the intensity of a superlative adjective, this expression implies that there are no competitors or contenders within reach of this description.

> You are far and away the greatest scoundrel I ever saw. (William E. Norris, *Thirlby Hall,* 1883)

hands down See EFFORTLESSNESS.

in spades Definitely, emphatically, to the utmost degree; without restraint or qualification; no ifs, ands, or buts. This expression connoting extremeness derives from the fact that spades are the highest suit in some card games. *In spades* is used as an intensifier, as in the following citation from *Webster's Third:*

> [I] have thought him a stinker, in spades, for many years (Inez Robb)

in the bag Assured, certain. The most plausible and frequent explanation holds that the reference is to game which has been killed and bagged, i.e., put in the gamebag. One source claims a cockfighting origin for the term; since a live gamecock is literally brought to the pits in a bag, for the owner confident of victory, "It's in the bag."

lead-pipe cinch An absolute certainty; a certain success; something that is easily accomplished; a piece of cake. In this expression, *cinch* refers to a saddle girth, the beltlike strap used to secure the saddle on a horse. If the cinch were tight enough, the rider did not have to worry about the saddle's slipping; in fact, it was a certainty that the saddle would stay in place. Although the rationale for the inclusion of "leadpipe" in this expression is unclear, it is possible that the relative ease with which lead for (waste) plumbing could be worked (compared with cast iron) gave rise to *lead-pipe* as an intensifier.

> It is a double-barrelled lead-pipe cinch that you'll be more anxious to get it back than you ever were about a $10 loan overdue. (*Outing*, July, 1921)

on ice See ABEYANCE.

shoo-in A candidate, athlete, team, or other competitor considered to be a sure winner; the favorite. This expression employs the verb phrase *to shoo-in* 'to cause to go into' as a noun.

> In the [Republican presidential] preferential poll, Taft looked like a shoo-in over Stassen. (AP wire story, May 13, 1952)

sure as shooting Certainly without a doubt, most assuredly. This colloquialism of American origin appeared in print by the mid-1800s. It was probably a cowboy expression referring to one's need for *sure* 'accurate' shooting to avoid being shot dead in turn.

> Sure as shootin' . . . one of these days one of my customers will be coming in and telling me he caught a fish with one of your jackets. (*Field and Stream*, June 19, 1947)

CESSATION (See also TERMINATION, THWARTING.)

call off the dogs To ease up on; to lay off of; to discontinue some disagreeable line of conduct, conversation, inquiry, procedure, or the like. The reference is to hunting; when dogs are on the wrong track, they are called back.

Mexican stand-off A deadlock; a situation or contest in which neither party wins. Exactly what the word *Mexican* adds to this expression is unclear; most likely it was originally a racial slur. It has been conjectured that American cowboys used *Mexican stand-off* in referring to conflicts in which one could get away alive without engaging in serious fighting.

peter out To diminish gradually and then cease; to fade, die out, come to an end. In this expression, *peter* is derived from saltpeter (potassium nitrate), a component of explosives. Miners nicknamed these explosives "peter," and used them to expose veins of gold or other valuable minerals. When a vein was exhausted and could yield no more ore, it was said to have been "petered out." Eventually, *peter out* assumed its figurative meaning and has been in widespread use for more than a century.

> Human effort of all kinds tends . . . to "peter out." (*Saturday Review*, January 9, 1892)

stalemate A deadlock, standstill, impasse; a draw or stand-off; circumstances in which no action can be taken. This term originated in chess to describe a situation in which a player cannot make any moves without placing his king in check. As a result, the game ends in a draw, and neither player can claim a victory. *Stalemate* is derived from the old French *estal* 'a fixed position' and the Middle English *mat* 'helpless.'

> So far as the public can see, the match [between two armies] ended

in stalemate. (*Standard*, September, 1912)

CHALLENGE (See **DIFFICULTY**.)

CHAOS (See **DISORDER**.)

CHARITABLENESS

cast one's bread upon the waters To act charitably or generously without thought of return or personal profit. The reference is to Ecclesiastes 11:1:

Cast thy bread upon the waters; for thou shalt find it after many days.

sprout wings To do an act of charity; to perform a good deed. This expression is based on the conventional depiction of angels as winged beings. It is usually used jocularly to suggest that one is progressing toward a more angelic nature. The expression is occasionally extended to mean death, perhaps as an assumption that those bound for eternal bliss develop the wings of angels.

widow's mite A small amount of money, especially a small contribution that represents a great sacrifice from one with limited financial resources. This expression is Biblical in origin, *mite* referring to a coin of very little value, less than an eighth of a penny.

And there came a certain poor widow, and she threw in two mites, which make a farthing. . . . [And Christ said] this poor widow hath cast more in, than all they which have cast into the treasury: for all they did cast in of their abundance; but she of her want did cast in all that she had, even all her living. (Mark 12:42–44)

A commonly used variation is *mite*.

CHEATING (See **SWINDLING**.)

CLOSENESS (See **PROXIMITY**.)

CLOTHING

best bib and tucker Finery; Sunday-go-to-meeting clothes; glad rags. Though now applied to the dress of either sex, the phrase originally and properly described only that of women. Both items of clothing—bibs and tuckers—were lacy and frilly affairs worn about the bodice and neck in the 17th and 18th centuries.

brothel-creepers British slang for crepe-soled suede shoes. Such shoes were long associated in England with pimps, who were often seen to wear them. The term appeared in G. Smith's *Flaw in Crystal* in 1954:

"Poncing about the place in those brothel-creepers of his!" . . . He always wore plush suede shoes.

glad rags One's best or finest clothes; fancy or dressy clothes, especially formal evening dress; also *glad clothes* and *glads*. This self-evident American slang term has been in use since 1902. An equivalent but as yet unestablished slang term is *heavy threads*.

highwaters Unfashionably short trousers or slacks. This expression is derived from the humorous inference that one wearing blatantly short pants must be expecting a flood. Application of this phrase is obviously contingent upon the mandates of the fashion world.

monkey suit Formal clothes; a tuxedo; the full dress uniform of a serviceman, police officer, etc. This expression may be a modification of *monkey jacket*, a close-fitting coat formerly worn by sailors and similar in appearance to the stiff jacket worn by an organ-grinder's monkey. The phrase maintains some contemporary usage.

I . . . demothed my monkey-suit and borrowed some proper shoes. (Dylan Thomas, *Letters*, 1950)

soup-and-fish A man's formal clothing; a cutaway; white tie and tails. This term came to be jocularly applied to formal dress because soup and fish were so often served as the first courses of a formal dinner.

You will see more men informal than in soup and fish. (Jack Lait and Lee Mortimer, *New York Confidential,* 1948)

Sunday-go-to-meeting clothes   One's best or finest clothes; also *Sunday clothes, Sunday best,* and *Sunday-go-to-meetings.* The term, in use since 1831, is an expansion of *Sunday clothes,* and refers to the days when most people wore their finery only on Sunday, which was reserved for churchgoing and visiting.

CLUMSINESS   (See AWKWARD-NESS.)

COERCION   (See also EXTORTION.)

force [someone's] hand   To pressure someone into taking a stand or revealing his beliefs or intentions; to compel someone to act immediately and against his will. In print since the mid-19th century, this expression perhaps derives from card games in which one player forces another to play a particular card and thereby reveal the contents of his hand. Another possible theory is that *force [someone's] hand* is like *twist [someone's] arm,* suggesting that the present figurative use derives from actual physical force.

knobstick wedding   The forced marriage of a pregnant, unwed woman; a shotgun wedding. Churchwardens (lay officers who dealt with the secular affairs of the church and who were the legal representatives of the parish) formerly used their authority to ensure such marriages. The term *knobstick* 'a knobbed stick, cane, or club used chiefly as a weapon' refers to the churchwarden's staff, the symbol of his office, used as an instrument of coercion, or cudgel.

put the screws to   To compel action by exercise of coercion, pressure, extortion, blackmail, etc. The expression de-rives from an early method of torture involving the use of thumbscrews to extract confessions.

put the squeeze on   To pressure another for one's own purposes; to demand payment or performance by means of harassment or threats.

She hired me to put the squeeze on Linda for a divorce. (Raymond Chandler, *High Window,* 1942)

shotgun wedding   Any union, compromise, agreement, etc., brought about by necessity or threat; originally a wedding necessitated or hastened by the bride-to-be's pregnancy, a forced marriage; also *shotgun marriage.* The allusion is to an irate father attempting to protect his daughter's reputation by using a shotgun to threaten the man responsible for her condition into marrying her. Use of the expression dates from at least 1927.

Werdel . . . characterized the Brannan plan as a "shotgun wedding between agriculture and labor." (*California Citrograph,* January, 1950)

when push comes to shove   See EX-ACERBATION.

COMBAT

battle royal   A free-for-all; an encounter of many combatants; a heated argument or altercation. The term derives from the type of endurance contest, especially common in cockfighting, in which the ultimate victor is determined by a process of elimination through survival of many trial heats. The badly wounded survivor of these repeated pairings is often barely alive at battle's close. Another type of battle royal from which the expression might derive was the custom of entering a number of pugilists into the ring at once, who fought each other in random and brutal fashion until only one remained conscious. Ralph Ellison includes a graphic description of the barbarous practice in *Invisible Man.*

broach [someone's] claret To give someone a bloody nose. This euphemistically elegant expression for a very inelegant action and its result plays on the meaning of *broach* 'to draw liquor from a cask' and on claret as a red wine of Bordeaux.

donnybrook A wild fight or brawl, a melee or free-for-all; also *Donnybrook Fair.* For centuries, an annual two-week fair was held each summer in Donnybrook, Ireland. Invariably, vast amounts of whiskey were consumed and the huge crowds got out of control, turning the fair into a massive drunken brawl. Because of such consistently riotous behavior, the Donnybrook Fair was abolished in 1855, although to this day its name denotes any type of wild, general fighting.

fight like Kilkenny cats To fight fiercely and bitterly until both sides have been destroyed; to argue or debate viciously and with determination. Several marginally plausible legends surround this expression, the most popular of which holds that in the Irish Rebellion of 1798, some sadistic soldiers stationed in Kilkenny enjoyed the "sport" of tying two cats together by their tails and hanging them over a clothesline so that, face to face, they would fight to the death. When an officer approached to break up this daily activity, a soldier cut off the cats' tails with his sword, and the cats escaped. When confronted by the officer, the soldier insisted that the cats had fought so viciously that they had eaten each other, leaving only the tails behind. A more likely explanation, however, is that the cats are allegorical symbols for two rival towns, Kilkenny and Irishtown, which for more than 300 years waged a bitter border dispute. By 1700, both towns were devastated and impoverished. A similar expression is *as quarrelsome as Kilkenny cats.*

introduce the shoemaker to the tailor To kick someone in the buttocks or rear end; to kick someone in the pants. This euphemism is a British colloquial expression.

knock for a loop See CONFUSION.

knock galley-west To incapacitate, to put someone out of action; to give such a severe blow as to cause unconsciousness; to knock for a loop, to throw off balance, to disorient or confuse. *Galley-west* is an alteration of the British dialectal *colly-west* 'awry, askew.' This colloquial Americanism dates from the latter part of the 19th century. The phrase is not limited in application to physical combat; it can also apply to mental or emotional disorientation resulting from the debunking of one's ideas, arguments, or beliefs.

> Your verdict has knocked what little [critical penetration] I did have galley-west! (Mark Twain, *Letters,* 1875)

knock the tar out of To thrash, whale, or beat senseless; also often *beat the tar out of.* The precise origin of the phrase is unknown. A plausible conjecture says it derives from the former practice of caulking a ship's bottom with tar, which would require an extremely severe shock or blow to loosen.

lay out in lavender See REPRIMAND.

lead a cat and dog life To fight or bicker constantly; to be contentious, quarrelsome, or argumentative on a regular basis. This expression alludes to the snapping and vicious battling associated with these two animals whenever they encounter each other.

lock horns To enter into conflict; to clash; to contend. Various species of mammals have horns for self-defense, and the reference is probably to the locking of bucks' horns when they "duel." The expression suggests a vehement entanglement between two people.

make [someone] see stars To hit someone on the head with such force that he

COMEDY □ 42

experiences the illusion of brilliant spots of light before his eyes; to knock someone out.

make the fur fly To cause a ruckus or commotion, to create a disturbance, to shake things up; also *make the feathers fly*. The allusion is to animals or game-cocks engaged in such a violent struggle that they tear out each other's fur or feathers. Both expressions date from at least the 19th century.

> Al Hayman is going to make the fur fly when he gets back from Europe. (*New York Dramatic News,* July, 1896)

measure swords To fight or do battle either physically or verbally; to compete or contest, to match wits with, to pit one's strength against. This expression originated when dueling was the gentlemanly method of settling disputes and defending honor. Swords chosen as weapons were measured against each other to guarantee that they were of the same length and that neither party had an advantage. Although measuring swords was originally a preliminary to a duel or fight, by extension it came to mean the fighting itself. The equivalent French expression is *mesurer les épées*. Shakespeare uses the phrase in *As You Like It* (V,iv):

> And so we measured swords and parted.

pull caps To quarrel and wrangle in an undignified manner. *Cap* refers to 'headgear.'

> Our lofty Duchesses pull caps,
> And give each other's reputation raps.
> (Thomas Perronet Thompson, *Exercises, Political and Others,* 1842)

This obsolete expression dating from the 18th century reputedly applied only to women, although *OED* citations indicate that men also "pulled caps."

> Men are exhorted to struggle and pull caps. (John Wolcott, *Lyric Odes to the Royal Academicians,* 1785)

take up the hatchet To begin or resume fighting, to prepare for war; also *dig up* or *unbury the hatchet, ax,* or *tomahawk.* To symbolize the resumption of hostilities, North American Indians would dig up war weapons, which had been buried as a sign of good faith when concluding a peace.

> Three nations of French Indians . . . had taken up the hatchet against the English. (George Washington, *Daily Journal in 1751–52*)

The expression, now obsolete, dates from the late 1600s. See also **bury the hatchet,** PEACE.

tan [someone's] hide To whip, beat, or thrash soundly; to knock the tar out of someone. Theoretically, severe, repeated beatings would harden or toughen one's skin, just as the tanning process does to hide in converting it to leather. The expression has been used in this figurative sense since the 17th century.

wigs on the green A fight, altercation, fracas, fray; a commotion; a difference of opinion that could lead to fisticuffs. This expression stems from the days when British gentlemen wore powdered wigs and often settled differences "in manly fashion" on the public greens. Since their wigs were likely to be pulled off during the pugilistics, *wigs on the green* became a euphemistic reference to a scuffle or brawl.

> Whenever they saw them advancing, they felt that there would be wigs on the green. (Sir Montagu Gerard, *Leaves From the Diaries of a Soldier and Sportsman,* 1903)

COMEDY (See HUMOROUSNESS.)

COMMENDATION (See also FLATTERY.)

blurb A short, often witty, advertisement or laudatory recommendation; a descriptive paragraph on a book jacket;

a squib or plug. The American humorist and illustrator F. Gelett Burgess (1866–1951) coined the term in 1907 when he humorously dubbed the alluring woman adorning a comic book jacket Miss Blinda Blurb. Today, the term is commonly applied to short radio and television advertisements as well as to the descriptive paragraphs on book jackets.

hats off A command to pay respect; a cheer or call to honor or salute a person, a noble ideal, etc. This expression dates from the mid-19th century and is said to derive from the custom of removing one's hat as a sign of respect or deference.

> "Hats off to them." "Yes, of course. Hats off to all the dead." (M. Farhi, *Pleasure of Your Death*, 1972)

See also **cap in hand**, DEFERENCE.

praise from Sir Hubert The highest compliment; the greatest possible praise. This expression, now languishing in oblivion, originated in Thomas Morton's comedy *A Cure for the Heartache* (1797):

> Approbation from Sir Hubert Stanley is praise indeed.

take one's hat off to To recognize the preeminent achievements of another; to praise or extol the superlative accomplishments of another. This common expression is derived from the custom of removing one's hat as a sign of respect.

> We should take off our hats to them and wish them godspeed. (*Harper's Magazine*, June, 1886)

COMMUNICATION

bush telegraph or **jungle telegraph** A jocular reference to the communications system employed by African natives in which coded messages are sent over long distances by the beating of a drum or hollow log.

call one's shots To verbalize what one intends to do or in what manner one intends to act; to inform others of one's plans. This phrase probably derives from various billiards games in which a player must call out the shot he plans to make before attempting it. The similar expression *call the shots* shifts the emphasis from one's personal domain to a larger frame of reference in which an individual attempts to direct or control events, to be in charge, or to be in the driver's seat. *Call the shots* may derive from the director's role in film making.

get one's signals crossed To be involved in a mutual misunderstanding, to fail to communicate. This current expression may have derived from the telephonic "crossing" of circuits which can result in accidental connections, though the use of various types of signals for communication is so pervasive as to preclude a precise origin for the phrase. Figurative use of the expression plays on the idea of an "accident," implying mutual misunderstanding with no one at fault.

> Can we by any chance have got the wires crossed? . . . It *was* the idea, wasn't it, that we should pile on to a pot of tea together? (P. G. Wodehouse, *Hot Water*, 1932)

Today *signals* is heard more frequently than *wires*, perhaps reflecting technological advances which facilitate the transmission of signals without wires.

grapevine The route by which a rumor circulates. During the American Civil War, *grapevine telegraph* expressed the term's current figurative sense while *grapevine* referred to the rumor itself.

> Just another foolish grapevine. (B. F. Willson, *Old Sergeant*, 1867)

The expression attained its gossip circuit connotation by analogy to the labyrinthine network of branches characteristic of the climbing grape plant.

> The art world grape-vine buzzed with rumors. (*New Yorker*, October, 1970)

Irish hint A broad hint, an unsubtle intimation or insinuation. This rarely used Americanism appeared in Henry J. Nott's *Novellettes of a Traveller* (1834):

> Various young men, . . . intimated, in what might be called Irish hints that they had espied the worthy Mr. Hunt.

The reputed bluntness of the Irish may have given rise to the expression.

powwow A conference or meeting. This expression originally referred to the festive tribal ceremonies of American Indians. The term is commonly used today for any important council or convention.

> The Abolitionists are having a great pow-wow here as to whether they shall or shall not maintain their organization. (*Daily Telegraph,* May, 1865)

COMPARABILITY

hold a candle to To be comparable in degree or kind; to be equal to, or on the same level with; to compare favorably with. This expression dates from the 16th century. At that time, it was the custom for a servant to carry a candle to light the way for his master on a nighttime walk. This subordinate position required familiarity with the layout of a town. A servant who did not know his way around was considered unfit or unable to hold a candle to his master. Figurative use of this expression— heard almost exclusively in the negative—suggests that the disparity between two people or things is so great as to render comparison impossible. One who can not or does not hold a candle to another is considered inferior.

> Edith is pretty, very pretty; but she can't hold a candle to Nellie. (William E. Norris, *No New Things,* 1883)

huckleberry above one's persimmon Beyond one's ability or capacity; also *the persimmon above one's huckleberry.* This expression, of unknown ori-

gin, dates from the early 19th century. A huckleberry is a small edible fruit; a persimmon is a plum-sized fruit. Perhaps it is this concrete contrast in physical size that gave rise to the abstract contrast in ability implied in this and similar expressions. Thomas Bangs Thorpe uses the phrase in describing the hunting exploits of one of the characters in *The Mysteries of the Backwoods* (1846):

> It was a huckleberry above the persimmon of any native of the country.

stack up against To compare with; to correlate with or compete with. This expression alludes to the common method of evaluation in which contrasting items are set side by side in piles, and examined for quantitative comparison. The phrase is quite common in the United States.

> For it tells him the productivity of his store, how one department stacks up against another. (*Business Week,* April, 1950)

COMPETENCE

answer the bell To meet demands, requirements, or requests; to respond to a challenge, to pick up the glove or gauntlet. The allusion is to a boxing match in which a bell is sounded to signal the beginning of each round. If a boxer is too hurt to continue the fight, however, he will not answer the bell, i.e., come out of his corner to start the next round.

cut the mustard To meet or exceed performance requirements; to succeed or accomplish. Several marginally plausible derivations have been proposed, one of which relies on the definition of *mustard* as the strong spice considered by many chefs to be the finishing touch to several culinary masterpieces. As with most flavor enhancers, mustard is cut into the food, that is, added in small amounts. Another source suggests that the original expression may have been *cut the muster,* implying that a soldier passed inspection with flying colors.

> I looked around and found a proposition that exactly cut the mustard. (O. Henry, *Heart of the West,* 1907)

In contemporary usage, the expression is often employed in a negative phrase such as *can't cut the mustard* or *doesn't cut the mustard.*

earn one's wings To prove oneself proficient and reliable in a given skill or ability. The allusion is to the wing-shaped badges worn by pilots and other aircraft crew members upon completion of rigid requirements and strict training. Such badges are symbolic of competence.

pass muster To pass inspection; to meet or surpass certain standards; to be approved or accepted; to succeed. *Muster* is a military term for an assemblage of troops for inspection or some other purpose. Thus, in its original context, *pass muster* indicated that a soldier had successfully undergone an inspection. The expression soon expanded into more figurative applications, and continues in widespread use.

> [She has] enough good looks to make her pass muster. (William Thackeray, *The Newcomes; Memoirs of a Most Respectable Family,* 1855)

toe the mark To conform to rules or standards, to come up to scratch, to shape up; to fulfill one's obligations, to perform one's duty; also *to toe the line.*

> To-day they had decided to toe the line with the progressive workers of the country. (*Daily News,* March, 1910)

Originally and literally *to toe the mark* meant to line up in a row with the toes touching a mark or line. It was probably used in reference to runners at the starting line of a race or to military personnel arrayed for inspection. The earliest recorded written use of the expres-

sion was in James K. Paulding's *The Diverting History of John Bull and Brother Jonathan* (1813).

up to scratch Meeting specified standards; acceptable, satisfactory. The *scratch* of the expression was the line drawn on the ground in various sporting events: prize fighting, cockfighting, foot racing, and others. Contestants who came "up to [the] scratch" were worthy competitors, ready to undertake the challenge and prove their mettle. Thus the expression is similar in origin and current meaning to *toe the mark.* Today it is used primarily for performance evaluation, but may be varied in context to specify any type of judgmental standard.

> Bulls . . . that are not up to scratch as to size. (*Farmer's Weekly* [South Africa], cited in *Webster's Third*)

up to snuff Satisfactory, acceptable; up to par; meeting performance standards. *Webster's Third* cites W. H. Whyte:

> If your work wasn't up to snuff . . . you'd hear about it quick enough.

The British require more than mere acceptability for "up to snuff," however; for them it means 'alert, sharp, shrewd, not easily duped.' Etymologically related to the German verb for *to smell,* the phrase *up to snuff* describes one who is quick to "smell out" a situation or to "be on the right scent;" one who is percipient and discerning.

> Queer start, that 'ere, but he was one too many for you, warn't he? Up to snuff, and a pinch or two over. (Charles Dickens, *Pickwick Papers,* 1837)

up to the mark Passing the test, meeting the requirements. There is little evidence to support the theory that the *mark* here is specifically that fixed by the Assay Office as the standard for gold and silver. *Mark* has so many applications relevant to criteria that none can be definitively cited as the sole origin. It is quite possible that this *mark* is the same as that of *toe the mark,* and as such is also the equivalent of *scratch* in *up to scratch*.

walk the chalk To pass the test, to meet the requirements. Literally the phrase refers to the sobriety test formerly given seamen: walking between parallel lines chalked on deck. The expression is little used today.

win one's spurs To achieve recognition for one's accomplishments, to distinguish oneself in one's field, to prove one's worth or ability. This expression, dating from the 14th century, originally meant to attain the rank of knight, since a newly dubbed knight was presented with a pair of gilt spurs as a symbol of his chivalry. In order to become a knight, one first had to distinguish oneself by performing acts of bravery, usually on the battlefield. The expression is still current.

> Among them are David Giles *(Richard II)*, Who won his spurs with *The Forsyte Saga*. (*Saturday Review*, February, 1979)

COMPETITION

the Devil take the hindmost Every man for himself; survival of the fittest; similar to the more current phrase *the last one in is a rotten egg*, popular among children. This expression is said to have derived from an old legend concerning the Devil's school at Toledo where students were instructed in the art of black magic. Each year, as a sort of test, the graduating class was made to run through an underground hall. The last one, if caught by the Devil, would then become his servant. The phrase was used as early as 1611.

give [someone] a run for [his] money To provide keen and tough competition, thereby inciting one's opponent to go all out, to "give it all he's got" to win. Dating from the 19th century, this expression was originally racing slang. The then current *have a run for one's money* was suggestive of a determined struggle and subsequent victory or payoff. Today *to give [someone] a run for his money* means to make that person work for what would otherwise have been an easy victory.

jockey for position To maneuver or compete within the ranks for an advantageous position; to manipulate or pull strings to gain a more favorable position. The allusion is to horse racing and the jockeys' skillful maneuvering. The expression is now frequently applied to any kind of competitive maneuvering although it has been used in reference to sports since the early part of this century.

> In Alberta when there was no jury, congestion was caused by lawyers jockeying for position in order to appear before the right judge. (*The Times*, July, 1955)

keeping up with the Joneses Trying to maintain the social standing of one's neighbors; creating the impression that one is on an equal social or economic stratum as one's neighbors. This expression was coined in 1913 by Arthur "Pop" Momand, a cartoonist for the *New York Globe*, who satirized his own social pretensions in his long-running comic strip. The surname *Jones* was undoubtedly picked to represent the average American of Anglo-Saxon descent.

> Why . . . does John Doe choose to speculate on margin? . . . An ages-old desire to get something for nothing; keeping up with the Joneses. (E. C. Harwood, *Cause and Control of Business Cycles*, 1932)

rat race See **FRENZIEDNESS**.

take up the gauntlet To accept or undertake willingly any challenging task; to accept an offer to fight or duel. Similarly, *throw down the gauntlet* means to challenge one to a fight or duel. Gauntlets were the armored gloves worn by knights in medieval times. A knight wishing to joust with another would cast his gauntlet to the ground as a challenge to combat. The other knight would pick up the gauntlet to show the challenge was accepted.

Making a proclamation, that whosoever would say that King Richard was not lawfully king, he would fight with him at the utterance, and throw down his gauntlet. (Hall, *Chronicles of Richard III*, 1548)

throw one's hat into the ring To enter a competition, to become a candidate for public office, to accept a challenge. This expression, dating from the mid-19th century, is said to derive from the custom of throwing a hat into the ring to signal the acceptance of a pugilist's challenge.

When Mr. Roosevelt threw his hat into the ring the other day, he gave the signal for a contest the like of which has not been seen before in this country. (*Nation*, March 7, 1912)

up for grabs Open to competition; available, free. This U.S. expression made its appearance in slang dictionaries by the 1940s; it is now quite commonly used in informal writing, often in reference to positions, candidacies, etc.

Right now every position is up for grabs. Every player is going to get a shot. (*Boston Globe*, April, 1967)

While the phrase carries the connotation of wide-open competition, it also implies the necessity of effort and competence to attain the goal. A possible but totally conjectural origin is that *up for grabs* derives from the jump ball in basketball.

COMPLACENCY

look like the cat that swallowed the canary To look smug; to appear very self-satisfied or pleased. This self-evident expression has been in use since 1871.

resting on one's laurels To be content with one's present or past honors, accomplishments, or prestige. The *laurels* in this expression have long been a sym-

bol of excellence or success in one's field of endeavor. *Resting* indicates self-satisfaction and complacency with the implication that no further efforts will be expended to acquire additional figurative laurels. It is interesting to note that ancient philosophers and poets sometimes kept laurel leaves under their pillows for inspiration, a concept almost totally opposite to the phrase's contemporary meaning.

snug as a bug in a rug Extremely comfortable and content. This common expression of obvious derivation was purportedly used by Benjamin Franklin in 1772. The phrase enjoys frequent use in the United States.

COMPLAINT (See GRIEVANCE.)

COMPLETION (See also CESSATION, CULMINATION, TERMINATION.)

go through-stitch To go through with; to finish or conclude; to follow through. This expression alluding to the work of a tailor was popular in the 17th century but is no longer heard today.

For when a man has once undertaken a business, let him go through-stitch with it. (*The Pagan Prince*, 1690)

in for a penny, in for a pound Once involved in a matter, however slightly, one must carry it through whatever the consequences. The metaphor comes from the monetary units of Great Britain: formerly, the penny was $\frac{1}{12}$ of a shilling and the pound 20 shillings or 240 pence; since decimalization, the pound is 100 new pence.

sign off To complete or end a performance, project, or other matter; to terminate; to withdraw. In the 9th century and for several hundred years thereafter, a person could change his religious affiliation simply by "signing off," i.e., by signing a legal paper that ended his membership in one religious organization and, if he so desired, enrolled him in another.

The revolution . . . broke up the State Church and gave to every man the liberty of "signing off" as it was called, to any denomination that pleased him. (Harriet Beecher Stowe, *The Poganuc People, Their Loves and Lives,* 1878)

Beginning in the late Middle Ages, *sign off* usually referred to a creditor's releasing a debtor from financial obligation by "signing off," i.e., by affixing his signature to a document to that effect. A contemporary variation that refers to this practice of canceling a debt or amortizing an asset is *write off.*

The company wrote off the loss as a bad debt. (*Law Times,* 1891)

Since the 1930s, *sign-off* (as a noun) most commonly applies to a radio or television station's ending its broadcast day.

Because of the earlier sign-off required by the Federal Communications Commission . . . (*ABC Radio,* 1949)

tie up the loose ends To conclude or settle matters; to answer all questions and account for any seemingly superfluous details. *Loose ends* in this expression refers to the last bit of unfinished business, the apparently irrelevant or contradictory details of a plan, arrangement, project, etc. This figurative use may derive from the practice of tying the ends of thread that hang loose after a cloth is woven or a garment is knitted.

COMPLICATION

can of worms A situation or specific problem which threatens to cause trouble and have unresolvable complications for all concerned; a sore spot; a sensitive topic better left unexplored. A can of worms might pass for an acceptable product before it is opened. However, *to open a can of worms* means to instigate trouble, to broach a subject or do something questionable which has uncontrollable, complex, and negative repercussions.

Pandora's box A source of afflictions and complications which plague one without warning; a loaded situation; something which appears in a positive light but is negative in effect. In Greek mythology, Pandora, the first woman, was showered with gifts from the gods, among them a magnificent box presented her by Zeus which she was told never to open. Disobeying the gods, she opened it, and unwittingly allowed all of the human ills contained within to escape. Only Hope remained. The term appeared as early as the mid-16th century.

I cannot liken our affection better than . . . to Pandora's box, lift up the lid, out flies the Devil; shut it up fast, it cannot hurt us. (Stephen Gosson, *The School of Abuse,* 1579)

red tape Excessive formality and petty routine, preventing expeditious disposal of important matters. The term derives from the literal red tape with which official and legal documents were formerly bound and sealed. Though its use has proliferated along with the proliferation of bureaucracy and departmentalization, its current figurative meaning is by no means recent:

All the morning at the customhouse, plagued with red tape. (Henry Wadsworth Longfellow, *Life,* 1869)

COMPOSURE

cool as a cucumber Calm, cool, and collected; self-possessed, composed. Cucumbers have long been used in salads and relishes for their refreshing, cooling quality. This popular simile dates from 1732.

cool your jets Relax, calm down, take it easy; used chiefly as an admonition. This recent American slang expression is perhaps an extension of the 1950s slang term *cool it.* The *jets* in the phrase may refer to the jet engines of a plane which get extremely hot before takeoff, and are thus comparable to the feverishly excited condition of an individual to whom this remark would be addressed.

count to ten To take a deep breath, calm down, and gird oneself to do something difficult or trying; to pause and consider before acting impetuously; to redirect one's energy and attention to avoid becoming enraged. This common expression is often used by someone who is violently angry and on the verge of losing his temper. It is a warning to another person to behave in a certain manner or suffer the consequences when the counter reaches "ten."

hold your horses Hold on, be patient, keep calm, don't get excited; nearly always used in the imperative. The allusion is to the way a driver holds his horses back by pulling up on the reins in order to slow them down. Of U.S. origin, this expression is thought to have first appeared in print in its figurative sense in the *New Orleans Picayune* (September, 1844):

Oh, hold your hosses, Squire. There's no use gettin' riled, no how.

keep one's powder dry To keep cool, to keep control, to remain calm and ready for action. This expression is military in origin and refers to the reputed final words of Sir Oliver Cromwell to his troops before they crossed a river to attack on the opposite side:

Put your trust in God; but be sure to keep your powder dry.

keep your shirt on Stay calm, keep cool, don't get worked-up; also *hold on to your shirttail;* both expressions nearly always used in the imperative. Men usually remove their shirts before engaging in a fistfight; whence the expression. George W. Harris used this U.S. slang phrase in the *Spirit of the Times* (N.Y., 1854):

I say, you durned ash cats, just keep yer shirts on, will ye?

on an even keel Steady, stable, balanced; even-tempered; maintaining composure or equilibrium. *Keel* is a nautical term for a "central fore-and-aft structural member in the bottom of a hull" *(Random House Dict.)* which affects a vessel's stability. Nautical use of *on an even keel,* as in the following quotation from James Greenwood's *A Rudimentary Treatise on Navigation* (1850), has given rise to current figurative use of this expression.

A ship is said to swim on an even keel when she draws the same quantity of water abaft as forwards.

roll with the punches See ENDURANCE.

without turning a hair Without batting an eyelash, showing no sign of excitement or emotion; completely calm and composed, unperturbed, unflustered.

When I tried her with a lot of little dodges . . . she never turned a hair—as the sporting people say. (Richard D. Blackmore, *Dariel,* 1897)

The earliest recorded literal use of the expression is found in Jane Austen's *Northanger Abbey* (1798) in allusion to a horse which, though hot from racing, did not become sweaty or ruffle its hair.

CONCEALMENT (See also SECRECY.)

all one's geese are swans See EXAGGERATION.

cover one's tracks To hide or conceal one's actions or motives, to cover up, to get rid of the evidence. The allusion is to the practice of American Indians, backwoodsmen, and such, who erased or otherwise obliterated their footprints to avoid being followed. See Indian file, ARRANGEMENT.

In corresponding, I endeavored to cover my tracks as far as possible. (Albert D. Richardson, *The Secret Service, the Field, the Dungeon, and the Escape,* 1865)

gild the pill To mask or ease an offensive or onerous task by providing attractive incentives; to cloak in euphemism. This expression is derived from the sugary coating applied to pills to make them more palatable.

> Palmerston must go . . . There was no attempt to gild the pill, since on reflection it seemed better that he should not lead the Commons. (Philip Guedalla, *Palmerston*, 1926)

put up a smoke screen To camouflage or conceal one's intentions, motives, or actions from one's rivals or opponents, or from the general public. A smoke screen is a cover of dense smoke produced to camouflage a ship, plane, or area from the enemy during top-secret military operations.

> A reply which General Waters considers was a skilful smoke-screen to conceal a refusal. (*The Observer*, June, 1928)

sweep under the carpet To cover up or conceal something embarrassing or disagreeable in the hope that it will escape notice or be forgotten; also *to push under the carpet.*

> It would be self-deception to think that unemployment could be dealt with by emergency measures and pushed under the carpet. (*The Times*, January, 1963)

Of fairly recent coinage, this expression refers to the lazy person's stepsaving trick of literally sweeping dirt under the rug instead of picking it up.

under the counter In a clandestine, often illegal manner; out of sight, set apart from the regular stock; having to do with money changing hands unofficially or illegally. The counter or table is the one over which money is exchanged for merchandise. *Under-the-counter* or *under-the-table* practices or products are often connected with the black market. The expression was popular during World War II when certain luxury items were in demand but accessible only "under the counter." Banned

books have also been popular "under-the-counter" items.

> Chief goods to "go under the counter" are fully fashioned silk stockings, watches, and silk handkerchiefs. (*Evening Standard*, December 20, 1945)

Under the counter is usually used interchangeably with *under the table,* though the latter is heard more often to describe payment made but not officially recorded, thus evading taxes.

whitewash To cover up defects, faults, or mistakes, especially to deceive the public about the disreputable goings on of a public figure; to make the guilty look innocent or to condone a reprehensible action, by hiding or manipulating the facts and creating a façade of respectability. To whitewash is literally to whiten with a composition of lime and water, or ground chalk. Figuratively, this Americanism means to exonerate or give a clean slate to an unethical or guilty person. Also used substantively, the term is commonly heard in political contexts.

> Several Republican senators reported that the report was a "whitewash" of [Senator] McCarthy's charges. (AP wire story, July 20, 1950)

CONCLUSION (See CESSATION, COMPLETION, CULMINATION, TERMINATION.)

CONFRONTATION

beard the lion in his den To confront face-to-face; to oppose another boldly and openly on his turf; to challenge. W. S. Gilbert used this expression in *Iolanthe* (1882).

bell the cat To dare to confront danger at its source, despite overwhelming odds. The allusion is to a fable recounted in Langland's *Piers Plowman* (1377). A group of mice continually harassed by a certain cat met to decide what to do about the problem. One old mouse suggested that a bell hung around the cat's neck would serve to warn the mice of the feline's approach. This idea was greeted with much enthusiasm until a bright young mouse brought up the question, "But who will bell the cat?"

come to grips with To face up to a problematic situation and deal or cope with it; to tackle a problem head-on in an attempt to get it under control; to grapple or struggle with a dilemma or difficulty. The idea of confronting an opposing force suggests that the expression may derive from a sport such as wrestling. This theory is highly conjectural, however, because the many meanings and uses of *grip* allow for a variety of possible explanations.

face the music To confront stoically the consequences of one's deeds; to face up to an unpleasant or trying experience. This expression may have originated in the theater, where actors and actresses nervously awaited their cues to come onstage and thus "face the music" in the pit. Another origin may lie in the military practice of mustering soldiers in full battle regalia for inspection, often at the call of a bugle. Figuratively, this term refers to a personal confrontation for which one must gather courage.

in the teeth of In direct opposition to; straight against, without a buffer; confronting, face to face; in defiance or in spite of. This expression of unknown origin dates from the 13th century. The oldest examples of its use describe direct confrontation between two forces:

A Hector, who no less desires to meet them in the teeth. (Arthur Hall, tr., *Ten Books of Homer's Iliad,* 1581)

Since the 18th century, *in the teeth of* has broadened in its applicability to include confrontations of a less physical or tangible nature, such as between contradictory ideas.

A judge has no right to enter judgement in the teeth of the finding of a jury. (*Law Times,* June 13, 1885)

The expression can also mean 'in the face or presence of.'

They were in fact in the very teeth of starvation. (Charles Lamb, *Elia,* 1825)

showdown A decisive confrontation between opposing parties to settle a dispute; a revelation of facts and other information, usually in hopes of resolving an issue. In poker, a showdown is the laying down of one's cards, face up, to determine the winner of that hand. *Showdown* has assumed its figurative implications by extension.

The opening game of the showdown Yankees-Red Sox series . . . (AP wire story, September 24, 1949)

square off To take on a defensive stance; to gird up one's loins. This phrase originated and is still used as a boxing term for the initial positions that boxers assume at the beginning of a round. The expression maintains widespread figurative use.

The bow appeared to be rearing up to square off at the midday sun. (J. H. Beadle, *Undeveloped West,* 1873)

take the bull by the horns To attack a problem head-on; to confront without fear or evasiveness; to face up to danger, difficulty or unpleasantness without shrinking. In bullfighting, a matador grasps the horns of a bull about to toss him. Jonathan Swift used the expression in 1711:

To engage with France, was to take a bull by the horns. (*Conduct of Allies*)

CONFUSION

at loose ends Unsettled, undecided, lacking direction or goal; uncommitted to one's present position and uncertain of one's future status. A loose end is anything that is left hanging or not properly attached, as a piece of fabric or a seemingly superfluous detail. A person is "at loose ends" when his life lacks coherence or a sense of direction as exemplified in the following fragment quoted in *Webster's Third:*

> . . . feeling himself at loose ends—no job, no immediate prospects. (Dixon Wecter)

See also **tie up the loose ends,** COMPLETION.

at sea Confused, perplexed; without direction, design, or stability; in a state of uncertainty. Figurative use of this expression dates from the mid-18th century and is based on an analogy to a ship lost at sea, having no bearings and out of sight of land. *At sea* can refer to a person or state of affairs. *All adrift* is an analogous nautical expression with a similar figurative meaning 'aimless, confused.'

knock for a loop To disorient someone by saying or doing something shocking or unexpected; to strike a blow and cause one to lose balance and fall. The *loop* in this modern slang expression derives from the aeronautical term for the mid-air maneuver of an airplane. To knock someone for a loop is to hit that person hard enough to make him do a somersault. The feeling of dizziness and disorientation is carried over into the more common figurative use.

> That little charade of hers had knocked him for a loop. (D. Ramsey, *Deadly Discretion*, 1973)

Also current is *throw for a loop.*

> I was really confused. That memorandum threw me for a loop. (E. Ambler, *Intercom Conspiracy*, 1969)

knock galley-west See COMBAT.

lose one's bearings To become lost; to lose all sense of direction; to become hopelessly disoriented, confused, or bewildered. In this expression, *bearings* carries the literal meaning of reference points or directions in relation to one's position; thus, the term's use to describe a person who is lost or disoriented.

not know if one is afoot or on horseback So completely confused as to not know what one is doing, thoroughly befuddled or mixed-up; not to know whether one is coming or going. This self-evident American colloquialism dates from the late 19th century.

> "Fay Daniels!" gasps the girl, which don't know if she's afoot or horseback—and neither did *I.* (*Collier's,* October, 1927)

not to know if one is coming or going Not to know what one is doing; extremely confused or mixed-up; not to know which end is up; ignorant, stupid.

> There's nobody at the Town Hall could take it on. Town Clerk doesn't know whether he's coming or going. (J. B. Priestley, *Fest. Frabridge,* 1951)

Use of the phrase dates from at least 1924.

not to know which end is up See IGNORANCE.

not to make head nor tail of See **make head or tail of,** DIFFERENTIATION.

slaphappy See FATUOUSNESS.

CONSEQUENCES

the devil to pay See PUNISHMENT.

domino theory The belief that if one of a cluster of small, neighboring countries is taken over by communism or some other political system the others will soon follow suit; the phenomenon of political chain reaction. This theory takes its name from the chain-reaction effect created when one in a line of standing dominoes topples, bringing the rest down, one after the other. The concept arose during the 1950s and was popular during the 60s as the expression most representative of the basis for American involvement in Southeast Asia at that time.

he that lieth with dogs riseth with fleas
A person is known by the company he keeps; associate with riffraff and you'll soon be one of them. This well-known proverb appeared as early as 1640 in George Herbert's *Jacula Prudentum.*

pay the piper To bear the consequences of one's actions or decisions; to pay the cost of some undertaking; to foot the bill. This expression probably alludes to the 13th-century legend of the Pied Piper of Hamelin in which the piper, upon being refused the payment promised for ridding the town of rats, played his pipe again; this time, however, it was the children who were led out of town to their deaths. Thus, the residents suffered the consequences of their decision, having "paid the piper" with their children's lives. One source suggests that the derivation may be more literal, that is, it was customary to pay a piper or other street musician for the entertainment he supplied.

> After all this dance he has led the nation, he must at last come to pay the piper himself. (Thomas Flatman, *Heraclitis Ridens,* 1681)

A common variation is *pay the fiddler.*

sow the wind and reap the whirlwind
A proverb implying that if a person acts in a self-indulgent, hedonistic, or dissolute manner, he will have to suffer the calamitous consequences. This adage is Biblical in origin, appearing in Hosea 8:7 as a warning to the Israelites to emend their iniquitous ways. *Sow the wind* implies senseless or unproductive activity, while *whirlwind* alludes to a violent and destructive force, the fate of one who "sows the wind."

stew in one's own juice To suffer the unhappy consequences of one's own unfortunate actions, to reap what one has sown; also *to fry in one's own grease.* According to the *OED, to fry in one's own grease* dates from the 14th century when it was applied to persons burned at the stake. The phrase appeared in

the prologue to *The Wife of Bath's Tale* by Chaucer:

> In his own grease I made him fry,
> For anger, and for very jealousy.

To stew in one's own juice, although the most popular form of the expression today, did not appear until approximately 300 years later. The equivalent French phrase is *cuire dans son jus* 'to cook in one's juice.'

CONSERVATISM

blimp See POMPOSITY.

Dame Partington and her mop Stubborn and futile opposition to the inevitable, particularly to economic, political, or social reform. This infrequently used expression is derived from English newspaper stories of November 1824 which tell of a woman who used only a mop in attempting to rid her nearly inundated seaside home of water during a raging storm. The woman eventually gave up her struggle and sought safety elsewhere. In October 1831, Rev. Sydney Smith compared the rejection of a reform bill by the House of Lords to the plight of Dame Partington.

die-hard See PERSEVERANCE.

hard-hat A working-class conservative, so called from the protective metal or plastic helmet worn by construction workers. *The Sunday Mail* (Brisbane, June, 1970) offers the following explanation of the term:

> A "Hard Hat" is a construction worker, but his helmet symbolises all those beefy blue-collar workers who have suddenly become the knuckleduster on the strong right arm of President Nixon's silent majority.

redneck An ultraconservative. This disparaging term usually refers to the poor white farmers of the Southern backwoods who are notorious for their purported intolerance of liberals, intellectuals, Blacks, and hippies. *Redneck,* originating as an allusion to a farmer's perennially sunburned neck, is now an epithet for any person who shares similar prejudices.

right-wing Reactionary, conservative; averse to change, die-hard. The term reputedly arose from the seating arrangement of the French National Assembly of 1789, in which conservatives sat on the right side, or wing, of the chamber. As used today, *right-wing*, like *left-wing*, has pejorative connotations of extremism—in this case, of bigotry, prejudice, moneyed interests, anti-humanitarianism, etc. Both terms are used primarily to denigrate and stigmatize one's opponents; a political conservative would not call himself a *right-winger*, just as a liberal would not call himself a *left-winger;* yet each might well label the other with the appropriate epithet.

CONSPIRACY

hand in glove Intimately associated, on very familiar terms; closely related or connected; in cahoots, in conspiracy. Literary use of the expression dates from the late 17th century when it was properly *hand and glove*, a form now rarely heard. In contemporary usage the expression often carries connotations of illicit or improper association.

in cahoots In league or in partnership; in conspiracy; also *to go in cahoots* or *cahoot with*, meaning to join up with, to become partners; and *go cahoots* meaning to share equally. This U.S. slang expression, dating from 1829, is said to have derived from the kind of partnership that was expected of early American pioneers who shared a frontier cabin, or engaged in a joint venture. Originally, the phrase may have come from the French *cahute* 'cabin, hut,' although Dutch *kajuit* and German *kajüte* have also been suggested as possibilities.

CONSTANCY

dyed-in-the-wool Confirmed, inveterate; complete, thorough, unmitigated, out-and-out. When wool is dyed before being made into yarn, its color is more firmly fixed and lasting. A variant of this expression appeared in Sir Thomas North's translation of Plutarch's *Lives of the Noble Grecians and Romans* (1579):

He had . . . through institution and education (as it were) died in wool the manners of children.

hard-and-fast Ironclad, binding, strict, rigid, unbending. The literal, nautical sense of the term denotes a ship on shore or aground, stuck and immovable. It is probably this sense that gave rise to the figurative meaning in popular use today. Both the figurative and literal meanings date from the late 19th century.

man for all seasons A reliable, steadfast male; a man of principle who retains his integrity regardless of the situation. This expression alludes to a man who is unruffled by vicissitudes and who remains constant despite changing circumstances, like the weather. The phrase was popularized when Robert Bolt used it as the title of his dramatization of the life of Sir Thomas More (1960).

regular brick An agreeable, sincere male; a regular guy. This expression, referring to the solid, unvariegated constitution of a brick, describes a man who is genuinely amiable, unaffected, and reliable.

I don't stick to declare Father Dick . . . was a regular brick. (Richard H. Barham, *The Ingoldsby Legends,* 1845)

through thick and thin Through difficulties or adversity, in spite of any or all obstacles; faithfully, unwaveringly. According to the *OED*, *thick and thin* was originally *thicket and thin wood*. Thus this expression denoted an actual physical obstacle, as in the following quotation from Spenser's *Faerie Queene:*

His tireling jade he fiercely forth did push

Through thick and thin, both over bank and bush.

Currently *through thick and thin* is used figuratively as well, referring to any conceivable obstacle, and in context, connoting faithfulness.

There's five hundred men here to back you up through thick and thin. (T. H. Hall Caine, *The Manxman*, 1894)

true-blue Loyal, faithful; steadfast, staunch, unwavering, constant.

The Old Beau is true-blue, to the high-flown principles [of] King Edward's First Protestant Church. (Edmund Hickeringill, *Priest-craft*, 1705)

The color blue has long been the symbol of truth and constancy. Some conjecture the association arose because of the renowned fastness of Coventry blue dye. According to the *OED*, true-blue was applied to the Scottish Presbyterian or Whig party of the 17th century, the Covenanters having assumed blue as their partisan color in opposition to the royal red. Their doing so may have been connected with Numbers 15:38 of the Bible, in which the Lord commands Moses to have the Israelites put a blue ribbon on the fringes of the borders of their garments as a reminder to keep His commandments.

CONTEMPLATION (See THOUGHT.)

CONTRAPTION

Heath Robinson A proper name applied to ingenious but overly complicated and impractical mechanical contraptions. Heath Robinson (1872–1944) was a British caricaturist whose name became associated with his popular drawings of complicated mechanisms made out of every imaginable piece of junk and held together by the most unconventional means. This British phrase is most often used adjectivally and is similar to the American *Rube Goldberg*.

This "Heath-Robinson" jumble of wooden sheds, sluices, and water troughs looks ridiculous, yet it works all right. (*Discovery*, November, 1934)

Rube Goldberg Any mechanical contrivance which is unnecessarily complex and impractical; used adjectivally, makeshift or improvised, jerry-built. Reuben Goldberg was an American cartoonist born in the late 19th century. His name evokes images of cartoons depicting ridiculously complex mechanical contrivances, and is used in referring to elaborate but ineffective repair work, inventions, etc. A "Rube Goldberg job" looks impressive but is unreliable.

CONTROL (See also DOMINATION, MANIPULATION.)

call the shots See **call one's shots**, COMMUNICATION.

carry the ball To assume responsibility for the progress of an undertaking; to be in charge and bear the burden of success or failure. This metaphorical expression stems from the role of the ball carrier in American football.

corner the market To possess, have access to, or be in control of something which is in demand; from the financial practice of attempting to secure control over particular stocks or commodities. This U.S. expression, dating from the mid-19th century, was originally heard only in financial contexts; however it is now heard in noncommercial contexts as well. In financial terms, a "cornering" involves one party buying all of one kind of stock or commodity, thereby driving potential buyers and sellers into a corner because they have no option but to acquiesce to the price demands of those controlling the stock.

have the ball at one's feet See ADVANTAGE.

have the world on a string See ELATION.

hold the fort To take charge, often to act as a temporary substitute; to remain at one's post, to maintain or defend one's position. This expression is attributed to General Sherman, who in 1864 is said to have signaled this message to General Corse. In modern use, *fort* can refer to a place or a philosophical position.

> Elizabeth and her archbishops . . . had held the fort until their church had come . . . to have an ethos of its own. (A. L. Rowse, *Tudor Cornwall*, 1941)

hold the line To try to prevent a situation from becoming uncontrollable or unwieldy; to maintain the status quo. This Americanism probably comes from the game of football. It is frequently heard in an economic context, as in "to hold the line on taxes" or "to hold the line on prices."

hold the purse strings To determine how much money shall be spent and how much saved; to regulate the expenditure of money. *Purse strings* refers literally to the strings at the mouth of a money pouch which can be tightened or loosened, thereby controlling the amount of money put in or taken out. By extension, this term also refers to the right to manage monies. To "hold the purse strings" is to be in charge of the finances.

the one who pays the piper calls the tune An adage implying that a person has control of a project or other matter by virtue of bearing its expenses. The figurative use of this expression is derived from its literal meaning, i.e., someone who pays a musician has the right to request a certain song.

> Londoners had paid the piper, and should choose the tune. (*Daily News*, December 18, 1895)

See also **pay the piper, CONSEQUENCES.**

run a tight ship To maintain good order and firm discipline; to manage a project or organization so that its interdependent parts and personnel function smoothly together, with machinelike efficiency and precision. A literal tight ship is one which is both watertight and well-run, in that officers and crew carry out their respective roles with an absence of friction. Though *to run a tight ship* may have connotations of martinetlike strictness, it is usually used positively to compliment an efficient administrator.

COOPERATION (See also **ASSISTANCE, RECIPROCITY.**)

chip in To make a contribution, either of money or of time and effort; to interrupt or butt in. This expression probably derives from the game of poker in which chips, representing money, are placed by players in the "pot." Putting chips in the "pot" is equivalent to entering the game. Figurative uses of the phrase play on the idea of "entering the game"—that is, becoming involved. Ways of "chipping in" range from giving money to a charity or participating in a joint enterprise to "putting one's two cents in." Such uses of the phrase gained currency in the second half of the 19th century. Only the 'interrupt, butt in' meaning is uncommon today.

go Dutch To have each person pay his own way, to share or split the cost; to go fifty-fifty or halves. Although the exact origin of this expression is not known, it is perhaps an allusion to the qualities or independence and thrift characteristic of the Dutch people. The phrase *to go Dutch* probably arose from the earlier combinations of *Dutch lunch, party,* or *supper,* events or meals to which each person contributed his share, similar to today's potluck suppers or B.Y.O.B. parties where the guests furnish the food and drink. The oldest related "Dutch" combination is apparently *Dutch treat,* which dates from about 1887, and is closest in meaning to *to go Dutch.*

> To suggest a free trade area to any of them in such circumstances looks rather like proposing to a teetotaller that you and he go dutch

on daily rounds of drinks. (*The Economist,* October 1957)

The expression dates from the early part of the 20th century.

in cahoots See CONSPIRACY.

in there pitching See EXERTION.

keep one's end up To do one's fair share, do one's part; to hold one's own; to share the responsibilities involved in an undertaking. In print since the mid-19th century, this expression probably derives from the image of two people balancing a heavy load. It is widely heard today.

Colonel Baden-Powell and his gallant garrison will have to keep their end up unassisted. (*Westminster Gazette,* November 24, 1899)

kick in To contribute, to put in, to donate or give, to pay one's share; usually in reference to money. This American slang expression probably derives from the poker slang meaning of *to kick* 'to raise or up an already existing bet.'

The lawyer guy kicked in with the balance of the ten thousand. (K. McGaffey, *Sorrows of Show-Girl,* 1908)

pick up the slack To compensate, offset or counterbalance. The expression usually indicates that a person or group must put forth extra effort to make up for another's absence, weakness, or low output.

play ball To work together toward a common goal; to cooperate; to act justly and honestly. This expression is perhaps derived from the set of rules agreed upon by youngsters before they play a game together or from the necessity of team effort and cooperation in athletic contests. The expression is heard throughout the English-speaking world.

The police of Buffalo are too dumb —it would be redundant, I suppose, to say "and honest"—to play ball with the hold-up mobs. (C. Terrett, *Only Saps Work,* 1930)

pull one's weight To do one's rightful share of the work; to effectively perform one's job. This expression apparently originated from rowing, where an oarsman who does not apply all his strength to each stroke is considered a burden rather than an asset. Similarly, one who figuratively pulls his weight makes himself a valuable contributor to a team effort. In contemporary usage, the expression is often used in discussing the value or usefulness of an employee.

If the office boy is really pulling his weight . . . he is providing me with 3¾ days per week. (J. P. Benn, *Confessions of a Capitalist,* 1927)

Tinker to Evers to Chance John Tinker, John Evers, and Frank Chance formed the famous double play combination of the Chicago Cubs in the early part of the 20th century. The line "D.P. (double play): Tinker to Evers to Chance" appeared so often in box scores of that time that it became a permanent part of American idiom. The expression is used currently to describe any cooperative effort with the fluidity and speed of a Tinker to Evers to Chance double play.

CORPULENCE

bay window Paunch, protruding belly, pot-belly. The visual image is of the type of window which projects outward in curved form, creating a bay or recess within. The term is an Americanism of long standing.

Since his bay window began to form . . . (Cimarron *News,* November 27, 1879)

beer-belly A protruding abdomen, supposedly caused by excessive indulgence in beer. The term has been in popular slang use since 1920.

black-silk barge British slang for a stout woman. This uncomplimentary comparison of a woman's physique to a large, flat-bottomed vessel generally used for transporting freight needs no further explanation.

broad in the beam Having disproportionately large hips or buttocks; hippy; steatopygous. The greatest breadth of a ship is called its 'beam,' from its transverse timbers or 'beams.' The term is thus similarly applied to the width of a person's hips or buttocks. Though most often used of women, early citations show the word was first used descriptively of men.

He stood watching disgustedly Bigges' broad beam. (H. Walpole, *Hans Frost*, 1929)

butterball A plump or chubby person, especially a short one. Used figuratively since 1892, this mildly derogatory term compares a person's physique to an individual serving of butter molded in the form of a ball.

German goiter A bulging stomach, usually the result of excessive beer intake; a beer-belly. Goiter is a thyroid gland disorder manifested by protuberant swelling about the neck. Similarly, *German goiter* is a distention of the stomach due to the consumption of copious amounts of beer, a beverage that Germans particularly enjoy.

pot-belly A protruding abdomen; a person with same. This common term, coined by analogy to the rounded pot, dates from the early 18th century.

spare tire A roll of fat about one's middle; paunch, pot-belly. Such an excess of adiposity visually resembles a tire. The term has been around since 1925.

tun-bellied Extremely obese, gargantuan, elephantine. In this obsolete expression, *tun* 'tub, vat' alludes to rotundity. The phrase appeared in William Cartwright's *The Royal Slave* (1639):

Some drunken hymn I warrant you towards now, in the praise of their great, huge, rowling, tun-bellyed god Bacchus as they call him.

CORRECTNESS (See also PRECISION, PROPRIETY.)

get hold of the right end of the stick To have the proper grasp or perspective on a situation. The expression is more common in Britain than in the United States. See also **get hold of the wrong end of the stick**, FALLACIOUSNESS.

hit the white To be right, to be right on target, to hit the bull's-eye. The allusion is to archery and the inner circle of the target or the bull's-eye, formerly of a white color. Since bull's-eyes are now usually painted or outlined in black, it is easy to see why this expression is rare or obsolete today.

'Twas I won the wager, though you hit the white. (Shakespeare, *The Taming of the Shrew*, V,ii)

on the beam On the right track; correct; accurate. The reference is to a radio beam used to direct the course of an aircraft. Thus, an airplane on the beam is right on the proper course. The phrase appeared as early as 1941 in the *Daring Detective*.

right as a trivet See GOOD HEALTH.

right as rain Very right, exactly correct or accurate, quite right. This simile, although not as common today as formerly, is still popularly used to emphasize degree of correctness. Its origin would appear to be simply from alliteration.

COST (See also PAYMENT.)

an arm and a leg An exorbitant amount of money; a popular American hyperbole.

bleed See EXTORTION.

for a song Cheaply, inexpensively, at low cost, for little or nothing. *A song* meaning 'a trifle or thing of no consequence' may stem from the supposed retort of Baron Burleigh on being ordered by Elizabeth I to give Edmund Spenser an annuity of 100 pounds for having composed the *Faerie Queene:*

All this for a song?

In any event, *a song* as an insignificance dates from Elizabethan times, for Shakespeare uses it in this sense in *All's Well That Ends Well* (1601).

for love or money At any price; by any means available. This phrase is most frequently used in the negative expression *not for love or money* to imply that someone or something is unobtainable at any price—either financial or emotional.

> He let me . . . use . . . Anglo-Saxon texts not elsewhere to be had for love or money. (Francis March, *A Comparative Grammar of the Anglo-Saxon Language*, 1870)

highway robbery Exorbitantly or outrageously high prices. The allusion is to highwaymen, the holdup men of yesteryear who roamed the public roads robbing travelers. This expression is often used to express indignation at ridiculously high prices which one is nevertheless forced to pay for lack of an alternative, just as the victims of highwaymen had no choice but to surrender their money and goods at the risk of their lives. The expression has been in figurative use since at least 1920.

> Nothing on the wine list . . . under two-pound-ten. Highway robbery by candlelight. (J. B. Priestley, *It's Old Country*, 1967)

pay through the nose To pay an exorbitant price, financially or otherwise, unwittingly or through coercion. Many variations on one story line are cited as sources for this expression. The most popular is that the Danes in the 9th century imposed a "nose tax" on the Irish. Those who neglected to pay were punished by having their noses slit. Some say the Swedes or Norwegians were the oppressors. Others say the Jews rather than the Irish were the oppressed. However, *pay through the nose* derives from the punishment, irrespective of who inflicted the punishment on whom. The phrase was used as early as

1672 and is commonly heard today, often implying an unawareness or naiveté on the part of the person "paying through the nose."

pay too dearly for one's whistle To pay more for some desired object than it is worth; to expend a great deal of time, effort, or money for something which does not come up to one's expectations; to indulge a whim. This expression is based on Benjamin Franklin's *The Whistle* (1799), which tells of his nephew's wanting a certain whistle so much that he paid its owner four times its value. As soon as the whistle had been acquired, however, it lost its appeal of the unattainable, leaving the boy disappointed with his purchase.

> If a man likes to do it he must pay for his whistle. (George Eliot, *Daniel Deronda*, 1876)

COUNTENANCE (See VISAGE.)

COURAGE (See BRAVERY.)

COWARDICE

cold feet A feeling of fear or uncertainty; a loss of confidence or nerve; cowardice; usually *to get* or *have cold feet*. This expression, in popular use since at least 1893, is said to have come from Ben Jonson's play *Volpone*, produced in London in 1605.

lily-livered Cowardly, pusillanimous, craven. This expression is a variation of *white livered, lily* 'pure white' serving to emphasize the color. According to ancient Roman and Greek custom, an animal was sacrificed before each major battle. If the animal's liver was red and healthy-looking, it was considered a good omen; if the liver was pale or white, it portended defeat. This tradition was based on the belief that the liver was the seat of love and virile passions such as bravery and courage. It was further believed that the liver of a poltroon contained no blood, either through a prenatal fluke of nature or more often as the result of a cowardly act.

> For Andrew, if he were opened, and you find so much blood in his liver as will clog the foot of a flea, I'll eat the rest of the anatomy. (Shakespeare, *Twelfth Night* III,ii)

show the white feather To act in a cowardly, craven, dastardly fashion; to lack courage; to be fearful in the face of danger. This expression alludes to the gamecocks used in the sport of cockfighting. A purebred gamecock has only red and black feathers, while a crossbreed, usually a poor fighter in the pit, often has white feathers in its tail. Though these white feathers are usually covered by the colored ones, when one of these inferior hybrids knows its defeat is imminent, its tail droops, clearly showing the white feathers.

> No one will defend him who shows the white feather. (Sir Walter Scott, *Journal,* 1829)

turn turtle See VULNERABILITY.

weak sister A person (male or female) who is unreliable or timorous, especially during emergencies; a group member whose support cannot be counted on under pressure or in a crisis.

> There is always a weak sister who turns yellow or overplays his game through nervousness. (*Saturday Evening Post,* October, 1925)

yellow belly A coward, a craven. *Yellow* has been a common American colloquialism for 'cowardly' since the mid-19th century. *Yellow-bellied* followed, a coinage perhaps due to the initial rhyming sounds. Both are still more frequently heard than the noun *yellow belly.* Reasons for the long association of the color yellow with cowardliness are unknown; they may simply lie in its connotations of sickliness and consequent lack of force and vigor.

CRIMINALITY

bootlegger A smuggler; a dealer in illicit goods; originally, a dealer in contraband whiskey, so-called because the bottles were often carried hidden in the legs of his tall boots. Though the term gained currency during the era of Prohibition (1920–33), it dates at least from the mid-19th century. It was much used in the dry states of Kansas and Oklahoma in the 1880s. Back formation yielded *bootleg,* both verb and adjective.

cutpurse A pickpocket, a thief. This term, in use since the 14th century, originally described those who stole by cutting purses off the belt or girdle from which they were hung. Since purses or money-holders are now carried in pockets rather than worn at the waist, the term *pickpocket* has all but replaced its older counterpart *cutpurse.*

Dick Turpin Any especially daring or flagrant highway robber or bandit. Dick Turpin (1706–39) was an infamous English highwayman renowned for his criminal derring-do. He appears as a character in William Harrison Ainsworth's romance *Rookwood* (1834), as well as in various thriller novels.

five-finger A thief, pickpocket. In this expression, the obvious reference is to the hand and its role in stealing something or in picking someone's pocket. A similar expression, *five-finger discount* is used to describe shoplifting, the implication being that by virtue of one's five fingers, a 100% discount has been obtained. Other similar expressions dealing with the hand's role in theft are *light-fingered, sticky-fingered,* and *itchy palm.*

fly-by-night A temporary and usually unethical business; a poor credit risk; a person or enterprise of dubious reputation or questionable merit. This expression originally referred to a person who defrauded his creditors by hurriedly and furtively leaving town in the dead of night, thus flying (or fleeing) by night. In its usual context, however, *fly-by-night* is used adjectivally to describe a business which accepts orders and money but folds before delivering any goods or services, leaving both creditors and customers in the lurch. The expression is sometimes used in a more general sense to describe anyone or anything of uncertain character.

footpad A thief or other criminal who operates on foot. This expression refers to the padded shoes worn by a criminal to muffle his footsteps as he stealthily approaches a victim.

> Roads in the neighborhood of the metropolis were infested by footpads or highwaymen. (Charles Dickens, *Barnaby Rudge,* 1841)

hanky-panky See MISCHIEF.

hatchet man A hired assassin; any writer or speaker, especially a journalist, who manipulates words in order to ruin someone's reputation. The former meaning dates from the mid-1800s when professional murderers actually carried hatchets.

> Some of them are called hatchetmen. They carry a hatchet with the handle cut off. (G. B. Densmore, *Chinese in California,* 1880)

The current figurative meaning, in use since the mid-1900s, refers to character assassination rather than actual murder. Related phrases include *hatchet job* and *hatchet work.*

> Exuberant hatchet jobs were . . . done on Foster Dulles because of his Wall Street connections. (*Time,* October 23, 1944)

horn-thumb A cutpurse; a pickpocket or purse-snatcher. This obsolete term derives from a thief's practice of wearing a thimble of horn on the thumb for protection against the edge of his knife. The term appears in the 17th-century play *Bartholomew Fair:*

> I mean a child of the horn-thumb, a babe of booty, boy, a cut-purse.

jailbird A convict or prisoner; an ex-convict or ex-prisoner. This expression, derived from the iron cages to which inmates were formerly confined, usu-

ally refers to a prisoner who has spent the better part of his life behind bars.

> The one thing dreaded by the old jailbird is work requiring bodily exertion. (*Contemporary Review,* August, 1883)

jaywalker A person who crosses a street without heeding the traffic laws; a presumptuous pedestrian. This expression, derived from the belligerent and defiant jaybird, is commonplace throughout the United States and Great Britain.

> Realizing his mistake, [he] pulls back quickly, narrowly missing the jaywalker. (*Police Review,* November, 1972)

lully prigger A thief of the lowest, most despicable sort. The origin of this expression is unknown; however, *lully prigger* originally referred to a thief who stole wet clothing from a clothesline, and *prigger* alone meant 'horse thief' as early as the 16th century. Today this chiefly British phrase describes any thief.

plug-ugly A hoodlum, thug, miscreant, or larrikin; a gangster; a boisterous, uncouth, physically unattractive person. This term was first used as the self-assumed name of a 19th-century gang that terrorized the city of Baltimore:

> The class of rowdies who originated this euphonious name . . . [said] it was derived from a short spike fastened in the toe of their boots, with which they kicked their opponents in a dense crowd, or, as they elegantly expressed it, "plugged them ugly." (*Times,* November 4, 1876)

Although the gang is long since gone, the expression lives on in figurative contexts:

> His friends were alternately the "plug-uglies" of Sixth Avenue and the dudes of Delmonico's. (*The Pall Mall Gazette,* July 4, 1884)

scofflaw A person who disregards the law. This term is clearly a combination of *scoff* 'mock, jeer' and *law.* The expression, used during Prohibition for a patron of a speakeasy, now usually refers to someone who ignores traffic regulations or refuses to pay traffic fines.

skulduggery Deceitful or dishonest conduct; underhanded scheming. Derived from the Scottish *skulduddery* 'illicit sexual intercourse; obscenity,' *skulduggery* is, by extension, often used to describe fraudulent or surreptitious business practices.

> The United States Courts . . . are now very busy affixing the penalties for violations of the national banking laws and for general skulduggery in the management of institutions. (*Columbus* [Ohio] *Dispatch*, December 22, 1893)

tenderloin See LOCALITY.

wetback An unauthorized immigrant. Although in its widest sense this term may refer to any person who illegally enters the country, *wetback* is most often applied disparagingly to Mexican laborers who wade or swim across the Rio Grande to the United States in search of temporary employment.

> How do these "wetbacks" who slip across the border near Calexico, California manage to swim the Rio Grande? (*Newsweek*, May, 1950)

Wetback is also frequently used as an offensive epithet for any Mexican-American. In addition, "wet" is sometimes prefixed to the names of various animals which are illegally imported from Mexico by American ranchers.

> Pierce once brought three hundred Mexican ponies, "wet ponies," into Texas, at a cost of two dollars and fifty cents a head. (Douglas Branch, *The Cowboy and his Interpreters*, 1926)

CRITERION (See also TEST.)

acid test Any crucial or conclusive test to judge value or genuineness; the "real" test. The term is an extension of a chemical test using nitric acid or aqua fortis, as it is sometimes called, to determine the gold content of jewelry. Used literally in 1892 in G. F. Gee's *The Jeweller's Assistant,* the expression was first used in its figurative sense in 1912:

> Few professional beauties could have stood, as this woman did, the acid test of that mercilessly brilliant morning. (L. J. Vance, *Destroying Angel,* 1912)

Aunt Sally See VICTIMIZATION.

bench mark A standard or touchstone against which to measure; a criterion or test. A bench mark is literally a surveyor's arrow-shaped mark indicating a given elevation used as a point of reference in measuring other elevations. According to the *OED* the name comes from the way a surveyor's angle-iron forms a bracket or bench to support the leveling-staff when taking a reading. The term was used figuratively as early as 1884 in *Science:*

> These star-places . . . are the reference-points and benchmarks of the universe.

landmark decision A verdict issued by a high court (e.g., the Supreme Court) which determines the direction or disposition of a previously untried issue; a precedent-setting ruling. Traditionally, a landmark is a guide for direction in one's course, or, metaphorically, an event that marks a turning point in history. As an adjective, *landmark* has come to describe any decision or legislation of such significance that it will serve as a guide or criterion in similar matters in the future.

play in Peoria To be accepted by the common man of "Middle America." Peoria, a small town in central Illinois, has come to represent traditional, down-to-earth American values, perhaps originally from the experiences of traveling theater troupes in playing to small town audiences. Today the expression is most often heard in the political context; "playing in Peoria" successfully has become the touchstone for determining an idea's appeal to the American public at large.

Procrustean bed An arbitrary system or standard to which ideas, facts, etc., are forced to conform. In Greek mythology, the robber Procrustes made his victims fit the length of his bed by stretching or amputating their limbs. Thus, to *stretch* or *place on the bed of Procrustes* is to produce conformity by violent, irrational means. Figurative use of *Procrustean bed* dates from the 16th century.

> Neither must we attempt to confine the Platonic dialogue on the Procrustean bed of a single idea. (Benjamin Jowett, tr., *The Dialogues of Plato,* 1875)

the proof of the pudding is in the eating A proverbial admonition against passing judgment on something without first examining the evidence or facts; often shortened to *the proof of the pudding.* Another popular proverb conveying basically the same message is the imperative *don't judge a book by its cover.*

rule of thumb A rough guide or approximate measurement; a practical criterion or standard. The thumb's breadth was formerly used in measurements to approximate one inch. Since such reckoning was imprecise and unscientific, *rule of thumb* has come also to indicate a guideline resulting from instinct rather than from scientific investigation. The phrase has been in figurative use for nearly three centuries.

> What he doth, he doth by rule of thumb, and not by Art. (Sir William Hope, *The Compleat Fencing-Master,* 1692)

sounding board A person to whom new concepts and ideas are presented for his reaction or opinion. A sounding board is a structure which reflects sound back to an audience. Its figurative usage was illustrated in *Atlantic,* as cited by *Webster's Third:*

> . . . use the newspapermen merely as a sounding board.

touchstone A criterion or test; a standard or measure. A touchstone is literally a smooth, black, siliceous stone used to test the purity of gold and silver alloys. By rubbing the alloy on the stone and analyzing the color of the streak on the stone, the gold or silver content can be determined. The term was used both literally and figuratively as early as the mid-15th century.

trial balloon Literally, a balloon which is used to test air currents and wind velocity. By extension, a trial balloon is any specific proposal, statement, etc., used to test public reaction by provoking feedback.

CRITICISM (See also **FAULTFINDING.**)

blue-pencil To delete or excise, alter or abridge; to mark for correction or improvement. Used of written matter exclusively, *blue-pencil* derives from the blue pencil used by many editors to make manuscript changes and comments.

damn with faint praise To praise in such restrained or indifferent terms as to render the praise worthless; to condemn by using words which, at best, express mediocrity. Its first use was probably by Alexander Pope in his 1735 *Epistle to Dr. Arbuthnot:*

> Damn with faint praise, assent with civil leer.

peanut gallery See **INSIGNIFICANCE.**

pot shot A random, offhand criticism or condemnation; a censorious remark shot from the hip, lacking forethought and direction. *Webster's Third* cites C. H. Page's reference to

> subjects which require serious discussion, not verbal potshots.

Pot shot originally referred to the indiscriminate, haphazard nature of shots taken at game with the simple intention of providing a meal, i.e., filling the pot. By transference, the term acquired the sense of a shot taken at a defenseless person or thing at close range from an advantageous position.

slings and arrows Barbed attacks, stinging criticism; any suffering or affliction, usually intentionally directed or inflicted. The words come from the famous soliloquy in which Hamlet contemplates suicide:

Whether 'tis nobler in the mind to suffer
The slings and arrows of outrageous fortune,
Or to take arms against a sea of troubles
And by opposing end them. (III,i)

As commonly used, the expression often retains the *suffer* of the original phrase, but usually completes the thought by substituting another object for *outrageous fortune,* as in the following:

En route to the United States the enterprise has suffered the slings and arrows of detractors as diverse as George Meany and Joseph Papp. (Roland Gelatt, in *Saturday Review,* February, 1979)

stop-watch critic A hidebound formalist, whose focus is so riveted on traditional criteria or irrelevant minutiae that he fails to attend to or even see the true and total object of his concern. Laurence Sterne gave us the term in *Tristram Shandy.*

"And how did Garrick speak the soliloquy last night?" "Oh, against all the rule, my lord, most ungrammatically. Betwixt the substantive and the adjective, which should agree together in number, case, and gender, he made a breach, thus—stopping as if the point wanted settling; and betwixt the nominative case, which, your lordship knows, should govern the verb, he suspended his voice in the epilogue a dozen times, three seconds and three-fifths by a stop-watch, my lord, each time."

"Admirable grammarian! But in suspending his voice was the sense suspended likewise? Did no expression of attitude or countenance fill up the chasm? Was the eye silent? Did you narrowly look?" "I looked only at the stop-watch, my lord." "Excellent observer!"

CULMINATION

last hurrah A final moment of glory or triumph; a last fling; a swan song. This expression refers to *hurrah* 'hubbub, commotion, fanfare' and was popularized by Edwin O'Connor's novel, *The Last Hurrah* (1956), which dealt with a big-city political boss apparently modeled after James M. Curley, long-time mayor of Boston.

the straw that broke the camel's back
The last in a series of cumulative irritations, unpleasant tasks, responsibilities, or remarks, especially a seemingly minor one that pushes a person's patience and endurance beyond their limits; a final setback, one which demoralizes someone or destroys an enterprise or other matter. The camel, a beast of burden, stubbornly refuses to move if given too heavy a load to bear. Although a single straw on a camel's back has an insignificant weight, many straws can produce a burden which may be too heavy to bear, figuratively breaking the camel's back. By implication, then, a person subjected to one too many misfortunes or vexations may be pushed beyond his limits and respond suddenly and explosively in a manner which seems disproportionate to the provocation. This expression has several variations, the most common of which is *the last straw.*

swan song The last work, words, or accomplishment of a person or group of persons, especially of a poet, writer, or musician; a final gesture, such as that of a politician or other public figure before retirement or death. This common expression is based on the ancient belief (cited by Aristotle, Plato, Euripides,

Cicero, and others) that swans sing their most beautiful songs just before they die.

> Will you not allow that I have as much of the spirit of prophecy in me as the swans? For they, when they perceive that they must die, having sung all their life long, do then sing more lustily than ever, rejoicing in the thought that they are going to the god they serve. (Plato, *Dialogues,* circa 360 B.C.)

Although the song of a swan is actually somewhat unpleasant to the ear, and no evidence has ever supported the theory that its final song is unusually beautiful, the legend has persisted for centuries and has been incorporated into the works of Shakespeare, Byron, Chaucer, and many other literary masters.

> The Phoenix soars aloft, . . . or, as now, she sinks, and with spheral swan song, immolates herself in flame. (Thomas Carlyle, *Sartor Resartus,* 1831)

CURIOSITY (See also MEDDLE-SOMENESS.)

eavesdropper One who clandestinely listens in on private conversations; a fly on the wall, a snoop or spy. It was formerly the practice of such persons to listen in on private conversations by standing under the eaves of the dwelling in which they occurred. The *dropper* part of the term seems to have some connection with rain dripping off the eaves and onto the listener standing under them, as indicated by the following passage describing the punishment prescribed by the Freemasons for a convicted eavesdropper:

> To be placed under the eaves of the house in rainy weather, till the water runs in at his shoulders and out at his heels.

The term dates from 1487.

fly on the wall An eavesdropper, an unseen witness. In this expression, the implication is that a small, inconspicuous fly that has settled on a wall is able to witness events without being noticed. The phrase is nearly always heard as part of a person's expressed desire to see and hear certain conversations or goings on ("I'd love to be a fly on the wall"); rarely is it used in contexts implying actual clandestine behavior. This same concept, that is, a small, unobtrusive insect acting as a witness, may have given rise to *bug* 'a concealed recording device or microphone.' However, it is more likely that *bug* was used to describe the tiny microphone, which resembles an insect.

rubberneck A person who gapes and gawks; one who stares intently at something or someone; a curious observer; a tourist. This expression alludes to the elasticlike neck contortions of one trying to view everything in sight. Although the phrase sometimes carries a disparaging implication of unjustified curiosity, *rubberneck* is more often applied humorously to conspicuous sightseers in an unfamiliar locale who gaze wonderingly at scenes taken for granted by the natives.

> They are the nobility—the swells. They don't hang around the streets like tourists and rubbernecks. (G. B. McCutcheon, *Truxton King,* 1910)

take a gander To glance at; to look at out of curiosity. This expression, derived from the inquisitive male goose, enjoys widespread use in the United States and Great Britain.

> Take a gander at the see-through door below. See that corrugated piece of steel? (*Scientific American,* October, 1971)

D

DANGER (See also **PRECARIOUS-NESS, PREDICAMENT, RISK, VULNERA-BILITY**.)

beware the ides of March See **SUPERSTITION**.

cat ice Flimsy ground, precarious condition. Cat ice is extremely thin ice formed on shallow water which has since receded. It owes its name to the belief that it could not support even the weight of a cat. The phrase has been in use since 1884.

nourish a snake in one's bosom To show kindness to one who proves ungrateful. The allusion is to the Aesop fable in which a farmer, finding a snake frozen stiff with cold, placed it in his bosom. The snake, thawed by the warmth, quickly revived and inflicted a fatal bite on its benefactor.

> I fear me you but warm the starved snake,
> Who, cherished in your breasts, will sting your hearts.
> (Shakespeare, *II Henry VI*, III,i)

snake in the grass A sneak, dastard, skulker; a suspicious, treacherous, or disingenuous person; a traitor or craven; any lurking danger. This expression is derived from a line in Virgil's *Third Eclogue* (approx. 40 B.C.), *Latet anguis in herba* 'a snake lurks in the grass,' alluding to the potential danger posed by a poisonous snake that is hidden in the grass as if in ambush.

> There is a snake in the grass and the design is mischievous. (Thomas Hearne, *Remarks and Collections*, 1709)

sword of Damocles The threat of impending danger or doom; also *Damocles' sword*.

> Little do directors and their companies know of this sword of Damocles that hangs over them. (*Law Times*, 1892)

The allusion is to the sycophant Damocles, invited by Dionysius of Syracuse to a lavish banquet. But Damocles could not enjoy the sumptuous feast because Dionysius had had suspended over his head a sword hanging by a single hair. He dared not move lest the sword fall and kill him. See also **hang by a thread, PRECARIOUSNESS**.

DEATH

big jump An American cowboy who dies is said to have taken the big jump.

bite the dust To die; to come a cropper; to suffer defeat; to fail. The image created by the phrase is one of death: a warrior or soldier falling from a horse and literally biting the dust. In 1697, Dryden used the phrase in his translation of Virgil's *Aeneid*.

> So many Valiant Heros bite the Ground.

Western stories popularized the phrase in expressions such as "many a redskin bit the dust that day" *(Webster's Third)*. It is also said to have gained currency during World War II in R.A.F. circles. Today the phrase is used figuratively in reference to the defeat, disaster, or failure of a person or something closely associated with a person. One who is defeated is said to bite the dust, but rarely is the phrase used seriously in regard to someone's death.

bless the world with one's heels To suffer death by hanging. The *bless* of the expression carries its obsolete meaning 'to wave or brandish,' a meaning Dr. Johnson conjectured derived from the action of benediction when the celebrant blesses the congregation with the monstrance. In somewhat similar fashion a hanging man blesses the world with his heels.

buy it To be killed; to die prematurely as a result of a tragedy. *Buy it* is a witty way of saying "pay for it with one's life." The phrase dates from the early 19th century when it was used primarily in military circles.

> The wings and fuselage, with fifty-three bullet holes, caused us to realize on our return how near we had been to "buying it." (W. Noble, *With Bristol Fighter Squadron,* 1920)

Today this British slang phrase is used in nonmilitary contexts as well.

buy the box To die, or be as good as dead. Many people buy their own coffins in order to spare their families the expense and trauma of the funeral and burial arrangements. The irony of "preparing for death" probably gave rise to this irreverent slang expression, the implication being that once a person "buys the box," he might as well be dead.

buy the farm To die; to be shot down and killed. The origin of this British slang phrase has been attributed to British pilots who were wont to say that when "it was all over," they were "going to settle down and buy a farm." Many pilots were never able to realize this dream because they were shot down and killed. Thus, *buy the farm* became a euphemism for 'die' because of the glaring disparity between the idealized dream cherished by the pilots and the tragic reality of the death they experienced.

cash in one's chips To die, to pass on or away. Also *cash* or *pass* or *hand in one's checks.* In use since the 1870s, this expression is a reference to the card game of poker, in which a player turns in his chips or checks to the banker in exchange for cash at the end of the game.

cross the Great Divide To die; to go west; to cross the Styx. *Cross over* is a euphemistic way of saying 'to die.' *Cross the Great Divide* is a longer, more emphatic, but still euphemistic way of saying the same thing. Here the "Great Divide" is being used figuratively to refer to the illusory line between life and death. At one time, the unsettled area referred to as the "West"—across the Great Divide or Continental Divide —represented the "Great Unknown," and heading in that direction came to mean risking one's life.

curtains See **TERMINATION.**

dance on air To be hanged; also *dance on nothing.* A person who is hanged may undergo involuntary muscle contractions. These jerky movements resemble dancing of a sort. Similar expressions include *dance in the rope* and *dance the Tyburn jig,* the latter in reference to Tyburn, a place for public executions in London, England.

> If any of them chanced to be made dance in the rope, they thought him happy to be so freed of the care and trouble [that] attends the miserable indigent. (Sorel's *Comical History of Francion,* 1655)

> Just as the felon condemned to die . . .
> From his gloomy cell in a vision elopes,
> To caper on sunny greens and slopes,
> Instead of the dance upon nothing. (Thomas Hood, *Kilmansegg, Her Death,* 1840)

dead as a doornail Dead, very dead, deader than dead; inoperative with no hope of repair. Many houses formerly had a heavy metal knocker on the front door. A doornail was a large, heavy-headed spike sometimes used as a striker plate against which the knocker was struck to increase its loudness and prevent damage to the door. Since the doornail was continually being struck on the head, it was assumed that nothing could be deader.

> Old Marley was as dead as a doornail. (Charles Dickens, *A Christmas Carol,* 1843)

As knockers (and doornails) became less common, the word *doorknob* was often substituted in the expression. Other expressions such as *dumb as a doornail* and *deaf as a doornail* imply that someone is extremely stupid or stone deaf, respectively.

debt to nature Death. The implication is that life is a loan and, with or without interest, it must be paid off with death. *Pay one's debt to nature* means to die. Both these expressions, common since the Middle Ages, have been used as euphemistic epitaphs on tombstones, particularly those from the early 20th century.

> Pay nature's debt with a cheerful countenance. (Christopher Marlowe, *Edward II*, approx. 1593)

die for want of lobster sauce See EXCESSIVENESS.

die in harness To die while working or while in the middle of some action, especially while fighting. The allusion may be to a horse who drops dead while still in harness, as a plowhorse working a field. Another possibility is that *harness* is used in the archaic sense of armor for men or horses, as in the following passage from Shakespeare's *Macbeth:*

> At least we'll die with harness on our back. (V,v)

Two similar phrases are to *die in the saddle* and to *die with one's boots on.* The latter dates from the late 19th century and formerly meant to die a violent death, especially by hanging. To *die in the saddle* brings to mind cavalry or mounted soldiers while to *die with one's boots on* conjures up images of foot soldiers, as in the following citation:

> They died with their boots on; they hardly ever surrendered. (*Listener Magazine*, 1959)

die like Roland See HUNGER.

feed the fishes To die by drowning.

food for worms A dead and interred body; a corpse or carcass. The source of this saying is obvious. Another expression of similar zoological origin is *food for fishes,* referring to one dead from drowning.

> He was food for fishes now, poor fellow. (Rider Haggard, *Mr. Meson's Will,* 1894)

give up the ghost To die, to expire, to breathe one's last. *Ghost* refers to one's soul or spirit, the essence of life. The expression is Biblical in origin:

> But man dieth, and wasteth away: yea, man giveth up the ghost, and where is he? (Job 14:10)

go belly up An American slang expression meaning to die and float belly up in the manner of dead fish. It is used figuratively for any failure or nonsuccess, just as *death* is.

go the way of all flesh To die. This expression is of Biblical origin:

> And, behold, this day I am going the way of all the Earth. (Joshua 23:14)

The phrase's evolution to its present form with *flesh* substituted for *the Earth* is not fully understood by modern scholars. The expression appeared in *The Golden Age* by Thomas Heywood (1611):

> Whether I had better go home by land, or by sea? If I go by land and miscarry, then I go the way of all flesh.

go west To expire, die. This expression, obviously derived from the setting of the sun in the west, may be traced to the ancient Egyptian belief that their dead resided west of the Nile River. In addition, whites who traveled west of the Mississippi during the frontier days were considered fair game for Indians; hence, in the United States "going west" became synonymous with dying. The use of this expression has decreased since its heyday during World War I.

> I shall once again be in the company of dear old friends now 'gone west.' (E. Corri, *Thirty Years as a Boxing Referee*, 1915)

have [someone's] number on it See
DESTINY.

join the majority To die; to pass on or
away. Also *join the great majority, go* or
*pass over to the majority, death joins us
to the great majority*. Based on the
Latin phrase *abiit ad plures*, this expression and variants have been in use
since the early 18th century.

kick the bucket To die. Although several explanations as to the origin of this
expression have been advanced, the
most plausible states that the phrase
came from an old custom of hanging
slaughtered pigs by their heels from a
beam, or *bucket*, as it is known in parts
of England. In use since 1785, this irreverent synonym for *to die* is popular in
both England and America. Shorter
variations include *kick, kick off,* and
kick in.

leap in the dark An action of unknown
consequences; a blind venture; death.
The last words of Thomas Hobbes, philosopher and translator (1588–1679),
are reputed to have been:

Now am I about to take my last
voyage—a great leap in the dark.

make a hole in the water To commit
suicide by drowning. The hole in this
expression refers to a grave. To make a
hole in the water, then, is to go to a
watery grave intentionally. This slang
phrase, rarely heard today, dates from
the mid-19th century.

Why I don't go and make a hole in
the water I don't know. (Charles
Dickens, *Bleak House,* 1853)

make [someone's] beard See DOMI-
NATION.

necktie party A lynching or hanging;
also *necktie social, necktie sociable,
necktie frolic*. This euphemistic and irreverent American slang expression,
popularized by western movies, is an
extension of the slang *necktie* 'hangman's rope.'

Mr. Jim Clemenston, equine
abductor, was on last Thursday
morning, at ten sharp, made the
victim of a neck-tie sociable.
(*Harper's Magazine,* November,
1871)

[one's] number is up A person is about
to die—one is done for, one's time has
come. At an earlier date, *number* referred to one's lottery number; currently, the full expression refers euphemistically to death.

Fate had dealt him a knock-out
blow; his number was up. (P. G.
Wodehouse, *Girl on Boat,* 1922)

This expression was common among
American soldiers who may have
been the first to use it in speaking of
death.

peg out To die; to bite the dust. In
cribbage, the game is finished when a
player pegs out the last hole. This expression is among the less frequently
heard euphemisms for death.

Harrison . . . was then 67 . . . and
actually pegged out in 1841. (H. L.
Mencken, in *The New Yorker,*
October 1, 1949)

push up daisies To be dead and buried
in one's grave; also *turn one's toes up to
the daisies* and *under the daisies*. The
reference is to the flowers often planted
on top of new graves. The expression
and variants have been in use since the
mid-19th century.

sprout wings See CHARITABLENESS.

step off To die; to be married. The expression's latter sense, often extended
to *step off the carpet*, refers to the conclusion of the bride's procession to the
altar. The phrase's former, more common, meaning is an allusion to the last
footstep of life.

The old man and I are both due to
step off if we're caught. (Dashiell
Hammett, *Blood Money,* 1927)

take for a ride To murder; to deceive
or cheat; to pull someone's leg. This underworld euphemism for 'murder'
dates from the early 1900s. Gangsters
first abducted their victims, then took

them to a secluded area where they were murdered.

> The gang believes he is getting yellow or soft, and usually takes him for a ride. . . . (Emanuel H. Lavine, *The Third Degree*, 1930)

Take for a ride also means 'deceive, cheat' because the driver is in a position to manipulate or trick. The expression is often used of one who leads another on and then fleeces him.

> But the one who really took my friend for a ride was the electrician. He used more . . . cable . . . than . . . it takes to build a battle ship. (Roger W. Babson, in a syndicated newspaper column, 1951)

turn one's face to the wall To die; more precisely, to make the final gesture of acquiescence indicating that one is about to give up the ghost. The origin is Biblical (2 Kings 22:2); when Hezekiah was informed his death was imminent:

> He turned his face to the wall, and prayed unto the Lord.

The expression appears in works as varied as *Narratives of the Days of the Reformation* (1579):

> He turned his face to the wall in the said belfry; and so after his prayers slept sweetly in the lord.

and *Tom Sawyer* (1876):

> He would turn his face to the wall, and die with that word unsaid. (Mark Twain)

DECADENCE

bread and circuses Free food and entertainment, particularly that which a government provides in order to appease the common people. Such is reputed to bring about a civilization's decline by undermining the initiative of the populace, and the term has come to mean collective degeneration or debauchery. According to Juvenal's *Satires, panem et circenses* were the two things most coveted by the Roman people. *Bread and Circuses* was the title

of a book by H. P. Eden (1914). Rudyard Kipling used the expression in *Debits and Credits* (1924):

> Rome has always debauched her beloved Provincia with bread and circuses.

the primrose path The route of pleasure and decadence; a frivolous, self-indulgent life. In Shakespeare's *Macbeth* the drunken porter, playing at being the tender of Hell gate, says:

> I had thought to have let in some of all professions that go the primrose way to the everlasting bonfire. (II,iii)

The expression connotes a colorful, blossomy course of luxury and ease, but as commonly used also includes the implication that such a carefree, self-gratifying life cannot be enjoyed without paying a price.

> Never to sell his soul by travelling the primrose path to wealth and distinction. (James A. Froude, *Thomas Carlyle*, 1882)

wine and roses Wanton decadence and luxury; indulgence in pleasure and promiscuity; la dolce vita. This expression, often extended to *days of wine and roses*, alludes to the opulence as well as the depravity of the primrose path. The longer expression was popularized by an early 1960s film and song so entitled.

DECEPTION (See MENDACITY, PLOY, PRETENSE, SWINDLING, TRICKERY.)

DECISIVENESS

burn one's bridges To cut oneself off from all possible means of retreat, literal or figurative; to make an irrevocable statement or decision from which one cannot withdraw without considerable embarrassment, humiliation, or disgrace; also *burn one's boats* or *ships*. This expression, in figurative use since the late 1800s, is said to have come from the military practice of burning the troop ships upon landing on foreign soil in order to impress upon the soldiers the fact that only a victorious campaign would ensure them a safe return to their own country.

cross the Rubicon To take a decisive, irrevocable step, especially at the start of an undertaking or project; also *pass the Rubicon.* This expression, which dates from 1626, refers to the decision of Julius Caesar in 49 B.C. to march with his army across the Rubicon, the ancient name of a small stream in northern Italy forming part of the boundary with Cisalpine Gaul. The decision was tantamount to declaring war, since there was a law forbidding a Roman general to cross the stream with armed soldiers. Caesar's crossing did in fact mark the beginning of the war with Pompey. Another phrase with a similar meaning is *the die is cast* (Latin *alea jacta est*)—the words said to have been uttered by Caesar during the crossing.

fish or cut bait A request or demand that someone take definitive action, resolve a situation, or make a choice. The implication here is that one cannot both fish and cut bait at the same time, and, if he is not going to fish, he should step aside and give someone else a chance while he cuts bait. A similar common expression is *shape up or ship out.*

flat-footed See CANDIDNESS.

leave the door open To decide not to commit oneself or to limit one's options. Figurative use of *door* is as old as the literal. This particular expression dates from at least 1863.

> Which left open a door to future negotiation. (Alexander W. Kinglake, *The Invasion of the Crimea,* 1863)

put one's foot down To take a firm stand; to decisively embrace a point of view. The stance assumed by literally putting one's foot down reflects a men-

tal attitude of determination and will power. Such decisiveness is often the response to having been pushed to the limits of endurance or patience.

put your money where your mouth is To back up one's words with action; to support one's assertions by willingness to risk monetary loss. This expression, perhaps of gambling origin, implies that certain statements are worthless unless the assertor is willing to reinforce them with a cash bet. The expression is now in wide use throughout the United States and Great Britain.

> The squadron betting book the barman keeps . . . for guys who are ready to put their money where their mouth is. (A. Price, *Our Man in Camelot,* 1975)

take the plunge To make an important and often irrevocable decision despite misgivings; to choose to act, usually after much deliberation or a bout of indecision. The allusion is to a swimmer who dives into the water, in spite of doubts or fear.

DEFERENCE

after you, my dear Alphonse This popular catch phrase is the first half of the complete expression "After you, my dear Alphonse—no, after you, my dear Gaston." It first appeared in the Hearst (King Features) comic strip *Happy Hooligan* written by F. Opper. The strip ran throughout the 1920s and for part of the 1930s. The characters Alphonse and Gaston were two extremely debonair Frenchmen who were so polite that they would jeopardize themselves in times of danger by taking the time to courteously ask each other to go first. Today, when two people go to do the same thing at the same time, one might humorously say to the other, "After you, my dear Alphonse."

cap in hand Submissively; with a deferential air or manner. The phrase alludes to the image of a rustic or servant who self-consciously and humbly takes off his cap and holds it, usually against his chest, while speaking to someone of higher social status.

give the wall To yield the safest place; to allow another to walk on the walled side of a street. This expression is derived from an old custom which compelled pedestrians to surrender the safer, inner path bordering a roadway to a person of higher social rank. Modern social etiquette still requires a man to walk on the streetside of a female when walking along a sidewalk. A related expression, *take the wall*, describes the adamant perambulator who assumes the safer path closer to the wall. The inevitable friction between "givers" and "takers" is discussed by James Boswell in his *Journal of a Tour of the Hebrides* (1773):

> In the last age . . . there were two sets of people, those who gave the wall, and those who took it; the peaceable and the quarrelsome. . . . Now it is fixed that every man keeps to the right; or, if one is taking the wall, another yields it, and it is never a dispute.

strike sail See SUBMISSION.

DEGENERATION

go to hell in a handbasket To indulge in petty or sporadic dissipation; to carouse occasionally, in a small way; to degenerate bit by bit; gradually to go downhill morally. This slang expression is often used to describe typically adolescent anti-social behavior, usually of a temporary nature. However, it sometimes carries connotations of more serious and permanent moral decline. Its origin is unknown but it is interesting to speculate that it may be related to *go to heaven in a wheelbarrow* 'to be damned'—*handbasket* replacing *wheelbarrow* to indicate the relative smallness of one's sins; *hell* replacing *heaven* to accommodate more literal minds. See **go to heaven in a wheelbarrow**, PUNISHMENT.

go to pot To deteriorate, to go downhill, to degenerate, to fall into a state of disuse or ruin. Although the exact origin of this expression is unknown, it may be related to the earlier phrase *go to the pot*, literally 'to be cut into pieces like meat for the pot,' and figuratively 'to be ruined or destroyed.'

> If it were to save the whole empire from going to pot, nobody would stay at home. (*Pall Mall Gazette*, February, 1884)

go to rack and ruin To degenerate, to deteriorate, to decline, to fall apart; also *to go to rack* and *to go to ruin*. *Rack* 'destruction' is a variant of *wrack* and *wreck*. The expression dates from at least 1599.

> Everything would soon go to sixes and sevens, and rack and ruin. (Elizabeth Blower, *George Bateman*, 1782)

go to the dogs To degenerate morally or physically, to deteriorate, to go to ruin. The expression, which dates from at least the early 17th century, is thought to have come from the earlier Latin phrase *addicere aliquem canibus* 'to bequeath him to dogs.'

> Rugby and the school-house are going to the dogs. (Thomas Hughes, *Tom Brown's School Days*, 1857)

on the high-road to Needham On the road to poverty or ruin; on the skids; suffering a mental, moral, or financial decline. This British expression, of infrequent occurrence, simply puns on *need* without reference to a specific locality.

on the skids On the road to poverty, ruin, disgrace, or oblivion; in a state of rapid deterioration or decline. *The skids* as denotative of a moral condition may derive from *Skid Row*. (See LOCALITY.) It appears frequently in longer phrases such as *hit the skids* 'start on the downward path' or *put the skids under* 'cause the ruin or decline' of a person or plan.

By 1929 Bix [Beiderbecke] was on the way down—not yet on the skids, but the good time and the big time was behind him. (Stephen Longstreet, *The Real Jazz Old and New*, 1956)

the seamy side The most disagreeable, unsavory, and offensive aspect; the sordid, perverse, degenerate, or immoral features. Literally, *the seamy side* refers to the wrong, or underside, of pieced fabric which shows the rough edges and seams of an otherwise acceptable article of clothing, tapestry, etc. The figurative use of *the seamy side* was pioneered by Shakespeare:

Oh fie upon them! Some such squire he was
That turned your wit the seamy side without,
And made you to suspect me with the Moor.
(*Othello*, IV,ii)

A commonly used derivative is *seamy*.

DEGREE (See EXTENT.)

DEJECTION (See also GRIEVING.)

crestfallen Dispirited; lacking in confidence, spirit, or courage; humbled; in a blue funk. In use since the 16th century, this term is said to allude to the crests of fighting cocks which reputedly become rigid and deep-red in color during the height of battle but flaccid and droopy following defeat. This theory regarding the term's origin is unlikely, however, since the crests of fighting cocks are cut off.

down in the mouth Sad, dejected, disappointed, in low spirits, down in the dumps. This expression, dating from the mid-17th century, derives from the fact that the corners of a person's mouth are drawn down when he is sad or despondent.

The Roman Orator was down in the mouth; finding himself thus cheated by the money-changer. (Bp. Joseph Hall, *Resolutions and Decisions of Diverse Practical Cases of Conscience*, 1649)

eat one's heart out See eat one's heart, SELF-PITY.

in the doldrums See STAGNATION.

in the dumps In a dull and gloomy state of mind; sad, depressed, joyless, long-faced. No one knows the exact origin of *dump*, in use since the 16th century. One suggestion is that it derives from the Dutch *domp* 'exhalation, haze, mist,' and that this meaning gave rise to its association with mental haziness. An even less convincing theory is that *dumps* is an allusion to King Dumops of Egypt, who, after building a pyramid, died of melancholia. Thus, one who suffers from melancholia, like King Dumops, is said to be "in the dumps." This expression, still current, and *in doleful dumps* were in use in the 17th century. *Down in the dumps* is another popular variant.

no joy in Mudville Pervasive sadness or disappointment, especially that accompanying the unexpected defeat of a local sports team. This expression, generally limited to use by sports reporters, is derived from "Casey at the Bat," a poem which tells of the untimely failure of the hometown baseball hero to save the day:

Oh! somewhere in this favored land the sun is shining bright;
The band is playing somewhere, and somewhere hearts are light;
And somewhere men are laughing and somewhere children shout,
But there is no joy in Mudville— mighty Casey has struck out.
(Ernest Thayer, "Casey at the Bat," 1888)

off one's feed See ILL HEALTH.

a peg too low Moody, listless, melancholy. The drinking bouts of medieval England occasionally turned to brawls when one of several men drinking from the same tankard accused another of taking more than his share. This problem was remedied by the legendary St.

Dunstan, who suggested that pegs be placed at equal intervals inside the cup to indicate each man's portion. Apparently, the expression evolved its figurative meaning in allusion to the dismay of one whose remaining portion was depressingly small. The phrase usually implies a desire for another go at "the cup that cheers."

the pits An extraordinarily poor state of mind; the depths of despond; the nadir; the worst of anything. This expression, alluding to an extremely deep shaft or abyss, enjoys widespread slang use in the United States. Columnist Erma Bombeck recently punned on the expression in entitling a collection, *If Life Is a Bowl of Cherries, What Am I Doing In the Pits?* (1978).

slough of despond A feeling of intense discouragement, despair, depression, or hopelessness. In John Bunyan's *Pilgrim's Progress* (1678), the Slough of Despond was a deep, treacherous bog which had to be crossed in order to reach the Wicket Gate. When Christian, the pilgrim, fell into the Slough, he might have been totally consumed had not his friend Help come to his assistance. Eventually, *slough of despond* became more figurative, describing the seemingly helpless and hopeless predicament of being enmired in despair.

> I remember slumping all [of] a sudden into the slough of despond, and closing my letter in the dumps. (Thomas Twining, *Recreations and Studies of a Country Clergyman of the 18th Century,* 1776)

touch bottom To reach one's lowest point; to sink to the depths of despair; to know the worst; to feel that everything has gone wrong and nothing worse can happen. In print at least as early as the mid-19th century, this expression probably derives its figurative use from the nautical use referring to a ship which scrapes its bottom and is temporarily or permanently disabled.

waterworks Tears, crying, the shedding of tears; often to *turn on the waterworks;* also to *turn on the faucet.*

> Harry could not bear to see Clare cry. "Hold up!" he cried. "This will never do. Hullo! no waterworks here, if you please." (*F. Leslie's Chatterbox* [New York], 1885–86)

By implying that the flow of tears can be turned on and off virtually at will, these phrases place doubt on the sincerity of the tears being shed. This facetious use of the term dates from the 17th century.

DEPARTURE (See also ESCAPE.)

cut and run To leave as quickly as possible; to take off without further to-do; in slang terms, to split or cut out. These figurative meanings derive from the nautical use of *cut and run* which dates from the 18th century. According to a book on sailing entitled *Rigging and Seamanship* (1794), *cut and run* means "to cut the cable and make sail instantly, without waiting to weigh anchor." By extension, this expression can be used to describe any type of quick getaway.

> The alternative was to go to jail, or as the phrase is, to cut and run. (H. H. Brackenridge, *Modern Chivalry,* 1815)

Both nautical and figurative uses are current today.

cut one's stick To be off, to go away, to depart, to leave; also *to cut one's lucky,* although the sense here is more to decamp, to escape. This British slang expression, which dates from the early 19th century, is said to have come from the custom of cutting a walking stick prior to a departure.

do a moonlight flit To leave a hotel or other accommodation without paying the bill. This expression, often used jocularly in England, has a self-evident application and is sometimes applied to any situation in which someone is said to evade his responsibilities.

hoist the blue peter To indicate or advertise that departure is imminent. A "blue peter" is a flag of the International Code of Signals for the letter "P," used aboard vessels to signal that preparations are being made for departure. A blue flag with a white square in the center, it is a signal for hands on shore to come aboard and for others to conclude business with the crew. It dates from about 1800. By 1823, figurative use of *hoist the blue peter* gained currency, as exemplified in the following quotation from Byron's *Don Juan* (1823):

> It is time that I should hoist my "blue Peter,"
> And sail for a new theme.

Blue peter is also the name for a move in whist in which one plays an unnecessarily high card as a call for trumps.

make tracks To leave rapidly; to hotfoot it; to flee or escape. This expression alludes to the trail or tracks created by the passage of human beings or animals through woods, snow, etc. The phrase has been in widespread use since the early 19th century.

> I'd a made him make tracks, I guess. (Thomas Haliburton, *Clockmaster*, 1835)

pull up stakes To move or relocate; to leave one's job, home, etc., for another part of the country.

> They just pulled up stakes and left for parts unknown. (*The New Orleans Times-Picayune Magazine*, April, 1950)

Stakes are sticks or posts used as markers to delimit the boundaries of one's property. In colonial times, literally pulling up stakes meant that one was giving up one's land in order to move on, just as driving them in meant that one was laying claim to the enclosed land to set up housekeeping.

shake the dust from one's feet To depart resolutely from an unpleasant or disagreeable place; to leave in anger, exasperation, or contempt.

> I then paid off my lodgings, and "shaking the dust from my feet," bid a long adieu to London. (Frances Burney, *Cecilia*, 1782)

The expression, which implies a certain abruptness, is found in Matthew 10:14 where Jesus is speaking to the disciples before sending them out to preach the Word:

> And whosoever shall not receive you, nor hear your words, when ye depart out of that house or city, shake off the dust of your feet.

take to the tall timber To depart unexpectedly and with little to-do; to escape. *Tall timber* originally referred to a heavily timbered, uninhabited area in the forest. This colloquial Americanism, often used literally, dates from the early 1800s.

> I fell off *three times;* finally the disgusted critter took to the tall timber, leaving me to hike onward and to get across the frigid stream as best I could. (*Sky Line Trail*, October 18, 1949)

Variants of this expression include *break* or *strike* or *pull for tall timber.*

DEPENDABILITY (See **CONSTANCY.**)

DEPENDENCE

close as the bark to the tree See **FRIENDSHIP.**

hang on [someone's] sleeve To be completely dependent on someone for support or assistance; to rely on someone else's judgment. The allusion is perhaps to children hanging onto their mother's sleeve. This expression, now obsolete, dates from at least 1548. It appears in Samuel Hieron's *Works* (1607):

> You shall see . . . a third hanging upon some lawyer's sleeve, to plot and devise how to perpetuate his estate.

hooked Addicted; entangled in a difficult situation; under someone else's power or influence; devoted to or obsessed by a person, occupation, or other matter. This expression refers to the plight of a fish that has been captured, or hooked, by a fisherman, a fate which usually leads to the animal's destruction. *Hooked* or the related *on the hook* often describes a person who is addicted to or dependent on drugs, alcohol, cigarettes, or some other potentially harmful habit; but it is used equally often in reference to one's consuming hobby or interest.

> "Poor Caudle!" he said to himself; "he's hooked, and he'll never get himself off the hook again."
> (Anthony Trollope, *The Small House At Arlington*, 1864)

See also **get someone off the hook**, **RESCUE**.

meal ticket One's main source of income; a person, skill, or talent upon which one depends for his livelihood. This familiar expression originally referred to a prize fighter who was virtually the breadwinner for his agent and manager. Today, the phrase is usually used in reference to a working spouse.

> He was her meal-ticket. Why should she want him sent to the pen? (H. Howard, *Nice Day for a Funeral*, 1972)

on a string Dependent, easily manipulated, psychologically or financially tied to another person; unable to stand on one's own two feet. This expression dates from the 1500s although it is antedated by use of the single word *string* referring to a leash or other inhibiting tie or connection.

> Make him put his slippers on,
> And be sure his boots are gone,
> And you've got him on a string, you see. (*Circus Girl*, 1897)

Currently *on a string* is often heard in the context of relationships where one person is subject to the whims of another.

on [someone's] coattails Dependent upon or as a consequence of another's effort. The image is of a swallow-tailed coat, whose tapered ends naturally follow its body as sort of secondary appendages. The term is usually derogatory, implying a lack of ability to fare for oneself or to gain an undeserved benefit. Its most frequent use, as well as its origin, is probably political: to *ride in on someone's coattails* means to be carried into office because a popular candidate led the ticket. Abraham Lincoln used the term in 1848:

> Has he no acquaintance with the ample military coat tail of General Jackson? Does he not know that his own party have run the last five Presidential races on that coat tail? *(Congressional Globe)*

tied to [someone's] apron strings Completely under someone's thumb, totally dominated by or dependent on another person; usually used in reference to a husband or son's relationship with his wife or mother, respectively. The allusion is probably to the way small children cling to their mother's skirts for support and protection. Thomas Babington Macaulay used the expression in *The History of England from the Accession of James II* (1849):

> He could not submit to be tied to the apron strings even of the best of wives.

DERISION (See **INSULT**, **RIDICULE**.)

DESIRE (See also **LUST**.)

big eyes A great lust or desire for a person or object. This jazz term, in use since the 1950s, may have come from the older, less picturesque to *have eyes for* 'to be attracted to or desirous of,' used as early as 1810 in *The Scottish Chiefs* by Jane Porter. *Big eyes* has a corresponding negative expression, *no eyes*, also in use since 1950s, meaning 'lack of desire, or disinclination.'

forbidden fruit A tempting but prohibited object or experience; an unauthorized or illegal indulgence, often of a sexual nature. The Biblical origin of this phrase appears in Genesis 3:3:

But of the fruit of the tree which is in the midst of the garden, God hath said, Ye shall not eat of it, neither shall ye touch it, lest ye die.

The expression has been used figuratively for centuries.

The stealing and tasting of the forbidden fruit of sovereignty. (James Heath, *Flagellum,* 1663)

give one's eyeteeth To gladly make the greatest sacrifice to obtain a desired end; to yield something precious in exchange for the achievement of one's desire. The eyeteeth, so named because their roots extend to just under the eyes, are the two pointed canines which flank the front teeth of the upper jaw. Since excruciating pain accompanies their extraction, this expression came to imply making a painful sacrifice.

He'd give his eye-teeth to have written a book half as good. (W. S. Maugham, *Cakes & Ale,* 1930)

give one's right arm To be willing to make a great sacrifice or to endure great pain or inconvenience; to trade something as irreplaceable as part of one's body for an object of desire. In our predominantly right-handed society, to forfeit one's right arm signifies a great loss. This phrase has been popular since the early 1900s. Earlier, in the late 19th century, *willing to give one's ears* was a common expression. It is said to allude to the ancient practice of cutting off ears for various offenses.

Many a man would give his ears to be allowed to call two such charming young ladies by their Christian names. (William E. Norris, *Thirlby Hall,* 1883)

go through fire and water To be willing to suffer pain or brave danger in order to obtain the object of one's desire; to undergo great sacrifice or pay any price to achieve a desired end; to prove oneself by the most demanding of tests. The expression is thought to derive from ordeals involving fire and water which were common methods of trial in Anglo-Saxon times. To prove their innocence, accused persons were often forced to carry hot bars of iron or to plunge a hand into boiling water without injury. The phrase is now used exclusively in a figurative sense, as illustrated by the following from Shakespeare's *Merry Wives of Windsor:*

A woman would run through fire and water for such a kind heart. (III,iv)

itching palm Avarice, greed, cupidity; an abnormal desire for money and material possessions, often implying an openness or susceptibility to bribery. The expression apparently arose from the old superstition that a person whose palm itches is about to receive money. The figurative sense of *itching* 'an uneasy desire or hankering' dates from the first half of the 14th century. Shakespeare used the phrase in *Julius Caesar:*

Let me tell you, Cassius, you yourself
Are much condemned to have an itching palm. (IV,iii)

make the mouth water To excite a craving or desire, to cause to anticipate eagerly. This expression has its origin in the stimulation of the salivary glands by the appetizing sight or smell of food. Both literal and figurative uses of the phrase date from the 16th century.

[She would] bribe him . . . to write down the name of a young Scotch peer . . . that her mouth watered after. (Daniel Defoe, *The History of D. Campbell,* 1720)

my kingdom for a horse! An expression used when one would gladly trade an obviously valuable possession for one of seemingly lesser worth, usually because the lack of the latter renders the former meaningless or useless. It was the cry of Shakespeare's Richard III at Bosworth Field:

A horse! A horse! My kingdom for a horse! (V,iv)

wait for dead men's shoes To covetously await one's inheritance; to eagerly anticipate the position or property that another's death will bring. This expression, infrequently used today, derives from the former Jewish custom surrounding the transfer or bequeathing of property, as related in Ruth 4:7. A bargain was formally sealed by removing and handing over one's shoe. Similarly, inheritance due to death was signaled by pulling off the dead man's shoes and giving them to his heir. *Dead men's shoes* was often used alone to indicate the property so bequeathed or so awaited.

yen A craving or strong desire; a yearning, longing, or hankering. One theory regarding the origin of this expression claims that *yen* is a corruption of the Chinese slang term *yan* 'a craving, as for opium or drink.' Another theory states that *yen* is probably an altered form of *yearn* or *yearning*. The term dates from at least 1908.

> Ever get a yen to "take off" a day or two and see the country? (*Capital-Democrat* [Tishomingo, Oklahoma], June, 1948)

DESPERATION

any port in a storm See EXPEDIENCE.

at the end of one's rope or **tether** At the end of one's endurance or resources, out of options; exasperated, frustrated. The rope or tether is generally conceded to be that formerly attached to a grazing animal, restricting his movement and area of pasturage.

> He was at the end of his rope when he had consumed all the provender within reach.

climb walls To be stir-crazy from confinement; to feel trapped or hemmed-in; to suffer from a lack of options. One who is "climbing the walls" suffers from a claustrophobic feeling of confinement—physical or mental—from which there is no apparent relief. The image is of a person trapped in a room with no doors or windows—the only way for releasing his pent-up energies being to climb the walls.

forlorn hope A desperate hope or undertaking; an expedition in which the survival of the participants is doubtful. This phrase is homonymously derived from the Dutch *verloren hoop* 'lost troop,' and formerly referred to the front line of soldiers in a military confrontation:

> Called the forlorn hope, because they . . . fall on first, and make a passage for the rest. (*Gaya's Art of War*, 1678)

grasp at straws To seek substance in the flimsy or meaning in the insignificant; to find ground for hope where none exists. In common use since the 18th century, the expression derives from the even older self-explanatory proverb: "A drowning man will catch at a straw."

last-ditch Made in a final, desperate, all-out attempt to avoid impending calamity; fought or argued to the bitter end, using every available resource. This expression has the military overtones of continuing one's efforts even though disaster seems imminent and all but the last line of defense (e.g., a ditch or foxhole) has been overcome. Its initial use is credited to William, Prince of Orange, who, in 1672, was asked if he expected to see his country (England) defeated by the French in the war that was raging at the time. He replied, "Nay, there is one certain means by which I can be sure never to see my country's ruin. I will die in the last ditch." He then rejected all offers of peace, intensified his efforts, and was victorious in 1678, not dying in the last ditch, but becoming King William III. A variation, derived from William's quote, is *die in the last ditch*. In contemporary usage, *last ditch* is not limited to military affairs, but is used to describe any all-out, no-holds-barred effort.

> Charlton himself surely was offside before McNab made his last ditch effort to recover the situation. (*Times*, August 27, 1973)

push the panic button To overreact to a situation, to react in a wildly impulsive, confused, or excessive manner, often because of pressures of work. Literally, a panic button is a control button or switch which can trigger the pilot's ejection from an aircraft in an emergency; thus, figuratively, a last resort to be used only when all else has failed.

tear one's hair out To be visibly distressed or agitated; to show signs of extreme anger or anguish. Originally referring to a gesture of mourning or intense grief, this expression, dating from the 16th century, is no longer used literally. It continues to be said, however, of one who is extremely frustrated, or going through an intensely painful emotional experience.

> Sir Ralph the Rover tore his hair
> And curst himself in his despair.
> (Robert Southey, *Inchcape Rock*, 1802)

DESTINY

[one's] cup of tea See PREFERENCE.

handwriting on the wall See OMEN.

have [someone's] number on it To be the instrument of one's fate, usually the agent which causes someone's death. Apparently this expression originated from a superstition that one need not fear any bullet unless it has one's *number* 'code by which one may be identified' on it.

> I'm as safe here as . . . anywhere . . . if it's got your number on it, you'll get it, no matter where you are! (C. Fremlin, *By Horror Haunted*, 1974)

Currently the expression is also heard in broader contexts where the stakes are not always as high as life and death.

in the cards Likely to happen; probable; a sure bet, foreordained; sometimes *on the cards*. The phrase derives from either cartomancy or card playing. The earliest citations are from the beginning of the 19th century.

> It don't come out altogether so plain as to please me, but it's on the cards. (Charles Dickens, *Bleak House*, 1852)

in the wind Imminent, about to happen; astir, afoot. Dating from the 16th century, this expression may have originally referred to something nearby which can be perceived by means of the wind carrying its scent.

> There's a woman in the wind. . . . I'll lay my life on it. (Charles Kingsley, *Westward Ho!*, 1855)

However, *in the wind* refers more often to time than to physical distance.

> There must be something in the wind, perhaps a war. (Benjamin Disraeli, *Vivian Grey*, 1826)

kiss of death A relationship or action, often appearing good and well-meaning, which in reality is destructive or fatal; the instrument of one's downfall or ruination. This expression is a derivative of the earlier phrase *Judas kiss*, the kiss Judas Iscariot gave Jesus in betraying Him to the authorities in the Garden of Gethsemane and which ultimately led to His death by crucifixion. It has been in use since at least 1948.

> Let us hope that the critics' approval does not, at the box-office, prove a kiss of death. (*The Guardian*, December, 1960)

See **Judas kiss**, BETRAYAL.

that's the way the ball bounces See RESIGNATION.

DESTRUCTION (See DOWNFALL, RUINATION, THWARTING.)

DETERIORATION (See DEGENERATION.)

DETERMINATION (See PERSEVERANCE.)

DICTION

BBC English The speech of the announcers of the British Broadcasting Corporation, generally accepted as the epitome of correct British English pronunciation until the early 1970s, when announcers ("presenters" in England) with regional accents were allowed on the air. The term is often used disparagingly due to its connotations of affectation and pretentiousness:

> Critics who enjoy making fun of what they are pleased to call "B.B.C. English" might with profit pay occasional visits to the other side of the Atlantic, in order to hear examples of our language as broadcast where there are no official "recommendations to announcers." (*Listener*, 1932)

The expression is rapidly losing its significance.

the King's English Perfectly spoken English; also, *the Queen's English*. The British monarch has long been considered the paragon of flawless diction, notwithstanding the fact that many of the kings and queens spoke with heavy accents. The expression was used in Shakespeare's *Merry Wives of Windsor:*

> Abusing of God's patience, and the King's English. (I,iv)

Received Pronunciation British English as spoken at Oxford and Cambridge, and in England's public schools; often abbreviated RP. This term describes the speech of England's cultured, educated class; it has no dialectal or regional characteristics or boundaries but is recognized throughout the country as the hallmark of the educated Englishman.

DIFFERENCE (See **DISSIMILARITY**.)

DIFFERENTIATION

funny-peculiar or funny ha-ha Most often heard interrogatively, this expression serves to distinguish between two meanings of the word *funny*—'peculiar' and 'amusing or humorous.' In 1938, I. Hay used this expression in a play entitled *Housemaster.* Since then,

funny-peculiar or funny ha-ha has gained currency and is frequently heard today.

know a hawk from a handsaw See **PERCEPTIVENESS**.

know chalk from cheese See **PERCEPTIVENESS**.

make head or tail of To make sense of, to understand or decipher; also *make heads or tails of.* The head and the tail are opposite sides of a coin. Tossing a coin is a common method of deciding by chance; the outcome is determined by which side is up when the coin lands. It is easy to see how a coin landing in such a way that it cannot clearly be called either heads or tails gave rise to the frequently heard negative *not make head nor tail of,* implying confusion and senselessness.

> Pray what is the design or plot? for I could make neither head nor tail on't. (Henry Fielding, *The Author's Farce,* 1729)

DIFFICULTY (See also **PREDICAMENT**.)

a hair in the butter An American cowboy expression for a delicate or ticklish situation. The difficulty of picking a single hair out of butter makes this analogy appropriate.

a hard nut to crack A poser, a puzzler, a stumper; a hard question, problem, or undertaking; a difficult person to deal with, a tough cookie; also *a tough nut to crack.*

> You will find Robert Morris a hard nut to crack. (James Payn, *The Mystery of Mirbridge,* 1888)

hard row to hoe A difficult or uphill task, a long haul, a hard lot, a tough situation; also *a long row to hoe.* This American expression is an obvious reference to the dispiriting task of hoeing long rows in rocky terrain.

> I never opposed Andrew Jackson for the sake of popularity. I knew it was a hard row to hoe, but I stood

up to the rack. (David Crockett, *An Account of Col. Crockett's Tour to the North and down East,* 1835)

have one's work cut out To be facing a difficult task; about to undertake a demanding responsibility of the sort that will test one's abilities and resources to the utmost; to have one's hands full. This common expression is a variation of the earlier *cut out work for,* meaning simply to prepare work for another, may have a sense that its origins in tailoring; it apparently carried no implications of excessiveness in quantity or difficulty. Perhaps it is the nature of superiors to be exceedingly demanding, or at least for underlings to assume so; in any event, when the expression "changed hands," so to speak, it took on these added connotations, along with the frequent implication that the person who "has his work cut out for him" has more than he can capably manage.

hold an eel by the tail To try to grasp something slippery and elusive; to try to control an unmanageable situation; to encounter or deal with a deceitful, unreliable person. In use since the early 16th century, this expression exemplifies what any angler knows: holding an eel by the tail is a near impossibility; the squirmy, twisting, slippery creature will wrench itself from the grasp of anyone who attempts the feat.

> He may possibly take an eel by the tail in marrying a wife. (Thomas Newte, *A Tour in England and Scotland in 1785,* 1791)

hot potato A controversial question; an embarrassing situation. This familiar saying is of obvious origin.

> The Judge had been distressed when Johnny agreed to take the case, was amazed at first at the way he handled it—hot potato that it was. (Carson McCullers, *Clock Without Hands,* 1961)

The term is often used in the expression *drop like a hot potato,* meaning to swiftly rid oneself of any unwanted thing or person.

> They dropped him like a hot potato when they learned that he had accepted a place on the Republican Committee of the State. (B. P. Moore, *Perley's Reminiscences,* 1886)

sticky wicket A difficult predicament; a perilous plight; an awkward situation requiring delicate, cool-headed treatment. This expression, primarily a British colloquialism, alludes to the sport of cricket and describes the tacky condition of the playing field near the *wicket* 'goal' after a rainstorm. Because of the sponginess and sluggishness of the ground, the ball does not roll and bounce as predictably as on a dry field, and the player must therefore adapt to the situation by being exceptionally accurate and careful. The phrase is often used in expressions such as *bat on a sticky wicket, be on a sticky wicket.*

DIRECTION

as the crow flies In a straight line; by the most direct route. This expression stems from the widely held belief that a crow flies in a straight line from one point to another. *Sporting Magazine* used the phrase as early as 1810.

bolt upright Straight up; stiffly upright; on end. This expression derives from *bolt* meaning 'projectile, arrow.' It was used as early as 1386 in Chaucer's *Reeve's Tale.*

follow one's nose See INTUITION.

from pillar to post Aimlessly or futilely from place to place; purposelessly from one thing to another; from predicament to predicament, often with the sense of being beleaguered or harassed. The expression is among the oldest in the language, first appearing as *from post to pillar.*

> Thus from post to pillar was he made to dance. (Lydgate, *Assembly of Gods,* 1420)

There is little agreement regarding its origin. One theory holds that it stems from tennis but fails to explain how. Other sources see its roots in manège: the pillar being the column at the center of the riding ground, the posts those that in pairs mark its circumference. Yet another hypothesizes that it derives from the custom of bloodthirsty crowds following convicted persons "from pillory to whipping-post." Today the phrase most often describes a lack of direction or purpose or the futility of receiving the runaround, as with bureaucratic red tape. It also exists as an adjective.

The pillar-to-post travels from one official to another. (*Pall Mall Gazette*, August, 1887)

go around Robin Hood's barn To arrive at one's destination by a circuitous route; to proceed in a very roundabout way. The origin of the expression is unknown. It has no logical association with the legendary Robin Hood, who, of course, had no barn, though it may have been formed by analogy with other possessives whose meanings are connected with that figure's exploits: *Robin Hood's mile* 'one several times the recognized length'; *Robin Hood's bargain* 'a cheap purchase.' The expression appeared in print at least as early as the 18th century.

I can sell them abundantly fast without the trouble of going round Robin Hood's barn. (Mason Locke Weems, *Letters*, 1797)

make a beeline See PACE.

DISADVANTAGE (See also PREDICAMENT, VULNERABILITY.)

behind the eightball At a disadvantage; in a jam or difficult situation. Originally American, this expression is said to have come from the game of Kelly pool. In one variation of this game, all the balls except the black eightball must be pocketed in a certain order. If, in the course of play, another ball strikes the eightball, the player is penalized. Thus, a player finding the eightball between the cueball and the one he intends to pocket is indeed in a disadvantageous position. John O'Hara used the phrase in *Appointment in Samarra* (1934):

You get signing checks for prospects down at the country club, and you wind up behind the eightball.

get the short end of the stick See VICTIMIZATION.

have two strikes against one To be at a disadvantage, and thus have less chance of successfully reaching one's goal or following through with one's plans. This expression comes from baseball, where a batter has three chances to hit a ball in the strike zone. Sometimes this expression alludes to a disadvantage over which one has no control, such as one's sex, race, or ethnic background.

on the hip At a disadvantage, in an extremely vulnerable or helpless position, over a barrel. There is some dispute as to whether this expression derived from hunting or from wrestling. The wrestling theory seems more plausible and is supported by the *OED*. The phrase, now archaic, dates from the latter half of the 15th century. It appeared in Shakespeare's *The Merchant of Venice:*

If I can catch him once upon the hip,
I will feed fat the ancient grudge I bear him. (I,iii)

play with loaded dice To undertake a project or other matter in which the odds are against success; to have little chance. Literally, loaded dice are those which have been fraudulently weighted to increase the chances of throwing certain combinations—usually losing ones—in craps or other games of chance. Figuratively, then, to *play with loaded dice* is to engage in some undertaking in which the odds are fixed so that there is little chance of success. A related expression, *play with a stacked deck*, has the same implications and refers to cheating by stacking a deck of cards, i.e., arranging them in a certain order to force a desired result.

suck the hind teat See VICTIMIZATION.

underdog A person in an inferior position; one who is expected to be defeated in a race, election, etc.; a dark horse. This expression may allude to a canine skirmish, in which both dogs vie for the more advantageous top position. The familiar phrase, while retaining its sense of an unlikely victor in a competition, is often used today to describe the victim of social conventions, government bureaucracy, and other virtually omnipotent institutions.

> The mission of the Democratic party is to fight for the under-dog. (*Daily Chronicle*, June, 1892)

DISARRAY (See DISORDER.)

DISCONTINUITY

lose the thread To lose one's train of thought in a discussion; to have the continuity of one's thoughts or words interrupted. *Thread* in this phrase is the central thought connecting successive points, a continuous flow which is carried on in spite of digressions or interruptions. This figurative use of thread dates from the mid-17th century.

> We laughed so violently . . . that he could not recover the thread of his harangue. (Frances Burney, *Diary and Letters*, 1782)

side-track To diverge from the main subject, course, or road; to go off on a tangent; to shelve or otherwise delay consideration of some matter. Literally, to *side-track* means to shunt a train onto a siding, off the main track, hence its figurative implications.

> The business of the minister is to preach the gospel, not . . . to side-track on great moral issues. (*Advance* [Chicago, Illinois], June, 1893)

A related expression which also employs railroad terminology is *off the track*.

table In U.S. parliamentary procedure this verb means to 'postpone action on':

> The amendment which was always present, which was rejected and tabled and postponed. (*The Century XXXVII*, 1873)

In British parliamentary procedure, it means to 'present for discussion':

> If any more "Old Residents" wish to be heard, they must table their names. (*Pall Mall Gazette*, Jan. 3, 1887)

This is a confusing state of affairs and must be watched carefully by those encountering the term in what may be foreign contexts.

DISCOVERY (See ADVANTAGE.)

DISDAIN (See HAUGHTINESS.)

DISFAVOR

black sheep One who is rejected and scorned as a result of being different from other members of a group; a disreputable character, a bad apple. In a flock of white sheep, a black sheep represents an undesirable deviation from the norm. Some say shepherds dislike the black sheep because of its lesser value; others say because it is an eyesore; still others associate black with badness, evil, and the devil. The label is applied to any person who has flagrantly violated or even slightly deviated from the social norms of a particular group. A black sheep is considered a disgrace and is therefore ostracized from the group. Black sheep have been considered objectionable creatures for at least four centuries:

> Till now I thought the proverb did but jest,
> Which said a black sheep was a biting beast.
> (Thomas Bastard, *Chrestoleros*, 1598)

foul ball One whose personal philosophy or behavior is unacceptable to the mainstream of society; a nonconformist or eccentric. In baseball, a foul ball is one outside the field of play, which is hit or rolls outside of the designated "fair" area. The transference of this expression to an individual whose principles are outside the realm of established social standards is apparent.

hit list Any list of people in disfavor with someone in power; literally, a list of those scheduled to be murdered, usually by the hit man or hired gun of a crime syndicate. This 20th-century Americanism was originally gangster lingo but is no longer limited to underworld use.

in Dutch In trouble, in disgrace, out of favor, in the doghouse; often in the phrase to *get in Dutch*. No satisfactory explanation has yet been offered as to why one gets in Dutch as opposed to some other nationality, although this expression may have some connection with the older phrase to *talk to [someone] like a Dutch uncle*. This American slang term has been in use since at least 1912. See also **talk to like a Dutch uncle**, REPRIMAND.

in [someone's] black books Out of favor; in disgrace. Nicholas Amherst, in his *Terrae Filius: or The Secret History of the University of Oxford* (1721), speaks of the college's black book, pointing out that no student whose name appeared there could receive a degree.

in the doghouse In disfavor or disgrace. Though most commonly applied to misbehaving husbands, the phrase also refers to general disaffection or rejection:

> Several big stars are in studio doghouses because of their political affiliations. (*Daily Ardmoreite* [Ardmore, Oklahoma], April 19, 1948)

This figurative use is considered American in origin, though in James M. Barrie's *Peter Pan* (1904) Mr. Darling literally lived in a doghouse as penance until his children returned from Never Never Land. He was responsible for their departure since he had chained up their nurse-dog, Nana, the night they ran off with Peter Pan.

[one's] name is mud A discredited or disreputable person; one who is ineffective, not respected, or untrustworthy; one held in low esteem; a pariah. In this expression, *mud* implies the worst part of something, the dregs, scum. Since many people consider their name (with its attendant reputation and other abstract qualities) their most important possession, they are loath indeed to have it likened to mud.

> If tha' doan't put ring on finger shortly, my lad, tha' name will be mud in Mountaindale. (D. Robins, *Noble One*, 1957)

DISILLUSIONMENT

burst [someone's] bubble To disabuse; to open someone's eyes; to shatter someone's illusions; also *pop* or *break [someone's] bubble* and to *prick* or *put a pin in [someone's] balloon*. This expression refers to the fragile nature of both soap bubbles and human illusions.

cut the ground from under See RUINATION.

everything tastes of porridge An expression used to inject a note of reality into our daydreams. The point is that no matter how grandiose our schemes or how successful our self-delusions, the taste of porridge or the reality of our domestic affairs will always be there to impinge on our fantasies. Porridge, formerly a staple in every household, is a most appropriate symbol of the practical, basic nature of home life.

pull the rug out from under See RUINATION.

DISMISSAL   (See EXPULSION.)

DISORDER

at sixes and sevens In a state of disorder and confusion; higgledy-piggledy; unable to agree, at odds. Originally *set on six and seven*, this expression derives from the language of dicing and is said to be a variation of *set on cinque and sice*. This early form of the expression dates from the time of Chaucer when it often applied to the hazardous nature of one's fate in general. By the 18th century, the plural *sixes* and *sevens* was standard; earlier, the expression had undergone other changes: the verb *set* was dropped, *at* replaced *on*, and the applicability of the expression broadened to accommodate any situation or state of affairs. Although the *OED* authenticates the dicing theory as the source of this expression, many stories—some more plausible than others—have been related to explain its origin.

> If I was to go from home . . . everything would soon go to sixes and sevens. (Mrs. Elizabeth Blower, *George Bateman,* 1782)

bollixed up Thrown into disorder or confusion; chaotic, topsy-turvy; messed up, bungled, flubbed. *Ballocks* 'testes' dates from 1000 and its variant *bollocks* from 1744. *Bollix* is close in pronunciation and related in meaning to *bollocks* although the former is used as a verb and the latter only as a noun. As a verb, *bollix* is akin to *ball up* 'make a mess, bungle.' The change in meaning from 'testes' to 'confusion, nonsense' is itself confusing and is a relatively recent development (late 19th century). *Bollix* and *bollixed up* date from the early 1900s.

> Watch your script. . . . You're getting your cues all bollixed up. (J. Weidman, *I Can Get It For You Wholesale,* 1937)

catch-as-catch-can See UNRESTRAINT.

confusion worse confounded See EXACERBATION.

go haywire To go out of control, to go awry, to run riot; to go crazy, to go berserk, to go out of one's mind. One source hypothesizes that the phrase derived from the unmanageability of the wire used in binding bales of hay. More reputable sources see its origin in the adjective *haywire* 'poor, rough, inefficient' (from the use of haywire for makeshift or temporary repairs). The phrase dates from at least 1929.

> Some of them have gone completely haywire on their retail prices. (*The Ice Cream Trade Journal,* September, 1948)

higgledy-piggledy In a confused state; topsy-turvy; helter-skelter. This amusing expression may have derived from the disheveled appearance of a pig sty.

> In a higgledy-piggledy world like this it is impossible to make very nice distinctions between good luck and good work. (*Daily News,* January, 1890)

hugger-mugger See SECRECY.

hurrah's nest A confused jumble, an unholy mess. The first recorded use of this expression *(hurra's nest)* appears to have been in Samuel Longfellow's biography of his poet-brother (1829). No clear explanation of its origin has been found, though it seems likely the term is related to the matted, tangled branches of the hurrah bush. S. W. Mitchell in an 1889 issue of *Century Magazine* parenthetically defined a *hurrah's nest* as:

> a mass of leaves left by a freshet in the crotch of the divergent branches of a bush.

By that time, however, the expression had already attained its figurative meaning.

> Everything was pitched about in grand confusion. There was a complete hurrah's nest. (R. H. Dana, *Two Years Before the Mast,* 1840)

kettle of fish A confusing, topsy-turvy state of affairs; a predicament; a contretemps. Literal use of this originally British expression refers to the kettle of fish served at a riverside picnic, and by extension, to the picnic itself.

> It is customary for the gentlemen who live near the Tweed to entertain their neighbours and friends with a Fete Champetre, which they call giving "a kettle of fish." Tents or marquees are pitched . . . a fire is kindled, and live salmon thrown into boiling kettles. (Thomas Newte, *A Tour in England and Scotland in 1785*, 1791)

Some believe that *kettle* is a corruption of kiddle 'a net placed in a river to catch fish.' However, neither this suggestion nor the many other theories offered to account for the figurative use of *kettle of fish* are plausible.

> Fine doings at my house! A rare kettle of fish I have discovered at last. (Henry Fielding, *The History of Tom Jones*, 1749)

Fine, pretty, nice, and *rare* are frequently heard in describing *kettle of fish.* Ironic use of these adjectives serves to highlight the implied confusion and disorderliness.

make a hash of To botch, spoil, or make an unholy mess of. *Hash* is literally a hodgepodge of foods cooked together. By extension, it applies to any incongruous combination of things; and carried one step further, *make a hash of* is to inadvertently create a confused chaotic mess in an attempt to deal with the particulars of a situation or plan.

> Lord Grey has made somewhat of a hash of New Zealand and its constitution. (R. M. Milnes Houghton, *Life, Letters, and Friendships*, 1847)

mare's nest A state of confusion or disarray; a spurious and illusionary discovery. A mare's nest would indeed be a bogus discovery since horses do not display nesting habits.

> Colonel S.'s discovery is a mere mare's nest. (*Times*, October, 1892)

Perhaps as an allusion to the bewilderment which would accompany the finding of a *mare's nest,* the expression now denotes a jumbled or chaotic state of affairs.

no man's land An area, literal or figurative, not under man's control; a scene of chaos or disorder; a desolate, hostile, or uninhabitable tract of land.

> Until the Dutchman Yermuyden came to the scene . . . to control . . . the river Great Ouse . . . much of the region was a marshy no-man's-land through which . . . the only means of transport was by boat. (*Country Life*, June, 1975)

The expression is used in a similar sense to describe a land area sandwiched between two contending armies. Recently, however, *no man's land* acquired the new figurative meaning of a sphere of human undertaking marked by complexity and confusion.

> One question chased another . . . question that got lost in a no-man's-land of conjecture. (H. Carmichael, *Motive*, 1974)

out of joint Disordered, confused; out of kilter. In literal use, this phrase describes a dislocated bone. Figuratively, *out of joint* applies to operations, conditions, and formerly, to individuals in relation to their behavior. The phrase has been in print since the early 15th century, and is especially well known from Shakespeare's *Hamlet:*

> The time is out of joint. Oh cursed spite
> That ever I was born to set it right! (I,v)

pell-mell See IMPETUOUSNESS.

the right hand doesn't know what the left hand is doing Confusion, disorder, disarray. Now used derogatorily to indicate a lack of coordination, organization, or direction, in its original New Testament context (with hands reversed) the phrase denoted a desirable state. In his Sermon on the Mount, Jesus tells His listeners not to broadcast their good deeds, but to keep them to themselves:

> But when thou doest alms, let not thy left hand know what thy right hand doeth: that thine alms may be in secret. (Matthew 6:2–4)

The current meaning apparently stems from the fact that in different circumstances keeping something to oneself is undesirable, leading to a lack of communication, which in turn brings on chaos, confusion, and disorganization.

topsy-turvy Upside-down, helter-skelter, in a state of utter confusion and disarray. The expression appeared in Shakespeare's *I Henry IV:*

> To push against a kingdom, with his help
> We shall o'erturn it topsy-turvy over. (IV,i)

Although the expression is of obscure origin, etymologists have conjectured that its original form was *topside, turnaway,* from which evolved *topsideturvy,* and then finally *topsy-turvy.* The modern form, dating from 1528, retains its figurative meaning of dislocation or chaos.

> A world of inconsistencies, where things are all topsy-turvy, so to speak. (Robert M. Ballantyne, *Shifting Winds,* 1866)

DISPOSAL

deep-six To destroy, discard, or hide embarrassing or incriminating material; to reject or shelve an unwanted proposal or project; to get rid of anything undesirable. Originally an informal U.S. Navy expression for burial at sea, *deep-six* referred to the regulation that the water at the burial site had to be at least 600 feet (100 fathoms) deep. Eventually, *deep-six* referred to throwing anything overboard. Also, since many states require that the dead be buried at least six feet underground, *deep-six* sometimes referred to any burial. Thus, *deep-six* usually means to put a rejected object, scheme, matter, etc., in a place where it will receive little, if any, further notice and will be, figuratively, if not literally, buried. Since the Watergate scandal and trial (1971–75), however, *deep-six* often implies a political cover-up, that which is *deep-sixed* being not merely undesirable, but politically sensitive and potentially dangerous as well.

> To destroy all incriminating documents, [the Watergate conspirators] . . . planned to deep-six a file in the Potomac. (Jack Anderson, *New York Post,* August 22, 1973)

file 13 A wastebasket; a figurative place where something will receive no further consideration. This expression enjoyed limited popularity during World War II. It has, for the most part, been replaced in contemporary usage by *circular file.* The use of "13" probably stems from the negative qualities associated with that number by superstitious people, and its consequent omission in number sequences denoting floors, rooms, restaurant tables, etc. Thus, to put something in *file 13* is to put it in a nonexistent place.

DISSENSION

apple of discord An object or source of dispute; a bone of contention. Eris, Greek goddess of discord, angry at not having been invited to the wedding of Peleus and Thetis, sought to foment discord among the wedding guests. She threw into their midst a golden apple inscribed "for the fairest." When Hera, Pallas Athena, and Aphrodite each laid claim to the apple, Paris was called upon to decide the issue. He awarded the apple to Aphrodite, thus bringing upon himself the vengeance of the other two goddesses, to whose spite is attributed the fall of Troy.

at loggerheads At odds, in disagreement, quarreling. Although numerous explanations have been offered, the origin of this expression remains obscure. The *OED* suggests that a loggerhead (a long-handled instrument for melting pitch and heating liquids) may have been formerly used as a weapon.

> I hear from London that our successors are at loggerheads. (John W. Croker, *The Croker Papers*, 1831)

at sixes and sevens See DISORDER.

bone of contention A subject of disagreement or dispute; a cause of discord. This expression is an expanded version of the simpler *bone* from the phrase *cast a bone between*. The discord created when a single bone is thrown among several dogs is the obvious source.

a crow to pluck A dispute or disagreement; a bone to pick. Of unknown origin, this expression appeared as early as 1460 in the Towneley mysteries; its earliest version was *a crow to pull*.

> No, no, abide, we have a crow to pull.

DISSIMILARITY

apples and oranges Unlikes; any two sets of objects, items, concepts, or ideas of essentially different natures, such as to render comparison meaningless or combination impossible. As used in context, this commonly heard phrase implies an inability to perceive crucial distinctions; it is often employed to counter an argument or destroy an opponent's point. Its origin is unknown; but the longer, less-frequently heard *you can't add apples and oranges* suggests that its antecedents may lie in grade-school arithmetic problems requiring children to perform various mathematical functions in terms of concrete objects or associations.

a far cry Very different, totally dissimilar; a long way, a good distance away; usually *a far cry from*. This expression, which dates from 1819, probably derived from a crude means of measuring distance, such as how far away one's cry or call could be heard. The phrase appeared in *Tait's Magazine* (1850):

> In those days it was a "far cry" from Orkney to Holyrood; nevertheless the "cry" at length penetrated the royal ear.

a horse of another color Something totally different; something else altogether. Precisely why the color of a horse should be indicative of the essence of a matter is somewhat puzzling, but the phrase has existed in the language for several centuries. *A horse of a different color* is heard equally often today, but the variation *a horse of the same color* has little frequency. In Shakespeare's *Twelfth Night*, Maria, scheming with Sir Andrew and Sir Toby against Malvolio, says:

> My purpose is indeed a horse of that color. (II,iii)

Today the expression denotes difference almost exclusively, but it remains popular at all levels of speech and writing.

> A horse of a somewhat different colour is that tycoon of the brush, pop-man Salvador Dali. (*The Listener*, May, 1966)

DISSIPATION (See DECADENCE, DEGENERATION.)

DISTANCE (See EXTENT.)

DISTINCTION (See ACCOMPLISHMENT.)

DOCILITY (See SUBMISSIVENESS.)

DOMINATION (See also MANIPULATION, VICTIMIZATION.)

browbeat To intimidate by stern looks or words; to bully; to push around. Dating from about 1600, this term refers to the brows of the beater and not the beaten, as is commonly supposed today. However, it is unclear whether *to beat* in the expression means to beat figuratively with one's brows or 'to lower' one's brows at, i.e., to frown at.

crack the whip To command or control; to run a tight ship; to be strict with. The allusion is to the threatening crack of a whip used to keep horses and slaves moving or in line.

have by the short hairs To have complete mastery or control over, to have someone right where you want him. The British equivalent of this expression, *to have by the short and curlies,* makes this rather obvious reference to pubic hair more explicit. Use of the phrase dates from the latter half of the 19th century.

Those Chinhwan really did seem to have got the rest of the world by the short hairs. (*Blackwood's Magazine,* February, 1928)

have by the tail To be in control, to be in the driver's seat; to be certain of success. *Tail* in this phrase refers to the buttocks and backside. This American slang expression appeared in S. Longstreet's *The Pedlocks* (1951):

Oh, I know all young people are sure they can have it by the tail, permit me that indelicate phrase, but can you and Alice really be happy?

have one's foot on [someone's] neck To be in a superior, dominating position; to have someone at one's mercy; to have complete control over another person. This expression owes its origin to the following Biblical passage:

Come near, put your feet upon the necks of these kings . . . for thus shall the Lord do to all your enemies against whom ye fight. (Joshua 10:24–25)

A similar phrase is *have under one's thumb.*

lead by the nose To completely dominate another, particularly one who is weak-willed or easily intimidated. This expression refers to the practice of leading some animals by their noses; horses and asses, for example, are guided by

means of a bit and bridle, while cattle and camels frequently have a ring through the nose. Thus, the implication in this expression is both demeaning and derisive, i.e., that a person led by the nose has the intelligence, initiative, and decisiveness of a beast of burden.

Because thy rage against me, and thy tumult, is come up into mine ears, therefore will I put my hook in thy nose, and my bridle in thy lips, and I will turn thee back by the way by which thou camest. (Isaiah 37:29)

The Moor is of a free and open nature
That thinks men honest that but seem to be so,
And will as tenderly be led by the nose
As asses are.
(Shakespeare, *Othello,* I,iii)

make [someone's] beard To have a person totally under one's control or at one's mercy. This obsolete expression, dating from the 14th century, derives from the fact that a barber who is making (i.e., dressing) a man's beard has complete control over him. The longer expression *make [someone's] beard without a razor* carries this power to the limit—it is a euphemism for 'behead.'

If I get you . . . I shall deliver you to Joselyn, that shall make your beard without any razor. (John Bourchier Berners' translation of Froissart's *Chronicles,* 1525)

ride herd on To dominate completely, to tyrannize; to crack the whip, to whip into line or shape, to maintain strict order and discipline; to drive hard, to oppress, to harass. The expression comes from the practice of driving cattle by riding along the outer edge of the herd, thus keeping their movement and progress under tight control. *Webster's Third* cites Erle Stanley Gardner's figurative use of the phrase:

Here comes an officer to ride herd on us.

Though *ride herd on* most often connotes the use of pressure, harassment, or coercion, occasionally it is used in the milder sense of simple oversight—keeping an eye on another's performance.

ride roughshod over To treat abusively; to trample on or walk all over; to tyrannize, suppress, or dominate; to act with total disregard of another's rights, feelings, or interests. The expression usually implies that one is ruthlessly advancing himself at another's expense and hurt. A horse is roughshod when the nails of its shoes project, affording more sure-footed progress but also damaging the ground over which it travels. Robert Burns used the phrase in 1790; it remains in common currency.

> 'Tis a scheme of the Romanists, so help me God!
> To ride over your most Royal Highness roughshod.
> (Thomas Moore, *Intercepted Letters,* 1813)

rule the roost To be in charge or control, to dominate. Though the expression makes perfect sense when seen as stemming from the imperious habits of gamecocks, its origin more likely lies in a corruption of *rule the roast,* common in England since the mid-16th century but itself of uncertain origin. As used in some early citations, *roast* appears to suggest a council or ruling body of some sort. Though this latter form is rarely heard in the U.S., it remains more common in England than *rule the roost. Webster's Third* cites W. S. Gilbert's use of the phrase:

> Wouldn't you like to rule the roast, and guide this university?

settle [someone's] hash To subdue, control, suppress, or otherwise inhibit; to squelch someone's enthusiasm; to give a comeuppance; to make mincemeat of; to get rid of or dispose of someone. This expression alludes to hash as a jumbled mess; therefore, *to settle [someone's] hash* originally meant to kill someone, implying that his murder

settles, once and for all, the jumble of his mental and emotional woes.

> My finger was in an instant on the trigger, and another second would have settled his hash. (Edward Napier, *Excursions in Southern Africa,* 1849)

The expression has been extended somewhat to include less drastic means of subdual.

Simon Legree A cruel, heartless taskmaster; an employer, foreman, or overseer. Simon Legree was the villainous slave dealer in Harriet Beecher Stowe's *Uncle Tom's Cabin.* Nowadays, the expression is often applied somewhat humorously to any taskmaster.

> At least $20 is going into a kitty to help Lewis pay for some dead horses which he has managed to scrape up during his tenure as the miner's Simon Legree. (*Retail Coalman,* November, 1949)

take in tow See GUIDANCE.

wear the pants To be the dominant member; to be in control. This expression alludes to the stereotypic male dominance over women. In common usage, the expression usually refers to a domineering wife who, in essence, controls the household.

with a high hand Overbearingly, arbitrarily, arrogantly, imperiously, tyrannically, dictatorially. The expression originally meant 'triumphantly' as illustrated by this Biblical passage describing the delivery of the Israelites from Egyptian bondage:

> On the morrow after the passover the children of Israel went out with an high hand in the sight of all the Egyptians. (Numbers 33:3)

The phrase apparently entered the English language with John Wycliffe's translation of the Bible in 1382. There is, however, no explanation as to how or why the expression shifted in meaning from the original sense of 'triumphantly' to today's exclusive meaning of 'arrogantly' or 'imperiously.'

DOUBT   (See SKEPTICISM.)

DOWNFALL   (See also FAILURE.)

come a cropper   To fail badly in any undertaking, particularly after its apparent initial success; to encounter a sudden setback after an auspicious beginning. This figurative meaning derives from the literal *come a cropper* 'to fall or be thrown headlong from a horse.' Although the precise origin of the expression is not known, it may be related to the earlier phrase *neck and crop* meaning 'bodily, completely, altogether.' Both literal and figurative uses of the expression date from the second half of the 1800s.

Custer's last stand   An all-out, noble effort that ends in utter, embarrassing failure. In June of 1876, U.S. General George A. Custer's troops were annihilated by Sioux warriors under Sitting Bull at the Battle of Little Big Horn. Since then, *Custer's last stand* has gained currency as a phrase used in comparisons to emphasize those aspects of a given situation which fit the pattern of an all-out effort negated by total defeat, as established by the historical Custer's last stand.

hoist with one's own petard   See REVERSAL.

meet one's Waterloo   To suffer a crushing and decisive defeat; to succumb to the pressures of a predicament, tragedy, or other unfavorable situation; to meet one's match; to get one's comeuppance. This expression alludes to the Battle of Waterloo (1815) in which Napoleon was decisively vanquished by the Duke of Wellington.

Every man meets his Waterloo at last. (Wendell Phillipps, in a speech, November 1, 1859)

DRESS   (See CLOTHING.)

DRUNKENNESS   (See also FOOD AND DRINK, TIPPLING.)

all mops and brooms   Intoxicated; half-drunk. In use since the early 19th century, the phrase is of uncertain origin. One conjecture is that the *mop* of the expression derives from that word's use in some districts of England for the annual fairs at which servants were hired, and at which much drinking was done. Women seeking employment as maids reputedly carried mops and brooms to indicate the type of work sought. Thomas Hardy's use of the expression in *Tess of the D'Urbervilles* (1891) makes its meaning clear:

There is not much doing now, being New Year's Eve, and folks mops and brooms from what's inside 'em.

barfly   A hanger-on at a bar; an alcoholic or heavy drinker; a barhopper. This U.S. slang phrase was in print as early as 1928.

Andy Jackson, Kit Carson and General Grant—all good American barflies in their day. (B. de Casseres, *American Mercury*, August, 1928)

This early use of *barfly* implies a good-natured backslapping attitude, without the stigma attached to heavy drinking. Today, calling someone a barfly is an insult; the label is often used judgmentally to describe a woman who flits from one bar to another.

drink like a fish   To drink excessively, particularly alcoholic beverages; to drink hard. The allusion is to the way many fish swim with their mouths open, thus seeming to be drinking continuously. This popular simile, dating from at least 1640, is usually used to describe a drinker with an extraordinary capacity to put away liquor.

drunk as a fiddler   Highly intoxicated, inebriated; three sheets to the wind. In the past, fiddlers received free drinks as payment for their services. Thus, their predictable and notorious overindulging gave rise to this popular expression.

drunk as a lord Intoxicated, soused, blind or dead drunk, pickled. In the 18th and 19th centuries, not only was gross intoxication prevalent, but men prided themselves on the amount they could consume at one sitting. It was considered a sign of gentility to overindulge. Thus, it was not an uncommon sight to behold dinner guests helplessly sprawled under the table in front of their chairs, having successfully drunk each other "under the table."

feel as if a cat has kittened in one's mouth To have an extremely distasteful sensation in the mouth as a result of drunkenness; the morning-after blues. This expression, one of the more graphic and picturesque, is used to describe the taste in one's mouth that often accompanies a hangover. It is first cited in the 1618 play *Amends for Ladies* by Nathaniel Field, a British playwright.

fishy about the gills Suffering the aftereffects of excessive drinking; hung over. In this expression, *gills* carries its figurative meaning of the skin beneath the jaws and ears, a place where the symptoms of crapulence are often manifested. The phrases *blue around the gills* and *green around the gills* carry similar meanings, often extended to include the deleterious consequences of gross overeating.

full as a tick Extremely drunk, loaded, smashed; also *full as an egg* or *bull*. A tick is a bloodsucking parasite that attaches itself to the skin of men and certain animals. It buries its head in the flesh and gradually becomes more and more bloated as it fills up with blood. This Australian and New Zealand slang expression dates from the late 19th century.

half-cocked Partially drunk; tipsy. This American colloquialism, often shortened to merely *cocked*, is of unknown origin, though it may have some relationship to *half-cocked* 'foolish, silly.'

See **go off at half-cock**, IMPETUOUS-NESS.

half seas over Thoroughly drunk, intoxicated; having had a few too many, a mite tipsy. Authorities agree that the term's origin is nautical, but they have widely divergent explanations of its meaning. Those who say the expression means 'half-drunk' move from its early literal meaning of 'halfway across the sea' to the later figurative 'halfway to any destination' or 'halfway between one state and another.' Others see in it the image of a ship nearly on its side, about to founder and sink; hence, they consider the term descriptive of one decidedly unsteady due to drink, lurching and staggering, barely able to maintain his balance and likely to fall at any minute.

have a jag on To be drunk, to be inebriated or intoxicated, to be loaded. This U.S. slang expression apparently derives from the dialectal and U.S. sense of *jag* 'a load, as of hay or wood, a small cartload.' By extension, *jag* came to mean a "load" of drink, or as much liquor as a person can carry.

> Others with the most picturesque "jags" on, hardly able to keep their feet. (*The Voice* [N.Y.], August, 1892)

have a package on Drunk; loaded; having really tied one on. More common in Britain than in the U.S., this expression may have arisen as a variation of *tie a bag on*.

have the sun in one's eyes To be intoxicated or drunk, to be under the influence; also the slang phrase *to have been in the sun*. The expression may be a euphemistic explanation of the unsteady walk of one who has had a few too many, implying that his stagger is due to sun blindness. Another possibility is that the phrase refers to the red color one's complexion acquires or the bloodshot eyes resulting from too much sun as well as from too much drink. The expression dates from at least 1770.

Last night he had had "the sun very strong in his eyes." (Charles Dickens, *The Old Curiosity Shop*, 1840)

in bed with one's boots on Drunk, extremely intoxicated; passed out. The reference is, of course, to one so inebriated that he cannot take his boots off before going to bed.

in one's cups Intoxicated, inebriated. This expression has been common since the 18th century. Because of its literary and euphemistic tone, it is now often employed jocularly. Jeremy Bentham used the phrase in an 1828 letter to Sir F. Burdett:

> I hear you are got among the Tories, and that you said once you were one of them: you must have been in your cups.

An early variant, now obsolete, is *cupped.*

> Sunday at Mr. Maior's much cheer and wine,
> Where as the hall did in the parlour dine;
> At night with one that had been shrieve I sup'd,
> Well entertain'd I was, and half well cup'd.
> (John Taylor, *Works,* approx. 1650)

in the altitudes Light-headed; giddy; drunk. *In the altitudes,* as opposed to *having both feet planted on the ground,* is one of many similar expressions meaning drunk. Attributed to the British dramatist and poet Ben Jonson, it is clearly analogous to contemporary expressions such as *high, spacey, flying,* and *in the ozone.*

in the bag Drunk; often *half in the bag.* This may be a shortened version of the now infrequently heard *tie a bag on,* which may itself be related to *bag* as nautical slang for 'pot of beer.' The precise origin is unknown.

jug-bitten Intoxicated. This obsolete expression is derived from the figurative sense of the liquid contents of a jug.

When any of them are wounded, potshot, jug-bitten, or cup shaken, . . . they have lost all reasonable faculties of the mind. (John Taylor, *Works,* 1630)

like an owl in an ivy bush See VISAGE.

loaded for bear See READINESS.

one over the eight Slightly drunk, tipsy; one alcoholic drink or glass too many. One could infer from this British colloquial expression that a person should be able to drink eight pints or glasses of beer without appearing drunk or out of control. *One over the eight* appeared in print by 1925.

on the sauce Drinking heavily and frequently, boozing it up, hitting the bottle; alcoholic, addicted to alcoholic beverages; also to *hit the sauce* 'to drink excessively.' *Sauce* has been a slang term for hard liquor since at least the 1940s.

> He was already as a kid (like General Grant as a boy) on the sauce in a charming school-boy way. (S. Longstreet, *The Real Jazz Old and New,* 1956)

pie-eyed Drunk, intoxicated, inebriated, loaded.

> He is partial to a "shot of gin," and on occasion will drink till he is "pie-eyed." (*T. P.'s and Cassell's Weekly,* September, 1924)

The origin of this term is confusing, since drunkenness tends to cause the eyes to narrow, just the opposite of what *pie-eyed* implies.

put to bed with a shovel To be extremely drunk, dead drunk; to bury a corpse. The more common, former sense of the phrase refers to an extraordinarily intoxicated person who requires much assistance in getting home to bed. The latter, less figurative meaning, from which the former probably derives, is an obvious allusion to burial of a corpse. The expression is rarely used.

queer in the attic See ECCENTRICITY.

shoot the cat See ILL HEALTH.

three sheets in the wind Very unsteady on one's feet due to excessive indulgence in drink; barely able to stand or walk without weaving and lurching and swaying about. Though *three sheets to the wind* is more commonly heard today, *three sheets in the wind* is the more accurate term. This expression for drunkenness is another creation of some metaphorically minded sailor—*in the wind* being the nautical term describing the lines or 'sheets' when unattached to the clew of the sails, thus allowing them to flap without restraint. Older ships often had three sails, and if the sheets of all three were "in the wind," the ship would lurch about uncontrollably. The currency of *three sheets to the wind* may be due to the erroneous belief that the sheets are the sails, rather than the lines that control them. This expression has been used figuratively to mean drunkenness since the early 19th century.

tie one on To go on a drunken tear; to get drunk. This very common American slang expression is probably an elliptical variation of *to tie a bag on,* which in turn could have spawned the phrase *in the bag,* all of which have the same meaning. It is uncertain whether they are related to the supposed nautical slang use of *bag* 'pot of beer.'

under the table Drunk, intoxicated to the point of stupefaction; not only too drunk to stand, but too drunk to maintain a sitting position. The expression derives from the days when excessive consumption of liquor was the mark of a gentleman. In subtle oneupmanship the lords would vie in "drinking each other under the table."

under the weather See ILL HEALTH.

up to the gills Drunk, intoxicated; really soused, pickled. When used in reference to human beings, *gills* refers to the flesh under the jaws and ears. So one who has consumed liquor "up to the gills" has imbibed a considerable quantity.

walk the chalk See COMPETENCE.

DURATION (See also TIME.)

a coon's age A long time; a blue moon; usually in the phrase *in a coon's age.* This U.S. expression dates from 1843. Although its exact origin is not known, it may have derived from the raccoon's habit of disappearing for long periods of sleep during the winter months when it would not be seen out for "ages."

long haul An extended period of time; a great distance, especially one over which material is transported. This latter use probably gave rise to the former figurative one referring to time. *In* or *over the long haul,* both currently popular, suggest a broad, inclusive perspective, one that sees everything as part of an ongoing process.

a month of Sundays An unspecified but usually prolonged period of time; a seemingly endless interval of time. Sunday, the Christian Sabbath, was observed in the 19th century with the utmost dignity and decorum. All entertainment and frivolity were strictly taboo; thus the day seemed never ending. As used today this expression describes a period of time experienced as longer than it actually is because of tediousness or boredom.

> I ain't been out of this blessed hole . . . for a month of Sundays. (Rolf Bolderwood, *Robbery Under Arms,* 1888)

pissing-while A brief span of time; a few minutes. This obsolete expression, clearly derived from the short period of time required to urinate, appeared in Shakespeare's *The Two Gentlemen of Verona:*

> He had not been there a pissing-while, but all the chamber smelt him. (IV,iv)

till the cows come home For a long time, forever. This expression, dating from the 17th century, apparently first indicated shamefully late or early morning hours, as in this citation from Alexander Cooke's *Pope Joan* (1610):

> Drinking, eating, feasting, and revelling, till the cows come home, as the saying is.

A possible explanation as to the origin of the phrase is found in the English satirist Jonathan Swift's literal use of it in *Polite Conversation* (1738), where it refers to a slugabed who did not get up until it was time for the cows to come home for the evening milking:

> I warrant you lay abed till the cows come home.

E

EAGERNESS   (See ZEALOUSNESS.)

EASE   (See EFFORTLESSNESS.)

ECCENTRICITY   (See also UNCON-
VENTIONALITY.)

barmy on the crumpet   Eccentric; a bit
daft; wacko. This picturesque British
expression plays on *barmy* 'balmy, foolish' and *barmy* 'yeasty'—a crumpet
being a breadlike muffin, here metaphorically standing for one's head.

have a moonflaw in the brain   To be a
lunatic; to behave in a very bizarre or
peculiar manner. A *moonflaw* is an abnormality or idiosyncrasy ascribed to
lunar influence. This now obsolete expression appeared in Brome's *Queen
and Concubine* (1652):

> I fear she has a moonflaw in her
> brains;
> She chides and fights that none can
> look upon her.

have a screw loose   To be eccentric,
crotchety, or neurotic; to be irregular
or amiss. As early as 1884, the phrase
loose screw was used figuratively to
apply to a flawed condition or state of
affairs.

> I can see well enough there's a
> screw loose in your affairs. (Charles
> Dickens, *The Life and Adventures
> of Martin Chuzzlewit*, 1884)

A more recent and increasingly common figurative meaning applies *have a
screw loose* to states of mind or mental
health. This slang meaning is used in
regard to whimsical, unusual behavior
rather than to disturbed or sick behavior, although the phrase tends to conjure up images of "falling apart" or
"breaking down." A British variant is
have a tile loose.

have bats in one's belfry   To be eccentric, bizarre, crazy, daft. The erratic
flight of bats in bell towers interferes
with the proper ringing and tone of the
bells, just as crazy notions darting about
one's brain weaken its ability to function. The slang term *batty* is a derivative of this phrase, which appeared as
early as 1901 in a novel of G. W. Peck:

> They all thought a crazy man with
> bats in his belfry had got loose.
> *(Peck's Red-Haired Boy)*

The analogy between sanity and finely
tuned bells is an old one; its most famous expression is in Ophelia's description of the "mad" Hamlet:

> Now see that noble and most
> sovereign reason,
> Like sweet bells jangled, out of
> tune and harsh. (III,i)

off one's trolley   Crazy, demented; in a
confused or befuddled state of mind; ill-
advised; senile. This expression alludes
to the once-common spectacle of a mo-
torman's attempts to realign the contact wheel of a trolley car with the overhead wire. Since this contact wheel is
also called a "trolley," *off one's trolley*
may refer either to the conductor's actions or to the fact that when the wires
are "off the trolley," the vehicle no
longer receives an electric current and
is, therefore, rendered inoperative.

> The medium is clear off her trolley,
> for my father has been dead [for]
> three years. (Warren Davenport,
> *Butte and Montana Beneath the
> X-Ray*, 1908)

A similar expression is *slip one's trolley*
'to become demented.' In the more
widely used variation, *off one's rocker,*
rocker is most often said to refer to the
curved piece of wood on which a cradle
or chair rocks. But since both *off one's
trolley* and *off one's rocker* became popular about the time streetcars were in-
stalled in major American cities, and
since *rocker*, like *trolley*, also means the
wheel or runner that makes contact
with an overhead electricity supply, it is

more likely that the *rocker* of the expression carries this latter meaning.

> When asked if he had swallowed the liniment, he said, "Yes, I was off my rocker." (*Daily News*, June 29, 1897)

queer in the attic Eccentric or feeble-minded; intoxicated. In this expression, attic carries its British slang meaning of 'the mind'; thus, this colloquialism alludes to stupidity, insanity, or drunkenness, all of which may generate bizarre behavior.

round the bend Insane, crazy. In this British expression, *bend* describes one's mental faculties as being 'out of alignment, bent, or out of kilter.'

> Right round the bend . . . I mean . . . as mad as a hatter. (John I. M. Stewart, *The Guardian*, 1955)

Related expressions are *go round the bend* and *be driven round the bend*.

EFFECTIVENESS

blockbuster Something extremely forceful, violent, or effective; a success, a winner, a hit. The term owes its origin to the name given the highly destructive bombs dropped on industrial targets in Britain during World War II.

corker A clincher or a sockdolager, something that settles the question or closes the discussion; also, a lollapalooza; something striking, astonishing, or extraordinary. In use since 1837, this slang term probably derives from the image of a cork "capping a bottle" (the first three meanings) or flying off a champagne bottle with a bang (the latter meanings). *Corker* was also a baseball term in the late 19th century.

haymaker Any extremely forceful or effective argument, statement, ploy, maneuver, etc., especially a decisive and culminating one. The term is boxing slang for a violent punch or knockout blow. Hay is grass or alfalfa which has been cut or mowed down. Similarly, the recipient of a haymaker in a pugilistic encounter is "cut down." *Mow (someone) down* is a related expression.

> I deliberately pulled my right back and swung "haymakers" at Choinyski, intending to miss him. (J. J. Corbett, *Roar of the Crowd*, 1925)

the old one-two Any especially effective combination of two persons or things; a double whammy. The reference is to boxing and the highly effective combination punch consisting of a left jab immediately followed by a hard right cross, usually to the opponent's jaw and intended as a knockout blow.

put teeth into To make effective or enforceable; to give meaning or substance to. *Webster's Third* cites a contemporary use by E. O. Hauser:

> . . . started turning out the arms which would put teeth into neutrality.

The expression is most often used with reference to legislation.

sledge-hammer argument A single statement or ploy which completely dissolves the opposition in a disagreement; a clincher. A sledge-hammer is a large, weighty hammer which, if used as a weapon, can easily incapacitate the victim. This expression is heard infrequently today.

EFFICIENCY

cooking with gas Operating at maximum efficiency; performing well, functioning smoothly; really in the groove or on the right track. The expression probably comes from the efficiency of gas as a cooking medium (as contrasted with coal, wood, kerosene, electricity, etc.). Occasionally the phrase is jocularly updated by variants such as *cooking with electricity* or *cooking with radar*.

hit on all six To run smoothly; to function properly; to work to one's fullest capacity; to be in physically fit and trim condition. This Americanism was originally used in speaking of internal combustion engines, specifically the functioning of the cylinders, which often misfired in earlier cars. When the figurative use gained currency, the word *cylinder* was dropped from the end of the expression. Variants include *hit on all four* and other multiples of two.

> Modern science offers you a *natural* means to keep you "hitting on all six"—every minute of the day. (*Saturday Evening Post*, March 10, 1928)

in the groove In full swing, functioning smoothly, in top form. This U.S. slang expression was coined in the jazz age. *Groove* originally referred to the grooves of phonograph records. In the 1930s and '40s, *in the groove* meant to play jazz music fervently and expertly, or to appreciate such music and by association be considered "hep" and sophisticated.

> The jazz musicians gave no grandstand performances; they simply got a great burn from playing in the groove. (*Fortune,* August, 1933)

Eventually *in the groove* and *groovy* grew to mean 'up-to-date' or 'fashionable,' although this use is now being phased out of current slang. When *in the groove* is used, as in the following quotation from *Webster's Third,* it emphasizes the quality of being in top form, rather than sophistication or fashionableness.

> It made no difference, when he was in the groove, what he chose to talk about. (Henry Miller)

just like New York This American slang expression, usually an isolated comment on successful performance, has a wide range of equally vague equivalents such as *right on, great, nice going, way to go.* The reference is to New York City as the epitome of success, society, and fashion.

EFFORTLESSNESS

duck soup An easy task; a breeze, a cinch, a snap. This expression, originally and chiefly American slang, probably derived from the phrase *sitting duck* 'an easy mark or target,' literally a duck resting on the water and thus very likely to end up in duck soup. See also **sitting duck, VULNERABILITY.**

hands down Easily, effortlessly; unconditionally, incontestably; beyond question, undoubtedly. The original expression was the horse racing phrase *to win hands down,* an allusion to the way a jockey, certain of victory, drops his hands, thus loosening his grip on the reins. The term dates from at least 1867.

lead-pipe cinch See **CERTAINTY.**

like water off a duck's back Easily, harmlessly; to no effect, without making any impression.

> I had taken to vice like a duck to water, but it ran off me like water from a duck's back. (C. Day Lewis, *Buried Day,* 1960)

This self-evident expression dates from at least 1824.

no sweat No problem, no trouble or bother, no difficulty; a cinch, a piece of cake. Working up a sweat and working hard have long been synonymous. Use of this American slang expression dates from at least 1955. It has lost its former crude associations and is now used readily in most informal contexts.

> No sweat, mate . . . We're not looking for trouble. (R. Giles, *File on Death,* 1973)

a piece of cake Any task requiring little or no effort; a cinch, a snap, a breeze; a pleasant or enjoyable experience. This expression, in use since at least 1936, obviously refers to the simple, pleasurable experience of eating cake.

plain sailing Easy going, without obstruction or interruption; according to plan. In nautical terminology, plane sailing is the supposedly uncomplicated art of determining a ship's position based on the assumption that the earth's surface is a plane and not spherical.

Plane-sailing is so simple that it is colloquially used to express anything so easy that it is impossible to make a mistake. (William Henry Smyth, *The Sailor's Word-book,* 1867)

Nautical use of this expression appeared in print by the late 17th century and shows *plain* used interchangeably with *plane.* Figuratively, as applied to any plan or course of action, *plain sailing* is the standard form.

So far all was plain sailing, as the saying is; but Mr. Till knew that his main difficulties were yet to come. (Francis E. Paget, *Milford Malvoisin,* 1842)

Today *clear sailing* is heard as often as *plain sailing.*

ELATION

cock-a-hoop In a state of elation or exultation; also to *make cock-a-hoop* and the now obsolete phrase to *set cock a hoop* or *cock on hoop* 'to drink and make merry.' Although this expression is of obscure origin there have been several attempts to explain it. One such explanation maintains that *cock* formerly referred to the spigot on a barrel of ale. Supposedly, this cock was removed and placed on the hoop of the barrel, so that the free-flowing ale could be drunk with abandon. Thus, the drinkers were said to be cock-a-hoop. A somewhat more tenuous explanation uses the 'male fowl' meaning of *cock* and relates *hoop* to *whoop,* thus comparing the boisterous merrymaking to a cock whooping or crowing. Variants of the expression have been in use since 1529.

feel one's oats To feel spry, lively, and chipper, sometimes to the point of feistiness; to feel important or special. This expression refers to horse-feed which usually contains oats as one of its major components. A well-cared-for and well-fed horse is active and lively, or "feeling its oats."

You know that, and you feel your oats, too, as well as anyone. (Thomas Haliburton, *Attache,* 1843)

happy as a clam at high tide Quite happy, delighted, well-pleased, content; also *happy as a clam, happy as a clam at high water,* and other variants. The allusion is probably to the relative safety a clam enjoys at high tide when water hides its mud flat habitat from clam-diggers. Apparently the original version of this U.S. colloquial expression was simply *happy as a clam,* since it appears as such in the earliest citations of the phrase which date from the early 19th century.

Now I'm in business and happy as a clam at high tide. (*New York Evening Post,* June, 1907)

have the world on a string To be in high spirits, to be on top of the world, to be "sitting pretty"; to feel as if one has life completely under control, that the forces of the world are waiting to be manipulated for one's pleasure. The word *string* referring to a tie of dependency or a means of controlling a person or animal dates from the 14th century. By the 16th century, *have the world in a string* appeared in print.

Those that walk as they will, . . . persuading themselves that they have the world in a string, are like the ruffian Capaney, . . . (Brian Melbancke, *Philotimus,* 1583)

Today *in* has been replaced by *on,* but the expression continues to enjoy widespread use.

in fine feather In an excellent physical and mental state; in superb condition; also *in high feather.* The origin of these expressions is associated with the molting and subsequent new growth of a bird's plumage. Thomas Hardy uses the phrase "summer days of highest feather" in *Return of the Native* (1878).

in fine fettle In splendid condition; in a jubilant state of mind. The Old English *fetel* 'belt, girdle' is the likely ancestor of this expression, which apparently first referred more to physical appearance than mental state. One "in fine fettle" was well dressed and smartly attired. The transference of the term's application from external appearance to inner state of mind is easily seen in light of the fact that one's manner of dress is still considered to reflect and express one's emotional state. In this phrase, *fine* is occasionally replaced by another modifier to describe other states or conditions.

> I'm in terrible poor fettle with the toothache. (Henrietta Lear, *Tales of Kirkbeck*, 1850)

in merry pin Happy, cheerful, elated, light-hearted; in a good mood or frame of mind. The *pin* in this expression probably refers to the pegs which are used to tune a stringed musical instrument. One source suggests that *pin* may allude to the pegs on a peg-tankard, for which there were a number of uses. One use provided a favorite alehouse pastime: trying to drink only to the next lower pin on the tankard. If this were not done exactly, and it rarely was, the drinker had to try again and again until successful—attempts which inevitably led to intoxicated merriment and mirth.

> The calendar, right glad to find
> His friend in merry pin,
> Return'd him not a single word,
> But to the house went in.
> (William Cowper, *John Gilpin*, 1782)

A variation is *in jolly pin*.

in seventh heaven Intensely happy, blissful, ecstatic. Muslims believe in a seven-tiered heaven—as did the ancient Jews and Babylonians, whose highest—or heaven of heavens—was the abode of God and the highest angels. The Muslims' seventh heaven is ruled by Abraham and peopled by numberless mythical-type inhabitants ceaselessly chanting the praises of the Most High. The now common figurative use of the term appears as early as 1824 in the work of Sir Walter Scott.

like a dog with two tails Delighted, elated, overjoyed; pleased as punch; tickled pink. This expression refers to the fact that a dog shows its happiness by wagging its tail. By implication, if a dog had two tails, both of which were wagging, it would be safe to assume that the animal was very happy indeed.

> Ned came in . . . looking scared. He was not at all like a dog with two tails. (P. H. Johnson, *Impossible Marriage*, 1954)

on cloud nine Blissful, euphoric; enraptured, transported. The precise origin of the term is unknown; it may have begun as a variation on and subsequent intensification of *seventh heaven*, since *A Dictionary of American Slang* cites the phrase *on cloud seven*—no longer heard—as having the same meaning. The same source also indicates that *on a cloud* is commonly used to mean 'high,' i.e., under the influence of narcotics. Being "on cloud nine" may be akin to being "way out" or "spaced out."

> I don't like strange music, I'm not on Cloud Nine. (*Down Beat*, 1959)

pleased as Punch Very pleased or happy; delighted, elated, euphoric; tickled pink. This expression alludes to the cheerful singing and self-satisfaction which characterized the star of the "Punch and Judy" puppet show created by the Italian comedian Silvio Fiorillo in the early 1600s.

> I am as pleased as Punch at the thought of having a kind of denizenship if nothing more, at Oxford. (James Lowell, *Letters*, 1873)

The expression persists in contemporary usage, perhaps most notably as one of the favorite sayings of Hubert Humphrey (1911–78) during his political career as Senator and Vice President.

slaphappy See FATUOUSNESS.

tickled pink Delighted, elated, glad. This common expression alludes to the convulsive laughter as well as the pink skin tone produced by excessive tickling.

tickled to death Very happy, highly pleased, delighted, thrilled.

> They stopped as if they were tickled to death to see her. (Jonathan Slick, *High Life in New York*, 1844)

This expression is a simple combination of two earlier components: *to tickle* 'to please, to excite agreeably' plus the intensifier *to death* 'to an extreme degree, thoroughly.'

with bells on Dressed up and in high spirits; ready for a good time. The phrase may come from the following Mother Goose Rhyme:

> Ride a cock-horse to Banbury Cross,
> To see a fine woman upon a white horse;
> With rings on her fingers and bells on her toes,
> She shall have music wherever she goes.

ENDURANCE (See also PERSEVERANCE.)

bite the bullet To suffer pain without expressing fear; to grit one's teeth and do what has to be done. This phrase derives from the supposed practice of giving a wounded soldier a bullet to bite on to channel his reaction to intense pain. This practice preceded the first use of anesthesia (in the U.S.) in 1844. By 1891, the phrase was used figuratively.

> Bite on the bullet, old man, and don't let them think you're afraid. (Rudyard Kipling, *The Light that Failed*, 1891)

It is analogous to other phrases describing rituals such as *take a deep breath* and *grit your teeth*, which refer to preparing oneself or pulling oneself together in order to experience or do something unpleasant.

roll with the punches To endure with equanimity, not to be thrown by the blows of fate; to be resilient, bending slightly under pressure then bouncing back; to have the balanced perspective that comes of experiencing hardship. This common metaphor obviously owes its origin to pugilism.

stand the gaff To endure punishment, criticism, or ridicule; to sustain oneself through a period of stress or hardship; to keep one's chin up. In this expression, *gaff* may refer to the steel spurs worn by fighting cocks, or it may derive from a Scottish term for noisy and abusive language.

> Neil has got to stand the gaff for what he's done. (W. M. Raine, *B. O'Connor*, 1910)

take it on the chin To face adversity courageously; to withstand punishment, to persevere against the odds; to bounce back from hardship with an undefeated attitude. This American slang expression originated in boxing.

> I liked the Williams' because of the way they took life on the chin. (D. Lytton, *Goddam White Man*, 1960)

ENJOYMENT

get a bang out of To derive pleasure from, to get a thrill from, to get a charge out of. In this common American expression, *bang* carries its slang meaning of intense exhilaration.

> He seems to be getting a great bang out of the doings. (Damon Runyon, *Guys and Dolls*, 1931)

get a charge out of To become physically or mentally exhilarated; to enjoy greatly; to get a kick out of. This expression, derived from the physical jolt caused by an electric charge, is commonplace in the United States, but is somewhat less frequently heard in Great Britain.

> It seems to me that people get a bigger charge out of their grandchildren than they did from their own offspring. (*New York Times Magazine*, May, 1963)

lick one's chops To eagerly anticipate, especially in reference to food; to take great delight or pleasure in, to relish. In this expression, *chops* refers to the mouth or lips. *Lick* refers to the action of the tongue in response to the excessive salivation that often precedes or accompanies the enjoying of food. By extension, one can "lick one's chops" over any pleasurable experience.

music to the ears Pleasing or agreeable news, good tidings, just what one wanted to hear; usually in the phrase *that's music to my ears*. Good news is as pleasant to hear as sweet music.

tickle one's fancy To appeal to someone, to please, to make happy, to delight, to amuse.

> Such . . . was the story that went the round of the newspapers at the time, and highly tickled Scott's fancy. (John G. Lockhart, *Memoirs of the Life of Sir Walter Scott*, 1837)

Tickle in this phrase means 'to excite agreeably' and *fancy* is equivalent to 'imagination.' Figurative use of this popular expression dates from about the late 18th century.

warm the cockles of the heart To induce sensations of joy, comfort, or love. The cockle, a palatable mollusk, was often compared to the heart by early anatomists because of its shape and valves. Furthermore, the scientific name for cockle is the Greek *cardium* 'heart.' The phrase enjoys frequent use today, usually in reference to the kindling of pleasurable emotions.

> An expedition . . . which would have delighted the very cockles of your heart. (Scott, in Lockhart, *Letters*, 1792)

ENTHUSIASM (See ZEALOUSNESS.)

ENTICEMENT

drawing card An attraction; a person or thing noted for its drawing power—the ability to attract a great deal of attention or patronage. This expression has been in use since the 1800s, although *drawing* 'attractive' dates from the 16th century.

> The Falls City team is the best drawing card here of any in the Association. (*Courier-Journal*, May 4, 1887)

A variant of *drawing card* is *selling card*.

Fata Morgana A mirage or illusion that entices one into danger or destruction; also, an alluring woman, a seductress. *Fata Morgana* often refers specifically to the mirage of a great city that appears occasionally in the treacherous Straits of Messina, and which has led many a sailor to an untimely death on the jagged rocks bordering the Straits. The term combines the Italian *fata* 'fairy' and *Morgana*, derived from Morgan le Fay, an enchantress of Arthurian fame believed to be the sister of King Arthur and the student of the magician Merlin. She was reputed to live in Calabria, an area of Italy adjacent to the Straits of Messina, where, with her enticing illusions of pleasure and grandeur, she lured unwary men to their destruction.

jail bait One who serves as a temptation to commit crime, esp. an alluring female who has not reached the age of consent. This common expression of obvious origin usually refers to a young girl with whom sexual contact is the foundation for a statutory rape charge. A variant is *San Quentin Quail*.

> I'm not interested in little girls. Particularly not in jail-bait like that

one. (J. Braine, *Room at the Top*, 1957)

lead up the garden path To deceive or mislead; to entice or beguile; to tempt with less than honorable intentions. Though no longer limited to affairs of the heart, this expression refers to the proclivity of many casanovas and coquettes to stroll among the flowers with a sweetheart in search of romantic privacy.

> They're cheats, that's wot women are! Lead you up the garden [path] and then go snivellin' around cos wot's natcheral 'as 'appened to 'em. (Ethel Mannin, *Sounding Brass*, 1926)

ENTIRETY (See **INCLUSIVENESS, THOROUGHNESS, TOTALITY**.)

ENVIOUSNESS (See **RESENTMENT**.)

EPITHET (See **NICKNAMES**.)

EPONYMS

Alibi Ike See **EVASIVENESS**.

Annie Oakley A free ticket to a performance; a meal ticket. Annie Oakley (1860–1926) was the famous trick-shot artist who traveled with Buffalo Bill's Wild West Show. Her reputed ability to throw a playing card into the air and shoot it full of holes before it fell to the ground supposedly explains how an *Annie Oakley* came to mean a free pass or meal ticket. A playing card riddled with bullet holes resembles a perforated ticket or punched meal ticket. The meal ticket use of the word is obsolete, and the free pass meaning is now rarely heard, although both were popular earlier in the 20th century.

> A newspaper circulation man gave him two "Annie Oakleys" to a boxing match. (*Life*, June 17, 1946)

Baron Münchhausen See **MENDACITY**.

blimp See **POMPOSITY**.

blurb See **COMMENDATION**.

craps A game of chance using dice. This American term, which dates from 1843, is thought by some to be a French variant of the 18th-century English slang term *crabs* 'the lowest throw at hazard [a dice game], two aces.' Other less scholarly sources maintain that *craps* is short for Johnny *Crapaud*, the nickname given to the Creole Bernard Marigny, who is said to have first introduced dice-playing to the largely French city of New Orleans about 1800.

Dick Turpin See **CRIMINALITY**.

dunce See **IGNORANCE**.

Goody Two Shoes See **PRUDISHNESS**.

Grub Street See **LETTERS**.

Jack Ketch An appellation for a hangman or executioner. Jack Ketch is said to be the name of the notorious English hangman in the 17th century who barbarously executed William Lord Russell, Duke of Monmouth, and other political offenders. Another conjecture is that this name derived from "Richard Jaquette," Lord of the Manor of Tyburn, where executions were performed until 1783. Another suggestion is that *Jack* is a common name and *Ketch* plays on the verb "catch."

> He is then a kind of jack-catch, an executioner-general. (John Wesley, *Works*, 1755)

Jim Crow See **RACISM**.

John Hancock A person's signature or autograph, especially on legal documents; also *John Henry*. The allusion is to John Hancock's bold, legible signature, the first on the Declaration of Independence. The variation *John Henry* was originally a cowboy term. Both expressions are American in origin as well as in use. Although *John Hancock* as a synonym for signature dates only from the early part of this century, a reference to the bold style of his hand was made as early as 1846.

After he got through filling in the blank spaces with his John Hancock, he didn't have a window to hoist or a fence to lean on. (Ade, *People you Know*, 1903)

little Lord Fauntleroy See INEXPERIENCE.

malapropism See LANGUAGE.

maverick See INDEPENDENCE.

Meddlesome Matty See MEDDLESOMENESS.

Molotov cocktail A weapon consisting of a bottle containing a combustible liquid and a wick that is lit before the device is thrown. These makeshift fire bombs, named for V. M. Molotov, the wartime foreign minister of Russia, were used by Russian civilians against the invading Nazi stormtroopers in 1941. This phrase has been in common use since World War II.

Stationary tanks can be disabled by dropping grenades or Molotov cocktails through the ventilating openings. (T. Gorman, *Modern Weapons of War*, 1942)

Peck's bad boy See MISCHIEF.

peeping Tom See SEXUAL ORIENTATION.

Pollyanna See IDEALISM.

pooh bah See POMPOSITY.

Simon Legree See DOMINATION.

soapy Sam See EXHORTATION.

son of Belial See EVIL.

son of thunder See EXHORTATION.

Uncle Tom See SUBMISSIVENESS.

EQUIVALENCE

neck and neck Even, equal, on a par; abreast, at the same pace. Based on available citations, figurative use of this expression is as old as the literal horse-racing one, both dating from the early 19th century. It still finds frequent application.

Production ran neck and neck in the studios, but the second version . . . reached the public screen last. (*The Times*, June, 1955)

nip and tuck So close as to be of uncertain outcome; neck and neck, on a par, even; up in the air, questionable. This chiefly U.S. term is of puzzling origin and inconsistent form, appearing in print in the 1800s as *rip and tuck, nip and tack*, and *nip and chuck*, before assuming its present *nip and tuck*. Its original restriction to contexts describing close contests, usually athletic, lends credence to the claim that it originated as a wrestling term (Barrère and Leland, *Dictionary of Slang*, 1890). The expression is now employed in much broader contexts, indicative of any kind of uncertainty.

It is nip and tuck whether such a last great achievement of the bipartisan foreign policy can be ratified before . . . the Presidential race. (*The Economist*, May, 1948)

ERRONEOUSNESS (See also FALLACIOUSNESS.)

all wet Totally mistaken, in error; perversely wrong. This slang expression dates from the early 1930s and is still in common use.

Alfalfa Bill Murray may be all wet in his state-line bridge and oil production controversies. (*Kansas City Times*, August 29, 1931)

Although the exact origin of *all wet* is unknown, *wet* as a negative word is familiar in phrases such as *wet blanket* and in the British use of *wet* to mean 'feeble or foolish.'

back the wrong horse To be mistaken in one's judgment, to support a loser. The expression, originally a reference to betting on a losing horse, is now used popularly to denote the support or backing of any losing person or cause.

bad-ball hitter A person of questionable judgment, so-called from the baseball term for a batter who swings at pitches well outside the strike zone.

bad break An unfortunate piece of luck, bad luck. This American slang term is conjectured to have come from billiards, where to make a bad break is to cause the racked billiard balls to scatter in such a way that further shots are difficult. This meaning dates from the late 19th century and, though still occasionally encountered, has been largely displaced by the currency of *break* meaning 'a stroke of luck or fortune.'

bark up the wrong tree To pursue a false lead; to be misled or mistaken. This Americanism clearly comes from hunting; specifically, according to some, nocturnal raccoon hunting in which the dogs would often lose track of their quarry.

> I told him . . . that he reminded me of the meanest thing on God's earth, an old coon dog, barking up the wrong tree. (*Sketches and Eccentricities of Col. David Crockett*, 1833)

miss the cushion To make a mistake; to fail in an attempt. It has been hypothesized that *cushion* is another word for 'target' or 'mark'; thus, the expression is thought to derive from the unsuccessful attempt of an archer to hit the mark. Now obsolete, *miss the cushion* dates from the early 16th century.

> Thy wits do err and miss the cushion quite. (Michael Drayton, *Eclogues*, 1593)

off base Badly mistaken, completely wrong. In baseball, a runner leading too far off the base is likely to be thrown out. This expression is also obsolete slang for 'crazy or demented.'

out in left field Wildly mistaken, absolutely wrong; disoriented, confused. This American slang term refers to the left outfield position in baseball, a game in which the infield is the center of activity. Nothing inherent in the game, however, makes the left field position more appropriate than the right for

inclusion in the expression. Perhaps the negative associations of *left* (clumsiness, backwardness) account for its use.

overshoot the mark See EXCESSIVENESS.

pull a boner To make an obvious, stupid mistake, to blunder; to make an embarrassing, amusing slip of the tongue. This originally U.S. slang expression dating from the turn of the century may have derived from the antics of the two end men, Mr. Bones and Mr. Tambo, of the old minstrel shows. The interlocutor would carry on humorous conversations with the end men who sometimes provoked laughter by "pulling a boner."

> Got his signals mixed and pulled a boner. (*American Magazine*, September, 1913)

A common variant is *make a boner*.

> This Government has made about every boner possible. (*Spectator*, October 7, 1960)

slip of the tongue See EXPOSURE.

take in water To be flawed or weak; to be invalid or unsound. This obsolete expression, dating from the late 16th century, alludes to a vessel that is not watertight. By extension, it applies to flawed ideas or statements.

> All the rest are easily freed; St. Jerome and St. Ambrose in the opinion of some seem to take in water. (Bishop Joseph Hall, *Episcopacie By Divine Right Asserted*, 1640)

See also **hold water, VALIDITY**.

wide of the mark Inaccurate, erroneous, off base; irrelevant, not pertinent. Dating from the 17th century, this expression most likely derives from the unsuccessful attempt of an archer to hit the "mark" or target. Variants of this expression include *far from the mark* and *short of the mark*. See **beside the mark, IRRELEVANCE**.

ESCAPE   (See also **DEPARTURE**.)

fly the coop   To escape, as from a prison; to depart suddenly, often clandestinely. In this expression, *coop* is slang for a prison or any other confining place, literal or figurative. Thus, while the phrase is commonly applied to prison escapes, it is sometimes used to describe a child who has run away from home or an employee who quits suddenly because of the pressures and restrictions of his job.

give leg bail   To run away; to escape from confinement on foot. Literally, bail is the surety, often provided by a third party, which allows a prisoner temporary liberty. In this rather droll expression, however, the prisoner is only indebted to his legs for his escape from custody.

> I had concluded to use no chivalry, but give them leg-bail instead of it, by . . . making for a deep swamp. (James Adair, *History of the American Indian*, 1775)

give the guy   To give someone the slip, to escape; also *to do a guy* and *to guy* 'to run away, to decamp.' Although of unknown origin, *guy* in these phrases means 'a decampment, a running off on the sly.' All three of these British slang expressions date from the late 19th century.

give the slip   To elude or to escape from a person; to steal away or slip away unnoticed. *Slip* as an intransitive verb meaning 'to escape or get away' dates from the 14th century; transitive use dates from the 16th century. No explanation for the change to the substantive in *give the slip* is very plausible. One possibility is that the expression derives from the nautical *slip* which means 'to allow the anchor-cable to run out when trying to make a quick getaway.' Another theory suggests that the expression alludes to the image of an animal "slipping" its collar in order to run free. Neither theory is convincing, however, since it is difficult to determine accurately which use came first.

on the lam   Escaping, fleeing, or hiding, especially from the police or other law enforcement officers. This popular underworld slang expression, in use since at least 1900, first received general acceptance and popularity during the 1920s. *Lam* probably derives from the Scandinavian *lemja* 'to beat' or, in this case, 'to beat it, flee.' A similar expression is *take it on the lam*.

> He plugged the main guy for keeps, and I took it on the lam for mine. (No. 1500, *Life in Sing-Sing*, 1904)

show a clean pair of heels   To escape by superior speed; to outrun; to run off; also *show a fair pair of heels* or *a pair of heels*. This expression, in use since 1654, is said to have derived from the ancient sport of cockfighting. Since Roman times gamecocks have fought wearing heels or metal spurs. If a rooster ran away instead of fighting, he was said to have shown his rival a clean pair of heels, since his spurs were unsullied by the blood of combat.

ESSENCE

in a nutshell   Concisely, tersely, pithily; briefly, simply, in few words; containing much of substance in a small space, as nutmeat within a nutshell. *Nutshell* as representative of conciseness has been in use since the 17th century; the phrase *in a nutshell* since shortly thereafter.

> A great complex argument, which . . . cannot by any ingenuity . . . be packed into a nutshell. (John Henry Newman, *Grammar of Assent*, 1870)

nature of the beast   The essence of a person or thing; human nature; the qualities and characteristics common to human beings and other animals. This expression combines *nature* 'essential qualities or properties' and *beast* 'any animal,' implying that there is a certain crudeness common to all animals, both human and nonhuman. It is often used in the context of explaining or excusing the behavior of someone who acts or has acted in an inappropriate or boorish manner. Such usage is illustrated in a 1683 letter by Jules Verney:

> I'm very sorry [that] John my coachman should be so great a clown to you . . . but 'tis the nature of the beast. (*Letters and Papers of the Verney Family*, 1899)

In recent years, the usage of *nature of the beast* has been extended to describe the negative qualities often inherent in inanimate objects, bureaucratic systems, and other matters.

part and parcel An integral or essential component; a vital part of a larger entity. In this expression, common since the 14th century, *part* and *parcel* are synonymous, their juxtaposition serving to emphasize the importance of a given constituent to the whole.

> The places referred to are, for all intents and purposes, part and parcel of the metropolis. (John McCulloch, *A Descriptive and Statistical Account of the British Empire*, 1846)

sixty-four-dollar question The crux of the matter; the basic or critically important question; the remaining unknown whose answer would provide the ultimate solution of a problem. This expression refers to the prize awarded for correctly answering the last and most difficult in a series of questions asked of a contestant on "Take It or Leave It," a popular radio quiz show in the 1940s. With the advent of television, the stakes were raised considerably in "The $64,000 Question" (1955–58), giving rise to the updated variation, *sixty-four-thousand-dollar question*.

ESTABLISHMENTS

barrelhouse A cheap, disreputable saloon; also, a loud, forceful, unpolished type of jazz. The name *barrelhouse* probably came from the practice of serving beer from kegs or barrels in less expensive bars. Of American origin, this word appeared in its slang sense in 1883 in *Peck's Bad Boy* by George W. Peck. The musical sense of the term, however, which derived from the style of piano entertainment associated with such places, did not appear until 1926 in H. O. Osgood's *So this is Jazz.*

but-and-ben A Scottish term for a two-room dwelling; a cottage. In use as early as 1724, the term is a combination of the Scots *but* 'outer or front room' and *ben* 'inner or back room.' R. Burton explains the term as follows:

> Each house has two rooms, a "but" and a "ben" separated by a screen of corncanes. . . . The but, used as parlour, kitchen, and dormitory, opens upon the central square; the ben . . . serves for sleeping and for a storeroom. (*Central Africa*, in *Journal*, 1859)

the cooler A jail or prison, especially a solitary confinement cell. This U.S. slang term, which dates from 1884, originally referred to isolated cells where drunk or violent inmates were kept in order to "cool off." The expression has since become more generalized and is now used popularly to mean simply jail or prison.

flea bag A dingy, squalid residence; a decrepit hotel or rooming house. The term alludes to a small, confined area infested with roaches, fleas, and other vermin. In modern usage, *flea bag* usually refers to a run-down building where low-cost rooms are available to destitute people.

> The flea bag where I was living did not permit dogs. (John O'Hara, *Pal Joey*, 1939)

fleshpot A luxurious establishment offering its customers wanton pleasure and depravity; a brothel or house of ill repute. In the Old Testament (Exodus 16:3) this term describes the plenty of Egypt so sorely missed by the wandering Israelites. Its modern figurative meaning is decidedly different.

He would sally out for the flesh-pots to enjoy a hell raising binge. (W. R. and F. K. Simpson, *Hockshop,* 1954)

honky-tonk A disreputable nightspot; a tawdry cabaret; a chintzy establishment featuring cheap entertainment and music.

Others of possibly less talent were doing stalwart work as accompanists to the blues singers in the honky-tonks of New Orleans and St. Louis. (S. Traill, *Concerning Jazz,* 1957)

The origin of this expression lies in the tinny, honklike sounds of ragtime piano playing heard in cheap nightclubs and brothels; hence, the term's adjectival use describing the pianos on which such music is played, or the music itself.

Happy, beery men thumping honky-tonk pianos. (*Drive,* Spring, 1972)

speak-easy A restaurant, bar, or nightspot where alcoholic beverages are sold illicitly. While the expression may have originated from the 19th-century British underworld's *speak-softly shop* 'a smuggler's home or business establishment,' it is more likely derived from the ease with which a tipsy person engages in conversation. The phrase was particularly commonplace during Prohibition, when it referred to the many clandestine establishments serving bootleg whiskey and moonshine.

Moe Smith and Izzy Einstein were the most dreaded prohibition agents who ever closed down a speakeasy. (*Life,* January 2, 1950)

ETIQUETTE (See PROPRIETY.)

EUPHEMISMS

blankety-blank See PROFANITY.

dickens See PROFANITY.

love-brat A child born out of wedlock; a bastard. This obsolete expression, the equivalent of the modern *love-child,* appeared in the 17th-century *Old Chapbook:*

Now by this four we plainly see
Four love brats will be laid to thee:
And she that draws the same shall wed
Two rich husbands, and both well bred.

pillars to the temple British slang for a woman's legs. The sexual allusion in this coy euphemism is obvious.

pooper-scooper A shovellike device used to daintily pick up the feces of dogs or other pets. The expression, as well as the devices, has become especially popular since the mid-1970s when New York and other cities enacted laws requiring dog owners to clean up after their pets.

Sam Hill Hell. The person to whom this euphemistic expletive apparently refers is unknown. The *Random House Dictionary* suggests that *Sam* may be derived from *salmon,* a variation of *Sal(o)mon* 'an oath,' and that *Hill* may be a variation of *hell.* The term usually appears in expressions like "What the . . . ," "Who the . . . ," etc.

He wondered who the Sam Hill the "senator" was. (*Salt Lake* [City, Utah] *Tribune,* December 18, 1948)

see a man about a dog To go to the men's room; to go out for a drink; to visit a prostitute. This slang Americanism appears to have been coined in the mid-to-late 19th century as a Victorian euphemism to avoid direct reference to bodily functions or frowned-upon activities.

Although they were all out, at the bases, and the rest of our nine having gone to see a man, there was nobody to take the bat. (*The Ball Players' Chronicle,* September 12, 1867)

The appearance in print of the inverted *see a dog about a man* and the variant *see a man about a horse* attests to the nonsensicalness of the original expression.

> I'm in a rush—gotta see a dog about a man. (*Chicago Tribune,* March 21, 1948)

See a man about a dog is also used as an evasive response to almost any inconvenient or embarrassing question.

son of a gun An evil person, a miscreant; a rogue, scamp, or scalawag; any person; a disagreeable or odious task or other matter; as an interjection, an exclamation of surprise, disappointment, or dismay. It has been suggested that *son of a gun* originated during the 18th century when nonmilitary women were permitted to live aboard naval ships. When one of these women gave birth to a child without knowing which of the sailors had fathered it, the paternity was logged as "gun" and the child as "son of a gun," alluding either to the sexual implications of *gun* or to the midship gun which was located near the makeshift maternity room. In any case, the expression is a popular and somewhat less offensive alternative to *son of a bitch,* which also intimates that a person is of uncertain paternity and that his mother was less than virtuous. Over the years, however, both expressions have lost much of their derogatory connotations and are often applied in jocular and familiar contexts.

EVASIVENESS (See also **SECRECY**)

Alibi Ike One who repeatedly makes excuses; a shirker. This label, popularized in the U.S. during the 1930s and '40s, is the name of the main character in a 1924 Ring Lardner short story of the same title. By the time he coined the phrase, *alibi* had acquired its informal meaning of 'any excuse, pretext, or plea of innocence,' as opposed to the specific plea that one was elsewhere when an alleged act took place (from the Latin *alibi* 'elsewhere'). Lardner's choice of the name Ike was probably

due simply to the catchy sound and rhythm of *Alibi Ike.*

beat around the bush To approach cautiously or in a roundabout way; to be evasive; to refuse to come to the point. Nocturnal bird hunters in 15th-century Britain checked for birds lurking in bushes by cautiously beating around a bush with a bat and a light. The saying is now used figuratively in regard to discourse and can be expressive of timidity at one extreme or dishonesty at the other.

bury one's head in the sand To avoid reality; to hide from the truth; to ignore the facts. In times of danger ostriches lie on the ground with their necks stretched out in order to escape detection. It is presumably this behavior that gave rise to the myth that ostriches bury their heads in the sand when pursued, and, no longer able to see their enemies, believe themselves secure from danger.

do an end run To evade or circumvent; to outmaneuver or outfox. This American slang expression is a figurative extension of the football term *end run* or *sweep,* a running play in which the offense blocks to center while the ball carrier runs toward the sideline and slips around the opposing blockers.

fimble-famble A trivial excuse or explanation; balderdash, fiddle-faddle, nonsense. This British expression is probably a dialectal variant of skimble-skamble, which appears in Shakespeare's *I Henry IV:*

> . . . and such a deal of skimble-skamble stuff
> As puts me from my faith. (III,i)

fire one's pistol in the air To purposely avoid offending or injuring an opponent in an argument or debate. This expression harkens back to the days when dueling was the gentleman's way of defending his honor. A dueler who did not want to injure his opponent would fire his pistol into the air—a harmless way of discharging his debt. In current usage, the expression is employed figuratively to indicate that someone deliberately avoids a direct personal attack on an opponent during the discussion of issues.

give the run-around To avoid personal contact by being perpetually unavailable; to avoid direct, open communication by evasive, misleading responses; to postpone action, or to employ dilatory tactics. In any case, the words *run* and *around* are suggestive of avoidance and evasion. *Give the run-around* appeared in print by the turn of the century.

> Pitts is satisfied that he is the victim of the grandest run-around ever put over on a boxing promoter. (*Chicago Herald,* December 2, 1915)

hem and haw To speak evasively; to avoid answering a question directly; to procrastinate. This familiar expression is an onomatopoeic rendering of the unintelligible muttering of a noncommittal mugwumpian. The phrase, as used by Clifford Aucoin, is cited in *Webster's Third:*

> Hem and haw and put it off, apparently in the hope that things will pick up.

in soaped-pig fashion Vaguely, ambiguously, equivocally; used in reference to speaking or writing of this nature.

> He is vague as may be; writing in what is called the "soaped-pig" fashion. (Carlyle, *The Diamond Necklace*)

In former times, at fairs and carnivals, great sport was had chasing after and trying to catch the pig that was turned out among the crowd for their diversion. Before the pig was loosed, however, it was soaped in order to heighten both the difficulty and the fun.

Mickey Mouse around To avoid confronting a major issue or problem by wasting time; fooling around; indulging in trivial activities. The reference is to the animated persona that made its debut in Walt Disney's *Steamboat Willie* (1928), the first cartoon with sound, and the allusion is to the playful though insignificant activities which characterize most Mickey Mouse cartoons.

> We can't Mickey Mouse around while faced with technological challenges from other countries. (R. G. Hummerstone, in *Fortune Magazine,* May, 1973)

A common variation is the shortened *Mickey Mouse.*

See also **Mickey Mouse, INSIGNIFICANCE.**

pull punches To be evasive, hedge, or weasel; to pussyfoot and be mealymouthed; to lessen the impact of a disclosure or to discuss a sensitive topic with discrimination. This expression originated as boxing slang for an intentionally weak blow. It is most often used negatively as an implicit compliment to candor and openness, as in the following by Sara H. Hay, cited in *Webster's Third:*

> She has pulled no punches in coming directly to the extreme issues involved.

EVIL   (See **UNSCRUPULOUSNESS, WICKEDNESS.**)

EXACERBATION   (See also **AUGMENTATION.**)

add fuel to the fire To make a bad situation worse; to intensify; to say or do something to increase the anger of a person already incensed. Literally adding fuel to a fire increases the strength with which the flames blaze, just as metaphorically adding "something that serves to feed or inflame passion, excitement, or the like . . . especially love or rage" (*OED*), intensifies the passion.

add insult to injury To heap scorn on one already injured. The phrase is from the Aesop fable of a baldheaded man who, having been bitten on his pate by a fly, tries to kill the insect. In doing so, he gives himself a painful blow. The fly jeeringly remarks:

> You wished to kill me for a mere touch. What will you do to yourself, since you have added insult to injury?

confusion worse confounded Chaos compounded or made greater than before. John Milton uses the expression in *Paradise Lost* (1667):

> With ruin upon ruin, rout on rout, Confusion worse confounded.

The unusual syntactical structure of this expression may be clarified by noting that the obsolete or archaic meaning of *confound* was 'to overthrow, to bring to ruin' while the obsolete meaning of *confusion* was 'overthrow, ruin.' Thus, the line *confusion worse confounded* follows the pattern of repetition found in the previous line.

cut off one's nose to spite one's face To cause one's own hurt or loss through spiteful action; to cause injury to oneself or one's own interests in pursuing revenge. This proverbial expression first appeared in print in 1785, when it was defined in Francis Grose's *A Classical Dictionary of the Vulgar Tongue:*

> He cut off his nose to be revenged of his face. Said of one who, to be revenged on his neighbour, has materially injured himself.

This saying is believed to have come from the French *se couper le nez pour faire dépit à son visage.*

escape the bear and fall to the lion To be free of one predicament only to get involved in another more trying, complex, or dangerous one; to go from bad to worse. In use as early as the beginning of the 17th century, this expression suggests that there is danger to be met at every turn.

heap Pelion upon Ossa To make matters worse, to compound or aggravate things; also, to indulge in fruitless or futile efforts. The allusion is to the Greek myth of the giants who unsuccessfully tried to get to Olympus, home of the gods, by stacking Mount Pelion on Mount Ossa.

Job's comforter One who either intentionally or unwittingly adds to another's distress while supposedly consoling and comforting him. The allusion is to the Biblical Job's three friends who come to commiserate with him over his misfortunes and who instead of consoling him only aggrieve him more by reproving him for his lack of faith and his resentful attitude. The term has been in use since at least 1738.

> You are a Job's comforter with a vengeance. (Mrs. B. M. Croker, *Proper Pride*, 1885)

out of the frying pan into the fire From bad to worse, from one disastrous situation to one even worse.

> If they thought they could get away from the State by disestablishment, they would find that they were jumping out of the frying-pan into the fire. (*The Guardian*, October, 1890)

Use of the expression dates from the early 16th century.

rub salt in a wound To maliciously emphasize or reiterate something unfavorable or disagreeable with the express purpose of annoying someone; to continually harp on a person's errors or shortcomings, especially those of which he is acutely conscious. Since salt, when placed on an open wound, causes painful stinging and discomfort, to actually *rub* salt into a wound would be excessively cruel and sadistic. Although recent medical research has shown that salt (such as in seawater) actually helps wounds to heal with minimal scarring, it is safe to assume that a person who figuratively rubs salt in a wound is not motivated by therapeutic concern. A popular and more widely used variation is *rub it in.*

Ye needn't rub it in any more.
(Rudyard Kipling, *Captains Courageous,* 1897)

when push comes to shove When a situation goes from bad to worse; when worse comes to worst; when the going gets tough. In this expression *shove* refers to an exaggerated—bigger and harder—push. Thus, *when push comes to shove* refers to the point at which subtlety gives way to flagrancy.

EXAGGERATION

all one's geese are swans A proverbial expression said of one who is prone to overexaggeration and overestimation. Geese are rather unattractive, common birds in comparison to the rarer, more elegant swans; thus, to *turn one's geese to swans* is, figuratively speaking, to color reality considerably. Use of this phrase, which is infrequently heard today, dates from at least the early 17th century.

The besetting temptation which leads local historians to turn geese into swans. (*Saturday Review,* July, 1884)

draw the longbow To exaggerate or overstate, to lay it on thick; to stretch the truth, to tell tall tales. The longbow, a weapon drawn by hand, was of central importance in the exploits of Robin Hood and his band. The farther back one stretched the bowstring, the farther the arrow would fly. It is easy to see how this literal stretching of the longbow came to mean a figurative stretching of the truth. This expression, in use since at least the latter part of the 17th century, appears in Lord Byron's *Don Juan* (1824):

At speaking truth perhaps they are less clever,
But draw the long bow better now than ever.

fish story A tall tale, an exaggeration; an absurd or unbelievable account of one's exploits. This colloquialism, in use since at least the early 19th century, derives from the propensity of many, if not all, fishermen to exaggerate the size of their catch. An important element in many fish stories is the angler's lament, "You should have seen the one that got away."

ham See OSTENTATIOUSNESS.

hyped-up Overblown, overly touted, inordinately promoted or publicized; artificially induced; bogus, contrived. The term's origin stems from the use of a hypodermic injection to stimulate physiological response. In a 1950 syndicated column Billy Rose said of a movie:

No fireworks, no fake suspense, no hyped-up glamour.

The term has now given rise to the truncated form *hype,* used disparagingly both as noun and verb.

lay it on See FLATTERY.

make a mountain out of a molehill To make a to-do over a minor matter, to make a great fuss over a trifle. Although this particular expression did not appear until the late 16th century, the idea had been expressed centuries earlier by the Greek writer Lucian in his *Ode to a Fly;* it subsequently became the French proverb *faire d'une mouche un éléphant* 'make an elephant of a fly.'

[This is] like making mountains out of molehills. (James Tait, *Mind in Matter,* 1892)

megillah See ANECDOTE.

shoot the bull See TALKATIVENESS.

snow job See MENDACITY.

song and dance A misleading, false, or exaggerated story designed to evoke sympathy or to otherwise evade an issue; a rigmarole; a snow job. Though the derivation of this expression is unclear, it probably alludes to the "song and dance" acts that introduced or filled in between the main attractions in a vaudeville show.

Labor leader Preble . . . was not impressed by the song and dance about [Stefan's] mother and sister being persecuted and murdered. (*Time*, September 5, 1949)

spin a yarn To tell a story, especially a long, involved, exaggerated account of one's exploits and adventures, both real and imagined; to tell a tall tale. Originally, *spin a yarn* was a nautical term that meant 'to weave hemp into rope.' Since this was a tedious, time-consuming task, sailors often traded tall tales and adventure stories to help pass the time. Thus, these stories came to be known as *yarns*, and their telling as *spinning a yarn*, by association.

Come, spin us a good yarn, father. (Frederick Marryat, *Jacob Faithful*, 1835)

talk through one's hat To talk nonsense, to lie or exaggerate, to make farfetched or unsupported statements.

But when Mr. Wallace says that . . . he is talking through his hat. (*The Chicago Daily News*, December, 1944)

Use of this expression, whose origin as yet defies explanation, dates from the late 19th century.

talk through the back of one's neck To use extravagant, flowery language, often sacrificing accuracy; to make unrealistic, illogical, or extraordinary statements.

"Don't talk through yer neck," snarled the convict. "Talk out straight, curse you!" (E. W. Hornung, *Amateur Cracksman*, 1899)

Through the back of one's neck is here opposed to *straight*, which connotes directness, straightforwardness, and truthfulness.

Anybody who gets up in this House and talks about universal peace knows he is talking through the back of his neck. (*Pall Mall Gazette*, 1923)

EXASPERATION (See **DESPERATION**.)

EXCELLENCE

A1 or A one Superior, excellent, first-rate. The term dates from the 1830s. Lloyd's *Register of British and Foreign Shipping* used letters to indicate the condition of a ship's hull, and numbers to designate the state of the cables, anchors, etc. The highest attainable rating was A1. In the United States the colloquial phrase *A-number one* is often heard.

bear away the bell See **VICTORY**.

bear the bell To be in the foremost position; to take the lead; to be the best. This expression refers to the bell worn on the neck of the bellwether, the leading sheep of a flock. It can be used quantitatively to mean the first in a series, or qualitatively to mean the best. Chaucer used it in the former sense:

And, let see which of you shall bear the bell
To speak of love aright? (*Troilus and Criseyde*, 1374)

The judgmental use of *bear the bell* is more current today.

blowed-in-the-glass First-rate, superior, high quality. This American hobo slang expression alludes to the fact that the better liquors often had the brand name blown into the glass of the bottle.

blue ribbon The highest order of excellence; preeminence in a given area; first prize. The term may come either from the blue ribbon worn by members of the Order of the Garter, the highest order of British knighthood, instituted in the mid-14th century; or from the blue ribbon (*cordon bleu*) worn by members of the Order of the Saint Esprit, the highest order of knighthood in France, instituted in the late 16th century. The French term *cordon bleu* remains in use primarily for chefs of distinction. The first figurative use of *blue ribbon* has been attributed to Disraeli, who termed the Derby "the Blue Ribbon of the Turf" (1848).

cat's meow Someone or something excellent, first rate, remarkable; the acme. Introduced in the early 1900s, this was among the most popular fad expressions of the Roaring 20s. It is rarely used now. *Cat's pajamas,* another popular phrase of the era, derives from the fact that pajamas had just been introduced and were still considered somewhat daring nighttime attire. The word *cat* is also used in expressions such as *cat's whiskers, cat's cuff links, cat's eyebrows, cat's galoshes, cat's roller skates,* and *cat's tonsils.*

In the 1920s, it was all the rage to combine an animal with an inappropriate body part or clothing item, e.g., *ant's pants, bee's knees, clam's garters, eel's ankles, elephant's instep, gnu's shoes, leopard's stripes, pig's wings, sardine's whiskers,* and *tiger's spots.*

corker See EFFECTIVENESS.

enough to make a cat speak Said in reference to something extraordinarily good, usually superior drink. The point is that the liquor is so good it will loosen even a cat's tongue. A variant of this expression appears in Shakespeare's *The Tempest* (II,ii):

Here is that which will give language to you, cat; open your mouth.

hunky-dory In a fine state; in superb condition; A1 or A-OK. This American expression, derived from the Dutch *honk* 'goal, home,' as in the children's games of tag or hide and go seek, implies feelings of success, contentment, or satisfaction.

I thought everything was hunkydory and you were well on the way to being a big executive. (D. M. Dakin, *Sullen Bell,* 1956)

of the first water Perfect, consummate; pure, unblemished. The transparency, color, or luster of a diamond or pearl is its water. Diamonds are rated of the first, second, or third water. The phrase came to be applied to jewels in general, and subsequently to any person or object of outstanding quality. It is frequently used in negative contexts as an intensifier—*pure* as 'unmitigated, out-and-out, thoroughgoing, complete.'

He was a . . . swindler of the first water. (Scott, *Journal,* 1826)

purple patches Passages in a literary work that are marked by ornate writing, especially as interlarded with an overuse of dramatic, exaggerated literary effects; inappropriately laden with rhetorical devices. In this expression, *purple* means 'gorgeous.'

A few of the purple patches scattered through the book may serve as a sample of the rest. (*Academy,* April, 1881)

the real McCoy See GENUINENESS.

round as Giotto's O Said of a task, project, or other matter that is completed quickly, effortlessly, and with a high degree of perfection. According to legend, Pope Boniface VIII sent a messenger to secure the services of the famous Italian artist Giotto (c. 1266–1337). Seeking proof of Giotto's skill, the messenger asked for a sample of his work, whereupon the artist quickly drew a perfect circle on a sheet of paper. The pope was impressed, and the expression and its variants soon became almost proverbial in Italy and elsewhere.

I saw . . . that the practical teaching of the masters of Art was summed up by the O of Giotto. (John Ruskin, *The Queen of the Air,* 1869)

Rounder than the O of Giotto is sometimes said of a work that epitomizes perfection, one that is more perfect than perfect.

to a fare-thee-well Perfectly, to the utmost degree or fullest extent, to the maximum; also *to a fare-you-well.* This American expression, which dates from the latter part of the 19th century, comes from the parting phrase *fare you well,* used to express good wishes to one about to leave on a journey. Perhaps the connection lies in the finality of departure.

top-drawer Of the highest rank; usually in reference to social class. Conjecture is that the term stems from keeping one's most valuable possessions in the top drawer of a chest.

top-shelf Of superior quality, used especially in relation to social class or standing, as in *top-shelfer.*

> The frontiersman calls them, as we have heard, "top-shelfers"; they are accompanied by their servants from England. (Baillie-Grohman, *Camps in the Rockies,* 1882)

Top-shelf items are out of easy reach, for use or wear only on rare occasions; extraordinary or fine as opposed to everyday. One theory holds that *top-shelf* derives from the saloon keepers' practice of placing the most expensive, and consequently the least requested, brands of liquor on the higher shelves. The more frequently ordered house-brands were kept more readily accessible.

tough act to follow Said of a presentation, performance, project, or other matter that has been completed successfully and with a high degree of excellence, especially one that has received much acclaim. In variety shows, theatrical performances, concerts, etc., it has become customary to save the best act for last lest the audience become disappointed and leave before the entire show has been completed. *Tough act to follow* implies that the standards set by a previous performer will be difficult, if not impossible, to meet or exceed.

EXCESSIVENESS

baker's dozen Thirteen; a dozen plus one. Bakers at one time reputedly gave an extra roll for every dozen sold in order to avoid the heavy fines levied against those who short-changed their customers by selling lightweight bread.

The phrase appeared in the early 17th century in *Tu Quoque* by John Cooke.

barnburner See ZEALOUSNESS.

break a butterfly on a wheel To employ a degree of force or energy disproportionate to the needs of a situation; to overkill. The wheel was formerly an instrument of torture upon which a criminal was stretched and beaten to death. Considering the fragile nature of a butterfly, the analogy is self-evident. The phrase appears in Alexander Pope's *Epistle to Dr. Arbuthnot:*

> Satire or sense, alas! can Sporus feel?
> Who breaks a butterfly upon the wheel?

die for want of lobster sauce To die or suffer greatly on account of some minor disappointment, irritation, or disgrace. This expression is said to have had its origins in a sumptuous banquet given by Louis II de Bourbon (the great Condé) for Louis XIV at Chantilly. Legend has it that when the chef was informed that the lobsters which he had intended to make into a sauce had not been delivered in time for the feast, he was so overcome with humiliation that he committed suicide by running upon his sword.

drug on the market A commodity which is no longer in demand; anything which is so readily available that it tends to be taken for granted or undervalued; a glut on the market. *Drug* alone was used as early as the 1600s; *in the market* was introduced in the 1700s. The phrase "a drug in the market of literature" appeared in Thomas Walter's *A Choice Dialogue Between John Faustus, A Conjurer, and Jack Tory his Friend* (1720). Today *drug on the market* is more frequently heard. Perhaps this expression derives from the fact that drugs induce a dulling effect similar to that caused by too much of anything—in other words, by any type of overindulgence.

enough [something] to choke Caligula's horse A lot, a great deal, plenty, more than enough. Caligula, Roman emperor from 37–41 A.D., was thought to be insane because of his extravagant claims, his wholesale murdering and banishment of his subjects, and his wild, foolish spending. It is perhaps in reference to this last quality that the expression *enough [something] to choke Caligula's horse* arose. There is, however, no evidence to substantiate this theory, and no theory at all regarding the rest of the phrase.

gingerbread Garish or tasteless ornamentation; superfluous embellishments. This term is derived from the ornate decorations a baker uses to adorn a gingerbread house. Figuratively, *gingerbread* describes excessive or tacky furnishings and decorations.

Some people would have crammed it full of gingerbread upholstery, all gilt and gaudy. (Lisle Carr, *Judith Gwynne*, 1874)

go overboard To go to great extremes; to express either overwhelming opposition to or support for a person or cause. One who shifts all his weight to one side of a small boat may literally go overboard. Likewise, one who radically directs all his energies toward one thing figuratively "goes overboard." This very common phrase as used by Dwight MacDonald is cited in *Webster's Third:*

. . . went overboard for heroes and heroines who don't seem so heroic today.

out Herod Herod See OUTDOING.

overshoot the mark To exceed or go beyond prescribed limits; to be off base, irrelevant, or inappropriate. Literally, a missile or other projectile "overshoots the mark" when it misses its target by going above or beyond it. Figuratively, this expression is said of any attempt or idea which errs on the side of excess. Such use dates from the late 16th century.

The greatest fault of a penetrating wit is not coming short of the mark but overshooting it. (*The English Theophrastus*, 1702)

paint the lily To adorn or embellish an already beautiful object, thereby destroying its delicate balance and rendering it gaudy and overdone; to detract from the natural, full beauty of an object by trying to add ornamentation where none is required. This expression derives from Lord Salisbury's speech in Shakespeare's *King John:*

Therefore, to be possess'd with double pomp,
To guard a title that was rich before,
To gild refined gold, to paint the lily,
To throw a perfume on the violet,
To smooth the ice, or add another hue
Unto the rainbow, or with taper-light
To seek the beauteous eye of heaven to garnish,
Is wasteful, and ridiculous excess.
(IV,ii)

Gild the lily is actually more familiar to most people, although few are aware that it is a corruption of *gild refined gold* and *paint the lily*.

run into the ground To overdo, to continue beyond a period of effectiveness to the point of counter-productivity; to beat to death. The expression frequently appears in contexts dealing with argument or with utilization of material objects. One runs a topic into the ground when he undermines a point already effectively made because his persistence and long-windedness antagonize his listeners. Objects are "run into the ground" when a user wrings the last ounce of service from them. In either case, what is "run into the ground" is effectively buried.

sow one's wild oats Indulge in excesses during one's youth; behave in a profligate manner. The origin of this expression is obscure, but it may have reference to the Biblical "Whatsoever a man soweth, that shall he also reap." (Galations 6:7), with the implicit warning against irresponsible behavior, wild oats being utterly useless.

We meane that wilfull and unruly age, which lacketh rypeness and discretion, and (as wee saye) *hath not sowed* all *theyre wyeld Oates.* (*Touchstone of Complexions,* 1576)

tempest in a teapot A great commotion, disturbance, or hubbub over a relatively insignificant matter; excessive agitation or turmoil caused by something of trifling importance. This expression and variations thereof have been common at least since the time of Cicero (106–43 B.C.), as evidenced in *De Legibus:*

Gratidius raised a tempest in a ladle, as the saying is.

The implication, of course, is that something as small as a teapot (or ladle) is hardly an appropriate place for a *tempest* 'violent or stormy disturbance.'

What a ridiculous tea-pot tempest. (*Peterson Magazine,* January, 1896)

Common variations are *tempest in a teacup* and *storm in a teacup.*

M. Renan's visit . . . to his birthplace in Brittany has raised a storm in the clerical teacup. (*Pall Mall Gazette,* September 19, 1884)

throw out the baby with the bath water To reject the essential or valuable along with the unimportant or superfluous. This graphic expression appeared in print by the turn of the century. It is frequently used in reference to proposals calling for significant change, such as political and social reforms or large-scale bureaucratic reorganization.

Like all reactionists, he usually empties the baby out with the bath. (George Bernard Shaw, *Pen Portraits and Reviews,* 1909)

EXCLAMATIONS (See also LANGUAGE.)

for crying out loud This U.S. colloquial exclamation expressing impatience, astonishment, or perturbation is a minced equivalent of similar profane ejacula-

tions such as *for Christ's sake, Holy Christ,* and *Jesus H. Christ.*

For crying out loud, why did you do it? (R. West, *Black Lamb,* 1941)

Geronimo An exclamation of surprise or delight. This Americanism was a battle cry used by World War II paratroopers as they jumped from planes. Military use of the term derived from the American Apache Indian Chief, Geronimo (1829–1909), whose name carried associations of savage killing. After the war, *Geronimo* became a popular term in nonmilitary contexts, retaining the flavor of surprise and exhilaration.

God save the mark This parenthetic phrase can be used as an exclamation of contempt, impatience, or derision; as a formula spoken to avert an evil omen; or as a phrase serving to soften or lessen the offensiveness of something said. Contrary to popular belief that this expression was originally used by archers, it is now believed to have been originally used by midwives at the birth of a child bearing a "mark." Shakespeare popularized the phrase and its variant *bless the mark* in his plays.

He had not been there (bless the mark) a pissing while, but all the chamber smelt him. (Shakespeare, *Two Gentlemen of Verona,* 1591)

In modern use, *save the mark* is most often heard as an ironic expression of contempt.

The crisis of apathetic melancholy . . . from which he emerged by the reading of Marmontel's Memoirs (Heaven save the mark!) and Wordsworth's poetry. (William James, *The Varieties of Religious Experience,* 1902)

hit the deck An exclamatory warning to fall to the ground; to take cover; (in nautical use) to get out of bed.

The whole House fell on its knees or went prone behind desks, as one Pacific veteran shouted out: "Hit the deck, you damn fools!"

(*Manchester Guardian Weekly*, March 4, 1954)

This citation supports the theory that *hit the deck* had a nautical wartime origin. This expression, however, is also used in boxing to mean to fall or be knocked down in the ring. Yet another (nonnautical) use of *hit the deck* refers to going to bed.

> I'm going to hit the deck now, and I'm going to turn the lamp out. (J. Hackston, *Father Clears Out*, 1966)

These different uses have no common origin but share the connotations of speed and impact.

holy mackerel An exclamation expressing surprise or wonder. The only plausible explanation for this curious expression is that it was once felt to be vaguely anti-Catholic, since Catholics were enjoined from eating meat on Fridays and often partook of mackerel instead. Thus, the mackerel acquired a jocularly sacred character. A similar expression, *Holy cow*, evidently sprang up in reference to the sacred cows of Hinduism.

my eye Stuff and nonsense, bunk, baloney—an emphatic exclamation of disbelief. *My eye* is a current truncated version of *all my eye and Betty Martin*. The most popular and most far-fetched story offered to explain the origin of this expression tells of a sailor who overheard a poor Italian beggar cry out, "Ah mihi, beate Martini" which means "Ah, grant me, Blessed Martin." In relating the story to his friends, the sailor's faulty recollection of the beggar's words gave rise to the expression as it stands today: "All my eye and Betty Martin." Undermining the plausibility of this story is its attribution to "Joe Miller"—meaning that it was probably from a book of jests called *Joe Miller's Jest-Book*. (See **Joe Miller, ANECDOTE**.) Other sources scoff at this explanation and suggest that the phrase derives from a gypsy named "Betty Martin"

who gave a black eye to a constable who unjustly accused her of committing a crime. Obviously the exact origin of this expression is unknown although the former explanation is most often cited.

> That's all my eye, the King only can pardon, as the law says. (Oliver Goldsmith, *The Good Natured Man*, 1767)

my foot An exclamation of contradiction, usually spoken directly after the word or phrase being questioned, as in the following:

> Cooperation my foot. You're trying to trap me into admitting a motive for doing the old girl in. (L. A. G. Strong, *Othello's Occupation*, 1945)

The origin of this phrase is unknown. It appeared in print by the turn of the century.

shiver me timbers An interjection, sometimes used as a mock oath. This expression is associated with buccaneers and old salts because of its popularity in comic fiction and children's stories, where it frequently appears as an epithet used by a pirate or other villain. *Timbers* here refers to a ship's structural hull; literally, *shiver me timbers* means to deliver a severe shock to a ship's hull so as to imperil its safety, as from having run aground; figuratively, it means to rattle one's ribs.

> I won't thrash you, Tom. Shiver my timbers if I do. (Frederick Marryat, *Jacob Faithful*, 1835)

EXERTION (See also **OVERWORK**.)

blood, sweat, and tears Adversity, difficulty; suffering, affliction; strenuous, arduous labor. The now common expression is a truncated version of that used by Winston Churchill in addressing the House of Commons shortly after his election as Prime Minister.

> I say to the House, as I said to the Ministers who have joined this Government, I have nothing to offer but blood, toil, tears and sweat. (May 13, 1940)

The phrase gained additional currency when it was adopted as the name of a music group popular in the late 1960s.

buckle down To adopt a no-nonsense attitude of determination and effort; to set aside frivolous concerns or distractions and concentrate on the task at hand. *Buckle down to* dates from 1865, and appears to be but a variation on the earlier *buckle to* or *buckle oneself to,* both of which probably have their antecedents in the act of buckling on armor to prepare for battle.

cleanse the Augean stables See REF-ORMATION.

elbow grease Strenuous physical effort or exertion; hard physical work or manual labor; vigorous and energetic rubbing, muscle. This self-evident expression dates from at least 1672. A hint of its original meaning is provided by the definition found in *A New Dictionary of the Terms Ancient and Modern of the Canting Crew* (1700): "a derisory term for sweat."

get one's teeth into To work with vigor and determination; to come to grips with a task or problem; also, *sink one's teeth into.* This expression may be derived from the greater effort required to chew food than to sip it. Similarly, one who gets his teeth into something of substance is directing a great deal of physical or mental effort into completing the task.

in there pitching Putting forth one's best effort; working energetically and diligently; directing one's energy and talent toward a specific goal. Current since the early 1900s, this colloquial Americanism derives from the game of baseball, specifically the role of the pitcher.

> Everybody on the system is in there pitching, trying to save a locomotive or piece of locomotive. (*Saturday Evening Post*, June 26, 1943)

put one's shoulder to the wheel To strive, to exert oneself, to make a determined effort, to work at vigorously. The reference is to the teamster of yesteryear who literally put his shoulder to the wheel of his wagon when it got stuck in a rut or in mud in order to help his horses pull it out.

work up to the collar To labor diligently; to perform strenuous tasks energetically. A beast of burden is not considered to be working at its utmost capacity unless its collar is straining against its neck. This expression sees little use today.

EXHORTATION

one for the Gipper A highly emotional appeal for an all-out effort; an exhortation to give it one's all for the sake of some emotionally charged cause; a sentimental pep talk. "The Gipper" was George Gipp (1895–1920), a football player at Notre Dame during the era of the renowned Knute Rockne. When it was learned that "the Gipper," no longer on the active roster, was suffering from a fatal illness, Rockne reportedly aroused his "Fighting Irish" with the charge, "Let's win this one for the Gipper." As used today, the phrase more often carries associations of weepy sentimentality than of true poignancy.

soapbox orator An impassioned street orator, a vehement haranguer, a ranting, emotional speaker; also a *soapboxer.*

> Midday crowds gathered in the sun to hear soapbox speakers supporting labor solidarity. (*Time,* July 25, 1949)

Wooden boxes or crates such as those in which soap was once packed were formerly used as temporary, makeshift platforms by street orators declaiming to crowds.

soapy Sam A smooth, honey-tongued orator. This term was first applied to

Samuel Wilberforce, the Anglican Bishop of Oxford. The Cuddeson College student body, wishing to honor the bishop as well as their principal, Alfred Pott, placed floral arrangements in the form of the initials S.O.A.P. (Samuel, Oxford, Alfred, Pott) upon two pillars. The bishop was shocked to see this rather satiric display, which ultimately served to perpetuate his already common nickname. According to legend, a young girl once inquired of the bishop why he had such an unusual sobriquet. Wilberforce replied "Because I am often in hot water, and always come out with clean hands." The expression still maintains some use as an epithet for a moralistic, unctuous speaker.

son of thunder An orator who bellows forth his beliefs in spellbinding manner; a vociferous demagogue. This expression is of Biblical origin:

And James, the son of Zebedee, and John, the brother of James; and he surnamed them Boanerges, which is, the sons of thunder. (Mark 3:17)

The phrase alludes to the resonant, reverberating tones produced by a powerful speaker; originally, it carried no negative connotations. The expression is little used today.

tub-thumper A haranguer or ranter; an emotional, emphatic preacher or orator.

An honest Presbyterian tub-thumper, who has lost his voice with bawling to his flock. (*Letters from Mist's Journal*, 1720–21)

The allusion is to a declamatory speaker, especially a preacher, who repeatedly thumps the *tub*, a humorous and disparaging term for a pulpit. Use of this derogatory British colloquialism dates from the 17th century.

EXONERATION

come out smelling like a rose To escape the negative consequences of one's own actions; to emerge in a positive light, or at least unscathed, after having been embroiled in an unpleasant controversy. The expression usually implies that others are suffering the censure or opprobrium properly due the "innocent" one who "smells like a rose." Despite the phrase's implied vulgar origins, it is now commonly considered inoffensive and frequently appears in a variety of informal contexts.

get off scot-free To escape deserved punishment; to be excused from paying the appropriate fine or penalty; to be released without castigation or just punishment. This expression originated from *scot and lot* 'tax allotment,' which was formerly levied on all English subjects according to their ability to pay. Hence, a person who went scot-free was not required to pay the proper tribute. This expression now implies the legal but morally wrong release of someone from a deserved admonishment or penalty.

. . . the notorious offender has got off scot free. (William Black, *Green Pastures and Piccadilly*, 1877)

EXPEDIENCE

any port in a storm Any refuge in a difficulty; any recourse in an emergency. The nautical meaning of this expression has given way to its figurative use, which implies that pressure limits choice, forcing one to abandon plans, principles, or standards.

Band-aid treatment See FLIMSINESS.

by hook or by crook By any means necessary—direct or indirect, right or wrong, fair or foul. Most of the stories invented to explain the origin of this phrase are not plausible because of chronological inconsistencies; however, one recurring story stands out as being more convincing. Apparently, there was an ancient forestal custom giving manorial tenants the right to take as much firewood as could be reached by a crook and cut with a billhook. Various sources state that this "right" appears in old records: "a right, with hook and crook, to lop, crop, and carry away fuel." However, the following citation from the late 14th century seems to be the earliest recorded use of the phrase and may predate the "forestal right" story.

So what with hepe and what with croke
They [false Witness and Perjury] make her maister ofte winne.
(John Gower, *Confessio Amantis*, 1390)

catch-as-catch-can See UNRESTRAINT.

cut corners To take the shortest, most convenient route; to do something in the quickest, easiest way possible; to choose a particular course of action in the hopes of saving time, money, or effort. This expression is used almost literally when describing driving habits.

The careless driver . . . cuts corners or tries to pass another car at the top of a hill. (*Kansas City Times,* November 7, 1931)

Figuratively, *cut corners* often refers to any effort or behavior which represents a compromise for the sake of expediency, often without regard for quality or sincerity.

He could cut a sharp corner without letting it bother his conscience. (S. Ransome, *Hidden Hour,* 1966)

However, *cutting corners* can also be used positively to describe the most viable and efficient mode of action.

fair-weather friend A person who is friendly only when convenient; someone who is a friend during favorable times and an acquaintance (at best) during adverse times.

Am I to be only a fair-weather wife to you? (Rhoda Broughton, *Nancy,* 1873)

jury-rigged See FLIMSINESS.

know on which side one's bread is buttered To be aware of what is and what is not in keeping with one's own best interests; to recognize what is to one's advantage in a given situation. This ex-

pression appears in John Heywood's *Works* (1562):

I know on which syde my bread is buttred.

The implication is that a person will take care not to offend or alienate someone who has the power to grant or withhold favors. One who knows on which side his bread is buttered will do nothing to jeopardize his position.

paper over the cracks To use stopgap or makeshift measures to give the outward appearance that all is well; to create an illusion of order or accord by means of a temporary expedient while ignoring the basic questions or issues. The expression is usually attributed to Otto von Bismarck, who reputedly used it in regard to the temporary nature of the Austro-Prussian settlement reached at the Convention of Gastein in August, 1865; war broke out between the two countries the next year.

Mr. Bevan agreed to paper over the cracks for the period of the election. (*Annual Register,* 1952)

politics makes strange bedfellows An adage implying that expedience—political or otherwise—often dictates the formation of alliances, however temporary, between two or more highly unlikely parties. In the Middle Ages, it was not unheard of for political allies to share the same bed, especially after long hours of negotiations or strategic planning. As a result, these collaborators came to be known as "bedfellows," a term which persisted even when this custom fell into disfavor. Popularized by Charles Dudley Warner in *My Summer in a Garden* (1870), *politics makes strange bedfellows* is no longer limited to application in political contexts. The expression is sometimes used jocularly to describe a romance between disparate people whose sole attraction seems to be shared political or activist interests.

pull out all the stops See UNRESTRAINT.

rob Peter to pay Paul To take from one person to give to another; to satisfy one obligation by leaving another unsatisfied. The popular theory explaining the origin of this expression is that in 1550, the Order which had advanced the Church of St. Peter to the status of a cathedral was revoked, and St. Peter's was not only reunited with St. Paul's Cathedral in London, but its revenues went toward the expenses of the latter. However, a chronological inconsistency refutes this theory, since Wyclif used the expression almost 200 years earlier in his *Selected Works* (1380):

> How should God approve that you rob Peter, and give this robbery to Paul in the name of Christ.

Peter and Paul were popular apostles and saints, but even this fact does little to explain the use of their names in this expression.

trim one's sails See ADAPTATION.

EXPENSE (See COST.)

EXPERIENCE (See KNOWLEDGE.)

EXPLOITATION (See also VICTIMIZATION.)

all is fish that comes to his net See ABILITY.

butter one's bread on both sides See IMPROVIDENCE.

feather one's nest To look after one's own interests; to accumulate creature comforts, money, or material possessions either through one's own efforts or at the expense of others; to be completely selfish, totally unconcerned with the well-being of others. This expression stems from the fact that many birds, after building a nest, line it with feathers and hair to make it warm and more comfortable. The expression *line one's nest* is a variation.

fish in troubled waters To take advantage of adversity, stress, or unrest for personal gain; to make the best of a bad situation. Fishermen often experience their greatest success when the water is rough. In its figurative use, the phrase implies that though things may be troubled on the surface, at a deeper level, the situation holds potential for gains.

grist for the mill Any experience, fact, discovery, or object with potential for one's personal profit; a seemingly worthless item employed to one's personal gain or benefit. Grist is unground grain to be converted to meal or flour by milling. In the figurative expression, *grist* is anything that serves as the raw material which a person's talents or abilities transform into something of value.

make hay while the sun shines To make the most of an opportunity, to take full advantage of an occasion for profit, to be opportunistic. Hay is made by spreading mown grass in the sun to dry, an impossibility if the sun is not shining both when the grass is cut and when it is set out to dry. A variant of the expression dates from at least 1546. It is often used as an admonition to be provident, as it was by an unknown American author in 1788:

> It is better to make hay while the sun shines *against* a rainy day. (*The Politician Out-witted*)

milk To extract all potential profit from a person or situation, often with connotations of excessiveness or victimization. Used figuratively as early as the beginning of the 16th century, this term derives from the literal act of extracting milk from an animal by manipulating its udder.

> This their painful purgatory . . . hath of long time but deceived the people and milked them from their money. (John Frith, *A Disputation of Purgatory,* 1526)

Unlike *bleed* (see EXTORTION), *milk* is not limited in its figurative use to money-related matters.

> To overplay an audience for applause is called milking the

audience. (Hixson and Colodny, *Word Ways*, 1939)

To milk someone usually implies taking unfair advantage, and is often heard in the expression *to milk [someone] for all he is worth.*

play the field To remain open to multiple opportunities by not restricting one's role; to engage in a variety of activities, causes, etc., instead of focusing on just one; to socialize with no one person exclusively.

Japan Plays the Field. Peace and Trade with Everyone. (*The New Republic*, March, 1966)

In baseball, the outfielders have the largest area of ground to cover and therefore the widest range of playing room, a fact which probably gave rise to the expression. In addition, an outfielder often rotates among all three outfield positions. This American phrase has been in use since at least 1936.

seize the day To make the most of the day, to live each day to the fullest, to enjoy the present to the utmost; originally, Latin *carpe diem*. This proverbial expression of Epicurean philosophy was apparently first used by the Roman poet and satirist Horace. Both the original Latin and the later English version remain in common use.

The reckless life of Algeria . . . with . . . its gay, careless carpe diem camp-philosophy. (Ouida, *Under Two Flags*, 1867)

strike while the iron is hot To lose no time in acting when an opportunity presents itself, to seize an opportunity to one's advantage, to act when the time is right. A blacksmith heats the iron he is working on until it is red-hot and most malleable before hammering it into the desired shape. The equivalent French phrase is *il faut battre le fer pendant qu'il est chaud.* A variant of the expression dates from at least 1386.

It will become us to strike while the iron is hot. (W. Dummer, in *Baxter Manuscripts*, 1725)

take time by the forelock To act quickly in seizing an opportunity, to take full and prompt advantage of an opportunity for gain or advancement. Phaedrus, a Roman fable writer, describes Father Time (also called Father Opportunity) as an old man, completely bald at the back of his head but with a heavy forelock. Thus, a person who takes time by the forelock does not wait until Opportunity passes before taking advantage of what it offers. The expression has been attributed to Pittacus of Mitylene, one of the seven sages of Greece. Variants of the expression date from the late 16th century.

work both sides of the street To avail oneself of every opportunity to attain a given end; to seek support from opposing camps, to court the favor of rival interests; to walk a tightrope or to play both ends against the middle. The phrase probably derives from salesmen's lingo. Currently it is said of one who compromises principle in an attempt to garner some desideratum, who slants his approach or his pitch to align with what his listeners will "buy."

In a crucial election year . . . was shrewdly working both sides of the street. (*Time*, cited in *Webster's Third*)

EXPOSURE

another lie nailed to the counter An Americanism referring to something false or misleading which is publicly exposed to forewarn possible future offenders and con artists. The popular story explaining the origin of this expression is that the keeper of a general store used to nail counterfeit coins to the counter to discourage future customers from trying to perpetrate the same fraud.

blow the gaff To divulge a secret; to reveal a plot; to blab, peach, or give convicting evidence. *Blow the gaff* is the British slang equivalent of *spill the beans.* As early as 1575, *blow* was used to mean 'expose or betray.' *Blow the gab* appeared in print in 1785, followed by *blow the gaff* in 1812. According to the *OED,* the origin of *gaff* is obscure, though *gaffe* 'blunder' is a common modern borrowing from French.

> I wasn't going to blow the gaff, so I told him, as a great secret, that we got it [the gun] up with a kite. (Frederick Marryat, *Peter Simple,* 1833)

blow the whistle To expose or threaten to expose a scandal; to put a stop to, put the kibosh on; to inform or squeal. This expression may come from the sports referee's whistle which stops play when a foul or violation has been committed or at the end of the game; or from the policeman's whistle which calls attention to a traffic or civil offense.

cackling geese Informers, warners; saviors, protectors, defenders. According to legend, the cackling of the sacred geese alerted the Roman garrison when the Gauls were attacking the Capitol, enabling them to save the city.

come out in the wash See OUTCOME.

debunk To expose the falseness or pretentiousness of a person or his attitudes, assertions, etc.; to divest of mystery, thereby bringing down from a pedestal; to destroy the illusions perpetuated by clever talk and feigned sincerity; to reveal the true and nonsensical nature of something. The root *bunk* is a shortened form of *buncombe* 'nonsense, gobbledygook.' Thus, to "debunk" is to eliminate the nonsense, or as below, to "burst the bubble."

> Michael, after drifting round the globe, becomes a debunking expert, a pricker of bubbles. (*Nation,* October 10, 1923)

See also **bunkum, NONSENSE.**

Freudian slip A slip of the tongue; a seemingly innocent statement which has a concealed psychological significance. This expression comes from the psychoanalytical theories of Sigmund Freud, some of which hold that a person often reveals his true psyche in less than obvious ways, such as through slips in speech or through forgetfulness. In its contemporary usage, however, *Freudian slip* has been carried to extremes and is often used to call attention to any slip of the tongue, especially if such attention might be embarrassing (in a questionably humorous sort of way) to the speaker.

> It was an odd little slip of the tongue . . . They call them Freudian slips nowadays. (N. Blake, *Deadly Joker,* 1963)

let the cat out of the bag To divulge a secret, often accidentally. Most accounts claim that this expression derives from the county fairs once common in England and elsewhere at which suckling pigs were sold. After being purchased, the pigs were sealed in a sack. Occasionally, an unscrupulous merchant would substitute a cat for the pig and try to sell the sealed bag to an unsuspecting customer at a bargain price. If the buyer were cautious, however, he would open the sack before buying its unseen contents, thus "letting the cat out of the bag." This expression has enjoyed widespread figurative use ever since.

> We could have wished that the author . . . had not let the cat out of the bag. (*The London Magazine,* 1760)

See also **pig in a poke, SWINDLING.**

a little bird See INTUITION.

murder will out The truth will manifest itself in time; the secret will be disclosed. Chaucer uses this expression in *The Nun's Priest's Tale:*

> Murder will out, that see we day by day.

A later version appears in Shakespeare's *Hamlet:*

Murder, though it have no tongue,
will speak
With most miraculous organ. (II,ii)

It was once believed that a dead body would bleed if touched by the murderer. This and similar myths popular in the 16th century reinforced the belief embodied in this expression.

put the finger on To identify; to inform on; to point out one person to another who seeks him, such as a victim to a hit man or a criminal to a police officer; sometimes simply *finger.*

> Frank Lee . . . had fingered many, many dealers to the Feds. (*Flynn's,* December 13, 1930)

A related expression, *fingerman,* refers to an informer, one who puts the finger on someone else. *Fingerman* sometimes describes the person who cases (i.e., surveys or examines) a prospective victim or location and relays information to criminals such as thieves or kidnappers.

show one's true colors To reveal one's real character or personality; to strip oneself of façades and affectations; to expose one's true attitude, opinion, or position. Originally, *colors* referred to the badge, insignia, or coat of arms worn to identify and distinguish members of a family, social or political group, or other organization. Thus, to *show one's colors* was to proudly display a sign of one's ideology or membership in an organization. With the rise in piracy, however, the expression took on implications of exposure after attempted or successful deception. More specifically, showing one's true colors involved lowering the bogus colors (i.e., the flag of a victim's ally) and raising the skull-and-crossbones. Used figuratively, this expression carries intimations of asserting oneself after having vacillated; used literally, it means exposure after deception. Variations are *come out in one's true colors* and *show one's colors.*

> Opponents who may find some difficulty in showing their colors.

(William Gladstone, in *Standard,* February 29, 1884)

See also **sail under false colors, PRETENSE.**

sing in tribulation To confess under torture; to act as an informer, especially when threatened with or subjected to bodily harm; to squeal. In the Middle Ages, a person who had previously refused to inform or reveal information was said to "sing in tribulation" when extreme suffering and torture finally loosed his tongue.

> This man, sir, is condemned to the galleys for being a canary-bird . . . for his singing . . . for there is nothing more dangerous than singing in tribulation. (Miguel de Cervantes, *Don Quixote,* 1605)

A related expression from the same work is *sing in agony.*

> One of the guards said to him, "Signor Cavalier, to sing in agony means, in the cant of these rogues, to confess upon the rack."

A widely used variation is the slang *sing* 'to inform.'

slip of the tongue An inadvertent remark, an unintended comment; a verbal mistake, a faux pas. This colloquialism plays on the idea of a tongue having a mind of its own. Or, as in *Freudian slip,* it is implied that the *slip* reflects one's unconscious thoughts or desires.

> It was a slip of the tongue; I did not intend to say such a thing. (Frances Burney, *Evelina,* 1778)

The following anonymous verse advises how to avoid the problem:

> If you your lips
> Would keep from slips,
> Of these five things beware:
> Of whom you speak,
> To whom you speak,
> And how, and when, and where.

A similar expression is *slip of the pen,* referring to a written mistake. According to *OED* citations, this expression appeared in print by the mid-17th century, antedating *slip of the tongue* by 65 years.

spill one's guts To reveal one's most intimate thoughts and feelings; to lay bare one's soul; to divulge secret information, usually damaging to another; to confess or to inform on. In this expression, *guts* means bowels, in the latter's senses of deepest recesses and profoundest feelings. This common phrase often implies that the revealed information was obtained through coercion, as in the interrogation of a person suspected of a crime or a prisoner-of-war.

spill the beans To divulge a secret; to prematurely reveal a surprise, often by accident. This expression is one of the most common in the English speaking world, but no plausible theory of its origin exists.

> "Tell me the truth," she says. "Spill the beans, Holly, old man!" (E. Linklater, *Poet's Pub*, 1929)

tell tales out of school To utter private information in public; to indiscriminately divulge confidential matters; to gossip. In this expression dating from the mid-16th century, *school* represents a microcosm, a closed society having its own standards and codes of behavior. The family unit is another such microcosm. These and similar groups usually encourage confidentiality. Thus, to tell tales out of school is to share with members outside of the group information privy to it.

> A very handsome . . . supper at which, to tell tales out of school, . . . the guests used to behave abominably. (Thomas A. Trollope, *What I Remember*, 1887)

tip one's hand To reveal one's intentions, motives, or plans before the proper moment, to unintentionally or unwittingly give oneself away; also to *show one's hand*.

> He was perilously near showing his whole hand to the other side. (*Bookman*, October, 1895)

The allusion is to the inadvertent display of one's hand to the other players in a card game.

wash one's dirty linen in public To discuss domestic problems with mere acquaintances; to reveal personal concerns to strangers; to expose the skeleton in the family closet. This common expression seems to have come to English via the French *Il faut laver son linge sale en famille* 'One should wash one's dirty linen in private [at home, within the household].'

> I do not like to trouble you with my private affairs;—there is nothing, I think, so bad as washing one's dirty linen in public. (Anthony Trollope, *The Last Chronicle of Barset*, 1867)

EXPULSION (See also **REJECTION**.)

the bum's rush The forcible removal or expulsion of a person, usually from a public place, especially by lifting him by the shirt collar and the seat of his pants to a walking position and propelling him toward the door; an abrupt dismissal; the sack. The image evoked is of the way a bum, having had too much to drink, is unceremoniously "escorted" to the door of a bar. A synonymous American slang term is *French walk*. Eugene O'Neill uses the phrase in *The Hairy Ape* (1922):

> Dey gimme de bum's rush.

fire To discharge someone from a job, usually suddenly and unexpectedly. This expression derives from *fire* in the ballistic sense of ejecting violently and forcefully just as a bullet is fired from a gun.

> He that parts us shall bring a brand from heaven,
> And fire us hence like foxes. (Shakespeare, *King Lear*, V,iii)

get (or **give [someone]**) **the sack** To be dismissed, fired, or expelled. This expression may have originated from the ancient Roman custom of eliminating undesirables by drowning them in sacks. Figuratively, the phrase often implies that the grounds for a person's dismissal are justifiable.

If . . . the solicitor by whom he was employed, had made up his books, he [the plaintiff] would have been "sacked six months ago." (*Daily Telegraph*, 1865)

give [someone] running shoes To discharge an employee; to end a business association; to jilt a suitor. The figurative use of this expression implies that the dismissed person should make a speedy departure.

go fly a kite Go away; get lost; buzz off. Similar to other trite insults (such as *go jump in the lake, go play in traffic,* and *dry up and blow away*), *go fly a kite* is used as a command, usually issued with disdain, ordering someone to leave. Whereas the contemptuous element of the other phrases is transparent, precisely why flying a kite should carry the same scorn remains puzzling. Attempts to relate *go fly a kite* with *fly a kite* (see **SWINDLING**) are unconvincing.

go peddle your papers Get lost, scram, don't bother me. This imperative putdown implies that the person addressed, suited only for trifling pursuits, is interfering in matters of greater moment. Billy Rose used the expression in a syndicated column in 1949:

He had been told to peddle his papers elsewhere.

go to Jericho Begone; get out of here. The Biblical origin (II Samuel 10:5) of this obsolete expression concerns a group of David's servants who, having had half their beards shaved off, were banished to Jericho until their beards were presentable. Figuratively, *go to Jericho* implies a command to go elsewhere and not return until physical or mental growth has occurred, or, more simply, to get lost.

He may go to Jericho for what I care. (Arthur Murphy, *Upholsterer,* 1758)

kick upstairs To get rid of someone by promoting him to an ostensibly higher position of greater prestige. This euphemistic expression, dating from at least 1750, implies a correlation between the importance of one's position and the physical location of one's office.

The plot was devastatingly simple— Dibdin was to be kicked upstairs and Albert was to take his place. (W. Cooper, *Struggles of Albert Woods,* 1952)

pink slip A notice of discharge from employment; notification to a worker that he has been fired or laid off. It has long been the custom of personnel departments to formally notify an employee that he is being discharged by giving him a standard letter of termination. Since such a letter is often enclosed in an envelope with the worker's paycheck, many companies print the letter on colored (sometimes pink) paper so that it will be readily noticed.

All 1,300 employees got pink slips today. (*Associated Press,* May 29, 1953)

In recent years, *pink-slip* has sometimes been used as a verb, and its meaning has occasionally been extended to include jocular reference to interpersonal relations, such as the jilting of a sweetheart.

ride on a rail See **PUNISHMENT.**

send to the showers To reject; to send away or expel; also, *knock out of the box.* This expression originated in baseball, where a player, removed from the game because of poor performance or rudeness to the umpires, is sent to the locker-room for a shower. In contemporary usage, the phrase usually carries a mild suggestion of castigation or admonishment.

twenty-three skidoo Go away! Hit the road! Make yourself scarce! A rather implausible theory suggests that this expression developed at the turn of the century in New York City. Twenty-third Street was a favorite haunt of the city's flirtatious dalliers, and the police reputedly dispersed these wolfish loiterers with the command "twenty-three skidoo!" The expression, which caught on in the 1920s, remains associated with that period. At that time *twenty-three skidoo* was more often a noncommittal greeting or an exclamation of surprise than an order of expulsion. Although general use of the term has significantly declined since its Roaring 20s heyday, it does retain some jocular use.

> When she swished past, this leering beast in human form would boldly accost her with such brilliant greetings as "Oh, you kid!" or "Twenty-three skiddoo." (*Houston Post,* June 14, 1948)

walk Spanish To physically eject from a public place; to bounce, force, or throw out; to give the sack. Although the exact origin of the phrase is unknown, it is said to refer to the way in which pirates of the Spanish Main compelled their captives to walk the plank. The expression appeared in February, 1815, in the *American Republican* (Downington, Pa.):

> The vet'ran troops who conquer'd Spain,
> Thought they our folks would banish;
> But Jackson settled half their men,
> And made the rest walk Spanish!

walk the plank To be forced or drummed out of office; to be unceremoniously discharged or compelled to resign. The expression derives from the 17th century pirate practice of forcing blindfolded prisoners to walk off the end of a plank projecting from the side of the vessel in order to dispose of them.

EXTENT

by a long chalk By a large amount, by a great degree, by far. This colloquial British expression derives from the practice of using chalk marks to keep score in various games. Thus, a "long

chalk" would be a large number of marks or points—a high score. The equivalent American expression is *by a long shot* and both are frequently heard in the negative—*not by a long chalk* or *shot.*

by a long shot By a great deal, by far, by a considerable extent. This U.S. expression was in print as early as the 1870s.

> That's more'n I'd done by a long shot. (Edward Eggleston, *Hoosier Schoolmaster,* 1872)

A long shot is a contestant in any competition, most commonly athletic or political, with little chance of winning; therefore, with high odds in the betting. By extension, the phrase has come to refer to any bet or undertaking having little chance of success but great potential should the unexpected occur. *Long shot* connotes greatness of quantity or quality, if only in potential. Therefore, *by a long shot* means 'by a large amount or degree,' and the negative *not by a long shot* means 'not at all,' 'in no way, shape or form,' or 'hopelessly out of the question.'

by a long sight By a considerable amount; a great deal; to a large extent. *Sight* in this expression may carry its meaning of 'range or field of vision,' and hence, indicate distance. By further extension, *long sight* in this Americanism refers to great quantity or degree rather than spatial distance. This expression dates from the early 19th century and is most frequently heard in the negative. Other variants are interchangeable with *long,* as in the following quotation from Mark Twain's *Huckleberry Finn:*

> I asked her if she reckoned Tom Sawyer would go there, and she said not by a considerable sight.

by a nose By an extremely narrow margin, just barely, by a hair or whisker. The allusion is to a horse race in which the winner crosses the finish line only a nose ahead of his rival. This

U.S. slang expression dates from the early part of the 20th century.

Flying Cloud slipped by the pair and won on the post by a nose in one forty nine! (L. Mitchell, *New York Idea,* 1908)

higher than Gilderoy's kite Very high, higher than a kite, out of sight.

She squandered millions of francs on a navy . . . and the first time she took her new toy into action she got it knocked higher than Gilderoy's kite—to use the language of the Pilgrims. (Mark Twain, *The Innocents Abroad,* 1869)

This chiefly U.S. expression is apparently a truncated version of *hung higher than Gilderoy's kite* 'to be punished more severely than the very worst of criminals.' The allusion is to the hanging of the notorious Scottish highwayman, Patrick Macgregor, nicknamed Gilderoy, and five of his gang in Edinburgh in 1636. According to legal custom at the time, the greater the crime, the higher the gallows, and so it was with the gallows of Gilderoy that towered above those of his companions. As for the *kite* in the expression, two explanations have been offered. One is that Gilderoy was hung so high that he looked like a kite in the sky. The other, more scholarly, is based on the fact that *kite* or *kyte* meant 'the stomach, the belly' in Scottish and by extension was probably used to denote the whole body.

out of all scotch and notch Beyond all bounds or limits; incalculable, immeasurable, unlimited, unbounded. Rarely heard today, this expression is said to refer to the boundary lines, or scotches, and the corners, or notches, used in the children's game of hopscotch.

The pleasure which you have done unto me, is out of all scotch and notch. (Martin Marprelate, *Hay any Work for Cooper,* 1589)

room to swing a cat Plentiful space; ample room; a large area. This expression has several possible origins, none of them particularly plausible. One theory alludes to the sailors' pastime of twirling a cat about by the tail, while another possibility refers to the former training exercise in which a cat was suspended in a bottle and shot at for target practice. *Cat* was also an old Scottish word for rogue; thus, the expression may have derived from the amount of room necessary to hang a wrongdoer. In any case, the phrase is often applied negatively to describe a lack of space or cramped quarters.

June, I am pent up in a frowzy lodging, where there is not room enough to swing a cat. (Tobias Smollett, *Expedition of Humphry Clinker,* 1771)

EXTORTION

badger game Extortion, blackmail, intimidation achieved through deception; most specifically, the scheme in which a woman entices a man into a compromising situation, and then victimizes him by demanding money when her male accomplice, often pretending to be the enraged husband, arrives on the scene, threatening violence or scandal. The expression, in common use in the United States since the early 1900s, arose from the cruel sport of badger baiting, in which a live badger was placed in a hole or a barrel so that it could be easily attacked by dogs. Thus, *to badger* came to mean 'to worry, pester, or harass,' and, more intensively, in the sense above, 'to persecute or blackmail.' The woman decoy in the badger game is called the *badger-worker.*

bleed To extort money from an individual or an organization; to pay an unreasonable amount of money; to pay through the nose. This slang term has been in use since the 17th century, at which time bleeding was a common surgical practice. Whether bleeding was natural or surgically induced, loss of blood was significant. The significance of money to most people, and the fact that it can be paid out with or without force, makes the figurative use of *bleed* relating to money a logical extension of the literal meaning.

fry the fat out of To obtain money by high-pressure tactics or extortion; to milk, put the squeeze on. Just as the frying process removes excess fat, so does extortion or high-pressure fund-raising tactics remove the "fat" or excess wealth from the affluent. This now little-used U.S. slang expression dates from the late 19th century.

> His main qualification is admitted to be that of a good collector of funds. No one could, in the historic phrase, fry out more fat. (*The Nation*, April, 1904)

put the bite on To solicit money from, to hit up for a loan; also, to do so through force, thus, to extort money from, to blackmail. Both uses play on the idea of extracting by exerting pressure. The alternate *put the bee on* is usually limited to the less forceful borrowing sense. *Webster's Third* cites Hartley Howard:

> . . . some smooth hoodlum puts the bee on his daughter for two thousand bucks.

The stronger meaning is the more common, however:

> Or did he just happen to see what happened and put the bite on you and you paid him a little now and then to avoid scandal? (Raymond Chandler, *High Window,* 1942)

shakedown Extortion, blackmail; a forced contribution, as for protection. This term originally referred to a method of getting fruits and nuts out of a tree. In its figurative applications, *shakedown* conjures images of a person's being turned upside down and shaken to forcefully remove the money from his pockets.

> He [a New York City policeman] was fined 30 days' pay because he would not stand for a "shakedown," which means that he had refused to give from time to time upon demand 5 or 10 dollars from his meagre salary to his superiors to be used for purposes unknown. (A. Hodder, *The Fight For The City,* 1903)

Shake down 'to extort, plunder' is frequently used as a verb phrase.

> For only last week they were shook down for five hundred by a stray fellow from the Department. (J. Barbicon, *Confessions of a Rum-Runner,* 1927)

EXTRAVAGANCE (See **IMPROVIDENCE.**)

F

FAILURE (See also **DOWNFALL, IRRETRIEVABILITY**.)

back to the drawing board An acknowledgment that an enterprise has failed and that one must begin again from scratch, at the initial planning stages. The drawing board in question is the type used by draftsmen, architects, engineers, etc., for blueprints and such schematic designs. A similar phrase is *back to square one,* by analogy to a games board. Its meaning is the same—"We've got to start all over, from the very beginning."

bite the dust See **DEATH**.

[one's] cake is dough One's project or undertaking has failed, one's expectations or hopes have come to naught; one never has any luck. A cake which comes out of the oven as dough is clearly a total failure. Shakespeare used this now obsolete proverbial expression in *The Taming of the Shrew* (V,i):

> My cake is dough; but I'll in among the rest,
> Out of hope of all but my share of the feast.

damp squib An enterprise that was to have been a great success, but fizzled out; a lead balloon; a dud. In this British colloquialism, *squib* is another name for a firecracker. If it is damp, it will not explode as expected. It may fizzle or, in some cases, turn out to be a dud.

flash in the pan An instant but short-lived success; a brief, intense effort that yields no significant results; a failure after an impressive beginning. This expression refers to the occasional misfiring of the old flintlock rifles which caused a flash, or sudden burst of flame, as the gunpowder in the pan burned instead of exploding and discharging a bullet. The expression appears in an 1802 military dictionary edited by Charles James:

> *Flash in the pan,* an explosion of gunpowder without any communication beyond the touch-hole.

go belly up See **DEATH**.

goose egg A term used figuratively for lack of success in any endeavor; an instance of not scoring or of missing a point, so-called from the slang term for the numeral "0." As far back as the 14th century, things were compared to goose eggs because of a similarity in shape and size. By the mid-1800s, the term was used in scoring at athletic contests.

> At this stage of the game our opponents had fourteen runs—we had five large "goose eggs" as our share. (*Wilkes' Spirit of Times,* July 14, 1866)

Goose egg can also be used as a verb.

> I now had twenty-two consecutive World Series innings in which I goose-egged the National League. (*Saturday Evening Post,* February 28, 1948)

go up in smoke To come to naught, to be wasted or futile; to be unsuccessful, to fail or flop; also *to end up in smoke* and other variants.

> One might let him scheme and talk, hoping it might all end in smoke. (Jane Welsh Carlyle, *New Letters and Memorials,* 1853)

Use of this self-evident expression dates from the 17th century.

lay an egg To flop or bomb, especially when performing before an audience; to fail miserably. During World War I, *lay an egg* was Air Force terminology for 'drop a bomb,' *egg* probably being associated with *bomb* because of its similar shape. In addition, *egg* or *goose egg* is common slang for 'zero, cipher,' also because of their similar shapes. Thus, to *lay an egg* is 'to bomb' (figuratively), or to produce a large zero, i.e., nothing in terms of a favorable response from an audience, supervisor, or other persons evaluating a performance.

> You would just as well come wearing a shell if you ever took a job [singing] in a spot like this, that is how big an egg you would lay. (John O'Hara, *Pal Joey,* 1939)

lead balloon A failure, fiasco, or flop; an attempt to entertain or communicate that fails to elicit a desirable response. This phrase is relatively new, having appeared in print no earlier that the mid-1900s. *Lead balloon* was originally heard in the verb phrase *to go over like a lead balloon,* an obvious hyperbolic expression for failing miserably. Today the phrase is used alone substantively or adjectivally. Thus, a joke, plan, etc., can be called a "lead balloon."

> *What the Dickens?* was a lead balloon literary quiz wherein the experts showed only how little they knew. (*Sunday Times,* April 19, 1970)

lemon An object of inferior quality; a dud; something that fails to meet expectations. This expression alludes to the lemons painted on the reels of slot machines or "one-armed bandits." Whenever a lemon appears on one of the reels, regardless of what appears on the other reels, the gambler automatically loses his money. *Lemon* was in popular use by 1905, less than ten years after slot machines were invented. The expression remains almost ubiquitous, particularly in its most common current application, i.e., in reference to automobiles which experience almost constant mechanical difficulties.

> Mechanics are less than delighted to see lines of lemons converging on their service departments. (*Saturday Review,* June 17, 1972)

See also **one-armed bandit**, NICK-NAMES.

lose one's shirt To be financially devastated. This common expression implies that a shirt is the last of one's possessions to be lost in a financial upheaval.

a miss is as good as a mile A proverb implying that it does not matter how close one comes to hitting or attaining a goal, a near miss is still a miss, a near success is still a failure, etc. This expression is probably a corruption of an earlier, more explicit adage, "An inch in a miss is as good as an ell." (An ell is a unit of measurement; in England, 45 inches.) It has also been suggested that the original expression was "Amis is as good as Amile," alluding to two of Charlemagne's soldiers who were both heroes, both martyrs, and both saints—thus, to many people, they were virtually indistinguishable.

> He was very near being a poet— but a miss is as good as a mile, and he always fell short of the mark. (Sir Walter Scott, *Journal,* 1825)

miss the boat To miss out on something by arriving too late, to lose an opportunity or chance; to fail to understand; also *to miss the bus.* These phrases bring to mind the image of someone arriving at the dock or bus stop just in time to see the boat or bus leaving without him. Although both expressions date from approximately the early part of this century, *to miss the boat* is by far the more common.

> Some firms were missing the boat because their managements were not prepared to be adventurous. (*The Times,* March, 1973)

my Venus turns out a whelp See RE-VERSAL.

take a bath To be ruined financially, to lose everything, to go to the cleaners; usually used in reference to a specific financial venture. This figurative American slang use of *to take a bath,* meaning 'to be stripped of all one's possessions,' plays on one's physical nakedness when bathing.

washed out To have met with failure or financial ruin; disqualified from social, athletic, or scholastic pursuits. One theory suggests that this phrase originated as an allusion to the former military custom of whitewashing a target after shooting practice, but the connection is difficult to discern. In modern usage, this expression is often applied in an athletic context to one who, because of injury or inferior ability, can no longer compete. In addition, the expression often implies a total depletion of funds.

> I would sit in with . . . hustlers who really knew how to gamble. I always got washed out. (Louis Armstrong, *Satchmo, My Life in New Orleans,* 1954)

wither on the vine To fail to mature, develop, or reach fruition; to die aborning; to go unused, to be wasted. The expression describes lost opportunity, unrealized ambitions or talents, unfulfilled plans, etc. It often implies negligence or oversight; if such had been properly tended and nourished, they would have blossomed. An obvious antecedent of the expression appeared in the 17th century:

> Like a neglected rose
> It withers on the stalk with
> languish't head.
> (John Milton, *Comus,* 1634)

FAIRNESS

a cat may look at a king Even an inferior has certain rights in the presence of a superior. This proverb, which dates from 1562, was used by Robert Greene in *Never Too Late* (1590):

> A cat may look at a King, and a swain's eye has as high a reach as a lord's look.

even break An equal or fair chance; no advantage or handicap; as much or little chance as the next person. Of American origin, this colloquial expression may derive from the custom whereby opponents break a stick to determine who will have the advantage in a given situation. The long end is the preferable portion; the short goes to the loser. However, if the break is even, neither party has an advantage—each party has an equal chance. *Even break* dates from the early part of this century.

> The chances in the "quartermile" seem to give the Americans only an even break for a first place. (*Daily Express,* July 11, 1928)

every dog has his day Just as "the meek shall inherit the earth," everyone will come into a period of power or influence. This proverbial expression dates from the time of the Greek poet Pindar in the 5th century B.C.

> Thus every dog at last will have his day—
> He who this morning smiled, at night may sorrow;
> The grub today's a butterfly tomorrow.
> (*Odes of Condolence*)

fair shake Just, equitable, unbiased treatment; an even break. In this expression, *shake* refers to a throw of the dice. Unscrupulous gamblers often use shaved or loaded dice to increase their chances of winning. A fair shake implies that no cheating or other undue influence has been employed to affect a situation, and that the situation has been resolved justly.

a place in the sun See FAME.

FAITHFULNESS (See CONSTANCY.)

FALLACIOUSNESS (See also ERRONEOUSNESS.)

get hold of the wrong end of the stick To be mistaken, to have the story wrong or the facts twisted; to attack or approach a problem from the wrong direction. This expression is more common in Britain than in the United States. The similar *get the wrong end of the stick* may have the identical meaning or be equivalent to *get the short end of the stick* (VICTIMIZATION).

put the cart before the horse To reverse priorities; to be illogical; to have an erroneous perspective; to do things backwards. Similar sayings exist in numerous languages. This one appears to have its direct antecedents in Latin and French expressions; it appeared in English by the 13th century and has been common ever since. In Shakespeare's *King Lear* the Fool puns:

> May not an ass know when the cart draws the horse? (I,iv)

skin an eel by the tail To do something the wrong way, to do something backwards. The usual method of skinning an eel involves slitting its body just under the head and pulling downward to remove the skin. The reverse simply does not work.

FAME

in good odor In favor, in good repute; highly regarded, esteemed. *Odor* in this phrase means 'repute, estimation.' *In good odor* appeared in print as early as the mid-19th century. Also current is its opposite *in bad* or *ill repute* 'out of favor, disreputable.'

> When a person is in ill odour it is quite wonderful how weak the memories of his former friends become. (Charles Haddon Spurgeon, *The Treasury of David*, 1870)

in the limelight In the public eye; famous or infamous; featured; acclaimed; exalted. Before the discovery of electricity, theater spotlights burned a mixture of hydrogen and oxygen gases in a lime (calcium oxide) cylinder. This produced an intense light which could be focused by lenses on a featured actor or actress, thus drawing the audience's attention to that performer.

> The town hardly gets its full share of the limelight because of the hero. (Aldous Huxley, *Letters*, 1934)

name in lights Fame, notoriety, recognition, acclaim. In the world of theater, the name of a well-known or featured actor or actress may be displayed in lights on the marquee over the theater's entrance, thus drawing the public's attention and, it is hoped, their patronage.

> I couldn't wait to get up there with the best of them and see my name up in lights—topping the bill at the Palladium. (*Guardian*, January 15, 1972)

In contemporary usage, this expression is sometimes employed figuratively, and is no longer strictly limited to performing artists.

a place in the sun A position of favor, prominence, or recognition; a nice, warm, comfortable spot; a share in the blessings of the earth. Theoretically every individual is entitled to the benefits symbolized by the sun—life, growth, prosperity. The expression has been traced back to Pascal's *Pensées*, translated as follows:

> This dog's *mine*, says the poor child: this is *my* place, in the sun. (Bishop Kennett, *Pascal's Thoughts*, 1727)

put on the map To establish the prominence of a person or place; to make well known or famous. This expression originally referred to an obscure community which, following the occurrence of a newsworthy event, was noted on maps. The common phrase now describes a happening that thrusts a person or object into the public limelight.

> "The Fortune Hunter," the play that put Winchell Smith on the dramatists' map. (*Munsey's Magazine*, June, 1916)

set the world on fire To achieve far-reaching success and renown; to make a name for oneself. This expression originated from the British *set the Thames on fire*, in which *Thames* is sometimes mistakenly thought to be derived homonymously from *temse* 'sieve,' through feeble allusion to a hard worker who uses a sieve with such celerity that the friction causes a fire. This theory is discounted by the fact that the

French, Germans, and Italians all have similar sayings in regard to their own historic waterways, sayings which predate the English phrase. Thus, *set the Thames on fire* is undoubtedly the English version of the foreign expressions. When the phrase reached the United States, it was apparently Americanized to *set the river on fire*. As worldwide commerce and communication evolved, the phrase assumed its more cosmopolitan but somewhat less phenomenal form of *set the world on fire*. While the expression today usually implies the success of a vital and ambitious person, it is also applied negatively to the nonsuccess of a slow or lazy person. The term perhaps gained greater popularity through its incorporation into the lyrics of Bennie Benjamin's song *I Don't Want to Set the World on Fire* (1941).

FANTASY (See **ILLUSION**.)

FASHION (See **STYLISHNESS**.)

FATE (See **DESTINY**.)

FATUOUSNESS (See also **ECCENTRICITY**.)

ding-a-ling A person who repeatedly makes silly mistakes or foolish and inappropriate remarks; one whose behavior is unconventional or eccentric. A *ding-a-ling* is literally one who behaves as if he hears bells in his head. The implication is that a head full of ringing bells must be devoid of brains and sense. A newer and equivalent American slang term is *dingbat*.

full of beans Uninformed, ignorant, stupid; silly, empty-headed. This use of *full of beans* may have derived from an indirect reference to a bean's small value. Thus, to be "full of beans" is to be full of insignificance and inanity.

have windmills in one's head To be full of dreamlike illusions; to live in a fool's paradise. This obsolete expression implies the circulation of fanciful ideas in the vacuity of a daft mind.

He hath windmills in his head.
(John C. Clarke, *Paroemiologia*, 1639)

See **tilt at windmills, ILLUSION**.

in the ozone In a daze, in another world; spacey, spaced-out. The ozone layer or ozonosphere is a region in the upper atmosphere characterized by a high concentration of ozone and a relatively high temperature due to the assimilation of ultraviolet solar radiation. Hence, *in the ozone* is equivalent to *out in space*. This American slang expression appears to be of very recent coinage.

not have all one's buttons To be whimsical, odd, or crazy; to be out of it or not all there. In the 19th century, this expression was used to describe unintelligent, irrational behavior. It is now considered a slang phrase which emphasizes the eccentric, idiosyncratic aspects of behavior rather than characteristics indicative of stupidity or dullness.

slaphappy Severely confused or befuddled; cheerfully irresponsible; giddy; happy or elated, as if dazed. This term alludes to the apparent exhilaration which sometimes accompanies a concussion caused by a series of blows to the head, such as might be inflicted in a boxing match.

A sample [of talk] designed to knock philologists slap-happy.
(*Newsweek*, May 23, 1938)

A related expression which, like *slaphappy*, employs an internal rhyme is *punch-drunk*. A variation is *punchy*.

FAULTFINDING

armchair general A person removed from a given situation who thinks he could do a better job of directing it than those actually in charge. Although the phrase *armchair general* did not come into popular usage until World War II, similar combination forms *(armchair politician, armchair strategist, armchair critic)* have been in existence since 1858, with *armchair* clearly connoting a position of comfort and relaxation, remote from the hurly-burly or pressures attendant on those who must act. Consequently the term carries the negative implications of theorizer, speculator, or academician—one ignorant of practical realities, an observer rather than a doer.

back-seat driver A kibitzer; a giver of unsolicited advice or criticism; one who tries to direct a situation which is not his responsibility and over which he has no real control. The term is an extension of the name given to a person, usually sitting in the back seat of a car, who interferes with the driver's concentration by volunteering unnecessary warnings and directions. The phrase appeared as early as 1926 in *Nation* magazine.

a jaundiced eye See **PREJUDICE.**

Monday-morning quarterback One who criticizes the actions or decisions of others after the fact, and uses hindsight to offer his opinions on what should have been done. The phrase is an extension of the name given to football buffs who spend their Monday mornings rehashing the particulars of the weekend games.

mote in the eye See **IMPERFECTION.**

pick holes in To find fault with, to destroy the credibility or reputation of. The original expression *to pick* or *make a hole in someone's coat* was based on the notion that such a flaw in one's appearance would damage one's respectability or standing. The phrase is now used more often to apply to arguments than to persons, though this usage is itself very old.

> The lawyers lack no cases . . . Is his lease long . . . Then . . . let me alone at it, I will find a hole in it. (Thomas Wilson, *The Art of Rhetoric*, 1553)

the pot calling the kettle black Said of a person who criticizes or blames someone else for a failing of which he is also, and usually more, guilty. First used by Miguel de Cervantes in *Don Quixote, Part II* (1615), this proverb is based on the idea that since both a pot and a kettle are carbonized (i.e., blackened) by exposure to a cooking fire, neither can accuse the other of being black without acknowledging its own blackness. This expression usually implies the presence of an unjustified holier-than-thou attitude on the part of the accuser.

> I've been as good a son as ever you were a brother. It's the pot and kettle, if you come to that. (Charles Dickens, *The Life and Adventures of Martin Chuzzlewit*, 1844)

raise an eyebrow To show disapproval; to register a look of disapprobation or skepticism; to appear mildly shocked or put off. Popular since the early part of this century, *raise an eyebrow* derives from the fact that such a gesture is often an instinctive reaction, a natural response to being taken by surprise. However, the look of surprise is often tinged with disapproval or skepticism, as if it registered a value judgment rather than an instinctive reaction.

> Brown, though he raises his eyebrows a little at the usage, by no means condemns it outright. (G. H. Vallins, *The Pattern of English*, 1956)

strain at a gnat and swallow a camel See **HYPOCRISY.**

trigger-happy See **IMPETUOUSNESS.**

FAVORITISM

apple of one's eye A prized or cherished possession, an object of special devotion or attention; a favorite or beloved person. The literal apple of the eye is the pupil, formerly thought to be a solid globular body. The figurative phrase, perhaps derived from the priceless value placed on vision, appears to be as old as the language itself, having been used by King Alfred in his translation of Boethius' *Consolation of Philosophy* (approx. A.D. 885). The expression also appears in Deuteronomy 32:10.

He kept me as the apple of his eye.

button of the cap The top; the most favored. This expression comes from the use of different types of buttons or knobs on the top of the caps worn by Chinese mandarins to distinguish various degrees of rank. Shakespeare used the phrase in *Hamlet* (II,ii):

On Fortune's cap we are not the very button.

fair-haired boy A person being groomed for a position of leadership; a favorite of those in power. Throughout Western mythology and folklore, the hero, an embodiment of goodness and beneficence, is traditionally pictured as having a light complexion, blue eyes, and light-colored or blond hair. In many cultures, both past and present, a fair-haired person is considered to be a god, godlike, or in some way superior to dark-haired people in the same culture. Thus, the expression describes anyone, not necessarily only a blond male, destined for leadership in a given field.

Joe Mooney . . . a blind [jazz pianist] . . . is the latest "fair-haired boy" of the musical world. (Dave Bittan, Temple University *News*, January 24, 1947)

Vishinsky was Stalin's newest fair-haired boy. (*Time*, March 14, 1949)

Similar expressions include *fair-haired girl, blue-eyed boy* or *girl, blonde-haired boy* or *girl*, and *white-haired boy* or *girl*. In recent years, such terms have sometimes been used derogatorily to describe an employee who attempts to curry favor with his superiors.

handle with kid gloves See CAUTIOUSNESS.

make chalk of one and cheese of the other To show favoritism; to treat one thing or person better than another. The terms *chalk* and *cheese* are often found in opposition to one another in proverbial expressions, where *chalk* stands for something worthless and *cheese* symbolizes something of value. Thus, *to make chalk of one and cheese of the other* means to treat two things or persons unequally, to favor one over the other.

make fish of one and flesh of another To favor one thing or person over another, to make unfair distinctions between similar things or persons; also *to make fish of one and fowl of another*. The allusion is to the practice of dividing meat into the categories of fish, flesh, and fowl. Thus, to make fish of one and flesh or fowl of another is to discriminate unnecessarily and unfairly between basically similar things or persons, to show partiality. Use of this expression, rarely heard today, dates from the early 18th century.

This is making fish of one and fowl of another with a vengeance. (*The Manchester Examiner*, May, 1885)

red-carpet treatment Preferential or royal treatment; also the phrase *to roll out the red carpet* 'to give someone preferred or royal treatment.' The reference is to the literal plush strip of red carpet traditionally laid out for the entrances and exits of kings and other heads of state.

sacred cow Any person, idea, or object held sacrosanct and consequently immune from attack or criticism. As commonly used, *sacred cow* carries the implication that inviolability is unwarranted, but that considerations of political expedience prevent dispassionate evaluations or judgments of merits. The expression is derived from the Hindu belief that cows are sacred; thus, they are never slaughtered, and are allowed to roam about freely.

FEAR (See also ANXIETY.)

have one's heart in one's mouth To be frightened or scared, fearful or afraid, anxious or tense. The allusion is to the supposed leaping of the heart into the mouth upon experiencing a sudden jolt or start.

> Having their heart at their very mouth for fear, they did not believe that it was Jesus. (Nicholas Udall, *Erasmus upon the New Testament*, translated 1548)

make the hair stand on end To terrify, to scare or frighten, to fill with fear. The allusion is to the way an animal's hair, especially that on the back of the neck, involuntarily stiffens and becomes erect in the face of danger.

> As for the particulars, I'm sure they'd make your hair stand on end to hear them. (Frances Burney, *Evelina*, 1778)

shake in one's shoes To be petrified, terrified, panic-stricken; to be scared out of one's wits. The expression is often applied figuratively to corporate as well as individual bodies.

> It had set the whole Liberal party "shaking in its shoes." (*Punch*, March 15, 1873)

Variations are *quake* or *shake in one's boots.*

shake like an aspen leaf To tremble, quake; to shiver, quiver. This metaphor derives from the aspen tree with its delicate leaves perched atop long flexible stems that flutter even in the slightest breeze. The expression was used as early as 1386 by Chaucer in his *Canterbury Tales.*

FEAT (See ACCOMPLISHMENT.)

FIGHTING (See COMBAT.)

FINANCE (See also INDEBTEDNESS, MONEY, SUBSISTENCE.)

feel the draught See **feel a draft, PERCEPTIVENESS.**

feel the pinch To sense one's precarious financial position; to be in a tight spot. In this expression, *pinch* carries its figurative meaning of an internal twinge of emotional discomfort. The expression most often refers to an economic situation which warrants austerity measures.

grubstake Money advanced in exchange for a share in a venture's expected return. The term, dating from at least 1863, originally referred to money "staked" to prospectors for "grub" and other provisions in return for a part of the profits from their finds.

> The farmer realizes the . . . plight of the out-of-work who . . . is left without a grubstake between himself and hunger. (*The Atlantic Monthly*, March, 1932)

in the black Making a profit; out of debt. This Americanism is so called from the bookkeeping practice of entering profits in black ink. It is synonymous with *out of the red.*

> This time she appeared at the Italian Village, and within two weeks she had pulled it out of the red ink and into the black. (*American Mercury*, July, 1935)

on a shoestring Dependent upon a very small sum of money; relying on a meager amount of money as capital in a working investment. This colloquial meaning of *shoestring* has been common in the U.S. since the early part of the century, though precisely how it acquired this sense is unclear. Perhaps *shoestring* was equivalent to "the cost of a shoestring."

> They accomplished their elegance on a shoestring, too. (*Ward County* [North Dakota] *Independent*, July, 1944)

play the papers To gamble. This obsolete Americanism was current in the 19th century.

> Poor Kit was in a bad way one hour before we parted. The fact is, you know, he'd bin playin' the papers (meaning gamblin') and had lost everything. (De Witt C. Peters, *The Life and Adventures of Kit Carson*, 1858)

A similar expression with specific reference to horse racing is *play the ponies.*

prime the pump To attempt to rejuvenate an enterprise by channeling money into it; to try to maintain or stimulate economic activity through government expenditure. A pump is primed or prepared for use by pouring water into it to produce suction. The expression was used figuratively by T. W. Arnold, as cited in *Webster's Third:*

> This spending has not yet primed the pump.

salt away To save or hold in reserve money or other valuables for future use; to build a nest egg. The figurative meaning of this expression is derived from its literal one, i.e., preserving meat or other perishables by adding salt.

> [There is] no one to hinder you from salting away as many millions as you can carry off! (R. W. Chambers, *Maids of Paradise,* 1902)

sock away To set aside money in a savings account; to save or put money in reserve. This American expression implies that the money is being stowed away for some future investment. It may derive from the days when socks were a common storage receptacle for one's savings. The phrase appeared in *Life,* as cited by *Webster's Third:*

> (He) has socked away very little of his earnings with which to buy a ranch.

FLAMBOYANCE (See **OSTENTATIOUSNESS.**)

FLATTERY (See also **COMMENDATION, OBSEQUIOUSNESS.**)

applesauce See **NONSENSE.**

blarney Flattery, soft soap, cajolery. The expression comes from the Blarney Stone located high in the wall of Blarney Castle near Cork, Ireland. Legend has it that an Irish commander of the castle by his cleverly evasive communiqués successfully duped an English commander demanding its surrender. A similar gift of forked or honeyed speech is thus said to come to whoever kisses the stone. The verb usage of *blarney* dates from 1803; the noun usage from shortly thereafter.

court holy water Flattery, hollow promises, fair but empty words; also court-water and court-element. The French equivalent phrase is *eau bénite de la cour.* According to Le Roux's *Dictionnaire Comique,* unfounded promises or empty compliments were called court holy water because there was no lack of fair promises in court, just as there is no lack of holy water in church. This obsolete proverbial expression dates from 1583.

flannelmouth A smooth talker; a silver-tongued devil; a flatterer or braggart; a person who talks incessantly and says nothing; one who mumbles or speaks with a thick accent. In this expression, *flannel,* a smooth, soft fabric, refers to a person's manner of speech: it may be smooth and soft like flannel, or it may be mumbled and confusing, as though the speaker had a mouthful of flannel.

lay it on To flatter or criticize excessively; to act or speak in an exaggerated manner. This expression alludes to the manual-labor trades such as masonry and painting where one might add more and more mortar, paint, etc., in an attempt to produce a superior product when, in actuality, a small amount would be just as, if not more, effective. As a result of such excessiveness, the final product is often messy and of questionable value. The figurative implications are obvious. Related expressions include *lay it on thick, lay it on with a shovel,* and *lay it on with a trowel.*

> Well said; that was laid on with a trowel. (Shakespeare, *As You Like It,* I,ii)

soft-soap To wheedle or cajole; to win over or persuade by means of flattery; to butter someone up for ulterior motives. In use since the early 18th century, the verb and corresponding noun are thought to derive from *soft soap,* the semiliquid soap whose oiliness might well be linked with unctuousness.

FLIMSINESS

band-aid treatment Temporary, inadequate patching over of a major difficulty demanding radical treatment; makeshift or stopgap measures which temporarily relieve a problem without solving it. *Band-aid* is a trade name for a small adhesive bandage used on minor cuts and scrapes. The expression is American slang and apparently of fairly recent coinage.

half-baked Insufficiently planned or prepared, not well thought out, ill-considered; unrealistic, flimsy, unsubstantial, incomplete; sloppy, shoddy, crude; not thorough or earnest. It is easy to see how the literal sense of *half-baked* 'undercooked, doughy, raw' gave rise to the figurative sense of 'inadequately prepared or planned.' The use of this term in its figurative sense dates from the early 17th century. The expression appeared in this passage from *Nation Magazine* (August 1892):

> The half-baked measures by which politicians try so hard to cripple the Australian system.

house of cards Any insecure or unsubstantial structure, system, or scheme subject to imminent collapse; also *castle of cards.* The allusion is to the card-castles or houses children often build, only to blow them down in one breath a few moments later.

> Painted battlements . . . of prelatry, which want but one puff of the King's to blow them down like a paste-board house built of court-cards. (John Milton, *Of Reformation Touching Church Discipline in England,* 1641)

jerry-built Cheaply made, poorly constructed, flimsy, unsubstantial, slapdash, haphazard, makeshift. The most plausible of the many theories as to the origin of this term relates it to the Jerry Brothers, Builders and Contractors of Liverpool, England, in the early 19th century. This company was apparently so notorious for its rapidly and cheaply constructed, though showy, houses that its name became synonymous with inferior, shoddy building practices. Of British origin, this expression dates from at least 1869.

> It would soon be overspread by vulgar jerry-built villas. (George C. Brodrick, *Memories and Impressions,* 1900)

jury-rigged Makeshift, stopgap, temporary; a nautical term applied to a ship that leaves port partially, rather than fully- or ship-rigged, with rigging to be completed at sea; or to one temporarily rigged as a result of disablement. Though the *jury* has been said to derive from the French *jour* 'day' (hence rigged for the/a day only), the *OED* says the origin is unknown.

rope of sand Something of no permanence or binding power; an ineffective, uncohesive union or alliance; a weak, easily broken bond or tie. The phrase, of British origin, has been used metaphorically since the 17th century to describe worthless agreements, contracts, etc.

> Sweden and Denmark, Russia and Prussia, might form a rope of sand, but no dependence can be placed on such a maritime coalition. (John Adams, *Works,* 1800)

FOCUS

draw a bead on To aim at carefully, to line up in the sight of one's gun; to zero in on a person or thing. The reference is to the bead or front sight of a rifle. George Catlin used the expression literally in his treatise on North American Indians (1833).

zero in on To focus one's attention on a specific person, proposal, issue, or other matter; to aim at; to set one's sights on. Originally, *zero in* referred to adjusting the sights of a gun to the zero or horizontal line so that when aimed and fired at a target, the projectile will hit it dead center. Though this meaning persists, the expression has been extended to include figurative application in various nonballistic contexts as evidenced in this example by J. N. Leonard cited in *Webster's Third:*

> . . . bird-dogs zeroing in on coveys of hidden quail.

FOOD AND DRINK

belly-timber Food or nourishment; provisions. According to *Brewer's Dictionary of Phrase and Fable,* there is a connection between the French phrase *carrelure de ventre* 'refurnishing or resoling the stomach,' and the origin of *belly-timber.* Apparently Samuel Butler and his contemporaries were the last to use the term seriously.

> . . . through deserts vast
> And regions desolate they pass'd
> Where belly-timber above ground
> Or under, was not to be found.
> (Samuel Butler, *Hudibras,* 1663)

firewater Whiskey; hard liquor. This expression is a literal translation of the Algonquin Indian *scoutiouabou* 'liquor.' The reference, of course, is to the burning sensation caused by the ingestion of strong liquor and, since most liquor at that time was of the clear "moonshine" variety, its waterlike appearance. *Firewater* was commonly used in the pioneer and Wild West days, but is now mainly a humorous colloquialism.

> He informed me that they [the American Indians] called the whiskey fire water. (John Bradbury, *Travels in the Interior of America,* 1917)

a hair of the dog that bit you A cure identical to the cause of the malady; usually and specifically, another drink of the liquor that made you drunk or sick the previous night, or caused your present hangover. The expression derives from the former belief that the only effective antidote for a mad dog's bite was its own hair, a belief based on the homeopathic principle *similia similibus curantur* 'likes are cured by likes.' The expression dates from at least 1546.

L. L. Whisky A high-quality whiskey. The initials *L. L.* stand for "Lord Lieutenant." Apparently, the Duke of Richmond, Lord Lieutenant from 1807 to 1813, requested that a cask of his favorite whiskey be preserved. The cask was labeled "L. L.," and since then, *L. L. Whisky* has referred to any whiskey of a comparable high quality.

Mickey Finn A drink to which a drug such as a narcotic, barbiturate, or purgative has been added, sometimes as a joke but usually with the intention of rendering an unsuspecting person unconscious or otherwise causing him discomfort; the drug itself; knockout drops, especially chloral hydrate. This eponymous term purportedly refers to a notorious underworld character who lived in Chicago in the 19th century. Although originally a nickname for a horse laxative, *Mickey Finn* has, since the 1930s, been expanded to include a much wider range of drugs used as adulterants. It is commonly shortened to *Mickey* and frequently appears in expressions such as *slip someone a Mickey* [*Finn*].

> She had been about to suggest that the butler might slip into Adela's bedtime ovaltine what is known as a knockout drop or Mickey Finn. (P. G. Wodehouse, *Old Reliable,* 1951)

moonshine Illegally distilled liquor. This expression is derived from the clandestine nighttime manufacture of whiskey, an industry particularly widespread during Prohibition (1920–33).

The phrase was figuratively used prior to that era, however, especially in reference to the homemade spirits of the Appalachian backwoods.

> The manufacture of illicit mountain whiskey—"moonshine"—was formerly, as it is now, a considerable source of income. (*Harper's Magazine*, June, 1886)

mountain dew Liquor, particularly scotch whisky, that is illegally distilled; moonshine. This expression is derived from the illicit manufacture of spirits in stills that are concealed in the mountains.

> The distilled spirits industry . . . wages an expensive propaganda campaign against . . . mountain dew. (*Times*, October, 1970)

mountain oysters The testicles of sheep, calves, or hogs when used as food. This expression originated perhaps as an analogy to the shape of oysters.

> I have consumed mountain oysters and prairie dancers that are actually poetic. (E. Paul, *Springtime in Paris*, 1951)

nightcap A bedtime drink, usually alcoholic, consumed to help one sleep; a final drink of the evening. This expression has two suggested derivations, one of which alludes to the nightcap, a now obsolete article of sleepwear worn on the head. Since for many people two essential somniferous activities were donning a nightcap and downing an alcoholic drink as a soporific, the latter came by association to be also called a *nightcap*. Since the decline in the popularity of nightcaps as headgear, *nightcap* now refers almost exclusively to a drink. A second possibility is that *cap* is used in the sense of 'to complete or finish.' Thus, one could conceivably cap off an evening's activities with a drink before retiring.

> I neither took, or cared to take, any wine with my dinner, and never wanted any description of "nightcap." (Thomas Trollope, *What I Remember*, 1887)

In recent years, however, *nightcap* has been expanded to include any prebed beverage—alcoholic or nonalcoholic—consumed to aid one's falling asleep.

> "Ovaltine" . . . The world's best "nightcap" to ensure sound, natural sleep. (*Daily Telegraph*, April 9, 1930)

potluck See MIXTURE.

red-eye Low quality liquor; cheap, strong whiskey. This expression is plausibly derived from the alcohol-induced dilation of blood vessels in the eye. The now infrequently used phrase usually referred to bootlegged whiskey during its Prohibition heyday.

> This fellow paid a thousand dollars for ten cases of red-eye that proved to be nothing but water. (Sinclair Lewis, *Babbitt*, 1922)

rotgut Low quality liquor; bootlegged whiskey; red-eye. This expression is derived from the deleterious effects that such intoxicants have on one's insides. The phrase is widely used in Great Britain as well as in the United States.

> It's the real stuff—pure Prohibition rot gut. (H. A. Smith, *Putty Knife*, 1943)

sneaky pete Cheap wine, usually laced with alcohol or with a narcotic. Although this phrase is of unknown origin, it may perhaps refer to the slowly creeping inebriation caused by such spirits. Today, the expression often refers specifically to cheap wine.

> . . . A pint of forty-cent wine known under the generic title of "Sneaky Pete." (*Commonwealth*, December, 1952)

tiger's milk British slang for gin; also sometimes for whisky or for brandy and water. This term, apparently originally army slang, appeared as an entry in George R. Gleig's *The Subaltern's Log-Book*, published in 1828.

torpedo juice Homemade alcoholic beverages of the lowest quality. This expression originated during World War II, when soldiers who desperately craved intoxication developed makeshift beverages to substitute for the unavailable quality whiskey. The expression itself arose from the grain alcohol drained from torpedos, although alcohol was also extracted from fuel, hair tonics, and medications. Usually, this alcohol was combined with fruit juice, resulting in a somewhat palatable concoction.

FORCE   (See COERCION.)

FORCEFULNESS   (See EFFECTIVENESS, INTENSITY.)

FRAGILITY   (See FLIMSINESS.)

FREEDOM

carte blanche   Full discretionary power, unrestricted freedom, blanket permission; a blank check; literally, white paper or chart. In its original military usage, the term referred to the blank form used to indicate unconditional surrender, on which the victor could dictate his own terms. The phrase is now used only figuratively, and has been so used for some time:

> Mr. Pitt, who had carte blanche given him, named every one of them. (Lord Chesterfield, *Letters*, 1766)

The figuratively synonymous *blank check* refers literally to an executed check on which the amount is left unspecified to be filled in by its bearer or receiver.

the coast is clear   Nothing stands in the way of one's progress or activity; there is little danger that anyone in authority will witness or interfere with one's actions; "Go ahead, nobody's looking." This expression was originally used by smugglers to indicate that no coast guard was in the vicinity to prevent their landing or embarking. Its use is still largely limited to contexts implying

wrongdoing, though such may range from mischievous misbehavior to criminal activity.

give a wide berth to   To allow latitude, leeway, or freedom; to shun, to stay clear of; to remain a discreet distance from. Dating from the 17th century, *berth* is a nautical term which refers to a sufficient amount of space for a ship at anchor to swing freely, or enough distance for a ship under sail to avoid other ships, rocks, the shore, etc. *Give* or *keep a wide berth* gained currency in the 1800s and has since been used in nautical and nonnautical contexts.

> I recommend you to keep a wide berth of me, sir. (William Makepeace Thackeray, *The Newcomes*, 1854)

give enough rope   To give someone a considerable amount of freedom with the expectation that he will act in an embarrassing or self-destructive way; to grant just enough leeway that a person may set and fall into his own trap. This expression has been in use since the 17th century and is equally familiar in the longer version—*give [someone] enough rope and [he'll] hang himself.* A rope is often used as a leash or rein to control freedom of movement. Perhaps this expression derives from the fact that it is easy to trip or become entangled by too much rope. The second half of the expression plays on the idea of a rope as a cord for hanging a person.

> Give our Commentator but Rope, and he hangs himself. (Elkanah Settle, *Reflections on Several of Mr. Dryden's Plays*, 1687)

no strings attached   No stipulations or restrictions; no fine print. This common expression, perhaps an allusion to puppets that are controlled by strings, implies the lack of catches or hidden conditions in an undertaking or purchase. The phrase may be varied to assume its opposite sense.

> The corporation . . . made its offer to California—an offer good for six

months only, and having several untenable strings attached. (*Sierra Club Bulletin*, January, 1949)

FRENZIEDNESS

have kittens To give vent to one's emotions—anger, fear, excitement, surprise, etc.; to flip one's lid, to blow one's top or stack. This U.S. slang expression dates from the turn of the century. Why *kittens* rather than *pups* or any other animal is not apparent.

My doctor nearly had kittens when I suggested my being dropped to the *maquis* by parachute. (W. Plomer, *Museum Pieces*, 1952)

in a flap In a dither, all hot and bothered; excited, agitated. This primarily British expression was coined by analogy with the flapping and fluttering of birds when disturbed.

Now don't go and get into a flap or anything, Mother, but Joan's broken her arm. (*Punch*, August, 1939)

In the 1920s, *flap* saw navy use as a term for a high-pressure emergency; in air force parlance it denoted an air raid.

like a chicken with its head cut off Frenzied, frantic, harried; disoriented, disorganized; driven, moving erratically from one spot to another or from one task to another with no sense of order, direction, or control. This common simile, often part of the longer *running around like a chicken with its head cut off*, describes the behavior of one at an extreme emotional pitch—but the emotion engendering the behavior may vary from eager anticipation to raging anger to acute anxiety. The image derives from the fact that a decapitated chicken often continues to flutter his wings and flap about wildly for several seconds before succumbing to the fatal blow that has been dealt.

rat race Frenzied but unproductive activity; ceaseless and unrewarding struggle to get ahead; meaningless endeavor engaged in at a frenetic pace. The

image of laboratory rats on a treadmill gave rise to this expression. The comparison of men to rodents also underscores the nastiness and viciousness that can erupt in competitive situations. *Webster's Third* cites Frances G. Patton:

Life was a rat race . . . no time for gracious living or warm family feeling.

FREQUENCY (See also **DURATION, TIME.**)

once in a blue moon Very rarely. A *blue moon* occurs when there is a full moon twice in the same month, an unusual event, but one that takes place from time to time.

rare as hen's teeth See **scarce as hen's teeth, ABSENCE.**

when two Fridays come together Never. Since two Fridays never come together, this expression is usually used as a sarcastic quip when one is asked when he intends to do something of an onerous nature such as complete a project, pay back a personal loan, or the like.

FRIENDSHIP (See also **LOVE.**)

close as the bark to the tree Intimate, close; interdependent, symbiotically related, mutually sustaining. The phrase is used particularly of the closeness between husbands and wives. Though occasionally used to indicate physical proximity, the expression usually carries implications that such is indicative of a spiritual or psychological intimacy or dependency.

She would stick as close to Abbot as the bark stuck to the tree. (Cotton Mather, *The Wonders of the Invisible World*, 1692)

The "bark and the tree" as symbolic of "husband and wife" was in print as early as the mid-16th century. The analogy assumes that spouses interrelate in the interdependent, mutually nourishing patterns characteristic of the relationship between a tree and its bark. See also **go between the bark and the tree, MEDDLESOMENESS.**

eat [someone's] salt To share someone's food and drink, to partake of someone's hospitality. Among the ancient Greeks to eat another's salt was to create a sacred bond of friendship between host and guest. No one who had eaten another's salt would say anything against him or do him any harm. *Salt,* as it is used in this phrase, symbolizes hospitality, probably because it once was of considerable value. (cf. the etymology of *salary*). The first *OED* citation given for this expression is dated 1382.

hand in glove See CONSPIRACY.

hobnob To be chummy, familiar, or intimate with; also, *hob and nob.* This expression originated as *hab-nab* 'have or have not,' 'give or take.' Shakespeare employed this early sense in *Twelfth Night:*

He is a devil in private brawl. . . . Hob, nob, is his word, give't or take't. (III,iv)

The 'give or take' sense of this expression was subsequently extended to include the exchange of toasts as a sign of comradeship. Consequently, the phrase evolved its contemporary figurative meaning of being on friendly or familiar terms.

It cannot be her interest to hob and nob with Lord Fitzwilliam. (Lady Granville, *Letters,* 1828)

the mahogany The dining room table, as symbolic of sociability, conviviality, friendship, conversation, etc. This popular 19th-century British colloquial term usually appeared in phrases such as *around the mahogany, over the mahogany,* or *with one's feet under the mahogany.*

I had hoped . . . to see you three gentlemen . . . with your legs under the mahogany in my humble parlour. (Charles Dickens, *Master Humphrey's Clock,* 1840)

Currently *mahogany* is a colloquial term for a bar.

From the moment Mr. Primrose appeared behind his own mahogany and superseded the barmaid, he dominated everything. (N. Collins, *Trinity Town,* 1936)

rub shoulders To mingle or socialize; to hobnob. This expression is derived from the bumping and grazing of bodies against each other at social gatherings. The phrase quite often describes the mingling of persons of diverse background and social status at cocktail parties, political gatherings, and the like.

thick as thieves Intimate, familiar, friendly; close, tight. This expression is thought to derive from the French *ils s'entendent comme larrons en foire* 'as thick as thieves at a fair,' where *thick* means 'crowded, densely arranged.' When *at a fair* was dropped from the expression, the figurative jump to *thick* 'close, intimate' occurred; Theodore Hook used the truncated form in *The Parson's Daughter* (1833):

She and my wife are as thick as thieves, as the proverb goes.

Pickpockets, cutpurses, and their kind frequented fairs and other large gatherings where the prospects of gain and escape were both high.

FUNDAMENTALS (See also ESSENCE.)

down to bedrock Down to basics or fundamentals; down to the essentials. Bedrock is literally a hard, solid layer of rock underlying the upper strata of soil or other rock. Thus, by extension, it is any foundation or basis. Used literally as early as 1850 in Nelson Kingsley's *Diary,* the phrase appeared in its figurative sense by 1869 in *Our New West* by Samuel Bowles.

get down to brass tacks To get down to business; to get down to the essential or fundamental issues. Although the precise origin is unknown, this expression is said to have been originally a nautical phrase referring to the brass nails exposed during the cleaning of the hulls on early sailing ships. Brass was used to resist the corrosion of sea water in fastening metal sheathing to the hull. The phrase appeared as early as 1897 in *Liars* by H. A. Jones.

meat-and-potatoes Basic, fundamental, essential, main. Meat and potatoes have long been the basic ingredients of a traditional hearty meal.

It's the meat-and-potatoes appeal—the old pull at the heartstrings—that'll put us over at the box office. (S. J. Perelman, *Listen to the Mocking Bird*, 1949)

nitty-gritty The heart of a matter. This American slang term first appeared in 1963 as part of the Black militant slogan *get down to the nitty-gritty.*

The Negroes present would know perfectly well that the nitty-gritty of a situation is the essentials of it. (*Time*, August, 1963)

The phrase is conjectured to be an oblique reference to the small hard-to-remove nits or lice that are often found attached to the hair and scalp of poor ghetto-dwellers because of unclean living conditions.

nuts and bolts Basics, brass tacks, the nitty-gritty, the heart of the matter. Since literal nuts and bolts are essential parts of virtually any machine, it is only logical that figuratively they symbolize the essence or core of something, the practical basics. This expression, apparently of fairly recent coinage, dates from at least 1960.

His preference was for journalism. He learnt the nuts and bolts of his profession with the Montreal *Gazette*. (*The Times*, June, 1971)

FURTIVENESS (See SECRECY.)

FURY (See also ANGRINESS, ILL TEMPER, IRRITATION, VEXATION.)

bite [someone's] head off To answer curtly or sharply out of anger or annoy-

ance, to snap at in reply; also *to bite* or *snap [someone's] nose off.* Although the nose was apparently the original object of the biting or snapping in this expression (predating *head* by nearly three centuries) *head* is more commonly heard today.

I . . . ask'd him if he was at leisure for his chocolate, . . . but he snap'd my nose off; no, I shall be busy here these two hours. (Susanna Centlivre, *The Busybody*, 1709)

blow a fuse To lose one's temper; to become angry or violent; to respond emotionally and dramatically. These figurative meanings of *blow a fuse* allude to the fact that a fuse will blow if there is an overload on an electrical circuit. By the same token, a person can only stand so much before "reaching the breaking point" and "blowing up."

Relax . . . or you'll blow a fuse. (S. J. Perelman, *Listen to the Mocking Bird*, 1949)

To have or *be on a short fuse* is to be short-tempered, to be quick to blow a fuse.

blow a gasket To lose one's temper. When the gasket sealing an automobile cylinder wears out, pressure in the cylinder cannot be contained and the contents spurt out. So too, when life is not running smoothly and patience has worn thin, the result is often uncontrollable, angry outbursts.

blow off steam To discharge suppressed feelings, especially resentment; to release tension by loud talking or shouting. This phrase alludes to actual steam engines, boilers, etc., which allow pressure to build up to a certain point, after which it is released forcibly and noisily. Figurative use of the phrase dates from the early 19th century.

The widow . . . sat . . . fuming and blowing off her steam. (Frederick Marryat, *The Dog-Fiend*, 1837)

blow one's stack To be unable to contain oneself; to lose control. As a smokestack discharges smoke and soot, a fired-up person gives vent to angry, resentful words.

blow one's top To lose control; to fly off the handle; to be unable to contain oneself; also *blow one's lid.* This slang phrase plays on an analogy comparing the top of one's head to a lid. When a container is about to burst because of the internal pressure, the lid will fly off to allow the pressure to escape. Similarly, when one can no longer bear the pressure of intense emotions building up, one "loses one's head."

> He blew his top and lost his job and came bellyaching to Loraine. (John Steinbeck, *The Wayward Bus,* 1947)

duck-fit An outburst or fit of anger, a conniption fit. This American slang term, in use since at least 1900, is probably an allusion to the loud quacking of a mad duck.

fly off the handle To become furious, often suddenly and without warning; to lose self-control. The tendency of an ax blade to fly off its handle when forcefully struck against an object is the apparent origin of this expression. The current use of the phrase is almost exclusively in reference to loss of temper.

> He reckoned you would . . . get good and mad, fly off the handle . . . (C. E. Mulford, *Orphan,* 1908)

hit the ceiling To be enraged, agitated, or violently angry; to lose one's temper, to blow one's top. This slang expression dates from the early 1900s. Currently, *hit the roof* is a frequently employed variant.

> Larry hit the ceiling and said he *had* to come along, that he'd spoil everything if he didn't. (E. Dundy, *Dud Avocado,* 1958)

slow burn Gradual intensification of anger; escalation from a low level of displeasure to a high pitch of rage. This originally U.S. colloquial phrase dates from the early 1900s. Wentworth and Flexner (*Dictionary of American*

Slang) attribute the phrase to the 1930s comedian Leon Carroll who was apparently well known for his facial expression of that name. *Slow burn* referred to the gradual reddening of his face as he took on the image of an enraged man.

> His slow burn at a Minnesota prof's constant use of the name when he was a student. . . . (*New Yorker,* March 3, 1951)

This phrase is often heard in the longer expression *do a slow burn.*

FUTILITY (See also **EXTRANEOUSNESS.**)

bark at the moon To labor or protest in vain; to choose an ineffectual means to achieve a desired end, or to attempt the impossible, thereby making any effort futile by definition; also often *bay at the moon.* The phrase refers to the common practice of dogs to bay at the moon, as if to frighten or provoke it. Connotations of the foolishness of barking at the moon, based on the disparity between the earthly dog and the mystical moon, are carried over into the figurative usage, as if to imply that barking at the moon is like banging one's head against the wall.

beat one's head against the wall To attempt an impossible task to one's own detriment; to vainly oppose an unyielding force; also *to hit, knock,* or *bang one's head against the wall,* often *a stone wall.* The allusion is to the futility and frustration, not to mention injury, caused by such an action.

beat the air To strike out at nothing, to labor or talk idly or to no purpose; to shadowbox. The phrase may well derive directly from the last definition, as suggested by its use in the King James Version of the New Testament:

> I therefore so run, not as uncertainly; so fight I, not as one that beateth the air. (I Corinthians 9:26)

the blind leading the blind Ignorance on the part of both leaders and followers; lack of guidance and direction resulting in certain failure; futility. The phrase is of Biblical origin. Speaking of the Pharisees, Jesus says:

> They be blind leaders of the blind. And if the blind lead the blind, both shall fall into the ditch. (Matthew 15:14)

The expression is also the title of a famous painting by Pieter Breughel the Elder (1568).

cast stones against the wind To labor in vain; to work without accomplishing anything.

> I see I swim against the stream, I kick against a goad, I cast a stone against the wind. (Grange, *Golden Aphrodite*, 1577)

cry for the moon To desire the unattainable or the impossible, to want what is wholly beyond one's reach; also *to ask* or *wish for the moon*. Although some sources conjecture that this expression comes from children crying for the moon to play with, that theory seems a bit forced. The moon has long typified a place impossible to reach or object impossible to obtain, and was so used by Shakespeare in *Henry VI, Part II* (1593):

> And dogged York, that reaches at the moon,
> Whose overweening arm I have plucked back. (III,i)

A similar French expression is *vouloir prendre la lune avec les dents* 'to want to take the moon between one's teeth.'

Dame Partington and her mop See CONSERVATISM.

flog a dead horse To attempt to rekindle interest in a worn-out topic, flagging discussion, doomed or defeated legislation, or other matter; to engage in futile activity. The figurative use of this expression is closely related to the literal, i.e., it is useless to attempt to revive or stimulate something that is dead.

> In parliament he again pressed the necessity of reducing expenditure. Friends warned him that he was flogging a dead horse. (John

Morley, *The Life of Richard Cobden,* 1881)

A variation is *beat* or *whip a dead horse.*

from pillar to post See DIRECTION.

kick against the pricks See REBELLION.

make bricks without straw To try to accomplish a task without the proper materials or essential ingredients. The current sense of this expression is due to a misinterpretation of the Biblical story (Exodus 5:6–19) from which it comes. The Israelites were not ordered to make bricks without straw at all, as is popularly believed. Rather, they were told that straw for the sun-dried mud-and-straw bricks they were required to make would no longer be provided for them, and that they would have to go out and gather it themselves. Making bricks without straw would be an impossible task since straw was the essential element in holding the sundried mud bricks together. Use of the expression dates from the mid-17th century.

> It is often good for us to have to make bricks without straw. (Sir Leslie Stephen, *Hours in a Library,* 1874)

milk the ram To engage in an activity destined to fail, to try in vain to do something which cannot be done; also *to milk the bull.* A ram is a male sheep and a bull is a male bovine. The old proverb "Whilst the one milks the ram, the other holds under the sieve" probably spawned this phrase; it appeared in *Several Tracts* by John Hales in 1656.

a nod is as good as a wink to a blind horse An obsolete proverb of obvious explicit literal meaning. Figuratively, this phrase implies that regardless of how obvious a hint or suggestion may seem, it is useless if the person to whom it is directed is not aware of it. Thus, subtlety and tact can, at times, be inappropriate, particularly when dealing with a person known for his obtuseness.

It is likely that this adage had been current for several centuries before its earliest literary usage in 1794 by William Godwin in *The Adventures of Caleb Williams.*

pile Pelion upon Ossa See EXACERBATION.

plow the sands To engage in fruitless or futile labor, to waste one's time trying to do an impossible or endless task.

> All our time, all our labour, and all our assiduity is as certain to be thrown away as if you were to plough the sands of the seashore, the moment that the Bill reaches the Upper Chamber. (Herbert Henry Asquith, *Speech at Birmingham,* 1894)

In *Richard II* (II,ii) Shakespeare used a similar expression with the same meaning:

> Alas, poor Duke! The task he undertakes
> Is numbering sands and drinking oceans dry.

put a rope to the eye of a needle To attempt the impossible. To explain would be to belabor the obvious.

roast snow in a furnace To pursue ludicrous or meaningless activities; to engage in futile, pointless tasks. The figurative implications of this expression are obvious.

seek a knot in a bulrush See NIT-PICKING.

shoe the goose To engage in aimless, trivial, unnecessary, or futile activities; to do busy work; to waste time. As this expression implies, putting shoes on a goose is as ludicrous and pointless as it is futile.

> Yet I can do something else than shoe the goose for my living. (Nicholas Breton, *Grinello's Fort,* 1604)

sleeveless errand Any aimless or futile activity; an endeavor that is sure to be unprofitable or unsuccessful. In this expression, *sleeveless* is probably derived from *sleave* 'knotted threads' such as on the ends of woven fabrics, implying that the task or errand has loose ends which are not tied together in any significant or worthwhile manner. Most popular in the 16th and 17th centuries, *sleeveless errand* commonly referred to a false mission or other bogus activity which would keep a person occupied, and therefore out of the way, for a period of time. Variations such as *sleeveless words, sleeveless reason,* etc., have appeared in works by Chaucer, Shakespeare, Milton, and others.

> He was employ'd by Pope Alexander the third upon a sleeveless errand to convert the Sultan of Iconium. (Myles Davies, *Athenae Britannicae,* 1716)

square the circle To engage in a futile endeavor; to undertake an impossible task. Early mathematicians struggled to find a circle and a square with equal areas. This is an impossibility since a principal factor in the area formula for a circle is π (3.1416 . . .), an irrational number, whereas the factors in the area formula for a square are always rational numbers. The expression can now be applied to the attempting of any impossibility.

> You may as soon square the circle, as reduce the several Branches . . . under one single Head. (Thomas Brown, *Fresny's Amusements,* 1704)

throw straws against the wind To vainly resist the inevitable, to sweep back the Atlantic with a broom. A similar expression appeared in John Taylor's *Shilling* (1622):

> Like throwing feathers 'gainst the wind.

Both straw and feathers are very light and no match for the force of the wind.

wash a brick To work in vain, to engage in utterly useless or futile labor, to plow the sands.

> I wish I could make him feel as he ought, but one may as well wash a

brick. (Warner in John Heneage Jesse's *George Selwyn and his Comtemporaries,* 1779)

Rarely heard today, this self-evident expression is the English equivalent of the old Latin proverb *laterem lavare.*

wild-goose chase An impractical and ill-advised search for something nonexistent or unobtainable; a foolish and useless quest; a futile or hopeless enterprise. Originally, a wild-goose chase was a horse race where the second and all succeeding horses had to follow the leader at definite intervals, thus resembling wild geese in flight. Since the second horse was not allowed to overtake the first, it would become exhausted in its futile chase. It has alternately been suggested that *wild-goose chase* may refer to the difficulty of capturing a wild goose, implying that even if caught, the prize is of little value.

"I see you have found nothing," exclaimed Lady Gethin. . . . "It was a wild goose chase," he replied with a weary look. (Mrs. Alexander, *At Bay,* 1885)

G

GENEROSITY   (See **CHARITABLE-NESS.**)

GENUINENESS

all wool and a yard wide Genuine, authentic, bona fide; sincere, trustworthy, straightforward. Apparently the term was an early sales pitch used by yard goods merchants confronted with wary buyers. The earliest known print citation applying the phrase figuratively is from George W. Peck:

> You want to pick out (as the "boss combination girl" of Rock Co.) a thoroughbred, that is, all wool, a yard wide. (*Peck's Sunshine*, 1882)

hallmark A mark or stamp of superior quality or genuineness; a distinctive characteristic or feature, a trademark. The term takes its name from Goldsmiths' Hall in London where Goldsmiths' Company stamped its gold and silver pieces with an official plate mark indicating their grade of purity. Eventually the literal meaning of *hallmark* 'a symbol of the standard of quality of precious metals' became generalized so that it now represents any mark of excellence or distinguishing characteristic. Literal use of the term dates from the early 18th century while figurative use dates from the latter half of the 19th century.

the real McCoy Genuine, authentic; unadulterated, uncut; hence, excellent, of superior quality. Numerous attempts to account for the term's origin testify to the failure of any to be convincing. Among the more popular are those relating the phrase to a boxer, Kid McCoy, a former welterweight champion (1898–1900). These vary from simple transference by association (the champion is "the best," superior) to the hypothetical existence of a lesser pugilist with the same surname; to clearly apocryphal anecdotes concerning Kid McCoy's barroom exploits. It does seem certain, however, that this American colloquialism did come into usage shortly after his championship fame, and that it gained frequency during Prohibition when it described genuine, uncut whiskey. Stuart Berg Flexner (*I Hear America Talking*) conjectures the existence of a McCoy brand, since *the clear McCoy* was in use by 1908 to describe good whiskey. *The real McCoy* remains one of our most popular and puzzling picturesque phrases. During the strike of bagel bakers in December, 1951, a *New York Times* article said:

> Toasted seeded rolls, Bialystok rolls . . . and egg bagels, a sweeter variety but not the real McCoy, were being thrown into the bagel void with varying degrees of reception.

simon-pure Real, veritable, authentic; as a noun, the genuine article. In Susannah Centlivre's comedic play, *A Bold Strike For a Wife* (1718), Simon Pure was a Quaker who was temporarily impersonated by Colonel Feignwell. When Feignwell had won the hand of Miss Lovely, Simon returned and, after much difficulty, proved that he was, in fact, the real Simon Pure and that Feignwell was the actual imposter.

> If we would come with him the other way he would show us the real mummy, the Simon Pure. (William C. Prime, *Boat Life in Egypt*, 1860)

GIBBERISH

abracadabra See **MAGIC.**

Dutch Unintelligible gibberish, meaningless talk or writing; also, *double Dutch;* often in the phrase *it's Dutch to me.* The allusion is probably to the meaningless jumble of sounds any foreign language seems to those who do

GLUTTONY □ 152

not understand it. *High Dutch* was apparently the oldest variant of this expression since it appeared in the earliest *OED* citation from 1789; however, *Dutch* and *double Dutch* are the only forms in use today. An illustration of the use of this term is found in Charles Haddon Spurgeon's *Sermons* (1879):

> The preacher preaches double Dutch or Greek, or something of the sort.

Greek Gibberish, unintelligible or meaningless language; usually in the phrase *it's Greek to me.* The allusion is most likely to the unintelligible and senseless sound of any foreign language to those who do not understand it. The expression dates from about 1600; it is found in Shakespeare's *Julius Caesar:*

> But, for my own part, it was Greek to me. (I,ii)

mumbo jumbo Meaningless chanting and ritual; nonsensical or pretentious language. This expression evolved as an English rendering for the African deity *Mama Dyumbo,* whom the Mandingo tribes venerated with mystical rites incomprehensible to the European explorers. The expression is now frequently used to describe senseless or ostentatious language contrived to obscure a topic or befuddle the listener.

> A mumbo jumbo of meaningless words and phrases. (*Times,* May, 1955)

ubble-gubble Nonsensical talk, drivel, prattle. This uncommon expression, perhaps derived as a rendering of inarticulate vocalizations, appeared in W. B. Johnson's *Widening Stain* (1942).

GLUTTONY (See GOURMANDISM.)

GOOD HEALTH

fit as a fiddle Healthy, very fit, in good physical condition. There are several possible derivations of this expression, one of which holds that a properly tuned fiddle looks and sounds so impressive that it is a compliment for a person to be compared to it. Two other possibilities claim that the original expression was *fit as a fiddler* in which *fiddler* was a nickname applied either to a boxer with fancy footwork or to the person who played the fiddle at lively Irish dances, most of which lasted from dusk to dawn without any breaks. In both cases, the fiddler would have to be physically fit and have great stamina to last throughout the event. Similar expressions are *fine as a fiddle* and *face made of a fiddle,* the latter used to describe someone who is exceptionally attractive.

> I arrived at my destination feeling fit as a fiddle. (Harrington O'Reilly, *Fifty Years on the Trail,* 1889)

in fine feather See ELATION.

in fine fettle See ELATION.

in the pink In excellent health; robust. This familiar expression, derived as a shortening of the phrase *in the pink of condition* 'the most perfect state of something,' probably developed its current figurative sense as an allusion to the rosy complexion of a healthy person.

> I am writing these lines to say I am still in the pink and hoping you are the same. (John B. Priestly, *Good Companion,* 1929)

right as a trivet Stable, solid, sound; in good health or spirits, fine, very well; thoroughly or perfectly right.

> "I hope you are well, sir." "Right as a trivet, sir," replied Bob Sawyer. (Charles Dickens, *The Pickwick Papers,* 1837)

The allusion is to a literal trivet, a three-legged stand or support, which stands firm on nearly any surface.

right as ninepence Perfectly well, in excellent health or spirits, in fine fettle, in good condition or shape.

> I thought I was as right as ninepence. (Rolf Boldrewood, *A Colonial Reformer,* 1890)

The ninepence was originally a British shilling minted under Queen Elizabeth I and intended for circulation in Ireland. The coin so depreciated in value, however, that it was used as a ninepenny piece in England. Considering the unhealthy background of the ninepence, the expression's current meaning is somewhat ironic.

sound as a bell Healthy, fit, in fine fettle; secure or stable. The phrase appeared in Shakespeare's *Much Ado About Nothing* (III,ii):

He hath a heart as sound as a bell.

This expression is based on the fact that even the slightest imperfection markedly affects the tone of a bell. Although the expression may refer to the quality and condition of an inanimate object, it is more often applied to the soundness of the human mind and body.

A single man . . . with prospects, an' as sound as a bell . . . is not to be had every day. (*Pall Mall Magazine*, July, 1898)

GOOD LUCK (See also **SUPERSTITION**.)

born with a caul on one's head Immune to death by drowning; charmed; lucky. The caul is part of the fetal membrane sometimes present on the heads of newborns. The superstition regarding its magical properties was at one time so strong that such membranes, or some material claimed to be such, were sold. Mariners in particular sought them, for obvious reasons.

carry a rope in one's pocket To be extremely lucky at cards. This expression is an allusion to the superstition that a piece of a hangman's rope carried in the pocket brings the bearer good luck at cards.

the devil's own luck Unbelievable or amazing good luck; also *the devil's luck*. This expression, in use since at least the mid-19th century, may have derived

from the former belief that lucky people had consorted with the Devil.

hit the jackpot To win a large prize; to have a remarkable stroke of good luck; to achieve great success; to strike it rich. *Jackpot* is a poker term for the kitty or pot that accumulates until a player can open the betting with the required cards. Thus, *jackpot* has come to mean 'a prize; success or luck,' often of an extraordinary nature because it has been long awaited and its value has accumulated over a period of time.

We saw our first American audience-participation show. The prizes included a diamond wrist watch . . . The jackpot was 1,250 dollars! (*Radio Times*, July 15, 1949)

The expression *to hit the jackpot* probably derives from slot machine usage.

There is always the chance that one or other number or artist will hit the jackpot. (*Sunday Times* Supplement, June 10, 1962)

manna from heaven A stroke of good fortune; a windfall; a boon or blessing, particularly one resulting from divine intervention. This expression comes from Exodus (16:15):

And when the children of Israel saw it, they said one to the other, It is manna: for they wist not what it was. And Moses said unto them, This is the bread which the Lord hath given you to eat.

strike oil See **SUCCESS**.

windfall An unexpected acquisition or gain, such as a legacy; a sudden stroke of good luck, especially financial; a godsend; a bonanza. This term may stem from post-medieval England where laws prohibited the people from cutting down trees because all lumber was earmarked for use by the Royal Navy. If a tree were felled by the wind (literally, a windfall), however, it was excluded from this restriction and could be used by the property owner as he wished, thus being considered exceptional and unexpected good fortune. One source suggests that *windfall* may refer to a fruit or other edible delight which is blown from a tree by the wind without requiring active exertion on the part of the recipient.

> [He] kept little windfalls that came to him by the negligence of customers— . . . loose silver, odd gloves, etc. (Maria Edgeworth, *Moral T. Forester,* 1802)

GOODNESS (See VIRTUOUSNESS.)

GOURMANDISM

belly-god A glutton or gourmand; one who makes a god of his belly. The term was in use in the mid-16th century.

chowhound A glutton; a hearty eater, a gourmand. The word combines the U.S. slang term for food with the aggressive and uncouth eating habits of a dog. J. B. Roulier describes a "chowhound" in *Service Lore: Army Vocabulary* (1943):

> He is not necessarily a prodigious eater; his unpopularity is usually caused by his roughshod methods in getting first to the best of the food.

The term enjoyed wide use among the Armed Forces in World War II and is now commonly heard in civilian speech.

eat out of house and home To deplete another's supply of food or money by excessive gluttony, to batten on one's host or hostess to the point of their ruination. In Shakespeare's *Henry IV, Part II* (II,i), Mistress Quickly uses this expression when answering the Lord Chief Justice's question as to why she had Sir John Falstaff arrested:

> He hath eaten me out of house and home; he hath put all my substance into that fat belly of his.

live like fighting cocks To gorge oneself, to eat too much rich food, to overindulge. This British colloquialism, dating from the early 19th century, is puzzling since gamecocks were kept on strictly controlled diets much like boxers and wrestlers. However, since the phrase means to have the best food as well as to have an abundance of it, perhaps the reference is to a fighting cock's diet as compared to that of an ordinary chicken.

> [They] live like fighting-cocks upon the labour of the rest of the community. (William Cobbett, *Rural Rides,* 1826)

play a good knife and fork To eat heartily. This expression plays on the image of dining utensils in constant motion as someone eats a hearty meal. It appeared in print by the turn of the 19th century in Benjamin Malkin's 1809 translation of LeSage's *Adventures of Gil Blas:*

> Domingo, after playing a good knife and fork . . . took himself off.

GRAFT (See also BRIBERY, EXTORTION.)

feather one's nest See EXPLOITATION.

line one's pockets To profit, especially at the expense of others; to receive money or other favors through bribery, blackmail, or graft. This expression reputedly stems from the English tailor who, hoping to become the clothes designer for the famous fashion plate, Beau Brummel (1778–1840), sent him an ornate coat, the pockets of which were lined with money. Although Beau sent a letter of thanks and added that he especially admired the lining, it is not known whether the tailor received any more of his business.

a piece of the pie See ALLOCATION.

pork barrel Legislation providing federal funding for local projects designed to put congressmen in the good graces of their constituents. Thus, the pork barrel is, metaphorically speaking, the federal treasury viewed as a source of monies for "pet" local projects. The connection between this figurative, political sense of *pork barrel* and the literal keg is not clear, although it may derive from pork considered as *fat,* a slang term for excess wealth, riches. Use of this U.S. slang expression is restricted to politics and dates from the early part of this century.

> The River and Harbor bill is the pork barrel par excellence, and the rivers and harbors are manipulated by Federal machinery and not by State machinery. (*The New York Evening Post,* May, 1916)

shoe one's mule To embezzle; to misuse or steal money entrusted to one's care and management. Some unscrupulous blacksmiths and grooms reputedly once engaged in the fraudulent practice of charging a horse (or mule) owner for shoeing the steed, and then either kept the money without performing the promised work, or used the money to buy shoes for their own animals.

> He had the keeping and disposal of all the moneys, and yet shod not his mule at all. (*Sorel's Comical History of Francion,* 1655)

A variation is *shoe one's horse.*

GREED (See DESIRE.)

GRIEVANCE

ax to grind A private or selfish motive, a personal stake; a grievance or complaint, especially a chronic one. The phrase stems from an 1810 story by Charles Miner in which a gullible boy is duped by a flattering stranger into turning a grindstone for him. According to the *Dictionary of Americanisms,* the frequent but erroneous ascription of the phrase's origin to Benjamin Franklin is due to confusion between *Poor Richard's Almanac* and *Essays from the Desk of Poor Robert the Scribe,* the collection in which the story appeared.

a bone to pick A complaint or grievance; a point of disagreement or a difference to settle. Formerly, the expression *have a bone to pick* meant to be occupied, as a dog is with a bone. It was used in this sense as early as 1565. The

similar French phrase uses a different metaphor, *une maille à partir* 'a knot to pick.'

a chip on one's shoulder See BELLIGERENCE.

grumble in the gizzard To complain or grouse, to be dissatisfied or annoyed. In this British expression, which dates from the late 17th century, *gizzard* 'a bird's stomach' is applied jocularly to a human being's throat or craw.

> I was going home, grumbling in the gizzard. (Thomas Flloyd, *Gueullette's Tartarian Tales,* translated 1764)

GRIEVING (See also DEJECTION.)

come home by Weeping Cross To suffer disappointment or failure; to mourn, to lament; to be penitent and remorseful. The origin of this now rarely heard expression is obscure. There are several place names of this designation in England, but the common explanation that they were the site of penitential devotions is without substance. Use of the expression may have given rise to the explanation, rather than vice versa; for example, the following passage from Lyly's *Euphues* (1580):

> The time will come when coming home by weeping cross, thou shalt confess.

in sackcloth and ashes In a state of remorse and penitence; contrite, repentant; in mourning, sorrowful. This expression alludes to the ancient Hebrew custom of wearing sackcloth, a coarse fabric of camel's or goat's hair, and ashes (usually sprinkled on the head) to humble oneself as a sign of sorrow or penitence. Among the Biblical references to this custom is that in the Book of Daniel (9:3):

> Then I turned my face to the Lord, God, seeking him by prayer and supplications with fasting and sackcloth and ashes.

The expression has been used metaphorically for centuries.

He knew that for all that had befallen she was mourning in mental sackcloth and ashes. (Hugh Conway, *A Family Affair*, 1805)

A common variation is *wearing sackcloth and ashes.*

wear the willow To mourn the death of a mate; to suffer from unrequited love. The willow, especially the weeping willow, has long been a symbol of sorrow or grief. Psalm 137:1–2 is said to explain why the branches of the willow tree droop:

By the rivers of Babylon, there we sat down, yea, we wept, when we remembered Zion. We hanged our harps upon the willows in the midst thereof.

Wear the willow appeared in print by the 16th century but is rarely, if ever, heard today.

There's . . . Marie . . . wearing the willow because . . . Engemann is away courting Madam Carouge. (Katharine S. Macquoid, *At the Red Glove*, 1885)

GUIDANCE

bear leader The traveling tutor or guardian of well-heeled, aristocratic youths of the 18th century. Horace Walpole used the term in his *Letters to Sir Horace Mann* (1749):

She takes me for his bear-leader, his travelling governor.

The phrase is said to have come from the old practice of leading muzzled bears around the streets and having them perform in order to attract attention and money.

hand on the torch To pass on or transfer the tradition of enlightenment and knowledge to succeeding generations. The allusion is to the ancient Greek torch races, precursors of the Olympics, in which a lighted torch was passed from one runner to the next in the manner of modern-day relay races. Because of the brilliance of its light, the torch has long been symbolic of enlighten-ment and learning. The expression dates from at least 1887.

lick into shape To make suitable or presentable; to develop, mold, or give form to. This expression refers to the belief, prevalent until the 17th century, that bear cubs are born as amorphous masses that assume the normal ursiform appearance only if they are licked into shape by their mother. This mistaken assumption was based on information in *The History of Animals* by Aristotle (384–327 B.C.) and *The Canon of Medicine* by Avicenna (979–1037), an Arab physician. Despite its unsound origin, the expression is extremely common.

Their proposals . . . would be licked, by debate . . . into practicable shape. (*The Spectator,* December 12, 1891)

The French expression *ours mal léché* 'an improperly licked bear' is used colloquially to describe a boorish person. *Whip into shape* and *beat into shape* are variations of *lick into shape* which refer to a different definition of *lick,* i.e., 'to strike or hit,' yet they retain the connotation of the original expression.

take in tow To guide, lead, take charge of, or assume responsibility for. Originally said of pulling a vessel through water with a rope, this expression applies figuratively to one person leading another. This use of *take in tow* dates from the 18th century.

A young lama . . . took me in tow, and conducted me to all the tents. (James Gilmour, *Among the Mongols,* 1883)

Current usage frequently implies a need for discipline and control.

take under one's wing To protect, care for, or watch over; to nourish or nurture; to rear, teach. This expression alludes to a mother hen's protecting her chicks by taking them under her wing.

I have gathered thy children together, even as a hen gathereth her chickens under her wings . . . (Matthew 23:37)

They fled for their lives to find safety under Pompey's wing in Capua. (James Froude, *Caesar; A Sketch*, 1879)

Although implying protection, *take under one's wing* is most often applied in contexts where an experienced person takes it upon himself to show a neophyte "the ropes."

GUILT

caught with one's hand in the cookie jar Taken by surprise in the process of wrongdoing; caught red-handed. This expression implies that the person caught is not only surprised, but is also in possession of self-incriminating material. Though the image is that of a mischievous child atop a counter engaged in normal childhood activities, in context the phrase is often used for serious adult wrongdoing, particularly political graft.

caught with one's pants down See VULNERABILITY.

cry peccavi To confess one's guilt; to openly acknowledge one's fault or wrongdoing. The origin of this expression is the Latin *peccavi* 'I have sinned.' Both *peccavi* 'an acknowledgement of guilt' and *cry peccavi* date from the 16th century.

> Now lowly crouch'd, I cry peccavi,
> And prostrate, supplicate *pour ma vie.*
> (Jonathan Swift, *Sheridan's Submission*, 1730)

dead to rights See CERTAINTY.

red-handed In the act, with clear evidence of guilt, *in flagrante delicto*. This term evolved from the earlier *with red hand* and *with bloody hand*.

tarred with the same brush See SIMILARITY.

with bloody hand Guilty; caught red-handed or *in flagrante delicto*. According to the Forest Law of ancient Britain, a man found with bloody hand was presumed guilty of having killed the king's deer.

with egg on one's face See HUMILIATION.

H

HAPPINESS (See ELATION.)

HARASSMENT

dun See SOLICITATION.

from pillar to post See DIRECTION.

get off [someone's] back To stop bothering, irritating, or criticizing another person; similar to the currently popular *get off [someone's] case*. This expression is usually spoken in the command form by a desperate victim of incessant nagging or harassment.

> Then stop picking on me, will you? Get off my back, will you? (Joseph Heller, *Catch-22*, 1961)

the heat's on The police are hot on one's trail; the pressure is on. *Heat* can refer to a gun, a policeman, or other external source of pressure. In this originally U.S. slang expression dating from the early 20th century, *heat* combines the latter two meanings.

> But the word went out that the government heat was on. The FBI was known to be relentless in its pursuit. (H. Corey, *Farewell, Mr. Gangster*, 1936)

The heat's on currently applies to any pressure-ridden situation, though its most frequent usage is still police-related.

make it hot for To make things very uncomfortable or unpleasant for someone, especially through repeated harassment or persecution; to make trouble for. This expression and the variant *to make it too hot for* were precursors of the American slang phrase *to turn the heat on* 'to apply pressure to.'

> Caesar Augustus thought good to make that practice too hot for them. (Edmund Bolton, *The Roman Histories of Lucius Julius Florus*, translated 1618)

play cat and mouse with To tease, toy with, or torment; to be engaged in a power struggle in which one takes the role of cat, or oppressor, and victimizes the mouse, or weaker party; to outwit one's opponent; to take part in a round of near capture and escape. The Cat-and-mouse Act, a nickname for the Prisoners Act of 1913 which enabled hunger strikers to be released temporarily, popularized use of the phrase *cat and mouse* in the early 1900s.

> The Administration played a curious cat-and-mouse game with the Jewish self-defence organization. (Arthur Koestler, *Promise and Fulfillment*, 1949)

ride herd on See DOMINATION.

HARDSHIP (See ADVERSITY.)

HAUGHTINESS (See also POMPOSITY.)

bridle To tuck in the chin and throw the head back as in vanity or scorn; to put on an air of disdain or offense; sometimes *bridle up* or *back*. The allusion is to the upward movement of a horse's head when the reins are abruptly pulled. In use since 1480, the term appeared in Henry Fielding's *Amelia* (1751):

> "Is she," said my aunt, bridling herself, "fit to decide between us?"

high-hat To act in an aloof, snobbish, or condescending manner.

> Denver's dignity was mistaken by some for "high-hatting." (Noel Coward, *Australia Revisited*, 1941)

This expression, alluding to the tall headgear formerly worn by the wealthy, usually refers to a manner of behavior, although it is also often used as a moniker for a pompous or pretentious person.

look down one's nose To regard in a condescending manner; to view with disdain or disgust. A person who literally looks down his nose bears a countenance of disapproval or arrogance. The expression carries a strong suggestion of snobbery or haughtiness.

It is getting more difficult for a lawyer to look down his nose at the courtroom, with consequent impairment of the prestige of the courts. (*Baltimore Sun,* October, 1932)

on one's high horse With one's nose in the air; pretentious, arrogant, affected; also *to ride* or *mount the high horse, to get down off one's high horse,* and other variants. In royal pageants of former times persons of high rank rode on tall horses, literally above the common people. Use of the expression dates from the late 18th century.

Only his mother felt that Mayo was not a rude boy, but his father frequently asked Mayo to get down off his high horse and act like everybody else. (William Saroyan, *Assyrian & Other Stories,* 1950)

toffee-nosed Stuck-up, with one's nose in the air, conceited, pretentious, stuffy. Although the origin of this British slang term is not certain, it may be related to the stickiness of the candy.

HEALTH (See GOOD HEALTH, ILL HEALTH.)

HINDRANCE (See IMPEDIMENT.)

HOPELESSNESS (See FUTILITY.)

HUMILIATION

cut [someone's] comb To humiliate or humble; to degrade, to take down a peg or two. This expression, which dates from the mid-1500s, is said to allude to the supposed practice of cutting the fleshy red combs of roosters in order to humble their pride.

eat crow To be forced to do or say something distasteful and humiliating; to eat one's words or eat humble pie; to be compelled to confess wrongdoing or to back down. This colloquial expression of American origin and its variant *eat boiled crow* were used as early as the mid-19th century. The most popular story explaining this expression tells of an American soldier in the War of 1812 who killed a crow for sport. Its owner reacted by forcing him to eat the dead crow at gunpoint. After a few bites, the soldier was released, whereupon he turned his gun on his foe and forced him to eat the remaining portion. Later, the soldier's only comment was that he and the other party had "dined" together. Today, *eat crow* continues to be a popular picturesque expression.

eat humble pie To come down off one's high horse, swallow one's pride, and submit to mortification and humiliation; to be forced to apologize and defer to others; to eat crow, to eat dirt, or to eat one's words. In this expression, *humble* derives from the obsolete *umbles* 'heart, liver, and entrails of the deer.' Apparently these parts were considered leftovers suitable only for the huntsman and other servants. When the lord and his company feasted on venison, the others ate the umbles that had been made into a pie. Thus, "umble pie" was suggestive of poverty and lowly status. Since *humble* also connotes lowliness and subservience, the simple fact of confusion gave rise to *eat humble pie,* used as early as the beginning of the 19th century.

eat one's words See RECANTATION.

go to Canossa To humble oneself, to submit oneself to humiliation. In January of 1077, Pope Gregory VII stayed for a time at the castle of Canossa in Italy on his way to Germany to take action against the excommunicated Henry IV, emperor of the Holy Roman

Empire. To forestall this event, Henry IV made the pilgrimage to Canossa where he was kept waiting outside, exposed to the harshness of the elements, for three days before receiving absolution from the Pope. This example of secular submission to Church authority gave rise to the expression in question, now used in the general sense of submitting oneself to humiliation.

put [someone's] nose out of joint To arouse someone's anger or resentment by replacing him in the affection or esteem of another; to humiliate, to spoil or upset someone's plans, to thwart.

> The King is pleased enough with her: which, I fear, will put Madam Castlemaine's nose out of joint. (Samuel Pepys, *Diary*, 1662)

It is easy to see how the literal *out of joint* 'dislocated, out of place' gave rise to the figurative 'supplanted, superseded.'

rub [someone's] nose in it To persistently humiliate a person by reminding him of a fault or error. This expression may have derived from the canine housebreaking technique of placing the pet's nose close to its mistake in hope of discouraging future indoor accidents. As used today, the expression implies unmerciful harping and castigation over a relatively minor mishap.

> I'm sorry. I've said I'm sorry. Don't rub my nose in it. (P. M. Hubbart, *Flush as May*, 1963)

take down a peg To humble, to lower someone in his own or another's estimation; to snub or put down. In print since the 16th century, this expression is said to derive from the raising or lowering of a ship's colors, or flag, by pegs, to mark the importance of an occasion—the higher the colors, the greater the honor, and vice versa. Another theory is that *peg* originally referred to the notches inside a cup to indicate each person's share. To take someone down a peg meant to drink his share.

Today *take down a notch* is a common variant.

> I must take that proud girl down a peg. (Mrs. Humphrey Ward, *Marcella*, 1894)

with egg on one's face Embarrassed or humiliated by some mistake; in the wrong, guilty. The origin of this expression is unknown. It may have derived from an audience's practice of throwing rotten eggs at actors during an especially poor performance. Another possible derivation is of a more agrarian nature. Weasels, foxes, and other such animals are known for their habit of sneaking into henhouses at night to suck eggs. To come out with egg on their faces would display to all the evidence of their wrongdoing.

with one's tail between one's legs Ashamed, humiliated, disgraced, embarrassed; cowed, dejected, beaten; afraid, scared.

> We shall have you back here very soon . . . with your tail between your legs. (William E. Norris, *Thirlby Hall*, 1884)

A dog, disgraced by having lost the scent on a hunt or embarrassed at being caught doing something forbidden, returns to its master with its tail hanging between its legs instead of triumphantly wagging on high.

HUMOROUSNESS

funny as a barrel of monkeys Very funny, hilarious, uproarious, riotous. Monkeys are known for their humorous antics; a barrel of them would undoubtedly serve to heighten one's amusement. But, since too many monkeys would not be funny for long, the expression is also used sarcastically to mean not funny at all.

funny-peculiar or funny ha-ha See DIFFERENTIATION.

in stitches Doubled over with laughter, in pain from laughing so hard.

Stitch dates from the 11th century as a term for a sharp, spasmodic, localized pain. *In stitches* refers to the analogous spasms produced by uncontrollable laughter. Shakespeare used the phrase in *Twelfth Night* (III,ii):

> If you desire the spleen, and will laugh yourself into stitches, follow me.

laugh like a drain To guffaw or horselaugh; to laugh loudly and boisterously. This British colloquialism refers to the sound made by water as it gurgles down the drain, and is frequently used in the context of laughing in derision at another's discomfiture.

> Old Hester would laugh like a drain if she could see us singing hymns over her. (K. Nicholson, *Hook, Line and Sinker*, 1966)

merry-andrew One who amuses others through buffoonery or zaniness; a droll, witty person; a clown. This expression may have derived from the learned traveler and physician to Henry VIII, Andrew Borde, though the evidence for this theory is flimsy at best. In an attempt to instruct the common English people, Borde spoke at fairs and other festivals, often interjecting witticisms and puns into his rather unpretentious lectures. The many people who imitated him were thus called merry-andrews. The expression is still used today for an amateur comedian or a buffoon.

> Richter is a man of mirth, but he seldom or never condescends to be a merry-andrew. (Thomas Carlyle, *Tales by Musaeus, Tieck, and Richter*, 1827)

slapstick A type of comedy characterized by boisterousness, farcical facial expressions, and horseplay, and quasi-violent actions such as throwing pies, striking or tripping one another, etc. This comedic genre takes its name from the *slapstick* 'flexible lath or stick' used by clowns and harlequins to deliver a loud but painless blow to another actor.

Slapstick comedy was perhaps epitomized by the Keystone Cops and other silent-film characters created by Mack Sennett (1884–1960). Even during its heyday in the early 1900s, but especially after the introduction of sound in motion pictures in the late 1920s, slapstick was considered by some to be a low, if not base, form of humor because of its exaggerated visual effects and rampant, though innocent, acts of violence.

> It was a musical show—one of those . . . slap-stick affairs which could never by any possibility satisfy a cultivated audience. (T. K. Holmes, *Man From Tall Timber*, 1919)

wear the cap and bells To willingly play the clown or buffoon, to act the fool, to be the life of the party; also, to serve as foil to the straight man, to be the butt of others' jokes. This now little-used expression derives from the headgear formerly worn by court jesters, a cap with bells attached.

HUNGER

die like Roland To die from hunger or thirst. Legend has it that Roland, after having escaped the massacre at Roncevalles, ironically died of starvation and thirst while trying to cross the Pyrenees.

dine with Duke Humphrey To go hungry; to partake of a Barmecide feast. According to the usual but perhaps apocryphal account, the expression derives from the practice of London's poor who, come the dinner hour when the streets began to empty of those preparing to dine, were wont to wander the aisles of St. Paul's claiming to be in search of the monument to Duke Humphrey. Humphrey, Duke of Gloucester, was renowned for his hospitality, and at his death it was rumored that there was to be a monument to his bounty erected in St. Paul's. None such was ever built; thus, to dine with Duke

Humphrey is to have no place at which to dine, to wander idly while others eat.

A cadaverous figure who had been invited for no other reason than that he was pretty constantly in the habit of dining with Duke Humphrey. (Nathaniel Hawthorne, *Mosses from an Old Manse*, 1854)

Another explanation holds that the phrase originally meant to dine well; after the Duke's death, its meaning naturally became inverted to the current one.

narrow at the equator Hungry, ravenous, famished. In this expression, purportedly used by American cowboys in the Old West, *equator* refers to a person's waist which, in cases of extreme or prolonged hunger, might be narrower than usual.

sup with Sir Thomas Gresham To go hungry. London's layabouts and idle poor commonly frequented the Exchange, which was built by Sir Thomas Gresham. Thus, those who had nowhere to dine, or no money with which to dine, were often said to sup with Sir Thomas Gresham. The phrase is not nearly so common as its near synonym *to dine with Duke Humphrey.*

HYPOCRISY (See also PRETENSE.)

carry fire in one hand and water in the other To be duplicitous, to engage in double-dealing; to be two-faced, to speak with forked tongue. The expression comes from Plautus; it continues "to bear a stone in one hand, a piece of bread in the other." Thus, the expression indicates that a person is prepared to act in totally contradictory ways to achieve his purposes.

crocodile tears Pretended or insincere tears, hypocritical weeping, false sorrow. Legend has it that a crocodile sheds tears and moans in order to lure passers-by into its clutches, and then, still weeping, devours them. A person who feigns deep sorrow in order to impress others or gain their sympathy is thus said to cry crocodile tears. This expression, in use since 1563, is found in Shakespeare's *Henry VI, (Part II):* Gloucester's show

Beguiles him, as the mournful crocodile
With sorrow snares relenting passengers. (III,i)

give pap with a hatchet To do or say a kind thing in an unkind way; to administer punishment under the guise of an act of kindness or generosity. This expression derives from the title of an anonymous pamphlet published in 1589 and attributed to John Lyly. The image of an infant being fed with a hatchet gives the phrase its obvious ironic tone. The recipient experiences more harm than good, thus undercutting any illusion of good intentions and suggesting the possibility of duplicity at play.

He that so old seeks for a nurse so young, shall have pap with a hatchet for his comfort. (Alexander Niccoles, *A Discourse of Marriage and Wiving*, 1615)

This expression usually indicates a disparity between reality and appearances, intentions, or expectations.

mote in the eye See IMPERFECTION.

odor of sanctity See VIRTUOUSNESS.

strain at a gnat and swallow a camel To make a great commotion about an insignificant matter while accepting grave faults and injustices without a murmur; to complain vociferously about minor transgressions while committing deplorable offenses. This expression originated in Christ's castigation of the hypocritical Pharisees:

Ye blind guides, which strain at a gnat, and swallow a camel. Woe unto you . . . for ye make clean the outside of the cup and platter, but within they are full of extortion and excess. (Matthew 23:24–25)

In this expression, *gnat* alludes to some-thing small and insignificant, while *camel* refers to something large or bulky which is difficult to "swallow" or accept.

Can we believe that your government strains in good earnest at the petty gnats of schism, when it makes nothing to swallow the Camel heresy of Rome. (John Milton, *Church Government*, 1641)

talk out of both sides of one's mouth
To espouse conflicting, contradictory points of view; to be inconsistent and hypocritical. This expression can be said of one who is two-faced or wishy-washy and afraid to take a stand.

I

IDEALISM

bullish Optimistic, hopeful, confident. In the world of finance, a "bull" is an investor who speculates in stocks or commodities in anticipation of a profit to be realized when the market prices increase. Thus, the "bull" believes that the general business climate is or will soon be favorable. *Bullish* is used in other, non-monetary contexts as well.

A related term, *bearish,* also derived from stock market jargon, describes a pessimistic outlook. Since a "bear" believes financial conditions are worsening, he may try to sell short, hoping to repurchase the stocks or securities at a lower price at some future date. Since both "bulls" and "bears" often buy the rights to trade stocks on margin, i.e., at a percentage of their true market value, the "bear" may, in effect, sell what he has not yet purchased. It has therefore been conjectured that the origin of *bear* may lie in the proverb *to sell the bear-skin before one has caught the bear.* As early as 1721, Nathan Bailey's *Universal Etymological English Dictionary* included the following: "to sell a bear: to sell what one hath not."

hitch one's wagon to a star To aim high, to have high ideals, to be idealistic. Ralph Waldo Emerson apparently coined this metaphor which appeared in his *Society and Solitude* (1870):

> Now that is the wisdom of a man . . . to hitch his wagon to a star.

look through rose-colored glasses To be cheerfully optimistic; to see things in a bright, rosy, favorable light. The color of a rose has long connoted optimism, cheerfulness, and promise.

> Oxford was a sort of Utopia to the Captain. . . . He continued . . . to behold towers, and quadrangles, and chapels, . . . through rose-coloured spectacles. (Thomas Hughes, *Tom Brown at Oxford,* 1861)

Implicit in this expression is the suggestion that a rosy view is unwarranted, perhaps even detrimental.

Pollyanna An incurable optimist. This expression comes from Eleanor Porter's book *Pollyanna,* in which the title character was a cheery little girl whose blitheness and buoyancy raised the spirits of all whom she met. In contemporary usage, however, this term is often applied disparagingly to one who exists in a fool's paradise.

IDLENESS (See also INDOLENCE.)

bench warmer See SUBORDINATION.

boondoggle To engage in work of little or no practical value; to look busy while accomplishing nothing.

> They boondoggled when there was nothing else to do on the ranch. (*Chicago Tribune,* October 4, 1935)

This U.S. slang term of uncertain origin gained currency in the 1930s with the proliferation of public-sector jobs created to combat the extensive unemployment of the Depression. As a noun the term is still primarily used for windfall government contracts awarded to appease certain constituencies despite the project's questionable value. The *boon* of the term 'a favor or gift freely bestowed' clearly relates to its meaning, but the *doggle* element is puzzling. One source says that *boondoggle* is a Scottish word for a marble received as a gift, without having worked for it.

goldbrick A shirker, a loafer, a boondoggler, a scrimshanker. This enlisted man's term of disparagement for a second lieutenant appointed from civilian life probably derived from the gold bar insignia of these officers. Now this U.S. slang term is applied to military or civilian workers in sinecures, or to those who discharge their responsibilities in an inefficient or lackadaisical manner.

In the ranks, billeted with the stinking, cheating, foul-mouthed goldbricks, there were true heroes. (John Steinbeck, *Once There Was War*, 1958)

The slang use of this term dates from the early part of this century.

have lead in one's pants To think or act very slowly or ponderously; to be lethargic, apathetic, or lazy. The implication here is that one whose pants are weighted down with lead moves very slowly. Several related expressions were used as commands during World War II and for several years thereafter, but are rarely heard today. These include *get the lead out* and *get the lead out of one's pants*.

She knows I'm in imminent danger of dying of malnutrition unless she takes the lead out of her pants and gets a move on with that picture. (P.G. Wodehouse, *Frozen Assets*, 1964)

Mickey Mouse around See EVASIVENESS.

monkey around See MISCHIEF.

on the beach Unemployed; without a job. This American slang term originally referred to seamen out of work; either retired or unemployed. It is probably an extension of the verb *to beach*, 'to haul [a ship] up on the shore or beach.' The phrase appeared in 1903 in *People of Abyss* by J. London.

rest on one's laurels See COMPLACENCY.

rest on one's oars See RESPITE.

sit on one's hands To do nothing, especially when the circumstances dictate that action be taken; to withhold applause or to applaud weakly. Originally a theater expression, *sit on one's hands* implies that the people in an audience

are so cold (i.e., unresponsive) that they are sitting on their hands for warmth, and are thus unable to applaud.

Well, they were sitting on their hands to-night, all right. Seemed they would never warm up. (Edna Ferber, *Show Boat*, 1926)

By extension then, *sit on one's hands* is often applied figuratively to describe a person's inactivity in a situation where action would be more appropriate.

twiddle one's thumbs To idle away the time; to be extremely bored. This expression refers to the indolent pastime of playing with one's own thumbs. The common phrase, while occasionally implying a state of involuntary inactivity, more often describes mere goofing off.

You'd have all the world do nothing half its time but twiddle its thumbs. (Douglas Jerrold, *Mrs. Caudle's Curtain Lecture*, 1846)

IGNORANCE (See also FATUOUSNESS.)

blockhead A dimwit, a numskull. The term comes from the dummy head used by wigmakers and hatters.

cork-brained Light-headed; giddy. This phrase plays with the analogy between cork cells which are dead, air-filled cells and one's brain. *Cork-brained* appeared in print as early as 1630.

dunce A dull-witted, stupid person; a dolt, blockhead, or ignoramus. This term makes use of the name of a scholastic theologian of the late 13th century, John Duns Scotus. Originally the term referred to a caviling sophist, derived from the fact that Scotus' doctrines were criticized as a conglomeration of hairsplitting distinctions. Such a person would be full of useless information and perhaps even opposed to progress and learning, as Scotus was regarded.

A dunce, void of learning but full of books. (Thomas Fuller, *The Holy and Profane State*, 1642)

Dunce also referred to one who is uneducated or incapable of learning.

> But now in our age it is grown to be a common proverb in derision, to call such a person as is senseless or without learning a Duns, which is as much as a fool. (Raphael Holinshed, *The First Volume of the Chronicles of England, Scotland, and Ireland,* 1577–87)

Today *dunce* has lost its connotations of overrefinement and pedantry; it means simply 'stupid, doltish, ignorant.'

dunderhead A thickheaded, stupid person; a numskull, blockhead, or dullard. The origin of this term is obscure, but it has been speculated that *dunder* is a corruption of the Spanish *redundar* 'to overflow' and is the name given to the lees or dregs of cane juice used in the fermentation of rum. Thus, a "dunderhead" is a head full of dregs, overflowing with this worthless substance. This term has been in use since the early 17th century.

not know A from a windmill To be extremely ignorant or stupid. This expression is said to have been originally suggested by the similarity between the shape of a capital A and that of a windmill. This theory is further reinforced by the now rare or obsolete definition of windmill found in the *OED:* "a figure of a windmill; a sign or character resembling this, as a cross or asterisk." In popular usage until the late 19th century, the phrase appeared as early as 1402 in the Rolls of Parliament.

not know B from a battledore To be illiterate, ignorant, or obtuse. *Battledore* is an obsolete word for a hornbook used as a child's primer. Not to know the letter from the book signified utter ignorance.

> He knew not a B from a battledore nor ever a letter of the book. (John Foxe, *Acts and Monuments of These Latter and Perilous Days,* 1553–87)

Many alliterative variations of the phrase exist, substituting *broomstick, bull's foot,* or *buffalo's foot* for *battledore.*

not know if one is coming or going See CONFUSION.

not know one's ass [or *Brit.* arse] from one's elbow Not know the first thing about something, not know what's what, completely ignorant or naïve.

> I wish I'd had a crowd like that for my first crew. We none of us knew arse from elbow when they pushed me off. (N. Shute, *Pastoral,* 1944)

not know shit from shinola To be totally stupid or ignorant. *Shinola* is the brand name of a formerly popular shoe polish little used today. Because of its vulgar origin and implications, the phrase is somewhat limited in written usage.

not know which end is up Not know what's going on; ignorant, stupid; totally confused or mixed up.

out to lunch Stupid, daft, or flaky; socially incompetent. This expression relates physical absence to mental vacuity. The common phrase often describes a person whose social ineptness or exceedingly poor judgment is due to a severe lack of common sense.

> A girl who would be attracted to Bud's mean streak and bad temper must be a little out to lunch. (*Toronto Daily Star,* June, 1966)

ILLEGALITY (See CRIMINALITY.)

ILL HEALTH

charley horse Muscular cramp or stiffness in an arm or leg. Reliable sources say the origin of this term is unknown. Nevertheless, a story is told of a limping horse named Charley who used to draw a roller in the White Sox baseball park in Chicago. Thus, the (apocryphal) origin of the term is based on the resemblance between the posture of an athlete suffering from a leg cramp and a limping horse.

Toward the close of the season Mac was affected with a "Charley-horse" and that ended his ball-playing for 1888. (*Cincinnati Comm. Gazette,* March 17, 1889)

Current today, this North American slang phrase has been popular since the 1880s.

[one's] days are numbered Dying, almost dead; with little time remaining, nearing the end. This expression is usually used to describe someone who is critically ill and has but a short time to live; so short, in fact, that one could count the days remaining. The phrase is also frequently used to describe the imminent end of anything, particularly one's employment.

feed the fishes To be seasick. Herbert Meade used this humorous metaphor in *A Ride through the disturbed districts of New Zealand* (1870):

His first act was to appease the fishes . . . by feeding them most liberally.

a frog in one's throat Temporary hoarseness or thickness in the voice; an irritation in the throat. This colloquial expression dates from at least 1909 and is an obvious allusion to the hoarse, throaty croaking of frogs.

have one foot in the grave Near death, at death's door, dying. This common expression often refers to one afflicted by a lingering, terminal illness.

He has twenty thousand a year . . . And one foot in the grave. (J. Payn, *Luck Dorrells,* 1886)

in the straw In labor or giving birth; in childbed; pregnant. This expression probably refers to the ancient custom of placing straw on the doorstep of a house to muffle the footsteps of visitors so as not to disturb a woman in parturition. One source, however, suggests that *in the straw* may allude to the straw-filled

mattresses once common among the poor.

In the phrase of ladies in the straw, "as well as can be expected." (Thomas DeQuincey, *Confessions of an Opium-Eater,* 1822)

A related expression said of a woman who has just given birth is *out of the straw.*

Montezuma's revenge Diarrhea, particularly when it afflicts foreigners in Mexico. This expression is named for the last Aztec emperor, Montezuma, who lost his empire in 1520 through the trickery of the Spanish conquistadors. American and European tourists in Mexico are still plagued by this condition, perhaps as a reaction to spicy Mexican food or from dysentery generated by impure water. This expression and some humorous variations appeared in *Western Folklore XXI* (1962):

The North American in Mexico has coined a number of names for the inevitable dysentery and diarrhea: "Mexican two-step," "Mexican foxtrot," "Mexican toothache," and, less directly if more colorfully, "Montezuma's revenge," the "Curse of Montezuma," and the "Aztec hop."

In keeping with the tradition of *Montezuma's revenge,* various euphemisms for diarrhea have been coined by persons who travel to Egypt, India, Burma, and Japan, as delineated in this citation from an April, 1969, *Daily Telegraph:*

Prevent gippy tummy. Also known as Delhi belly, Rangoon runs, Tokyo trots, Montezuma's revenge.

off one's feed To be ill; to suffer from loss of appetite; to be depressed or disconsolate. This expression, originally a reference to an ailing horse, usually describes a person whose physical or emotional state effects a repulsion to food.

on one's last legs Moribund; in a state of exhaustion or near-collapse; about to break down or fail. In this expression, *legs* is usually used figuratively to describe that part of a person, machine, project, or other item which allows it to move forward or continue. *Last legs* implies that the person or object is tired and will be unable to function at all within a short time.

on the blink Unwell, in ill health, out of condition; in disrepair, not in working order, *on the fritz*. This common slang expression is of unknown origin. Two possible but highly conjectural theories relate it to the dialectal meaning of *blink* 'milk gone slightly sour,' and to the U.S. fishermen's use of the term for mackerel too young to be marketable.

out of sorts See ILL TEMPER.

the runs Diarrhea. This slang expression is derived not only from the fluid consistency and movement of the feces, but also from the celerity and frequency with which one so afflicted reaches a bathroom. The phrase is commonplace in both the United States and Great Britain. A similar term is *the trots*.

a shadow of one's former self See PHYSICAL APPEARANCE.

shoot one's cookies To vomit. This expression and innumerable variations euphemistically describe the regurgitation of recently eaten food.

> If I'm any judge of color, you're goin' to shoot your cookies. (Raymond Chandler, *Finger Man*, 1934)

Among the more popular variants are *toss one's cookies, shoot one's breakfast* or *lunch* or *dinner* or *supper, return one's breakfast* or *lunch*, etc., *lose one's breakfast* or *lunch*, etc., *blow lunch, spiff one's biscuits*, etc.

shoot the cat To vomit, especially as a result of excessive alcoholic indulgence. This British colloquialism alludes to a cat's purported tendency to vomit frequently.

> I'm cursedly inclined to shoot the cat. (Frederick Marryat, *The King's Own*, 1830)

Variations include *cat, jerk the cat, whip the cat*, and *sick as a cat*.

under the weather Not feeling well, ill; intoxicated; hung over. This expression is derived from the common but unproven belief that atmospheric conditions and health are directly correlated. The phrase usually suggests the affliction of minor ailments.

> They have been very well as a general thing, although now and then they might have been under the weather for a day or two. (Frank R. Stockton, *Borrowed Month*, 1887)

The expression is often extended to include drunkenness and its aftereffects.

ILL TEMPER (See also ANGRINESS.)

get up on the wrong side of the bed To be grouchy, peevish, or ill-tempered. Most probably this is another holdover from ancient superstitions associating the right side with good omens and fortune, the left with evil and ill luck. The transference to temperament and mode of arising is centuries old:

> Thou rose not on thy right side, or else blest thee not well. (*Gammer Gurton*, 1575)

have a worm in one's tongue To be quarrelsome or dyspeptic; to be irritable or grouchy. Dogs suffering from worms are unfriendly and disagreeable just as one with a figurative "wormy" tongue is spiteful and surly. This obsolete expression was used by Samuel Butler in *Upon Modern Critics:*

> There is one easy artifice
> That seldom has been known to miss—
> To snarl at all things right or wrong,

Like a mad dog that has a worm in 's tongue.

like a bear with a sore head Irritable, peevish; in a disagreeable mood. The analogy here is self-evident:

He grumbles and growls like a bear with a sore head. (John Davis, *Travels,* 1803)

This phrase seems to have been shortened at some point to the more common *sorehead.*

out of sorts Irritable, short-tempered; low-spirited, depressed; under the weather, slightly unhealthy. The origin of this expression is unknown. Some speculate that it derives from the literal typographical *out of sorts* meaning 'out of type.' Only a considerable stretch of the imagination renders this explanation plausible. *Out of sorts* has been popular since the early 17th century.

He was extremely out of sorts because there was some company in the room who did not please him. (Madame D'Arblay, *The Early Diary of Frances Burney,* 1775)

This expression can also refer to things and situations, implying that something is amiss or not functioning properly.

serpent's tongue A shrewish disposition; a tendency toward vicious, vitriolic speech marked by scathing sarcasm. This expression appeared in Shakespeare's *Midsummer Night's Dream* (V,i):

Now to scape the Serpent's tongue, We will make amends ere long.

This phrase, clearly referring to a snake's forked, venomous tongue, was frequently employed in 18th- and 19th-century poetry.

She is not old, she is not young, This woman with the serpent's tongue. (Sir William Watson, *The Prince's Quest,* 1880)

sorehead A poor loser; one who is disgruntled or dissatisfied. The term seems to be an abbreviated version of the phrase *like a bear with a sore head.* The current meaning of this word is said to have come into use during the presidential campaign of 1848.

ILLUSION

Barmecide feast An illusion of plenty; any illusion. In *The Arabian Nights,* Barmecide, a wealthy Persian noble, invited the beggar Schacabac to dine with him at a banquet table laden with dishes, all empty of food. The host feigned indulgence in the illusionary banquet, and when the beggar followed suit with gusto, Barmecide repented of his joke and served the pauper a sumptuous repast. This latter aspect of the story does not figure into the meaning of the phrase; *Barmecide feast* retains only that aspect of the story dealing with the nonexistent fare.

cast beyond the moon To indulge in fanciful, outlandish thoughts about the future; to imagine the impossible. One definition of *cast* is "to calculate or conjecture, to anticipate, to forecast" (*OED*). The moon was considered a mysterious force of inexplicable power. *Beyond the moon* reinforces the idea of a realm where nothing is impossible. The phrase appeared as early as the mid-16th century.

But oh, I talk of things impossible, and cast beyond the moon. (Thomas Heywood, *A Woman Killed with Kindness,* 1607)

castles in Spain Fanciful notion; pipe dream—the opposite of all that is practical, reasonable, and grounded in common sense. The phrase appeared in English in *The Romance of the Rose* (approx. 1400).

Thou shalt make castles then in Spain, And dream of joy, all but in vain.

Château en Espagne, the French equivalent, dates from the 13th century. The *OED* attributes the reference to Spain to the fact that it represents a "foreign country where one had no standing-ground." *Spain* was superseded by the now current *air* or *sky*.

castles in the air Visionary projects; daydreams or fantasies; impractical, romantic, or whimsical schemes; half-baked ideas without solid foundation. This phrase, common since 1575, is equivalent to *castles in the sky*.

> Things are thought, which never yet were wrought,
> And castles built above in lofty skies.
> (George Gascoigne, *The Steele Glas*, 1575)

Fata Morgana See ENTICEMENT.

fool's paradise A self-deceptive state of contentment or bliss; a mental condition in which one's happiness is generated by delusions and false hopes. The expression is derived from the Latin *limbus fatuorum*, a quasi-limbo where the mentally feeble went after death. The phrase has evolved to mean the fantasy world inhabited by certain daft individuals.

> You have been revelling in a fool's paradise of leisure. (James Beresford, *The Miseries of Human Life*, 1807)

pie in the sky An illusion of future benefits and blessings which will never be realized; an unattainable state of happiness or utopia. This expression, probably alluding to the concept of *pie* as something sweet and desirable, and *sky* as in the air, beyond one's reach, was popularized in a World War I song often attributed to Joe Hill (1927):

> You will eat, bye and bye,
> In the glorious land above the sky!
> Work and pray,
> Live on hay,
> You'll get pie in the sky when you die!

pipe dream An unrealistic and often fantastic plan, goal, or idea. One source suggests that this expression alludes to the dreams and schemes which may inspire an opium addict after he has smoked a pipeful of the drug.

tilt at windmills To combat imaginary evils, to fight opponents or injustices that are merely the figments of an overactive imagination. The allusion is to Cervantes' *Don Quixote de la Mancha*, in which the hero Don Quixote imagines the windmills he has come upon to be giants and proceeds to do battle, with the result that both the knight and his horse are injured and his lance destroyed. At this Quixote's squire Sancho Panza says that anyone who mistakes windmills for giants must have windmills in his head, i.e., suffer delusions, be crazy. The equivalent French phrase is *se battre contre les moulins à vent*. A variant of the expression appeared in Frederic W. Farrar's book on Christ:

> Dr. Edersheim is again—so far as I am concerned—fighting a windmill.

IMBIBING (See TIPPLING.)

IMITATION (See SIMILARITY.)

IMMATURITY (See INEXPERIENCE.)

IMPATIENCE (See also IMPETU-OUSNESS.)

champ at the bit To show impatience; to wait restlessly or anxiously to begin. This expression, in figurative use since 1645, refers to the way a horse, eager to be off, chews on the bit in his mouth and stamps the ground with his hooves. Similar phrases with the same meaning are *to bite the bridle*, used figuratively since 1514, and *to strain at the leash*.

cool one's heels To impatiently await the promised and supposedly imminent arrival of one or more persons, especially when the arrival has been intentionally and rudely delayed. Dating from the early 1600s, this expression is an allusion to the fact that one's feet, hot from walking, are cooled by waiting in a stationary position.

Well, if we're not ready, they'll have to wait—won't do them any harm to cool their heels a bit. (John Galsworthy, *Strife*, 1909)

sit upon hot cockles To be very impatient or restive; to be on pins and needles. "Hot Cockles" is the name of an ancient children's game in which a blindfolded child tried to guess who had just struck him on the buttocks. Since *sit on* can mean 'to await' or 'to be seated upon,' to *sit on hot cockles* probably alludes either to one's fidgety anticipation of the blow, or to the squirming discomfort of one who sits down after having been struck by an enthusiastic player.

He laughs and kicks like Chrysippus when he saw an ass eat figs; and sits upon hot cockles till it be blazed abroad. (Thomas Walkington, *The Optick Glasse of Humors*, 1607)

soft fire makes sweet malt A proverbial expression meaning that reckless hurriedness often spoils an undertaking or project.

Soft fire, They say, does make sweet Malt, Good Squire. (Samuel Butler, *Hudibras*, 1663)

Malt is burnt and its sweetness lost by too intense a fire. This expression, synonymous with the common phrase *haste makes waste*, is now rarely heard.

IMPEDIMENT (See also THWARTING.)

albatross around the neck See BURDEN.

ball and chain See BURDEN.

bottleneck A narrow passage; an impasse; congestion or constriction; a traffic jam. The reference is to the thin, narrow neck of a bottle, which is necessarily constrictive. By extension, the word is used for any point at which passage or flow becomes impeded because the volume of a larger area must move into a smaller. The equivalent French term is *embouteillage*. The word appeared in print by 1907 in the *Westminster Gazette*.

choke-pear Something difficult or impossible to "swallow"; something "hard to take"; a difficulty. The figurative sense of this term is an extension of its literal meaning, i.e., a variety of pear with a harsh, bitter taste. Samuel Collins used the expression in *Epphata to F.T.* (1617):

S. Austens testimony . . . is a choke-pear that you cannot swallow.

The term has been used literally since 1530 and figuratively since 1573.

cooling card Anything that diminishes or lessens a person's ardor or enthusiasm; a damper. According to the *OED*, *cooling card* is apparently a term of some unknown game and is used figuratively or punningly with the meaning above. This expression, now obsolete, dates from 1577. In Henry Dircks' *Life* the Marquis of Worcester is quoted as using it thus in 1664:

It would . . . prove a cooling card to many, whose zeal otherwise would transport them.

fly in the ointment A triviality which ruins an otherwise enjoyable occasion; a negative element or consideration. The Biblical origin of this expression appears in Ecclesiastes (10:1):

Dead flies cause the ointment of the apothecary to send forth a stinking savour.

In modern usage, the phrase implies minor inconvenience or untimeliness:

The present situation is not without its 'fly in the ointment' for those motorists who have patriotically lent the assistance of their cars to the military authorities. (*Scotsman*, September, 1914)

a lump in the throat A choked-up or tight feeling in the throat at times of deep emotion. A person usually gets a lump in his throat when he is very touched and on the verge of tears—either from happiness or from sadness. A literal lump in the throat would inhibit speech and swallowing. The figurative expression has been in use since the latter half of the 19th century.

> A lump always comes into my throat when I think of it. (Princess Alice, *Biographical Sketch and Letters*, 1878)

The similar expression *have the words stick in one's throat* implies an inability to express oneself due to intense emotion.

a new wrinkle See ADVANCEMENT.

red tape See COMPLICATION.

skeleton at the feast A source of gloom or sadness at an otherwise festive occasion; a wet blanket, a party pooper; something that acts as a reminder that life holds sorrow as well as joy. According to the *Moralia,* a collection of essays by Plutarch (A.D. circa 46–120), the Egyptians always placed a skeleton at their banquet tables to remind the revelers of their mortality.

> The skeleton of ennui sat at these dreary feasts; and it was not even crowned with roses. (George Lawrence, *Guy Livingstone,* 1857)

It was also common practice for many monastic orders to place a skull or death's head on the refectory table to remind those present of their mortality.

there's the rub Said of an impediment, hindrance, or stumbling-block, especially one of an abstract nature; the crux of a problem. In this expression, *rub* alludes to the rubbing of a spoon inside a mixing bowl, an occurrence which interferes with smooth stirring. Although *rub* in this sense had been in use for some time before Shakespeare, he popularized the phrase by incorporating it into Hamlet's famous soliloquy:

> To be, or not to be: that is the question . . .
> To sleep: perchance to dream: ay, there's the rub. (III,i)

A variation is *here lies the rub.*

third wheel See EXTRANEOUSNESS.

wet blanket A discouraging or dampening influence on others' enjoyment of a party or similar pleasurable occasion; a person who is habitually grouchy or depressed; a kill-joy, party pooper, spoilsport. Literally, a wet blanket is one that has been soaked in water and is used to smother or quench a fire. The figurative implications are obvious.

> Sometimes he called her a wet blanket, when she thus dampened his ardor. (Margaret Oliphant, *Annals of a Publishing House,* 1897)

IMPERFECTION

crack'd in the ring Flawed or imperfect at the perimeter or edge; of little value or use; (of women) nonvirginal. This expression, popular during Elizabethan times, is no longer used today. It was limited in application to money, artillery, and (figuratively) to women.

diamond in the rough One whose unrefined external appearance or ungraceful behavior belies a good or gentle character and untapped potential. This expression derives from the disparity between a diamond in its natural state, before being cut and polished, and in its refined state, when it has become an impressive gem. Analogously, graceful manners and social amenities can be learned. *Diamond in the rough* dates from the early 17th century.

feet of clay An unforeseen blemish in the character of a person hitherto held above reproach.

> The woman . . . finds that her golden-headed god has got an iron body and feet of clay. (Anthony Trollope, *Fortnightly Review,* 1865)

This expression originated with Daniel's interpretation of Nebuchadnezzar's dream in the Old Testament (Daniel 2:31–45). The Babylonian king had dreamed of an image completely made of precious metals, except for its feet, which were made of clay and iron. Daniel explained that the feet represented man's vulnerability to weakness and destruction.

Homer sometimes nods An erudite way of saying, "Nobody's perfect." The expression is often used to indicate that an artistic performance or endeavor has fallen below expectations or has not been of consistently high quality. The phrase's origin lies in lines from Horace's *De Arte Poetica* usually translated as: "I think it shame when the worthy Homer nods; but in so long a work it is allowable if drowsiness comes on."

mote in the eye A fault or imperfection observed in a person by one who is guilty of something equally or more objectionable. This phrase comes from Matthew 7:3:

And why beholdest thou the mote that is in thy brother's eye, but considerest not the beam that is in thine own eye?

Mote refers to a small particle, as a bit of sawdust; *beam* refers to a glance, or eyebeam, formerly thought to be emitted from, rather than received by the eye. Shakespeare makes use of the allusion in *Love's Labor's Lost:*

You found his mote, the King your mote did see,
But I a beam do find in each of three. (IV,iii)

An analogous proverbial exhortation is "People who live in glass houses shouldn't throw stones."

a rift in the lute A flaw or imperfection, particularly one that endangers the integrity of the whole; the one rotten apple that spoils the whole barrel. The expression, more familiar to British than American ears, comes from Alfred, Lord Tennyson's *Idylls of the King* (1885):

It is the little rift within the lute,
That by and by will make the music mute,
And ever widening slowly silence all.

rough edges Characteristics or manners indicating a lack of polish, refinement, or completion. Use of *rough* meaning 'lacking in culture or refinement' dates from at least the time of Shakespeare. It is difficult to pinpoint exactly when *edges,* probably originally referring to the edges of sawed lumber which have not been trimmed or sized, was added to make the new phrase. In current use, *corners* is a common variant of *edges.*

IMPERMANENCE (See **FLIMSINESS.**)

IMPETUOUSNESS

early days Premature, overhasty; too early or soon; jumping the gun. In use since the 16th century, this British expression has a self-evident meaning but may sound awkward to American ears.

As regards the current year, it is early days to express any considered opinion, but trading conditions are bad. (*Times,* December 23, 1957)

from the hip Impulsively, impetuously, without preparation or thought; spontaneously, extempore. This expression is an abbreviated version of *to shoot from the hip,* literally to fire a handgun from the hip immediately upon drawing it from the holster and without taking formal aim.

. . . second thoughts about letting their man shoot from the hip quite so much as his nature prompted him to. (R. L. Maullin as quoted in *Webster's 6,000*)

go off at half-cock To start prematurely; to leave unprepared; to act rashly, impetuously, or ill-advisedly;

also, *go off half-cocked.* In this expression, *half-cock* refers to a position of a gun's hammer which renders the weapon inoperable; thus, one is unprepared if the gun happens to go off at half-cock. Figuratively, the phrase implies acting on a whim with no preparatory measures.

> Poor Doctor Jim! What disasters he brought down upon his country and his company by going off at half-cock. (*Westminster Gazette,* January, 1896)

Half-cocked is used adjectivally to mean 'ill-prepared, ill-considered' and by extension 'foolish, silly, inane.'

head over heels See **INTENSITY.**

jump the gun To begin prematurely; to start early with the prospect of gaining an advantage. This expression's origin lies in the false starts made by runners before the firing of the pistol that signals the race's start. The phrase maintains common usage in the United States and Great Britain.

> The Prime Minister has jumped the gun by announcing that it will take the form of government advances to building societies. (*Economist,* November, 1958)

on the spur of the moment See **SPONTANEITY.**

pell-mell In a recklessly hurried fashion; in a confused or disordered manner. This expression is derived from the medieval French sport *pelle-melle,* in which the object was to knock a ball through a hoop suspended at the end of an alley. Known as *pall-mall* in England, this sport involved much reckless, headlong rushing of the players into the alley, inspiring the coinage of the term *pell-mell* to describe this frenzied scurrying.

> We were an absurd party of zealots, rushing pell-mell upon the floes with vastly more energy than discretion. (Elisha Kane, *The U.S. Grinnell [First] Expedition in Search of Sir John Franklin,* 1853)

take the ball before the bound See **ALERTNESS.**

trigger-happy Impetuous, reckless, rash, irresponsible; overanxious, overeager; overly critical, quick to point out mistakes and faults in others. This term originally referred to an overeager gunman just itching to pull the trigger of his gun and cut somebody down. The term has since become generalized and is now applied to anyone inclined to hasty or ill-advised actions.

IMPROBABILITY

as a pig loves marjoram Not at all. This now rarely heard emphatic rejoinder derives from the maxim of the Roman poet Lucretius: *Amaricinum fugitat sus* 'swine shun marjoram.'

Chinaman's chance No chance at all; little or no prospect of gaining, achieving, or reaching one's immediate goal; the near certainty of being thwarted. It is assumed that the phrase derives from the days of the California gold rush (1849) when the Chinese immigrants were victims of discrimination and illtreatment. Minorities, specifically the Chinese, were denied the opportunity of "striking it rich" and partaking of the "American Dream."

dark horse An unlikely winner, a long shot; an unfamiliar or unexpected candidate for political office; a person whose abilities and potential are unknown. The term originally referred to a horse whose ability and promise were kept secret until the day of the race. The evolution of the phrase's figurative meaning in American politics is obvious. A political candidate whose nomination is the result of a compromise is often called a *dark horse.*

in a pig's eye No way, not on your life, fat chance. The phrase carries the conviction of absolute certainty, in the negative sense; it is often spoken with a degree of disgust or contentiousness, in response to another's expression of optimism or likelihood. No origin or explanation of this frequently used phrase has been found. A remote possibility is that it relates to a once popular shipboard game "placing the pig's eye," in which the figure of a pig was outlined on the deck, and blindfolded passengers or crew had to place an object representative of a pig's eye in the proper anatomical position. Their chances of success were slim at best.

a snowball's chance in hell No chance at all, absolutely no possibility; also, *a snowflake's chance in hell;* usually in the phrase *as much chance as a snowball in hell.* This self-evident American slang expression has been in use since 1931.

IMPROPRIETY

beyond the pale Beyond the limits of propriety or courtesy; outside the bounds of civilized behavior. The word *pale* comes from the Latin *palus* 'stake' (cf. *palisade*), hence an enclosing or confining barrier; limits or boundaries. The phrase originally had a more literal meaning (still sometimes used today) 'outside an enclosed area' and by extension, 'outside one's jurisdiction or territory.'

cross [someone's] bows See VEXATION.

do you know Dr. Wright of Norwich?
A mildly sarcastic comment made to someone at a dinner party who does not pass the decanter, preventing other guests from helping themselves to wine. The popular story which gives the background for this British expression involves a man known as Dr. Wright of Norwich, a charming guest and gifted conversationalist. Asking a dinner guest, "Do you know Dr. Wright of Norwich?" implies that the person is holding up the decanter, as Dr. Wright was wont to do, but unlike the good Doctor, not compensating for this breach of manners by entertaining the company with enlivening conversation.

gate crasher One who attends a social affair, athletic event, etc., without the proper admission credentials; an uninvited, unwanted guest. This expression has entered into wide use among the youthful, concert-going crowd in reference to their more belligerent peers who sneak or force their ways into crowded rock concerts. The term is literally used for persons who gain entry to an event by actually smashing down barriers. The phrase has been in use for most of this century.

> "One-eyed Connolly," the champion American "gate crasher" (one who gains admittance to big sporting events without payment.) (*Daily News,* June, 1927)

pigs in clover Well-to-do and supposedly refined people who act in a boorish manner; parvenus. Figuratively, a pig is a person with the characteristics or habits commonly associated with that animal, while *in clover* implies luxury or wealth; hence the expression. See also **in clover,** AFFLUENCE.

put one's foot in one's mouth To say something inappropriate, gauche, or indiscreet; to commit a verbal faux pas. This expression implies that by saying something out of line, a person has figuratively put his foot in his mouth, an imprudent and untoward activity in any situation. A variation is *put one's foot in it.*

> I put my foot into it (as we say), for I was nearly killed. (Frederick Marryat, *Peter Simple,* 1833)

A related, more contemporary expression is *foot-in-mouth disease,* a play on hoof-and-mouth disease of cattle, and a jocular reference to an affliction in which a person exhibits a marked tendency to constantly "put his foot in his mouth."

sail close to the wind To act in a manner that verges on the illegal, immoral, or improper; to say or do something that borders on being in bad taste; to observe the letter but not the spirit of the law. Literally, to sail close to the wind is to head one's ship into the wind at enough of an angle to keep the sails filled. This is a risky tactic as the ship is in constant danger of being in irons if there is even a slight change in the wind direction. Figuratively, this expression implies that one's words or actions put him in a precarious position because they are so close to the limits of propriety.

> A certain kind of young English gentleman, who has sailed too close to the wind at home, and who comes to the colony to be whitewashed. (Henry Kingsley, *The Hillyars and the Burtons*, 1865)

A variation is *sail near to the wind*.

step on toes To upset, offend, or irritate, especially by encroaching on someone's territory; to overstep one's bounds. Literally stepping on someone's toes is a violation of space or territory. On a figurative level, the "territory" usually refers to one's area of responsibility or realm of authority. The expression is often said of an upstart who prematurely assumes authority or responsibility delegated to someone else. An *OED* citation dates the expression from the 14th century, but whether the use was literal or figurative is difficult to determine.

IMPROVEMENT (See **REFORMATION**.)

IMPROVIDENCE

butter-and-egg man See **OAFISHNESS**.

butter one's bread on both sides To be wasteful or extravagant; also, to gain favor from two sides at once, to work both sides of the street. The two different figurative meanings of this expression, which dates from 1821, neatly express the two sides of the single literal action to which it refers, i.e., unnecessary indulgence and prudent foresight.

from hand to mouth See **PRECARIOUSNESS**.

pay too dearly for one's whistle See **COST**.

penny wise and pound foolish Said of a person who is prudent or thrifty in small or trivial matters but careless in large or important ones. This expression, with its obvious implications, refers to two denominations of British money, the penny and the pound.

play ducks and drakes with To waste or squander, to spend foolishly or recklessly; also *to make ducks and drakes of*; usually in reference to money or time.

> His Majesty's Government never intended to give over the British army to the Governors of this Kingdom to make ducks and drakes with. (Arthur Wellesley, Duke of Wellington, *Dispatches*, 1810)

Ducks and drakes is the name of a game or pastime which consists of skipping flat, smooth stones across the surface of water. Thus, to play ducks and drakes with one's money is to throw it away, as if using coins instead of stones. Also, to spend one's time playing ducks and drakes is to waste one's time in idle pleasure. Use of the expression dates from at least 1600.

scattergood A spendthrift, squanderer, profligate; a big spender. This term is a combination of *scatter* 'to throw loosely about' and *good[s]* 'valuables.'

> You have heard what careless scattergoods all honest sailors are. (Richard Blackmore, *Tommy Upmore*, 1884)

send the helve after the hatchet To be reckless; to throw away what remains because the losses have been so great; to send good money after bad; also *throw the helve after the hatchet*. The allusion is to the fable of the woodcutter who lost the head of his ax in a river, and then, in disgust, threw the helve, or handle, in after it. John Heywood used the phrase in a collection of proverbs published in 1546.

spare at the spigot and spill at the bung To be frugal in inconsequential matters while being wasteful in important affairs. This expression alludes to the foolishness of a person who halts the outflow of a cask at the spigot while allowing the orifice through which the cask is replenished to remain open. The saying, synonymous with the common phrase *penny wise and pound foolish,* is now virtually obsolete.

spend money like a drunken sailor To spend money extravagantly or foolishly, to throw money away. This self-evident expression enjoys widespread popular use.

IMPRUDENCE (See also **IMPROVI-DENCE.**)

cast pearls before swine To offer something precious to those who are unable to appreciate its worth; to give a valuable gift to someone who responds by abusing or defiling it. The phrase, which derives from the Sermon on the Mount, is still current today.

> Give not that which is holy unto the dogs, neither cast your pearls before swine, lest haply they trample them under their feet, and turn and rend you. (Matthew 7:6)

put new wine in old bottles To take inappropriate action; to fail to make the measures fit the need; to impose greater stress than the recipient can bear. Though this expression most often refers to the imposition of newness or change where age will resist it, the phrase's application is not restricted to contexts of time disparity. Old wineskins lack the extensibility of new and consequently burst under the pressure of fermentation. The *wineskins* of the original Biblical context in the course of time became *bottles,* to the detriment of the phrase's clarity of meaning.

> Neither is new wine put into old wineskins; if it is the skins burst, and the wine is spilled and the skins are destroyed: but new wine is put into fresh wineskins, and so both are preserved. (Matthew 9:17)

reckon without one's host To act, plan, or conclude without adequate consideration of significant factors or circumstances; to fail to take into account the role of others, particularly those whose position would make their input determinative. The expression was originally literal; to reckon without one's host was to calculate food or lodging expenses without first consulting the innkeeper. This early meaning, dating from the 17th century, has been totally lost in the now figurative one indicating shortsightedness, improvidence, or lack of foresight.

> He reckoned strangely in this matter, without the murderous host into whose clutches he had fallen. (John A. Symonds, *The Renaissance in Italy,* 1886)

a rolling stone gathers no moss A proverb meaning that one with nomadic tendencies is unlikely to prosper. This expression, equivalents of which exist in numerous other cultures, was popularized in the English language following its use in Thomas Tusser's *Five Hundred Points of Good Husbandrie* (1573). A stationary stone accumulates moss which protects it from erosion and weathering. Likewise, one who settles down is more likely to amass a fortune than one whose life is spent wandering from place to place. The expression maintains widespread usage today.

> The sudden turning up of Jack as a roving brother, who, like a rolling stone, gathered no moss. (Sarah Tytler, *Buried Diamonds,* 1886)

send a sow to Minerva A proverb said of one who presumes to teach another, more learned person something that he already knows. This expression is derived from an ancient Latin adage, *sus Minervam docet* 'a pig teaching Minerva,' alluding to the inappropriateness of something as ignorant as a pig trying to instruct the goddess of wisdom.

> In Latin they say *sus Minervam* when an unlearned dunce goeth about to teach his better or a more learned man, . . . or as we say in English, the foul sow teach the fair lady to spin. (Edward Topsell, *The History of Four-Footed Beasts*, 1607)

swap horses in midstream To change leaders during a crisis; to change the rules after the game has started; to change one's approach, to alter one's method at an unpropitious time. This Americanism is attributed to Abraham Lincoln. On June 9, 1864, after his renomination to the presidency, Lincoln delivered a speech in which he alluded to the fact that he was reelected even though many felt that he had mismanaged the War Between the States:

> . . . they have concluded it is not best to swap horses while crossing the river, . . . I am not so poor a horse that they might not make a botch of it in trying to swap.

The expression nearly always appears as part of an admonition not to do so.

teach one's grandmother to suck eggs A proverb, said of one who tries to teach or advise an older and more experienced person. This adage, similar in spirit to *teach a bird to fly* and *teach a fish to swim*, alludes to the inappropriateness of trying to teach a person something which he already knows. It is usually used in derisive reference to someone, particularly an adolescent, who is presumptuous enough to think that his new-found knowledge is so unique that his elders could not possibly be privy to it and so takes it upon himself to educate them. Specifically, this expression refers to the technique— usually passed from generation to generation—of sucking out the contents of an egg through a small hole in one end

without breaking the shell, a skill important to one who wishes to decorate Easter eggs, for example. An anonymous English poem captures the sentiments of this ancient proverb:

> Teach not a parent's mother to extract
> The embryo juices of an egg by suction:
> The good old lady can the feat enact
> Quite irrespective of your kind instruction.

Although the expression had fallen into disuse by the mid-1900s, it was revitalized in 1978 by its inclusion in one of the routines of comedian Steve Martin.

IMPULSIVENESS (See **IMPETUOUSNESS**.)

INAPPROPRIATENESS

carry coals to Newcastle To bring something to a place where it is naturally abundant; hence, to do something wholly superfluous or unnecessary. Newcastle lies in the heart of England's great coal-mining region. The equivalent French expression is *porter de l'eau à la rivière* 'carry water to the river.'

caviar to the general Something too sophisticated or subtle to be appreciated by hoi-polloi; beyond the taste of the general public. This expression derives from Shakespeare's *Hamlet:*

> The play, I remember, pleased not the million; 'twas caviar to the general. (II,ii)

In this line, "general" refers to the general public, the common people. Caviar, of course, is the very expensive gustatory delicacy prepared from sturgeon roe. It is a food appreciated only by those who have acquired a taste for it.

send owls to Athens To do something completely useless, unnecessary, or extraneous; to carry coals to Newcastle; also *to carry owls to Athens.*

I may be thought to pour water into the sea, to carry owls to Athens, and to trouble the reader with a matter altogether needless and superfluous. (Henry Swinburne, *A Brief Treatise of Testaments and Last Wills*, 1590)

The owl, as emblem of the Greek goddess Athena, patron of Athens, was naturally plentiful in that area.

INANITY (See FATUOUSNESS.)

INCLUSIVENESS (See also THOROUGHNESS, TOTALITY.)

across-the-board General; all-inclusive and comprehensive; treating all groups or all members of a group equally and without exception. The term refers to the board used to display the betting odds and totals at race tracks. An across-the-board bet is a combination wager in which the same amount of money is bet on a single horse to win, place, or show, thereby ensuring a winning ticket if the horse places at all. The original sporting use of the term dates from about 1935; the more general usage dates from about 1950.

all along the line At every point; in every particular or detail; entirely, completely. Common variants include *all down the line* and *right down the line*. What the original line was, if indeed one did exist, is uncertain. The expression does, however, seem to presuppose some sort of actual line, be it a line of soldiers going into battle, a geographical line of some kind, or any of the other sundry types of lines that exist. Charles Haddon Spurgeon used the phrase in *The Treasury of David* (1877).

bag and baggage With all one's personal belongings; completely, totally. This phrase was military in origin and applied to the possessions of an army as a whole (baggage), and of each individual soldier (bag). The original expression *to march out [with] bag and bag-* *gage* was used in a positive sense to mean to make an honorable retreat, to depart without having suffered any loss of property. The equivalent French expression was *vie et bagues sauves.* The term is now used disparagingly, however, to underscore the absolute nature of one's departure; it implies quite the opposite of an honorable retreat. Used in the original military sense in 1525 by John Bourchier Berners in his translation of Froissart's *Chronicles,* the phrase did not appear in its more contemporary sense until the early 17th century in Thomas Middleton's *The Witch.*

every man Jack Every single person without exception. The precise origin of this phrase is unknown. A plausible but not entirely convincing theory traces the source of *every man Jack* to the early form *everych one* 'every one,' which in the 16th and 17th centuries was often written as *every chone.* By corruption, *every chone* became *every John,* and since *Jack* is the familiar form of *John,* the phrase was corrupted once again giving rise to the current form *every man Jack.* Thackeray used the phrase in *Vanity Fair.*

Sir Pitt had numbered every "Man Jack" of them.

Thackeray's use of quotation marks and capitalization of *man* casts doubt on the theory of the origin of *every man Jack* presented above.

everything but the kitchen sink Everything imaginable, everything under the sun; also *everything but the kitchen stove.* Both expressions date from the first half of this century, although *everything but the kitchen stove* predated *everything but the kitchen sink* by about twenty years according to the *OED* citations. In his *Dictionary of Forces' Slang* (1948) Partridge says that *kitchen sink* was "used only in the phrase indicating intense bombardment—'They chucked everything they'd got at us, except, or including the kitchen sink.' " In other words, every possible kind of missile, including kitchen sinks.

from Dan to Beersheba From one outermost extreme or limit to the other; everywhere. This expression is based on a Biblical reference:

Then all the children of Israel went out, and the congregation was gathered together as one man, from Dan to Beersheba. (Judges 20:1)

Judges 19 and 20 discusses the reasons that all of the Israelite nations gathered to attack the Benjamites. Dan was the northernmost city in Israel, Beersheba the southernmost. Thus, from Dan to Beersheba implied the entire kingdom. In more contemporary usage, this expression is often employed by political writers to describe the extent of a person or issue's popularity.

from soup to nuts From A to Z, from first to last; everything, usually in the phrase *everything from soup to nuts.* This American slang expression alludes to an elaborate multicourse meal in which soup is served as the first course and nuts as the last.

Today's drug stores may have everything from soup to nuts, but they can't boast fascinating remedies like Gambler's Luck, Virgin's Milk, . . . or Come-Follow-Me-Boy. (*New Orleans Times-Picayune Magazine,* April, 1950)

from stem to stern Completely; entirely; from one end to the other. On ships the stem is the forward part of the vessel, and the stern is the rear. The phrase maintains common figurative use.

I had him stripped and washed from stem to stern in a tub of warm soapsuds. (Elizabeth Drinker, *Journal,* 1794)

ragtag and bobtail See STATUS.

right and left From all directions at once, everywhere you look, on all sides; every time, repeatedly. This phrase implying inclusiveness or ubiquity dates from the beginning of the 14th century.

Webster's Third cites both current usages:

troops looting right and left. (A. N. Dragnich)

social events . . . have been rained out right and left. (*Springfield Daily News*)

run the gamut To include the full range of possibilities; to extend over a broad spectrum; to embrace extremes and all intermediate degrees of intensity. The gamut is the whole series of notes recognized by musicians. The term was used figuratively by the 18th century; Hogarth referred to "the painter's gamut."

The stocks were running . . . up and down the gamut from $1 to $700 a share. (*Harper's Magazine,* 1883)

The vitriolic wit of Dorothy Parker once described an actress's performance as "running the gamut of emotion from A to B."

Tom, Dick, and Harry Men, or people in general; everyone, everyone and his uncle. The phrase, usually preceded by *every,* has been popular in America since 1815, when it appeared in *The Farmer's Almanack.* Tom, Dick, and Harry are all very common men's first names and so are used in this expression to represent average, run-of-the-mill people. Although first used only in reference to men, the phrase is currently applied to everyone, male or female.

the whole kit and caboodle The whole lot, the whole bunch; the entire outfit; also *the whole kit and boodle, the whole kit and biling, the whole kit, the whole boodle, the whole caboodle.* The word *caboodle* or *boodle* in this expression is probably a corruption of the Dutch *boedel* 'property, possessions, household goods.' The phrase has been in use since 1861.

the whole shooting match Everyone and everything, the whole shebang; the entire matter or affair, the whole deal, the whole ball of wax.

You are not the whole shooting match, but a good share of it. (*Springfield* [Mass.] *Weekly Republican*, March, 1906)

A literal shooting match is a contest or competition in marksmanship, but how it gave rise to this popular American slang expression is unclear.

INDEBTEDNESS (See also **POVERTY**.)

in the hole In debt; in financial difficulties. The story behind this U.S. slang expression has to do with proprietors in gambling houses taking an amount of money out of the pots as a percentage due the "house." When money must be paid up, one "goes to the hole" with a check. The "hole" is a slot cut in the middle of the poker table leading to a locked compartment below. All the checks "in the hole" become the property of the keeper of the place. The gamblers' losses were the keeper's gain. *In the hole* has been popular since the 1890s, although *put [someone] in the hole* 'to swindle or defraud' dates from the early 1800s.

How in the world did you manage to get in the hole for a sum like that? (P. G. Wodehouse, *Uncle Fred in Springtime*, 1939)

in the ketchup Operating at a deficit; in debt; failing to show a profit. *Ketchup* is a more graphic term than *red* but the meaning of *in the ketchup* is synonymous with *in the red*. The former, a slang expression of U.S. origin, dates from the mid-1900s.

Ridgway . . . has wound up in the ketchup trying to operate a gym. (Dan Parker, *Daily Mirror*, September 11, 1949)

in the red Operating at a deficit; in debt. This 20th-century colloquial Americanism is so called from the bookkeeping practice of entering debits in red ink. The opposite *out of the red* 'out of debt' (or *in the black*) is also current.

Rigid enforcement of economies in running expenses will lift the club's balance sheet out of the red where it now is. (*Mazama*, June 1, 1948)

lame duck See **INEFFECTUALITY**.

lose one's shirt See **FAILURE**.

on the rocks Ruined, especially financially; hence, bankrupt, destitute. The concept, but no record of the actual phrase, dates from the days when a merchant's wealth depended on the safety of ships at sea. Shipwreck—or going on the rocks—meant financial disaster. In Shakespeare's *Merchant of Venice*, Salarino asks Antonio:

Should I . . . not bethink me straight of dangerous rocks,
Which touching but my gentle vessel's side
Would scatter all her spices on the stream,
Enrobe the roaring waters with my silks—
And, in a word, but even now worth this,
And now worth nothing? (I,i)

over one's head See **PREDICAMENT**.

take a bath See **FAILURE**.

washed out See **FAILURE**.

INDECISIVENESS (See **INEFFECTUALITY, VACILLATION**.)

INDEPENDENCE (See also **SELF-RELIANCE**.)

independent as a hog on ice Cockily self-assured; pigheadedly independent.

He don't appear to care nothing for nobody—he's "independent as a hog on ice." (*San Francisco Call*, April, 1857)

It has been unconvincingly conjectured that this American expression, popular since the 1800s, derives from the Scottish ice game of curling in which *hog* refers to a pucklike stone that stops short of its goal, thus coming to rest and sitting sluggishly immovable on the ice.

But no other proffered explanation appears plausible either. The puzzling simile nevertheless continues on in popular usage.

> They like to think of themselves as independents—independent as a hog on ice. (*Time*, August, 1948)

lone wolf A loner; one who, although leading an active social life, chooses not to divulge his personal philosophies; a person who pursues neither close friendship nor intimate relationships. Although most wolves live in small packs, some choose to live and hunt solitarily. The expression's contemporary usage often carries an implication of aloofness to or disillusionment with the mainstream of society.

> An individualist to be watched unless he should develop into too much of a lone wolf. (G. F. Newman, *Sir, You Bastard*, 1970)

march to the beat of a different drummer To follow the dictates of one's own conscience instead of prevailing convention; to act in accord with one's own feelings instead of following the crowd; also, to be odd or eccentric. This expression comes from these now famous words of Henry David Thoreau in *Walden, or Life in the Woods* (1854):

> If a man does not keep pace with his companions, perhaps it is because he hears a different drummer. Let him step to the music which he hears, however measured or far away.

If one man in a marching column is out of step, it may look as if he is marching to the beat of another drummer, or as if he is simply "out of it." Such a one is considered either an independent or an eccentric.

maverick An intractable or refractory person; a person who adheres to unconventional or unpopular ideals that set him apart from society's mainstream; a dissenter, a loner. This expression is credited to the early 19th-century Texas rancher Samuel Maverick, who consistently neglected to brand his cattle, and it still maintains its meaning of an unbranded cow, steer, or calf. Through allusion to these unmarked cattle, *maverick* evolved its now more common nonconformist sense by the late 1800s:

> A very muzzy Maverick smote his sergeant on the nose. (Rudyard Kipling, *Life's Handicaps*, 1892)

In the United States the expression has developed the additional meaning of a politician who resists affiliation with the established political parties, or whose views differ significantly from those of his fellow party members.

> One Republican Senator, and by no means a conspicuous maverick, pointed out that the Senate might have acted. (*Chicago Daily News*, 1948)

mugwump A politically independent person; a person who is indecisive or neutral on controversial issues. This expression is derived from the Algonquian Indian word *mogkiomp* 'great man, big chief,' and was first used by Charles A. Dana of the *New York Sun* in reference to the Republicans who declined to support their party's 1884 presidential candidate, James G. Baine. The term thus evolved its current figurative sense of a political maverick.

> A few moments after Secretary Wallace made his pun, he hastened to add that he himself had been a mugwump. (*Tuscaloosa News*, March, 1946)

A jocular origin is ascribed to the word: a *mugwump* is one who sits on the fence, with his *mug* on one side and his *wump* on the other. In addition to its political sense, the British use *mugwump* to describe a self-important person who assumes airs and behaves in an aloof or pompous manner.

sail against the wind To think or act independently of popular or accepted convention, opinion, trends, etc.; to march to the beat of a different drummer. This expression refers to the difficulty of sailing into a wind in order to reach one's destination. Although *sail against the wind* is sometimes applied figuratively to a person who is inflexible and stubborn, it more often refers to one who does not succumb to peer or social pressure, but rather pursues his own course irrespective of the opinions and customs of others.

INDETERMINATENESS

between hawk and buzzard Hovering in the balance between two extremes; caught in the middle; neither one nor the other. The early uses of this phrase, dating from the early 17th century, were based on the disparity between a hawk and a buzzard, although they are both birds of prey. According to the *OED,* the buzzard is an inferior type of hawk, useless for falconry. Elsewhere, the hawk is referred to as a "true sporting bird," and the buzzard is called a "heavy lazy fowl of the same species." Thus, *hawk* has positive connotations and *buzzard* negative. Brewer's 1895 edition of *The Dictionary of Phrase and Fable* makes reference to tutors, governesses, etc., as being "between hawk and buzzard" because they are neither masters and mistresses nor lowly servants. The phrase is also sometimes used in referring to twilight, which is neither day nor night. Therefore, anything that is caught in the tension between two extremes, such as good and bad, light and dark, high and low, is "between hawk and buzzard."

between hay and grass Neither one thing nor the other; indeterminate; in an in-between and undefinable stage. Just as a hobbledehoy is neither a man nor a boy, something is between hay and grass when it cannot be categorized or fitted into a slot.

neither fish nor flesh nor good red herring Neither this nor that; a person of uncertain or oscillating principles. This phrase originated in medieval England, where, on certain fast days, all strata of society abstained from their staple foods; monks abstained from fish, the general populace abstained from meat, and beggars abstained from herring. In its figurative sense, this term refers to a nondescript object or a wishy-washy person.

> Damned neuters, in their middle way of steering,
> Are neither fish nor flesh nor good red herring.
> (John Dryden, "Epilogue" to *The Duke of Guise,* 1682)

INDIFFERENCE

have other fish to fry To have other, more important matters to attend to; to have better things to do or more pressing business to occupy one's time and attention. A stock phrase used to give someone the brush-off, this expression dates from the 17th century. It implies that one has no time to waste on unimportant (usually someone else's) concerns.

> "I've got other things in hand . . . I've got other fish to fry." (Margaret Oliphant, *A Poor Gentleman,* 1889)

not give a continental To be so scornful as to refuse to give something even so worthless as a continental. The continental was paper scrip issued by the Continental Congress during the American Revolution and was considered to be of virtually no value as a medium of exchange.

not give a damn Not to care, not to be concerned, to have no interest or stake in. *Damn* is a mild obscenity which has no connection with the practically worthless old Indian coin, a dam, as has been repeatedly and mistakenly conjectured.

> It was obvious, as one angry young woman remarked, that he didn't give a damn—and so they were enraged. (J. Cary, *Captive and Free,* 1959)

not give a fig To be indifferent or actively hostile toward. The term *fig* has been in use since 1450 to denote a worthless or insignificant object. Some trace this meaning to ancient Greece where figs were so plentiful as to be worth little or nothing. Others relate it to the *fig* or *fico* of the phrase *to give the fig* (INSULT). Shakespeare plays on the two senses of the term in *Henry V:*

A figo for thy friendship!—
The fig of Spain. (III,iv)

not give a hoot To be indifferent toward, to be totally unconcerned about. *Hoot* in this expression is short for *hooter,* which in turn is thought to be a corruption of *iota* 'a whit, a jot.' Although the abbreviated form *hoot* did not appear until the early 20th century, *hooter* was in use in this and similar phrases during the 19th century. *Not give a hoot* has combined with the similar expression *not give a continental* to form the currently popular *not give a continental hoot.* See **not worth a continental, WORTHLESSNESS.**

I do not give a hoot if it's colder, and I do not give two hoots what any given cabbie thinks about it. (*The Chicago Sun,* November, 1947)

not give a rap Not to care or be concerned about. A rap was a counterfeit coin worth about half a farthing which was circulated in Ireland during the 18th century due to the shortage of genuine currency. The worthlessness and neglibility of the literal rap gave rise to the figurative expression.

For the mare-with-three-legs [the gallows], boys, I care not a rap. (William Harrison Ainsworth, *Rookwood,* 1834)

not give a tinker's dam To care so little as not to give even something without value; also, *not give a tinker's damn.* Conflicting views are current as to the origin of this expression. A *dam* is a worthless bit of metal used (by tinkers, among others) to keep molten solder in a certain place till it has cooled and solidified. On the other hand, itinerant tinkers were considered of the lowest

class, traditionally ill-mannered and given to the use of foul language. To such a one, *damn* may have been so mild an obscenity as to have no meaning in a string of invective.

INDIVIDUALITY

bag Personal style; special interest or point of view; manner of playing jazz. *Bag* was originally a jazz term referring to a particular musical conception, style, attack, etc. By extension, it came to be applied to any aspect of a person's characteristic style, such as one's values, interests, motivations, or actions. It is probably an abbreviation of *bag of tricks.*

I dig everything about this lady, but what was her bag? (B. B. Johnson, *Death of a Blue-Eyed Soul Brother,* 1970)

See also **bag of tricks, PLOY.**

the cut of one's jib One's outward appearance or manner, a person's characteristic demeanor or countenance; often in the phrases *to like* or *dislike the cut of one's jib.* This expression, which dates from at least 1823, is of nautical origin. A jib is a triangular foresail by which sailors formerly identified the nationality of passing ships and thus recognized them as friend or foe.

a fine Italian hand A distinctive or characteristic style; subtle craftiness. The literal Italian hand is the graceful penmanship which replaced the heavy Gothic script of northern Europe in the 17th century, and is now used throughout Western Europe and America. Figuratively, *a fine Italian hand* may refer to that characteristic or distinguishing quality of an object or work of art which identifies its creator. In its more negative sense, however, this expression describes a cunning scheme in which the plotter's identity is revealed through his subtle yet intrinsic design.

hallmark See **GENUINENESS.**

INDOLENCE   (See also IDLENESS.)

bed of roses   A situation or state of ease, comfort, or pleasure; the lap of luxury. This phrase and its variants *bed of down* or *flowers* were used as early as the first half of the 17th century by Shakespeare and Herrick, among others. The rose is a symbol of perfection and completeness, giving it more weight than *down* or *flowers*, which may account for why *bed of roses* is the preferred form today. The expression is often used in the negative, as *no bed of roses*, to emphasize the disparity between what is and what could be.

dolce far niente   Delightful idleness, carefree indolence; relaxation, peacefulness, tranquillity. Attesting to the great appeal of such a lifestyle is the fact that equivalent phrases have appeared in different languages dating back to the Roman writer Pliny. English use of the Italian *dolce far niente* 'sweet doing nothing' dates from at least the turn of the 19th century.

> It is there . . . that the dolce far niente of a summer evening is most heavenly. (Henry Wadsworth Longfellow, *Life*, 1830)

live in cotton wool   See INEXPERIENCE.

lotus-eater   An idle dreamer, one who lives a life of indolence and ease. The lotus-eaters or lotophagi are a mythical people found in Homer's *Odyssey*. Odysseus discovers them in a state of dreamy forgetfulness and contentment induced by their consumption of the legendary lotus fruit. Having lost all desire to return to their homelands, they want only to remain in Lotus-land living a life of idle luxury. Use of the term dates from the first half of the 19th century.

> A summer like that of 1893 may be all very well for the lotus-eater, but is a calamity to people who have to get their living out of English land. (*The Times*, December, 1893)

woolgathering   Daydreaming, idle imagining or fantasizing; absent-mindedness, preoccupation, abstraction; often *to go woolgathering.*

> Ha' you summoned your wits from wool-gathering? (Thomas Middleton, *The Family of Love*, 1607)

Although the practice of woolgathering (wandering about the countryside collecting tufts of sheep's wool caught on bushes) is virtually obsolete, the figurative term is still current.

INEFFECTUALITY   (See also FUTILITY.)

all talk and no cider   All talk and no action; much ado about nothing; great cry and little wool. This colloquial Americanism dates from the turn of the 19th century. The popular story explaining its origin tells of a party supposedly organized for the purpose of sharing a barrel of superior cider. Apparently the subject of politics was introduced and its talk supplanted pleasure and drinking as the focal point of the party. Disappointed guests left the gathering with the complaint of "all talk and no cider."

> Fine stories are cold comfort, when it is as they say "All talk and no cider." (Nelson Kingsley, *Diary*, 1849)

beat one's gums   See TALKATIVENESS.

cut no ice   To have no effect or influence; to fail to impress; to carry no weight, to mean nothing; also *to cut ice* meaning 'to impress, to make an effect,' although the phrase is almost exclusively used in the negative. In common usage since the late 19th century, the expression apparently owes its coinage to the fact that only keen and strong instruments can make an impression on the hard and glossy surface of ice.

go in one ear and out the other   To be heard but not heeded; to be ignored or forgotten; to make no impact or impression. The implication here is that whatever is being said does not stay inside the listener's head because he is empty-headed; information just passes straight through to the other side. A variant of this expression dates from 1400.

great cry and little wool Much ado about nothing; a lot of fuss and bother with little or nothing to show for it; also *more cry than wool.* Stephen Gosson relates the proverbial origin of this expression in *The School of Abuse* (1579):

As one said at the shearing of hogs, great cry and little wool, much ado and small help.

A similar current phrase is *all talk and no action.*

guinea pig See VICTIMIZATION.

lame duck An elected public official who is completing his term in office but has not been reelected; a stockbroker or speculator who has lost a great deal of money, or who has committed himself (through stock options, buying on margin, etc.) to more than he can afford; an inefficient or injured person. In the United States, this expression is usually political in nature, while in England, it is financial. *Lame duck* refers to an injured bird which is unable to care for itself and waddles around aimlessly as it awaits its imminent death. The implication is that a lame duck politician has, in essence, been rendered impotent; he is without a constituency and without bargaining clout—thus totally ineffective.

A "lame duck" Administration was in power, and a "lame duck" Congress still in being. (*Times,* December 14, 1932)

In 1933, Congress approved the 20th Amendment to the Constitution of the United States, popularly known as the *Lame Duck Amendment* because it provided that newly elected Senators and Representatives would assume office on January 3 instead of March 4, thus reducing the length of the Congressional lame duck period. The Amendment also set the date for the presidential inauguration on January 20 instead of March 4.

like water off a duck's back See EFFORTLESSNESS.

man of straw See VICTIMIZATION.

mealy-mouthed Indecisive; compromising or vacillating; namby-pamby; afraid or disinclined to assert oneself; timidly soft-spoken or mincing; avoiding plain and direct language. This expression alludes to the concept of *meal* 'ground grain' as dry, soft, and crumbly, lacking form or substance. A common variation is *mealy.*

He was not mealy-mouth'd, but would . . . have talked his mind to knights, or anybody. (Tom Ticklefoot, *Some Observations Upon the Late Trials of Sir George Wakeman,* 1679)

milk-and-water Insipid or jejune; lackluster, wishy-washy. This expression, alluding to the bland, vapid mixture that results when milk is diluted with water, is used to describe a person or thing virtually devoid of any interest, character, or vitality.

Change the milk-and-water style of your last memorial; assume a bolder tone. (*Journal of the American Congress,* 1783)

milksop A man who lacks courage and spunk; a spiritless, babyish man or youth. This term alludes to the obsolete meaning of *milksop* referring to an infant fed on only milk. Chaucer used the label figuratively in the 14th century. Today it sees little use except in literary contexts.

I ought to be d—n'd for having spoiled one of the prettiest fellows in the world, by making a milk-sop of him. (Henry Fielding, *Tom Jones,* 1749)

namby-pamby Wishy-washy; insipid, lacking character or strength; weak or indecisive; childishly cute or affectedly sentimental. This expression was first used in a 1726 poem nicknaming and ridiculing Ambrose Philips (1674–1749), who purportedly had written a children's verse employing affected, "cutesy" language.

Namby Pamby's little rhymes,
Little jingle, little chimes.
(Henry Carey, *Namby Pamby,* 1726)

Namby is a baby-talk corruption of the name Ambrose, and *pamby* is simply a nonsensical rhyming word. The expression received almost immediate acceptance and popularity. Though now extended to contexts such as affected or effeminate behavior, *namby-pamby* (or the unhyphenated *namby pamby*) is still most commonly used to describe inferior writing.

At a very advanced age he condescended to trifle in namby pamby rhymes. (James Boswell, *The Life of Samuel Johnson,* 1791)

paper tiger A person or thing that seems impressive or powerful but is, in actuality, weak or ineffectual; a sheep in wolf's clothing. Figuratively, a *tiger* is a brave or forceful person, one with the qualities associated with the feline tiger. Since *paper* implies flimsiness, *paper tiger* refers to any person or thing whose impressiveness is actually a façade, whose bark is worse than his bite. This expression, part of an ancient Oriental proverb, first received public attention in 1946 when Mao Tse-tung, leader of Communist China, accused the United States of being a "paper tiger." He repeated the charge during the Korean War, specifically in reference to President Truman. Although now applied in widely varying contexts, *paper tiger* remains an effective political invective:

I disagreed with nearly all of Mr. Hoffer's conclusions but one. That is where he stated that the Negro is doing battle with a paper tiger

when he aims his wrath at the white liberal. (*New York Times Magazine,* April 25, 1965)

wishy-washy Indecisive, insipid, vacillating, weak; namby-pamby; lacking quality, character, or strength. Originally, *wishy-washy* referred to a weak, watered-down drink or to soup that was so watery that it was devoid of substance. Eventually, the expression was applied in other contexts to describe persons or ideas of weak and unimpressive character.

A weak, wishy-washy man who had hardly any mind of his own to speak of. (Anthony Trollope, *The Last Chronicle of Barset,* 1867)

write on water To leave no lasting record, to make no permanent impression; also *to write in the dust, on sand,* or *on the wind.* The equivalent Latin phrase is *in aqua scribere.* This expression, a comment on the ephemerality of human life and works, is found in the epitaph of the English poet John Keats.

Here lies one whose name was writ in water.

INEXPERIENCE

babe in the woods A naive, unsuspecting person; one easily duped or victimized. Attempts to trace the term to a popular pantomime story well-known in Norfolk, England, are unconvincing. The conventional figurative associations of both *babe* (innocence, ingenuousness) and *woods* (complexity, darkness) seem explanation enough; the phrase's origin remains unknown.

first-of-May Novice, inexperienced, uninitiated. This expression dates back to the early part of this century when circuses toured the country throughout the late spring, summer, and fall. After the winter layover, the circus had to hire many new laborers and performers to assure that the tour would run smoothly and successfully. Generally, these people would be hired by the first of May so that they could be trained before the tour began; hence the expression *first-of-May*.

> These first-of-May guys are a little off time. (R. L. Taylor, in *The New Yorker*, April 19, 1952)

greenhorn An unsophisticated, inexperienced, or naive person; a dupe or fall guy; an immigrant or newcomer, an uninformed person. In the 15th century *greenhorn* applied to a young ox whose horns had not yet matured. By the 1700s the word referred to a raw, inexperienced person, and not until the turn of the century did *greenhorn* mean 'immigrant.' Today the term is most often used contemptuously to refer to any novice or unsuspecting person.

> I suppose you are not hoaxing us? It is, I know, sometimes thought allowable to take a greenhorn in. (Sir H. Rider Haggard, *King Solomon's Mines*, 1885)

little Lord Fauntleroy A naïve and unsophisticated child of gentle nature; an impeccably mannered and fastidiously dressed child. This eponym comes from the hero of Frances Hodgson Burnett's novel *Little Lord Fauntleroy* (1885). It is usually employed in an ironic tone, as in the following:

> Some little Lord Fauntleroy who had just found out there were rotters in the world. (D. Powell, *Time to be Born*, 1942)

Fauntleroy can also stand alone as an adjective describing a particular style of children's dress or hair style popularized in the book.

> Myself aged seven—thicklipped, Fauntleroy-haired. (Dylan Thomas, *Letters*, 1933)

live in cotton wool To be naïve, to lead a sheltered, protected existence. Cotton wool or absorbent cotton is the kind used as padding or wadding. In this British colloquial expression it symbolizes insulation from the harsh realities of life. The phrase was used earlier as a metaphor for superfluous comfort or luxury—insulation, once again, from the difficulties of everyday life.

> Letty would never be happy unless she lived in clover and cotton-wool. (Dinah M. Mulock, *The Woman's Kingdom*, 1869)

low man on the totem pole See STATUS.

pigeon See VICTIMIZATION.

salad days See AGE.

tenderfoot A greenhorn, a novice; a raw, inexperienced person.

> We saw a man in Sacramento when we were on our way here, who was a tenderfoot, or rawheel, or whatever you call 'em, who struck a pocket of gold. (*American Speech*, 1849)

This term originated in the American West where it was used to describe newcomers unaccustomed to the hardships of rugged life. It now applies to a person inexperienced in any area or endeavor.

wet behind the ears Immature, inexperienced, green; naïve, unsophisticated, innocent; also *not dry behind the ears*.

> Married! You're still wet behind the ears. (Ben Ames Williams, *It's a Free Country*, 1945)

At birth most animals are literally wet from the amniotic fluid previously surrounding them. The recessed area behind the ears is one of the last to become dry.

> They aren't dry behind the ears, so to speak, but still believe in Santa Claus. (*The Chicago Daily News*, August, 1945)

INFIDELITY

backdoor man An illicit lover; a person with whom one is having an affair. Such a one presumably enters by the back door to avoid being seen.

bedswerver An adulteress; a woman who strays from the marriage bed. Shakespeare used the term in *The Winter's Tale:*

> That she's
> A bedswerver, even as bad as those
> That vulgars give bold'st titles. (II,i)

cuckold This term for the unwitting husband of an unfaithful wife supposedly derives from the cuckoo bird's habit of depositing its eggs in other birds' nests. The theory would have more plausibility if the word were *cuckoo* itself and were applied not to the injured party but to the adulteress, as is the case in several other languages. According to Dr. Johnson, the cry of "cuckoo" was formerly used to inform the husband, who subsequently came to be dubbed by the term himself. But even this does not account for the transformation from *cuckoo* to *cuckold.* A possibly more plausible explanation may be that the suffix *-wold,* akin to *wild,* was coupled with *coke* 'cock' to create a compound meaning 'horn-mad,' which may well describe a frustrated husband's condition, in the circumstances. Compare **wittol.**

false as Cressida Unfaithful, perfidious; pledging love and fidelity while practicing cuckoldry and adultery; two-faced, hypocritical; traitorous. According to legend set during the Trojan War, Cressida, the daughter of a Trojan priest, had exchanged a pledge of everlasting love and fidelity with Troilus, her beloved. When Cressida was offered to the Greeks in exchange for a group of prisoners, the pledge of fidelity was renewed and sealed with an exchange of gifts. But Cressida had barely arrived in the Greek camp when she succumbed to the charms of Diomedes. To make her abandonment of Troilus even more bitter, she wanted Diomedes to wear Troilus' gift of a sleeve during their frequent encounters. The legend has been immortalized by Chaucer in *Troilus and Criseyde* and by Shakespeare:

> "Yea," let them say, to stick the heart of falsehood,
> "As false as Cressid."

(Troilus and Cressida, III,i)

hanky-panky See **MISCHIEF.**

wear the bull's feather To be cuckolded. The bull's feather was a symbol of cuckoldry. A 17th-century song entitled "The Bull's Feather" popularized this expression.

> It chanced not long ago as I was walking,
> An eccho did bring me where two were a talking,
> Twas a man said to his wife, dye had I rather,
> Than to be cornuted and wear a *bulls feather.*

wear the horns To be made a cuckold, to have an unfaithful wife. The association of horns with cuckoldry appears in many European languages, but no totally satisfactory explanation of the link has been offered. The most plausible relates the cuckold's "horns" to the spurs of a castrated rooster, formerly implanted at the roots of the excised comb where they reputedly grew into appendages resembling horns. The fact that the German word for *cuckold* formerly meant 'capon' lends considerable credence to this otherwise questionable account. Since the deceived husband has been symbolically stripped of his manhood, the association is logical as well. Whatever the connection, the usage was pervasive. The following appeared in *Hickscorner,* a pre-Shakespearean drama.

> My mother was a lady of the stews' blood born,
> And, . . . my father wore a horn.

wittol A husband who knows of—and tolerates—his wife's infidelity. The word is modeled on the older *cuckold,* with *wit-*'knowledge' as a prefix. Both *cuckold* and *wittol* trace back to Middle

English; the latter—at least the word—
is archaic. Compare **cuckold**.

INFORMATION

get a line on To obtain knowledge
about; to receive news of. In this expression, *line* often means an anticipated
tidbit of information:

> If you want to get a line on how
> she feels, she gave me a letter to
> give you . . . Here it is. (P. G.
> Wodehouse, *Luck of Botkins*, 1935)

The phrase is occasionally used by po-
licemen or journalists to indicate a hot
tip or lead obtained clandestinely.

get wind of To acquire advance information about something hitherto unknown; to get a hint of something about
to happen. This expression is derived
from the olfactory ability of animals to
detect the airborne scent of other animals. The phrase often refers to the at-
tainment of foreknowledge which warrants special action.

> They retreated again, when they
> got wind that troops were as-
> sembling. (Princess Alice, *Memoirs*,
> 1866)

low-down The inside scoop; the bare
facts. This common American colloquialism implies that the unadorned facts
lie at the bottom of a situation.

> One of the minions will . . . give
> me the official low-down on Fisher.
> Possible police record, etc. (M.
> Mackintosh, *King and Two Queens*,
> 1973)

scuttlebutt Gossip, hearsay; a vague,
unconfirmed rumor; also, *water-cooler
talk*. This expression originated in the
United States Navy, where the *scuttlebutt* 'water pail, drinking fountain'
was the scene of much idle chitchat.
The expression was carried over to civilian life, where it describes office rumors, many of which are created
around the water-cooler.

> And worry about a slump,
> according to business scuttlebutt, is
> making some unions concentrate on

share-the-job plans. (S. Dawson, AP
wire story, March, 1953)

stable push The inside scoop; information from reliable or important people.
This expression originated and is still
virtually confined to the horse-racing
world, where it refers to hot tips from
knowledgeable people concerning a
horse's prospects for victory.

straw vote An opinion poll; an unofficial vote taken to ascertain the relative
strength of political candidates or the
general trend of opinion on a given
issue. In the 19th and early 20th centuries in the United States, informal polls
were taken by handing out a piece of
straw to each of the voters who would
break the straw to signify a "nay" vote,
or leave it intact to signify approval.

> Straw votes, which have recently
> been taken in the New York State
> campaign, indicate that Mr. Hearst
> will be badly beaten. (*Daily
> Chronicle*, October 24, 1906)

A somewhat cynical evaluation of the
validity of a straw vote was once offered
by O. Henry in *Rolling Stones* (1913):

> A straw vote only shows which way
> the hot air blows.

white paper A government bulletin
which establishes the official position on
a specific topic. This term is derived
from the white binding of such publications. The expression is commonly used
in the United States and Great Britain
for the vast number of government re-
ports released to the public.

INGRATITUDE

bite the hand that feeds you To repay
the kindness of a benefactor with ill will
or injury; to act ungratefully. This expression, which dates from 1770, probably refers to the way a surly dog snaps
at the hand of the one who offers it food.

don't look a gift horse in the mouth
Don't be ungrateful or unapprecia-
tive, don't criticize or find fault with a
gift. The allusion is to someone so

rudely ungrateful that he would look into the mouth of a horse given to him as a present to check its age and condition.

> He would be a fool . . . to look such a gift horse in the mouth. (James Payn, *The Mystery of Mirbridge,* 1888)

A variant of this proverbial expression dates from at least 1546.

INITIATION (See also **BEGINNINGS.**)

baptism of fire An extremely trying initial experience; a first encounter which tests one to the utmost. The phrase applies literally to the first time a soldier faces battle fire, but even that usage was originally figurative. The expression has its origin in the early Christian belief that an as yet unbaptized believer who suffered martyrdom by fire was thereby baptized, i.e., received into the community of the faithful and consequently saved. A synonymous term for other kinds of martyrdom is *baptism of blood.* Conventional baptism is called *baptism of water.*

break the ice To initiate a conversation or make a friendly overture; to overcome existing obstacles, prepare the way; begin, dive in, get started. In the late 16th century, *break the ice* meant literally to facilitate a ship's passage by breaking the ice. Soon after, it was used figuratively in regard to any efforts made to begin a new project or to upset the status quo of a stalemate, deadlock, impasse or such. In modern figurative use, *break the ice* is heard mostly in the context of interpersonal relationships. Any attempt to cut through another person's reserve is considered "breaking the ice."

> I availed myself of a pause in the conversation to break the ice in relation to the topic which lay nearest my heart. (Henry Rogers, *The Eclipse of Faith,* 1853)

get one's feet wet To get a start in or begin something new; to get one's first

taste of, to get the feel of. The allusion is probably to the way a bather tests the water by putting his toes or feet in before committing himself to total immersion.

get the ball rolling To initiate or begin; to assume active leadership of a project, event, or other matter; to set an activity in motion. This expression probably originated in the ancient British game of *bandy,* a hockeylike sport in which players kept a ball in constant motion as they attempted to score points by getting it in the goal of the opponent. A variation is *start the ball rolling.*

A related expression, *keep the ball rolling,* is probably also derived from bandy. It means to continue or to spark renewed interest and enthusiasm in an activity or project already underway. One source credits the popularity of this expression to the 1840 presidential campaign of William Henry Harrison whose followers wrote political slogans on a huge paper ball and then pushed it from city to city shouting, "Keep the ball rolling."

get under way To get started, begin moving. This is borrowed from an old nautical idiom *under way* 'in forward motion.'

pave the way See **PREPARATION.**

ring up the curtain on To begin or initiate a project, plan, or activity; to start the ball rolling. Originally limited to use in the theater, this expression referred to raising the curtain on cue (usually the ringing of a bell) to mark the start of a performance. Though still used in this theatrical context, *ring up the curtain on* is often applied figuratively to describe the inauguration of a project or other endeavor.

> Before the curtain was rung up on the great spectacular drama of Vaal Krantz . . . (M. H. Grant, *Words by an Eyewitness; The Struggle in Natal,* 1901)

A variation is the shortened *ring up.*

Look sharp below there, gents, . . . they're a-going to ring-up. (Charles Dickens, *Sketches by Boz,* 1837)

See also **ring down the curtain on, TERMINATION.**

INNOVATION (See **ADVANTAGE.**)

INSANITY (See **ECCENTRICITY, IRRATIONALITY, UNCONVENTIONALITY.**)

INSIGNIFICANCE (See also **WORTHLESSNESS.**)

anise and cumin Insignificant matters, petty concerns. The term is usually found within a context implying that one ought to be about more important work or focus his attention on larger concerns. The origin of the phrase lies in Jesus' reproach to the Scribes and Pharisees:

Ye pay tithe of mint and anise and cummin, and have omitted the weightier matters of the law, judgment, mercy, and faith; these ought ye to have done, and not to leave the other undone. (Matthew 23:23)

Anise and cumin are aromatic herbs often used in both cookery and medicine.

a drop in the bucket An absurdly small quantity in relation to the whole; a contribution so negligible or insignificant that it makes no appreciable difference; also *a drop in the ocean.* The expression appears in the following passage from the King James version of the Bible:

Behold, the nations are as a drop of a bucket, and are counted as the small dust of the balance. (Isaiah 40:15)

A drop in the ocean was apparently coined by analogy. It dates from the early 1700s.

fly in amber An unimportant person or incident remembered only through association with a person or matter of significance. The origin of this phrase is credited to certain extinct pine trees that produced a resin called amber which, while flowing down the trees, trapped and preserved small insects, thus fossilizing organisms of virtually no scientific interest.

Full-fledged specimens of your order, preserved for all time in the imperishable amber of his genius. (C. Cowden Clarke, *Shakespeare-characters,* 1863)

Mickey Mouse Cheap or inferior; small, insignificant, worthless; petty, trivial; simple, easy, childish. The allusion is to the cartoon character created by Walt Disney in 1928. Because this character is internationally famous, *Mickey Mouse* has been applied figuratively in innumerable and widely varied contexts. The connotation of cheapness and inferiority probably originated in the mid-1930s when the Ingersoll Watch Company marketed a popular wristwatch, with Mickey Mouse on its face and his arms serving as pointers or hands, which sold for $2. The watch was not made well enough to last long, hence the allusion to flimsiness and poor quality.

One reason for the AFL's reputation as a Mickey Mouse league is that it gave new life to NFL rejects. (J. Mosedale, *Football,* 1972)

At Michigan State [University] . . . a "Mickey Mouse course" means a "snap course." (Maurice Crane, "Vox Box," in *American Speech,* October, 1958)

See also **Mickey Mouse around, EVASIVENESS.**

no great shakes Unimportant or unimpressive; not exceptional or extraordinary; common, dull, boring. There are several suggested derivations of this expression: a low roll on a shake of the dice, a negative appraisal of someone's character made on the basis of a weak handshake, or a negligible yield resulting from shaking a barren walnut tree.

Alternate meanings of *shake* are also cited: 'reputation,' 'a shingle from the roof of a shanty,' or 'plant stubble left after harvesting.' One source alludes to the Arabic *shakhs* 'man.' At any rate, *no great shakes* has long implied that a person or thing is common, unimportant, or of no particular merit or ability.

[He] said that a piece of sculpture there was "nullae magnae quessationes" ['of no great shakes'] and the others laughed heartily. (Lord Henry Broughton, *Recollections*, 1816)

one-horse town An extremely small, insignificant town. A farmer whose plow was pulled by one horse instead of two was considered small-time and of limited resources. Similarly, a one-horse town refers to a small, often rural community which could presumably survive with only one horse. The phrase maintains common usage in the United States despite the fact that horses are no longer the principal means of transportation.

In this "one-horse" town, . . . as our New Orleans neighbors designate it. (*Knickerbocker Magazine*, 1855)

peanut gallery A source of unimportant or insignificant criticism; in a theater, the section of seats farthest removed from the stage. In many theaters, peanuts and popcorn were sold only to the people in the least expensive seats, usually those in the rear of the balcony, hence the nickname *peanut gallery*. Since these seats are traditionally bought by those of meager means and, by stereotypic implication, those with a minimal appreciation of the arts, comments or criticisms from people in the *peanut gallery* carried little, if any, weight, thus the expression's more figurative meaning.

pebble on the beach An insignificant or unimportant person, especially one who was once prominent; a face in the crowd, a fish in the sea. This expression is one of many that minimize the importance of someone by virtue of the fact that he is just one of a multitude. It usually follows phrases such as "There's more than one . . ." and "You aren't the only . . . ," and is most commonly used in situations involving a jilted sweetheart.

penny-ante Insignificant or unimportant; strictly small-time; involving a trifling or paltry amount of money. Originally, *penny ante* was a poker game in which the ante or limit was one penny. Though this literal meaning persists, the term is used figuratively as well.

Compared to the man Bilbo, 63-year-old John Rankin is strictly penny ante and colorless. (*Negro Digest*, August, 1946)

Podunk Any hick town; the boondocks, the sticks; the middle of nowhere. This name, of Indian origin, may refer either to the Podunk near Hartford, Connecticut, or to that near Worcester, Massachusetts. But how either gained the notoriety necessary to make it representative of all such insignificant, out-of-the-way towns is unknown.

He might just as well have been John Smith of Podunk Centre. (*Harper's Weekly*, September, 1901)

small potatoes An inconsequential, trivial person; an irrelevant or unimportant concept or notion; a small amount of money. This familiar saying is evidently derived from the short-lived satiation of one who has eaten a small potato. Although the expression retains its human application, *small potatoes* more often describes an insignificant amount of money, especially when such a pittance is compared with one's projected future earnings or with a much greater cash sum.

The $7 billion was of course pretty "small potatoes" compared to the vast inflationary borrowings of the federal government. (*Proceedings of the Academy of Political Science,* May, 1948)

INSTANTANEOUSNESS (See also PACE, SPEEDING.)

at the drop of a hat At the slightest provocation; at once, promptly, without delay; immediately, instantly. In use since at least 1854, this expression is said to have derived from the early American frontier custom of dropping a hat to signal the beginning of a fight. The downward sweep of a hat has also been used to signal the start of races.

> When in a bad temper [he was] ferocious and ready to quarrel "at the drop of a hat," as the American saying goes. (M. Roberts, *Western Avernus,* 1887)

before you can say "Jack Robinson" Instantly, immediately. There are two common but equally unsubstantiated theories as to the origin of this phrase. One holds that a rather mercurial gentleman of that name was in the habit of paying such brief visits to neighbors that he was gone almost as soon as he had been announced. The other sees the source in these lines from an old, unnamed play:

> A warke it ys as easie to be done
> As tys to saye, Jacke! robys on.

In popular use during the 18th century, the expression appeared in Fanny Burney's *Evelina* in 1778.

before you can say "knife" Very quickly or suddenly; before you can turn around. This colloquial British expression is equivalent to *before you can say "Jack Robinson."* Mrs. Louisa Parr used it in *Adam and Eve* (1880).

in a jiffy In a trice, in a minute, right away. Although the exact origin of this expression is unknown, it is thought by some to be the modern spelling of the earlier *gliff* 'a glimpse, a glance,' and by extension 'a short space of time, a moment.' The phrase dates from the late 18th century.

They have wonderful plans for doing everything in a jiffy. (Charles Haddon Spurgeon, *John Ploughman's Pictures,* 1880)

in a pig's whisper In a short time; soon. A pig's whisper was originally a short grunt, one so brief that it sounded almost like a whisper.

> You'll find yourself in bed, in something less than a pig's whisper. (Charles Dickens, *Pickwick Papers,* 1837)

in two shakes of a lamb's tail Immediately, right away; instantly. Although the exact origin is unknown, this expression is thought by some to be an enlargement of the older phrase *in a brace* or *couple of shakes,* which appeared in Richard H. Barham's *The Ingoldsby Legends* (1840). However, anyone familiar with sheep knows the quivering suddenness with which those animals twitch their tails.

one fell swoop All at once; with a single blow or stroke. The *swoop* of the phrase may carry its obsolete meaning of 'blow,' or refer to the sudden descent of a bird of prey; *fell* carries its meanings of 'fierce, savage, destructive.' Macduff uses the phrase in Shakespeare's *Macbeth* when he learns that his wife, children, and servants have all been killed. In doing so, he plays on its associations with birds of prey:

> All my pretty ones?
> Did you say all? Oh Hellkite! All?
> What, all my pretty chickens, and their dam
> At one fell swoop? (IV,iii)

Contemporary usage does not restrict the phrase to serious contexts of fatal destruction; in fact, the expression is so often used lightly that it has generated the common spoonerism *one swell foop.*

on the double Instantly; without delay; right off the bat. This expression originated as military jargon for double-time marching. The term's current civilian use is commonplace in the United States.

> They came with me on the double. (James M. Cain, *The Postman Always Rings Twice,* 1934)

p.d.q. Immediately, at once. This widely used abbreviation of "pretty damn quick" was coined in 1867 by Don Maginnis, a Boston comedian.

> He changed her mind for her p. d. q. (John O'Hara, *The Horse Knows the Way,* 1964)

right off the bat Immediately; at once; instantaneously. This very common expression is of obvious baseball origin.

> You can tell right off the bat that they're wicked, because they keep eating grapes indolently. (*The New Yorker,* May, 1955)

The less frequently heard synonymous *right off the reel* may derive from the specific sports use of *reel* in fishing, though many of the more general uses of *reel* could account equally well for its origin.

INSTIGATION (See **PROVOCATION.**)

INSTINCT (See **INTUITION.**)

INSULT (See also **RIDICULE.**)

barrack To boo or hiss; to voice loudly one's disapproval of a player, performer, or team at a public event. This British term is thought by some to be a back formation of the cockney word *barrakin* 'senseless talk,' although the *OED* claims an Australian origin. The word appeared in use in the late 19th century. The term *to barrack for* has the opposite meaning: 'to cheer for, or support vocally.'

bite one's thumb at To insult or show contempt for someone. The gesture, as defined by the 17th-century English lexicographer Randle Cotgrave, meant "to threaten or defy by putting the thumb nail into the mouth, and with a jerk [from the upper teeth] make it to

knack [click or snap]." A famous use of the phrase is from Shakespeare:

> I will bite my thumb at them; which is a disgrace to them, if they bear it. (*Romeo and Juliet,* I,i)

catcall A harsh, whistling sound, something like the cry of a cat, used by theater and other audiences to express their disapproval, displeasure, or impatience; the whistlelike instrument used to make this sound. This term dates from the mid-1600s.

cock a snook A British slang expression for the gesture of putting one's thumb on one's nose and extending the fingers, equivalent to *thumb one's nose.* The origin of *snook* is obscure, and based on citations from as early as 1879, it can refer to other derisive gestures as well. An earlier form of this phrase is *to take a sight.*

> "To take a sight at a person" a vulgar action employed by street boys to denote incredulity, or contempt for authority, by placing the thumb against the nose and closing all the fingers except the little one, which is agitated in token of derision. (John C. Hotten, *A Dictionary of Modern Slang, Cant, and Vulgar Words,* 1860)

A current variant of *snook* is *snoot,* a slang term for the nose.

fork the fingers To use one's digits in a disdainful motion toward another person. This self-explanatory expression is heard less often now than in past centuries.

> His wife . . . Behind him forks her fingers. (Sir John Mennes and J. Smith, *Witts Recreations,* 1640)

give the bird To hiss or boo; to dismiss or fire; to receive unsupportive, hostile feedback. The original phrase was *give the goose,* a theater slang expression dating from the beginning of the 19th century. *Goose* or *bird,* and currently *raspberry* or *Bronx cheer,* refer to the hissing sound made by an audience mimicking the similar sound made by a goose. It expresses disapproval, hostility, or rejection, and was directed at a performer or the play. Today it is a popular sound effect used by crowds at sporting events, although *give the bird* is also heard in other unrelated contexts. For example, an employer who dismisses an employee is said to *give the bird*, akin to *give the sack*. And in interpersonal relationships, *the bird* is analogous to *the brush-off* or *the gate*.

She gave him the bird—finally and for good. So he came to Spain to forget his broken heart. (P. Kemp, *Mine Were of Trouble*, 1957)

A familiar vulgar meaning of *give the bird* is to make the obscene and offensive gesture of extending the middle finger.

give the fig To insult; also *the fig of Spain* and the now obsolete *to give the fico*. The fig or Italian *fico* is a contemptuous gesture which involves putting the thumb between the first two fingers or in the mouth. English versions of both expressions date from the late 16th century. The equivalent French and Spanish phrases are *faire la figue* and *dar la higa* respectively.

give the raspberry To show ridicule or disapproval by making a vulgar noise; to respond in a scornful, acrimonious manner. *Raspberry*, a slang term dating from the turn of the century, refers to any expression of disapproval or scorn.

The humorist answered them by a gesture known in polite circles as a "raspberry." (T. Burke, *Nights in Town*, 1915)

Convict son totters up the steps of the old home and punches the bell. What awaits him beyond? Forgiveness? Or the raspberry? (P. G. Wodehouse, *Damsel in Distress*, 1920)

However, the most common raspberry is the sound effect known also as the *bird, goose,* or *Bronx cheer. Razz,* short for *raspberry,* is a slang verb meaning 'to ridicule or deride,' akin in use to the verb *tease.*

make horns at To insult by making the offensive gesture of extending the fist with the forefinger and pinkie extended and the middle fingers doubled in. This now obsolete derisive expression implies that the person being insulted is a cuckold.

He would have laine withe the Countess of Nottinghame, making horns in derision at her husband the Lord High Admiral. (Sir E. Peyton, *The Divine Catastrophe of the . . . House of Stuarts,* 1652)

See **wear the horns, INFIDELITY.**

a plague on both your houses An imprecation invoked upon two parties, each at odds with the other; often a denunciation of both of America's two leading political parties. Shakespeare coined this expression in *Romeo and Juliet* (III,i):

I am hurt.
A plague o' both your houses! I am sped.
Is he gone, and hath nothing?

a slap in the face A stinging insult; a harsh or sarcastic rejection, rebuke, or censure. This expression alludes to a literal blow to the face, a universal sign of rejection or disapproval. The implication is that a verbal blow, particularly an unexpected one, can be just as painful and devastating as a physical one.

[He] could not help feeling severely the very vigorous slap on the face which had been administered to him. (Thomas Trollope, *La Beata,* 1861)

thumb one's nose Literally, to put one's thumb to one's nose and extend the fingers, a gesture expressive of scorn, derision or contempt. This U.S. phrase came into use concurrently with *give the raspberry* in the early 1900s and is popular today. The gesture is considered offensive, but not as vulgar as the gesture known as *the bird.*

He thumbed his nose with both thumbs at once and told me to climb the Tour d'Eiffel and stay there. (B. Hall, *One Man's War*, 1916)

INTELLECTUALITY (See SCHOLARLINESS.)

INTENSIFICATION (See EXACERBATION.)

INTENSITY

back and edge Wholeheartedly, vigorously; entirely, completely. The allusion is to the thin sharpened side of a blade, or "edge," and the blunt side of the same blade, or "back." Together the two sides constitute the whole of the blade; thus the figurative extension in meaning to 'completely,' 'wholeheartedly,' 'with one's entire self.'

blow up a storm To engage in any activity with such enthusiasm and vigor as to effect a noticeable change in one's surroundings; also with the implication of being so caught up in the activity as to get carried away oneself. The most plausible explanation says the term comes from jazz trumpeting; another holds it stems from the storm of dust raised from the pit floor by the spectacular beating of wings and flurry of movement in a cockfight. Though *blow up a storm* appears to be the oldest and still most frequently heard form, *up a storm* itself is now commonly appended as an adverbial intensifier to many verbs of physical activity—one can work "up a storm," sing "up a storm," dance "up a storm," and so on.

full blast Maximum capacity, strength, volume, or speed; full swing; often in the phrase *in* or *at full blast.* In use as early as the 1830s, this phrase apparently originally connoted exaggerated or extreme behavior, appearance, etc., based on the following quotation from Frederick Marryat's *Diary in America II* (1839):

"When she came to meeting, with her yellow hat and feathers, wasn't she in full blast?"

Although the expression's origin is unknown, it may be related to the use of *blast* in relation to machinery: air forced into a furnace by a blower to increase the rate of combustion.

full tilt At maximum speed, force, strength, or capacity; straight at or for, directly. This expression is said to have come from the way knights rode straight for one another at full gallop and with lances tilted when jousting. The phrase, which dates from about 1600, appears in Frederic E. Gretton's *Memory's Harkback through Half-a-century* (1805–58):

The Earl rode full tilt at him as though he would have unhorsed him.

go great guns See PROSPERING.

go to town See PROSPERING.

hammer and tongs Forcefully, violently, strenuously; energetically, vigorously, wholeheartedly. A blacksmith uses tongs to hold the hot iron as he pounds and hammers it into shape. To go at anything hammer and tongs is to exert similar strength and force to accomplish a goal.

head over heels Intensely, completely, totally; rashly, impetuously. This expression, dating from the late 18th century, is a corruption of *heels over head,* which dates from the 14th century; both relate literally to body movement, as in a somersault. A similar phrase dating from the late 19th century is *head over ears,* a corruption of *over head and ears* 'completely or deeply immersed or involved.'

like a house afire See PACE.

swear like a trooper See PROFANITY.

to beat the band Vigorously, enthusiastically, intently, rapidly. To perform any activity with great force and gusto, so as to drown out or exceed the tempo of the band, as it were. The expression dates from the turn of the century.

tooth and nail Fiercely, vigorously, with all one's powers and resources. Despite its physical connotations of clawing, biting, and scratching, this phrase is almost always used figuratively. Such usage dates from the 16th century.

with might and main Vigorously, strenuously; using one's powers and resources to the utmost. The obsolete *main* is synonymous with *might* 'power, strength' and continues in the language only in this phrase as an intensifier—*with might and main* being a bit more forceful and somewhat more formal than *with all one's might.*

INTOXICATION (See **DRUNKENNESS.**)

INTUITION

by ear Relying on an innate sense of what sounds or feels right; without referring to, or depending upon prescribed procedures or written music. This use of *ear,* referring to an ability to recognize musical intervals, dates from the early 16th century. At that time, *play it by ear* meant to sing or play an instrument without printed music. By the 19th century, the same phrase came to mean to proceed one step at a time, trusting intuition and a subtle sense of timing, rather than a prearranged plan, to determine the proper course of action.

> "What happens then?" "I don't know. . . . We're playing it by ear at the moment." (A. Smith, *East-Enders,* 1961)

Both this figurative use and the earlier one heard in musical contexts are current today.

by the seat of one's pants By instinct or intuition; just barely, narrowly. This expression was originally an aviation term meaning to fly without instruments, and thus to be forced to rely upon the instincts acquired through past experience. The sense of 'just barely, narrowly' would seem to be an outgrowth of this aviation use, since a pilot flying by the seat of his pants is apt to escape disaster by a very narrow margin.

feel in one's bones To intuit; to sense something before it becomes apparent. This expression probably stems from the ability of people who suffer from bone diseases such as arthritis and rheumatism to predict changes in the weather because of increased pain. This ability is due to the fact that changes in atmospheric pressure and humidity may affect the bones and joints of such individuals. Since changes in pressure and humidity often precede a change in the weather, these people seem to sense the change before it becomes apparent. In its current usage, *feel in one's bones* is no longer limited to people with bone disorders or to changes in the weather.

follow one's nose To be guided by instinct, to play it by ear. The expression clearly derives from an animal's keen and usually unerring sense of smell. The phrase was used figuratively as early as 1692 by Richard Bentley in one of his Boyle lectures:

> The main maxim of his philosophy was, to trust to his senses, and follow his nose.

The expression also has the similar but somewhat less figurative meaning of 'go straight forward, continue on in a direct course.'

know which way the wind blows See **SHREWDNESS.**

a little bird An undisclosed source; a secret witness; intuition. This phrase refers to the ubiquitous yet unobtrusive nature of a small bird that, theoretically at least, is able to observe many covert goings-on as it flies through the air. Since the beginning of recorded history (and no doubt before), birds have been respected and, at times, revered for their godlike powers of flight and sight. Many Greek and Roman soothsayers cited their purported understanding of avian language as a source of their knowledge and intuitive or psychic abilities. According to the *Koran,* the sacred book of Islam, Solomon was advised of Queen Sheba's activities by a tiny lapwing, and Muhammad himself was counseled by a pigeon. In addition, some early religious woodcuts show various popes listening to the whispered advice of a small bird. These and many other legends have given rise to the almost universal adage, *a little bird told me,* an expression indicating that the speaker knows a secret or other confidential matter by virtue of intuition or some undisclosed source.

> Curse not the king, no not in thy thought; and curse not the rich in thy bedchamber: for a bird of the air shall carry thy voice, and that which hath wings shall tell the matter. (Ecclesiastes 10:20)

> We bear our civil swords and native fire
> As far as France. I heard a bird so sing,
> Whose music, to my thinking, pleased the king.
> (Shakespeare, *Henry IV, Part II* V,v)

my little finger told me that See OMEN.

rule of thumb See CRITERION.

a shot in the dark A wild guess; a random conjecture. This widely used expression combines *shot* 'an attempt' with the phrase *in the dark* 'uninformed' to imply that a given conjecture is made without the benefit of relevant information or assistance. In most cases, however, a "shot in the dark" does involve an element of intuitive reasoning. "Shot in the Dark" was the title of an amusing 1964 movie that starred Peter Sellers as the bumbling Inspector Jacques Clouseau.

INVALIDATION   (See RUINATION.)

INVESTIGATION

fishing expedition An investigation conducted without definite purpose,

plan, or regard to standards of propriety, in hopes of acquiring useful (and usually incriminating) evidence or information; apparently aimless interrogation designed to lead someone into incriminating himself. This expression refers to the literal fishing expedition in which, armed with basic equipment, one goes after his prey without knowing exactly what, if anything, he will catch. The more skillful and experienced the fisherman, though, the better are his chances of successfully catching his quarry.

> I am not going to permit counsel to go on a fishing expedition. (Erle Stanley Gardner, *The Case of the Bigamous Spouse,* 1961)

go over with a fine-tooth comb See THOROUGHNESS.

leave no stone unturned See THOROUGHNESS.

shakedown A thorough search, as of a prison cell in hopes of finding hidden weapons or other contraband. This expression alludes to shaking a tree to expose and acquire fruits or nuts which might be hidden within the foliage, and implies that something is turned upside-down and shaken to reveal the desired items. The expression is often used as a verb, to *shake down.*

> A couple of patrolmen to shake down the neighborhood . . .
> (Richard Starnes, *And When She Was Bad She Was Murdered,* 1951)

As an adjective, *shake-down* is often applied to a cruise or flight undertaken to expose any mechanical flaws and to orient the crew while breaking in and adjusting the new equipment. See also **shakedown,** EXTORTION.

take soundings To investigate, to try to find out what is going on or how things stand; to psych out a situation. To take soundings is literally to measure the depth of water by letting down a line with a lead attached to the bottom. Figurative use of *sounding* appeared in print during the time of Shakespeare.

Old Dan bears you no malice, I'd lay fifty pounds on it! But, if you like, I'll just step in and take soundings. (Charles J. Lever, *The Martins of Cro' Martin*, 1856)

the third degree Intensive, prolonged interrogation, often in conjunction with physical abuse, to obtain information or force a confession. Usually used in the context of a prisoner's being questioned by the police, *third degree* refers to the severity of the techniques employed. Just as a third-degree burn is the most damaging and extreme type of burn, so is a "third degree" the most drastic form of interrogation.

He was at first arrested merely as a suspicious person, but when put through the "third degree" at the station, admitted that he entered the house last night. (*New York Times*, July 6, 1904)

INVOLVEMENT

finger in the pie See MEDDLESOMENESS.

in the swim Actively involved in current affairs or social activities, in the middle or thick of things; abreast of the current popular trends in fashion, business, society, politics; in the know; also the opposite, *out of the swim.*

The second category of companies is usually so managed that the originators do pretty well out of it whether those of the shareholders who are not "in the swim" gain a profit or lose their capital. (*The Graphic*, November, 1884)

In angling a swim is that part of a river much frequented by fish, and consequently that in which an angler fishes. Figurative use of this expression dates from the 19th century.

a piece of the action Active, and usually remunerative, involvement in any undertaking; a share in the profits, a piece of the pie; personal and immediate participation in any activity. *Webster's 6,000* cites Charlie Frick:

Guys . . . rubbing their hands slowly together with dollar signs in their eyes. . . . Managers and agents and producers and all the others that had a piece of the action.

a piece of the pie See ALLOCATION.

IRRATIONALITY (See also FRENZIEDNESS.)

beside oneself In an intensely emotional state; unable to control or contain one's feelings; highly excited. Though one may be beside oneself with feelings ranging from pleasure to rage, the essence of the state is irrationality—being out of one's wits. The phrase is akin to the French *hors de soi,* and both relate to the concepts of being possessed or transported. Caxton used the expression in the late 15th century.

coop-happy Insane from confinement; stir-crazy; punch-drunk from being cooped up. *Coop* 'a confined area,' is also a slang term for jail. *Happy* is used euphemistically in this phrase to mean dull-witted or "feeling no pain," whence the term.

flip one's lid To react wildly or enthusiastically; to be delighted or outraged; to be knocked off one's feet or bowled over with shock; to lose one's head. This relatively new slang phrase of American origin plays with the idea that a "lid" serves to prevent something from escaping—in this case one's common sense and control. Thus, to "flip one's lid" is to lose self-control, leaving one unbalanced or crazed.

Present war emergencies plus strain and stress seem to have been too much for local governmental officials. I fear they have flipped their lids. (Letter to the editor, Ithaca, N.Y., *Journal*, January 30, 1951)

Currently, *flip* is heard more frequently than the longer *flip one's lid.*

Our food and service are great. Our decor's delightful. Your club treasurer will flip over our low rates. (*Boston Globe*, May 18, 1967)

Another variant, *flip out*, implies a more serious degree of losing control, as from drugs, a nervous breakdown, etc. It is analogous to *freak out* and *go off the deep end* in flavor and usage.

go bananas To go wild with excitement or rage, to act in an irrational or uncontrollable manner. The phrase supposedly comes from the chattering antics of a hungry monkey at the sight of a banana. It is nearly always used hyperbolically to indicate reason temporarily overcome by emotion; rarely would it be used to describe true mental derangement or disturbance.

go haywire See DISORDER.

go off the deep end To overreact, to get inappropriately angry or excited; to go overboard, to overdo it; to go in over one's head; to freak out. The "deep end" refers to the end of a swimming pool at which the water is deepest. Floundering unprepared and confused in the "deep end," one is apt to behave wildly and without a sense of propriety or concern for appearances. Dating from the early 1900s, this expression most often describes emotional outbursts, including occasionally those severe enough to be classified as mental breakdown.

lose one's head To lose one's equilibrium or presence of mind; to be out of control, off balance, or beside oneself. The head is associated with reason, sense, and rationality. Thus, to "lose one's head" is to become irrational and out of control. Its figurative use dates from the 1840s.

It has now and then an odd Gallicism—such as "she lost her head," meaning she grew crazy. (Edgar Allan Poe, *Marginalia*, 1849)

The phrase is often used to explain behavior (such as a temper tantrum or show of affection) that would otherwise be considered out of character or inappropriate.

lose one's marbles To go crazy; to act or speak in an irrational manner. Since the early 1900s, *marbles* has been equated with common sense and mental faculties. Therefore, to lose one's marbles is to lose one's wits, especially when there has been a sudden behavioral change which manifests itself in eccentric or irrational acts or babblings.

You lost your goddam' marbles? You gone completely crazy, you nutty slob? (J. Wainwright, *Take-Over Men*, 1969)

A related expression is *have some marbles missing*.

mad as a hatter Crazy, insane, demented; stark raving mad; violently angry, livid, venomous. It is probable that this expression is a corruption of *mad as an atter*, in which *atter* is an Anglo-Saxon variation of *adder* 'viper,' a poisonous snake. Thus, the original expression implied that a person was venomous, ready to strike with malicious intent. One source suggests that *mad as a hatter* may allude to the insanity and loss of muscular control caused by prolonged exposure to mercurous nitrate, a chemical once commonly used in the manufacture of felt hats. At any rate, in current usage, *mad as a hatter* refers to lunacy more often than to anger.

In that direction . . . lives a Hatter; and in that direction . . . lives a March hare . . . They're both mad. (Lewis Carroll, *Alice's Adventures in Wonderland*, 1865)

mad as a March hare Agitated, excited, worked up; frenzied, wild, erratic; rash; insane, crazy. This expression probably alludes to the behavior of hares during mating season when they thump the ground with their hind legs, and jump up and down, twisting their bodies in midair. Several sources suggest that the original expression may have been *mad* *as a marsh hare*, implying that due to lack of protective shrubbery in marshes, these hares act more wildly than others.

> As mad not as a March hare, but as a mad dog. (Sir Thomas More, *The Supplycacyon of Soulys*, 1529)

This expression was undoubtedly the inspiration for the March hare in Lewis Carroll's *Alice's Adventures in Wonderland* (1865). A common variation is *wild as a March hare*. The related term *harebrained* describes a person who is reckless or eccentric, or a plan, scheme, project, or other matter that is of dubious merit.

> Whilst they, out of hare-brained lunacy, desire battle. (John Stephans, *Satyrical Essays, Characters, and Others*, 1615)

stir-crazy To behave neurotically as a result of long-term imprisonment; to be climbing the walls; to act dull-witted or punch-drunk from confinement. *Stir* is a slang term for jail or prison. Although originating as underworld lingo, *stir* is now fairly common, especially in the phrase *stir-crazy* which is no longer limited in use to prison-related neurosis. Rather, any lack of activity or temporary isolation can make one stir-crazy. The term is rarely if ever used literally —almost always hyperbolically.

IRRELEVANCE

beside the cushion Irrelevant, beside the point; wrong. This obsolete expression dating from the 1500s is synonymous with *beside the mark*. Both expressions are thought to derive from archery. An idea or comment which misses the point or is "beside the cushion" is like an arrow which misses the target (cushion) entirely.

> He rangeth abroad to original sin altogether besides the cushion. (James Bell, *Walter Haddon Against Osorius*, 1581)

beside the mark Irrelevant, not to the point, inapplicable; off base, off target.

This expression is thought to derive from the unsuccessful attempt of an archer to hit the "mark" or target. *Beside the mark* appeared in print by the 1600s. *Miss the mark*, a verbal expression meaning 'to be irrelevant or far-fetched,' appeared in a slightly different form as early as the 14th century.

> But now has Sir David missed of his marks. (Laurence Minot, *Poems*, 1352)

IRRESPONSIBILITY

do a moonlight flit To evade responsibility by leaving town during the night; to fly by night. This common British colloquialism, the equivalent of the American *fly by night*, uses *flit* in the sense of moving from one residence to another, and *moonlight* to imply furtiveness associated with the move.

go between the moon and the milkman To leave town in order to evade creditors or other interested parties; to fly by night. This British colloquialism, the equivalent of the American *fly by night*, implies that, to avoid his personal and financial obligations, a person may depart clandestinely sometime between the rising of the moon (dusk) and the arrival of the milkman (dawn).

let George do it Let someone else do the work or assume the responsibility; pass the buck. This American colloquial expression dates from the turn of the century. *George* is a male generic term which derives from the Greek word for husbandman or farmer. By the 1920s this term was used by the British to refer to an airman, corresponding to *Jack* for a sailor (bluejacket) and *Tommy* for a soldier. *George* is also a British slang term for an automatic pilot in an aircraft or ship.

pass the buck To evade responsibility or blame by shifting it to someone else. Originally, *pass the buck* was a poker expression that meant handing the "buck" (a buckskin knife or other inanimate object) to another player in order to avoid some responsibility (such as dealing, starting a new jackpot, etc.) which fell on whoever possessed the "buck."

> I reckon I can't call that hand. Ante and pass the buck. (Mark Twain, *Roughing It*, 1872)

As the expression became more figurative, it enjoyed widespread popular use, particularly in reference to bureaucratic procedures:

> The Big Commissioner will get roasted by the papers and hand it to the Deputy Commish, and the Deputy will pass the buck down to me, and I'll have to report how it happened. (William Irwin, *The Red Button*, 1912)

By the mid-1900s, *pass the buck* had become so intimately associated with governmental administration that during his presidency (1945–53), Harry Truman adopted the now-famous motto, "The buck stops here."

pay with the roll of the drum Not to pay; to evade or ignore a debt. In this expression, *roll of the drum* implies a soldier on the march, i.e., in active military service. Since in many countries a soldier on active duty cannot be arrested for debts incurred while a civilian, it was common practice for debtors to join the armed services to avoid either having to make good on the debt or going to prison. The military connotations have faded over the years so that in contemporary usage, *pay with the roll of the drum* is usually applied figuratively.

IRRETRIEVABILITY

by the board Ruined, disregarded, forgotten; over and done with; literally, by or over a ship's side, overboard; usually in the phrase *go by the board*. This expression comes from the nautical sense of *board* 'the side of a ship.' The phrase was used literally in its nautical sense as early as 1630 but did not appear in figurative usage until 1859.

down the drain Wasted, lost, gone. The phrase, in use since 1930, probably refers to the way liquid disappears down a drainpipe. A more recent variant, equally popular today, is *down the tube*. The extended expression *pour down the drain* denotes an unnecessary or extravagant waste of time or money.

lost in the wash Lost in the confused and chaotic jumble of events, proceedings, etc. Considered literally, this expression brings to mind the occasional but mysterious disappearance of various articles of clothing in automatic washing machines. In this expression, however, *wash* refers not to laundry but to a body of water, as it does in the following lines from Shakespeare's *King John:*

> I'll tell thee, Hubert, half my power this night,
> Passing these flats, are taken by the tide.
> These Lincoln Washes have devoured them. (V,vi)

out the window Irretrievably lost or forfeited. The image conveyed by this American slang expression reinforces the idea of irretrievable loss, both of material possessions and emotional security, such as that provided by one's career, reputation, and the like.

up the spout Pawned, in hock; ruined, lost, gone. In a pawnbroker's shop the spout is the lift used to carry pawned items to an upper floor for storage. While the phrase was used literally as early as 1812, it did not appear in its figurative sense until 1853 in Dods' *Early Letters:*

> The fact is, Germany is up the spout, and consequently a damper is thrown over my hopes for next summer.

IRREVOCABLENESS

burn one's bridges See DECISIVENESS.

cross the Rubicon See DECISIVENESS.

cry over spilt milk To regret or bemoan what cannot be undone or changed, to lament or grieve over past actions or events. This proverbial expression, in common use in both America and Britain, was apparently first used by the Canadian humorist Thomas C. Haliburton in *The Clockmaker; or the Sayings and Doings of Samuel Slick of Slickville* (1835), in which a friend of the hero says, "What's done, Sam, can't be helped, there is no use in cryin' over spilt milk."

the die is cast A statement meaning that a decisive and irrevocable step has been taken, that the course has been decided once and for all and that there will be no going back. The original Latin *alea jacta est* would have more meaning for modern ears if rendered in the plural—'the dice have been thrown.' The phrase is attributed to Julius Caesar at the time of his famous crossing of the Rubicon. Although the *OED* dates this specific expression from 1634, Shakespeare's *Richard III* contains a similar concept:

I have set my life upon a cast,
And I will stand the hazard of the die. (V,iv)

the fat's in the fire What's done is done, and the negative consequences must be paid; usually used in reference to an irrevocable, potentially explosive situation; also *all the fat is in the fire*. The allusion is probably to the way fat spits when burning. This expression, in use since 1644, appeared in an article by William Dean Howells in the February, 1894, issue of *Harper's Magazine:*

The die is cast, the jig is up, the fat's in the fire, the milk's spilt.

let the dead bury the dead Let bygones be bygones; don't dwell on past differences and grievances. The implication in this expression is that one should not be tied down by things in the past, but should begin anew and look toward favorable prospects in the future.

Jesus said unto him, Follow me; and let the dead bury their dead. (Matthew 8:22)

point of no return A situation or predicament from which there is no turning back; a crucial position or moment in an argument, project, or other matter which requires total commitment of one's resources. This expression was first used by aircraft pilots and navigators to describe that point in a flight when the plane does not have enough fuel to return to its home base, and so must continue on to its destination.

that's water over the dam A proverbial phrase expressing the sentiment that what's past is past and nothing can be done about it; also *that's water under the bridge.*

IRRITABILITY (See **ILL TEMPER.**)

IRRITATION (See also **VEXATION.**)

flea in the ear Discontent or uneasiness caused by a broad hint or warning, especially one which arouses suspicion; restlessness caused by an unexpected or undesired reply, usually one which is a vicious or humiliating rebuff or reproach. Cited for centuries in literature from throughout the world, this expression refers to the restless and distressed behavior characteristic of a dog afflicted with a flea in its ear.

He went away with a flea in his ear,
Like a poor cur.
(Francis Beaumont and John Fletcher, *Love's Cure,* 1625)

gadfly A pest, nuisance, or bother; one who irritates, annoys, or tries to involve others in one's cockeyed schemes. Literally, a gadfly is an insect which bites and goads other animals, especially cattle. Figurative use of the term dates from the mid-17th century. Currently, *corporate gadfly* is frequently heard to describe one who disrupts corporate or stockholder meetings with unconventional questions and challenges. *To have* *a gadfly,* dating from the late 16th century, means 'to gad about,' or 'to rove idly.' *Gadfly* can also be used adjectivally, as in the British *gadfly mind,* denoting an inability to concentrate.

get in [someone's] hair To pester, annoy, irritate; to nag, henpeck; to be a nuisance. The persistent irritation of the scalp caused by hair lice is the probable source of this common expression.

> She got in my hair until I couldn't bear it another day. (J. Tey, *Shilling for Candles,* 1936)

get under [someone's] skin To irritate or annoy; to impress or affect deeply. This expression alludes to mites, ticks, and other small, parasitic arachnids and insects which embed themselves in the skin of a victim, causing itching, irritation, and inflammation. In contemporary usage, the phrase frequently implies deep affection or love, emotions exemplified in the classic Cole Porter song, "I've Got You Under My Skin" (1936).

pea in the shoe Any petty irritation or annoyance; a source of minor discomfort or distress; a thorn in the side. A literal pea in one's shoe is too small to seriously affect one's walking ability, but nevertheless large enough to be a source of considerable discomfort.

a thorn in the flesh A source of constant irritation, affliction, or inconvenience; a perpetual pain-in-the-neck. A sect of Pharisees used to place thorns in the hem of their cloaks to prick their legs in walking, and make them bleed. The expression no longer refers to self-imposed suffering, however, but to objectionable external conditions or parasitical acquaintances. St. Paul used *thorn in the flesh* in 2 Corinthians 12:7:

> And lest I should be exalted above measure through the abundance of the revelations, there was given to me a thorn in the flesh, the messenger of Satan to buffet me, lest I should be exalted above measure.

A common variant is *thorn in the side.*

> The Eastern Church was then, as she is to this day, a thorn in the side of the Papacy. (James Bryce, *The Holy Roman Empire,* 1864)

K

KNOWLEDGE

burn one's fingers To hurt oneself, physically or mentally, by meddling in other people's affairs or by acting impetuously. The expression usually implies that one has learned from the painful experience, and will avoid such situations or involvements in the future. The phrase has been in figurative use since 1710, often in proverbial statements like the following:

The busybody burns his own
fingers. (Samuel Palmer, *Proverbs*)

A similar current American slang expression is *get burnt,* which has the additional meaning of suffering financial loss.

by rote From memory; mechanically, automatically, unthinkingly, without understanding or feeling; usually as modifier of verbs such as *learn, get, know, recite.* Conjecture that *rote* comes from the Latin *rota* 'wheel,' and that *by rote* consequently relates to the repetitious turning round and round in the mind that accompanies memorizing, lacks solid etymological basis. George Gordon, Lord Byron, used the expression in *English Bards and Scotch Reviewers* (1809):

Take hackney'd jokes from Miller
got by rote.

cut one's eyeteeth To gain knowledge or understanding; to become sophisticated or experienced in the ways of the world; also *to have one's eyeteeth* meaning 'to be worldly-wise or aware.' This expression, which dates from the early 1700s, derives from the fact that the eyeteeth are cut late, usually at about the age of twelve. The implication then is that a person who has already cut his eyeteeth has reached the age of discretion. A similar phrase with the same meaning is *to cut one's wisdom teeth.* Wisdom teeth are cut even later than eyeteeth, usually between the ages of seventeen and twenty-five.

know one's beans To be generally knowledgeable and aware; to know a subject thoroughly; to be proficient, to have mastered a particular skill. Popular since the 19th century, this expression may be a contraction of the British *know how many beans make five,* an expression also used figuratively and said to derive from the practice of using beans to teach children how to count.

One has to know beans to be
successful in the latest Washington
novelty for entertainment at
luncheons. (*Chicago Herald,*
1888)

In the U.S., the negative construction *not to know beans* is more frequently heard, and may even antedate the other two.

Whatever he knows of Euclid and
Greek,
In Latin he don't know beans.
(*Yale Literary Magazine,* 1855)

Know one's onions is a common U.S. slang variant, as are *know one's stuff* and *know one's business.*

know the ropes To completely understand the operational methods of one's occupation or enterprise; to know the tricks of the trade. A sailor who understands the arrangement and functions of the numerous ropes on a ship is considered an invaluable crew member. Similarly, a person familiar with the ins and outs of his job or company establishes himself as a most valuable employee.

The circle was composed of men
who thought they "knew the

ropes" as well as he did. (John N. Maskelyne, *Sharps and Flats,* 1894)

under one's belt As a part of one's past experience, to one's credit, successfully completed or accomplished.

His wife had 135,000 miles driving in the States under her belt . . . but was still failed. (*The Manchester Guardian Weekly,* August, 1954)

Originally *under one's belt* 'in one's stomach' referred to food which had been taken in, digested, and finally assimilated into the body. Similarly, one's experiences are incorporated into one's personality.

L

LACK   (See **ABSENCE.**)

LANGUAGE   (See also **DICTION, GIB-BERISH, PROFANITY.**)

bombast   Pretentious speech; high-flown or inflated language. It is but a short step from the now obsolete literal meaning of *bombast* 'cotton-wool padding or stuffing for garments' to its current figurative sense of verbal padding or turgid language. Shakespeare used the word figuratively as early as 1588:

> We have received your letters full of love,
> Your favors, the ambassadors of love,
> And in our maiden council rated them
> At courtship, pleasant jest and courtesy,
> As bombast and as lining to the time.
> (*Love's Labour's Lost,* V,ii)

bumf   Official documents collectively; piles of paper, specifically, paper containing jargon and bureaucratese; thus, such language itself: gobbledegook, governmentese, Whitehallese, Washingtonese. This contemptuous British expression comes from *bumf,* a portmanteau type contraction for *bum fodder* 'toilet paper.' It has been used figuratively since the 1930s.

> I shall get a daily pile of bumf from the Ministry of Mines. (Evelyn Waugh, *Scoop,* 1938)

claptrap   Bombast, high-sounding but empty language. The word derives from the literal claptrap, defined in one of Nathan Bailey's dictionaries (1727–31) as "a trap to catch a clap by way of applause from the spectators at a play." The kind of high-flown and grandiose language actors would use in order to win applause from an audience gave the word its current meaning.

dirty word   A word which because of its associations is highly controversial, a red-flag word; a word which elicits responses of suspicion, paranoia, dissension, etc.; a sensitive topic, a sore spot. *Dirty word* originally referred to a blatantly obscene or taboo word. Currently it is also used to describe a superficially inoffensive word which is treated as if it were offensive because of its unpleasant or controversial associations. Depending on the context, such a word can be considered unpopular and taboo one day and "safe" the next.

gobbledegook   Circumlocutory and pretentious speech or writing; official or professional jargon, bureaucratese, officialese. The term's coinage has been attributed to Maury Maverick.

> The Veterans Administration translated its bureaucratic gobbledygook. (*Time,* July, 1947)

inkhorn term   An obscure, pedantic word borrowed from another language, especially Latin or Greek; a learned or literary term; affectedly erudite language. An inkhorn is a small, portable container formerly used to hold writing ink and originally made of horn. It symbolizes pedantry and affected erudition in this expression as well as in the phrase *to smell of the inkhorn* 'to be pedantic.' The expression, now archaic, dates from at least 1543.

> Irrevocable, irradiation, depopulation and such like, . . . which . . .were long time despised for inkhorn terms. (George Puttenham, *The Art of English Poesy,* 1589)

jawbreaker   A word difficult to pronounce; a polysyllabic word. This self-evident expression appeared in print as early as the 19th century.

You will find no "jawbreakers" in Sackville. (George E. Saintsbury, *A History of Elizabethan Literature,* 1887)

malapropism The ridiculous misuse of similar sounding words, sometimes through ignorance, but often with punning or humorous intent. This eponymous term alludes to Mrs. Malaprop, a pleasant though pompously ignorant character in Richard B. Sheridan's comedic play, *The Rivals* (1775). Mrs. Malaprop, whose name is derived from the French *mal à propos* 'inappropriate,' continually confuses and misapplies words and phrases, e.g., "As headstrong as an allegory [alligator] on the banks of the Nile." (III,iii)

Lamaitre has reproached Shakespeare for his love of malapropisms. (*Harper's Magazine,* April, 1890)

A person known for using malapropisms is often called a *Mrs. Malaprop.*

mumbo jumbo See GIBBERISH.

portmanteau word A word formed by the blending of two other words. *Portmanteau* is a British term for a suitcase which opens up into two parts. The concept of a *portmanteau word* was coined by Lewis Carroll in *Through the Looking Glass* (1872):

Well, 'slithy' means "lithe and slimy"
... You see it's like a portmanteau—
There are two meanings packed into one.

Carroll's use of *portmanteau* has been extended to include the amalgamation of one or more qualities into a single idea or notion. This usage is illustrated by D. G. Hoffman, as cited in *Webster's Third:*

Its central character is a portmanteau figure whose traits are derived from several mythical heroes.

red-flag term A word whose associations trigger an automatic response of anger, belligerence, defensiveness, etc.; an inflammatory catchphrase. A red flag has long been the symbol of revolutionary insurgents. *To wave the red flag* is to incite to violence. In addition, it is conventionally believed that a bull becomes enraged and aroused to attack by the waving of a red cape. All these uses are interrelated and serve as possible antecedents of *red-flag* used adjectivally to describe incendiary language.

LATITUDE (See FREEDOM.)

LAZINESS (See IDLENESS, INDOLENCE.)

LETTERS

climb Parnassus To pursue the arts, particularly poetry; to court the Muses. Parnassus, a mountain in central Greece near Delphi, was sacred to Apollo and the Muses. It is thus identified with literary endeavors such as the Muses would inspire.

Grub Street Literary hacks or drudges collectively. This expression takes its name from Grub Street (now Milton Street) in London. The area was once a haven for poor, inferior writers and literary hacks. *Grub Street,* which dates from at least 1630, is also used adjectivally to mean 'inferior, low-grade, poor.' Ralph Waldo Emerson used the expression in this passage from *Society and Solitude:*

Now and then, by rarest luck, in some foolish Grub Street is the gem we want.

hack A drudge, especially a literary one; a writer or artist who denies his creative talent and does inferior, unoriginal, dull work in an effort to attain commercial and financial success. An abbreviation of *hackney,* this term originally referred to a horse for hire as well as to the driver of a hackney coach or carriage. This last meaning of *hack* gave rise to the term's current meaning.

potboiler An inferior literary or artistic work executed solely for the purpose of *boiling the pot* 'earning a living'; a literary or artistic hack, such as produces potboilers.

> Such . . . was the singular and even prosaic origin of the "Ancient Mariner" . . . surely the most sublime of "potboilers" to be found in all literature. (Henry Duff Traill, *Coleridge,* 1884)

See also **boil the pot**, SUBSISTENCE.

LIKENESS (See SIMILARITY.)

LITERATURE (See LETTERS.)

LIVELINESS (See VITALITY.)

LOCALITY

asphalt jungle A big city. Also more recently, *concrete jungle.* The reference is both to the vast labyrinth of paved thoroughfares that make up any large city, and to the "law of the jungle" that rules its streets—might makes right, dog-eat-dog, and survival of the fittest. The term was used as early as 1920 in *Hand-Made Fables* by George Ade.

bedroom community A suburb; an outlying community whose inhabitants almost literally only sleep there, since most of their time is spent traveling to and from or working in a major metropolitan area. In England, such a colony is called a *commuting-town,* a *dormitory town,* or sometimes simply a *dormitory.*

the Big Apple Any large city, but especially New York City; the downtown area of a city. Also the title of a ballroom dance popular in the 1930s, the term is thought to have derived from its use in jazz meaning anything large, such as the earth, the world, or a big northern city, by analogy with the shape of the planet. In use since 1930, the term has recently spawned the derogatory variation *the Rotten Apple.*

borscht belt The Catskill region of New York State, particularly the resort hotels located there; also *borscht circuit.* In theater use since 1935, the expression was coined by entertainers who played there to the predominately Jewish clientele, to whose tastes the menu also catered by invariably featuring the borscht, or beet soup, popular with many eastern Europeans.

Hell's Kitchen A section of midtown Manhattan, from 42nd Street to 57th Street, west of Times Square, and including 8th through 11th Avenues. Until the 1940s, the elevated subway line on 10th Avenue turned the area into one notorious for its slums and high rate of crime. It is the site of Richard Rodgers's ballet, *Slaughter on Tenth Avenue* (1936).

neck of the woods Neighborhood, region, locality, territory; parts. *Neck* 'a narrow stretch' of land, woods, ice, etc. —by analogy with the shape of the neck —took on the additional *of the woods* in the United States to denote a settlement in a wooded area. However, it very quickly came to mean colloquially any neighborhood, for in his *Americanisms: the English of the New World* (1871), M. Schele DeVere writes:

> He will . . . find his neighborhood designated as a neck of the woods, that being the name applied to any settlement made in the well-wooded parts of the Southwest especially.

the old stamping ground The place of one's origin; one's home; an area or establishment that one frequents, a haunt or hangout. This expression apparently derives from the way in which an animal, upon determining where it will rest, tramples down the grass or brush so as to create a more comfortable spot for itself. Nowadays, the phrase often applies to the area where a person spent his childhood.

I made my way from Milledgeville to Williamson County, the old stamping ground. (H. R. Howard, *History of Virgil A. Stewart,* 1839)

one-horse town See INSIGNIFICANCE.

Podunk See INSIGNIFICANCE.

red-light district A neighborhood containing many brothels. This common expression is derived from the red lights which formerly marked houses of prostitution.

silk-stocking district The elegant section of an American city or town; a wealthy, posh neighborhood. The figurative sense of *silk-stocking* 'aristocratic, wealthy' was employed as early as 1812 by Thomas Jefferson. The expression maintains usage in the United States.

In as chairman . . . went 47-year-old Hugh Scott Jr., a three-term Congressman from a suburban "silk-stocking" district. (*Time,* July, 1948)

skid row A sleazy, dilapidated urban area inhabited by vagrants, alcoholics, and other of society's outcasts. This term is generally considered as having come from *Skid Road,* an unpaved road in Seattle over which loggers dragged logs from the forest to Yesler's mill in the 1850s. "Taverns, bawdy houses, and cheap hostelries clustered in the area to cater to the lumberjacks and sailors." (*The N.Y. Times,* March 23, 1975) The common American phrase usually describes an area where the buildings, commercial establishments, and residents have all reached an advanced state of deterioration.

The Bowery, . . . the gaudy, gory, sordid model for all this country's Skid Rows. (W. R. and F. K. Simpson, *Hockshop,* 1954)

tenderloin A city district where criminal activity flourishes; an area noted for vice and corruption. This Americanism was reputedly coined by a policeman named Williams in reference to the New York City police district west of Broadway between 23rd and 42nd Streets. In that area, the police were so well-heeled from graft that they could regularly enjoy tenderloin rather than a less expensive meat like hamburger.

Portland is not a puritanic city. In fact, its tenderloin is extensive and worse than anything in San Francisco. (*San Francisco Argonaut,* November 2, 1903)

whistle-stop A small, insignificant community; a one-horse town. This expression alludes to towns where trains stop only when a certain signal is given. The term gained general popularity as a result of the whistle-stop political campaigns, in which a candidate spoke briefly from the train's rear platform at each depot along the railroad line. The expression maintains common use today.

The frank, humorous, and, at the same time, challenging story of the men of the U.S. Foreign Service who represent America in the whistle-stops of the world. (*Saturday Review,* September, 1944)

a wide place in the road A one-horse town; Podunk; Hicksville. The expression, originally only in Western and truck driver use, attained greater popularity after it appeared as the title of an article in *Look* in 1956.

LOCOMOTION (See also VEHICLES.)

piggyback Carried on the back or shoulders like a pack; pertaining to the carrying of one vehicle by another. This term, like its 16th-century counterpart, *pick-a-back,* is of unknown origin. In contemporary usage, *piggyback* usually refers to carrying a child on one's shoulders or carrying a truck trailer on a railroad flatcar.

ride shanks' mare To walk; to go on foot. This expression employs a wry twist on *shanks* 'legs' to imply, especially to the uninitiated, that Shanks is actually the name of the owner of a horse which is to be used as a means of conveyance. Common variations substitute *pony, nag, horse*, etc., for *mare*. The closely allied *shank it* means 'to walk.' Related drolleries include *go by the marrow-bone stage* and *ride Walker's bus*.

LOOKS (See **PHYSICAL APPEARANCE**.)

LOSS (See **IRRETRIEVABILITY**.)

LOVE

get under [someone's] skin See **IRRITATION**.

heartthrob A lover, paramour, or sweetheart; a romantic idol. This common expression describes the exhilarating cardiac pulsations that supposedly accompany every thought, sight, or touch of one's true love. *Heartthrob* may also refer to a celebrity of whom one is enamored.

Rudolph Valentino was the great heartthrob of the silent screen in the nineteen-twenties. (*Listener*, June, 1966)

hold one's heart in one's hand To offer one's love to another; to make an open display of one's love. In Shakespeare's *The Tempest* (III,i), Ferdinand offers his hand to Miranda, to which she responds in kind:

And mine, with my heart in it.

Christopher Marlowe, a contemporary of Shakespeare's, also used this expression.

With this hand I give to you my heart. (*Dido*, III,iv)

look babies in the eyes To gaze lovingly into another's eyes; to look at closely and amorously. Two unrelated theories have been advanced as to the origin of this expression. One states that the reference is to Cupid, the Roman god of love, commonly pictured as a winged, naked baby boy with a bow and arrows. The other maintains that the phrase originated from the miniature reflection of a person staring closely in the pupils of another's eyes. In use as early as 1593, the term, now obsolete, was used to describe the amorous gaze of lovers:

She clung about his neck, gave him ten kisses.
Toyed with his locks, looked babies in his eyes.
(Thomas Heywood, *Love's Mistress*, 1633)

love-tooth in the head A propensity to love. This obsolete expression implies a constant craving for romance.

I am now old, but I have in my head a love-tooth. (John Lyly, *Euphues and His England*, 1580)

rob the cradle To date, marry, or become romantically involved with a significantly younger person. This self-explanatory expression, often substituted by the equally common term *cradlesnatch*, usually carries an implication of disapproval.

I don't usually cradlesnatch. But there was something about you that made me think you were older. (J. Aiken, *Ribs of Death*, 1967)

take a shine to To take a liking or fancy to, to be fond of, to have a crush on. This colloquialism of American origin dates from the mid-19th century. Perhaps *shine* refers to the "bright and glowing" look often attributed to love.

I wonst had an old flame I took sumthin of a shine to. (*Davy Crockett's Almanac*, 1840)

wear one's heart on one's sleeve To make no attempt to hide one's lovesickness; to plainly show that one is suffering from unrequited love; to publicly expose one's feelings or personal wishes. This expression is said to come from the practice of a knight wearing his lady's favor pinned to his sleeve when going into combat. In Shakespeare's *Othello* (I,i), the duplicitous Iago says:

For when my outward action doth
demonstrate
The native act and figure of my
heart
In compliment extern, 'tis not long
after
But I will wear my heart upon my
sleeve
For daws to peck at.

LOYALTY (See CONSTANCY.)

LUST (See also PROMISCUOUSNESS.)

cast a sheep's eye To look at amorously, longingly, covetously, or lustfully; to look at with bedroom eyes; to flirt. This expression alludes to the large, innocent, friendly eyes of a sheep.

Don Manuel cast many a sheep's
eye at my wife, and his good lady
at me. (William R. Chetwood, *The
Voyages and Adventures of Captain
Robert Boyle,* 1726)

dance the antic hay See REVELRY.

get one's ashes hauled To have sexual intercourse; to be sexually gratified; to experience sexual release. This expression appears in many blues lyrics, and may be of Black origin. In the Black community the term is used for both males and females; Whites relate *ashes* with *semen* and thus limit the expression's application to the male. No explanation of the term is entirely satisfactory. Blues lyrics also contain similar phrases with the same sexual implications: *empty my trash* and *my garbage can is overflowing,* giving rise to the *ashes/semen* equation. However, the many references to the use of ashes in casting voodoo spells has led to the conjecture that getting one's ashes hauled may originally have meant escaping the hex that had been put on one's sex life. Increasing cross-cultural interaction among Blacks and Whites has made the expression more familiar; and an increasing openness in speaking about sex in general has made the term, though not quite parlor talk, something less than taboo.

We'll get a box at the Comique,
then go get our ashes hauled.
Never had an Indian girl myself. (S.
Longstreet, *The Pedlocks,* 1951)

horny Sexually aroused; lustful; craving carnal pleasures. This American saying, derived from *horn* 'erect penis,' was formerly used only in reference to male libido.

You are a gorgeous lookin' piece,
Cass. Gets a guy all horny just
lookin' at you. (J. L. Herlihy,
Midnight Cowboy, 1965)

In contemporary usage, however, *horny* is extended to include female lasciviousness or desire.

hot to trot Sexually aroused, horny; lustful, lascivious. This currently popular slang expression was apparently coined by adding to the conventional *hot* 'desirous, eager' the rhyming *trot* as a pun on the slang meaning of *ride* 'to have sexual intercourse.'

proud below the navel Amorous; sexually excited. This uncommon expression is derived from the conspicuous manifestation of sexual arousal in males.

Whenever I see her I grow proud
below the navel. (William
Davenant, *Albovine, King of the
Lombards,* 1629)

roll in the hay To make love, to go to bed, to have sex; hence the noun *a roll in the hay* 'love-making.' This colloquial expression perhaps stems from bygone days when lovers often used hay for a bed.

He gets something out of it . . .
Maybe just a good roll in the hay.
(L. Lewis, *Birthday Murder,* 1945)

LYING (See MENDACITY.)

M

MAGIC

abracadabra A magical incantation or conjuration; any meaningless magical formula; nonsense, gibberish. Although the precise origin of this ancient rune is not known, it is said to be made up from the initials of the Hebrew words *ab* 'father,' *ben* 'son,' and *Ruach Acadosch* 'Holy Spirit.' Formerly believed to have magical healing powers, the word was written in triangular form on parchment and hung from the neck by a linen thread as a charm against disease and adversity. By extension, *abracadabra* is also commonly used to mean nonsense, jargon, and gibberish, as in:

> Leave him . . . to retaliate the nonsense of blasphemy with the abracadabra of presumption. (Coleridge, *Aids to Reflection*, 1824)

hocus-pocus A conjurer's incantation, a magic formula or charm; sleight of hand, legerdemain; trickery, deception; mumbo jumbo, gobbledegook, nonsense. The original 17th-century meaning of the term, now obsolete, was 'a juggler, a conjurer.' According to the *OED*, this use of the term was apparently an eponymic extension of a certain magician's assumed name. The name itself is thought to have derived from the mock Latin incantation which he used: 'Hocus pocus, tontus talontus, vade celeriter jubeo.' It has also been theorized that *hocus-pocus* was a corruption of the Latin words *hoc est corpus* 'here is the body,' uttered by priests at the consecration of the mass. Magicians and conjurers picked up the sounds in mocking imitation.

> These insurgent legions . . . which, by the sudden hocus pocus of political affairs, are transformed into loyal soldiers. (Washington Irving, *Life and Letters*, 1843)

magic carpet A means of transportation that defies conventional limitations such as gravity, space, or time; a means of reaching any imaginable place. Stories tell of legendary characters who owned magic silk carpets that could be ordered to take a rider wherever he wanted to go. Today the phrase is used figuratively to describe something which has a magical "transporting" effect, such as drugs, or as in the following quotation, a good book.

> His Magic Carpet is a book of travels, by means of which he is transported into lands that he is fated never to see. (*Times Literary Supplement*, August 20, 1931)

open sesame See SOLUTION.

MANIPULATION (See also DOMINATION, VICTIMIZATION.)

backstairs influence Indirect control, as of an advisor; power to affect the opinions of one in charge. *Backstairs* refers to the private stairways of palaces, those used by unofficial visitors who had true access to or intimate acquaintance with the inner circles of government. Connotations of deceit and underhandedness were natural extensions of the "indirect" aspect of the backstairs. Examples of this usage are cited as early as the beginning of the 17th century. Today *backstairs influence* has come to mean the indirect influence or sway that given individuals or groups are able to exert over persons in power.

brainwashing A method of changing an individual's attitudes or allegiances through the use of drugs, torture, or psychological techniques; any form of indoctrination. Alluding to the literal erasing of what is in or on one's mind, *brainwashing* used to be associated exclusively with the conversion tactics used by totalitarian states on political dissidents. This use of the word gained currency in the early 20th century.

Ai Tze-chi was Red China's chief indoctrinator or, as he was generally called, Brainwasher No. 1. (*Time*, May 26, 1952)

Today application of the phrase has been extended to include less objectionable but more subtle sources of control such as television and advertising.

in [someone's] pocket To be under another's influence or control; to be at the disposal or mercy of someone else. Dating from the turn of the 19th century, this expression evokes an image of one person being held in the pocket of another, much larger person, and thus conveys feelings of manipulation, insignificance, and helplessness.

Lord Gower . . . seemed charmed with her, sat in her pocket all the evening, both in a titter. (Countess Harriet Granville, *Letters*, 1812)

Although usually used in this interpersonal sense, *in [someone's] pocket* is applied to the control of inanimate objects as well.

He was sitting with the family seat in his pocket. (William Makepeace Thackeray, *The English Humorists*, 1851)

nose of wax A malleable or accommodating nature; a flexible or yielding attitude. This expression is clearly derived from the pliability of a waxen nose. Originally, the phrase alluded to the Holy Scriptures which, in 16th-century England, were subjected to multitudinous and often conflicting interpretations. The expression was later extended to include other controversial philosophies and laws that were subject to numerous explications.

Oral Tradition, that nose of wax, which you may turn and set, which way you like. (Anthony Horneck, *The Crucified Jesus*, 1686)

Although the expression's initial figurative meaning has been virtually obsolete since the 16th and 17th centuries, *nose of wax* is still occasionally used in describing a wishy-washy or easily manipulated person.

He was a nose of wax with this woman. (Benjamin Disraeli, *Endymion*, 1880)

play both ends against the middle To play two opposing forces off against each other to one's own advantage. According to several sources, "both ends against the middle" is a technique used to rig a deck of cards in dealing a game of faro; a dealer who used such a deck was said to be "playing both ends against the middle." His maneuvers ensured that competing players lost and that he (or the house) won.

play cat and mouse with See HARASSMENT.

play fast and loose To connive and finagle ingeniously but inconsiderately to gain one's end; to say one thing and do another; to manipulate principles, facts, rules, etc., irresponsibly to one's advantage. "Fast and Loose," also called "Pricking the Belt," was a cheating game from the 16th century practised by gypsies at fairs. The game required an individual to wager whether a belt was fast or loose. However, the belt would be doubled and coiled in such a way that its appearance prompted erroneous guesses and consequent losses. Shakespeare referred to the trick in *Antony and Cleopatra*:

Like a right gypsy hath at fast and loose
Beguiled me to the very heart of loss. (IV,xii)

And in *King John*, Shakespeare uses *play fast and loose* figuratively as it is also currently heard:

Play fast and loose with faith? So jest with heaven, . . . (III,i)

Procrustean bed See CRITERION.

pull [someone's] chestnuts out of the fire To be forced to save someone else's skin by risking one's own; to extricate another from difficulty by solving his problem; to be made a cat's paw of. This expression derives from the fable of the monkey and the cat. See **cat's paw**, VICTIMIZATION.

pull strings To influence or manipulate persons or things secretly to one's own advantage; used especially in reference to political maneuvering; also *to pull wires.*

> Lord Durham appears to be pulling at 3 wires at the same time—not that the 3 papers—the Times, Examiner and Spectator are his puppets, but they speak his opinions. (Samuel Rogers, *Letters to Lord Holland,* 1834)

The allusion is to a puppeteer who, from behind the scenes, controls the movements of the puppets on stage by pulling on the strings or wires attached to them. Although both expressions date from the 19th century, *to pull wires* apparently predated *to pull strings.* The latter, however, is more commonly used today.

twist [someone] around one's little finger To have complete control over, to have limitless influence upon, to have at one's beck and call; also *wind* or *turn* or *have [someone] around one's little finger. Twist* connotes the extreme malleability of the subject; *little finger,* the idea that the slightest movement or merest whim will suffice to manipulate him. The expression is often used of a woman's power over a man.

> Margaret . . . had already turned that functionary round her finger. (John Lothrop Motley, *Rise of the Dutch Republic,* 1855)

under [someone's] thumb Under the influence, power, or control of; subordinate, subservient, or subject to. This expression alludes to controlling someone in the same way one can control a horse by pressing his thumb on the reins where they pass over the index finger.

> She is obliged to be silent. I have her under my thumb. (Samuel Richardson, *The History of Sir Charles Grandison,* 1754)

work the oracle To wheel and deal, to scheme to one's own advantage, especially for money-raising purposes; to engage in artful behind-the-scenes manipulation of those in a position to grant favors. This British expression uses *oracle* as the means or medium through which desired information or goods are obtained.

> With . . . big local loan-mongers to work the oracle and swim with them. (John Newman, *Scamping Tricks,* 1891)

MARRIAGE

cheese and kisses Rhyming slang for *missis,* one's wife. This British expression is popular in Australia, where it is frequently shortened to simply *cheese.* It also enjoys some use on the West Coast of the United States. Ernest Booth used the phrase in *American Mercury* in 1928.

Darby and Joan A happily married, older couple; an old-fashioned, loving couple. According to one account, the pair was immortalized by Henry Woodfall in a love ballad entitled "The Joys of Love Never Forgot: A Song," which appeared in a 1735 edition of *Gentleman's Magazine,* a British publication. Darby is John Darby, a former employer of Woodfall's. Joan is Darby's wife. The two were inseparable, acting like honeymooners even into their golden years. *Darby and Joan* was also the name of a popular 19th-century song. *Darby and Joan Clubs* are in Britain what Senior Citizens' Clubs are in the United States. The word *darbies* is sometimes used as a nickname for handcuffs. The rationale is that handcuffs are an inseparable pair.

go to the world To be married or wed, to become man and wife. *World* in this expression refers to the secular, lay life as opposed to the religious, clerical life. The phrase, no longer heard today, dates from at least 1565. It appeared in Shakespeare's *All's Well that Ends Well:*

> But, if I may have your ladyship's good will to go to the world, Isbel the woman and I will do as we may. (I,iii)

jump over the broomstick To get married; said of those whose wedding ceremony is informal or unofficial. Variants include *to marry over the broomstick, to jump the besom,* and *to jump the broom.* This expression, which dates from the late 18th century, refers to the informal marriage ceremony in which both parties jumped over a besom, or broomstick, into the land of holy matrimony. Although neither the ceremony nor the phrase is common today, they were well-known to Southern Negro slaves, who were not considered important enough to merit church weddings, and so were married by jumping over the broomstick.

> There's some as think she was married over the broom-stick, if she was married at all. (Julian Hawthorne, *Fortune's Fool,* 1883)

mother of pearl Girlfriend or wife. This phrase is rhyming slang for *girl,* but applies almost exclusively to females who are girlfriends or wives.

my old dutch Wife. This expression of endearment is a British colloquialism for one's spouse. Here *dutch* is short for *duchess.*

plates and dishes Rhyming slang for *missis,* one's wife. *Plates and dishes* are a rather pointed reference to the household duties of a wife.

step off See DEATH.

trouble and strife Rhyming slang for *wife,* dating from the early 1900s. According to Julian Franklyn *(A Dictionary of Rhyming Slang),* this is the most widely used of the many rhyming slang phrases for *wife,* including *struggle and strife, worry and strife,* and the American equivalent *storm and strife.*

MEDDLESOMENESS (See also CURIOSITY.)

finger in the pie Meddlesome officiousness because of one's interest in a matter or concern; an interest or share in some endeavor or enterprise; a piece of the pie or the action. This expression may derive from the propensity of some children to taste "Mom's apple pie" by sticking a finger into it, often using "But I helped" as an excuse. Though the child may have had an interest or share in the project, his sticking a finger in does nothing to improve the final product. Though the expression may refer to legitimate or innocuous involvement, *finger in the pie* usually implies interference of a harmful or malicious nature.

> The devil speed him! no man's pie is freed
> From his ambitious finger.
> (Shakespeare, *Henry VIII,* I,i)

gatemouth One who knows and discusses the affairs of others; a gossip, busybody. This American expression, deriving from Black English, implies that the "gate" to the mouth of a gossipmonger is perpetually opening and closing.

go between the bark and the tree To intervene in the private concerns of intimates; most specifically, to meddle in the affairs of husband and wife.

> An instigator of quarrels between man and wife, or, according to the plebian but expressive apophthegm, one who would come between the bark and the tree. (Maria Edgeworth, *Modern Griselda,* 1804)

See also **close as the bark to the tree,** FRIENDSHIP.

guardhouse lawyer One who presumptuously gives advice; one who discusses matters of which he knows nothing. This expression is traced to soldiers who, deeming themselves authorities on military law, counsel their peers on a variety of military matters. Today, the term is often used disparagingly to describe a pretentious meddler.

Meddlesome Matty An officious meddler, a busybody; one with a finger in every pie and an ear to every keyhole. This epithet, from the title of a poem by Ann Taylor, has been in common American use since the early 1800s. *Webster's Third* cites a contemporary usage by Walter Lippmann:

> When men insist that morality is more than that, they are quickly denounced . . . as Meddlesome Matties.

Nosey Parker A busybody, a stickybeak. Apparently originally a descriptive term for one with an excessively large nose, *nosey* became in concept *nosy* 'inquisitive, prying' and the epithet is now restricted to that usage.

> "But Nosey Parker is what *I* call him," she said. "He minds everybody's business as well as his own." (P. G. Wodehouse, *Something Fresh*, 1915)

Paul Pry A busybody, a meddler; a nosy, interfering person. Paul Pry was the meddlesome hero of a play by the same name written by Englishman John Poole in 1825. A popular Briticism, the phrase is relatively unknown in the United States.

> The magistrate . . . ought to be a perfect jack-of-all-trades . . . Paul Pry in every house, spying, eaves-dropping, relieving, admonishing [etc.]. (Thomas Babington, Lord Macaulay, *Critical and Miscellaneous Essays*, 1829)

put in one's oar To interfere in another's affairs; to meddle in private matters; to intrude or butt in. This expression, a shortening of the original *put one's oar in another's boat*, is still heard occasionally.

> Now, don't you put your oar in, young woman. You'd best stand out of the way, you had! (Sir Walter Besant, *The Children of Gibeon*, 1886)

quidnunc A busybody or gossip. This expression, derived from the literal translation of the Latin *quid nunc* 'what now?', was first used in Arthur Murphy's *The Upholsterer, or What News?* (1757). The term maintains some frequency in the United States and Great Britain.

> He was a sort of scandalous chronicle of the quid-nuncs of Granada. (Washington Irving, *The Alhambra*, 1832)

stickybeak A busybody, quidnunc, or newsmonger. This Australian slang term clearly alludes to someone who thrusts his nose into everyone else's business.

MEEKNESS (See **SUBMISSIVENESS**.)

MENDACITY

Baron Münchhausen A teller of tall tales; one who embellishes and exaggerates to the point of falsehood; a creator of whoppers; a liar. Baron von Münchhausen (1720–97), a German who served in the Russian army, gained renown as a teller of adventurous war stories. These were collected by Rudolph Erich Raspe and published in 1785 as *Baron Münchhausen's Narrative of His Marvelous Travels and Campaigns in Russia.* His name has since become synonymous with tall tales and untruths, whether their intent be to entertain or to deceive.

cry wolf To give a false alarm; to use a trick or other deceitful stratagem to provoke a desired response. This well-known expression alludes to the equally well-known fable about a shepherd lad who often cried "wolf" to get the attention of his neighbors. When they finally grew wise to his trick, a real wolf appeared and the boy cried "wolf," to no avail—no one heeded his call. *OED* citations date the phrase from the late 17th century.

> She begins to suspect she is "not so young as she used to be"; that after

crying "Wolf" ever since the respectable maturity of seventeen—
... the grim wolf, old age, is actually showing his teeth in the distance. (Mrs. Dinah M. Craik, *A Woman's Thoughts About Women*, 1858)

Equivalent expressions and fables appear in many nations throughout the world.

draw the long bow See EXAGGERATION.

from the teeth outward To say but not mean; to speak insincerely. This archaic phrase implies that vocal protestations of friendship, trust, etc., are often of questionable value after their utterance.

Many of them like us but from the teeth outward. (John Udall, *Diotrephes*, 1588)

Lamourette's kiss See AGREEMENT.

lie through one's teeth To purposely tell flagrant and obvious falsehoods; to speak maliciously and untruthfully; to prevaricate with blatant disregard for the truth. The use of *teeth* in this expression serves to underscore the severity of the lie or lies. Variations include *lie in one's teeth, lie in one's throat,* and *lie in one's beard.*

out of whole cloth False, fictitious, fabricated, made-up; also *cut out of whole cloth.*

Absolutely untruthful telegrams were manufactured out of "whole cloth." (*The Fortnightly Review*, July, 1897)

The origin of this expression is rather puzzling in that literal whole cloth (i.e., a piece of cloth of the full size as manufactured, as opposed to a piece cut off or out of it for a garment) seems to lend itself to positive figurative senses rather than negative ones. It has been conjectured that the change in meaning came about because of widespread cheating on the part of tailors who claimed to be using whole cloth but who actually used pieced goods, or cloth stretched to appear to be of full width. Thus, ironic use of the phrase may have given rise to the reversal in meaning. On the other hand, it may come from the sense of 'having been made from scratch,' that is, 'entirely made up' or 'fabricated.' The expression dates from the late 16th century.

snow job An attempt to deceive or persuade, usually by means of insincere, exaggerated, or false claims; a line, particularly one used to impress a member of the opposite sex or a business associate; excessive flattery; a cover-up. Snow, especially in large amounts, tends to obscure one's vision and mask the true nature or appearance of objects on which it falls; thus, the expression's figurative implications.

a white lie A harmless or innocent fib; a minor falsehood that is pardonable because it is motivated by politeness, friendship, or other praiseworthy concern. This expression draws on the symbolism often associated with the color "white" (purity, harmlessness, freedom from malice). An interesting definition of *white lie* was offered in a 1741 issue of *Gentleman's Magazine:*

A certain lady of the highest quality ... makes a judicious distinction between a white lie and a black lie. A white lie is that which is not intended to injure anybody in his fortune, interest, or reputation but only to gratify a garrulous disposition and the itch of amusing people by telling them wonderful stories.

William Paley, on the other hand, presents a different view:

White lies always introduce others of a darker complexion. (*The Principles of Moral and Political Philosophy*, 1785)

window dressing Misrepresentation or deceptive presentation of facts, particularly those relating to financial matters, to give a false or exaggerated impression of success or prosperity. Literally, window dressing is a technique of attractively displaying goods in a store window. The expression is figuratively applied to any specious display, but is used most often in contexts implying financial juggling which borders on the illegal, usually obeying the letter, though certainly not the spirit, of the law.

> The promise of high duties against other countries deceives nobody: it is only political window-dressing. (*Westminster Gazette*, March 9, 1909)

MERRIMENT (See REVELRY.)

MISCHIEF

cut a dido To play clever pranks; to fool around or cavort about; to take part in monkey business; to cut a caper. An entertaining story which is held by some to be the origin of this expression concerns the mythical queen Dido, who founded the African city of Carthage. She obtained the land by the clever ploy of paying for only as much land as could be enclosed with a bull's hide. That amount, however, exceeded the seller's expectations when Dido cut the hide into thin strips and proceeded to encircle enough land to found the new city. *Dido* 'prank or caper' can stand alone; the U.S. slang *cut a dido* dates from at least as early as the beginning of the 19th century.

> A jolly Irishman, who cut as many didos as I could for the life of me. (J. R. Shaw, *Life*, 1807)

gremlin A mythical being fancied to be the cause of aircraft troubles; the personification of other inexplicable mishaps. This term, possibly derived from "goblin," was originally used by England's Royal Air Force in World War II. Its various meanings are discussed in the following citation:

> Gremlins are mythical creatures who are supposed to cause trouble such as engine failures in aeroplanes, a curious piece of

whimsy-whamsy in an activity so severely practical as flying. Now the gremlin seems to be extending its sphere of operations, so that the term can be applied to almost anything that inexplicably goes wrong in human affairs. (*American Speech XIX*, 1944)

hanky-panky Monkey business, shenanigans, mischief; any illegal or unethical goings-on; colloquially often used for philandering or adultery. The current British sense of this term 'legerdemain, jugglery, sleight of hand' was apparently the original meaning of *hanky-panky*, thought to be related to the similar rhyming compound *hocus-pocus* or its variant *hokey-pokey*. The expression dates from at least 1841.

monkey around To fool around; to waste time or loaf; to engage in aimless activities; also *monkey around with*, to tinker or play with something, usually out of curiosity; to interfere with; to tamper with. This expression and its alternative, *monkey about*, allude to the playful behavior and curiosity associated with monkeys.

> I don't see how you fellows have time to monkey around here. (Rudyard Kipling and Wolcott Balestier, *The Naulahka: A Story of West and East*, 1891)

> Any attempt to "monkey about" with the powers or composition of the Upper House would destroy the balance of the constitution. (*Times*, June 27, 1955)

monkey business Improper, unethical, or deceitful conduct or dealings; shenanigans, pranks, or mischief; hanky-panky. This expression refers to the frisky and often unpredictable behavior associated with monkeys.

> Because I've seen her talking with one of the neighbors isn't to say there was any monkey business between them. (H. Carmichael, *Naked to the Grave*, 1972)

"Monkey Business," the title of a 1931 movie, aptly described the zany antics of its stars, the Marx brothers.

monkeyshines Shenanigans, tomfoolery, high jinks; horseplay, monkey business; pranks, practical jokes. This term combines the informal meaning of *shine* 'foolish prank' with an allusion to the frolicsome antics often associated with monkeys.

> Why all the monkeyshines to get rid of Lucy? He'd been divorced before and he could be divorced again. (H. Howard, *Highway to Murder*, 1973)

A related expression, *cut up monkeyshines* 'to behave in a mischievous or frolicksome manner,' gave rise to other variations such as *cut monkeyshines, cut shines,* and *cut up.*

> People recognizing you and staring at you cutting up monkeyshines. (Sinclair Lewis, *Cass Timberlane,* 1945)

Peck's bad boy A mischievous child. This affectionate epithet for a naughty child derives from the main character in *Peck's Bad Boy and His Pa,* a book written in 1883 by George W. Peck.

play the devil To act in a mischievous way; or, more seriously, to act diabolically, in a destructive and harmful manner. This expression dates from the mid-16th century.

> Your firm and determined intention . . . to play the very devil with everything and everybody. (Charles Dickens, *The Life and Adventures of Nicholas Nickleby,* 1838)

play the goat To behave foolishly, to act in an irresponsible, uncontrolled manner. *Goat* has traditionally connoted a wide range of human folly or vice, with meanings ranging from 'butt' to 'lecher.' This colloquial expression dates from the 1800s. Variants include *play the giddy goat* and *act the goat.*

> You'll find some o' the youngsters play the goat a good deal when they come out o' stable. (Rudyard Kipling, *From Sea to Sea,* 1887)

when the cat's away the mice will play Subordinates will always take advantage of the absence of one in authority. This still common saying appeared in John Ray's *Collection of Proverbs* in the 17th century. It is based on a pessimistic view of human nature, one holding that external constraints are needed to insure proper behavior.

MISERLINESS

cheeseparing Penny-pinching, stinginess; excessive economy or frugality. This British expression, which dates from the mid-1800s, is a reference to the practice of taking excessive care when paring the rind from cheese so as to waste as little as possible.

close as a clam Close-fisted; parsimonious; stingy. This phrase alludes to the difficulty involved in opening a clam. One who is "close as a clam" hoards his possessions, making them inaccessible to others.

clutch-fist A miser; a close-fisted person; a stingy, ungenerous character. This obsolete phrase, as well as the truncated *clutch,* appeared in print as early as 1630. The image is of a hand selfishly grasping or clutching.

nickel nurser A miser, tightwad, or penny pincher. This expression, clearly alluding to the disproportionate amount of affectionate attention that a churl gives to his money, is infrequently used today.

penny pincher A miser, skinflint, or tightwad; a stingy or niggardly person; an overly thrifty or frugal person. In this expression, *penny* 'one cent' emphasizes the pettiness of *pincher* 'one who saves in a miserly manner.' A variation is *pinchpenny.* Similarly, *to pinch pennies* is to stint on expenditures, to economize.

piker A tightwad, a cheapskate. This Americanism appears to have originated during the Gold Rush, when the Forty-Niners applied this epithet to those among them who had come from Pike County, Missouri. By 1880, when *piker* denoted a two-bit gambler, its connotations were clearly derogatory, and the term was well on its way to its more general current application.

> My companion immediately produced the coin and not wishing to seem a piker, I followed suit. (Robert W. Service, *Ploughman of the Moon*, 1945)

skinflint A miser, penny pincher, tightwad; a mean, avaricious, niggardly person. This term is derived from the earlier *to skin a flint* which was based on the idea that only an excessively rapacious person would even attempt to remove and save the nonexistent skin of a rock such as flint. One source recounts the tale of an Eastern caliph who was so penurious that he issued his soldiers shavings that he had "skinned" from a flint to save the cost of their using complete flints in their rifles.

> It would have been long . . . ere my womankind could have made such a reasonable bargain with that old skinflint. (Sir Walter Scott, *The Antiquary*, 1816)

tight as the bark on a tree Extremely stingy or close-fisted. This American colloquialism conveys the idea of tightness, or miserliness, by using an image with the flavor of frontier life familiar to the early settlers.

> If you wasn't tighter than the bark on a tree, your wife wouldn't have to do her own washing. (*American Magazine*, November, 1913)

tightwad A miser, a cheapskate, a scrooge, a tight-fisted, stingy person.

> Pauline . . . despises the "tightwads" who have saved money. (E. Gilbert, *The New Republic*, 1916)

The allusion is to the way a miser, not wanting to part with his money, tightly clutches his wad or folded roll of bills. Use of this popular Americanism dates from about the turn of this century.

Vermont charity A now little used hobo term for sympathy—the implication being that Yankee frugality and independence would refuse handouts to those seeking them, offering instead only the inedible solace of sympathy.

MIXTURE (See also **AMALGAMATION**.)

cabbages and kings Anything and everything; odds and ends; assorted and diverse topics, items, etc. The expression comes from Lewis Carroll's *Through the Looking-Glass* (1871):

> "The time has come," the Walrus said,
> "To talk of many things:
> Of shoes—and ships—and sealing-wax—
> Of cabbages—and kings—
> And why the sea is boiling hot—
> And whether pigs have wings."

hodgepodge A heterogeneous mixture, a jumble, a farrago, a gallimaufry, a potpourri. This term is a corruption of the earlier *hotchpotch*, which in turn is a corruption of *hotchpot*, from the French *hochepot* (*hocher* 'to shake, to shake together' + *pot* 'pot'), a cookery term for a dish containing a mixture of many ingredients, especially a mutton and vegetable stew. *Hodge-podge* itself was used figuratively as early as the 15th century.

> They have made our English tongue a gallimaufry or hodgepodge of all other speeches. (E. K., *Epistle Dedicatory and Glosses to Spenser's Shepherds Calendar*, 1579)

mishmash A jumble, hodgepodge, or potpourri; a confused mess. *Mash* alone means 'confused mixture,' suggesting that *mishmash* may have originated as alliterative wordplay. It has also been suggested that *mishmash* comes from the Danish *mischmasch*. Still current, the term and its variants *mishmosh* and *mishmush* have been in print since the 16th century.

> The original *Panorama* had consisted of a mishmash of disconnected and frequently frivolous items. (*Listener*, October 30, 1975)

potluck Leftovers, odds and ends; pot-pourri, hodgepodge; an entity of uncertain composition. This expression is derived from, and still most commonly refers to, leftover food that has been placed in a pot, usually over a period of several days, and then served as a meal at a later date. The rationale for *luck* is that one takes his chances, that is, does not know what food to expect, when he is invited to partake of a potluck dinner. By extension, *potluck* can refer to any conglomeration from which a person makes a blind or indiscriminate selection.

> [He] took the same kind of pot-luck company in those days when he was not so shy of London. (Madame D'Arblay, *The Early Diary of Frances Burney,* 1775)

threads and thrums Odds and ends, scraps, fragments; a hodgepodge, a mishmash. Thrums are the unwoven portions of warp yarn which remain attached to the loom when the web is cut off, useless fragments of knotted threads.

> The confused and ravelled mass of threads and thrums, ycleped Memoires. (Thomas Carlyle, "Diderot," *Miscellaneous Essays,* 1833)

See also **thread and thrum, TOTALITY.**

MONEY

axle grease Australian slang for money, which greases the wheels of life, so to speak, helping things to run along more smoothly.

chicken feed Small change; a paltry or inconsequential amount of money. This American slang expression, which dates from 1836, is an allusion to the scraps and seeds fed to chickens.

fast buck Money acquired quickly and effortlessly, usually through illegal or unscrupulous methods. In this expression, *buck* carries the American slang meaning of dollar, making the origin of the term self-evident.

> Trying to hustle me a fast buck. (A. Kober, *New Yorker,* January, 1949)

filthy lucre Money; money or other material goods acquired through unethical or dishonorable means, dirty money. This expression was first used in an epistle by St. Paul:

> For there are many unruly and vain talkers and deceivers . . . who subvert whole houses, teaching things which they ought not, for filthy lucre's sake. (Titus 1:10–11)

a king's ransom A very large sum of money. This expression, perhaps familiarized by the hefty sum demanded for the release of the kidnapped King Richard the Lion-Hearted, maintains frequent usage.

> I couldn't look upon the babby's face for a king's ransom. (Mrs. Anna Hall, *Sketches of Irish Characters,* 1829)

loaves and fishes Monetary fringe benefits to be derived from public or ecclesiastical office; the personal profit one stands to gain from an office or public enterprise. This use of *loaves and fishes* derives from John 6:26:

> Jesus answered them and said, Verily, verily, I say unto you, Ye seek me, not because ye saw the miracles, but because ye did eat of the loaves, and were filled.

Today the phrase is also sometimes heard in referring to any unanticipated, miraculous proliferation or abundance. This emphasis on abundance rather than personal gain derives from the actual description of the miracle of the loaves and fishes (John 6:11–13).

mad money Money for frivolous purchases or little luxuries; money for a bit of riotous living-it-up. Originally mad money was that carried by a woman in the event her escort made advances prompting her to leave him in the lurch and finance her own return home. It subsequently came to be applied to money used for any emergency, but at some point took the grand leap from necessity to luxury. Perhaps today it might qualify as what economists call *discretionary income.*

monkey's allowance A trifling amount of money; a pittance; a paltry sum. This expression is derived from the saying, "He gets a monkey's allowance—more kicks than halfpence." At one time, trained monkeys performed tricks and then collected money from passers-by. If the monkey performed poorly, its owner often kicked or otherwise punished the animal. Thus, the monkey's allowance was frequently more abuse than money. By extension, a person who receives a "monkey's allowance" is one who works diligently but receives little, if any, payment for his labor. A related expression is *monkey's money* 'something of no value.'

nest egg Money saved, particularly a reserve fund for use in emergencies or retirement; a bank account or other form of investment which regularly increases in value by virtue of interest accrued or additional deposits made. Originally, a nest egg was a natural or artificial egg which was placed in a hen's nest to induce her to lay eggs of her own. Though the term retains this connotation, it has been extended to imply that once a person has saved a certain amount of money, he is likely to save more.

> A nice little nest egg of five hundred pounds in the bank. (John Ruskin, *Fors Clavigera,* 1876)

pin money A small amount of money set aside for nonessential or frivolous expenditures; an allowance given to a woman by her husband. When common or straight pins were invented in the 13th century, they were expensive and relatively scarce, being sold on only one or two days a year. For this reason, many women were given a regular allowance called pin money which was to be saved until the pins were once again available for purchase. In the 14th and 15th centuries, it was not uncommon for a man to bequeath to his wife a certain amount of money to be used for buying pins. Eventually, as pins became cheaper and more plentiful, the pin money was used for trifling personal expenses, but the expression persisted.

> If he gives me two hundred a year to buy pins, what do you think he'll give me to buy fine petticoats? (Sir John Vanbrugh, *The Relapse,* 1696)

rubber check A bad check; a check not covered by sufficient funds. A check issued for an amount greater than the account balance is said to bounce, because it is returned to its payee.

> She had bought the car and paid for it with a rubber check. (*This Week Magazine,* September, 1949)

a shot in the locker A reserve, usually financial; a last resource or chance. *Locker* is a nautical term for the compartment on board a vessel in which are stored ammunition, clothes, etc. *Shot in the locker* is literally stored ammunition; figuratively, it refers to a stash of money.

> As long as there's a shot in the locker, she shall want for nothing. (William Makepeace Thackeray, *Vanity Fair,* 1848)

This expression is often heard in the negative *not a shot in the locker,* meaning no money or means of survival.

small potatoes See INSIGNIFICANCE.

sugar and honey Rhyming slang for *money.* This expression dates from the mid-19th century. *Sugar* alone is a popular slang term for money, in Britain as well as in the United States, where most people are unaware that the term is a truncated version of a rhyming slang expression.

widow's mite See CHARITABLENESS.

N

NEATNESS

apple-pie order Excellent or perfect order. The phrase may seem "as American as apple pie," but its origin is British, and murky. The *OED*'s first citation is from Sir Walter Scott in 1813. Some theorize the expression derived from the French *cap-à-pie* 'from head to foot'; others see it as a corruption of the French *nappes pliées* 'folded linen.' The story that it gained popularity in the United States because of the systematic and orderly arrangement of apple slices in pies baked by New England women is at least as amusing as the others are credible.

clean as a whistle Very clean; completely clean; also *clear* or *dry as a whistle*. This proverbial simile, which dates from the 1780s, is said to have derived from the fact that a whistle must be clean and dry in order to produce a sweet, pure sound.

shipshape In good order, trim, tidy. The original nautical term meant fully rigged or ship-rigged, as opposed to temporarily or jury-rigged. The word often appears in the full phrase *all shipshape and Bristol fashion*, dating from the days when ships of Bristol, famous for its maritime trade, were held in high regard. An entry under "Bristol fashion and shipshape" in Smyth's *Sailor's Word-book* (1867) reads:

> Said when Bristol was in its palmy commercial days . . . and its shipping was all in proper good order.

spick and span Spotlessly clean, neat and tidy; a shortened form of the expression *spick and span new* meaning 'completely brand-new.' Although the exact origin of the expression is unknown, it has a possible connection with *span* 'a chip or piece of wood' and the obsolete meaning of *spick* 'spike-nail.' Thus, a brand-new ship would have all new spicks and spans. According to the *OED* the longer expression first appeared in the late 1500s, while the abbreviated term more popular today came into use about 1665. It would seem that in dropping the *new* from the expression the emphasis shifted from newness itself to those qualities usually associated with new things such as freshness, cleanliness, tidiness, and neatness.

spit and polish Meticulous attention given to tidiness, orderliness, and a smart, well-groomed appearance. This expression found its first widespread use in the armed forces, where it alluded to the common custom of spitting on a shoe or other leather item and buffing it to a high polish. While the phrase retains its military application, it now carries the suggestion of extreme fastidiousness in maintaining a sharp, scrubbed, disciplined appearance.

> To lessen the time spent in spit and polish to the detriment of real cavalry work. (*United Service Magazine,* December, 1898)

NEWNESS (See AGE.)

NICKNAMES

breadbasket Stomach, abdomen. This figurative slang term, whose literal origins are obvious, has been in common usage since the mid-18th century.

doughboy A U.S. Army infantryman. The exact origin of this colloquial term is unknown. It gained currency during World War I after seeing sporadic use during the Civil War. One of the many explanations for this term was put forth by E. Custer in *Tenting on Plains* (1887):

> A "doughboy" is a small, round doughnut served to sailors on

shipboard, generally with hash. Early in the Civil War the term was applied to the large globular brass buttons on the infantry uniform, from which it passed, by a natural transition, to the infantrymen themselves.

Another theory suggests a connection between *adobe*, a name used by Spaniards in the Southwest in reference to army personnel, and *doughboy*. The third most common explanation is that the infantrymen wore white belts, and had to clean them with "dough" made of pipe clay.

fire bug An arsonist, pyromaniac. In this expression, *bug* has the slang meaning of one who has great enthusiasm for something, in this case, for fire.

> It is believed there exists an organized band of firebugs. (*Pall Mall Gazette*, September 12, 1883)

fly trap The human mouth. This disparaging term of obvious origin is often shortened to merely *trap*.

> You can count on Angelo's keepin' his trap tight. (L. J. Vance, *Baroque*, 1923)

four-eyes A person who wears eyeglasses. The implication in this derisive expression is that a person has an extra pair of eyes by virtue of his spectacles. A similar expression, sometimes used by one who is putting on his eyeglasses, is *putting on one's eyes*, implying that without the glasses, he is, in essence, blind.

fruit salad Colorful ribbons or buttons worn as campaign decorations; medals or badges which adorn the uniforms of servicemen. The infrequently heard expression is derived from the motley colors present in a fruit salad.

grass widow A woman whose husband is away for an indefinite, extended period of time; a woman who is separated, divorced, or living apart from her husband. The oldest use of the term, now obsolete, dates from the early 16th cen-

tury. It referred to a discarded mistress. The expression gained currency in the United States during the California gold rush when it was used for the wives of the forty-niners. The popular theory that the term is a corruption of *grace-widow* 'a widow by grace or courtesy, not in fact' has been disproved by evidence of parallel forms in several other languages.

> Grass widows in the hills are always writing to their husbands, when you drop in upon them. (John Lang, *Wanderings in India*, 1859)

Jack Tar An appellation for a sailor. This name apparently derived from the fact that sailors tarred their pigtails. Sailors were called Jacks as early as the 1600s and by association were called Jack Tars by the mid-18th century. *Jack-tar* can also be used attributively, as in the following quotation:

> He had mixed it [brandy and water] on the Jack-tar principle of "half-and-half." (William Schwenk Gilbert, *Foggerty's Fairy and Other Tales*, 1892)

jock An athlete. This American slang expression is a shortening of *jockstrap*, the term for a supporter worn by men when participating in certain sports. It is most often applied to high school and college athletes, frequently with some degree of disparagement. In recent years the term has also been applied to females who actively participate in sports.

> Rocks for jocks, elementary geology course popular among athletes at Pennsylvania. (*Time*, October 2, 1972)

limey An Englishman; a Briton. This expression is a variation of *lime-juicer*, a somewhat derogatory nickname applied to English sailors, referring to the British regulation requiring all merchant vessels to carry a supply of lime juice to be used as a preventative measure against scurvy. Since scurvy is caused by a deficiency of Vitamin C, regular doses of lime juice (rich in Vitamin C) were used to prevent the disease.

"English, eh?" said the manager. "I ain't too keen on you limeys." (J. Spencer, *Limey*, 1933)

Nosey Parker See MEDDLESOMENESS.

the Old Lady of Threadneedle Street A popular British nickname for the Bank of England, located on Threadneedle Street. There is some confusion as to whether the epithet owes its origin to Gilray's caricature (1797) depicting "The Old Lady of Threadneedle Street in Danger" at a time when its financial solvency was in jeopardy, or to the essayist William Cobbett, who dubbed the bank's directors the Old Ladies of Threadneedle Street because of their conservatism. In any event, the phrase was well known less than a century later when in *Doctor Marigold's Prescriptions* (1865), Dickens referred to a bank note as:

a silver curl-paper that I myself took off the shining locks of the ever-beautiful old lady of Threadneedle Street.

old salt A sailor, particularly an old or experienced one; a sea dog. The allusion is to the salt in the seawater to which a sailor is constantly exposed.

If you want to hear about the sea, talk to an "old salt." (Charles Spurgeon, *Sermon XXIII*, 1877)

Common variations include *salt* and *salty dog*.

one-armed bandit A slot machine used for gambling. These popular devices are operated by placing a coin in the slot and pulling down on a lever or "arm" on the side of the machine. Since the odds are fixed against the player, usually causing him to lose more than he wins, slot machines soon came to be known as "one-armed bandits," and have been outlawed in most of the United States.

The machine that brought him from rags to riches was the notorious One Armed Bandit slot

machine. (*American Mercury*, September, 1940)

See also **lemon**, FAILURE.

pork chops American slang for sideburns or side whiskers, from the similarity in shape to the cut of the meat.

Saturday night special An inexpensive hand gun that is easily obtainable through a gun store or a mail order house. While the origin of this common expression is not documented, Robert Blair Kaiser, writing in a February, 1974, issue of *Rolling Stone*, offers a plausible explanation of its derivation:

Since a great many of these purchases were made to satisfy the passions of Saturday Night, Detroit lawmen began to refer to the weapons as Saturday Night specials.

scrambled eggs The gold decoration on the bill of a military officer's hat. The phrase's denotation is sometimes extended to include other gold garnishes on the uniform, though these are more properly denoted by the slang term *chicken guts*. Because such embellishments are reserved for senior officers only, enlisted men occasionally use the expression for the high-ranking officers themselves.

Tommy Atkins The nickname given to a typical, low-ranking soldier in the British armed forces. In 1815, the British War Office issued a manual to all military personnel in which each soldier was required to enter certain personal data, such as name, age, and medals received. Enclosed with each manual was a sample guide in which the fictitious name *Thomas Atkins* was employed. Before long, the manuals themselves were called *Tommy Atkins*, and subsequently, the epithet acquired its current application to any British soldier, particularly privates.

Some years ago, Lord Wolseley . . . said "I won't call him Tommy Atkins myself, for I think it a piece of impertinence to call the private soldier Tommy Atkins." (E. J. Hardy, in *United Service Magazine,* March, 1898)

The British have extended the term's application to include a private in any military force, or to the rank-and-file membership of a group or organization.

The Egyptian Tommy Atkins inspires one rapidly with feelings of sheer affection. (Francis Adams, *The New Egypt,* 1893)

Uncle Sam The personification of the United States; the American government, its prestige, or its citizenry.

The thirteen stripes turned vertically . . . thus indicating that a civil . . . post of Uncle Sam's government is here established. (Nathaniel Hawthorne, "Introduction," *The Scarlet Letter,* 1850)

This expression purportedly originated during the War of 1812, at Elbert Anderson's provisions stockyard in Troy, New York, where all shippable items were stamped E.A.—U.S., for Elbert Anderson—United States. Through allusion to the yard's chief inspector, Samuel Wilson, whose nickname was Uncle Sam, the workers suggested that U.S. actually stood for Uncle Sam. This epithet rapidly became a synonym for the United States, its usage being reinforced as a wartime rebuttal to Great Britain's trademark of John Bull. In 1868, Thomas Nast, the political cartoonist for *Harper's Weekly,* depicted Uncle Sam as he is familiarly known today. From the Civil War onward, Uncle Sam has appeared on military recruitment posters throughout the nation. The term has maintained frequent usage as a fond name for the United States.

Let patriots everywhere . . . prepare to do the clean thing by Uncle Sam and his bald headed eagle. (*Newton Kansan,* June, 1873)

NIT-PICKING

chop logic To argue, dispute, or to pettifog, to bandy words; split hairs. This expression, which dates from 1525, is most likely an extension of the now obsolete meaning of *chop* 'barter, trade, or exchange.' Shakespeare used the noun form *chop-logic* in *Romeo and Juliet:*

How, now! How, now! Chop-logic!
What is this?
"Proud," and "I thank you," and
"I thank you not,"
And yet "not proud." (III,v)

nit-pick To be overly concerned with picayune details; to look for inconsequential errors, often to the point of obsessiveness. A nit is the egg or larva of a louse or other parasitic insect. The task of removing all the nits from an infected person or animal can be almost overwhelming as it requires a millimeter-by-millimeter examination with a magnifying glass and tweezers. By extension, a pedantic person immersed in minutiae is often called a *nit-picker.*

When the nitpickers and parliamentary horse-traders had finished with it, the program had shrunk to much smaller proportions. (*Washington Post,* July 3, 1959)

seek a knot in a bulrush To look for errors or difficulties where there are none; to nit-pick; to pursue trivial, futile activities. Since knots occur only in woody plants, it would be both time-consuming and futile to try to find one in a bulrush, a grasslike, herbaceous plant.

Those that sought knots in bulrushes to obstruct the King's affairs in Parliament . . . (Roger North, *Examen; or An Enquiry Into the Credit and Veracity of a Pretended Complete History,* 1734)

split hairs To make gratuitously fine or trivial distinctions. This expression refers to the fineness of hair and the subsequent difficulty involved in splitting a single strand. The expression is in common use today.

wrangle for an ass's shadow To fight or bicker over trivial and insignificant matters; to nit-pick. This expression, once popular in England, is derived from a legend recounted by the Greek orator and statesman, Demosthenes (c. 384–322 B.C.). A traveler who had hired an ass to take him from Athens to Megara was in such discomfort from the noonday sun that he dismounted and sought relief by sitting in the shadow cast by the animal. The ass's owner, however, also wanted that shade and claimed that the traveler had rented the ass and not its shadow. The two men soon resorted to fisticuffs and the frightened animal fled, leaving both of them without any shade whatsoever. When the issue was pursued in the courts, the litigation was so lengthy and expensive that the two men were financially ruined. An earlier variation is *gone to the bad for the shadow of an ass.*

NONSENSE

applesauce Nonsense, balderdash, bunk; lies and exaggeration; flattery and sweet talk. The first of these meanings is now most common, and the last, least in use. According to a 1929 article in *Century Magazine*, however, the term originally meant "a camouflage of flattery" and derived from the common practice of boarding houses to serve an abundance of applesauce to divert awareness from the paucity of more nourishing fare. It seems equally plausible, though, that its origin might lie in the association of applesauce with excessive sweetness, mushiness, pulpiness, and insubstantiality.

balderdash Nonsense; a meaningless jumble of words. Used throughout most of the 17th century to mean a hodgepodge of liquors, this word began to be used in its current sense in the latter part of the same century.

banana oil Bunk, hokum, hogwash, nonsense. This American slang term for insincere talk derives from the literal banana oil, a synthetic compound used as a paint solvent and in artificial fruit flavors, itself so called because its odor resembles that of bananas. Its figurative use combines its characteristics of excessive sweetness and unctuousness.

bunkum Empty or insincere talk, especially that of a politician aiming to satisfy local constituents; humbug; nonsense; also *buncombe* or the shortened slang form *bunk;* sometimes in the phrase *talk* or *speak for* or *to Buncombe.* The term comes from a speech made by Felix Walker, who served in Congress from 1817 to 1823. It was so long and dull that many members left. The exodus of his fellow Congressmen did not bother Mr. Walker in the least since he was, in his own words, bound "to make a speech for Buncombe," a North Carolina county in his district. *Bunk,* the abbreviated slang version of *bunkum,* did not appear until 1900, although *bunkum* itself dates from much earlier:

"Talking to Bunkum!" This is an old and common saying at Washington, when a member of congress is making one of those hum-drum and unlistened to "long talks" which have lately become so fashionable. (*Niles' Register,* 1828)

cock and bull story A preposterous, improbable story presented as the truth; tall tale, canard, or incredible yarn; stuff and nonsense. Few sources acknowledge that the exact origin of this phrase is unknown. Most say it derives from old fables in which cocks, bulls, and other animals are represented as conversational creatures. In one of the Boyle Lectures in 1692 Richard Bentley says:

cocks and bulls might discourse, and hinds and panthers hold conferences about religion.

Matthew Prior's *Riddle on Beauty* clearly shows the nonsensical flavor of "cock and bull":

Of cocks and bulls, and flutes and fiddles, Of idle tales and foolish riddles.

The phrase is current today, as are the truncated slang forms—*cock* in Britain and *bull* in the United States—which mean 'nonsense.'

fiddlesticks Nonsense, hogwash, balderdash. This word is virtually synonymous with *fiddle-de-dee* and *fiddle-faddle*. Literally, a fiddlestick is the bow used to play a fiddle. Figuratively, it is often used as an interjectional reply to a totally absurd statement.

> Do you suppose men so easily damage their natures? Fiddlestick! (William Makepeace Thackeray, *Miss Tickletoby's Lecture,* 1842)

moonshine Nonsense, hogwash; foolish notions or conceptions. Moonshine is the light which, although appearing to be generated by the moon, is actually sunlight reflected off the lunar surface; hence, the expression's figurative connotation of illusion or fallacy.

> Coleridge's entire statement upon that subject is perfect moonshine. (Thomas DeQuincey, *Confessions of an Opium-Eater,* 1856)

tommyrot Nonsense, poppycock, balderdash. This expression combines *tommy* 'simpleton, fool,' with *rot* 'worthless matter' to form a word denoting foolish utterances.

> My fellow newcomers . . . thought nothing of calling some of our instructor's best information "Tommy Rot!" (Mary Kingsley, *West African Studies,* 1899)

O

bogtrotter Any rustic or country bumpkin; specifically, the rural Irish. The term, which dates from 1682, is most commonly used as an insulting epithet for unsophisticated countryfolk. *Bogtrotter* formerly referred to one who knew how to make his way around the bogs or swamps (which, the English maintain, abound in Ireland), or to one who fled to them for refuge.

butter-and-egg man A rich, unsophisticated farmer or small-town businessman who spends money freely and ostentatiously on trips to a big city. This American slang expression, which dates from the 1920s, is said to have had its origin in the heyday of Calvin Coolidge's administration, when highly paid workers and newly made millionaires threw their money around in wild splurges. *Butter-and-egg* is a rather pointed reference to dairy farming and serves to underscore the unsophistication of the men it is used to describe. *The Butter and Egg Man* is the title of a play by George S. Kaufman written in 1925.

clodhopper A rustic; a clumsy, awkward boor; a clown; a churl or lout; a plowman or agricultural laborer. Literally, a clodhopper is one who walks over plowed land among the *clods* 'lumps of earth or clay.' The common association of all that is unsophisticated, boorish, and gauche with simple countryfolk and farmers gives *clodhopper* its figurative coloring. The *OED* suggests that *clodhopper* is a playful allusion to *grasshopper*. By the early 18th century, *clodhopper* was used figuratively as an offensive epithet.

> Did you ever see a dog brought on a plate, clodhopper? Did you? (Susanna Centliver, *Artifice,* 1721)

Today, the literal use is rarely heard.

country bumpkin An unsophisticated, awkward, clumsy country person; a rube or hick. *Bunkin,* presumably a variant, was used humorously as early as the 16th century to mean a Dutchman, particularly a short, stumpy man. It is thought that the term derives from the Dutch *boomken* 'little tree' or *bommekijn* 'little barrel.' The word *country* is actually redundant and is often dropped from the phrase.

hayseed A humorous nickname for a farmer or rustic. The term is said to have originated in American politics where the delegates of rural constituencies were known as the hayseed delegation in state legislatures. The word appeared as early as 1851 in Herman Melville's *Moby Dick.*

rough edges See **IMPERFECTION**.

rough-hewn Uncultured, unrefined, unpolished; crude, coarse, gauche; blunt, tactless. Literally, *rough-hewn* refers to a piece of lumber that has been crudely and roughly shaped (by an ax or adze) without being finished or polished (by a mill). The expression is often applied figuratively to a person who lacks refinement or social grace.

> Smooth voices do well in most societies . . . when rough-hewn words do but lay blocks in their own way. (Gabriel Harvey, *Pierce's Supererogation, or A New Praise of the Old Ass,* 1593)

sodbuster A derogatory term for a farmer or one who works the soil. Originally Western slang, this word appeared in Carl Sandburg's *The American Songbag* (1927).

OBSCENITY (See **PROFANITY**.)

OBSEQUIOUSNESS

apple-polisher A sycophant or toady; an ingratiating flatterer. This informal

U.S. term stems from the schoolboy practice of bringing an apple to the teacher, supposedly to compensate for ill-prepared lessons. It has been in common student use since 1925 and has given us the now equally common verb phrases *apple-polish* and *polish* or *shine up the apple*, both meaning to curry favor with one's superiors.

ass kisser A fawning flatterer, especially one who is two-faced—submissively deferential to superiors in their presence but boldly badmouthing them in their absence. The once taboo, self-explanatory term has gained general currency in spoken usage where it is rapidly losing its literal associations. It has yet to become an acceptable word in the written language, however.

bootlick A self-explanatory but stronger term for an apple-polisher or toady. The phrase *to lick [someone's] boots* or *shoes* has the same connotation of abject servility and devotion.

brown-nose A fawning flatterer, an obsequious sycophant. The term is more strongly derogatory than *apple-polisher*, and was once considered vulgar owing to its derivation from the image of the ass kisser. Frequent use has rendered the term innocuous, though still insulting. Its corresponding verb form means to curry favor.

curry favor To seek to ingratiate oneself with one's superiors by flattery or servile demeanor. The original term *to curry Favel*, in use until the early 17th century, derived from a 14th-century French satirical romance in which the cunning, duplicitous centaur Fauvel granted favors to those who curried, or rubbed down, his coat. The natural English transition to *favor* appeared as early as 1510, and after a century of coexistence, totally replaced the earlier *favel*.

dance attendance on To be totally servile to another; to wait upon obsequiously. This expression originated from an ancient tradition that required a bride to dance with all the guests at her wedding. The phrase, found in literature dating from the 1500s, appears in its figurative sense in Shakespeare's *Henry VIII* (1613):

> A man of his place, and so near our favour,
> To dance attendance on our lordship's pleasure. (V,ii)

lickspittle The most servile of sycophants, the basest of groveling, parasitic toadies. An early use underscores the self-evident origin of the term:

> Gib, Lick her spittle
> From the ground. (Sir William Davenant, *Albovine,* 1629)

make fair weather To conciliate or flatter by behaving in an overly friendly manner; to ingratiate oneself with a superior by representing things in a falsely optimistic light. Shakespeare used this expression in *Henry VI, Part II;* however, it goes back even earlier to the turn of the 15th century.

> But I must make fair weather yet awhile,
> Till Henry be more weak, and I more strong. (V,i)

toad-eater A servile and obsequious attendant or follower; one who will go to any lengths to comply with a superior's wishes; a toady (whence the term) or sycophant. According to the *OED,* the original toad-eaters were charlatans' assistants who ate, or pretended to eat, poisonous toads, thus providing their mountebank masters with the opportunity to display their curative powers by expelling the deadly toxin.

tuft-hunter A self-seeking flatterer, particularly of the prestigious and powerful; one who attempts to enhance his own status by consorting with those of higher station. Formerly, titled undergraduates at Oxford and Cambridge were, in university parlance, called *tufts,* after the tuft or gold tassel worn on their mortarboards as an indication of their rank. Those of lesser standing who sought their attentions and company thus came to be known as *tuft-hunters*.

OBSESSION

have a bee in one's bonnet To be obsessed by a delusive notion or fantasy; to be preoccupied by a whimsical or perverse fancy; to be eccentric or crotchety. Variants of this phrase, such as *bees in the head* or *brains*, and *maggots in the head* or *brains*, were used as early as the beginning of the 16th century, although *bee in one's bonnet* is heard almost exclusively today. As for its origin, it seems evident that anyone with a live bee buzzing inside his hat would be preoccupied indeed. Perhaps the use of alliteration accounts for its currency.

one-track mind A mind completely obsessed with a single thought, idea, or desire; an extremely narrow point of view. This common expression alludes to a single set of railroad tracks on which trains can move in only one direction. As used today, the phrase often carries the disparaging implication that the possessor of such a mind stubbornly resists any consideration of alternative viewpoints.

> The persons with the one-track mind are the ones who usually have the most collisions. (*Kansas City Times*, May, 1932)

ride a hobbyhorse To pursue a favorite project or idea relentlessly and unceasingly; to be obsessed with a single notion or scheme. A *hobbyhorse* was the term given to a wickerwork horselike frame used in the old Morris dances, as well as to the stick toy with a horse's head ridden in mock fashion by children. The expression originally meant to play an infantile game of which one soon tired, since riding such a hobbyhorse involved little more than monotonous repetition of unvaried movements. In the 1700s John Wesley referred to *hobbyhorse* as "the cant term of the day."

OBSOLESCENCE

back number An old-fashioned person or outdated object; one whose mode of thought, dress, or behavior is generally regarded as passé. Issues of magazines are designated by number, and the literal term refers to those no longer current. The figurative meaning has been current, however, for almost a century.

> There is always some old back number of a girl who has no fellow. (George W. Peck, *Peck's Sunshine*, 1882)

nine days' wonder A person, object, or event that arouses considerable, but short-lived, interest or excitement; a flash in the pan. This expression probably derives from the activities surrounding the observation of major religious feasts during the Middle Ages. Usually nine days in length (hence the term *novena* 'a nine-day religious devotion'), these celebrations were accompanied by parades, festivities, and general merriment, after which the people returned to their normal lifestyles. One source suggests that the term may be derived from an ancient proverb: "A wonder lasts nine days, and then the puppy's eyes are open." This refers to the fact that dogs are born blind and do not realize their power of sight until they are about nine days old. It implies that the public is temporarily blinded by the dazzling sensationalism of a person or event, but once its eyes are opened, the wonderment soon fades. In Shakespeare's *Henry VI, Part III*, the King responds to Gloucester's playful charge that his marriage would be a "ten days' wonder" with

> That's a day longer than a wonder lasts. (III,ii)

old hat Old-fashioned; out of style; passé. This expression derives from dated headgear. The term is commonplace throughout the United States and Great Britain.

For that matter, tubular stuff [furniture] is now old hat. (*New Yorker*, October, 1949)

OBSTINACY

deaf as an adder Obstinate refusal to listen; stubborn unwillingness to pay attention. The origin of this phrase lies in ancient Oriental folklore. An adder was thought to protect itself against the music of a snake charmer by blocking one ear with its tail while pressing the other ear to the ground. This belief was mentioned in the Old Testament of the Bible:

> They are like the deaf adder that stoppeth her ear
> Which will not hearken to the voice of charmers, charming never so wisely.
> (Psalms 58:4–5)

OBVIOUSNESS

plain as a pikestaff Plain as day, obvious, clear-cut, evident. This proverbial expression, dating from the late 16th century, is a variant of the earlier, now obsolete, *plain as a packstaff*. The allusion is to the simple style and plain, smooth surface of a pikestaff, a type of walking stick with a metal point at the lower end.

> The evidence against him was as plain as a pikestaff. (Anthony Trollope, *The Last Chronicle of Barset*, 1867)

plain as the nose on your face Exceedingly obvious; extremely conspicuous. This concept was conveyed by Shakespeare in *The Two Gentlemen of Verona*:

> Oh jest unseen, inscrutable, invisible,
> As a nose on a man's face, or a weathercock on a steeple. (II,i)

The expression, clearly derived from the prominence of the nose on the human face, has maintained common usage through the centuries.

> It is as plain as the nose on your face that there's your origin.

(Thomas Hardy, *Pair Blue Eyes*, 1873)

point-blank See CANDIDNESS.

OCCUPATION

costermonger A street-vendor, a hawker of fresh fruits, vegetables, fish, etc.; also simply *coster*. This British expression comes from the earlier *costardmonger* 'apple-seller' (*costard* 'a large, ribbed variety of apple' + *monger* 'dealer, trader'). It has been in use since 1514.

flatfoot A police officer. This expression, in widespread use since the early 20th century, implies that a police officer on a beat becomes flatfooted from walking. *Flatfoot* and other expressions of derision became firmly entrenched in American speech during the Prohibition era (1920–33) when the general public was particularly contemptuous of those who enforced the law.

> He got sore as a boil and stepped up to the lousy flatfoot. (J. T. Farrell, *Studs Lonigan*, 1932)

flesh-tailor A surgeon. The derivation of this British colloquialism is obvious.

free-lance An unaffiliated person who acts on his own judgment; a writer or journalist who submits work to various publishers without actually being employed by any of them; a person hired on a part-time or temporary basis to perform tasks for which he has been specially trained. This expression dates from the Middle Ages when, after the Crusades, bands of knights offered their services to any country that was willing to pay. Also known as mercenaries or free companies, these bands were commonly called *free-lances* in reference to their knightly weapon, the lance. Eventually the term was applied to unaffiliated politicians. In contemporary usage, however, a *free-lancer* is anyone (though usually a writer) who offers his services on a temporary basis with payment upon completion of the work, as opposed to payment in the form of a salary or retainer.

> If they had to rely on the free-lance articles . . . they could close down tomorrow. (*Science News*, 1950)

gandy dancer Railroad slang for a section hand or tracklayer. The term, in use as early as 1923, derives from the rhythmic motions of railroad workers who laid tracks with tools made by the now defunct Gandy Manufacturing Company of Chicago.

ghost writer A person who is paid to write a speech, article, or book—particularly an autobiography—for another, usually more famous person who receives and accepts credit for its authorship; a hack writer. This expression alludes to the classic definition of *ghost* 'an unseen spirit or being existing among living persons.' The implication is that though a ghost writer exists, his presence is hidden from the general public; thus, his existence is unknown or unrecognized. A back formation is *to ghostwrite* or *to ghost* 'to write for another who accepts credit for the work.'

> The autobiographical baloney ghost-written by Samuel Crowther for Ford . . . (*New Republic*, February 10, 1932)

gumshoe A detective, plainclothesman, or police officer; so called from the rubber-soled shoes reputedly worn by those gentlemen in order to assure noiseless movement. Consequently *gumshoe* can also be used as a verb meaning 'to move silently; to sneak, skulk, or pussyfoot.'

ink-slinger A disparaging appellation for a writer, especially one who writes for his livelihood; also *ink-jerker, -spiller,* or *-shedder.* The reference is probably to a newspaper writer under such pressure to finish an article by a specified deadline that he "slings" the ink onto the paper without regard for the quality of writing. This American slang term dates from the latter half of the 19th century. The noun *ink-slinging* appeared in *The Spectator* (November, 1896):

> There is . . . no picturesque ink-slinging, as the happy American phrase goes.

pencil pusher An office worker who does a considerable amount of writing. This U.S. slang term is a disparaging comment on the lack of productive labor in office work. The phrase also implies that such work is menial and mechanical.

> The number of pencil pushers and typists has increased in the past 25 years out of proportion to the increase in factory workers. (Sam Dawson, AP wire story, July 9, 1952)

sawbones A surgeon; any doctor. The allusion in this term is gruesomely obvious.

> "What, don't you know what a Sawbones is, sir," enquired Mr. Weller; "I thought every body know'd as a Sawbones was a surgeon." (Charles Dickens, *Pickwick Papers*, 1837)

shrink A psychiatrist or psychoanalyst. This derogatory expression is a shortening of *headshrinker,* which may have been coined by analogy to the primitive tribal custom, practised by medicine men, of shrinking a decapitated head by removing the skull and stuffing the skin with hot sand.

> You talk like one of those head-shrinkers—a psychiatrist. (S. McNeil, *High-Pressure Girl*, 1957)

OLD AGE (See AGE.)

OLDNESS (See AGE.)

OMEN

handwriting on the wall A portent or prophecy of disaster, a sign of impending and unavoidable doom, an indication or sense of what is to come; often *the writing on the wall*. The allusion is to the Book of Daniel in the Bible, in which a hand mysteriously appeared and wrote a message on Balshazzar's palace wall foretelling his destruction and the loss of his kingdom.

my little finger told me that Pain or pleasurable sensation in the fingers was considered by the ancient Roman augurs a sign of evil or joy to come. The pricking of one's thumb was considered a portent of evil.

> By the pricking of my thumbs
> Something wicked this way comes.
> (Shakespeare, *Macbeth*, IV,i)

Thus, one's finger or thumb can be said to "tell" the future. Sometimes *my little finger told me that* is used to indicate that one has access to certain information, the source of which may be controversial and unscientific.

stormy petrel One whose arrival is seen as a harbinger of trouble. Stormy petrels *(Procellaria pelagica)* are the sea birds which sailors call Mother Carey's chickens. *Petrel* is derived from the Italian *Petrello* 'little Peter,' in allusion to the way these birds appear to walk on the sea, just as St. Peter walked on the Lake of Gennesareth. Stormy petrels are most often observed just prior to and during a storm; thus, their arrival portends deteriorating weather conditions. The expression may now be applied to anyone whose coming is inevitably followed by disaster or tragedy.

> Dr. von Esmarch is regarded at court as a stormy petrel, and every effort was made to conceal his visit to the German emperor. (*The World*, April, 1892)

See also **Mother Carey is plucking her chickens**, WEATHER.

weather breeder See WEATHER.

OPPORTUNENESS (See also TIMELINESS.)

field day A favorable time for accomplishment; a time rich with opportunity for enjoyment, profit, or success. This expression originally referred to a day scheduled for military maneuvers and war games. It still carries the literal meaning of a school day set aside for various outdoor activities and amusements, such as sports, games, or dances. The phrase was used figuratively by Aldous Huxley in his *Letters* (1953):

> Industrial agriculture is having a field day in the million acres of barren plain now irrigated.

the goose hangs high Things are looking good, everything is rosy, the future looks promising. No satisfactory explanation has yet been offered to account for the origin of this expression. The theory that the phrase was originally *the goose honks high*, based on the unsubstantiated notion that geese fly higher on clear days than on cloudy ones, must be discounted for lack of evidence. This expression, which dates from at least 1863, was used to describe fine weather conditions before it was applied to the state of affairs in general.

> If you believe there is a plethora of money, if you believe everything is lovely and the goose hangs high, go down to the soup houses in the city of New York. (*Congressional Record*, February, 1894)

pudding-time A favorable or opportune time; not too late; often in the phrase *to come in pudding-time*. This expression, now obsolete, literally means in time for dinner since pudding was at one time served at the start of this meal. The term dates from 1546.

strike while the iron is hot See EXPLOITATION.

OPTIMISM (See IDEALISM.)

ORATORY (See EXHORTATION.)

OSTENTATIOUSNESS

cut a swath To show off or attract attention to oneself; to make a pretentious display; to cut a dash. This expression, which dates from 1843, is a figurative extension of *swath* 'the strip or belt cut by the sweep of a scythe.'

English Any extra something that gives flourish or pizzazz to an otherwise ordinary movement or gesture; side spin on a ball. The following explanation of the origin of this American term appeared in the *London Sunday Times* in April 1959:

> The story goes that an enterprising gentleman from these shores travelled to the United States during the latter part of the last century and impressed the Americans with a demonstration of the effect of "side" on pool or billiard balls. His name was English.

This expression, which dates from 1869, is most often used in reference to billiard or tennis balls, though it is sometimes used in other contexts.

flourish of trumpets An unnecessarily flamboyant introduction; a pretentious display. This expression is derived from the musical fanfare associated with the arrival of royalty or other distinguished, high-ranking officials. The expression is used figuratively to describe an inappropriate show of pomposity.

fuss and feathers Pretentious, ostentatious display; exaggerated concern and preoccupation with one's appearance. *Fuss and feathers* is reputed to have been the nickname given to U.S. General Winfield Scott by those who thought him finicky, vain, and self-important. According to the *OED*, this expression appeared in print by 1866, the year of Scott's death.

grandstand Done to impress onlookers; done merely for effect or attention, used especially of an athletic feat.

> It's little things of this sort which makes the 'grandstand player.' They make impossible catches, and when they get the ball they roll all over the field. (M. J. Kelly, *Play Ball,* 1888)

This common expression is sometimes extended to *grandstand play,* an athletic maneuver done to draw applause from the spectators, and *grandstand finish,* a thrilling, neck-and-neck finale to a sporting event.

ham A performer who overacts and exaggerates to show off on stage; an inexperienced, inferior actor; frequently extended to any person who enjoys being the focus of others' attention and behaves in such a way as to attract it; an exhibitionist or show-off. There are several different but related theories as to the origin of this phrase. One of the best known states that, for economic reasons, poorly paid performers used cheap ham fat instead of the more costly cold cream to remove their makeup, thus giving rise to the term *ham*. Similarly, the *OED* theorizes that *ham* is short for *hamfatter* 'an ineffective, low-grade actor or performer.' A related synonymous term is *hamfat man,* also the title of a popular minstrel song. All of these terms are U.S. slang and date from the 1880s.

hot-dog To show off, especially by performing flashy, difficult, intricate maneuvers in sports; to grandstand, to play to the crowd; also *to hot-dog it.* The verb *to hot-dog* is a back formation from the surfing slang terms *hot-dogging* 'riding a hot dog surfboard' and *hot-dogger* 'a surfer who rides a hot dog board.' A *hot-dog* surfboard is relatively small and probably got its name from its cigarlike shape, similar to that of a hot dog. Although the verb *to hot-dog* dates only from the 1960s, the noun *hot dog* 'hot shot, show-off' dates from the early part of this century. This figurative sense of the noun probably derived from the exclamation *hot dog!* 'great,

OUTCOME ☐ 238

terrific,' used originally in reference to the food.

> Looking good on a little wave is hard. If you can hot dog on two foot waves you are "king." (*Pix* [Australia], September, 1963)

play to the gallery To overact or overplay to get a rise out of the less refined and educated members of a group; to appeal to the vulgar tastes of the common man; to seek recognition by showy, overdramatized antics. This expression dates from the 17th century when the *gallery* referred to the less expensive seats in the theater where the "gallery gods" (**STATUS**) congregated to watch a play.

> His dispatches were, indeed, too long and too swelling in phrase; for herein he was always "playing to the galleries." (*Standard,* October 23, 1872)

Today *gallery* refers to any uncultured group of undiscerning judgment. An analogous expression deriving from baseball is *play to the grandstand.*

posh Sumptuously opulent; luxurious. Although the origin of this term is in dispute, many people still adhere to the expression's purported acronymous derivation from 'port out, starboard home,' a reference to the shady, more comfortable north side of a ship traveling between England and India. The phrase, originally a British saying, is now commonplace on both sides of the Atlantic.

> I'd like to have . . . a very cozy car, small but frightfully posh. (John B. Priestley, *The Good Companions,* 1929)

shoot one's cuffs To show off; to flaunt or strut one's stuff; to grandstand; to put on the dog. In the Middle Ages, affectedly ostentatious noblemen often wore shirts with large, flamboyant cuffs which protruded from the sleeves of their equally ornate coats. Since the display of this type of cuff was clearly intended to impress, these quasi-aristocrats were derisively said to be "shooting their cuffs." With the decline in the popularity of such garish forms of dress, the expression became figurative and still enjoys occasional contemporary use. A variation is *shoot one's linen.*

OUTCOME

bottom line The end result, the final outcome, the upshot; the net profit or loss of any transaction or undertaking, financial or otherwise. This accounting term for the final figure on a profit and loss statement has been incorporated into more general usage and extended in meaning as indicated above.

come out in the wash Work out for the best in the long run; turn out all right; become known. Just as dirt and stains are removed when clothes are washed, anything which hinders or serves to cloud the truth will be removed in the end.

pan out See **SUCCESS.**

spinoff A by-product or offshoot; a new company, invention, product, etc., that develops as a result of the success of a related, pre-existing concern. This expression has been popularized by its frequent application in the television industry to a new program centering around a supporting character from an already successful show. The expression also enjoys widespread use in the business and medical worlds.

> The vaccine is the result of a new type of ultra high-speed centrifuge that is a spinoff from atomic weapons work conducted here by the Atomic Energy Commission. (Richard D. Lyons, in the *New York Times,* February, 1968)

OUTDOING (See also **ADVANTAGE.**)

beat all hollow To surpass completely or thoroughly; to outdo; to excel. The exact origin of this phrase is unknown. *Hollow* is the key word, meaning 'thoroughly, out-and-out,' and *all hol-*

low is an American colloquial variant. Various forms of the phrase *(have* or *carry it hollow)* were used as early as the middle of the 17th century. Today the most frequently heard form is the full phrase *beat all hollow,* which appeared as early as 1785 in the *Winslow Papers:*

> Miss Miller . . . is allowed by your connoiseurs in beauty to beat Miss Polly Prince all hollow.

beat Banagher To outdo, excel, or surpass in absurdity, incredibility, or preposterousness. This Irish expression has been said to derive both from an actual town of that name, and from a hypothetical storyteller of that name, but no authenticating anecdote or evidence for either theory has been proffered.

beat the Dutch To astonish or surprise owing to excess of any sort; to outdo or surpass. The expression is an Americanism dating from the days of the early Dutch settlers. Some say it owes its origin to their reputation as merchants and traders offering the best bargains and fairest prices. Others see it as an outgrowth of the English-Dutch hostility in the New World. Either theory may be correct, since the phrase is used either positively or negatively.

knock the spots out of To surpass or excel by an exceeding degree; to prove superior in a given skill or talent. This phrase, common in the United States in the 19th century, is said to derive from the former practice of developing one's proficiency in the use of firearms by aiming at the spots on playing cards which had been nailed to a tree. A marksman able to hit any given spot from a regulation distance could "knock the spots out of" another or another's performance. In describing the Duke "learning" Hamlet's soliloquy to the King, Huck Finn says:

> All through his speech, he howled, and spread around, and swelled up his chest, and just knocked the spots out of any acting ever *I* see before. (Mark Twain, *The Adventures of Huckleberry Finn,* 1885)

out-Herod Herod To outdo in excessiveness or extravagance; to be more outrageous than the most outrageous. The expression first appeared in Shakespeare's *Hamlet:*

> I would have such a fellow whipped for o'erdoing Termagant— it out-Herods Herod. Pray you, avoid it. (III,ii)

In these lines Hamlet is admonishing the players to perform with restraint, warning that a bombastic style of acting is not to his taste. In medieval mystery plays Herod was conventionally presented as a roaring tyrant, much given to ranting and raving and extravagant gesture. Use of the expression *out-Herod Herod* dates from the early 19th century. While it still most often describes blustering behavior or speech, it is by no means limited to such contexts. A person may "out-Herod Herod" by going beyond any other in any particular.

> As for manner, he [Alexander Smith] does sometimes, in imitating his models, out-Herod Herod. (Charles Kingsley, *Miscellanies,* 1853)

Out-Herod often occurs alone, with the character and characteristic in question completed by context; e.g., "He out-Herods Muhammad Ali in fancy talk and footwork."

run rings around To be unquestionably superior; to easily surpass another's performance; to defeat handily. No satisfactory explanation of this very common phrase has been found. One source conjectures it stems from races in which one contestant could literally run around his opponent and still come out the victor. Another says the phrase derives from Australian sheep-shearing contests, but fails to provide a clear explanation of the relationship; however, the earliest known citation is from Australia, lending this latter theory a degree of credibility.

> Considine could run rings around the lot of them. (*Melbourne Argus,* October, 1891)

steal [someone's] thunder See THWARTING.

steal the show To be the outstanding or most spectacular person or item in a group, especially unexpectedly; to usurp or get the credit for. This expression is rooted in the theater and refers to an actor or actress whose performance is so impressive and striking that it is the most memorable element in a stage production. Although still used in theater, *steal the show* is applied figuratively in varied contexts to describe a person or thing whose extraordinary qualities totally overshadow those of other members of a group. One who or that which "steals the show" is often called a *show-stealer.*

take the cake To be conspicuously good or bad; to be so extraordinary or preposterous as to surprise or stun into momentary incredulity; to excel or surpass. Cakes were often prizes in competitions of different sorts in many cultures, but most theorists agree that this phrase comes from the Black American dance competition called the cakewalk, in which couples would promenade around a large cake, and the one judged most graceful would get the cake as a prize. Though originally used in this sense of "win the prize" or "bear away the bell," the expression is now almost always heard used ironically. *Take the cake* more often means to be the worst than to be the best.

> Pack up and pull out, eh? You take the cake. (Theodore Dreiser, *Sister Carrie,* 1900)

upstage To outdo or surpass; to be a standout; to steal public attention and acclaim from another; to ignore or snub, especially condescendingly. In theater, upstage is the back half of the stage. To upstage an actor, then, is to stand toward the rear of the stage foreing the other actor has to turn his back to the audience so that its attention is effectively diverted from one actor and focused on the one who is doing the upstaging. By extension, *upstage* is applied in many nontheatrical contexts where one person overshadows or otherwise diminishes the importance of another.

> Nada Nice has upstaged the Kid . . . at your order. (Harry Witwer, *The Leather Pushers,* 1921)

As an adjective, *upstage* means condescending, aloof, haughty, stuck-up.

> Although Costello . . . had definite ideas . . . in connection with his art, as he took pictures seriously, he was never the least bit "upstage" with us youngsters. (*Sunday Express,* May 10, 1927)

OVEREXTENSION

bite off more than one can chew To undertake more than one can handle; to overextend oneself. John H. Beadle used the phrase in *Western Wilds, and the Men Who Redeem Them* (1877).

burn the candle at both ends To overextend oneself; to overdo; to use up or squander in two directions simultaneously. The phrase often carries connotations of dissipation. It comes from the French expression *brusler la chandelle par les deux bouts,* and first appeared in Randle Cotgrave's *A Dictionary of the French and English Tongues* (1611).

lazy man's load A burden too heavy to be carried; a task too large to be completed. This expression alludes to the purported tendency of lazy people to overburden themselves on one trip rather than make two trips with loads of a reasonable size.

serve two masters To split one's energies between pursuits of good and evil, uprightness and decadence, kindness and cruelty, etc.; to attempt to adequately meet conflicting demands; to work against oneself. This expression, of

Biblical origin, alludes to the self-defeating nature of the impractical if not futile attempt to obey two opposing sets of ideologies, morals, or ethics.

No one can serve two masters; for either he will hate the one and love the other, or he will be devoted to the one and despise the other. You cannot serve God and mammon. (Matthew 6:24)

spread oneself thin To overextend oneself, to be involved in so many projects simultaneously that none receives adequate attention; to overdo, to have too many irons in the fire. This popular expression compares a person's limited capabilities and resources to a given amount of a literally spreadable substance, such as jam or butter, which can cover just so much bread before it becomes too thin to be tasted.

too many irons in the fire Too many projects requiring one's attention, to the detriment of them all; so many undertakings in progress that none gets adequate attention. This expression, in use as early as 1549, refers to the pieces of iron a blacksmith heats in the forge before working on them; they must be hammered into the desired shape at precisely the right temperature. If he tries to prepare several at once, his efforts become counterproductive: he either gives short shrift to working the metal, or risks overheating it so that its malleability is adversely affected. A similar phrase, *many irons in the fire*, has the more positive meaning of several alternative ways to achieve one's ends.

OVERWORK

burn the midnight oil To study or work late into the night; to lucubrate. In the days before electricity students and scholars who wished to read or study at night used oil lamps for light. The term

midnight oil for late-night study was in use as early as 1635; the entire phrase appeared somewhat later.

keep one's nose to the grindstone See PERSEVERANCE.

a lot on one's plate British slang for a lot to do, much to think or worry about.

moonlighting Working a job at night to supplement one's daytime income. Although it was formerly used in Ireland and other countries to describe nighttime excursions of violence, the expression's current figurative sense is of American origin. The term is now used frequently in the United States and Great Britain, always in reference to a second job.

Several attempts have been made to ban moonlighting on the ground that it robs the unemployed of jobs. (*Economist*, December, 1961)

salt mines One's place of employment; any unnamed place, real or imaginary, that represents habitual punishment, confinement, isolation, or drudgery. This expression alludes to the salt mines of Siberia (U.S.S.R.) where political and other prisoners were sent to serve sentences at hard labor. *Salt mines* often appears in *back to the salt mines*, a jocular and somewhat derogatory reference to returning to work.

snowed under Overwhelmed; inundated, buried, or overburdened by work or other responsibilities. This expression alludes to the fact that while a single snowflake seems completely innocuous, a large amount of snow can be totally overpowering.

What he stood for (and he came to stand for more all the time) came under the lash of many tongues, until a frailer man than he would have been snowed under. (F. Scott Fitzgerald, *This Side of Paradise*, 1920)

P

PACE (See also **INSTANTANEOUS-NESS, SPEEDING.**)

at a snail's pace Very slowly, at an exceedingly slow rate of movement or progress. According to one source which claims to have actually measured its speed, a snail moves at the rate of one mile in fourteen days. The snail, like the turtle, is one of the slowest-moving creatures on the earth and has symbolized extreme slowness, tardiness, and sluggishness for centuries.

> That snail's pace with which business is done by letters. (Madame D'Arblay, *Diary and Letters*, 1793)

blue streak See **talk a blue streak, TALKATIVENESS.**

faster than greased lightning At the highest possible speed; moving at a tremendous velocity. Lightning travels at the speed of light, considered by modern scientists to be the highest attainable. The concept of lubricating a lightning bolt to reduce its friction with the air and consequently increase its speed is the apparent origin of this American term.

> He spoke as quick as "greased lightning." (*Boston Herald*, January, 1833)

full tilt See **INTENSITY.**

hand over fist Left and right, by leaps and bounds, a mile a minute, rapidly; usually in reference to making money. The original expression, dating from at least 1736, was *hand over hand*, a nautical term with the literal meaning of advancing the hands alternatively, as when climbing up or down a rope or when raising or hauling in a sail. Still in nautical use, the phrase acquired the figurative sense of advancing continu-ously, as one ship gaining rapidly on another. It is in this sense that *hand over fist* was first used, about 1825, according to *OED* citations. The figurative use of *hand over fist*, the only form of this expression current today, dates from the 19th century.

hellbent See **ZEALOUSNESS.**

like a bat out of hell Very rapidly, swiftly, speedily. The precise origin or explanation is unknown. A plausible conjecture is that bats, because of their aversion to light, would beat a hasty retreat from the illuminating flames of the infernal regions. The phrase is of American origin.

> We went like a bat out of hell along a good state road. (John Dos Passos, *Three Soldiers*, 1921)

like a house afire Quickly, rapidly, like greased lightning; vigorously, enthusiastically, hammer and tongs. This expression refers to the swiftness with which a fire can consume a house, particularly one built of wood or other flammable materials.

make a beeline To proceed directly and with dispatch; to hasten, hurry; to rush, race, or make a mad dash toward. It is commonly believed that pollen-carrying bees return to the hive speedily and directly; hence *beeline* meaning 'the most direct route.' The term is believed to be originally American; it appeared in 1848 in *The Biglow Papers* by James Russell Lowell.

quick as a wink Very quickly, in no time at all; in the twinkling of an eye. This is an obvious metaphor referring to the split second it takes to blink the eye.

sell like hot cakes To sell very quickly; to be disposed of immediately and without effort, usually in quantity; to be in great demand; also *to go like hot cakes.* Originally, hot cakes referred to corn cakes, but the term now applies to griddlecakes or pancakes. Freshly baked cakes, still warm from the oven, would presumably sell quickly because people would want to "get 'em while they're hot." The expression dates from the early 19th century.

> Ice cream sold like hot cakes Saturday, and hot cakes didn't sell at all, as the temperature began to climb early in the morning and kept it up until 4:30 P.M. (*The Fort Collins Coloradoan,* June, 1946)

slap-bang See CARELESSNESS.

slapdash See CARELESSNESS.

slow as molasses in January Very slow, barely moving. Molasses, naturally thick and sluggish, becomes even more so in cold weather due to the crystallization of its high sugar content. Among the numerous variants are the expanded version *slow as molasses going uphill in January* and *slow as cold molasses.*

PACIFICATION (See PLACATION.)

PARADISE

Abraham's bosom The abode of the blessed dead. The phrase, of Scriptural origin, is usually confined to literary usage.

> And it came to pass that the beggar died, and was carried by the angels into Abraham's bosom. (Luke 16:22)

Resting one's head on another's bosom was an ancient gesture of close friendship; John the Beloved Disciple reclined on the bosom of Jesus at the Last Supper.

happy hunting ground Heaven, paradise; the abode of American Indian warriors after death, where game was plentiful. The phrase in this literal sense was first used by Washington Irving in

Bonneville in 1837. It has since come to mean any region of abundant supply or fertile yield:

> Marin County—naturalists' happy hunting ground—supplied the thirty nature subjects now displayed in . . . North American Hall. (California Academy of Sciences, *News Letter,* 1948)

kingdom come The next world, the afterlife; paradise; hades, hell.

> And forty pounds be theirs, a pretty sum,
> For sending such a rogue to kingdom come.
> (Peter Pindar, *Subjects for Painters,* 1789)

This term is an irreverent excision from the Lord's Prayer: "Thy kingdom come, thy will by done." It is still in common usage, as illustrated by a citation in *Webster's Third:*

> . . . the guns that would blow everyone to kingdom come. (Meridel Le Sueur)

land of milk and honey An area of unusual fertility, abundance, and beauty; a paradise; a mecca; Israel. This expression appears in the Bible (Exodus 3:8; 33:3; Jeremiah 11:5) as a description of the Promised Land (Israel), a place where Moses and the oppressed Hebrews would have freedom, peace, and abundant blessings.

> And I [God] am come down to deliver them out of the hands of the Egyptians, and to bring them up out of that land unto a good land flowing with milk and honey. (Exodus 3:8)

PARTIALITY (See FAVORITISM.)

PARTICIPATION (See COOPERATION, INVOLVEMENT.)

PATIENCE

patient as Griselda Extraordinarily patient, humble, and submissive. In Boccaccio's *Decameron* (1353), Griselda

was a common woman who married the
Marquis of Saluzzo, a wealthy nobleman who subjected her to numerous
tests of her womanly virtues. Griselda
endured these tests without complaint,
thus proving her patience, obedience,
and meekness. The Griselda personage
soon became the paragon of patience in
the medieval miracle plays, and was
further popularized by an appearance
in Chaucer's *Canterbury Tales*. The
name Griselda is still used in reference
to a persevering, exceedingly patient
woman.

sit tight To wait patiently; to bide one's
time; to await (sometimes anxiously) the
results of an earlier activity; to refrain
from voicing one's opinions or ideas.
This expression was originally a poker
term applied to a person who, when it
was his turn, neither bet nor threw in
his cards, choosing instead to await the
outcome of the game. Thus, while *sit
tight* once smacked of stinginess, in
contemporary applications, it usually
implies patience.

PAYMENT (See also **BRIBERY, COST,
EXTORTION, GRAFT, SOLICITATION.**)

cash on the barrelhead Immediate
payment; money on the spot. This
Americanism probably gained currency during the days when perishable
items were kept in barrels to retain
freshness. To purchase something, one
had to put "cash on the barrelhead."
Today the phrase is used to indicate
that no credit is extended.

No more divorces in Holt County
until there is cash on the
"barrelhead," is the edict. (*Kansas
City Times,* April 7, 1932)

foot the bill To pay or settle an account; to assume responsibility for expenses incurred by others. This expression stems from the custom of signing
one's name at the bottom, or foot of
a bill as a promise of payment. Over
the years, this phrase has come to describe someone who pays an entire

bill himself, rather than allow or force
it to be divided among the parties involved.

The annual bill we foot is, after all,
small compared with that of
France. (*Leeds Mercury,* July 18,
1891)

the ghost walks Salaries will be paid;
there is money in the treasury; it's
payday. This expression, inspired by
Shakespeare's *Hamlet,* has two possible explanations, one of which cites
Horatio's asking the ghost (of Hamlet's
father) if it walks because:

Thou hast uphoarded in thy life
Extorted treasure in the womb
of earth. (I,i)

A more plausible, and certainly more
colorful, theory tells of a 19th-century
British theater company that threatened to strike because their salaries had
not been paid for several weeks. The
ghost was played by the leader of the
company, a highly acclaimed actor.
During a performance, the ghost, in answer to Hamlet's exclamation, "Per-
chance 'twill walk again," shouted from
the wings, "No, I'm damned if the ghost
walks any more until our salaries are
paid!" Their salaries were paid and the
performance continued. From then on,
the actors met every payday to determine whether the ghost would walk,
i.e., whether they would be paid. This
expression gave rise to *ghost,* theatrical
slang for a paymaster or treasurer of a
theater or theater company.

go on tick To buy an item on credit; to
be indebted for what one purchases;
also, *get on tick.* In this expression, *tick*
is a shortening of *ticket,* where *ticket*
carries its obsolete meaning of a written
note acknowledging debt. Although the
phrase never attained great popularity
in the United States, it has been a commonplace expression in Great Britain
for centuries.

A poor wretch that goes on tick for
the paper he writes his lampoons
on. (William Wycherley, *Love in a
Wood,* 1672)

lay it on the line See RISK.

the never-never plan Installment buying, buying on credit; the layaway plan. This British colloquialism for their own *hire-purchase* is usually abbreviated to the slang *never-never*. It appeared in print as early as the 1920s, and continues in common usage.

> They've still not paid off their mortgage, you know, and I wouldn't mind betting that Rover of theirs is on the never-never. (J. Wilson, *Truth or Dare*, 1973)

nickel and dime to death To drain a person of his money bit by bit; to eat away at one's monetary resources a little at a time; to exhaust one's finances by an accumulation of small expenses. This U. S. colloquial expression has become common in recent years, probably because of continued inflation and "built-in obsolescence." It might appear in a context such as: "It's not the initial outlay or major maintenance that makes automobile ownership expensive, but they nickel and dime you to death with piddling repairs due to their own shoddy workmanship."

on the cuff On credit; on a special payment plan; on tick. Although the origin of this expression is obscure, a plausible derivation is that, at one time, storekeepers and bartenders kept track of debts by making marks on their shirt cuffs, which, till the 1920s, were available in Celluloid and, like collars, were not sewn to the shirt. Written on in pencil, they could easily be wiped clean. The phrase is used frequently today.

> Money was not important at all. All business was transacted on the cuff. (B. Macdonald, *Egg and I,* 1945)

on the nail On the spot, at once, immediately, right away or now; used in reference to money payments. Although the origin of this expression is obscure, it may be related to the French phrase *sur l'ongle* 'exactly, precisely' (literally, 'on the nail'). The expression appeared in Maria Edgeworth's *Popular Tales* in 1804:

> The bonnet's all I want, which I'll pay for on the nail.

No longer in common use, this phrase dates from the late 16th century.

on the nod On credit, on the cuff, with no money down. This expression, in use since the late 19th century, is said to have come from the practice of bidders at auctions, who signify their acceptance of a stated price with a nod of the head, on the understanding that the formalities of paying would be taken care of later. In any case, this gesture has long been used to show assent or agreement when entering into a bargain.

> Drunks with determined minds to get bacon, bread, cheese, on the nod. (*The Bulletin* [Sydney], July, 1934)

PEACE (See also PLACATION.)

all quiet on the Potomac A period of peace during a war; any time marked by the absence of fighting or quarreling. This expression (now used ironically or humorously) is generally thought to have originated and gained currency during the Civil War. It appeared as early as 1861 in an article by E. L. Beers in *Harper's Weekly.* Simon Cameron, then Secretary of War, frequently used the phrase in his bulletins reporting the state of the war. Its origin has also been attributed to General George McClellan.

all quiet on the Western Front Peaceful, calm. This phrase is an update of the earlier *all quiet on the Potomac.* It was the official statement issued each day by the War Department during the periods of relatively little trench fighting in World War I.

bury the hatchet To lay down arms, to cease fighting, to make peace; also *to bury the ax* or *tomahawk.* The allusion is to the North American Indian custom of burying tomahawks, scalping-knives, and war clubs as a sign of good faith when concluding a peace. The procedure is described by Washington Irving in *Adventures of Captain Bonneville* (1837):

> The chiefs met; the amicable pipe was smoked, the hatchet buried, and peace formally proclaimed.

The expression dates from the late 1600s. See also **take up the hatchet**, COMBAT.

calm before the storm A period of relative peacefulness preceding an outbreak of confusion and tumult; the quiet and sane minutes just before chaos erupts. A drop in the barometric pressure prior to a thunderstorm produces an uncomfortable, almost eerie feeling of calmness. This meterological phenomenon has given rise to the popular expression *calm before the storm.*

dove A pacifist, one who opposes war, in contrast to a "hawk," who advocates a belligerent, warlike policy; one who favors negotiation and compromise as a means of resolving differences. The dove has been a symbol of peace in art and literature since Noah sent a dove from the ark to see if the waters had abated (Genesis 8:8–12). *Dove* referring to an antiwar advocate gained currency in 1962 during the Cuban Missile Crisis, and eventually became the label for those advocating withdrawal of U.S. troops from Vietnam.

> The hawks favored an air strike to eliminate the Cuban missile bases. . . . The doves opposed the air strikes and favored a blockade. (Alsop and Bartlett in *Saturday Evening Post*, December 8, 1962)

halcyon days A time of peace and prosperity; palmy or golden days. The halcyon was a bird, usually identified as a type of kingfisher, which bred in nests floating on the sea. The ancients believed that these birds charmed the winds and waves of the sea into tranquillity during their breeding season. Thus, *halcyon days* originally referred to the two weeks of calm weather about the time of the winter solstice during which the halcyons bred. The current, figurative sense of *halcyon days* dates from the latter half of the 16th century.

hold out the olive branch To make an overture for peace; to indicate one's peaceful intentions. Long considered a token or symbol of peace, the olive branch was represented as such in Genesis 8:11:

> And the dove came in to him in the evening; and, lo, in her mouth was an olive leaf pluckt off: so Noah knew that the waters were abated from off the earth.

A more recent example of its use appears below:

> My mother . . . had first tendered the olive branch, which had been accepted. (Frederick Marryat, *Percival Keene*, 1837)

Today this phrase still frequently appears in formal contexts.

raise the white flag See SUBMISSION.

PENSIVENESS (See THOUGHT.)

PERCEPTIVENESS (See also ALERTNESS, SHREWDNESS.)

feel a draft To sense negative feelings of others toward oneself; to perceive subtle manifestations of hostility, often racial. This phrase, obviously based on the dual dimensions of physical and emotional coldness, originated in the jazz world.

> The black audience would send a draft toward the Negro leader who hired a white man instead of a black man of comparable talent and stylistic inclination. (*Downbeat*, May 16, 1968)

The British use the expression *feel the draught* to describe a sense of inconvenience or discomfort, often in relation to one's financial situation.

> With only so much national advertising to go round . . . the

oldest commercial stations are feeling the draught as well. (*Listener*, June, 1966)

have [someone's] number To know a person's real motives or intentions; to be a perceptive and astute judge of character; to size another up. The practice of assigning numbers to identify people is the probable source of this expression. Although one's "number" is a superficial designation, the expression connotes a deeper, more profound understanding of a person. *Have [someone's] number* dates from the mid-19th century and is current today.

Do you remember the day before when he made that crack at you in front of Miss Crozier? I had his number right then. (R. D. Paine, *Comr. Rolling Ocean*, 1921)

know a hawk from a handsaw To be capable of differentiating between two things; to be wise, not easily fooled or duped. *Handsaw* is a corruption of *heronshaw* 'a young heron.' Thus, to differentiate between two similar things implies a more refined intelligence than is suggested by the expression in its present form. Shakespeare used this expression in *Hamlet:*

I am but mad north-northwest. When the wind is southerly, I know a hawk from a handsaw. (II,ii)

It has also been conjectured that *hawk* refers not to the bird of prey but to a tool like a pickax. In that case, both *hawk* and *handsaw* would denote instruments.

know chalk from cheese To be able to differentiate between two things that are superficially alike but essentially dissimilar; to be discerning, to have a keen mind; to know the real thing from a counterfeit. As early as the 14th century, these two words were set apart as opposites.

Lo, how they feignen chalk for cheese. (John Gower, *Confessio Amantis*, 1393)

The implication is that "cheese" is superior to or finer than "chalk." Thus, to be as "different as chalk and cheese" is to be as different as black and white, or day and night, even though chalk and cheese are similar in appearance.

look beneath the surface To go beyond appearances to try to perceive the true nature of something; not to be fooled by superficial glitter or plainness. This proverbial saying is attributed to the Roman Emperor, philosopher, and writer Marcus Aurelius (121–180):

Look beneath the surface; let not the several quality of a thing nor its worth escape thee. (*Meditations*)

look through a millstone To be discerning and sharp-sighted; to exercise keen powers of perception. A millstone is a large, opaque stone used in grinding grains. Therefore the physically impossible challenge to see through a millstone can be met only figuratively by one of extraordinarily keen perception. The expression appeared in print by the mid-16th century.

Your eyes are so sharp, that you cannot only look through a Millstone, but clean through the mind. (John Lyly, *Euphues and his England*, 1680)

read between the lines To understand the implications of another's words or actions; to see beyond the explicit and be sensitive to the implications of subtleties and nuances; to get the underlying message, whether intended or not, regardless of the words that couch it or the actions that convey it. The phrase was once literal; methods of cryptogrammic communication included the use of invisible ink for writing "between the lines" or the practice of relating the secret message in alternate lines. Thus, "reading between the lines" was crucial to receiving the message sent. Today the expression often refers to an ability to sense an author's tone or a person's ulterior motives.

People who have not the shrewdness to read a little between the
lines . . . are grievously misled. (*The
Manchester Examiner,* January,
1886)

PERSEVERANCE (See also ENDUR-ANCE.)

come hell or high water Come what
may, no matter what; also *in spite of
hell or high water.* P. I. Wellman in
Trampling Herd (1939) claims the following as the origin of the expression:

"In spite of hell and high water"
. . . is a legacy of the cattle trail
when the cowboys drove their
hornspiked masses of longhorns
through high water at every river
and continuous hell between.

Whether originally a cowboy expression or not, *hell* and *high water* symbolize any difficulties or obstacles to be
overcome. The expression has been in
use since at least 1915.

die-hard A hard-core supporter; one
who struggles and resists to the bitter
end, particularly against change or innovation; literally one who dies hard.
This expression reputedly had its origin
in the Battle of Albuera (1811) where
the 57th Regiment of Foot of the British
Army fought desperately to maintain a
strategic position. In the midst of the
fighting, Colonel Inglis is said to have
urged his men on by shouting "Die
hard! 57th, die hard!" The last-ditch
courage and stamina with which the
57th fought that day earned them the
nickname the "Die-hards," by which
their regiment is known to this day. Use
of this term dates from at least 1844.

don't give up the ship Keep fighting or
trying, hang in there. Although this
expression was not new at the time
of the Battle of Lake Erie (September
10, 1813) when Commodore Perry
adopted it as his battle cry, it was he
who popularized the words and made
them memorable. The expression has
extended beyond its naval origins and
application and is now currently used to
give encouragement to people in all
walks of life.

happy warrior One who is undaunted
or undiscouraged by adversity, a die-
hard; often used of a politician who is a
perennial candidate for nomination or
election to high office. The nickname
"Happy Warrior" was first applied to
Alfred E. Smith, Democratic candidate
in the presidential election of 1928.

He [Alfred E. Smith] is the "Happy
Warrior" of the political battlefield.
(Franklin Delano Roosevelt, *New
York Times,* June, 1924)

The term was later applied to Hubert
Humphrey, Democratic candidate for
President in 1968 and many times a
candidate for the Democratic presidential nomination. The term was first used
in the conventional sense of an excellent soldier, a fighter—a meaning
which is reflected in its figurative application to political "warriors."

hold one's ground To firmly maintain
or defend one's position; to resist the
pressure to compromise one's ideals. Although this expression can refer to
maintaining ground literally, as in a
battle, it is more frequently heard in
regard to defending a philosophical
stance. The two levels of usage are
related, however, because even in war
there is a philosophical basis for defending one's *ground,* meaning territory,
land, etc. This expression and its variants *keep* or *stand one's ground* appeared in print by the 17th century.

It is not easy to see how it [Indi-
viduality] can stand its ground.
(John Stuart Mill, *On Liberty,* 1859)

keep a stiff upper lip To keep one's
courage when confronted with adversity, to remain resolute in the face of
great difficulties, not to lose heart. The
allusion is to the quivering of the upper
lip when a person is trying to maintain
control and keep from crying in the
face of danger or great emotional stress.

"What's the use o' boo-hooin'? . . .
Keep a stiff upper lip; no bones

broke—don't I know?" (John Neal, *The Down Easters*, 1833)

The expression dates from the early part of the 19th century.

keep one's chin up To maintain one's courage and resolve, to keep one's spirits up, to keep one's head held high. This American expression has been in use since at least 1938.

Keep your chin up honey. (I. Baird, *Waste Heritage*, 1939)

keep one's nose to the grindstone To persist in an unpleasant task; to labor continuously, especially at hard, monotonous work; to labor unceasingly; to drudge. The allusion is perhaps to laborers hovering over grindstones or whetstones to sharpen tools made dull from constant use. The expression and variants, which date from at least 1532, originally meant to oppress someone else by exaction of labor.

keep one's pecker up To keep one's chin up, to hold one's head high, to keep one's spirits or courage up. In this British slang expression *pecker* means 'spirits, courage.' It probably derives from the term *pecker* for a bird's beak or bill. Cockfighting is sometimes cited as the source of the phrase, since a gamecock's pecker or beak sinks when he is tired and near defeat. Thus, the expression literally means to keep up one's beak (British slang for *nose*). This of course cannot be done without keeping the head and chin up as well. The expression, which dates from at least 1853, is avoided in the United States, where *pecker* has an altogether different and vulgar slang meaning.

nail one's colors to the mast To fight or hold out until the bitter end; to refuse to compromise, concede, or surrender; to persist or remain steadfast, especially in the face of seemingly overwhelming opposition. It has long been nautical custom for a ship to signify its nationality or allegiance by flying that country's colors (i.e., flag) from its tallest mast. In battle, a captain could signal his surrender or defeat by lowering the flag. If the colors were nailed to the mast, however, they could not be lowered, implying that surrender was not possible.

If they catch you at disadvantage, the mines for your life is the word, . . . and so we fight them with our colours nailed to the mast. (Sir Walter Scott, *The Pirate*, 1821)

praise the Lord, and pass the ammunition Keep up the struggle, don't give up. This expression, although rarely used today, was the title of a popular song during World War II. It has been attributed to Chaplain Howell Forgy, who was on board the cruiser *New Orleans* in Pearl Harbor at the time of the Japanese attack in 1941. During the assault the chaplain helped fuel a counterattack by carrying ammunition to the ship's guns. He is purported to have said the now famous words "Praise the Lord, boys—and pass the ammunition."

stick to one's guns To stand firm, to persist in one's point of view, argument, or beliefs; not to yield or give in, to hold one's ground.

An animated colloquy ensued. Manvers stuck to his guns. (Mrs. Alexander, *Brown, V.C.*, 1899)

Of military origin, this phrase was originally *to stand to one's gun(s)*, meaning literally to stand by one's gun, to keep fighting no matter what.

PERSONAGE (See also **STATUS**.)

big brass V.I.P.'s; high-ranking officials, either military or civilian. The phrase, which appeared in the *Boston Herald* in 1899, referred to the gold braid or insignia on the uniforms of high-ranking military officers. The term is now commonly applied to both military and civilian officials, and often appears simply as *the brass*. A related term for military and naval officials is *brass hat*.

big shot An important or influential person. Although the exact origin is unknown, this expression is most likely a derivative of the earlier *big gun,* in use since 1834, and the phrase *to carry big guns,* since 1867. Still widely used today, this term dates from the 1930s.

big wheel An important or influential person. In use since 1950, this term is thought to have come from the mechanics' expression *to roll a big wheel* 'to be powerful or important.' Other similar phrases include *big bug* (since 1827), *cheese* or *big cheese* (since 1920), and the equivalent French term *grand fromage.* All but *big bug* are still in popular use today.

bigwig A person of importance and prominence, so called from the days when aristocrats and other men of note wore powdered wigs, somewhat more ponderous than those still worn by barristers and judges in England. According to one source, the larger the wig, the more important the person. The term is usually used contemptuously or humorously. It appeared in its present figurative meaning as early as the 18th century:

> Though those big-wigs have really nothing in them, they look very formidable. (Robert Southey, *Letters,* 1792)

chief cook and bottle washer One who manages a menial operation, wearing different hats to accomplish whatever needs to be done; often used in reference to the wife and mother of a family. The origin of *chief cook and bottle washer* is not known. It may have originated as service jargon, or, as has been speculated, the phrase may be a derivative of *chiff chark and bottle washer,* found occasionally as a listing in old Salem logs. "Chiff chark" is a name for a variety of Russian wine glass. The expression has been in use since the beginning of the 19th century.

chief itch and rub The most important person; head honcho; big wheel or big deal; the "alpha and omega." One

possible explanation for this phrase relates to the role of a leader as an instigator, one who stirs up interest and sees to it that what needs to be done is accomplished. In this capacity, a leader is considered a source of irritation, an "itch." *Rub* could be a synonym for *itch* (emphasizing the nagging, irritating characteristics of a leader), or it could mean 'to soothe or relieve an itch.' This would refer to the role of a leader as a mediator or reconciler. Another very different explanation is that having the problem and solution (itch and rub) contained in one person precludes the need for other people. Such a self-sufficient person would be recognized as leadership material, or in slang terms, "chief itch and rub."

fat cat A wealthy and influential person, especially one who finances a political campaign or candidate; a bigwig or name in any field. In this expression, *cat* is used in a mildly derogatory sense; *fat* implies that the wealthy lead lives of self-indulgence and thus tend toward obesity. In contemporary usage, however, *fat cat* does not always carry its original connotation of the stereo-typical wealthy politician's physical appearance.

> Hollywood celebrities and literary fat cats . . . (Bennett Cerf, *Saturday Review of Literature,* April 16, 1949)

high-muck-a-muck American slang for an important or high-ranking person, especially one who is pompous or conceited. The term is from Chinook Indian jargon *hiu muckamuck* 'plenty [of] food.' Its current figurative use dates from 1856.

his nibs A person of importance, often the boss, chief, or head honcho; a self-important person, a puffed-up egotist; also *her nibs.* The expression may derive from a little-used slang term of the mid-19th century: *nib* 'gentleman.' It is usually used contemptuously.

I wish I could just lie on a bed and smoke, like His Nibs. (H. Croome, *Forgotten Place*, 1957)

honcho The leader or boss; the person in charge; also *hancho* or *head honcho*. This American slang term was picked up by U.S. Armed Forces stationed in Japan during the occupation, and gained currency during the Korean conflict. It is from the Japanese *hanchō* (*han* 'squad' + *chō* 'chief') 'squad or group leader,' and has been in use since 1947.

kingpin The most critical person in a business or project; leader, chief. In bowling, the kingpin is the foremost, number one pin which, if hit correctly, causes the other nine pins to fall. Correspondingly, the expression is figuratively used in reference to a bigwig whose elimination would bring about the collapse of an enterprise or undertaking.

The owner of three shops was the kingpin behind a wholesale shoplifting plot. (*Daily Telegraph*, October, 1970)

leading light An important or influential person; a leader. *Leading light* is a nautical term for a lighthouse or other visible beacon (such as a buoy) that helps guide a sailor or pilot into port. The figurative implications are obvious.

a name to conjure with A person so powerful and influential that the mere mention of his name evokes awe and respect and can work magic. The term's conceptual origin lies in the notion that only the names of important personages could conjure up the spirits of the dead.

Write them together, yours is as fair a name;
Sound them, it doth become the mouth as well;
Weigh them, it as as heavy; conjure with 'em,
Brutus will start a spirit as soon as Caesar.
(Shakespeare, *Julius Caesar*, I,iii)

The actual wording *a name to conjure with* dates from the late 19th century; it is still widely used.

His name, little known to the public, is one to conjure with in Hollywood. (Iris Murdoch, *Under Net*, 1954)

straw boss An assistant boss or supervisor, especially one who gives orders but lacks the status, power, or authority to enforce them; a laborer who acts as leader or foreman of a crew of fellow workers. This expression originated with the custom of a boss's supervising the loading of grain into a thresher while his assistant, the straw boss, watches the end-products as they leave the machine—a nominal job at best, and one that involves little responsibility. The term is commonly applied in nonagricultural contexts to an immediate supervisor who oversees and often participates in the work, but who is himself answerable to a person in a higher position.

These employees . . . [having suffered] the continual oppression of the "straw bosses" . . . were in no condition to be trifled with by the Company. (William Carwardine, *The Pullman Strike*, 1894)

top banana The best in a particular field; the senior or leading comedian in musical comedy, burlesque, or vaudeville. This American slang term, in use since the 1950s, is said to have come from the soft, water- or air-filled banana-shaped club carried by early comedians. These were used in slapstick routines for hitting other comedians over the head.

top dog The boss, the person in charge; the best, number one.

V.I.P. An important or well-known person; a big shot. This widely used expression is an abbreviation of "Very Important Person." It was first used during World War II by an army officer who was arranging a secret flight of dignitaries to the Middle East. To avoid disclosing their identities, he listed each of them as "V.I.P." on his transport orders. This appellation became an almost overnight sensation and though most frequently used to describe an officer, executive, or politician, *V.I.P.* has, over the years, been applied to virtually anyone in a position of importance.

PERSPECTIVE (See also NIT-PICKING.)

by and large From an overall perspective; on the whole; in general; without going into details. The origin of this phrase and its current literal use are both nautical. It means to sail to the wind and slightly off it, or with the wind near the beam.

> Thus you see the ship handles in fair weather and foul, by and large. (Samuel Sturmy, *The Mariner's Magazine*, 1669)

By and large was used figuratively as early as 1706 in Edward Ward's *Wooden World Dissected.* The jump from literal to figurative use is difficult to follow. This method of sailing is generally faster, a bit safer and easier (it offers less chance of being "taken aback" than sailing directly "by the wind")—on the whole, better in the long run. It is the quality of being preferable 'on the whole' or 'in general' (even if a detailed analysis proved otherwise) that is transferred to nonnautical situations.

> The virtue of sound broadcasting was that, by and large, the content mattered more than anything else. (*Times,* May 23, 1955)

in the long run In the end, when all is said and done; from the perspective of knowing the outcome or end result. This expression alludes to a long distance race in which runners who start slowly and conserve their energy often pull ahead and win the race, as in the story of the tortoise and the hare.

not see the forest for the trees To be so concerned with details as to lose a sense of the larger whole; to ignore the obvi-

ous, to miss the main point; to have tunnel vision. This expression appeared in print by the 16th century, at which time *wood* was used instead of *forest.* Today *wood, woods,* and *forest* are used interchangeably.

number the streaks of the tulip To be overly concerned with details and thereby miss the main point. This expression derives from Imlac's dissertation on poetry in Johnson's *Rasselas,* in which he contends that a poet should be concerned with the general rather than the particular. A related current expression is *not see the forest for the trees.*

over the long haul See the long haul, DURATION.

stumble at a straw To become bogged down in petty details; to suffer a setback because of a minor or trifling incident. This expression is derived from a proverb cited in *Homilies* (1547):

> They were of so blind judgment, that they stumbled at a straw and leaped over a block.

The implication is that either as a result of misplaced priorities or poor judgment, a person may concentrate on the picayune while ignoring issues of greater significance.

> He that strives to touch the stars Oft stumbles at a straw. (Edmund Spenser, *The Shepheardes Calendar,* 1579)

trade off the orchard for an apple Not to see the forest for the trees, to be myopic; to be so concerned with details that one loses sight of the larger whole.

PETTINESS (See NIT-PICKING.)

PHYSICAL APPEARANCE (See also CORPULENCE, PHYSICAL STATURE, VISAGE.)

bald as a coot To be so bald as to resemble a coot. The coot has a straight and slightly conical bill whose base extends onto the forehead forming a broad white plate. Anyone whose pate resembles a coot's forehead is said to be "bald as a coot." This phrase was used as early as 1430, as cited in the *OED*.

flat as a pancake Flat; having a surface that is free from projections or indentations. Though usually used literally, this expression is sometimes employed in its figurative sense to describe something that is flatter than it should be or flatter than one would expect. In his play, *The Roaring Girl* (1611), Thomas Middleton used the expression to describe a woman with small breasts.

pilgarlic A bald-headed man; an unfortunate, pitiable wretch. Originally *peeled garlic,* the term was applied to one whose hair loss was due to disease (venereal by implication) and whose naked scalp supposedly resembled the flaky, shiny bulb of that plant. Eventually *pilgarlic* came to be applied to persons deserving of contempt or censure, probably because of the reputed source of the affliction. It was often used in a quasi-affectionate way, however; frequently for oneself, as in the following passage from Rabelais' *Pantagruel* (1532):

> Never a bit could poor pilgarlic sleep one wink, for the everlasting jingle of bells.

plug-ugly See CRIMINALITY.

a shadow of one's former self Said of one who has become extremely feeble or emaciated. This expression uses *shadow* in the sense of something that resembles the original but lacks substance, thus implying that a person has been reduced to a mere shadow, either through the ravages of disease, aging, stress, etc., or by choice. The expression is sometimes shortened to *shadow of oneself.*

> He appeared to wither into the shadow of himself. (Sir Walter Scott, *Guy Mannering; or The Astrologer,* 1815)

A shadow of one's former self is sometimes used complimentarily in good-natured reference to a formerly corpu-lent person who has lost weight as a result of dieting.

ugly duckling See REVERSAL.

PHYSICAL STATURE

dandiprat A dwarf, midget, or pygmy. This archaic word was originally the name of a three halfpence coin issued in 16th-century England. It took on its present meaning when Richard Stanyhurst referred to Cupid as a dandiprat in his 1582 translation of the *Aeneid.*

go-by-ground A very tiny person, a homunculus, a Lilliputian. This obsolete expression is obviously derived from the little distance between the earth's surface and a small person's head.

> I had need have two eyes, to discern so petit a go-by-ground as you. (*Copley's Wits, Fits, and Fancies,* 1614)

hop-o'-my-thumb A diminutive person, a midget or pygmy; a mean, small, contemptible person, fit only to be ordered about and looked down upon. In early usage the term was primarily one of contempt; but, perhaps through confusion with Tom Thumb, it has become increasingly descriptive and less offensive, indicative of small stature rather than lowly status.

knee-high to a grasshopper Very short or small, especially because of a young age. This popular American expression and its many variants are jocular extensions of the simpler term *knee-high,* in use about 70 years before the earliest extended variant.

> You pretend to be my daddies; some of you who are not knee-high to a grasshopper! (*The Democratic Review,* 1851)

PLACATION

let sleeping dogs lie To avoid any word or action that could disturb a person or situation which is, for the moment at least, peaceful and calm; to refrain from resurrecting an issue, discussion, argument, or other matter which had previously aroused heated emotional debate or controversy. The implication here is that if a sleeping dog is awakened, it may respond by snapping or biting.

> It is good therefore if you have a wife that is . . . unquiet and contentious, to let her alone, not to wake an angry Dog. (Edward Topsell, *The History of Serpents*, 1607)

mend one's fences See POLITICKING.

pour oil on troubled waters To calm or pacify with soothing words or acts.

> His presence and advice, like oil upon troubled waters, have composed the contending waves of faction. (Benjamin Rush, *Letters*, 1786)

Pouring oil on rough waters does indeed serve to quiet the waves, though perhaps not to the extent recounted by the Venerable Bede in his *Ecclesiastical History* (731). He relates the story of a priest sent to fetch the bride-to-be of King Oswy. Before the priest's departure, Saint Aidan warned him of a violent storm and gave him a bottle of oil that he was to pour on the sea when the water grew rough. As predicted, a great tempest came up during the voyage; when the priest poured his vessel of oil on the turbulent waters, they became calm.

smooth ruffled feathers To calm or soothe an upset or angry person; to assuage, pacify, placate; to help someone regain his composure; to reconcile. Alluding to the erect feathers of an angry bird, this expression describes the action of one who mediates a dispute or otherwise calms an agitated or angry person. See also **ruffle feathers**, VEXATION.

a sop to Cerberus See BRIBERY.

PLEASURE (See ENJOYMENT.)

PLOY (See also TRICKERY.)

ace up one's sleeve A surprise; something of special effectiveness that is held in reserve or hidden from others; a trump card; sometimes *card up one's sleeve*. Very similar to an *ace in the hole*, this expression comes from the cardsharper's stratagem of hiding needed cards (e.g., aces) in his sleeve until the most advantageous moment to play them. By extension, it has come to mean any secret asset or ploy.

bag of tricks All of one's resources; the means to an end. This phrase derives from La Fontaine's fable of the fox and the cat.

> But fox, in arts of siege well versed, Ransacked his bag of tricks accursed. (Elizur Wright, trans., *La Fontaine's Fables*, 1841)

Bag of tricks can refer to one's survival techniques in general, or to a specific design one might have up one's sleeve.

> Men were all alike. A woman didn't have to carry a very big bag of tricks to achieve her purpose. (L. C. Douglas, *White Banners*, 1936)

bottom of the bag The last resort or expedient in one's bag of tricks; a trump card held in reserve; an ace up one's sleeve. Thomas Burton used the phrase in his *Diary* in 1659:

> If this be done, which is in the bottom of the bag, and must be done, we shall . . . be able to buoy up our reputation.

have something up one's sleeve To have a secret scheme or trick in mind, to have a surprise planned. The allusion is probably to the way magicians use their sleeves as convenient hiding places for the articles employed in executing their feats of magic.

red herring A diversionary tactic or misleading clue, a subject intended to divert attention from the real issue; a false trail; from the phrase *draw a red herring across the trail*. In the 17th century, dog trainers followed this practice to sharpen the scent discrimination of hunting hounds. Smoked herring drawn across the trail of a fox is said to destroy or markedly affect the original scent. Figurative use of the term outside the complete phrase dates at least from the late 19th century.

> The talk of revolutionary dangers is a mere red-herring. (*Liverpool Daily Post*, July 11, 1884)

springes to catch woodcocks Snares for the unsuspecting; traps for the unwary. This expression appears in Shakespeare's *Hamlet* (I,iii), when Polonius warns Ophelia that Hamlet's protestations of affection are but the wily words of a youthful lover, meant to ensnare his naive victim: "springes to catch woodcocks," he calls them. The phrase usually refers to a deceitful ploy.

> Alas, poor woodcock, dost thou go a birding? Thou hast even set a springe to catch thy own neck. (John Dryden, *Wild Gallant*, 1663)

stalking horse Anything used to conceal a design or scheme, a pretext; a person who serves as a means of allaying suspicion or obscuring an ongoing activity; the agency through which an underhanded objective is attained. The expression appeared in Shakespeare's *As You Like It*:

> He uses his folly like a stalking horse, and under the presentation of that he shoots his wit. (V,iv)

In bygone days, hunters hid themselves behind a horse as they stalked to within shooting range of the game. The expression early carried its still current figurative sense of the intended concealment of plans, projects, or intentions.

> Do you think her fit for nothing but to be a Stalking-Horse to stand before you, while you aim at my wife? (William Congreve, *Double Dealer*, 1694)

The expression has evolved the extended political meaning of a person whose candidacy is intended to conceal the true candidacy of another, or whose place on the ballot is meant to split the opposition.

throw a curve or **a curve ball** To employ clever and often deceptive artifice in verbal dealings with another; to trick so as to entrap; to accomplish one's ends by indirection. The expression derives from baseball; a curve ball is a pitched ball which appears to the batter to be approaching outside the strike zone, but which breaks over the plate and is thus "right on target." As employed metaphorically, a curve ball is usually a verbal technique, such as a leading question or seemingly casual comment which aims to evoke a specific reaction or to elicit a revealing response, usually one in some way damaging to the respondent. It thus appears innocuous or irrelevant but in actuality it is highly manipulative, and "right on target."

throw a tub to the whale To create a diversion, or to mislead or bamboozle, in order to avoid an awkward, embarrassing, or dangerous situation.

> It has been common to throw out something to divert and amuse the people, such as a plot, a conspiracy, or an enquiry about nothing, . . . which method of proceeding, by a very apt metaphor, is call'd throwing out the tub. (Charles Molloy, *Select Letters taken from Fog's Weekly Journal*, 1728)

Jonathan Swift explains the origin of this expression in the preface to *A Tale of a Tub*:

> Sea-men have a custom when they meet a whale, to fling him out an empty tub, . . . to divert him from laying violent hands upon the ship.

Tale of a tub meaning 'an apocryphal story' dates from the 1500s. However, Swift's use of *throw a tub to the whale* in 1704 is the earliest cited use of the expression in the *OED*.

Trojan horse A snare or trap, a treacherous device or ploy, particularly one appearing as an attractive lure. The allusion is to the tale recounted in Homer's *Iliad*. The Greeks, pretending to abandon their siege of Troy, left at its gates a gigantic wooden horse, within which were concealed several Greek soldiers. Interpreting the horse as a gift or peace-offering, the Trojans brought it into the city, whereupon those within stole out during the night to admit the entire Greek force and thus conquer the city. See also **beware of Greeks bearing gifts**, PRETENSE.

trump card An ace in the hole; a decisive, winning argument, ploy, piece of evidence, etc.; a clincher.

> Justice . . . is the trump card of the western world. (*The Times Literary Supplement* as quoted in *Webster's Third*)

A trump card is literally any card of a suit which outranks the other three suits in a card game. *Trump* in this term is a corruption of the now obsolete *triumph* 'a trump card.'

POLITENESS (See DEFERENCE.)

POLITICKING

barnstorm To make a whirlwind campaign drumming up political support and enthusiasm. The term nearly always appears in its participle or gerund form. Its current political use shows up as early as 1896 in the *Congressional Record,* but its origin is theatrical, referring to itinerant troupes or players who performed in barns to appreciative (and unsophisticated) audiences. Hence it still carries the connotation that such campaigning is done in remote, rural areas or small towns.

filibuster See TEMPORIZING.

logrolling See RECIPROCITY.

mend one's fences To renew or reinforce one's position or esteem through diplomacy; to engage in political wirepulling. This American political slang purportedly originated just prior to the 1880 presidential elections, when John Sherman, an aspirant of the executive office, left Congress and retreated to his Ohio farm to develop campaign strategy. While he was repairing a fence one day with his brother-in-law Colonel Morton, a reporter approached Morton and inquired about Sherman's activi-

ties. Colonel Morton replied that Sherman was obviously mending his fences. Although the expression occasionally carries the nonpolitical sense of trying to make one's peace with another, its more common use describes the standard pre-election attempts of public officeholders to re-establish communication with the voters.

> An early adjournment of the session is deemed essential in order that the members may go home to mend their fences, as the saying is. (*Forum,* April, 1906)

mud-slinging See SLANDER.

politics makes strange bedfellows See EXPEDIENCE.

pork barrel See GRAFT.

take to the hustings To campaign or electioneer; to take to the stump; to barnstorm, to conduct a whistle-stop tour. The *hustings* of this expression refers to the platform from which political speeches are made; earlier it specifically meant the platform from which candidates for the British parliament stood for nomination. Its oldest antecedents are in the Norse word for the assembly hall of a king, from which the term came to be applied to assembly meetings in general. Today it is associated with political speechmaking exclusively.

> An unpopular candidate had frequently to beat a hasty retreat from the hustings. (Samuel C. Hall, *Retrospect of a Long Life,* 1883)

take to the stump To tour the country making political speeches; to harangue, to rant. This Americanism is from the days when the stump of a felled tree was used as a platform from which political speeches were delivered.

POMPOSITY (See also HAUGHTINESS, OSTENTATIOUSNESS.)

blimp A pompous reactionary; a dyed-in-the-wool Tory. This British colloquialism was given us by cartoonist David

Low and his creation Colonel Blimp, whose name and figure clearly derive from the air-filled dirigibles of the same name.

cock of the walk A leader; the ruling spirit of a group, especially one who is dominating and cocksure. Gamecocks being trained for fighting are put out on a walk with a small group of hens. Here the fighting instinct is developed to the point where one gamecock cannot stand the presence of another. Two placed together will fight to the death. Recorded use of the phrase dates only from the early 19th century, but it is likely that the expression was used long before then.

fuss and feathers See OSTENTATIOUSNESS.

high-muck-a-muck See PERSONAGE.

his nibs See PERSONAGE.

mugwump See INDEPENDENCE.

pooh bah A pompous individual. Pooh Bah, a character in Gilbert and Sullivan's *The Mikado* (1885), derived a feeling of superiority from the many positions he held. A few of his titles included "First Lord of the Treasury," "Lord Chief Justice," "Commander in Chief," and the all-inclusive "Lord-High-Everything-Else." Thus *pooh bah* is currently used of any self-important person who holds several positions at once.

the pope's mustard maker A pretentious, self-important person. This expression originated in the 14th-century Avignon court of Pope John XXII. The pontiff, whose propensity for luxurious living and exquisite dining was common knowledge throughout Europe, had a particular fondness for mustard seasoning and required all his meals to be so spiced. In order to guarantee that the spicing was done properly, the pope created the office of *Moutardier* 'mustard maker,' which he bestowed upon his nephew. The nephew was so enthralled with the glamor and dignity of the position that he eventually became the target of satire and droll witticisms. The expression *Moutardier du Pape* 'the pope's mustard maker' is still commonly used in France for a pompous person.

too big for one's britches Smart-alecky, wise, presumptuous, arrogant, swellheaded; also *too big for one's breeches, boots,* etc.

> When a man gets too big for his breeches, I say Good-bye. (David Crockett, *An Account of Col. Crockett's Tour to the North and down East,* 1835)

A person who has an inordinately high opinion of himself is said to have a swelled head. The same concept underlies this expression in spite of the different point of reference.

POSTPONEMENT (See ABEYANCE, TEMPORIZING.)

POVERTY (See also INDEBTEDNESS, SUBSISTENCE.)

beggar's bush Beggary, financial ruin, bankruptcy; often in the phrases *to go by beggar's bush* or *to go home by beggar's bush.* The allusion is to a certain tree on the left side of the London road from Huntingdon to Caxton, where beggars once frequently gathered. This British expression, rarely heard today, dates from the late 16th century.

> We are almost at Beggars-bush, and we cannot tell how to help our selves. (Andrew Yarranton, *England's Improvement by Sea and Land,* 1677)

down-at-the-heel Poor, destitute; of slovenly or shabby appearance; also, *out-at-the-heel.* The latter usually refers to holes in one's stockings; the former, to the run-down condition of one's shoes.

> Thus the unhappy notary ran gradually down at the heel. (Henry Wadsworth Longfellow, *Outre-Mer,* 1835)

Some rich snudges . . . go with their hose out at heels. (Thomas Wilson, *The Art of Rhetoric*, 1553)

from hand to mouth See PRECARIOUSNESS.

hard up In financial straits, short of cash, out-of-pocket. Originally nautical, this expression was usually used in the imperative, directing that the helm or tiller be pushed as far windward as it would go in order to turn the ship's bow away from the wind. Since this maneuver was usually necessitated by a storm or other potentially disastrous situation, the phrase took on the general sense of difficulty or straits. The nonnautical use of this expression dates from the early 19th century.

You don't feel nearly so hard up with elevenpence in your pocket as you do with a shilling. (Jerome K. Jerome, *The Idle Thoughts of an Idle Fellow*, 1886)

in Carey Street Penniless, flat broke, destitute. This British colloquial expression takes its name from Carey Street in London, the former location of the Bankruptcy Court. It has been in use since 1922.

in low water Financially hard up, strapped, broke, impoverished. Although the exact origin of this expression is unknown, it may be related to the precarious condition of a ship finding itself in low water or about to go "on the rocks." This expression dates from the latter half of the 18th century.

Law-breakers . . . who, having been "put away," and done their time, found themselves in low water upon their return to the outer world. (*Chambers's Journal of Popular Literature*, February, 1885)

See also **on the rocks, INDEBTEDNESS.**

on one's beam-ends In financial difficulties, in imminent danger of bankruptcy. The reference is to a vessel on her beam-ends, that is, on her side such that the beams—the transverse timbers supporting the deck—are practically touching the water. Obviously, any vessel in such a state is in immediate danger of overturning. The phrase has been used figuratively since the early 19th century.

on one's uppers Impoverished, down-and-out; shabby-looking, down-at-the-heel. This phrase, of U.S. origin, appeared in *The Century Dictionary* (1891). The *uppers* are the upper leathers of shoes or boots; a person "on his uppers" has worn through both sole and welt. Footgear as indicative of financial status is also found in the term *well-heeled* (though this is probably of unrelated origin), and in the above-noted *down-at-the-heel.*

The rumor whirled about the Street that Greener was in difficulties. Financial ghouls . . . said . . . "Greene is on his uppers." (*Munsey's Magazine*, 1901)

on the high-road to Needham See DEGENERATION.

out at elbows Shabbily dressed; down-and-out, poverty-stricken; in financial difficulties. A coat worn through at the elbows has long been a symbol of poverty. The expression appeared in print by the time of Shakespeare.

He was himself just now so terribly out at elbows, that he could not command a hundred pounds. (Mrs. Mary M. Sherwood, *The Lady of the Manor*, 1847)

poor as a churchmouse Extremely poor; impoverished, insolvent; poor but proud. This expression, popular since the 17th century, is probably derived from a tale which recounts the plight of a mouse that attempted to find food in a church. Since most churches, including that of the story, do not have kitchens, the proud mouse found it difficult to survive since its pickings were slim at best.

The owner, 'tis said, was once poor as a churchmouse. (*Political Ballads,* 1731)

poor as Job Poverty-stricken, indigent, destitute. The allusion is to the extreme poverty which befell the central character in the Book of Job. In spite of a series of devastating calamities, Job remained steadfast in his faith and trust in God, and has long been the personification of both poverty and patience.

I am as poor as Job, my lord, but not so patient. (Shakespeare, *Henry IV, Part II,* I,ii)

A related expression, *poor as Job's turkey,* is credited to Thomas C. Haliburton (1796–1865), a Canadian judge and humorist. Haliburton, using the pseudonym Sam Slick, described Job's turkey as so poor that it had only one feather, and so weak that it had to lean against a fence in order to gobble. Job, of course, never had a turkey—poor or otherwise—as the bird is a native of North America. A variation is *poor as Job's cat.*

POWER

come on like gangbusters To burst upon the scene with noisy exuberance; to come on with great power or force; to be officious or overbearing at first meeting. This expression derives from the blaring sound effects that opened a 1936 radio program called *Gangbusters.* These included the sounds of marching feet, machine-gun fire, and a screaming siren.

money talks Wealth means power; almost anything can be secured with money. This expression alludes to the way money and its procurement direct one's life, as well as to the automatic respect and deference given to the wealthy by the less affluent.

the powers that be The authorities; a group or individual exercising complete control and having the power to make decisions affecting large numbers of people. This phrase is Biblical in origin.

For there is no power but of God: the powers that be are ordained of God. (Romans 13:1)

It is implied that "the powers that be" are impersonal and inaccessible.

pull rank To make use of one's higher status in order to obtain a desired objective. This expression originated in the armed forces, where one of subordinate rank must comply absolutely with the orders of a superior. The term is now also applied to civilians, particularly in describing certain employer-employee interactions. In either case, the expression usually suggests the unexpected or unfair use of authority in resolving a dilemma or in demanding submission.

throw one's weight around To exert one's influence inappropriately or unfairly, to pull strings; to lord it over subordinates, to pull rank. *Weight,* meaning 'power or influence,' probably derives from the advantage of added pounds or extra weight in contact sports.

PRACTICALITY (See **EXPEDIENCE.**)

PRAISE (See **COMMENDATION, FLATTERY.**)

PRECARIOUSNESS (See also **DANGER, PREDICAMENT, RISK, VULNERABILITY.**)

behind the power curve In a very precarious position, in danger of imminent downfall. The expression is of aeronautical origin; the power curve is a graph of velocity versus the power needed to overcome wind resistance or "drag." To be behind the power curve is to have insufficient power to remain aloft —rather risky for an aviator. Like many phrases from sports and technology, this expression has found widespread application in political contexts, where it describes persons not up to date or not in synchrony with a superior's decisions and policies, and thus headed for a fall.

by the seat of one's pants See INTUITION.

by the skin of one's teeth Just barely; hardly; narrowly. The allusion is to Job 14:20:

I have escaped with the skin of my teeth.

Since teeth have no skin, the implication of this expression is clear.

close shave A narrow escape; a close call; rescue from impending harm or dire trouble; a narrow difference. This informal American expression dating from the mid-19th century is said to be based on the narrow margin between a smooth, closely shaven skin and a serious cut. However, one meaning of *shave* is 'a slight or grazing touch' (*OED*); therefore, the expressions *close* or *near shave* can be taken literally as well. This literal meaning might well have spawned the figurative meanings of *close shave* common today.

cut it close To succeed, but just barely; to squeak by; to just make it; to come within an ace of failure. This multi-purpose expression can describe just about anything achieved by a narrow margin, whether because of tight, rigid planning or because of a lackadaisical absence of planning. Since the *it* has an indefinite referent, and the *cut* and *close* each have a multitude of relevant meanings, whether taken singly or in combination, pinning down a precise origin for this phrase is impossible. The likelihood is, there is none. But for a possible relationship, see **cut corners, EXPEDIENCE.**

dicey Uncertain, unpredictable, like a throw of the dice; risky, dangerous, unreliable; touch-and-go. According to the *OED*, this 20th-century British slang term was originally Air Force lingo. An equivalent but less common English term is *dodgy*.

The river got a little dicey. I thought we'd wait for the moon. (P. Capon, *Amongst those Missing,* 1959)

from hand to mouth From day to day, precariously; improvidently; in imminent danger of starvation. This expression is an obvious allusion to someone so poor and starved that whatever food he gets goes immediately from his hand to his mouth. In a more general sense the phrase denotes consumption of one's resources, food, money, etc., as soon as they are obtained. Use of this expression dates from the early 16th century. William Cowper uses the phrase in his *Letters to Newton* (1790):

I subsist, as the poor are vulgarly said to do, from hand to mouth.

hang by a thread To be in a very precarious situation or perilous position.

But this hangs only upon the will of the prince—a very weak thread in such a case. (Thomas Starkey, *England in the Reign of Henry the Eighth,* 1538)

The expression comes from the story of the flatterer Damocles, who was invited by the tyrant Dionysius to experience the luxury he so envied and praised. When Damocles sat down to a sumptuous feast, he discovered a sword suspended over his head by a single hair. Fear that the sword would fall and kill him prevented him from enjoying the banquet. See also **sword of Damocles, DANGER.**

hang by the eyelids To have a very slight hold on something, to be just barely attached, to be in a dangerous or precarious position. This particularly vivid expression, although rarely heard today, requires no explanation. It dates from the latter half of the 17th century, and appeared in James T. Fields' *Underbrush* (1877):

A magic quarto . . . with one of the covers hanging by the eyelids.

on thin ice In a precarious position, in a risky situation, on shaky ground. This self-evident expression is often used of a person's arguments or reasoning. The similar *skate on thin ice* most often refers to one's behavior, and is indicative of questionable, dangerous, risk-taking conduct. The expression has been used figuratively for more than a century.

The incessant, breathless round of intermingled sport and pleasure danced on the thin ice of debt. (Ouida, *Fortnightly Review,* 1892)

touch and go Risky, precarious; not to be taken for granted, uncertain; flirting with danger, avoiding disaster by a narrow margin. A ship is said to "touch and go" when its keel scrapes the bottom without stopping the boat or losing a significant amount of speed. Another nautical use refers to the practice of approaching the shore to let off cargo or men without actually stopping, thus avoiding the involved procedure required to stop. It has been speculated that the great risk and uncertainty involved in this maneuver has spawned the current figurative use of *touch and go* which emphasizes motion—however slow, erratic, or precarious—rather than arrested movement. Examples of this expression used adjectivally date from the 19th century; however, the less common substantive use of *touch and go* dates from the 17th century, and the verbal use from the 16th century.

walk a tightrope See CAUTIOUSNESS.

PRECISION (See also CORRECT-NESS.)

bang on Exactly on; directly on; precisely as planned; apt or appropriate. This British slang phrase often appears as *bang on target,* popularized by bomber lingo during World War I.

It [a play] has enough quality and sense of the theatre to suggest that before long he will land one bang on the target. (*Oxford Magazine,* February 27, 1958)

By extension, the phrase also describes anything which is just right, apt, or appropriate.

As a realistic tale of low life in London, it is bang on. (*Spectator,* February 14, 1958)

Spot on is another British slang phrase which is used interchangeably with *bang on.*

dot one's i's and cross one's t's To be precise or meticulous down to the last or smallest detail; to particularize in detail so as to leave no room for doubt or uncertainty; to cite chapter and verse. This expression is said to have sprung from the possibility of confusing *i*'s with *t*'s if they are carelessly written without the respective dot and cross. The phrase has been in figurative use since the 1800s.

hit the nail on the head To do or say the most fitting thing; to cut through extraneous details and come right to the point; to make a clear, pithy statement. This expression has been in print since the 16th century. Hitting a nail properly—that is, squarely on the head—is likened to communicating effectively, or to the point. On the other hand, a bad hit which bends the nail is like rambling which fails to get to the crux of a matter.

At least they ignorantly hit the nail on the head, saying that the Devil was in him. (*Fryke's Voyage,* 1700)

Occam's razor The maxim that unnecessary facts or assumptions used to explain a subject must be eliminated. William of Occam, the 14th-century English scholastic philosopher known as "the Invincible Doctor," believed that general ideas have no objective reality outside the mind (nominalism). *Razor* in this expression is a metaphorical term for the precise, dissecting, incisive methods which characterize Occam's intellectual approach.

on the button Exactly, precisely; punctually, promptly; on the dot; often *right on the button.* This expression derives from the boxing slang use of *button* to mean the point of the chin. Literally then, *on the button* indicates a perfectly aimed punch to the chin or jaw area intended to knock a fighter out or at least seriously impair his ability to retaliate.

on the money At precisely the right time or place, right on target; often *right on the money*. This American slang expression appears to refer to money placed as a bet against a certain, previously stated outcome.

on the nose Precisely; right on target; on time. *On the nose* is old radio parlance describing the producer's gesture of putting his finger on his nose to signify that the program was running according to schedule. The phrase is now used especially in regard to time but can describe anything which is accurate, precise, or apt. *On the button* is akin to *on the nose* in meaning and usage, and both are American equivalents of the British phrases *bang on* and *spot on.*

to a T Exactly, precisely, perfectly.

> All these old-fashioned goings on would suit you to a T. (Harriet Beecher Stowe, *Dred,* 1856)

The *OED* dismisses as untenable the popular belief that this expression is an allusion to the T square, a draftsman's T-shaped ruler for the accurate drawing of right angles, parallel lines, etc. It conjectures instead that it was the initial of a word, perhaps *tittle* 'dot, jot,' since this was in use nearly a century before *to a T* in exactly the same constructions. Use of the expression dates from at least the late 17th century.

PREDICAMENT (See also **DANGER, DISADVANTAGE, INDEBTEDNESS, PRECARIOUSNESS, RISK, VULNERABILITY.**)

between a rock and a hard place In a tight spot, in an uncomfortable position; trapped, cornered, pressured, with no way out; with equally undesirable alternatives, hence no true choice at all. This relatively recent and seemingly prosaic phrase is often used in reference to one's financial plight; hence it may be conceptually related to *on the rocks* (**INDEBTEDNESS**).

between hawk and buzzard To be caught in a precarious position between two undesirable alternatives; to have a choice semantically, but actually no choice worth mentioning. Since hawks and buzzards are both birds of prey, to be literally between hawk and buzzard is a frightening and dangerous prospect. The phrase is used figuratively although it is rarely heard. There is, however, another meaning of *between hawk and buzzard* which is more current. See **INDETERMINATENESS.**

between Scylla and Charybdis To be in an extremely vulnerable position between two powerful and dangerous alternatives, either of which is difficult to avoid without encountering the other. This expression alludes to Homer's *Odyssey* in which the hero Odysseus had to sail between Charybdis, a raging whirlpool on the Sicilian coast, and Scylla, a rock personified as a ravenous sea monster on the Italian side of the Straits of Messina. Odysseus tried to save his crew and ship, only to lose both and barely save his own life. The following citations from *Webster's Third* show how the phrase is currently used.

> . . . the Scylla of incomprehensibility and the Charybdis of inaccuracy have both been avoided. *(Times Literary Supplement)*

> . . . between the Scylla of national parochialism and the Charybdis of complete exoticism. (Bernard Smith)

between the devil and the deep blue sea In a perilous position; having two equally undesirable and dangerous alternatives. *Devil* in this expression is literally a nautical term for a seam in the hull of ships, on or below the water line.

The location of this seam made repair work hazardous, and any sailor ordered to make necessary repairs was put in a precarious position. Today the phrase is used figuratively. It is a popular saying, although few people are aware that *devil* does not refer to Satan.

catch-22 A double-bind, a no-win situation; a seeming choice which is no choice; the dilemma of the single alternative. The term owes its origin and currency to *Catch-22*, a Joseph Heller novel of World War II popular in the 1960s. It is said to have been a coinage by Robert Gottlieb, Heller's editor. As used therein, *22* is the number of the regulation which contains the *catch* 'hidden trick or snag.' The regulation provided that an airman could request release from combat duty only on grounds of insanity; but to do so was itself considered proof of sanity, because no sane person would willingly risk his life in such insane fashion. So he had no out.

Hobson's choice The dubious choice of taking what is offered or nothing at all; the absence of any viable alternative, no real choice at all. The reference is to Thomas or Tobias Hobson (1544–1631), the owner of a Cambridge livery stable, who gave his customers the questionable choice of taking the horse nearest the stable door or none at all, despite the good selection usually in his stable. This proverbial expression dates from at least 1660.

> The Masters were left to Hobson's choice, to choose Bennet and no body else. (Anthony Wood, *Athenae Oxonienses*, 1691)

hold a wolf by the ears To be in a dangerous, precarious situation; to have no viable alternative; to be in a jam or predicament. The problematic nature of holding a wolf by the ears is well expressed in the following quotation from Francis Quarles's *The History of Samson* (1631):

> I have a Wolfe by th'eares; I dare be bold,
> Neither with safety, to let go, nor hold:
> What shall I do?

Originally an old Greek saying, this expression appeared in print by the mid-1500s.

in a jam In a difficult or awkward situation, in a fix, in a tight spot, in a bind. This expression, of American origin, dates from the early part of this century. It could have derived either from the verb *jam* 'press, push, wedge, squeeze' or the noun *jam* 'blockage, bottleneck,' as in log jam or traffic jam.

> Henare would give his whole-hearted sympathy and his last shilling to anyone in a bit of a jam. (R. D. Finlayson, *Brown Man's Burden*, 1938)

in a pickle In a sorry plight, in quite a predicament; in hot water, on the hot seat; usually used with a modifier such as *pretty, sad, fine, sweet*. The now colloquial expression was formerly used in more serious contexts:

> In this pickle lyeth man by nature, that is, all we that be Adam's children. (John Foxe, *Sermons*, 1585)

It has been conjectured that its origin lies in the Dutch *in de pekel zitten* 'sitting in pickle juice,' since such a position in the brinish, vinegary liquid would be unpleasant indeed.

in a scrape In trouble, in a fix, in a fine mess.

> I was generally the leader of the boys and sometimes led them into scrapes. (Benjamin Franklin, *Autobiography*, 1771)

Several explanations have been offered as to the origin of this expression, which dates from the early 18th century. One such explanation cites the holes that deer scrape in the ground during certain seasons, while another claims that in Scotland *scrape* was a term for a rabbit's burrow (a dangerous trap for a golfer's ball). The *OED*, however, conjectures that the verb *to scrape* gave rise to the noun form *scrape* as used in this expression. The most plausible explanation is the most obvious: a person in danger, who survives with a mere scrape, is better off than one who is more seriously injured. Hence, a *scrape* is a situation from which one escapes with his skin intact.

in chancery In a predicament; unable to extricate oneself from an embarrassing, awkward position. *In chancery* is also a wrestling term describing the position of the head when held under the opponent's left arm, thus the expression *have one's head in chancery*. This vulnerable position of the head has given rise to figurative use of the phrase referring to any predicament; however, the wrestling term itself alludes to the absolute control of the Court of Chancery which was notorious for holding up suits and subjecting involved parties to great inconvenience.

> When I can perform my mile in eight minutes or a little less, then I feel as if I had old Time's head in chancery. (Oliver Wendell Holmes, *The Autocrat of the Breakfast-table,* 1858)

in deep water In trouble, in a difficult or dangerous situation, in over one's head. *Deep waters* 'difficulties, troubles' is found in Psalm 69.

in hot water In big trouble, in Dutch, in a scrape. This expression, which dates from the first half of the 16th century, refers to the obvious discomfort caused by scalding hot water.

> This poor fellow was always getting into hot water. (Richard H. Dana, Jr., *Two Years before the Mast,* 1840)

in over one's head Beyond one's capability or resources; usually in reference to one's financial situation 'in debt, in the red.' The allusion is to a swimmer floundering about in water over his

head, without the stamina or the ability to reach the shore.

in the cactus An Australian term meaning in an uncomfortable or awkward situation.

in the soup In trouble, in hot water, in a difficult situation.

> After collecting a good deal of money, the scoundrels suddenly left town, leaving many persons in the soup. (*The Lisbon* [Dakota] *Star,* April, 1889)

Although several explanations have been proposed as to the origin and popularization of this U. S. expression, no substantial evidence has yet been found to support any of them, leaving the original meaning of the phrase as obscure as ever.

kettle of fish See DISORDER.

on the horns of a dilemma Compelled to choose between two equally undesirable alternatives; in dire straits. A person *on the horns of a dilemma* must select an alternative that will surely result in a negative outcome; he will be caught or impaled no matter his choice. The word *horn* is used singularly to denote either of the undesirable alternatives.

> This seems a smart dilemma at first . . . yet I think neither Horn is strong enough to push us off from our belief of the Existence of God. (Henry More, *Divine Dialogue,* 1668)

on the spot In a dangerous situation; in a life-threatening position; in a dire predicament; also, *put on the spot.* This common phrase is derived from the pirates of old, who used the one-spotted ace of spades as an indication to a stool pigeon or poltroon that his days were numbered. In contemporary usage, the expression often refers to a situation in which one is forced into a self-incriminating position.

> Some of the questions directed at him were obviously designed to put

Stassen on the spot. (*Chicago Sun-Times*, March, 1948)

up the creek In trouble, in a tight spot. This common U.S. euphemism (a truncated version of *up shit creek without a paddle*) first appeared in print in the 1930s. Most who use it are unaware of its vulgar origins.

"How 'bout writing a composition for me, for English? I'll be up the creek if I don't get the goddam thing in by Monday." (J. D. Salinger, *The Catcher in the Rye*, 1951)

Variations are *up Salt Creek* and *up Salt River*, though some sources claim the latter to be a totally unrelated expression, giving conflicting, geographically erroneous, and equally implausible accounts for its reputed limited application to losing political candidates.

PREFERENCE

bag See INDIVIDUALITY.

[one's] cup of tea Suited to one's interests, talents, or taste; that which hits the spot, does the trick, or suits one's fancy.

Broadway by night seemed to be my cup of tea entirely. (Noel Coward, *Present Indicative*, 1937)

A logical extension of this sense is the British *cup of tea* meaning 'one's fate or destiny.' However, if something is neither suited to one's interest, nor a matter of destiny, it may well be *another* or *different cup of tea;* in other words, something of an altogether different kind.

A Fred racked with ideals, and in the grip of Federal Union, was quite a different cup of tea from the old, happy-go-lucky Fred. (Nancy Mitford, *Pigeon Pie*, 1940)

a man of my kidney See SIMILARITY.

up one's alley Suited to one's natural capabilities or interests; one's concern or business; where one feels at home; sometimes *down one's alley*. *In* or *up one's street* has the same meaning, al-

though the exact origin of either expression is anybody's guess. Both are cited as early as 1929.

Fun's fun, but box-fighting's your trick and anything else is out of your alley. (Witwer, *Yes Man's Land*, 1929)

A great many of the books published today are, as the saying is, right up her street. (*Publisher's Weekly*, December 21, 1929)

Up one's alley is currently the more common American expression; *up one's street* is more frequently heard in Britain.

PREJUDICE (See also PREFERENCE, RACISM.)

a jaundiced eye A prejudiced perspective or point of view; a skeptical, critical attitude; distorted vision that perceives everything as faulty, inferior, or undesirable. The disease of jaundice gives a yellowish cast to the whites of the eyes. This phrase is based on the assumption that everything appears "yellow"—i.e., negative, distorted—to such eyes.

All seems infected that the infected spy,
As all looks yellow to the jaundiced eye.
(Alexander Pope, *An Essay on Criticism*, 1709)

look through blue glasses To see things in a preconceived, usually distorted light; to be biased, to be unable to see things for what they are. This expression plays on the negative connotations often carried by the color "blue." The image of spectacles gives tangible form to the nonmaterial prejudice which colors one's perceptions.

nothing like leather An expression mocking one who has a chauvinistic attitude toward his own craft or field. Attributed to an Aesop fable, *nothing like leather* was popularized by the following anonymous verse which explains its origin.

A town feared a siege, and held
consultation
Which was the best method of
fortification;
A grave, skilful mason said in his
opinion
Nothing but stone could secure the
dominion.
A carpenter said, "Though that was
well spoke,
It was better by far to defend it
with oak."
A currier, wiser than both these
together,
Said, "Try what you please, there's
nothing like leather."

PREPARATION   (See also **READI-NESS.**)

batten down the hatches To prepare for adversity, to ready one's defenses. The expression is of nautical origin: battens are narrow strips of wood nailed down to secure the edges of the tarpaulin over the hatchways during rough weather at sea. The phrase is commonly used figuratively for the precautions necessary to prepare a dwelling against a literal storm of any sort; and by further extension, to take defensive precautions when faced with any upcoming trial or ordeal.

bite the bullet See **ENDURANCE.**

boots and saddle A U. S. Army bugle call for mounted drill and formation. This expression denoting a cavalry trumpet sound is a corruption of the French *boutes la selle* 'put on the saddle,' and consequently has no semantic relationship with *boots.* However, since boots are logically associated with horsemen, whether cavalry or cowboys, *boots and saddle* has come to carry connotations of the American West more than of the military.

get oneself in gear To ready oneself to take whatever action is necessary; to stop lazing about and get ready to go. This expression may derive from the use of *gear,* as in *put in gear, gear up,* or *get in gear,* all of which in literal use

refer to the harnessing of an animal. Another possibility is a more modern use of *gear.* In this latter sense, *in gear* applies to the state of parts in which they are connected or meshed with each other. Both possibilities involve the idea of preparation and are plausible explanations for the current use of *get oneself in gear.* A variant expression is *gear oneself up* which refers to preparing oneself psychologically, or psyching oneself up to do something demanding or distasteful.

get up steam To get up energy, gear oneself up, psych oneself up, motivate oneself. The allusion is to the steam-operated engines formerly used to propel riverboats and locomotives. These engines were powered by boiler-generated steam, a certain amount of which had to be produced before the boat or locomotive could begin moving forward. Because of its use as a power source for engines, *steam* has come to be used figuratively to mean energy, vigor, drive. The expression appeared in Francis Francis Jr.'s *Saddle and Mocassin* (1887):

"And he [the bull] came for you?"
"When he got up the steam he
did."

gird up one's loins To prime oneself for a test of endurance or preparedness; to ready oneself for scrutiny. The expression appears in Proverbs 31:17:

She girdeth her loins with strength,
and strengtheneth her arms.

The phrase may have derived from the loose-fitting clothes of ancient people, which needed to be tucked in or "girdled," usually about the loins, in preparation for work.

It was necessary, therefore, to gird
up our loins and walk. (Leitch
Ritchie, *Wanderings by the Loire,*
1833)

The expression is the literary equivalent of the modern *get psyched up,* a colloquialism for putting oneself into a state of readiness.

grit one's teeth To steel oneself to do what has to be done, to ready oneself for an unpleasant task or experience; to clench or grind one's teeth in anger or determination; also *to set one's teeth*. This expression, which dates from the late 18th century, is an allusion to the involuntary, reflexive clenching of one's teeth in moments of extreme anger or stress.

> The duellist gritted his teeth as he cocked the gun a second time. (*The Southern Literary Messenger*, 1840)

pave the way To prepare the way for, to lead up to; to smooth the way, to facilitate or make easier; to be the first step toward. Literal paved roads are, of course, much smoother to travel on than those of dirt and gravel. A variant of the expression was in use as early as the 16th century.

> It was Einstein who paved the way for the big-bang theory. (*Newsweek*, March, 1979)

screw oneself up to concert pitch To prepare for a particularly challenging task; to ready oneself for superior performance; to psych oneself up. This expression is an extension of the literal meaning of concert pitch, i.e., the slightly higher-than-usual pitch to which instruments are tuned for a concert in order to heighten the effect and brilliance of the music.

square off See CONFRONTATION.

PRETENSE (See also HYPOCRISY.)

ass in a lion's skin A pretender; a fool posing as a sage. The allusion is to the fable of an ass that donned a lion's skin in an attempt to masquerade as the noble beast, but betrayed itself by its braying.

beware of Greeks bearing gifts Distrust the kindnesses of known enemies; suspect an ulterior motive when adversaries act as benefactors. This warning to look for guile lest one be made the victim of treachery is a variation on the words of Laocoön in Book II of Virgil's *Aeneid:*

> Whatever it is, I fear Greeks even when they bring gifts.

The lines were spoken in reference to the so-called Trojan horse, left outside the gates of Troy supposedly as a gift or peace-offering from the Greeks, with whom Troy was at war. Laocoön's advice went unheeded, however, and the horse was brought inside the city gates; the Greeks hidden therein thus successfully sacked Troy and razed it to the ground.

four-flusher A bluffer; a pretender; a deadbeat, particularly one who pretends to have money but sponges or borrows from others. This expression derives from the card game of poker in which a flush is a hand (set of five cards) with all cards of the same suit. A four-flush is a hand with four cards of one suit and one card of another suit—worthless in poker. A good bluffer, particularly one who is poker-faced, upon finding himself with a four-flush, might bet in such a way as to make the other players think he is holding a five-card flush—almost a certain winner. Since this kind of bluffing requires heavy betting and involves a substantial risk, many a four-flusher has overextended himself and been unable to cover his losses. Thus, the expression was extended from its poker reference to its current, more general application.

> So, perhaps, was a four-flushing holdup man named Gunplay Maxwell. (Wallace Stegner, *Mormon Country*, 1942)

fox's sleep Pretended indifference to what is going on; noticing or observing a person, situation, or event without seeming to do so. This expression refers to the belief that foxes sleep with one eye open. Although this is not true in the literal sense, foxes and many other animals seem to remain on a "stand-by alert" when they sleep, ready for action and totally awake on a moment's notice. A related expression is *sleep with one eye open.*

iron hand in a velvet glove Tyranny, harshness, or inflexibility hidden under a soft, gentle exterior. At least one source has attributed this expression, in use since about 1850, to Napoleon. One of the several variations of the expression appeared in *The Victorian Hansard* (January, 1876):

They [the Government] have dealt with the Opposition with a velvet glove; but the iron hand is beneath, and they shall feel it.

look as if butter wouldn't melt in one's mouth Used contemptuously to describe a person of deceptively modest appearance, a goody-goody. The implication is always that the person's true nature is something quite different from what it seems. Hugh Latimer uses the expression, which dates from the early 1500s, in his *Seven Sermons Made Upon The Lord's Prayer* (1552):

These fellows . . . can speak so finely, that a man would think butter should scant melt in their mouths.

method in one's madness A reason, plan, or orderliness that is obscured by a person's apparent or feigned insanity or stupidity. This expression developed from a line in Shakespeare's *Hamlet:*

Though this be madness, yet there is method in 't. (II,ii)

It has enjoyed widespread popular usage since the 17th century.

He may be mad, but there's method in his madness. There nearly always is method in madness. It's what drives men mad being methodical. (Gilbert K. Chesterton, *The Man Who Knew Too Much,* 1922)

paper tiger See INEFFECTUALITY.

play possum To deceive or dissemble; to sham illness or death. This expression alludes to the opossum's defense mechanism of feigning death to ward off predators. In contemporary usage, the common phrase often suggests the feigning of ignorance.

By last week, in the Senate investigation of Washington five-percenters, it became plain that John had been playing possum the whole time. (*Time,* September, 1949)

Quaker guns Empty threats; harmless barbs; all bark and no bite. This expression comes from the former use of counterfeit guns, simulated to bluff the enemy into thinking that a ship or fort was well-fortified. Such were described as "Quaker" owing to that sect's doctrine of nonviolence. This U.S. expression is rarely heard today.

"He's like a Quaker gun," said Haxall—"piles of appearance, but no damage done." (Ella L. Dorsey, *Midshipman Bob,* 1888)

ringer A person or thing entered in a contest under false pretenses; a person or thing bearing an uncanny resemblance to another. The expression's first sense usually implies the misrepresentation of the contender's identity or potential. Although this American term finds its principal use in the horse-racing world, it may be applied to human competitors as well.

As a ringer in the Sadie Hawkins race, she was last heard of pursuing a panic-stricken Dogpatcher. (*Newsweek,* November, 1947)

The phrase's meaning of two nearly identical persons or things, most often expressed as *dead ringer,* is quite common in the United States.

I saw once . . . an outlaw . . . who was a dead ringer for him. (O. Henry, *Options,* 1909)

sail under false colors To pretend or appear to be what one is not; to put up a false front or façade; to act or speak hypocritically. In the days when buccaneers plundered on the open seas, it was common practice for a pirate ship to hoist the colors (flag) of a potential victim's ally in order to sneak up on the ship without arousing suspicion. At the last moment, the pirates would lower the false colors, "show their true colors," the Jolly Roger, and attack. This expression and its variations are now used figuratively.

Our female candidate . . . will no longer hang out false colors. (Sir Richard Steele, *The Spectator,* 1711)

sly-boots See SHREWDNESS.

wolf in sheep's clothing One who hides his true evil intentions or character behind a façade of friendship; a hypocrite or deceiver. This expression derives from an Aesop fable in which a wolf, wrapped in the fleece of a sheep, enters the fold and proceeds to devour the unsuspecting lambs. *A wolf in a lamb's skin,* in use as early as 1460, seems to be an older variation of the current phrase, which did not appear until 1591. A well-known Biblical passage has served to increase the phrase's familiarity:

Beware of false prophets, who come to you in sheep's clothing, but inwardly are ravening wolves. (Matthew 7:15)

PROBABILITY (See DESTINY.)

PROCESSING

in the hopper In the works, in the making, in the process of realization. The hopper of this expression is the box on the desk of an official of a legislative body. It serves as the receptacle for proposed bills. Consequently anything "in the hopper" is on its way toward realization.

Your show is in the hopper and you might just as well . . . not worry. (E. J. Kahn, cited in *Webster's Third*)

in the pipeline Under way, in action or operation; in the works. This picturesque expression alludes to the use of pipelines for transporting oil. If oil is in the pipeline, it's well on the way to its destination.

PROFANITY

air one's lungs To curse or swear. American cowboy slang.

billingsgate Vulgar or obscene language. The reference is to the coarse language commonly heard at Billingsgate, a London fishmarket. The term was in use as early as the 17th century.

blankety-blank A euphemism for profane or four-letter words. This expression, in use since at least 1854, derived from the former practice of leaving dashes or blank spaces to represent unprintable, vulgar words, as h--- for *hell* or d----- for *damned.* M. Diver used the phrase in *The Great Amulet* (1908):

Colonel Stanham Buckley . . . inquired picturesquely of a passing official when the blank this blankety blank train was supposed to start.

dickens A euphemistic word for the devil or Satan, common in such exclamations as *why the dickens* and *what the dickens.* The derivation of this slang term is not known although it has been in use since the time of Shakespeare. *Dickens* is also used in mild imprecations such as *the dickens take you, raise the dickens,* and *go to the dickens. To play the dickens* means to be mischievous, or to instigate or stir up trouble and confusion.

dip into the blue To tell an off-color story; to speak of the erotic or obscene. *Blue* 'lewd, obscene, indelicate, offensive' has been in use since at least as early as the mid-19th century. *Dip into the blue* is a picturesque but rarely heard euphemism.

locker-room talk Vulgar ribaldry; obscene, scurrilous, or vile language; also, *bathroom talk.* This expression derives from the lewd conversations that males purportedly indulge in when in the confines of a locker-room or bathroom.

swear like a trooper To use extremely profane language. This simile, dating from the late 18th century, derives from the language reputedly used by British soldiers. It has become almost a cliché that the language of men in exclusively male company, e.g., soldiers and athletes, is riddled with profanities.

> Women *got drunk* and *swore* like troopers. (William Cobbett, *A Year's Residence in the United States of America,* 1819)

Today the expression *like a trooper* is often used with other verbs to indicate forcefulness, intensity, enthusiasm, etc. One can "sing like a trooper," "dance like a trooper," "play like a trooper," and so on.

Sweet Fanny Adams See ABSENCE.

talk the bark off a tree To express oneself in strong, usually profane, language. This informal Americanism dates from the 19th century.

> The tracker will be led, perhaps, for mile after mile through just the sort of cover that tempts one to halt and "talk the bark off a tree" now and then. (*Outing,* November, 1891)

PROFESSION (See OCCUPATION.)

PROFUSION (See ABUNDANCE.)

PROLIFERATION (See ABUNDANCE.)

PROMISCUOUSNESS (See also LUST.)

Athanasian wench A loose woman, one of easy virtue, ready to grant sexual favors to any man who desires them. This somewhat irreverent slang phrase has its origin in the opening words of the Athanasian creed—*quicumque vult* 'whoever desires.' The creed, a Christian profession of faith dating from the 5th century, emphasized the doctrines of the Trinity and the Incarnation to combat the Arian heresy which denied the divinity of Jesus Christ.

bank-walker Exhibitionist; flasher. This American dialect expression (Ap-palachian region) for a male who enjoys displaying his physical endowments comes from the supposed practice of such a youth to strut about the riverbank unclothed, while his companions quickly hid their nakedness by plunging into the old swimming hole with all deliberate speed.

blue gown A harlot, prostitute. This British expression came from the blue garb formerly worn by women in houses of correction. In the United States, however, it has no such meaning. Though nonexistent as a discrete term, the phrase would be associated by most people with the all-time popular song "Alice Blue Gown," from the 1919 hit musical *Irene.* As such it would carry connotations of gentility and demureness rather than of brazenness and promiscuousness.

group grope An assemblage of people engaging in sex play; an orgy, bacchanalia, or love-in. This American expression is also applied to the mental or physical probing that transpires during encounter sessions, with the implication that all are floundering about, the blind leading the blind.

high-kilted Obscene, risqué, or indecent in one's manner of dress; literally wearing one's kilt or petticoat too short or tucked up. This British and Scottish expression dates from the early 17th century.

> To dazzle the world with her precious limb,
> —Nay, to go a little high-kilted.
> (Thomas Hood, *Kilmansegg,* 1840)

laced mutton A prostitute, strumpet, trollop; a loose or promiscuous woman. The derivation of this expression is uncertain, but there is general agreement that *mutton* 'prostitute' refers to the sheep, an occasional victim of bestiality by shepherds. *Laced* may refer to the elaborately tied bodices worn by ladies of the evening from the 17th through the 19th centuries. One source suggests that the reference may be to *lacing* 'flogging,' a common punishment for harlots at that time. The most plausible explanation is that *laced* is a corruption of *lost,* and that the original expression was a variation or perhaps even a deliberate pun on *lost sheep.* This concept received the punning treatment of William Shakespeare:

> Ay, sir: I a lost mutton, gave your letter to her, a laced mutton; and she, a laced mutton, gave me, a lost mutton, nothing for my labor. (*Two Gentlemen From Verona,* I,i)

make time with To date a girl or woman for the sole purpose of having sexual relations; to indulge in such endeavors with another's sweetheart or wife. Literally, *make time* means to move swiftly so as to recover lost time. Figuratively, one trying to "make time" with another is attempting a quick seduction with little or no intention of forming a lasting relationship.

> At another table, two young men were trying to make time with some Mexican girls. (William Burroughs, *Junkie,* 1953)

masher A playboy or womanizer; a man who attempts to seduce any woman he meets. This expression, derived from *mash* 'flirtation,' originally referred to certain 19th-century Englishmen who feigned wealth and sophistication while pursuing female companionship at the fashionable society establishments.

> The once brilliant masher of the music hall. (Walter Besant, *Bells of St. Paul's,* 1889)

In modern usage, however, this term is used to describe any male flirt or libertine.

one-night stand A single sexual encounter; a casual, one-time sex partner. This American slang term comes from the expression's theatrical use to denote either the town in which a touring company gives only one performance, or the single performance itself.

painted cat A prostitute, harlot, strumpet, daughter of joy. This expression combines *painted* and *cat,* terms both associated with prostitutes: *painted woman, cathouse.* Its usage was limited to American cowboys in the Old West.

quench one's thirst at any dirty puddle To be promiscuous; to indiscriminately obtain partners for sexual activity. This self-explanatory expression is infrequently heard today.

> I had before quenched my thirst at any dirty puddle [of women]. (Davis, *Travels,* 1803)

roué A libertine or playboy; one who leads a life of frivolity and self-indulgence; one who follows the primrose path. This expression was first used figuratively in the early 18th century for the decadent cronies of the Duke of Orleans. *Roué* 'wheel' refers to the punishment for wrongdoers of that time; thus, the term implies that the Duke and his cohorts deserved such a penalty.

> I knew him for a young roué of a vicomte—a brainless and vicious youth. (Charlotte Brontë, *Jane Eyre,* 1847)

shack up To cohabit or live together (usually in reference to an unmarried couple); to have a relatively permanent sexual relationship; to have sexual intercourse. During World War II, this expression was a popular means of describing the living arrangements of a soldier who, with a local woman, rented and intermittently lived in an apartment or inexpensive house (shack) located near the base where he was stationed. Since the 1950s, the expression's major application has shifted somewhat from the idea of actually setting up housekeeping to its more contemporary implications of promiscuous, and oftentimes indiscriminate sexual behavior.

> If you drink and shack up with strangers you get old at thirty. (Tennessee Williams, *Orpheus Descending,* 1957)

sow wild oats To be sexually promiscuous, especially before marriage; to live in an immoral and dissolute manner, particularly in one's youth. This expression, common since the 16th century, refers to the senselessness of planting wild oats (i.e., weeds) when it would be much more prudent to expend that effort with high quality grain.

> The wild oats, fully sown, are a veritable road to ruin. (*Pall Mall,* November 12, 1892)

starkers Nude; in the altogether; also, *starko.* This British colloquialism, a variation of *stark naked* (itself a corruption of *start naked*), has been in use since about 1910.

> The salesgirl had taken away all her clothes and hidden them. It was only the threat of running starkers into the street that brought them back. (Brigid Keenan, in the *Sunday Times* [London], September, 1964)

PROPRIETY (See also **PRUDISH-NESS.**)

according to Cocker By the book; in strict accordance with the rules; proper, correct. This British expression comes from the name of Edward Cocker (1631–75), arithmetician and author of several books including a well-known *Arithmetick,* viewed by many as the last word on correctness. Despite the work's popularity and authoritativeness, it is thought to have been a forgery.

according to Gunter This is the American answer to the British expression *according to Cocker.* In use as early as 1713, it was taken from the name of Edmund Gunter (1581–1626), famed English mathematician, astronomer, and inventor. Apparently neither the British expression nor its American equivalent is very well known on the opposite side of the ocean.

> The average American may not know what we mean by *according to Cocker;* while the average Englishman may be unaware of the meaning of *according to Gunter.* (G. A. Sala, *Illustrated London News,* November 24, 1883)

according to Hoyle By the book; in strict accordance with standard usage or rules; absolutely correct. A close synonym of *according to Cocker* and *according to Gunter,* this expression derives from the name of Edmond Hoyle, an 18th-century English writer. Hoyle was one of the first experts on the card game whist, which he spent several years teaching, and he did much to improve the game. His *A Short Treatise on Whist,* published in 1743, established him once and for all as the leading authority on the rules of the game. He was later to put together a whole encyclopedia of the rules of numerous other games. By extension his name has come to mean 'by the rules; correct.'

cricket Fair play, gentlemanly behavior, honorable conduct; especially in the phrase *not cricket* 'unfair, not proper, ungentlemanly.' Cricket is a popular British sport whose name has become synonymous with fair play because of the honorable and proper conduct expected from players of this game. The term dates from 1851.

keep one's nose clean To behave properly or appropriately, to keep out of trouble, to maintain a spotless record. This expression, which dates from at least 1887, is thought to have a vulgar origin.

> Do what people tell you, keep your nose clean and work out your academic progress. (Neil Armstrong et al., *First on the Moon,* 1970)

mind one's p's and q's To act or speak in a proper and dignified manner; to be on one's best behavior; to mind one's own business. There are several suggested derivations of this expression, the most likely of which alludes to a child's difficulty in distinguishing the letter "p" from the letter "q" because of their similar appearance. One source suggests that the expression may have been originated by King Louis XIV of France who advised his formally dressed noblemen that they could avoid disturbing their ornate attire by minding their *pieds* 'feet' and *queues* 'wigs.' Another source postulates that barkeeps may have said, "Mind your p's and q's!" to remind an alehouse patron that he had chalked up a large bill by ordering pints (p's) and quarts (q's) on credit.

> He minds his P's and Q's—and keeps himself respectable. (William S. Gilbert, *Utopia Limited,* 1893)

put one's best foot forward To make a good impression, to show oneself off to advantage. This grammatically puzzling expression may have developed by merger of its earlier form *best side outward* with the expression *get off on the right foot* (BEGINNINGS).

> A conceited man, and one that would put the best side outward. (Samuel Pepys, *Diary,* 1663)

stick to one's last To keep to the field of one's prowess; not to meddle in affairs of which one is ignorant. In this expression, *last* refers to a foot model with which shoes are shaped. According to ancient legend, Apelles, a famous Greek artist, showed one of his paintings to a cobbler, who immediately detected an error in the artist's rendering of a laced shoe. After the artist corrected this flaw, the shoemaker overstepped himself by criticizing the artist's depiction of the legs. Apelles is purported to have replied "stick to your last." This legend is supported by the fact that the expression was originally *a cobbler should stick to his last* before it evolved its current form. The phrase's figurative sense was illustrated by Thomas Barbour, as cited in *Webster's Third:*

> Curators . . . shirk any responsibility for exhibits and . . . want to stick to their lasts in the research collections.

PROSPERING (See also SUCCESS.)

flourish like a green bay tree Thrive vigorously; succeed overwhelmingly. Every year, the bay tree is adorned with numerous new branches growing along the entire length of its trunk. This characteristic, from which the expression is derived, is alluded to in the Bible:

> I have seen the wicked in great power, and spreading himself like a green bay tree. (Psalms 37:35)

go great guns To proceed with great momentum toward one's goal; to be well on the way to success; to act with gusto or go full steam ahead. Dating from the early 15th century, *great gun* referred to a large fire-arm like a cannon, as opposed to a *small gun* 'musket, rifle.' By the late 1800s, these uses of *great* and *small* became obsolete—however, the exclamation *great guns* gained currency, perhaps alluding to the loudness, forcefulness, and bigness of cannon and other large fire-arms.

> But great guns! is a man obliged to blurt out everything he honestly thinks? (*Pall Mall Magazine,* August, 1895)

To go great guns appeared later and has since been current.

> A moment later Louvois shot out, passed Sanquhar and Fairy King, and going great guns . . . beat the favorite by a head. (*Field,* May 3, 1913)

go to town To be successful, to thrive or prosper; to work very hard or energetically. This American slang expression is thought to have originated among the rural inhabitants of the backwoods who really whooped it up when they went out on the town for a spree.

land-office business A highly successful, very profitable, rapidly expanding business or enterprise; any period of high-volume sales. Although this expression has been in use for well over a hundred years, its popularity increased when the United States Government Land Office, after the passage of the Homestead Act of 1862, was swamped with work as hundreds of thousands of families and speculators sought free or low-cost land. Though the onslaught had eased by 1900, the Homesteading

Program was not terminated until 1974. The phrase, however, has continued in widespread figurative use.

> A practical printer . . . could do a land-office business here. (*New Orleans Picayune*, April 2, 1839)

sail before the wind To be successful or prosperous; to proceed smoothly and easily, without outside interference; to breeze through a task, project, or other matter. This expression alludes to a sailing vessel's moving forward smoothly and rapidly when it has a following wind to fill the sails.

PROTECTION

ride shotgun To guard goods or protect persons susceptible to attack. The expression originated with the custom of having armed guards riding beside stagecoach drivers in the days when they were frequently held up by bandits. It gained new currency with books and films on organized crime, since gangsters' bodyguards were often spoken of as "riding shotgun." The phrase is now used not only for one who provides armed security, but also for one who plays any sort of protective role, as witness these citations from *Webster's Third:*

> Armed security forces . . . have ridden shotgun on every Israeli civilian flight since the Athens raid. (*Newsweek*)
> . . . a front-seat passenger riding shotgun and calling out road conditions ahead. (P. J. C. Friedlander)

run interference To protect or defend a person, his reputation, a project, or any other matter which has come under attack; to prepare the way or lay the groundwork for a potentially controversial plan, project, etc. This expression is derived from "running interference" in football, i.e., running ahead of a ball-carrier and blocking prospective tacklers out of the way. Though still commonly used in football, *run interference* is applied figuratively

in contexts in which one diverts or otherwise deals with opposition, often with the implication that by so doing, he may be placing himself in jeopardy.

take under [one's] wing See GUIDANCE.

PROTEST (See also REBELLION.)

anvil chorus Clamorous, vociferous protest on the part of many; clangorous complaining; squawking. The anvil is an imitative percussive instrument consisting of steel bars and a striker, used largely in opera, and then on the stage rather than in the orchestra. The musical composition often referred to as "The Anvil Chorus" is from Verdi's *Il Trovatore.*

hue and cry Public, popular protest or outcry; noise, hullabaloo, clamor, uproar. The original, legal sense of this expression was a shout or cry calling for the pursuit of a felon, raised by the injured party or by an officer of the law. The phrase came from the Anglo-Norman *hu e cri. Hue,* now obsolete in this sense except in this expression, means 'outcry, shouting, clamor, especially that raised by a multitude in war or chase;' it is the noun form of the French verb *huer* 'to hoot, cry, or shout,' apparently of onomatopoeic origin. It has been suggested that *hue* originally referred to an inarticulate sound, such as that of a horn or trumpet as well as that of the voice, and was therefore distinct from *cry.* The legal sense of this expression dates from the late 13th century, while the general sense dates from the late 16th century.

> The public took up the hue and cry conscientiously enough. (John Ruskin, *Modern Painters,* 1846)

raise Cain See BOISTEROUSNESS.

a voice in the wilderness A lone dissenter, a solitary protestor; one whose warnings are unheeded, whose exhortations are ignored, or whose attempts to rally others around a cause are unfruitful; a minority of one, or similar small minority; frequently *a voice crying in the wilderness.* The phrase owes its origin to the words of the prophet Isaiah:

The voice of him that crieth in the wilderness, Prepare ye the way of the Lord, make straight in the desert a highway for our God. (40:3)

According to Matthew 3:3, Isaiah was referring to John the Baptist heralding the coming of Jesus Christ.

PROVOCATION

firebrand One who incites others to strife or revolution, an agitator; any energetic and impassioned person who inspires others to action. Literally, a firebrand is a burning stick that is used to set other materials on fire. The development of its figurative use is obvious.

Our fire-brand brother, Paris, burns us all.
(Shakespeare, *Troilus and Cressida,* II,ii)

get a rise out of To tease or goad someone in order to evoke a desired response; to provoke a person to react; to bait. This expression was originally angling parlance—*rise* describes the movement of a fish to the surface of the water to reach a fly or bait. By the 1800s, expressions such as *get* or *take a rise out of* referred to teasing or making a butt of someone. Today the expression has a wider application and can refer to evoking any desired response.

ginger group A faction which serves as the motivating or activating force within a larger body; Young Turks; a splinter group. "Ginger" is a pungent and aromatic substance used as a spice and sometimes used in medicines as a carminative or stimulant. Its qualities have spawned figurative use of the word meaning 'animation, high spirits, piquancy.' Thus, "ginger group" is an animating, stimulating subgroup. This British colloquial expression dates from the turn of the century.

The appearance of ginger groups to fight specific proposals, is not necessarily a bad thing—particularly if the established bodies aren't prepared to fight. (*New Society,* February 5, 1970)

look at cross-eyed To do the least little thing wrong, to commit the tiniest fault which provokes a response all out of proportion to its significance. This expression has no connection with internal strabismus but merely means to look at someone "the wrong way." Use of the phrase dates from the mid-20th century.

make waves To disrupt or upset the equilibrium of a situation, to cause trouble, to stir things up.

An unimaginative, traditional career man who does not make waves. (Henry Trewhitt, cited in *Webster's Third*)

Another expression, *to rock the boat,* is probably the source of this phrase, since moving a small boat from side to side creates waves in otherwise smooth water. Literally rocking a boat, especially a canoe or kayak, is a rather risky action since these boats readily capsize.

Unfortunate publicity had a tendency to rock the boat. (Frederick Lewis Allen, *Only Yesterday,* 1931)

policy of pin pricks A strategy in which a series of petty hostile acts is meant to provoke the opposition; a course of trivial annoyances undertaken as a part of national policy. This expression, equivalent to the French *un coup d'épingle,* was first applied during the Fashoda incident, a period of strained Anglo-French relations in 1898:

Such a policy of "pinpricks" is beginning to be recognized by sensible Frenchmen as a grievous error. (*Times,* November, 1898)

While the phrase's usage has declined since the Fashoda incident, it retains occasional use in describing irritating, but usually harmless, government policies.

Russian provocation is at present but a policy of pin-pricks. (*Daily Telegraph*, March, 1901)

put a cat among the pigeons To start trouble by introducing a highly controversial topic of discussion; to arouse passions by bringing an inflammatory subject into a conversation. This British colloquial expression is equivalent to the American phrase *to put a match in a tinderbox*.

ringleader One who leads an insurrection; the head of a street gang or underworld syndicate; any instigator or fomenter of trouble. At the elegant soirées of the 16th century, the person who led off the dancing was called the ringleader. He was so named because the participants, prior to the start of the dance, arranged themselves in a circle. In contemporary usage, the term always carries negative connotations, so it is difficult to determine if the current sense did indeed derive from the earlier.

The conspiracy is so nicely balanced among them that I shall never be able to detect the ring-leader. (James Beresford, *Miseries of Human Life*, 1806–07)

sow dragon's teeth To incite a riot or other conflict; to foment revolution; to kindle the flames of war; to plant the seeds of strife. This expression is based on the ancient Greek myth of Cadmus, a legendary hero who, after slaying a dragon that had devoured his servants, was advised by Athena to plant the monster's teeth in the ground, apparently to placate Mars, the deity who owned the dragon. The teeth produced fully armed soldiers who fought among themselves until all but five had been killed. Thus, while Cadmus thought his actions would have a pacifying effect, they did, in fact, cause more strife—a concept often implicit in the figurative use of *sow dragon's teeth*.

Jesuits . . . sowed dragon's teeth which sprung up into the hydras of rebellion and apostasy. (John Marsden, *The History of the Early Pilgrims*, 1853)

stir up a hornets' nest To activate latent hostility, to ask for trouble; to provoke a great stir and commotion of an antagonistic or controversial nature. The hornet has been symbolic of a virulent attacker for centuries; the phrase *hornets' nest* appeared in Samuel Richardson's *Pamela* (1739); the now more common *stir up a hornets' nest* is widely used in both the United States and Britain:

Judges have stirred up a hornets' nest in the sacred territory of "the right to strike." (*The Listener*, August, 1966)

wave the bloody shirt To incite to vengeance or retaliatory action; to foment or exacerbate hostilities. Two plausible theories are offered as to the origin of this phrase. One traces it to the Scottish battle of Glenfruin recounted by Sir Walter Scott in *Rob Roy*, after which the widows of the slain rode before James VI bearing their husbands' bloody shirts on spears. The other traces it to the Corsican custom of mourning victims of feudal murder. The dead man's bloody shirt, hung above his head as wailing female mourners surrounded his body and armed men guarded them all, was suddenly snatched and brandished about by one of the women, amidst increasingly loud lamentation. The men echoed her cries and vowed vengeance. *Wave the bloody shirt* was much used in the United States during the period of Reconstruction after the Civil War in reference to those who exploited and perpetuated sectional hostilities.

PROXIMITY

cheek by jowl Side by side, in close proximity. *Cheek by jowl*, in use since 1577, is a variation of the older *cheek by* *cheek,* which dates from 1330. In modern English *jowl* means either 'jaw' or 'cheek,' although it is more often construed as the former. Shakespeare used the expression in *A Midsummer Night's Dream:*

Nay, I'll go with thee, cheek by jowl. (III,ii)

in spitting distance Close, at arm's length. This expression denoting a short distance is based on the simple crude idea that one can spit only so far.

a stone's throw A short distance; close by.

Three mighty churches, all within a stone's throw of one another. (Augustus Jessopp, *Coming of the Friars,* 1889)

This common expression obviously alludes to the limited distance that one can throw a small rock.

within an ace Within a hair's-breadth; very close; on the brink or verge; almost. This popular phrase, which dates from 1704, stems from the figurative use of ace to mean 'a minute portion, a jot.' Hence:

I was within an ace of being talked to death. (Thomas Brown, *Letters,* 1704)

PRUDENCE (See **CAUTIOUSNESS.**)

PRUDISHNESS

bluenose An ultraconservative in matters of morality; a puritan, prude, or prig.

That this picture may aggravate blue nose censors is not beyond the bounds of possibility. (*Variety,* April 3, 1929)

As early as 1809 Washington Irving used the adjective form *blue-nosed.* The form in the above citation and the noun *bluenose* appeared later. The color blue has long been associated with conservatism and strictness, though for what reason is not clear. In the mid-19th century, conservative students at Yale and Dartmouth were called *blues.*

I wouldn't carry a novel into chapel to read, . . . because some of the blues might see you. (*Yale Literary Magazine,* 1850)

The usage may derive from Connecticut's "blue laws"—stringent restrictions on moral conduct with harsh penalties for their infraction—which obtained in the 17th and 18th centuries. They were presumably so called because originally printed on blue paper.

Goody Two Shoes A goody-goody, a nice nelly; an appellation for a person of self-righteous, sentimental, or affected goodness; also *Miss Goody Two Shoes.* The original Little Goody Two Shoes was the principal character in a British nursery rhyme thought to have been written by Oliver Goldsmith and published by Newbery in 1765. According to the story, Little Goody Two Shoes owned only one shoe and was so delighted at receiving a second that she went around showing both to everyone, exclaiming "Two shoes!" Although it is not clear why the nursery rhyme character Little Goody Two Shoes came to symbolize self-righteous, excessive, and affected goodness, the term appeared in the writing of the 19th-century author Anthony Trollope in just such a context:

Pray don't go on in that Goody Two-shoes sort of way.

Mrs. Grundy The personification of conventional opinion in issues of established social propriety; a prudish, straight-laced person who becomes outraged at the slightest breach of decorum or etiquette. In Thomas Morton's *Speed the Plough* (1798), Mrs. Grundy was the unseen character whose opinions in matters of social propriety were of constant concern to her neighbors:

If shame should come to the poor child—I say Jummas, what would Mrs. Grundy say then.

The expression is still used figuratively as the embodiment of public opinion.

> And many are afraid of God—and more of Mrs. Grundy. (Frederick Locker, *London Lyrics,* 1857)

PRURIENCE

pin-up A photograph or poster of a provocatively posed, scantily attired woman, usually one of the latest sex symbols among female movie stars. The term was most popular during World War II when soldiers commonly pinned such photographs up on the barrack walls. An equivalent American slang term is *cheesecake,* which combines the conventional association of food and sex with the photographer's cliché "say cheese," used to make subjects smile. The male counterpart of *cheesecake* is *beefcake,* an American slang term for sexually provocative photographs of partially-clad men. *Centerfold,* the current term for such photographs, comes from the two-page spreads featuring nude or semi-nude models, popular in magazines such as *Playboy* and *Playgirl.*

skin flick A movie that emphasizes nudity; a pornographic film. This expression, obviously derived from the blatant and frequent nakedness of cast members, describes erotic motion pictures which luridly depict sexual activity.

PUNISHMENT

the devil to pay Consequences to be suffered; a dear price to be paid; trouble, confusion, or a "fate worse than death" to be endured. The first and most convincing of the three possible origins of this expression is that it alludes to the alleged bargains made between the devil and an individual such as Faust, the chief character in a medieval legend who traded his soul for knowledge and power. Another popular explanation is that many London barristers mixed work and pleasure in an inn called the Devil Tavern in Fleet Street. Their excuse for working was that they had to pay the "Devil" for their drinks. Still other sources cite the significance of the nautical use of *devil to pay* and the longer *devil to pay and no pitch hot.* The "devil" is a seam in a ship near the keel and "to pay" is to cover the seam with pitch. The difficulty of "paying the devil" is said to have given rise to the figurative uses of *the devil to pay.* This expression has been in print since the early 18th century. See also **between the devil and the deep blue sea,** PREDICAMENT.

get it in the neck To be reprimanded or disciplined; to be severely chastised; to bear the brunt. This expression has its origins in the punishment of decapitation, in which the guillotine's blade cleaved off one's head at the neck. Figuratively, the phrase usually refers to an undeserving victim of castigation or loss:

> It's the poor old vicar who gets it most in the neck. . . . He runs the risk of losing the best-kept-village competition because . . . the churchyard is looking its shaggiest. (*Guardian,* June, 1973)

The expression is not limited in application to that which has a neck, even a figurative one:

> You probably don't know what a village looks like when it has caught it in the neck. (D. O. Barnett, *Letters,* 1914)

get one's lumps See ADVERSITY.

go to heaven in a wheelbarrow To be damned to eternal suffering; to go to hell. This obsolete expression has been traced to a window in Gloucestershire, England, depicting Satan wheeling away a termagant woman in a wheelbarrow.

> This oppressor must needs go to heaven, . . . But it will be, as the by-word is, in a Wheel-barrow; the fiends, and not the Angels will take hold on him. (Thomas Adams, *God's Bounty,* 1618)

See also **go to hell in a handbasket, DE-GENERATION.**

heads will roll Those responsible will be held accountable; there's trouble in the offing. This American slang expression is of fairly recent vintage, though it alludes to former times when beheading was common and heads literally did roll as a result of an enraged monarch's fit of anger at his subjects' incompetence, betrayal, or rebelliousness.

kiss the rod See **SUBMISSIVENESS.**

lower the boom To punish; to severely chastise or discipline; to prohibit. This expression originally described a nautical maneuver by which one of the ship's booms was directed so as to knock an offending seaman overboard. The expression later developed into a prize fighting term for delivering a haymaker. In contemporary usage, the phrase is often applied to an activity which is abruptly terminated through anger or castigation.

> Just as they were about to pawn my studs . . . my patience evaporated and I lowered the boom on them. (*The New Yorker*, June, 1951)

pin [someone's] ears back See **REPRIMAND.**

ride on a rail To punish severely, to chastise mercilessly; to subject to public abuse and scorn; to banish, ostracize, or exile; in the latter sense usually *to ride out of town on a rail*. It was formerly the practice to punish a wrongdoer by seating him astride a rail, or horizontal beam, and then carrying him about town as an object of derision. Often he was then taken to the village limits and warned not to set foot in the town again under pain of yet more severe punishment.

> The millmen . . . [hesitated whether to] ride him on a rail, or refresh him with an ablution at the town-pump. (Nathaniel Hawthorne, *Twice Told Tales*, 1837)

run the gauntlet See **ADVERSITY.**

send up the river To send to prison. This American expression originally referred to the incarceration of an offender at Sing Sing—a notorious correctional facility located up the Hudson River from New York City. The phrase has now been extended to include any imprisonment.

> I done it. Send me up the river. Give me the hot seat. (*Chicago Daily News*, March, 1946)

stand the gaff See **ENDURANCE.**

send to Coventry To ostracize or exclude from society because of objectionable behavior; to refuse to associate with, to ignore. Several explanations have been proposed as to the origin of this expression. The most plausible was put forth by Edward Hyde Clarendon in *A History of the Rebellion and Civil Wars in England* (1647). It stated that citizens of a town called Bromigham were in the habit of attacking small groups of the King's men and either killing them or taking them prisoner and sending them to Coventry, then a Parliamentary stronghold. A less plausible explanation maintains that the inhabitants of Coventry so hated soldiers that any social intercourse with them was strictly forbidden. Thus, a soldier sent to Coventry was as good as cut off from all social relations for the duration of his stay.

take the bark off To flog or chastise, to give one a hiding. This 19th-century Americanism, implying a flogging or whipping so severe as to flay one's skin, likens the skin on a person to the bark on a tree.

> The old man's going to take the bark off both of us. (Johnson J. Hooper, *The Adventures of Captain Simon Suggs*, 1845)

take the rap To accept or be given the responsibility and punishment for a crime, especially one committed by another; to take the blame. Although this expression apparently employs *rap* in its sense of 'blame or punishment,' one source suggests that the phrase may in fact be a corruption of the theatrical *take the nap* 'to be dealt a feigned blow.'

> I don't think though, I shall be able to take the nap much longer. (*Era Almanach*, 1877)

> He carried the banner and took the rap for Roosevelt in the Senate for years. (*Saturday Evening Post*, July 2, 1949)

Related expressions are *bum rap* 'a frame-up; a conviction for a crime of which one is innocent,' and *beat the rap* 'to be acquitted or absolved of blame,' usually with the implication that one is indeed guilty.

> [Senator] Kefauver [and his Congressional committee] realize that as dope peddling and boot-legging are made more difficult, the crooks will start looking for new ways to beat the rap. (P. Edson, AP wire story, September, 1951)

Rap itself is often used as a synonym for an arrest, a trial, or a jail sentence.

> Gangs with influence can beat about 90% of their "raps" or arrests. (Emanuel Lavine, *The Third Degree: A Detailed Exposé of Police Brutality*, 1930)

tar and feather To punish harshly or castigate severely. This expression is derived from the brutal punishment in which the victim was doused with hot tar and subsequently covered with feathers. In 1189, this form of chastisement received royal sanction in England. While it was never ordained as a legal penalty in the United States, it nevertheless became a form of punishment by the masses for a crime or misdoing which fell outside the realm of the law. It retains frequent hyperbolic use.

throw the book at To give a convicted criminal the maximum penalty or sentence; to prosecute on the most serious of several charges stemming from a single incident, especially when it would be possible to try a person on a lesser charge; to accuse of several crimes. This expression conjures images of a judge's referring to a law book to compile a list of all possible wrongdoings of which a prisoner may be accused, or a list of the most severe penalties that may be assessed for the crime(s) of which a person has been convicted.

> He was formally charged with "breaking ranks while in formation, felonious assault, indiscriminate behaviour, mopery, high treason, provoking, being a smart guy, listening to classical music, and so on." In short, they threw the book at him. (Joseph Heller, *Catch-22*, 1962)

Q

QUALITY   (See EXCELLENCE.)

QUEST

go gathering orange blossoms   To search for a wife. This expression is derived from the snow-white orange blossom, a popular wedding decoration that symbolizes the innocence of a young bride. The development of this phrase's figurative sense is obvious. Its use by William E. Norris was cited by James M. Dixon in the latter's *Dictionary of Idiomatic English Phrases* (1891):

> "What has he come to this lovely retreat for? To gather orange blossoms?"

go in search of the golden fleece   To pursue one's destiny; to seek one's fortune; to embark on an adventurous quest. This expression's origin lies in the Greek myth of Jason and the Golden Fleece, in which Jason and a band of cohorts, called the Argonauts after their ship, set forth on a virtually hopeless quest to recover the golden fleece. Jason and his companions were victorious only after numerous perils. Figuratively, this expression is applied to a person who searches against great odds for great fortune.

pound the pavement   To walk the streets seeking employment, to be out looking for a job, to go from door to door in search of work; also *to pound* or *hit the sidewalks.* The allusion is to feet walking back and forth "beating" the paved street. This American slang expression appeared in one of its variant forms in O. Henry's *Options* (1909):

> I'm pounding the asphalt for another job.

set one's cap for   To try to gain the affections of someone to whom one is attracted; to set one's romantic sights on; to flirt with; to make a play for. In the days when ladies always wore hats in public, a woman would don her most alluring bonnet in hopes of attracting that certain man of her dreams.

> Instead of breaking my heart at his indifference, I'll . . . set my cap to some newer fashion, and look out for some less difficult admirer. (Oliver Goldsmith, *She Stoops to Conquer,* 1773)

wild-goose chase   See FUTILITY.

QUICKNESS   (See INSTANTANEOUSNESS, PACE, SPEEDING.)

R

RACISM

Jim Crow Racial discrimination; laws which forbid interracial contact, as in public places and schools; also, *Jim Crowism*. This term originated in the popular plantation song by Thomas D. "Daddy" Rice (1828):

Wheel about and turn about
And do jis so,
Ebry time I wheel about
I jump Jim Crow.

After the Civil War Reconstruction, the phrase was applied to the many laws which limited the rights of Blacks, and more loosely, to racial bigotry itself.

One hundred years of frustration and battle have not resulted in victory over Jim Crow and racism. (*Freedomways*, XIII, 1973)

The expression has also become a disparaging epithet for any Negro.

RANK (See STATUS, SUBORDINATION.)

RAPIDITY (See INSTANTANEOUSNESS, PACE, SPEEDING.)

READINESS (See also PREPARATION.)

all systems go All set, everything's ready, let 'er roll. This expression denoting readiness for an undertaking gained frequency following the televised space flights of the 1960s and 70s, but its popularity soon waned. As originally used, it indicated that all of a spacecraft's systems were functioning properly so the countdown could begin and the launching occur.

A-OK This recent (1960s) American version of *A1* gained currency from television coverage of the space flights. Astronauts used the term to denote the condition of a spacecraft's systems, or their own situation. In common usage its connotations are less of superiority and excellence than of preparedness or satisfactoriness.

Barkis is willin' Availability, willingness, readiness; eagerness, desirousness. Charles Dickens gave us the phrase in *David Copperfield*. Barkis is enamored of the maid to David's mother. On learning from the youth that she is not spoken for, he sends her the message, via David, that "Barkis is willin'."

loaded for bear To be prepared for any possibility; to be armed and ready to fight; to have girded up one's loins. This phrase originated during the westward movement, when a man was not considered ready for hunting unless he had enough ammunition to kill a bear. The expression, as used by E. G. Love, is cited in *Webster's Third:*

Learning that every outfit . . . was of full strength, sober, and loaded for bear.

The expression has recently acquired the additional meaning of being drunk, undoubtedly as a lengthening of the common term *loaded* 'to be intoxicated.'

the noose is hanging Everything is set; everyone is ready and waiting. This expression alludes to the restive anticipation of a crowd awaiting a public hanging. The phrase has never gained widespread popularity.

The noose is ready—All the musicians are primed for a real cutting session. (E. Horne, *For Cool Cats and Far-Out Chicks*, 1957)

raring to go Enthusiastically eager to begin; primed, psyched, ready. This American slang expression, of uncertain origin, has been in print since the early 1900s. *Raring* may be related to *roaring* or *rearing* (as of horses), but either connection is pure hypothesis.

Both sides are rarin' to go, and
they are not liable to touch their
peremptory challenges. (F. N. Hart,
The Bellamy Trial, 1923)

REBELLION

fly in the face of To recklessly defy or
challenge; to act in bold opposition to. A
bird or insect that flies in the face of a
predator is acting against its instincts
and thus courting trouble. The phrase is
often used figuratively to describe political or social opposition:

He had to fly in the face of adverse
decisions. (*Nations,* December,
1891)

Extensions of the expression include *to
fly in the face of danger* and *to fly in the
face of providence,* both of which carry
a sense of reckless or impetuous disregard for safety.

kick against the pricks To protest in
vain, to ineffectually resist a superior
force or authority, especially to one's
own detriment. This expression appears several times in the Bible. In Acts
9:5 Jesus answers Saul's question "Who
art thou, Lord?" by answering:

I am Jesus whom thou persecutest:
it is hard for thee to kick against
the pricks.

Prick in this case literally refers to a
sharp, pointed goad for oxen and figuratively to the voice of authority. To literally kick against the pricks then is a
painful and thoroughly futile act.

For the past ten years he has
known what it is to "kick against
the pricks" of legitimate Church
authority. (Marie Corelli, *God's
Good Man,* 1904)

kick over the traces To rebel, to resist
or rise up against the accepted order, to
throw off or defy conventional restraints. A harnessed horse literally
kicks over the traces when it gets a leg
outside the straps (traces) connecting its
harness to a carriage or wagon.

The effervescence of genius which
drives men to kick over the traces

of respectability. (Sir Leslie
Stephen, *Hours in a Library,* 1876)

left-wing Espousing radical or progressive political, social, or economic ideologies; favoring extensive political, social,
or economic reform; socialistic; Communistic. This expression arose as the
result of the French National Assembly
of 1789 in which conservatives were
seated in the right side, or wing, of the
hall, moderates in the middle, and radical democrats and extremists in the left
wing. This seating arrangement persists
in several contemporary legislatures including the British Commonwealth Assemblies where politicians with radical
or socialistic views usually sit to the left
of the presiding officer. After World
War II, and especially during the
McCarthy era, *left-wing* usually implied that one was a Communist or a
Communist sympathizer.

The left-wing challenge over
Europe is expected to unseat at
least one member of the Labour
Party National Executive Committee. (*Times,* September 5, 1972)

People or groups of people with left-
wing philosophies are frequently called
left wing, left-wingers, or *the Left.* The
radical political activists in the United
States in the late 1960s and early 1970s
were often called *the New Left* in an
attempt to dissociate them and their activities from intimations of Communist
influence or complicity.

sow dragon's teeth See **PROVOCATION.**

take the bit between one's teeth To
cast off external controls and take
charge of one's own life; to rebel against
unfair restraints or impositions. The *bit*
in this expression refers to the mouthpiece of a bridle, attached to the reins
used to control a horse. When a horse
takes the bit between his teeth, the pain
in his mouth is relieved and he becomes
more manageable. This expression, dating from the early 17th century, often
implies willful defiance. A variant is
take the bit in one's teeth.

young Turk An insurgent; one who advocates reform in a staid, conservative organization; a rebel; a political radical or liberal. In 1891, a group of reformists established the Young Turks, a political party dedicated to realigning the priorities of the Turkish Empire and instituting European ideologies and customs in governmental procedures. After inciting a revolt in 1908 in which the Sultan was deposed, the Young Turks remained a viable political force until the end of World War I. By extension, *young Turk* has assumed figurative implications as evidenced in this quote from John Gunther (1901–70), cited in *Webster's Third:*

> The young Turks . . . [are] opposed to the ossified conservatism of the older, so-called statesmen.

RECANTATION (See also **REVERSAL**.)

do a 180° turn To do an about-face, to suddenly and completely reverse one's previous position, approach, or point of view. A circle is 360°; to turn 180° is literally to turn halfway around and face the opposite direction. It is easy to see how this literal turnabout gave rise to the figurative sense of the expression as it is popularly used today.

draw in one's horns See **SUBMISSION**.

eat one's words To retract one's assertions; to be compelled to take back what one has said; to be forced to back down or eat humble pie, to be humiliated and proven wrong. This expression dates from the 16th century, and will probably be popular for as long as putting one's foot in one's mouth is a common practice.

> Unguarded words, which, as soon as you have uttered them, you would die to eat. (James Beresford, *The Miseries of Human Life,* 1806–07)

Indian giver One who recalls a gift, either simply from second thoughts or because of subsequent dissatisfaction with a gift received in return. Early American settlers attributed this practice to the natives. The term is now used primarily among children as a name-calling taunt when one decides to renege on a trade or bargain.

sing a different tune To do or say something different; to change one's position; to assume a new attitude or express a revised opinion, especially one that is more appropriate and suited to the circumstances at hand; also *sing another song.* The change in attitude or behavior can be motivated by expediency or, at the other extreme, humbleness. In 1390, John Gower used the phrase in *Confessio Amantis.*

> O thou, which has disseized the Court of France by thy wrong, now shalt thou sing an other song.

The phrase is current today, as is the analogous *change one's tune.*

turncoat See **BETRAYAL**.

RECIPROCITY (See also **COOPERATION**.)

ka me, ka thee Do a good deed for another and the favor will be returned. This expression appeared in print as early as the mid-16th century. The exact origin is unknown and many variants were used interchangeably with *ka,* such as *kaw, kae, k, kay,* and *kob. Scratch my back, I'll scratch yours* is a current analogous expression which like the proverbial *Do unto others as you would have them do unto you* implies reciprocity of service, flattery, or favors.

> Ka me, ka thee, one good turn asketh another. (John Heywood, *Works,* 1562)

logrolling The trading of votes or favors, especially among legislators, for mutual political gain; the policy of "you scratch my back and I'll scratch yours." In pioneer days a logrolling was a gathering at which neighbors helped each other roll and pile their logs to a particular spot for burning or other means of disposal. It was similar in nature to barn raisings and husking bees. Literal log-rolling also played an important part in lumber camps where members of different camps often joined forces in rolling their logs to the water's edge to catch the flood downstream. This U.S. term apparently came from the proverbial expression "you roll my log and I'll roll yours." Political use of the term dates from the early 19th century.

> Territorial supreme courts have long since become known as a kind of log-rolling machine, in which the judges enter in the business of "you tickle me and I will tickle you." (*Weekly New Mexican Review*, July, 1885)

one hand washes the other A proverbial expression originally denoting mutual cooperation in its positive sense only, but now carrying the negative connotations of backscratching, cronyism, and logrolling. It appeared as early as the 1500s in the former sense, but within a few centuries began to take on the latter dubious coloration.

> Persons in business . . . who make, as the saying is, "one hand wash the other." (*Diary of Philip Hone*, 1836)

RECOLLECTION

hark back See REPETITION.

on the tip of one's tongue On the verge of being remembered and spoken; known but unable to be retrieved from the recesses of memory. This expression plays on the idea that words awaiting utterance are poised on the tip of one's tongue.

ring a bell To serve as a reminder, to bring to mind; to have meaning or significance. Although the exact origin of this expression is not known, it may stem from the former practice of ringing church bells to signal the hour or to inform the populace of significant events, such as births, deaths, or weddings.

> The things we talked about meant nothing to them: they rang no bell. (Nicholas Monsarrat, *This Is Schoolroom*, 1939)

RECOVERY

cheat the worms To recover from a serious illness. The expression *food for worms* is used to describe a dead, decaying body. Thus, when someone recovers from a potentially fatal illness, these worms have been cheated.

eat snakes To recover one's youth and vigor, to be rejuvenated. This obsolete expression dates from at least 1603. It is perhaps an allusion to the snake's seasonal shedding of its old skin. The phrase appeared in John Fletcher's *The Elder Brother* (1625):

> That you have eat a snake, and are grown young, gamesome, and rampant.

get out from under To recoup one's financial losses, to settle one's debts; to remove oneself from a negative situation; to get back on one's feet. This common expression implies the removal of an oppressive financial or personal burden, allowing one to lead a freer, more comfortable life.

Indian summer See WEATHER.

out of the woods Having passed through the most difficult or dangerous aspect of any ordeal or endeavor; on the road to recovery; with success assured; safe, secure.

> When a patient reaches this stage [of convalescence], he is out of the woods. (Wister, *The Virginian*, 1902)

This expression, dating from the late 18th century, may be a shortened version of the older proverb *don't shout until you're out of the woods*, although the literal wood or forest has symbolized danger, confusion, and evil for centuries.

second wind A renewed source of energy, inspiration, drive, will power, etc.;

a second life, a second chance. *Wind* in this phrase means 'breath' both literally (air inhaled and exhaled) and figuratively (the life force or vitality). *Second wind* remains current on both literal and figurative levels: the former refers to an actual physiological phenomenon in which an athlete, after reaching a point of near exhaustion, regains even breathing and has a second burst of energy; the latter denotes renewed "life" where *life* has an unlimited range of possible meanings. The following appeared as an advertisement for the second edition of Thomas Hood's *Epping Hunt* (1830):

> I am much gratified to learn from you, that the *Epping Hunt* has had *such a run*, that it is *quite exhausted*, and that you intend therefore to give the work what may be called "second wind," by a new impression.

a shot in the arm A stimulant, incentive, or inducement; anything that causes renewed vitality, confidence, or determination; anything that helps a person toward success; an infusion of money or other form of assistance that gives new life to a foundering project or other matter. This expression alludes to the revitalizing effect of taking a *shot* 'a small amount of liquor' or 'a hypodermic injection of some drug.' In its contemporary usage, however. the expression is usually figurative.

> The United States Olympic Shooting Team received an $80,000 shot in the arm Thursday afternoon. (Tom Yantz in *The Hartford Courant*, March 9, 1979)

REFORMATION

clean house To purge an organization of corruption and inefficiency; frequently used of government agencies. This expression and its noun form *housecleaning* have been used figuratively since the early part of this century.

cleanse the Augean stables To wipe out a massive accumulation of corruption, to clean house; to perform any seemingly impossible, arduous, and extremely unpleasant task. According to classical mythology, Augeas, king of Elis, kept three thousand oxen in stables which had not been cleaned for thirty years. As one of the twelve labors for which he was to be granted immortality, Hercules was assigned the task of cleaning them in a single day. This he accomplished by diverting the river Alpheus through the stables. A variant of this expression appeared as early as 1599.

clean up one's act To make one's actions or outward behavior more presentable or acceptable to others; to shape up. Although the exact origin of this recent American slang expression is unknown, it may derive from the theater; an entertainer is sometimes told to delete offensive or obscene material from his performance. Similar recent American slang expressions are *to get one's act together* and the abbreviated *get it together*.

have scales fall from one's eyes See DISILLUSIONMENT.

turn over a new leaf To change one's ways for the better, to become a new and better person; to start fresh, to wipe the slate clean and begin anew.

> I will turn over a new leaf, and write to you. (Thomas Hughes, *Tom Brown at Oxford*, 1861)

Literally, this phrase means to turn to a clean, fresh page in a book. Since an open book is often figuratively used to represent a person's life, turning to a blank page in this book of life symbolizes the start of a new and better chapter in one's personal history. Use of this expression dates from the 16th century.

REFUGE (See SANCTUARY.)

REFUSAL (See also **REJECTION**.)

no dice No, no way, nothing doing, absolutely not; a negative response or result. Although many tales surround the derivation of this expression, it is likely that since *dice* often implies luck, *no dice* simply implies no luck.

> I was around at her bank this morning trying to find out what her balance was, but no dice. Fanny won't part. (P. G. Wodehouse, *Barmy in Wonderland*, 1952)

no soap No; usually said in refusal or rejection. The origin of this expression is unknown, but it may have been originally used to refuse a bribe, since a slang meaning of *soap* is 'bribe money.'

> If you don't know, just say, "No soap." (Marks, *Plastic Age*, 1924)

thumbs down Disapproval, disapprobation, rejection. This expression refers to making a fist and extending the thumb downward, a gesture which, in the days of gladiatorial combats in ancient Rome, indicated that the spectators thought a defeated gladiator had fought poorly and, as a result, should be slain by the victor. The expression is commonly used figuratively as evidenced in a quote from bacteriologist Paul de Kruif (1890–1971), cited in *Webster's Third:*

> The government thumbs-down on penicillin for [treating] endocarditis was published.

See also **thumbs up, APPROVAL.**

REJECTION (See also **EXPULSION**.)

blackball To exclude; to cast a negative vote against a candidate or applicant seeking admission to a select group. Such adverse votes were formerly cast by placing a black ball in the ballot box. Thus, the term came to mean to reject or exclude in any sense, though its most frequent application is still in reference to membership rejection by fraternities or other socially prestigious, exclusive organizations. It has been in use since 1770.

blacklist To bar or exclude from something as work or a club; also, the list of people so excluded; hence, those under suspicion, censure, or otherwise out of favor with the powers that be. The expression, in use since 1692, is said to date from the reign of Charles II of England, with reference to the list of individuals implicated in the trial and execution of his father, Charles I.

cut off with a shilling To disinherit, especially by bequeathing a shilling or other nominal sum to show that the disinheritance was deliberate. This expression is said to have arisen from the erroneous belief that English law was the same as Roman in assuming forgetfulness or unsoundness of mind on the part of the testator who neglected to name close relatives in his will. Out of this grew the practice of giving the scorned heir a shilling or other trifling sum to show that he had not been omitted as an oversight. Although this precise expression dates from 1834, the concept and practice date from much earlier:

> My eldest son John . . . I do disinherit and wholly cut off from any part of this my personal estate, by giving him a single cockle shell. (Joseph Addison, *The Tatler*, 1710)

The original sense of this phrase has been distorted in time and it is popularly misconstrued today as *to cut off without a shilling.*

Dear John letter A letter from a woman telling her boyfriend, fiancé, or husband that she is jilting him for someone else. Usually a Dear John letter is sent to a man who has been separated from the woman by both time and distance, as a soldier overseas.

> "Dear John," the letter began. "I have found someone else whom I think the world of. I think the only way out is for us to get a divorce,"

it said. They usually began like that, those letters that told of infidelity on the part of the wives of servicemen . . . the men called them "Dear Johns." (*Democrat and Chronicle* [Rochester, N.Y.], August 17, 1945)

get the hook To have one's performance abruptly terminated; to be fired; to receive or be subjected to dismissal. This expression recalls the days of vaudeville when more than a few marginally talented or outrageously untalented performers were forcefully removed from the stage by means of a long stick with a hooked end, somewhat like an elongated cane. In contemporary usage, however, *get the hook* and a variation, *give the hook,* are usually figurative.

give a basket To refuse to wed; to discard a fiancé. This expression, derived from the old German custom of placing a basket on the roof of a jilted sweetheart's house, is seldom heard today.

give the air To suddenly jilt a lover or sweetheart; to abruptly fire an employee; also, *give the wind.* Figuratively, this expression might imply either that a person is given nothing, or that he is propelled from another's presence by a blast of air.

> I couldn't change her views . . . nor could she convert me to hers, even when she threatened to give me the air. (R. Graves, *Seven Days in New Crete,* 1949)

give the bag To leave a paramour suddenly or unexpectedly; to discharge a person from his job or duties. This phrase carried a nearly reverse meaning, i.e., to 'quit a job without giving the employer proper notice,' before developing its current figurative usage as a reference to the plight of a jilted lover.

> Sent away, with a flea in your ear; some girl has given you the bag. (John Neal, *Brother Jonathan,* 1825)

give the cold shoulder To display indifference or disregard toward; to ignore or snub; also *to show the cold shoulder.* Although the exact origin of this expression is unknown, it has been suggested that *cold shoulder* refers to the cold shoulder of meat reputedly once served to unwelcome guests so as to discourage their return. The phrase has been in use since 1816.

give the gate To reject or dismiss; to give someone the brush-off; to fire, or let go from employment. This expression, as well as *get the gate* 'to be rejected or jilted,' is said to be an Americanism dating from the early 1900s. However, *grant the gate* 'to give leave to go' (*OED*) appeared in print as long ago as the middle of the 15th century.

> The King grantit the gait to Schir Gawane,
> And prayt to the grete God to grant him his grace.
> (*Golagros and Gawane,* 1470)

In the transition from *grant the gate* to *give the gate,* a significant change took place. Today one "gives the gate" in a spirit of disaffection and alienation, whereas based on the above quotation, good will and magnanimity inspired the King to "grant the gate" to Gawane.

> She billed you for an extra month because Monnie gave her the gate. (E. Fenwick, *Impeccable People,* 1971)

give the mitten To jilt a sweetheart; to reject a romantically inclined admirer; to discharge an employee. There are several possible sources of this expression: the medieval French custom of giving a mitten to an unsuccessful suitor; the custom of throwing down a glove to signify defiance or rejection; or a derivation from the Latin *mittere* 'to dismiss.'

> Some said that Susan had given her young man the mitten . . . she had signified that his services as a suitor were dispensed with. (Oliver

Wendell Holmes, *The Guardian Angel*, 1867)

gong [someone] To terminate a person's performance before its completion; to fire; to dismiss rudely. This expression stems from the custom in many local and national talent contests of ringing a bell or striking an Oriental-type gong to signify that, in the opinion of the judges, an act is so bad that it does not merit continuation. This concept has been popularized, if not vulgarized, by "The Gong Show," a television series of the late 1970s.

turn up one's nose at To regard with disdain, to show contempt for; to reject or refuse scornfully; snub.

> What learning there was in those days . . . turned up its nose at the strains of the native minstrels. (Bayard Taylor, *Studies in German Literature*, 1879)

Dating from the early 19th century, this expression is perhaps an allusion to the way one wrinkles up one's nose at a particularly distasteful odor, or to the way animals, especially dogs and cats, sniff at their food before eating and walk away if the smell fails to suit them. A similar phrase is *to have one's nose in the air* 'to be arrogant or condescending.' The gestural equivalent of the expression consists of putting the forefinger under the tip of the nose and pushing it up slightly.

whistle [someone] down the wind To forsake, abandon, or discard. This expression appeared in Shakespeare's *Othello*:

> If I do prove her haggard,
> Though that her jesses were my dear heartstrings,
> I'd whistle her off and let her down the wind,
> To prey at fortune. (III,iii)

In bygone days, a hawk was released against the wind when pursuing game. If the bird was being set free, however, it was released with the wind. In figurative usage, the expression often implies the jilting of a paramour.

> Having accepted my love, you cannot whistle me down the wind as though I were of no account. (Anthony Trollope, *Castle Richmond*, 1860)

RELAXATION (See RESPITE.)

REMEDY (See SOLUTION.)

REPETITION

hark back To revert, to go back, to retrace one's steps, to return to an earlier subject; to recall, to revive. This expression was originally used in hunting in reference to hounds who returned along the trail in order to pick up a lost scent. It has been used in its extended, figurative sense since the early 19th century.

> He has to hark back again to find the scent of his argument. (Robert Louis Stevenson, *Familiar Studies of Men and Books*, 1882)

harp on To dwell on tediously, to repeat endlessly and monotonously, to belabor, to beat into the ground; also *to harp on one* or *the same string*. Ancient harpists reputedly played on only one string in order to demonstrate more fully their skill on the instrument. The phrase appears in Richard Grafton's *A Chronicle at Large and Mere History of the Affairs of England* (1568), where it is attributed to Sir Thomas More:

> The Cardinal made a countenance to the Lord Haward that he should harp no more upon that string.

The expression and its variants date from the 16th century.

return to one's muttons To get back to the subject at hand, to return to the point at issue; to stick to the point, to get back on track. Little known in the U.S., this British expression derives from the French *Revenons à nos moutons* 'Let's get back to our sheep.' The line originated as an often repeated admonition in an early French play by Blanchet, *L'Avocat Pathelin*, in which the plaintiff continually tried to discredit the defense's lawyer by claiming he had stolen from him. The judge's attempts to concentrate on the charge against the defendant, that he had stolen sheep, were marked by addressing the line *Revenons à nos moutons* to the plaintiff. The phrase was much quoted by Rabelais, which accounts for its wider currency.

ride a hobbyhorse See OBSESSION.

ring the changes To repeat the same thing in different ways; to vary the manner in which one performs a routine task. Originally, *ring the changes* referred to performing all possible permutations in ringing a set of bells. The expression is commonly applied figuratively to describe changing the order of a series of words, restating a fact or opinion in several different ways, or varying one's technique in accomplishing an otherwise routine task.

> They shall only ring you over a few changes upon three words: crying, Faith, Hope and Charity; Hope, Faith and Charity, and so on. (John Eachard, *The Grounds and Occasions of the Contempt of the Clergy and Religion Enquired Into*, 1670)

run that by me again A somewhat rude request to have information repeated, usually (but not necessarily) similar in tone to "Come again." The likelihood is that the expression's origin lies in the electronic re-runs and re-plays made commonplace by tape recordings and videotape.

REPRIMAND (See also CRITICISM, FAULTFINDING.)

cast in [someone's] teeth To upbraid or reproach a person; to throw back at a person something he has said or done. Some say the phrase, popular in Shakespeare's time, is an allusion to knocking someone's teeth out by casting stones. It may be an earlier form of the current expression *throw in [someone's] face.*

> He casteth the Jews in the teeth that their fathers served strange Gods. (Thomas Timme, tr., *Commentary of John Calvin upon Genesis*, 1578)

chew out To reprimand, scold, or give someone a tongue-lashing. This American slang expression dates from the middle of this century.

> A verbal admonishing from a superior would be recorded by the victim with "I just got eaten out" or "I just got chewed out." (J. B. Roulier, *New York Folk Quarterly*, IV, 1948)

curtain lectures A wife's nighttime naggings; a shrew's bedtime harangues. The *curtains* refers to drapes on old four-posters; the *lectures* to a wife's supposed practice of showering her husband with sermons when he least wants to listen, i.e., when he wants to fall asleep. The expression, in use since the early 17th century, gained popularity when the English humorist Douglas William Jerrold published his fictional "Mrs. Caudle's Curtain-lectures" in *Punch* in 1846.

dressing down A severe, formal reprimand or reproof; a tongue-lashing; a sharp censure. *Dress* 'to treat someone with deserved severity, to give a thrashing or beating to' (*OED*) dates from the 15th century, and *dressing down* from the 19th century. However, the two theories which have been proffered to explain the origin of *dressing down* do not take this long obsolete use of *dress* into account. The first theory relates to the preparation of fish.

> The order was given [to] . . . fall to splitting and salting [fish]. This operation which is known as "dressing down," is performed on hogshead tubs or boards placed between two barrels. (*Harper's Magazine*, March, 1861)

The second theory claims that the coals refers at worst to severe criticism
phrase derives from the practice of or censure.
"dressing down" in ore mines which involves breaking up the ore and crushing and powdering it in the stamping
mill. It is plausible that either image—
of splitting and cutting up fish or breaking up and crushing ore—could have
given rise to the figurative *dressing
down.*

> If the Tories do not mend their
> manners, they will shortly be
> hauled over the coals in such a
> manner as will make this country
> too hot to hold them. (James C.
> Ballagh, ed., *The Letters of Richard
> Henry Lee,* 1911)

get the stick To be severely rebuked or
reprimanded, to be called on the carpet. This expression is British slang and
apparently derived from the former
practice of birching or caning, i.e., beating misbehaved schoolchildren with
sticks. With the demise of corporal punishment in schools, the phrase has become figurative in meaning and now
refers only to verbal punishment.

a lash of scorpions An extremely severe punishment; an unusually harsh,
vituperative, or vitriolic chastisement
or criticism. Though now used figuratively, this expression was once literal,
the *scorpion* being an ancient instrument of punishment, a whip or lash
with four or five "tails," each set with
steel spikes and lead weights. The allusion to the arachnoid scorpion with its
venomous, stinging tail is obvious.
Needless to say, a scourging with a scorpion was a heinous ordeal which inflicted intense pain and, in many cases,
permanent injury or even death.

give [someone] Jesse To punish or
scold; to reprimand or castigate. In this
expression, Jesse may refer to the father
of David (Isaiah 11:1, 10), a righteous
and valiant man. It is more likely, however, that the reference is to the sport
of falconry in which a jess, or jesse, a
strap used to secure a bird by its leg to
a falconer's wrist, was used as a punishment for poor performance.

> My father hath chastised you with
> whips, but I will chastise you with
> scorpions. (I Kings 12:11)

> Just as soon as I go home I'll give
> you jessie. (Alice Cary, *Married,*
> 1856)

**give [someone] the length of one's
tongue** To speak one's mind, especially in verbally abusive terms; to give
someone a piece of one's mind. A citation from the *OED* dates the phrase
from the turn of the 20th century.

lay out in lavender To chastise harshly
and in no uncertain terms; to give
someone a dressing down; to knock
someone down or unconscious; to kill
someone. Although the derivation of
lavender in this expression is uncertain,
lay someone out has long meant 'to
strike someone so hard as to knock him
to the ground.' One source suggests
that since both "lavender" and "livid"
are derived from the Latin *lividula* 'a
purplish-blue plant,' there may be the
common theme of intense anger. A
more plausible explanation is that
branches of the lavender plant were
once used to beat freshly washed
clothes, and that *lay out in lavender* alludes to this physical act of beating. In
contemporary usage, however, this expression usually refers to a verbal beating rather than a physical one.

haul over the coals To reprimand or
scold; to censure, to take to task. Current figurative use of this expression derives from the former actual practice of
dragging heretics over the coals of a
slow fire. In a 16th-century treatise, St.
Augustine was described as knowing
best "how to fetch an heretic over the
coals." No longer is the phrase used literally as in the above quotation. Today
haul or *rake* or *drag* or *fetch over the*

> If that woman gets the Republican
> nomination, . . . I will lay her out in
> lavender. (Vivian Kellems in a

syndicated newspaper column, September 15, 1952)

a lick with the rough side of the tongue
A harsh or merciless criticism, censure, or rebuke; a severe reprimand. In this expression, *lick* 'a blow or strike, as in a punishment' is used figuratively as is *rough side of the tongue*, with all of its attendant implications.

on the carpet Summoned before one's superiors for a reprimand; called to account; taken to task; usually in the phrase *to call on the carpet*. Although this expression did not appear in this sense until 1900, both the verb *to carpet* 'to call someone in to be reprimanded, to censure someone' and the phrase *to walk the carpet* date from the early 1800s. Both were said of a servant called into the parlor (a carpeted area) before the master or mistress in order to be reprimanded.

pin [someone's] ears back To reprimand severely or harshly; to deliver a scathing comeuppance; to abuse or punish physically. This expression implies that, figuratively at least, a person's ears can be forced back against his head by the strength of a particularly harsh verbal or physical beating.

> Pine was a flip-lipped bastard who should have had his ears pinned back long ago. (John Evans, *Halo in Blood,* 1946)

read the riot act To reprimand or chastise vehemently and vociferously; to issue an ultimatum, an or-else; to threaten with drastic punishment. The expression derives from Britain's Riot Act of 1715, which provided that a given number of assembled persons perceived to be causing a disturbance were liable to arrest as felons if they refused to disperse on command. Such command or warning was given by formal reading of the Riot Act.

skin alive To reprimand harshly; to verbally abuse or browbeat; to humble or subdue, especially in a venomous,

cruel, or merciless manner. The figurative implications of this expression are obvious. Also, *flay alive.*

talk to like a Dutch uncle To rebuke or reprove someone with unsparing severity and bluntness. Although an adequate explanation as to why the uncle in this expression is Dutch as opposed to any other nationality has yet to be found, a possible derivation has been proposed in regard to the term *uncle* itself. Apparently, in Roman times, an uncle was a strict guardian given to administering severe reproofs if his charge stepped out of line. The following passage from Joseph C. Neal's *Charcoal Sketches* (1838) illustrates the use of the phrase:

> If you keep a-cutting didoes, I must talk to you both like a Dutch uncle.

tell where to get off To rebuke, to accuse someone of being presumptuous or stepping on toes; to take down a peg, to "tell off." This slang expression of U.S. origin dates from the turn of the century. It may have derived by analogy with the forced ejection of unruly passengers from streetcars or trains. The expression implies that the person who tells another "where to get off" has reached the limits of his endurance and is in effect saying, "You've gone far enough."

> He said he was a gentleman, and that no cheap skate in a plug hat could tell him where to get off. (Ade, *More Fables,* 1900)

tongue-lashing A severe scolding or reprimand; a stinging rebuke or censure; a verbal whipping. Current since the 1880s, this phrase is a modernization of *tongue-banging* which was popular throughout the 1800s. An Anglo-Irish variation is *slap of the tongue.*

REPUGNANCE (See REPULSION.)

REPULSION

the gorge rises at it To find repugnant, to hold in revulsion; to feel disgust at; to be sickened or nauseated by; to turn one's stomach. The gorge is the craw or stomach, and, by metonymy, its contents. The phrase is yet another owing its popularity and quite possibly its origin to Shakespeare's *Hamlet.* On recalling the lively wit that once inhabitated the cold, decaying skull of Yorick then in his hands, Hamlet says:

How abhorred in my imagination it is! my gorge rises at it. (V,i)

The expression is still frequently encountered in literary or formal writing. *Webster's Third* cites a recent usage by Pearl Buck:

When he tried to eat the flesh of his ox his gorge rose.

set the teeth on edge To repel, offend, or disgust; to jar or grate on one's nerves, to irritate or annoy. This expression is derived from an ancient proverb as evidenced in Jeremiah 31:29–30:

In those days they shall no longer say: "The fathers have eaten sour grapes, and the children's teeth are set on edge." But every one shall die for his own sin; each man who eats sour grapes, his teeth shall be set on edge.

The allusion is to the unpleasant, tingling sensation caused by sour or acidic foods.

I had rather hear a brazen canstick turn'd,
Or a dry wheel grate on the axle-tree;
And that would set my teeth nothing on edge,
Nothing so much as mincing poetry.
(Shakespeare, *I Henry IV,* III,iii)

A variation is *put the teeth on edge.*

stick in the craw To be difficult to accept or reconcile; to rub the wrong way; to be irritating, offensive, or annoying. The concept of swallowing is often used metaphorically for the acceptance or rejection of ideas. In this expression, which appeared in print by the 18th century, nonacceptance is conveyed by the image of something

being stuck in one's craw (crop or gullet). Variants of this expression include *stick in the gullet* or *crop* or *throat.*

There is one or two things that stick in my Crop. (*The Deane Papers,* 1775)

REPUTATION (See **FAME.**)

RESCUE

deus ex machina An eleventh-hour deliverer, a last-minute rescuer; any contrived or unlikely means used to resolve a problem or untangle the intricacies of a plot. Literally 'a god from a machine,' this expression owes its origin to the ancient literary device of relying on divine intervention in the resolution of a plot. The machine in the phrase refers to a special piece of stage equipment used in ancient Greek theaters to lower actors playing the roles of gods onto the stage.

get [someone] off the hook To rescue a person from a difficult situation, particularly one involving trouble or embarrassment; to exonerate, clear, or vindicate; to absolve of responsibility. This expression refers to the plight of a fish that is hooked by a fisherman. If the fish is able to escape without help, it is by getting off the hook and swimming to freedom. Thus, to get [someone] off the hook is to extricate him from a potentially ruinous predicament.

"It's an idea," said Dr. Craig . . .
"It would get Hartley off the hook, sure enough." (J. Potts, *Go, Lovely Rose,* 1954)

pull out of a hat See **SOLUTION.**

pull out of the fire To extricate from danger, to save from destruction; to rescue or salvage; to turn threatened defeat into victory. Used in reference to plans, projects, situations, relationships, etc.—virtually anything that can be in jeopardy—the expression's derivation is obvious.

saved by the bell Delivered from an undesirable fate by a lucky accident or intervention. The reference is to the bell which signals the end of a round of boxing. At that instant, even if the referee is in the middle of counting out a prostrate fighter, the round is officially over and the count is void, thus giving a losing contestant a reprieve. The expression is used when a doorbell, telephone bell, or other ringing interrupts a potentially unpleasant or embarrassing situation.

RESENTMENT

dog in the manger A person who out of pure spite prevents others from using or enjoying something that he himself does not need or want. The allusion is to the fable of a dog who situated himself in a manger and selfishly would not allow the ox or horse to feed on the hay it contained. This expression has been in use since at least the late 1500s.

gall and wormwood Feelings of intense bitterness and deep resentment; rancor, hostility, or hardness of heart. Both *gall* and *wormwood* refer to bitter substances—the former to bile and the latter to a bitter herb. The earliest use of the phrase *gall and wormwood* appears in Lamentations 3:19.

> Remembering mine affliction and my misery, the wormwood and the gall.

Today the phrase is heard more often in literary contexts than in everyday speech.

the green-eyed monster Jealousy. This epithet was coined by Shakespeare; Iago uses it when warning Othello of the destructive nature of jealousy:

> Oh, beware, my lord, of jealousy.
> It is the green-eyed monster which doth mock
> The meat it feeds on. (III,iii)

Green-eyed 'jealous' and *green with envy* are common variants.

put [someone's] nose out of joint See **HUMILIATION.**

sour grapes Disdain or contempt affected as a rationale for that which one does not or cannot have; envy, resentment. This expression is derived from Aesop's fable of *The Fox and the Grapes,* in which a hungry fox, unable to reach a cluster of grapes after repeated attempts, finally gives up and leaves, justifying his failure by telling himself that the grapes were undoubtedly sour anyway.

> I have never been able to understand the fascination which makes my brother Philip and others wish to spend their entire lives in this neighbourhood. I once said as much to Hannah, and she replied that it was sour grapes on my part. (C. P. Snow, *Conscience of the Rich,* 1958)

RESIGNATION

give her the bells and let her fly To acquiesce to the inevitable, regardless of cost; to acknowledge reality or failure before risking further loss; to make the best of an unalterable situation. This expression originated in the sport of falconry, in which a worthless bird was released without bothering to remove the valuable bells attached to it.

like it or lump it To accept and put up with; to resign oneself to the inevitable; to make the best of an undesirable situation. The exact origin of this informal expression is difficult to determine. The most plausible suggestion is that *lump it* originally meant 'gulp it down' and was probably said in reference to distasteful medicine. Figurative use of the expression appeared in print by the early 1800s.

> I'll buy clothes as I see fit, and if anybody don't like it, why they may lump it, that's all. (Harriet Beecher Stowe, *Poganuc People,* 1878)

Sometimes *lump it* means simply 'dislike' as in the following quotation:

Whether we like him or lump him, he [the Interviewer] is master of the situation. (Grant Allen in *Interviews,* 1893)

Like it or lump it is usually heard in situations where no actual choice exists.

that's the way the ball bounces That's life; that's the way it goes; there's nothing to be done about it. Just as one cannot determine ahead of time how a ball will bounce, so too no one can predict or prevent the twists and turns of fate. This expression and the analogous *that's the way the cookie crumbles* are usually said in resignation to a fait accompli.

RESISTANCE (See **PROTEST, REBELLION.**)

RESPITE

busman's holiday A vacation or day off from work spent in an activity of the same nature as one's usual occupation. There are Britishers who say that the regular driver of a London bus actually did spend one of his days off riding as a passenger alongside the driver who was taking his place, but thus far no evidence has been found to substantiate the story. The expression has been in use since 1893.

come up for air To take a breather, take five, take time out; to relax, rest, or enjoy a respite. The phrase implies that one has been so inundated with work or immersed in work that he is in danger of drowning, figuratively speaking; like an underwater swimmer or a diver he must pause to refresh himself and recoup his powers for the next lap.

hang up one's hatchet See **RETIREMENT.**

pit stop A brief stop at a restaurant or rest area to break the monotony of an automobile trip and allow passengers to stretch their legs; a short stay at a place while en route to a distant destination.

This expression derives from the auto racing *pit* referring to the area alongside a speedway where cars stop to be serviced or refueled.

rest on one's oars To relax after strenuous exertion; to suspend one's efforts temporarily; to take it easy for a while. Often this boating phrase is extended to mean ceasing one's labors altogether, relying on the momentum of past performance to carry one along. In this sense it is virtually synonymous with *rest on one's laurels. Rest on one's oars* was used literally in the early 18th century, and figuratively shortly thereafter.

The managers of the usual autumn gathering of paintings . . . will rest on their oars. (*Athenaeum,* April, 1887)

RESULT (See **CONSEQUENCES, OUTCOME.**)

RETALIATION

an eye for an eye A law which sanctions revenge; to repay in kind. This line from Exodus 21:24 is part of a longer passage in which the Lord sets forth the judgments and laws according to which the people are instructed to live. However, this expression may be even older if, as some speculate, it was part of the Code of Hammurabi (approx. 1800 B.C.). The noted resemblances between Hammurabi's laws and ancient Mosaic laws make this theory plausible.

fight fire with fire To argue or fight with an opponent using his tactics or ground rules; to counter an attack with one of equal intensity. This expression refers to the method used to fight a rapidly spreading forest or grass fire. To control such a fire, a firebreak (an area cleared of trees, grass, and other flammable material) is often created some distance in front of the advancing flames. A backfire may then be set to burn the area between the major fire and the firebreak, thereby containing the fire within a limited area where it can be doused with water or dirt. Thus, fire is literally fought with fire in order to defeat it. In its figurative sense, *to fight fire with fire* is to contend with someone on his level, using his tactics to defeat him. The expression usually implies a lowering or abandonment of one's principles.

fix [someone's] wagon To get even with, avenge; to prevent, interfere with, or destroy another's success, reputation, or expectations; to injure or kill. This expression may stem from the days of the covered wagons when a person's entire family, possessions, and livelihood could be contained in one of these vehicles. An unscrupulous and vindictive enemy might "fix" the wagon in such a way as to assure that it would break down, causing injury to and possible destruction of both the wagon and its contents. The related expression *fix [someone's] little red wagon* is an updated version, and all the more insidious in its implication of harming a child.

give [someone] a taste of [his] own medicine To pay someone back in his own coin, to requite a wrong in kind; also *to give [someone] a dose of [his] own medicine*. Use of the expression dates from the late 19th century.

> In killing Bob Ollinger the Kid only gave him a dose of his own kind of medicine. (Charles A. Siringo, *Riata and Spurs*, 1927)

heap coals of fire on [someone's] head To repay hostility with kindness; to answer bad treatment with good, supposedly in order to make one's enemy repent. The allusion is Biblical:

> If thine enemy be hungry, give him bread to eat; and if he be thirsty, give him water to drink: For thou shalt heap coals of fire upon his head, and the Lord shall reward thee. (Proverbs 25:21–22)

The usual explanation is that the "coals of fire" supposedly melted a person's "iciness."

pound of flesh Vengeance; requital. This expression derives from Shakespeare's *Merchant of Venice*, in which Shylock agrees to lend money to Antonio only on condition that, if the sum is not repaid on time, he be allowed a pound of Antonio's flesh in forfeit.

> The pound of flesh which I demand of him is dearly bought, 'tis mine, and I will have it. (IV,i)

The expression implies that, while the demanded retribution is justified, the yielding of it would incapacitate or destroy the giver, just as the yielding of a pound of one's own flesh would certainly have deleterious consequences.

> All the other Great Powers want their pound of flesh from Turkey. (*Fortnightly Review*, January, 1887)

a Roland for an Oliver An eye for an eye, a blow for a blow; retaliation in kind. Roland and Oliver, two of Charlemagne's paladins, had adventures which were so extraordinarily similar that it was all but impossible to determine which was the more chivalrous. Eventually, the two men met face to face in combat on an island in the Rhine, where, for five days they fought fiercely, with neither gaining an advantage. The bout climaxed when both men met simultaneous untimely deaths.

> We resolved to give him a Roland for his Oliver, if he attacked us. (*The Life of Neville Frowde*, 1773)

serve the same sauce To retaliate in like fashion; to fight fire with fire; to repay in kind.

> They serve them with like sauce, requiring death for death. (Richard Eden, *The Decade of the New World or West India*, 1555)

Variations are *serve a sop* or *taste of the same sauce*.

tit for tat Blow for blow, an eye for an eye and a tooth for a tooth, reciprocal retaliation.

> Fair Traders, Reciprocity men, or believers in the tit-for-tat plan of dealing with other nations. (*Daily News,* July, 1891)

According to the *OED* this expression is probably a variation of the earlier *tip* 'light blow' for *tap* 'light blow.'

> Much greater is the wrong that rewards evil for good, than that which requires tip for tap. (George Gascoigne, *Works,* 1577)

Other conjectures claim that *tit for tat* came from the French *tant pour tant* 'so much for so much' or the Dutch *dit vor dat* 'this for that.' Use of the phrase dates from at least 1556.

RETIREMENT

apply for Chiltern Hundreds To resign from office; to abandon one's position or responsibility. This British expression alludes to the method used by an M.P. who wishes to resign before his term of office has expired, a forbidden practice. Also forbidden is the holding of paid office under the Crown while a member of Parliament. Consequently, the M.P. who wishes to resign applies for the Stewardship of the Chiltern Hundreds, a no longer extant Crown appointment. On receiving the appointment, he is forced to relinquish his seat in Parliament. Having done so, he at once resigns his Stewardship as well, thus leaving the fictitious post vacant for the next M.P. in need of the ploy.

hang up one's hatchet To quit working, to take a rest or break from one's work. The allusion is probably to a wood cutter or other person who uses a hatchet or ax in his trade and literally hangs it up when he stops working. This expression, no longer in use, dates as far back as 1327.

> When thou hast well done hang up thy hatchet. (Richard Hills, *Proverbs from the Common-Place Book,* 1530)

put out to pasture Retired, put on the shelf, put away. The expression originally referred to animals, such as workhorses, which, due to old age or poor health, had outlived their usefulness to their owners and were turned out to pasture for the rest of their days. Today the phrase is more commonly applied to older persons who, for the same reasons, have supposedly outlived their usefulness to society and are no longer allowed to play an active role in the affairs of the working world. The implication is that they are not accorded the dignity of human beings but are treated as animals whose only worth is in their work.

swallow the anchor To end one's seafaring days by obtaining an onshore job or retiring from a maritime occupation; to be released from service with the Navy. This expression, of obvious nautical derivation, was used by A. E. Marten, as cited in *Webster's Third:*

> [He] swallowed the anchor and stayed ashore.

The expression is occasionally extended to apply to retirement from any occupation.

RETORT (See also **EXCLAMATIONS**.)

Dick Tracy A mildly sarcastic retort to one who makes an obvious observation as if from penetrating insight. This expression derives from the popular comic strip *Dick Tracy* which features a detective of that name. *Dick Tracy* is analogous to such rhetorical comments as "Is the Pope Catholic?" and "No kidding, you don't say."

the Dutch have taken Holland An obvious statement, this expression is used sarcastically to put down someone who tells a piece of stale news as though it were new and exciting. *If my aunt had been a man she'd have been my uncle is* a similar British retort to someone who has laboriously explained the obvious.

Queen Anne is dead A sarcastic remark made to the bearer of stale news. A similar, current American phrase is *So what else is new?* Anne was Queen of Great Britain and Ireland from 1702–14. The expression dates from the 18th century.

touché Literally French for 'touched,' *touché* is a fencing term indicating a hit or score. In verbal fencing or argumentation the parry *touché* acknowledges accuracy and truth in an opponent's remark or retort.

RETRACTION (See **RECANTATION**.)

RETRIBUTION (See also **RETALIATION**.)

chickens come home to roost An expression indicating that one has received his just deserts or met with a comeuppance. Robert Southey makes reference to this proverbial expression in *The Curse of Kehama* (1810):

Curses are like young chickens:
they always come home to roost.

have the last laugh See **SUCCESS**.

laugh on the other side of one's face or **mouth** To experience a comedown or to undergo a radical change in mood from happiness to sadness, usually as a result of meeting one's comeuppance; to be sad, disappointed, or depressed; to fail after expecting or experiencing success, with the implication that such failure is deserved. Though the derivation of this expression is uncertain, it may refer to the fact that in a frown, the lips are turned down rather than up as in a smile.

We were made to laugh on the other side of our mouth by an unforeseen occurrence. (Benjamin Malkin, *LeSage's Adventures of Gil Blas of Santillane,* 1809)

A variation is *laugh on the wrong side of one's face* or *mouth.*

the mills of God grind slowly Retribution may be slow in coming, but justice will eventually triumph; sooner or later everyone will get what he deserves. This expression, a variant of which dates from the early 17th century, applies the metaphor of a mill grinding grain to the meting out of justice by the Almighty. The phrase appeared in the poem *Retribution* by Henry Wadsworth Longfellow:

Though the mills of God grind slowly, yet they grind exceeding small;
Though with patience He stands waiting, with exactness grinds He all.

the shoe is on the other foot See **REVERSAL**.

REVELATION (See **EXPOSURE**.)

REVELRY

beer and skittles Fun and games, amusement and pleasure. This British expression stems from the days when skittles, a game akin to ninepins, was often played in alleys adjacent to country inns. The phrase usually appears negatively in expressions such as *Life is not all beer and skittles.* In *Pickwick Papers,* Dickens used the phrase *porter and skittles.*

cakes and ale Pleasure and good times, with connotations of carousing and self-indulgence. In Shakespeare's *Twelfth Night,* the puritanical Malvolio is reproached by the bibulous Sir Toby Belch:

Dost thou think, because thou art virtuous, there shall be no more cakes and ale? (II,iii)

Somerset Maugham used the phrase as the title of his 1930 satirical novel of the lives of two writers, presumably Thomas Hardy and Hugh Walpole.

cock-a-hoop See **ELATION**.

cut a caper To perform a spirited, frolicsome dance step; to behave in a playful, frisky manner. *Caper* is said to derive from the Italian *capra* 'she-goat'; thus, *cut a caper* alludes to the frisky, erratic movements of goats. In Shakespeare's *Twelfth Night* (I,iii), a dialogue between Sir Toby Belch and Sir Andrew Aguecheek lends credence to this explanation. Sir Toby's response to the claim that Sir Andrew can "cut a caper" plays on the allusion to a goat by reference to a sheep.

And I can cut the mutton to it.

Today the figurative use is more common, shifting the emphasis from the actual dance step to similarly frolicsome and frisky behavior.

dance the antic hay To lead a hectic, pleasure-seeking life; to be a jet-setter, a hedonist. The hay was a lively English dance, somewhat like a reel. In an antic hay, the dancers wore masks of animal faces and moved with grotesque, uncouth gestures. The emphasis was on lustful and lecherous behavior.

My men, like satyrs, . . . shall with their goat feet dance the antic hay. (Christopher Marlowe, *Edward II* I,i, approx. 1593)

high jinks Unrestrained revelry; unbounded merrymaking; mischievous fun. *High jinks* was originally a 17th-century game in which a person, according to his dice throw, had to gulp down a drink, imitate a famous person, or perform some other prescribed task.

All sorts of high jinks go on on the grass plot. (Thomas Hughes, *Tom Brown at Oxford*, 1861)

kick up one's heels To frolic, gambol, or make merry; to enjoy oneself, to have fun. This self-evident expression may be related to either *heelkicking* or *kick-up*, 18th-century terms denoting a dance. Since dancing is often associated with merriment and high spirits, the activity became synonymous with the mood.

kill the fatted calf To rejoice or celebrate; to indulge in jubilant merrymaking; to entertain sumptuously. This expression's Biblical origin lies in the parable of the prodigal son (Luke 15: 23):

And bring hither the fatted calf, and kill it; and let us eat and be merry.

a night on the tiles An evening of carousing and merrymaking; a night on the town; a high old time. This British colloquialism comes by analogy with cats' nocturnal reveling and caterwauling on the tile rooftops of city dwellings.

paint the town red To carouse, go on a riotous spree; to take part in a reckless and boisterous celebration. This U.S. slang expression appears as early as 1884 in the *Boston Journal:*

Whenever there was any excitement or anybody got particularly loud, they always said somebody was "painting the town red."

Why red?

A "spectrophotometric study of pigments," by Professor Nicolls, is recommended to young men who intend to "paint the town red." (*Boston Journal*, 1884)

This tongue-in-cheek exhortation plays with the fact that red is the color at the extreme end of the visible spectrum, which perhaps accounts for its association with extremes or immoderation. However, red symbolizes many things, including passion, violence, and promiscuity, to name a few, and there is no evidence to verify that one explanation is more correct than another.

pub-crawl To move from one nightspot to another on a drinking bout; to barhop. This expression is commonplace in Great Britain, where *pub* is a shortening of *public house* 'bar, tavern.' The expression implies that the reveler will dawdle at each drinking-hole and that he may be moving on all fours before the evening is over.

red-letter day Any day marked by a memorable, happy, or significant event.

The Calendar of the Book of Common Prayer, as well as other liturgical calendars, marked festival and holy days in red, a practice retained on many secular calendars which designate Sundays and holidays in similar fashion. Figurative application to any noteworthy day dates from the 18th century.

> I used to dine and pass the evening with Dr. Jeune; and these were my red-letter days. (Thomas A. Trollope, *What I Remember*, 1887)

see the elephant To do the town, to visit the "big city"; to see the world, especially its seamy side. This American colloquialism probably stems from an old ballad that tells of a farmer whose horse was knocked over by a circus elephant as the two animals tried to pass each other on a narrow road. Though the horse was injured, and the milk and eggs which were to be sold at the market were ruined, the farmer took solace in the thought that at least he had seen the elephant. In common usage, the expression is usually employed somewhat facetiously.

> He makes his rounds every evening, while you and I see the elephant once a week. (O. Henry, *Four Million*, 1906)

sow wild oats See PROMISCUOUSNESS.

tear up the pea patch To go on a wild spree, to go on a rampage. According to Wentworth and Flexner *(A Dictionary of American Slang)*, baseball announcer "Red" Barber popularized this expression in his broadcasts of the Brooklyn Dodgers' baseball games (approx. 1945–55). An analogous Americanism is *go on a tear.*

trip the light fantastic To dance; to frolic or make merry. This expression is derived from John Milton's *L'Allegro* (1631):

> Come, and trip it, as you go,
> On the light fantastic toe.

Thus, *trip the light fantastic* combines *trip*, from the Middle English *trippen* 'to step lightly,' with *light fantastic*,

converted into a noun phrase by the omission of *toe* but retaining its original reference to movements of dancing.

> "You dance very nicely," she murmurs. "Yes, for a man who has not tripped the light fantastic for years." (Archibald C. Gunter, *Miss Dividends*, 1892)

REVENGE (See RETALIATION.)

REVERSAL

catch a tartar To experience a reversal of expectations, particularly in dealing with another person; to find intractable one anticipated to be docile; to meet one's match, often specifically to marry a shrew.

> What a Tartar have I caught!
> (John Dryden, *Kind Keeper*, 1678)

By extension the phrase may mean to have a bargain backfire, an advantage prove a liability, a gift becomes a curse, and similar reversals.

Frankenstein monster An invention or other creation that eventually works against or kills its creator; something that backfires or boomerangs. The expression comes from Mary Shelley's famous work *Frankenstein* (1818), in which the notorious monster turned against and destroyed its maker, Dr. Frankenstein. The phrase is used figuratively to describe a project or undertaking begun with good intentions, but which ultimately develops into an uncontrollable agent of destruction or evil.

> Is Great Britain creating for herself something of a Frankenstein monster on the Nile? (*Saturday Review*, April, 1907)

hoist with one's own petard To be defeated by a plan that backfires; to be caught in one's own trap. In this expression, *petard* refers to an ancient, short-fuzed time bomb or grenade. Obviously, a soldier who placed the charge was endangered not only by enemy fire, but also by the exploding petard if he did not get away soon enough or if the fuze were faulty. So many soldiers were killed by exploding petards that the expression came into widespread literal, and later, figurative, use.

Let it work;
For tis sport, to have the engineer
Hoist with his own petard; and it
shall go hard
But I will delve one yard below
their mines,
And blow them at the moon.
(Shakespeare, *Hamlet*, III,iv)

my Venus turns out a whelp An expression formerly used on experiencing a reversal of expectations, a failure instead of the anticipated success. The expression comes from dice: the highest roll, three sixes, was called a Venus; the lowest, three aces, a canis (dog). The aptness was reinforced by the association of Venus with beauty and divinity, and of whelp with cur and mongrel.

the shoe is on the other foot The situation is reversed. This expression, with its obvious allusion, is most often used in reference to a certain poetic justice that results from the exchange or reversal of disparate roles: the controller becomes the controlled, the oppressor becomes the oppressed, the critic becomes the criticized, and so on.

Recently, much to British chagrin, the shoe was on the other foot. (*The Nation*, March 17, 1945)

the tables are turned The situation is completely reversed, roles have been switched, positions interchanged; the exact opposite is now the case. The *tables* in this expression refers to the playing boards which, in certain games, are fully turned round, so that the relative positions of the adversaries are reversed. The phrase often implies that one now enjoys (or suffers) the perspective formerly held by an opponent. The following citation shows both figurative application and literal derivation:

Whosoever thou art that dost another wrong, do but turn the tables: imagine thy neighbour were now playing thy game, and thou his. (Bishop Robert Sanderson, *Sermons*, 1634)

It also illustrates the active use of the phrase, somewhat less common today, *turn tables* or *turn the tables on*.

turn the tide To reverse the current trend of events, especially from one extreme to the other; to turn the tables. *Tide* (literally the ebb and flow of the ocean waters) is used here figuratively to represent the course or direction in which any matter or concern is moving.

ugly duckling A homely or unpromising child who blossoms into a beautiful or accomplished adult; anything appearing to lack redeeming qualities that subsequently proves worthy of respect and notice. This expression comes from Hans Christian Andersen's *Ugly Duckling*, in which the title character, after struggling through a year of ridicule and hardship, develops into a glorious white swan. While the expression retains its human applications, it is also used for an inanimate object that is initially thought to be worthless but later proves to be a windfall. This figurative use of the phrase was illustrated by W. O. Douglas, as cited in *Webster's Third*:

From the beginning Alaska was treated pretty much as our ugly duckling.

RIDICULE (See also **INSULT**.)

give the gleek To poke fun at; to mock or ridicule. In this expression, *gleek* carries its archaic meaning of a joke or jest, thus giving the obsolete phrase its figurative sense of harmless teasing.

Sir Thomas, seeing the exceeding vanity of the man, thought he needed modesty, and gave him this gentle gleek. (Christopher Wordsworth, *Ecclesiastical Biography*, 1599)

laugh in one's sleeve To laugh surreptitiously; to be secretly amused or contemptuous; to ridicule in secret. This expression alludes to the popular 16th-century Englishman's garb which included sleeves large enough to hide a person's face so that he could smile or laugh covertly.

> If I coveted now to avenge the injuries that you have done me, I might laugh in my sleeve. (John Daus, *A Famous Chronicle of Our Times Called Sleidane's Commentaries*, 1560)

The French equivalent is *rire sous cape* 'laugh in one's cape,' referring to a French nobleman's cape which could serve the same purpose as an Englishman's sleeve. Another variation which arose in Spain at about the same time is *laugh in one's beard,* implying that a beard could be used to hide the expression on one's face.

laugh like a drain See **HUMOROUSNESS.**

nine tailors make a man An expression of contempt and derision, usually used in the context of ridiculing someone's physical stature. Since it was medieval custom to mark the death of a man with nine tolls of the church bell, a woman with six, and a child with three, this obsolete British invective is probably a corruption of *nine tellers mark a man, teller* being a variation of *toller* 'a knell.' As the expression became more common, however, the original meaning was lost, being replaced by the stereotypic concept of tailors as being so feeble and physically degenerate that it would take nine of them to equal one man of normal size and strength. The Scottish historian Thomas Carlyle (1795–1881) tells of Queen Elizabeth I (1533–1603) who, upon receiving a delegation of eighteen tailors, greeted them with royal wit: "Good morning, gentlemen both."

quote-unquote So-called; thus designated. This expression is currently becoming more widely used in American speech, usually in a sarcastic, derogatory, or denigrating reference to a person's or group's appellation, especially one that is self-assumed. *Quote-unquote* is a verbal representation of quotation marks (" ") which, in writing, are placed around usually complimentary word(s) that are intentionally used cynically or disparagingly. For example, the term might be heard in a context like "The politician dreaded the thought of again having to meet with the quote-unquote pillars of society."

roast To mock brutally or ridicule; to criticize severely or put down; to dress down, to take down a peg. This relatively recent American colloquialism is a term which, like *cook, burn,* and *heat,* is heard in expressions that create an image of discomfort or destruction.

> If he were to roast our Skinski it might hurt our business. (Hugh McHugh, *You Can Search Me*, 1905)

tongue in cheek Sarcastically, insincerely; not seriously, deadpan; mockingly, derisively. The origin of the term is uncertain.

> There was no speaking "with his tongue in the cheek." He spoke straight from the heart. (Sir E. W. Hamilton, *Gladstone*, 1898)

RISK (See also **DANGER.**)

dance on the razor's edge To tempt fate, to invite trouble, to skate on thin ice. The allusion is to the very sharp and very thin edge of a straight razor. This expression is apparently an extension of the earlier phrase *on the razor's edge* 'in a very precarious or dangerous position,' which dates from the early 17th century. George Chapman used the expression in his famous translation of Homer's *Iliad* (1611):

> Now on the eager razor's edge, for life or death we stand.

lay it on the line To risk something valuable such as one's career, reputation, or life; to speak or answer candidly, clearly, and categorically; to say precisely what one means; to give or pay money. In this expression, *line* is a figurative indication of demarcation between two extremes such as success and failure, clarity and obscurity, or debit and credit. Although originally limited to financial matters such as payment of debts, in contemporary usage *lay it on the line* usually refers to speaking frankly or risking something of importance.

> I'll lay it on the line for you, if you like. Are you thinking of asking my girl to marry you? (E. E. Sumner, *Chance Encounter*, 1967)

> It was clear to the President [Nixon] that his credibility was on the line with the leaders of Hanoi. (*Guardian*, May 9, 1970)

Variations include *put it on the line* and *on the line*.

leap in the dark See DEATH.

play with fire To trifle with or become involved in a serious or potentially dangerous matter. This expression uses *fire* figuratively to represent any situation or entity which can be beneficial or useful, but which always holds the potential for harm or disaster.

> I should like to sound a note of warning . . . one who plays with fire . . . can only expect to get burnt. (*Daily Chronicle*, October 9, 1907)

In contemporary usage, *play with fire* is often applied to romantic entanglements or sexual encounters which, by their very nature, carry the risk of moral or emotional distress.

> She led me on, she played with fire, but she wouldn't have me. (L. P. Hartley, *The Hireling*, 1957)

put one's head in the lion's (wolf's) mouth To court danger; to ask for trouble. In the Aesop fable which gave rise to the phrase, the mouth belonged to a wily wolf; a gullible crane inserted its head to extract a bone. At some point in the phrase's development, the wolf evolved into a lion—perhaps through confusion with *beard the lion in his den*, or perhaps because the size and ferocity of a lion seem more appropriate when the phrase is applied to human foolhardiness.

ride for a fall To invite injury or misfortune by reckless conduct; to court danger, ask for trouble; to behave so imperiously as to be headed for a comeuppance. One source conjectures a derivation from horse racing, saying a jockey "rides for a fall" when he deliberately loses a race, often by riding in such a way as to be thrown. Whether or not its origin is this specific, the literal phrase seems clearly to have its roots in horsemanship. The expression is now used almost exclusively in its figurative sense; conceptually it is akin to the well-known saying from Proverbs:

> Pride goeth before destruction, and an haughty spirit before a fall. (16:18)

Russian roulette A risky activity or predicament, especially one which endangers a person's life. In the game of Russian roulette, a revolver is loaded with one bullet, the cartridge cylinder is spun, the gun is pointed at one's own head, and the trigger is pulled. If the revolver can hold six bullets, the odds are one in six that when the trigger is pulled, the person will kill himself. This "game" took its name from roulette, another game of chance in which a small metal ball is spun onto a revolving wheel, coming to rest in one of thirty-seven or thirty-eight numbered compartments. Its "Russian" designation probably derives from its being a popular pastime among the nihilistic intelligentsia of 19th-century Russia. Although both roulette and Russian roulette are forms of gambling, the stakes in the latter are considerably higher. *Russian roulette* is applied figuratively in situations where one takes his life into his own hands; for example, "It's Russian roulette out there on the freeways at rush hour."

take the bear by the tooth Recklessly to risk danger; to provoke to attack. The phrase's meaning is self-evident, its origin unknown.

RUINATION (See also **THWARTING**.)

cut the ground from under To disprove or invalidate someone's argument, case, position, etc., by demonstrating that it has no foundation in fact; to devastate someone by destroying his belief in an idea or his faith in a person. In this expression, *ground* is what supports a person or his perceptions, whatever sustains him or informs his life.

flub the dub To ruin one's own chances of success by inept or evasive behavior; to think or act awkwardly, inefficiently, or slowly; to be slothful and indolent; to blunder or bungle. This expression enjoyed limited popularity during World War II, but *flub* has remained in fairly widespread contemporary use. Related expressions are *flubdub* 'pompous bombastic language inappropriate to a situation' and *fluba-dub* 'awkwardness, ineptitude.' It is interesting to note that Flubadub was the name of the awkward, bumbling, nondescript circus animal (puppet) in the original *Howdy Doody Show* (1947–60).

> Maybe Mike Todd or [Milton] Berle should take over the management of the conventions. . . . They would remove much of the amateur flub-dub. (*Daily Mirror,* July 8, 1952)

gum up the works To botch or mess things up, to screw things up; to spoil or ruin, to interfere with the smooth operation of things; also *to gum* or *gum up* and *to gum the game.* The allusion is to the clogging effect gum or a gummy substance has on machinery. The figurative use of this American slang expression dates from at least 1901.

> When it comes to you horning into this joint and aiming to gum up the works for me . . . well, that's something else again. (P. G. Wodehouse, *Hot Water,* 1932)

knock for six To demolish an argument or defeat an opponent utterly and completely; to knock for a loop or into a cocked hat. This primarily British expression derives from cricket; a batsman knocks for six when he knocks the ball over the boundary of the field and scores six runs. The feat is similar to hitting a homerun in baseball, a game more familiar to Americans.

knock into a cocked hat To demolish or defeat utterly; to destroy, upset, or ruin. Though it may refer to actual physical combat, the expression is more often used in reference to plans, arguments, theories, etc. Most sources agree it derives from a game similar to ninepins, popular in the United States in the 19th century. When only the three pins forming a triangle were left standing, they were said to have been "knocked into a cocked hat"—by analogy with the shape of the tricornered, brimmed hat worn during the American Revolution.

> A frigate of the modern type would knock a fort armed with obsolete guns into a cocked hat. (*Pall Mall Gazette,* January, 1888)

make mincemeat of To destroy or annihilate; to beat in a contest. This expression, dating from the 17th century, can be used in referring to actual physical destruction or to the destruction of a person's ideas or theories.

> I'll hew thee into so many Morsels, that . . . Thou shalt be Mince-meat, Worm, within this Hour. (Abraham Cowley, *Cutter of Colman-street,* 1663)

The use referring to beating an opponent in a contest seems to be a later development, appearing in print by the mid-19th century.

> Maniac made mincemeat of Smoker, who was so stiff that he could scarcely raise a gallop. (*Coursing Calendar,* 1876)

An equivalent slang expression is *make hamburger out of,* an Americanism which applies almost exclusively to severe physical beating or thrashing.

pull the rug out from under To cut the ground from under someone; to suddenly and effectively shatter another's position, argument, or belief by demonstrating its invalidity; to deflate someone by destroying his illusions.

> But if . . . Bazargan were to quit, authority in Iran would apparently rest solely with the Komiteh, the mullahs and other fervent Shi'ites whose grab for power has literally pulled the Persian rug out from under Bazargan's regime. (*Time,* March, 1979)

upset the applecart To ruin plans or arrangements, to botch things up, to spoil things, to blight someone's hopes. An applecart is a pushcart street vendors use to peddle apples. For a huckster who makes his living selling apples, the overturning of his cart would be disastrous since it would inevitably damage the fruit and thus ruin his business. A variant of the expression dates from at least 1788.

> If the Control had done more it might have upset the apple-cart altogether. (*Pall Mall Gazette,* October, 1883)

S

SADNESS   (See DEJECTION.)

SAMENESS   (See EQUIVALENCE, SIMILARITY.)

SANCTUARY

glory hole   A container for the storage of ornaments, personal effects, and other paraphernalia. This term originally referred to a room where the war medals and decorations of a former soldier were stored. The expression is used today to describe any receptacle filled with useless items of sentimental value.

> You can bring out your old ribbon-box . . . It's a charity to clear out your glory-holes once in a while. (Adeline Whitney, *We Girls*, 1871)

ivory tower   A condition of isolation or seclusion from worldly or practical affairs; a sheltered, protected existence removed from the harsh realities of life; an attitude of aloofness or distance from the mainstream of society. The original term appears to have been the French *tour d'ivoire* first used by the French literary critic Sainte-Beuve in reference to the French writer Alfred Victor de Vigny in his book *Pensées d'Août* (1837). The expression appeared in English in Brereton and Rothwell's translation of *Bergson's Laughter* (1911):

> Each member [of society] must be ever attentive to his social surroundings . . . he must avoid shutting himself up in his own peculiar character as a philosopher in his ivory tower.

The term has spawned the noun *ivory-towerism* and the adjectives *ivory-towerish* and *ivory-towered* 'impractical, theoretical, removed from reality.'

sanctum sanctorum   A hideaway; a room or other place where one can seek refuge from his everyday concerns; a haven or sanctuary. Literally, the *sanctum sanctorum* (Latin, 'sanctuary of sanctuaries') is the Holy of Holies, a room in Biblical tabernacles and Jewish temples which only the high priest is allowed to enter, and then only on Yom Kippur, the Great Day of Atonement. By extension, *sanctum sanctorum* has been applied to any private, peaceful place such as a cabin in the woods or the den in a house which is not to be violated by intruders.

> We went by appointment to the archbishop confessor's and were immediately admitted into his sanctum sanctorum, a snug apartment . . . (Peter Beckford, *Familiar Letters From Italy*, 1834)

SARCASM   (See RIDICULE.)

SCHOLARLINESS

bluestocking   A woman of intellectual attainments or pretensions. Most sources agree that the term originated in 18th-century Britain in reference to certain gatherings of both men and women at which literary discussion replaced the former usual cardplaying. However, sources do not agree on whose receptions or whose stockings actually gave rise to the phrase. Regardless of the wearer or wearers, *bluestocking* appears to have reflected the casual dress accepted in these intellectual circles, the blue worsted being in opposition to the formal conventional black silk. Little used today, the term was derogatory both in its reference to dress and in its subsequent reference to the women who sought intellectual parity with men. In the Colonial United States, however, the term was interchangeable with *blueblood* and simply meant one of aristocratic birth or superior social standing.

bookworm One who seems to be nurtured and sustained through constant reading; one whose nose is always buried in a book; a bibliophile. This term derives from different kinds of maggots that live in books and destroy them by eating holes through the pages. However, one source suggests that the term alludes to the Biblical passage in which an angel says to St. John in regard to a scroll:

Take it, and eat it up; and it shall make thy belly bitter, but it shall be in thy mouth sweet as honey. (Revelations 10:9)

The term appeared in print in its figurative sense as early as 1599. It is usually used negatively to connote those qualities characteristic of a pedant.

double dome An intellectual or scholar, a highbrow or longhair. This rather derogatory American slang expression is of fairly recent coinage and would appear to be a humorous takeoff on *dome*, slang for head since the late 19th century. *Double dome* not only brings to mind the notion of a double head, and thus twice the average intelligence, but also the image of a particularly high forehead, once believed to be a mark of higher-than-average intelligence.

egghead An intellectual or highbrow, an academician or longhair. This disparaging term for an intellectual owes its origin to the visual resemblance between the shape of an egg and the head of a person with a high forehead, the latter feature being considered a mark of superior intelligence. The term became popular during the 1952 presidential campaign when Adlai Stevenson was the Democratic candidate. His supporters, mostly members of the intelligentsia, were often labeled eggheads, perhaps in humorous reference to Stevenson's own unusually high forehead, further accented by his baldness.

highbrow An intellectually and culturally superior person; an advocate of the arts and literature. The origin of this expression lies in the belief that people with high foreheads have a greater intellectual capacity. The term is often used disparagingly to describe anyone with intellectual interests. Variations of this expression include *low-brow*, a person of no breeding and negligible mental capacity; *middle-brow*, a person of mediocre intelligence and bourgeois tastes; and the place name *Highbrowsville*, a rarely used term for Boston, Massachusetts, once considered the hub of American intellectual life.

The strangely disreputable lady "Jazz"—disreputable because she was not sponsored by the highbrows. (S. R. Nelson, *All About Jazz*, 1934)

SEARCH (See **INVESTIGATION, QUEST.**)

SECRECY

button one's lip To keep quiet or silent; to keep a secret; also *button up* and *button up one's face* or *lip*. The expression has been in use since 1868.

hugger-mugger Covert or clandestine behavior, secrecy, furtiveness; confusion or disarray. This expression, possibly derived from the Middle English *mokeren* 'to conceal,' appeared in Shakespeare's *Hamlet* regarding the manner of Polonius' burial:

And we have done but greenly In hugger mugger to inter him. (IV,v)

Although the expression maintains its furtive connotation, *hugger-mugger* now more frequently carries the meaning of jumbled confusion or disorganization, a meaning it assumed because clandestine activity is often hurried and haphazard.

You find matters . . . so clumsily set out, that you fare in the style called hugger-mugger. (William Jerdan, *Autobiography*, 1853)

in petto Undisclosed, kept secret; private, in one's own thoughts or contemplation. This expression is Italian for 'in the breast.' Citations dating from the 17th century indicate that *in petto* is applied almost exclusively to affairs of church or state.

> There are seven cardinals still remaining in petto, whose names the Pope keeps secret. (*London Gazette,* 1712)

little pitchers have big ears An exhortation or reminder to guard one's tongue because children may overhear words not intended for their ears. The handle of a pitcher is sometimes called its "ear." Thus, *pitchers have ears* is a pun on *ears,* and is analogous in meaning to *walls have ears.* This expression appeared in print by the mid-1500s; the later addition of *little* limits the kind of listeners to children.

> Surely Miss Gray, knowing that little pitchers have ears, would have corrected the mistake. (Sarah Tytler, *Buried Diamonds,* 1886)

mum's the word Remain silent; do not breathe a word of what was just said. Shakespeare conveyed this meaning in *Henry VI, Part II:*

> Seal up your lips, and give no word but—mum. (I,ii)

This expression may have derived from the m-m sound, which can be produced only with closed lips. The phrase is particularly commonplace in Great Britain.

> As to Cornwall, . . . between you and me, Mrs. Harper, mum's the word. (Dinah Mulock, *Agatha's Husband,* 1852)

on the q.t. Secretly, surreptitiously, covertly, clandestinely, on the sly. Q.t. is simply an abbreviation of the word *quiet* in the original expression *on the quiet.*

> It will be possible to have one spree on the strict q.t. (George Moore, *A Mummer's Wife,* 1884)

skeleton in the closet A family secret or scandal kept concealed to avoid public shame and disgrace; any confidential matter which, if revealed, could be a source of embarrassment, humiliation, or abasement. Though popularized in the writings of William Thackeray (1811–63), *skeleton in the closet* is reputedly based on an earlier legend that tells of a search for a truly happy person, one free from cares and woes. After such a person had apparently been found, she opened a closet and exposed a human skeleton. "I try to keep my troubles to myself," she explained, "but every night my husband compels me to kiss that skeleton." The skeleton, it seems, was that of a former paramour whom her husband had killed.

> Some particulars regarding the Newcome family . . . will show us that they have a skeleton or two in their closets. (William Thackeray, *The Newcomes,* 1855)

A British variation is *skeleton in the cupboard.*

sub rosa Under the rose—in secret, privately, confidentially. Attempts have been made to trace the origin of this phrase to classical times; however, the *OED* states that it has Germanic origins. In Germany, and later in England and Holland, it was a common practice to paint or sculpture roses on the ceilings of banquet halls. The rose was a symbol reminding the revelers to watch their words. The phrase appeared in print by the mid-16th century. The English version *under the rose* is also heard.

> Being all under the Rose they had privilege to speak all things with freedom. (James Howell, *Parables Reflecting Upon the Times,* 1643)

under one's hat Secret, private, confidential; between you, me, and the lamppost; usually *to keep something under one's hat.*

> I'd be very grateful . . . if you'd keep the whole affair under your hat. (N. Marsh, *Dead Water,* 1963)

Although the exact origin of this expression is not known, perhaps at one time the space under a person's hat was literally used to conceal things. Use of the phrase dates from the late 19th century.

walls have ears An admonition to be discreet in speech, implying that privacy is never certain and that no one is to be trusted. The expression is often linked with the so-called *auriculaires* of the Louvre Palace, tubes within the walls by means of which Catherine de Médicis reputedly learned of state secrets. There is no evidence, however, that the phrase actually owes its origin to these contrivances. A similar concept and personification appeared contemporaneously in Heywood's *Proverbs* (1562):

> Fields have eyes and woods have ears.

SELF-DISPARAGEMENT

carry coals To be put upon; to submit to degradation or humiliation; to put up with insults; also *bear coals*. This expression, which dates from 1522, refers to those servants considered the lowest of the low in any household, i.e., the coal and wood carriers, due to the dirty nature of their work. Shakespeare used the phrase in *Romeo and Juliet*:

> Gregory, on my word, we'll not carry coals. (I,i)

cry stinking fish To badmouth oneself, to belittle or disparage one's own efforts or character, to put oneself down; to cause others to think ill of oneself. *To cry* means 'to sell by outcry,' 'to offer for sale by auction,' or 'to announce' (*OED*). Obviously one who wishes to sell fish will not say it stinks. Crying "stinking fish" is self-defeating, and—inasmuch as what one sells is a reflection of oneself—self-deprecating as well. This picturesque expression has been in use since the mid-1600s.

dig one's own grave To bring about one's own downfall, to be the instrument of one's own destruction.

Of course any *apologia* is necessarily a whine to some extent; a man digs his own grave and should, presumably, lie in it. (F. Scott Fitzgerald, *Letters,* 1934)

hide one's light under a bushel To conceal or obscure one's talents and abilities, to be excessively modest or unassuming about one's gifts, to be self-effacing. The allusion is Biblical; in his Sermon on the Mount, Jesus urges his followers to let others benefit from their good qualities:

> Neither do men light a candle, and put it under a bushel, but on a candlestick; and it giveth light to all that are in the house. Let your light so shine before men, that they may see your good works, and glorify your Father which is in heaven. (Matthew 5:15–16)

Bushel in this expression indicates a vessel or container of this capacity and not the measure itself.

stand in one's own light To injure one's reputation through brazen conduct; to damage one's prospects for success through improper behavior. This self-evident expression is infrequently heard today.

> Take a fool's counsel, and do not stand in your own light. (Ben Johnson, *A Tale of a Tub,* 1633)

take eggs for money To allow another to take unfair advantage of oneself; to let oneself be cheated or imposed upon. The expression appears in Shakespeare's *The Winter's Tale:*

> Mine honest friend
> Will you take eggs for money? (I,ii)

This expression stems from the fact that eggs were once so plentiful and cheap that they were virtually worthless.

SELF-EFFACEMENT (See **SELF-DISPARAGEMENT**.)

SELF-PITY

crying towel An imaginary towel offered to the kind of person who chronically complains about ill fortune, minor defeats, or other adversities. The phrase can be used teasingly or judgmentally, implying that one who needs a "crying towel" is unnecessarily wallowing in self-pity.

cry in one's beer To overindulge in self-pity; to be inappropriately sentimental or maudlin; to feel sorry for oneself. This expression probably derives from the fact that many people tend to become sentimental, even teary-eyed, after a few drinks. The result of such self-indulgence is often sloppy behavior and a loose tongue.

cry on [someone's] shoulder To reveal one's problems to another person in order to get sympathy; to assail someone's ear with one's woes in an attempt to win pity or to get moral support. Although the image is of a distraught person literally crying in another person's arms, the expression is usually used hyperbolically and sometimes with a sarcastic edge undercutting the seriousness or gravity of the situation.

eat one's heart To suffer inconsolably; to have sorrow or longing dominate one's thoughts and feelings; to be in a constant state of mental and emotional disquietude. Spenser used this expression in *The Fairie Queene* (1596):

He could not rest; but did his stout heart eat.

More common today is the expression *eat one's heart out*. It is often heard as a playfully sarcastic command, very different in tone from the earlier serious version of the expression.

sob story See SENTIMENTALITY.

SELF-RELIANCE (See also INDEPENDENCE.)

carry a message to Garcia To accomplish one's assigned task in an independent, resourceful, self-sufficient manner; to do one's job without making a fuss. This Americanism alludes to Elbert Hubbard's article "A Message to Garcia," written during the Spanish-American War. The piece addressed itself to the inability of most people to act without quibbling and procrastinating, citing Major Andrew S. Rowan of the U.S. Army as an exemplary model for his behavior in carrying out the order to find and deliver a message to the Cuban General Garcia. The expression was popular in the early part of this century but is now less frequently heard.

What you have to do, young man, is to carry a message to Garcia. That's your task. You go back to the Research Laboratory and do it! (*American Mercury,* July, 1924)

A common variant is *take a message to Garcia.*

cottage industry A business which is partly or wholly carried out in the home, often based upon the family unit as a labor force. The connection between *cottage* and home and family is self-evident.

For generations now the sewing of gloves has been conducted largely as a cottage industry. (B. Ellis, *Gloves,* 1921)

every tub must stand on its own bottom Every man for himself, everyone must take care of himself, everyone must paddle his own canoe; sometimes *every tub on its own black bottom.* The *tub* of this expression may mean a vat or cask, or a slow, clumsy ship. *Bottom* may mean either the underside of a barrel or cask or of a ship. Depending on which of these alternative senses one chooses, a case can be made for either a nautical or a more general origin for this phrase. Either way the expression is said to have first become popular among southern Blacks before being adopted and reassigned by Black jazzmen to describe complete improvisation. The phrase dates from the early 18th century. Another similar expression is *to stand on one's own bottom* 'to be independent, to act on one's own or for oneself,' dating from the early 17th century.

hoe one's own row To make one's own way, to do one's own work, to be independent, to take care of oneself. This self-evident American expression dates from the first half of the 19th century.

> Our American pretender must, to adopt an agricultural phrase, "hoe his own row," . . . without the aid of protectors or dependents. (*The Knickerbocker,* 1841)

paddle one's own canoe To shift for oneself, to be self-reliant, to handle one's own affairs, to manage independently. This expression, which dates from at least 1828, appeared in a bit of doggerel published in *Harper's Magazine* in May, 1854. The first stanza was as follows:

> Voyager upon life's sea,
> To yourself be true,
> And, whate'er your lot may be,
> Paddle your own canoe.

It is sometimes facetiously rendered as *Pas de lieu Rhône que nous,* in macaronic French.

pull oneself up by one's own boot straps To better oneself by one's own efforts and resources; to improve one's status without outside help; to start at the bottom and work one's way up. A bootstrap is a loop sewn on the side of a boot to help in pulling it on. The expression is a jocular reference to the impossibility of hoisting oneself into the air, even by dint of the mightiest effort.

> I had no money, I could have got some by writing to my family, of course, but it had to be the bootstraps or nothing. (Doris Lessing, *In Pursuit of English,* 1960)

Also current are the variants *lift* or *raise oneself up by one's own bootstraps.*

> A poet who lifted himself by his own boot-straps from an obscure versifier to the ranks of real poetry. (Kunitz and Haycraft, *British Authors of the 19th Century,* 1922)

scratch for oneself To take care of oneself, to be self-reliant; to look out for one's own best interests. This American colloquialism appeared in print by the mid-19th century.

> Shaking off the other child, [she] told him to scratch for hisself a time, while she began to prepare the supper. (Alice Cary, *Married, not Mated,* 1856)

Scratch for oneself is infrequently heard today.

SELF-RESTRAINT (See **COMPOSURE.**)

SENSATIONALISM

blood and thunder Melodrama, sensationalism. Of U. S. origin, the expression capsulizes the stock terror-inducing devices and stage effects common to works of the genre.

> Mrs. Bill, left to herself, resumed reading a blood and thunder romance. (*Quinland,* 1857)

penny dreadful A cheap, sensational novel of adventure, crime, violence, or sex; a trashy, pornographic, or blood-and-guts magazine or newspaper. This British colloquialism is aptly defined by James Hotten in *The Dictionary of Modern Slang, Cant, and Vulgar Words* (1873):

> Those penny publications which depend more upon sensationalism than upon merit, artistic or literary, for success.

Although such writings no longer cost a penny, the expression persists. A collection of penny dreadfuls is sometimes sold in books nicknamed *shilling shockers.* A more modern American variation is *dime novel,* though even this expression has been dated by inflation.

yellow journalism Media coverage that concentrates on the gory and gruesome, blatantly appealing to the public's basest curiosities; flagrant bias and distortion in presenting the news, so as to attract purchasers or otherwise achieve personal gain for the publisher. Many employ the term rather loosely today in disparaging reference to any reporting they consider unfair or "nonobjective." Though the expression gained popularity during the era of muckraking, much of which was attributed to the Hearst syndicate, its origin is rather innocuous, deriving from an early experiment in color printing on newsprint. In 1895 *The New York World* published an edition containing a cartoon of a child in a yellow dress, captioned "The Yellow Kid." Such a novelty was naturally designed to attract buyers, but it was a far cry from tabloids catering to the market for mutilation and perversion—today's "yellow journalism."

SENSE

rhyme or reason Sense, justification, explanation, cause, motivation; reasonableness, reason. The *rhyme* of the phrase remains as a superfluous alliterative element, providing added emphasis. Apparently it originally referred to amusement or entertainment, since works written in verse were considered aimed toward those ends; the *reason* of the phrase meant instruction or enlightenment, the supposed province of prose. Today the words usually appear in negative structures or contexts denoting their absence: *without rhyme or reason, neither rhyme nor reason, what possible rhyme or reason?* The expression was used in this sense of 'reasonableness' only as early as 1664 by Henry More:

> Against all the laws of prophetic interpretation, nay indeed against all rhyme and reason. *(Mystery of Iniquity)*

An anecdote frequently recounted about Sir Thomas More, however, indicates that the phrase may have been in common parlance by the 15th century. A budding author, on requesting the learned man's opinion of a work, was told to convert it to rhyme. Having done so, he submitted it to Sir Thomas' judgment once again, upon which the scholarly wit devastatingly remarked, "That will do. 'Tis rhyme now, anyway, whereas before 'twas neither rhyme nor reason."

SENSITIVITY

close to the bone Deep; near to the heart; to the quick; close to home; also *near to the bone.* The deeper a physical wound, the closer it is to the bone. The phrase is usually used figuratively of mental or emotional sensation.

to the quick Where one is most sensitive and vulnerable; to the very heart or core; deeply; often *cut to the quick.* In this phrase *the quick* means 'the tender, sensitive flesh of the body, particularly that under the nails.' The expression dates both in literal and figurative usage from the 1520s, but is commonly used today to denote extreme mental or emotional pain.

SENTIMENTALITY

bleeding heart A person of excessive and emotive compassion; one of undue sentimentality, whose heart strings quiver at the slightest provocation. This figurative phrase is of relatively recent origin:

> You want to think straight, Victor. You want to control this bleeding-heart trouble of yours. (J. Bingham, *Murder Plan Six,* 1958)

hearts and flowers An expression or display of cloying sentimentality intended to elicit sympathy; sob stuff, excessive sentimentalism or mushiness; maudlinism. This American slang phrase was originally the title of a mawkishly sad, popular song of 1910.

> I believed all the hearts and flowers you gave me about being in love with your husband . . . (J. Evans, *Halo,* 1949)

one for the Gipper See EXHORTATION.

sob story A very gloomy story; a sad tale designed to elicit the compassion and sympathy of the listener; a tear-jerker. This common, self-explanatory expression often applies to an alibi or excuse. It also frequently describes the narrative recounting of the trials, frustrations, and disappointments of one's life.

How anyone could heed such a sob story is beyond me. (*Los Angeles Times,* June, 1949)

tear-jerker A book, play, or motion picture designed to induce gloominess or weeping, a sob story; a speaker or performer who is able to obtain the audience's compassion and sympathy. This common expression describes a work which dwells excessively on inconsolable grief, grave disappointment, tragic frustration, or excessive sentimentality.

William A. Brady in 1901 decided that New York's sophisticates would like to see the old tear-jerker [the play *Uncle Tom's Cabin*] with an all-star cast. (H. R. Hoyt, *Town Hall Tonight,* 1955)

SERENITY (See PEACE.)

SEXUAL ORIENTATION

AC/DC Bisexual; capable of being sexually aroused and satisfied by either sex. This slang term was coined by analogy to an electrical appliance which operates on either alternating current (AC) or direct current (DC). The phrase is often used non-judgmentally and appears to be losing even its slang stigma. Webster's *6,000 Words* (1976) cites R. H. Kuh:

. . . help the A.C./D.C. youngster to shape his actions in a heterosexual direction.

camp or **campy** See AFFECTATION.

kinky Perverse, deviant, or aberrant; sexually eccentric or depraved. This term's sexual sense, derived from *kink* 'flaw, abnormality,' enjoys widespread, contemporary use in the United States. Its antonym is *straight.*

In a moment of excessively kinky passion a husband strangles his mistress. (*Daily Telegraph,* July, 1971)

peeping Tom A voyeur; one who achieves sexual gratification through clandestine observation of sexual activity. This expression is named for the 11th-century peeping Tom of Coventry, a tailor who, when he peeked at Lady Godiva as she rode naked through town in protest of increased taxes, was purportedly struck blind. The evolution of the expression's current voyeuristic application is apparent.

switch hitter A bisexual. This recent American slang expression uses baseball terminology for a player who can bat from either side of the plate.

SHABBINESS

dog-eared Folded over or down, as the corner of a page in a book; used, worn, shabby. The term obviously derives from the fact that such a flap resembles a dog's ear. Since a book with many such pages has been read and acquired a shabby appearance in the process, the word *dog-eared* takes on its secondary 'used, worn' meaning.

down-at-the-heel See POVERTY.

like a dog's breakfast Sloppy, messy, disheveled, unkempt; showing little taste or style. This British colloquial expression means the opposite of *like a dog's dinner.* Why a canine's breakfast is associated with sloppiness and a canine's dinner with neatness and style is left unexplained.

SHREWDNESS (See also ALERTNESS, PERCEPTIVENESS.)

know what's o'clock To be cognizant of the true state of affairs, to know what's up; to be on the ball.

Our governor's wide awake . . . He knows what's o'clock. (Dickens, *Sketches by Boz,* 1836)

This expression is rarely heard in the United States, where the analogous negative is a familiar expression of ignorance: "He doesn't even know what time it is."

know which way the wind blows To be shrewdly aware of the true state of affairs; to have an intuitive sense of what will probably happen. The origin of this expression may have been nautical. One must know which way the wind blows in order to navigate a vessel. Variants of this expression appeared in print as early as the 15th century. Today it is used figuratively to indicate a commonsensical awareness of outside influences at work.

Philadelphia lawyer A shrewd, sharp lawyer well-acquainted with the intricacies and subtleties of the law; a very clever lawyer who uses his knowledge of legal technicalities and fine points to his advantage; a shyster. The reference is apparently to Alexander Hamilton, a former attorney general in Philadelphia. In a case of criminal libel in 1735, he obtained an acquittal for John Peter Zenger, the publisher of the *New York Weekly Journal*, in the face of what seemed to be irrefutable evidence. The decision established the principle of freedom of the press in America. Use of the term dates from the late 18th century.

> The new violation ticket will be in quadruplicate, and traffic officials say it takes a "Philadelphia lawyer" to fix it. (*The Daily Times* [Chicago], November, 1947)

sly-boots A cunning, sly, or wily person, especially one who gives the impression of being slow-witted. In this expression, *boots* probably refers to a servant, stereotypically a dullard, who polishes boots and shoes. Thus, a sly-boots is one who appears to be a dolt but who is actually shrewd and alert.

> That sly-boots was cursedly cunning to hide 'em. (Oliver Goldsmith, *Retaliation, A Poem*, 1774)

A variation is *sly as old boots*.

smart as a whip Extremely bright, alert, witty, or clever; very intelligent; sharp or keen. This commonly used expression may have originated as a humorous twist on *smart* 'sharp pain,' such as that caused by a whip.

> [He] was a prompt and successful business man, "smart as a whip," as the Yankees say. (*Mountaineer* [Salt Lake City, Utah], March 24, 1860)

too far north Too clever or shrewd, smart or knowing, extremely canny.

> It shan't avail you, you shall find me too far north for you. (Tobias Smollett, *The Adventures of Roderick Random*, 1748)

This British slang expression is an allusion to the reputed shrewdness of the inhabitants of northern counties such as Yorkshire and Aberdeen.

SILENCE (See also SECRECY.)

have an ox on the tongue See BRIBERY.

lose one's tongue To lose temporarily the power of speech, to be struck dumb. Such speechlessness is usually attributed to emotions such as shyness, fear, or surprise.

pipe down To become quiet or mute; to cease talking. In this expression, *pipe* may carry any of its numerous sound-related meanings, ranging from a shrill noise to the vocal cords themselves. In contemporary usage, the phrase is most often imperative.

> "Pipe down," replied the husband. "What do you expect for a $10 paint job, grand opera?" (*Kansas City Star*, March, 1932)

see a wolf To temporarily lose one's voice, to become tongue-tied. The phrase expresses the old belief that if a man saw a wolf before the wolf saw him, the man would temporarily lose the power of speech. The expression dates from the late 16th century.

> Our young companion has seen a wolf, . . . and has lost his tongue in

consequence. (Sir Walter Scott, *Quentin Durward,* 1823)

SIMILARITY (See also **EQUIVA-LENCE.**)

chip off the old block A son who resembles his father in appearance or behavior. The expression is reputed to have been coined by Edmund Burke (1729–97) addressing the British House of Commons, speaking in reference to Pitt the Younger. However, a citation from the *OED* dates a similar phrase from the early 17th century.

Am not I a child of the same Adam
. . . a chip of the same block, with
him? (bp. Robert Sanderson,
Sermons, 1627)

Chip off the old block is the modern form of the phrase; *chip of the old* or *same block* is the original. The allusion is obvious. A chip has the same characteristics as the block from which it comes. Any connection with "family tree" is amusing but doubtful.

copycat An imitator; one who copies another's style or work. The term has been in use since the turn of the century.

A good architect was not a
"copy-cat;" nor did he kick over
the traces. (*Oxford Times,* April 24,
1931)

Copycat is occasionally used as a verb meaning 'to imitate.'

follow in the footsteps To emulate; to follow the example or guidance of another; to imitate the performance of a predecessor. The implication here is that in order to be like a respected and admired person, one must follow his example, that is, follow in the figurative footsteps he took along his pathway to success.

You are obliged to follow the
footsteps of your predecessors in
virtue. (*Complaint of Scotland,*
1549)

A variation is *walk in the footsteps.* A similar expression dealing figuratively with the feet of a revered person is *big*

or *large shoes to fill,* implying that substantial effort will be required to meet the standards established by a predecessor.

follow suit To imitate or emulate; to act in the same manner as one's predecessor. This term is rooted in card games such as bridge or setback where rules dictate that, if possible, a participant must follow suit, that is, play a card of the same suit as that which was led.

get on the bandwagon To support a particular candidate or cause, usually when success seems assured and no great risk is entailed; often *climb aboard the bandwagon.* In the era of political barnstorming, bandwagons carried the parade musicians. Theory has it that as candidate-carrying wagons moved through a district, local politicos would literally jump aboard those of favorite candidates, thus publicly endorsing them. The figurative use of *bandwagon* dates from the early 1900s:

Many of those Democrats . . . who
rushed onto the Bryan band-wagon
. . . will now be seen crawling over
the tailboard. (*New York Evening
Post,* September 4, 1906)

Though still most commonly associated with politics, *bandwagon* is used in other contexts as well:

The next serious outbreak was a
three-cornered affair between the
gangs of Joe Saltis (who had
recently hopped on the Capone
band-wagon) and "Dingbat"
O'Berta. (Arthur B. Reeve, *The
Golden Age of Crime,* 1931)

a man of my kidney A person whose character and disposition are similar to one's own. In this expression, *kidney* carries its figurative meaning of nature, temperament, or constitution. The phrase appeared in Shakespeare's *Merry Wives of Windsor:*

Think of that, a man of my kidney;
. . . that is as subject to heat as
butter. (III,v)

This figurative use of *kidney* sometimes refers to kind or type of person.

It was a large and rather miscellaneous party, but all of the right kidney. (Benjamin Disraeli, *Endymion*, 1880)

play the ape To imitate, to copy someone's style, to counterfeit. This expression alludes to the way apes mimic the expressions and gestures of human beings. It appeared in print by the 1500s. Robert Louis Stevenson popularized the expression in his *Memories and Portraits* (1882):

> I have played the sedulous ape to Hazlitt, to Lamb, to Wordsworth, to Sir Thomas Browne. . . . That, like it or not, is the way to learn to write.

ringer See PRETENSE.

spit and image The exact likeness, image, or counterpart; a duplicate, a double; a chip off the old block. This expression implies that two people are so much alike (usually in appearance) that figuratively, at least, one could conceivably have been spit from the mouth of the other, an interesting concept especially in light of recent breakthroughs in the fields of genetics and cloning. Since an earlier expression was *the very spit, image* serves to emphasize the similarity in appearance.

> She's like the poor lady that's dead and gone, the spit an' image she is. (Egerton Castle, *The Light of Scartney*, 1895)

Variations are *spitting image* and *spitten image*.

take a page out of [someone's] book To follow another's example, to copy or imitate someone else; also *to take a leaf out of [someone's] book*. The allusion is to literary plagiarism, but the expression is now employed in a positive sense only.

> It is a great pity that some of our instructors in more important matters . . . will not take a leaf out of the same book. (Thomas Hughes, *Tom Brown at Oxford*, 1861)

tarred with the same brush All having the same shortcomings; each as guilty as the next. This expression derives from the practice of marking all sheep of the same flock with a common mark made by a brush dipped in tar. Some say the mark was for identification only; others claim it was to protect the sheep against ticks, or to treat sores. A variant of this expression is *painted with the same brush*. These expressions usually imply that what distinguishes a given group of individuals is their shared guilt or their similar negative characteristics.

Tweedledum and Tweedledee So similar as to be indistinguishable or undifferentiated. Though the names were popularized by the well-known pair in Lewis Carroll's *Through the Looking-Glass* (1871), the terms were coined in 1725 by John Byrom, who used them in a satirical poem about quarreling musicians. In doing so, he was obviously playing on the meaning of *tweedle* 'to produce shrill musical sounds.'

> Strange all this Difference should be,
> Twixt Tweedle-dum and Tweedle-dee!
> *(Handel and Bononcini)*

Even before Carroll's fictional creations were so christened, the terms were used figuratively in contexts concerning insignificant differences, petty squabbles, nitpicking arguments, etc., such as the following later application:

> A . . . war of words over tweedledees of subtle doctrinal differences and tweedledums of Church polity. (*Church Endeavor Times*, August, 1911)

SIMPLIFICATION

black and white One extreme or its opposite with no in-between possibilities, such as right or wrong, good or bad, etc.; absolute, inflexible, close-minded. The colors black and white, considered without all the shades of gray in between, represent a simplified and necessarily limited point of view that fails to see things in their full complexity. The phrase is commonly used to describe people's attitudes and opinions.

chew it finer To simplify; to put into simple, clear, unambiguous terms. Apparently the phrase, rarely heard today, was popular among American cowboys. The likelihood is that it stemmed from their practice of tobacco-chewing.

copybook Commonplace, conventional, unoriginal, stereotyped; platitudinous. To learn penmanship, students used to imitate specimen entries from copybooks. Today *copybook* is used adjectivally to describe complex subjects which are treated superficially and thus take on the triteness characteristic of the maxims used as specimens in old copybooks.

> Well provided with stores of copy-book morality. (George Lloyd, *Ebb and Flow*, 1883)

As used above, this term dates from the mid-19th century.

cracker-barrel Simple, direct, homespun; often in the expression *cracker-barrel philosophy*. This Americanism refers to the practice of local countryfolk gathering around a cracker barrel in country stores to discuss everything from crops and the weather to the political issues of the day.

> Politics, rum, riches, and religion— these were the favorite topics of American cracker-barrel debaters. (J. T. Flynn, *God's Gold*, 1933)

cut and dried All set, readily solved, having no loose ends or puzzling complexities; perfunctory, lacking spontaneity, boring, run-of-the-mill. This phrase, in use since the early 18th century, originally referred to those herbs sold in herbalists' shops; these were prepared ahead of time and thus lacked the freshness of growing herbs, newly picked.

SINCERITY (See also **CANDIDNESS**.)

in one's heart of heart In the deepest, innermost recesses of one's heart; in one's most private and pure thoughts or feelings. The first *heart* in this expression means 'core' and the second *heart* means 'seat of feeling, understanding, and thought.' Although the corrupted *heart of hearts* is frequently heard, the original expression as it appeared in *Hamlet* is *heart of heart*.

> Give me that man
> That is not passion's slave, and I will wear him
> In my heart's core—aye, in my heart of heart,
> As I do thee. (III,ii)

Today this expression is used to assure the veracity or sincerity of any statement of belief.

> In his heart of heart Froude would have admitted that. (*Quarterly Review*, October, 1895)

SIZE (See **PHYSICAL STATURE**.)

SKEPTICISM

doubting Thomas A skeptic, a doubter or disbeliever; one who believes only on the basis of firsthand proof or physical evidence. The original doubting Thomas was the apostle Thomas, who refused to believe that Christ had risen from the dead after His crucifixion until he saw Him for himself.

> But Thomas, one of the twelve, called Didymus, was not with them when Jesus came. The other disciples therefore said unto him, We have seen the Lord. But he said unto them, Except I shall see in his hands the print of the nails, and put my finger into the print of the nails, and put my hand into his side, I will not believe. (John 20:24-25)

from Missouri Skeptical, doubting, suspicious; unwilling to accept something as true without proof. Original use of the phrase *I'm from Missouri; you've got to show me* is generally attributed to Congressman Willard D. Vandiver of Missouri in a speech delivered to the Five O'Clock Club of Philadelphia in 1899. However, others have claimed that the expression was commonly known in parts of the country long before the Congressman popularized it by employing it in this speech.

tell it to the marines An expression of disbelief or skepticism, said in response to a tall tale, a fish story, or any far-fetched account. This originally British expression dates from the early 19th century. There are two popular explanations for its origin, one reflecting positively, the other negatively, upon the British Royal Marines. The more involved story is that Charles II said in response to a naval officer's claim that he had seen flying fish, "Go, tell that to the Marines." When accused of insulting the reputation of the Marines, Charles II responded that no slur was intended. To the contrary, he claimed that he would believe the story if the well-traveled and experienced Marines believed it. The second explanation, simple and more plausible, is that the Marines were proverbially gullible and would swallow any yarn. An analogous American slang expression is *tell it to Sweeney.*

with a grain of salt With skepticism; with reservations. This expression is based on the idea that a pinch of salt may make palatable something otherwise hard to swallow. Furthermore, Pompey (106–48 B.C.), a member of the first Roman triumvirate, once advocated the use of a grain of salt as an antidote against poison. One source suggests that the minuscule grain of salt may represent the amount of truth in a given statement, assurance, or other matter which has been accepted "with a grain of salt." The expression occurs in many western European languages, usually in its Latin form, *cum grano salis.*

SLANDER

hatchet man See CRIMINALITY.

mud-slinging The use of slander, calumny, or malicious gossip to publicly denigrate a person's character or ability. In its most common usage, *mud-slinging* (or *mud-throwing*) refers to the vituperative claims, counter-claims, and accusations which may be employed by one or more candidates in a vicious, no-holds-barred political campaign. The rationale for such tactics is well-stated in the proverbial statement, "If you throw enough dirt, some is sure to stick."

> This sweeping provision, if constitutional and enforceable, would have the effect of eliminating "mud-slinging" in political campaigns, perhaps indeed of revolutionizing campaign methods entirely. (*National Municipal Review,* 1914)

Mud-slinging is used in various other contexts, most of which involve slanderous comments made about a person who is in the public eye.

> A woman in my position must expect to have more mud thrown at her than a less important person. (Florence Marryat, *Under the Lilies and Roses,* 1884)

SLEEP

drive one's pigs to market To snore loudly, to log ZZZs. The allusion is probably to the snorting noises of swine being herded to market. This expression is apparently an elaboration of the phrase *to drive pigs* 'to snore,' dating from the early 19th century.

forty winks A brief nap; a short period of relaxation. This expression, clearly derived from the closed-eye position assumed during sleep, nevertheless implies that the resting person will not fall sound asleep. It is reputed that the first literary use of the phrase appeared in the November 16, 1872, issue of *Punch,* in which the writer surmised that the reading of the Thirty-nine Articles of faith by the communicants of the Anglican Church was indeed a somniferous ordeal:

> If a . . . man, after reading steadily through the Thirty-nine Articles, were to take forty winks. . . .

hit the deck See EXCLAMATIONS.

hit the sack To go to bed; to retire for the night; also, *hit the hay.* During World War II, *sack* was substituted for "bed" among American soldiers as an allusion to the sleeping bags or blankets they used as beds. J. J. Fahey used the expression in *Pacific War Diary* (1943):

> I hit the sack at 8 P.M. I slept under the stars on a steel ammunition box two feet wide.

Variations of the phrase include *sack time, sack drill,* and *sack duty,* all military slang for time spent asleep; *sack artist,* a soldier who is adept at obtaining extra sleep; and *sack out,* a common term for sleeping until fully refreshed.

in the arms of Morpheus In deep sleep; overcome with the desire to sleep. In Greek mythology Morpheus was the god of dreams. The narcotic morphine, which dulls pain and induces sleep, gets its name from the same deity.

in the Land of Nod Asleep; in dreamland. After Cain killed Abel, he was banished to wander in the Land of Nod (Genesis 4:16). *Land of Nod* did not mean sleep until Swift made a pun on the Biblical phrase in his *Complete Collection of Genteel and Ingenious Conversation* (1730). Today *Nod* retains the meaning of sleep.

> In the nighttime, when human beings . . . are absent in the Land of Nod. (Chambers, *Journal of Popular Literature,* 1900)

saw wood To sleep soundly; to snore. This expression came into popular use in the early 20th century primarily as a result of the commonly employed cartoonist's technique of representing sleep with a drawing of a saw cutting through wood, alluding, of course, to the sound of snoring.

shut-eye Sleep. A 20th-century American colloquialism.

> That shut-eye done me good. (Boyd Cable, *Old Contempt,* 1919)

sleep like a top To sleep soundly, like a log; to be dead to the world. The rationale for the seemingly anomalous reference to a top is explained by Anne Baker in *Glossary of Northhamptonshire Words and Phrases* (1854):

> A top sleeps when it moves with such velocity, and spins so smoothly, that its motion is imperceptible.

Likewise, when a Yo-Yo spins swiftly at the end of its string, it is said to "sleep," without apparent motion. By extension, then, though a person in a deep, peaceful sleep may seem totally motionless, his internal systems are actually working at a high level of efficiency.

> Juan slept like a top, or like the dead. (George Gordon, Lord Byron, *Don Juan,* 1819)

SLOVENLINESS (See **SHABBINESS.**)

SNOBBERY (See **HAUGHTINESS.**)

SOLICITATION

dun To badger someone to pay a debt; to importune for payment of a bill; to make repeated and insistent demands; to pester or assail relentlessly. Another term of uncertain origin, *dun* dates from the 1600s. Tradition has it that a man named Joe Dun, a London bailiff in the reign of Henry VII, was so successful in collecting bad debts that his name became synonymous with the practice of pursuing someone to deliver payment. *Dun* can also be used in nonfinancial contexts meaning to harass, badger, or plague. Another version offers that the word is cognate with *din* and acquired its metaphoric sense from the raising of a great to-do until the debtor paid up.

> I am so dun'd with the Spleen, I should think on something else all the while I were a playing. (*Shuffling, Cutting, and Dealing,* 1659)

fry the fat out of See EXTORTION.

panhandle To accost strangers on the street and beg money from them. Literally, a panhandle is the handle of a pan. Since the arm and hand project from the body somewhat like a handle from a pan, the act of holding one's hand out to solicit money came to be known as *panhandling*. Similarly, one who employs such techniques is known as a *panhandler*.

> The prisoners were members of a "panhandling" corporation which operated extensively throughout the district. (*New York Evening Post*, December 9, 1903)

pass the hat To solicit money, as for a charity; to take up a collection. It has long been the custom among minstrels and other street performers to collect contributions from the spectators by passing around a hat. In contemporary usage, *hat* has often become figurative, referring to any container into which people in a group or crowd are expected to put money. In fact, *pass the hat* is no longer limited to its original concept, i.e., voluntary payment for entertainment, and usually carries somewhat resentful or contemptuous implications, probably because of the subtle coercion involved.

> It was easy enough to make the hat go round, but the difficulty was to get any one to put anything in it. (Charles J. Matthews, in *Daily News*, September 11, 1878)

put the acid on To pressure someone for a loan; to place excessive demands on someone; to coerce someone into granting a favor. This expression alludes to the destructive potential as well as the sharp, bitter taste of an acidic solution. Although the expression's money-borrowing sense originated and is still used in Australia and New Zealand, the phrase is now applied in the United States and Great Britain to any situation in which an inappropriate amount of pressure is being exerted.

> They want to shift the ship at seven. That puts the acid on us. (J. Morrison, in *Coast to Coast*, 1947)

put the bite on See EXTORTION.

work the oracle See MANIPULATION.

SOLUTION

cut the Gordian knot To resolve a situation or solve a problem by force or evasive action; to take action quickly, decisively, and boldly.

> Turn him to any cause of policy,
> The Gordian knot of it he will unloose.
> (Shakespeare, *Henry V*, I,i)

According to Greek legend, Phrygia (now part of Turkey) was in need of a leader to end its political and economic woes. The local oracle foretold that a man fit to be king would enter the city in a cart. Shortly thereafter, Gordius, a peasant, rode into town in an ox-cart which was connected to the yoke by an intricate knot made of bark. After being proclaimed king, Gordius dedicated the cart to Zeus, whereupon the oracle predicted that whoever was able to undo the knot would rule over all of Asia. In 333 B.C., Alexander the Great reputedly entered the temple and cut the knot with his sword, thus fulfilling the prophecy. The expression *cut the knot* is a variation.

deus ex machina See RESCUE.

a hair of the dog that bit you See FOOD and DRINK.

hammer out To work out laboriously or with much intellectual effort; to figure out, to settle, to resolve. This verb phrase usually appears in a context implying that opposing and conflicting forces have resolved differences or tensions. The term was clearly coined as the figurative extension of the literal pounding and hammering of a blacksmith as he shapes metal objects.

just what the doctor ordered Something desirable or restorative. A product of our health- and medicine-conscious culture, this expression is said of anything—a person, a substance, an idea—which has a soothing, palliative, make-it-all-better effect.

> The waiter brought her a drink. "Just what the doctor ordered," she said, smiling at him. (Gore Vidal, *City and Pillar*, 1948)

open sesame Any agency through which a desired result is realized; the key to a mystery or other perplexing situation; any real or magic act that brings about wanted fame, acceptance, etc. This saying comes from *The Arabian Nights* (1785) where it was used by Ali Baba as the password to open up the door of a robber's hideaway.

> Ali Baba . . . perceiving the door, . . . said—"Open, sesame."

The expression was perhaps derived homonymously from *open-says-me.*

> Thy name shall be a Sesame, at which the doors of the great shall fly open. (Charles Calverley, *Verses and Translations*, 1862)

pull out of a hat To come up unexpectedly with a response or solution, often in the nick of time, when all else has failed. This expression appeared in print during the mid-1900s. It alludes to the magician's trick of pulling a rabbit out of a hat.

> I must say you've really pulled one out of the hat this time. (J. McClune, *Steam Pig*, 1971)

Rosetta stone The agency through which a puzzle is solved; something that provides the initial step in the understanding of a previously incomprehensible design or situation. The Rosetta stone, discovered in 1799 by the French engineer M. Boussard, is an ancient basalt table which bears inscriptions in two languages—Egyptian and Greek—and three alphabets—hieroglyphic, demotic (a cursive type of Egyptian hieroglyphics), and Greek. This archaeological windfall furnished the key to translating the hitherto indecipherable Egyptian hieroglyphics. The expression's current figurative use as a reference to the first clue in unraveling a mystery was illustrated by Ellsworth Ferris, as cited in *Webster's Third:*

> This book can be its own Rosetta stone and it is an interesting game to try to ferret out meanings by comparing passages till the puzzle is solved.

SPEEDING (See also **INSTANTANEOUSNESS, PACE.**)

ball the jack To travel at full speed; to go or act quickly; to stake everything on one attempt. In railroad terminology *ball* is a truncated form of *highball*, a railroad signal for a jack, or locomotive, to accelerate to full speed. The word derives from the signal itself—a raised pole with a metal ball attached to it. *Ball the jack* is a slang phrase now used to apply to swift action of any type. Perhaps the secondary meaning of staking everything on one attempt is related to the opening of the engine's throttle to reach maximum speed. Both are all-out, all-or-nothing, no-holds-barred efforts. "Ballin' the jack" is also the name of a dance and the title of a song by Chris Smith and Jim Burris, both of which were popular in the early 1900s.

burn up the road To drive or move extremely fast; to go at full speed; also *to burn the breeze* (primarily Southwestern use) or *earth* or *wind*. *To burn the earth* or *wind* dates from the late 1800s, while *to burn the road* and *to burn the breeze* did not appear until the 1930s. A similar popular American slang expression is *to burn rubber*, an allusion to the screeching of automobile tires and the streaks of burned rubber left on the road due to rapid acceleration.

go two-forty To move at a rapid clip; to run, race, or tear; to bustle, hurry, or rush. In horse racing, the former trotting record for a mile was two minutes and forty seconds. Early use incorporated this time record in phrases such as *at a pace* or *rate of two-forty,* but by the turn of the century *two-forty* had taken on its current adverbial function.

> He's going it two-forty a minute. (Mary Waller, *The Wood-Carver of 'Lympus,* 1904)

hotfoot To go with great speed, to hurry, to run; also *to hotfoot it.* Although the exact origin of this chiefly U.S. expression is unknown, it may refer to the heat generated by running fast. *Hotfoot* is also the name of a practical joke which consists of inserting a match between the sole and the upper of someone's shoe, and then lighting the match. However, this use of the term dates from only the 1930s, while the other was in use as early as 1896.

> When O'Dowd did hear . . . he would hot-foot out to Quilty and make the sale. (John O'Hara, *Appointment in Samarra,* 1934)

let her rip See UNRESTRAINT.

SPITEFULNESS (See RESENTMENT.)

SPONTANEITY

off the cuff Extempore, on the spur of the moment, spontaneously, impromptu; offhandedly, informally, unofficially. The allusion is to speakers whose only preparation is notes jotted on their shirt cuffs. Of U.S. origin, this expression dates from at least 1938.

> In that scene, shot off the cuff in a shockingly bad light, there leapt out of the screen . . . something of the real human guts and dignity. (*Penguin New Writing,* 1944)

off the top of one's head Offhandedly, unofficially, informally, without notes or preparation, extemporaneously. In this expression, the top of the head represents the superficial nature of the information being given. *Webster's Third* cites Goodman Ace's use of the expression:

> Countless conferences at which everyone talked off the top of their heads.

on the spur of the moment Impulsively, impetuously; spontaneously, extemporaneously; suddenly, without deliberation. In this expression, *spur* implies speed, alluding to the sharp, U-shaped device strapped to the heel of a boot and used by a rider to prod a horse.

> A speaker who gives us a ready reply upon the spur of the moment. (Robert Blakely, *Free-will,* 1831)

wing it To undertake anything without adequate preparation, usually with connotations of bluffing one's way through. The term originated in the theater, with reference to actors who would go on stage without knowing their lines, relying on the prompters in the wings to get them through. This literal usage appears as early as 1886 in *Stage Gossip.*

STAGNATION

in a rut Stuck in an established routine; mired in monotony; caught in a stultifying sameness. This figurative use of *rut* 'deep furrow or track' has been common since the mid-19th century.

> On his return to civilized life, he will settle at once into the rut. (Sir John Skelton, *Campaigner at Home,* 1865)

Today the expression carries the contradictory connotations of comfort and discontent, with emphasis on the latter: movement in a fixed course is smooth and easy but deadening.

in the doldrums Inactive, stagnant, nonproductive; depressed, in low spirits, in the dumps, in a blue funk. *Doldrum* derives from *dol,* an obsolete form of *dull,* and is itself an obsolete slang term for a dullard. Thus, *the doldrums* refers to a condition of dullness, low spirits, or depression.

I am now in the doldrums; but
when I get better, I will send you
. . . . (*Morning Herald,* April 13,
1811)

The doldrums also often refers to the
condition of a becalmed ship. By extension, not only ships, but the economy,
politics, trade, etc., can be "in the doldrums."

At the present moment the trade
appears to be in the doldrums. (Sir
T. Sutherland, *Westminster Gazette,*
July 11, 1895)

According to the *OED,* confusion as to
whether *the doldrums* referred to a
condition or a location gave rise to its
use as the name of that specific region
of calm near the Equator where neu-
tralizing trade winds often prevent
ships from making progress.

STARTING (See also BEGINNINGS,
INITIATION, PREPARATION.)

get a move on To get going, to proceed; move speedily or efficiently. This
original U.S. expression dates from the
late 1800s.

Come on! Come on! . . . Get a
move on! Will you hurry up! (C. E.
Mulford, *Bar-20 Days,* 1911)

A more picturesque variant is the
American slang *get a wiggle on,* current
since the turn of the century. This expression plays on the image of one's
posture while running or walking
quickly, a more defined image than that
conjured up by the word *move* in the
former expression.

get cracking To get moving, to get
started on; to hustle, hurry. Although
the origin of this slang expression is unknown, it may be related to a relatively
uncommon meaning of *crack* 'to move
or travel speedily, to whip along,' which
dates from the early 19th century. The
phrase *get cracking* itself, however, appears to be of fairly recent origin.

Come on, let's get cracking, we're
late now. (S. Gibbons, *Matchmaker,*
1949)

get on the stick To get on the ball, to
get started or going, to get a move on.
Although the meaning of *stick* in the
expression is not clear, the phrase
nevertheless enjoys widespread popularity. It is often used as an imperative.

Worrying what might happen if we
didn't get on the stick pretty fast.
(Tom Findley, as quoted in
Webster's 6,000)

get the show on the road To get any
undertaking under way, but most often
to start off on a trip of some kind; to hit
the road; usually used in reference to a
group of people and their belongings.
This expression probably derives from
traveling shows, such as theatrical
troupes, circuses, etc., which regularly
toured the countryside giving performances along the way.

let her go, Gallagher! Let's go; let's get
started without delay. The "Gallagher"
to whom this advice is given may be
one or none of the legendary people
cited in various folklore explanations.
He may have been a cab driver in
Australia, a hangman in Galveston
(Texas), a warden in St. Louis, the
owner of a broken-down nag (horse)
in Texas, a street-car operator in New
Orleans, St. Louis, Chicago, Galveston,
or Camden, New Jersey; or any of an
almost endless list of folk heroes named
Gallagher. Most likely, "Gallagher" was
chosen because it is close in sound to
"let 'er go." In spite of the amorphous
nature of this "Gallagher," the expression has enjoyed international popularity for more than a hundred years.

pull one's socks up To get on the stick
or on the ball, to get a move on, to shape
up, to show more stuff. This British colloquialism apparently had the earlier
sense of bracing oneself for an effort,
probably in reference to the way runners pull up their socks before starting
off on a race. Or the expression may
simply refer to making oneself presentable in appearance.

put one's hand to the plow To undertake a task, to get down to business; to embark on a course of action.

> It was time . . . to set his hand to the plow in good earnest. (George Hickes and Robert Nelson, *Memoirs of the Life of John Kettlewell,* 1718)

The allusion is to Jesus' admonishment of a man who said he would follow Him but only after bidding his family farewell.

> And Jesus said unto him, No man, having put his hand to the plough, and looking back, is fit for the kingdom of God. (Luke 9:62)

shake a leg To get a move on, to get going, to hurry up; to dance. This expression meaning 'to dance' dates from the 17th century. Currently, the other meanings are more common.

> . . . if you shake a leg and somebody doesn't get in ahead of you . . . (John Dos Passos, cited in *Webster's Third*)

step on the gas To speed up; also, *step on it.* This expression alludes to the speeding up of a car by depressing the accelerator. The phrase enjoys widespread use in the United States and Great Britain.

> Jazz it up. Keep moving. Step on the gas. (Aldous Huxley, *Jesting Pilate,* 1926)

The phrase is often used imperatively, directing a slothful or sluggish performer to increase his pace.

stir one's stumps To get a move on, to get into action; to shake a leg. In this expression, *stumps* alludes to the legs, or to the wooden prosthetic attachment fastened to a stump or mangled limb. Use of this rather indelicate phrase has declined since the 19th century.

> Come, why don't you stir your stumps? I suppose I must wait on myself. (Baron Edward Lytton, *Ernest Maltravers,* 1837)

STARVATION (See **HUNGER.**)

STATUS (See also **SUBORDINATION.**)

above the salt Among the distinguished or honored guests at a dinner; of high rank, important; also the opposite *below the salt.* Formerly a large saltcellar, i.e., a salt shaker or mill, was customarily placed in the middle of dining tables. The higher-ranking guests were seated at the upper or master's end of the table, above the salt, while those of lesser rank were seated at the lower end of the table, below the salt. The phrase has been in use since the late 16th century.

> Though of Tory sentiments, she by no means approved of those feudal times when the chaplain was placed below the salt. (James Payn, *The Luck of the Darrells,* 1885)

blueblood An aristocrat or noble; a thoroughbred. Fair-skinned Spaniards prided themselves on their pure stock, without Moorish or Jewish admixture. Their extremely light complexions revealed a bluish cast to their veins, which they consequently believed carried blue blood, as opposed to the supposed black blood of Moors and Jews.

bluestocking See **SCHOLARLINESS.**

born in the purple Of royal or exalted birth. Purple has long been associated with royalty because of its former scarcity and consequent costliness. It was obtainable only by processing huge quantities of a certain mollusk, which was harvested at Tyre, an ancient seaport of Phoenicia, and was called Tyrian purple. *Born in the purple* is a literal translation of Porphyrogenitus, a surname of the Byzantine Emperor Constantine VII (905–959) and his successors, most accurately applied only to those born during their father's reign; it was customary for the Empress to undergo childbirth in a room whose walls were lined with purple. Today *born to the purple* is more commonly heard.

born with a silver spoon in one's mouth Born to wealth and high station. It was formerly customary for godparents to give spoons as christening gifts. The child born to wealth could anticipate a silver one from the moment of his birth.

born within the sound of Bow bells A British expression denoting a Londoner, especially of the lower classes; a native of the East End district; a Cockney. The church of St. Mary-le-Bow, so called because of the bows or arches that supported its steeple, was known for the peal of its bells, which could be heard throughout the city. The phrase has been used to denote a Cockney since the early 17th century.

brown-bagger A person of inferior status or social standing. In the United States, the term derives from the practice of the less well-to-do, such as blue-collar workers, to carry their lunches in brown paper bags. In Britain, a brown-bagger is a nonresident student at public school or university; his brown bag is the attaché case in which he carries his books. Such students are usually looked upon with a degree of disdain or condescension by those in residence.

chief cook and bottle washer See PERSONAGE.

codfish aristocracy A disparaging appellation for the nouveau riche, originally those Massachusetts aristocrats who made their money from the codfishing industry; also *the codfish gentility.* This expression, which dates from 1849, was the title of a poem written in the 1920s by American journalist Wallace Irwin. The first stanza reads as follows:

Of all the fish that swim or swish
In ocean's deep autocracy,
There's none possess such haughtiness
As the codfish aristocracy.

the Four Hundred The social elite; the wealthy, refined people generally regarded as "high society." This term dates from 1889 when Ward McAllister,

a prominent New York socialite, was given the task of deciding who should be invited to a centenary celebration of the inauguration of George Washington. His list included the names of four hundred people whom he considered to be the true elite, the *crème de la crème,* as it were. Although the list received rapid acceptance and the term *the Four Hundred* became an overnight sensation, the number was raised to eight hundred in 1904 by Mrs. William Astor, the grande dame of New York society.

To social strivers she is the Queen of the 400. (*Coronet,* August, 1948)

gallery gods Those members of a theater audience occupying the highest, and therefore the cheapest, seats; those persons sitting in the balcony or gallery of a theater. The *OED* attributes this expression to the fact that persons occupying gallery seats are on high, as are the gods. However, another source credits the painting on the ceiling over the gallery in London's Drury Lane Theatre as the inspiration for this expression. The ceiling in question is painted to resemble a cloudy blue sky peopled by numerous flying cupids. Thus, it is in reference to the cupids painted on the ceiling above their heads that persons sitting in the gallery first became known as *gods* or *gallery gods.* The term dates from the latter half of the 18th century.

gentleman of the four outs A man without manners, wit, money, or credit —the four marks of a true gentleman. This subtle expression used by Englishmen to denote an upstart has been in use at least since the late 18th century. Sometimes the expression varies according to whether the "essentials" are considered more or less than four in number.

A gentleman of three outs—"out of pocket, out of elbows, and out of credit." (Edward Lytton, *Paul Clifford,* 1830)

grass roots The common people, the working class; the rank and file of a political party; the voters. At the beginning of this century the term was used to mean 'source or origin,' the fundamental or basic level of any thing. This figurative extension of literal grass roots later acquired the political dimension denoting the people of rural or agricultural sections of the country as a factional, economic, or social group. Finally, *grass roots* was extended to include not just farmers and inhabitants of rural areas but the common people in general, or the rank and file of a political party or social organization.

> "No crisis so grave has confronted our people" since the Civil War, Mr. Lowden told the grassroots convention at Springfield. (*Nation*, June, 1935)

the great unwashed The general public, the masses; hoi polloi. Although its coinage has been attributed to Edmund Burke (1729–97), this phrase has been in print only since the early 19th century.

> Gentlemen, there can be but little doubt that your ancestors were the Great Unwashed. (William Makepeace Thackeray, *The History of Pendennis*, 1850)

low man on the totem pole The lowest in rank, the least important or experienced person; a neophyte. A totem pole is a tree trunk with symbolic carvings or paintings one above the other. North American Indians placed such poles in front of their houses. The apparent hierarchical arrangement of the symbols may have given rise to the current meaning of *totem pole*, which retains only the idea of 'hierarchy.' Thus, the *low man on the totem pole* refers to one who is at the bottom in the ordering of rank. Its popularity is undoubtedly partly owing to a comic novel, *Low Man on the Totem Pole*, by humorist H. Allen Smith. The following citation from *Webster's Third* shows the corre-

sponding use of the phrase for one of superior rank:

> . . . entertain top men on the political totem pole. (Mary Thayer)

pecking order Hierarchy; the levels of authority within a group of people or an organization; one's relative degree of predominance, aggressiveness, or power in comparison to others. This expression alludes to dominance hierarchy—a zoological term for the instinctive vertical ranking among birds and social mammals, in which the stronger animals assert their dominance over the smaller, weaker ones. Among domestic fowl, particularly chickens, the hierarchy becomes virtually uncontested; thus, the bird highest on the barnyard totem pole can peck at the dominated without worry of retaliation. Hence, avian dominance hierarchy came to be known as pecking order and, by extension, *pecking order* developed its figurative application to the hierarchy of authority and domination in human affairs.

ragtag and bobtail The rabble, the riff-raff, the masses; also, everyone collectively, the whole lot, every man Jack, every Tom, Dick, and Harry. The term, of British origin, was originally *tag*, then *tag and rag*; later the two words were reversed; still later the addition of *bobtail* (credited by some to Samuel Pepys) completed the term as we know it. Its component words all relate to worthless shreds, tatters, remnants, etc. The expression is sometimes extended to indicate comprehensiveness—every last one—as it was in this passage from T. A. Trollope's *What I Remember* (1887):

> He shall have them all, rag, tag, and bobtail.

the rank and file The general membership of an organization, as distinct from its leaders or officers; the lower echelons; the common people in general, hoi polloi. The origin of the term is military, *rank and file* being used to denote common soldiers (privates and corporals as opposed to commissioned officers) since the 18th century; for these were the men commonly required to line up in such formation: *rank* 'a number of soldiers drawn up in line abreast'; *file* 'the number of men constituting the depth from front to rear of a formation in line' (*OED*). By the 19th century the term was popular in government and political circles, as it still is today.

One of the mere rank and file of the party. (John Stuart Mill, *Considerations on Representative Government*, 1860)

run-of-the-mill Average, common, routine; mediocre, ordinary, no great shakes. This commonly used adjective is derived from its application to lots of manufactured goods which have not been inspected and consequently not sorted and graded for quality. By extension the term describes persons lacking in originality or individuality, those who through blandness blend in with the masses.

salt of the earth A person or group of persons epitomizing the best, most noble, and most admirable elements of society; a paragon; the wealthy aristocracy. For centuries, salt has been used in religious ceremonies as a symbol of goodness, purity, and incorruptibility. Thus, it was praise of the highest order when, after preaching the Beatitudes at the Sermon on the Mount, Christ called His disciples the "salt of the earth."

You are the salt of the earth; but if salt has lost its taste, how shall its saltness be restored? It is no longer good for anything except to be thrown out and trodden underfoot by men. (Matthew 5:13)

top billing Stardom. A phrase describing the most prominent or important in a group of persons, events, etc. In theater advertisements and billboards, billing is the relative position in which a person or act is listed. "Top billing," then, is the most prominent position, usually above the name of the play, and is reserved for an actor or actress who has attained stardom, one whose name is readily recognized by the public.

He made his Broadway debut as Lancelot in Camelot, with billing below the title; now, he is returning to Broadway, with top billing. (*Globe & Mail* [Toronto], January 13, 1968)

Although still most commonly used in reference to the theater, the scope of *top billing* has been expanded to include application in other contexts as well.

top-drawer See EXCELLENCE.

top-shelf See EXCELLENCE.

to the manner born Destined by birth to observe certain patterns of behavior, usually those associated with good breeding and high social status; also, innately or peculiarly suited for a particular position. This latter use is becoming increasingly common. One "to the manner born" is a "natural" with an instinctive ability in a given area. The former meaning is still the more accurate, however. Shakespeare's Hamlet gave us the expression when he criticized Claudius' and Denmark's drinking customs:

But to my mind, though I am native here
And to the manner born, it is a custom
More honored in the breach than the observance. (I,iv)

upper crust The highest social stratum; the wealthy; the aristocracy. This expression originated from the former custom of serving the upper crust of a loaf of bread to the most distinguished guests. As used today, the phrase often carries a suggestion of snobbery.

He took a fashionable house and hobnobbed lavishly with Washington's tight-ringed upper crust. (*Newsweek*, July, 1946)

STUPIDITY (See IGNORANCE.)

STYLISHNESS

clotheshorse A person who delights in wearing and showing off fancy clothes; a fashion plate, dandy, or fop; an exhibitionist. A clotheshorse is literally a wooden frame on which clothes are hung out to air or dry. The figurative meaning plays on the connections between *horse* 'a frame, with legs, on which something is mounted' and a person. Figurative use dates from the mid-19th century; literal use from the early 19th century.

> She ordered her chauffeur to drive her to Fifi's, Shmifi's—a fancy French place for clothes horses. (J. Ludwig in *Canadian Short Stories,* 1962)

daffadowndilly A dandy or fop; one excessively concerned with his appearance; a coxcomb or narcissist. This 19th-century Briticism, also spelled *daffydowndilly,* originally was a name for the daffodil, a member of the genus of flowers called *Narcissus.* In Greek mythology, Narcissus was a young man overly impressed with his appearance. As punishment, the gods made him fall in love with his own reflection in a pool of water. He stayed by the pool until he died and was then turned into a flower, the narcissus (or daffodil). Thus, the nickname for a daffodil became the nickname for a narcissist.

dressed to kill Stunningly or impressively attired; provocatively dressed, specifically in such a way as to completely overwhelm someone of the opposite sex, or, in the words of a similar slang phrase, "to knock 'em dead." Dating from the early 19th century, this expression still enjoys widespread popularity.

dressed to the nines Dressed in one's best from head to toe, perfectly attired, dressed in the height of fashion or style; also *dressed up to the nines.* Apparently the original phrase, dating from the late 18th century, was simply *(up) to the nines* meaning 'to perfection, to the utmost degree or extent.' At some point in the evolution of its usage the expression came to apply to a person's dress; it is rarely heard outside of that context today. Although the exact origin of this expression is unknown, several varying theories have been proposed. One suggests that the phrase is actually a corruption of Middle English *to then eyne* 'to the eyes.' Another, less plausible but nonetheless pervasive theory holds that the expression is a reference to the nine Muses and to the magical power formerly attributed to the number nine.

fashion plate A person who always wears the latest styles, a clotheshorse; a tony dresser; a dandy or coxcomb. Literally, a fashion plate is a newspaper or magazine advertisement featuring chic, urbane models nattily attired in the most fashionable clothes. In its figurative sense, a fashion plate is anyone who seems to have stepped out of one of these advertisements.

the glass of fashion and the mold of form A male fashion plate; a style-setter; a well-dressed Adonis; a gentleman of excellent physique with exquisite clothes-sense. The expression is a verbatim description of Prince Hamlet by Ophelia (III,i).

in full feather Exquisitely dressed, in full regalia, dressed to the nines. The origin of this expression is associated with the molting and subsequent new growth of a bird's plumage.

> No words can describe the serene effulgence of the Heartsease appearance when in full feather and high spirits. (J. E. Cooke, *Ellie,* 1855)

like a dog's dinner Dolled up, dressed to kill, all decked out; stylish, natty, dapper. This British colloquial expression, the opposite of *like a dog's breakfast,* is of unknown origin.

little Lord Fauntleroy See INEXPERIENCE.

macaroni A coxcomb or dandy; one with pretensions of sophistication and intellectualism. This British term originally referred to members of the Macaroni Club—an 18th-century group of well-traveled Englishmen who, in affecting Continental mannerisms, became notorious throughout the British Isles for their decadent behavior and pomposity. The phrase is now used to describe conceited, insolent fops.

> The weak chin, . . . resolute brow,
> and good forehead, portray
> Sheridan to the life, as he
> appeared, a macaroni and brilliant
> lounger in Carlton House.
> (*Athenaeum*, November, 1881)

neat as a bandbox Conspicuously neat in appearance, spiffy, smart-looking, fresh, sharp; in the United States, usually *looking as if* [*he*] *just stepped out of a bandbox*. This American phrase appeared as early as 1833 in *The Knickerbocker* and has been in common use since, despite the impossibility of a bandbox ever containing a human being. A bandbox is a small receptacle for collars and millinery, much used in the 17th century for storing the ruffs, or bands, commonly worn then. The following citation hints at the elliptical process by which the person himself rather than the item of apparel came to be described as "neat as *or* out of a bandbox."

> Why, he is a genteel, delightful
> looking fellow, neat as a starched
> tucker fresh from a bandbox [*sic*].
> (Samuel Woodworth, *The Forest Rose*, 1825)

spit and polish See NEATNESS.

SUBMISSION (See also SUBMISSIVENESS.)

cry barley To call or cry out for a truce, especially in children's games; to wave the white flag, to surrender. This Scottish and Northern English dialectal expression, which has been in use since the early 19th century, is thought to be a corruption of *parley*.

cry uncle To admit defeat, to surrender, to give up; also *to say uncle*. Although the precise origin of this expression is unknown, an often repeated story claims that an early Roman, finding himself in trouble, cried out *patrue mi patruissime* 'uncle, my best of uncles.' The phrase first appeared in print early in this century.

draw in one's horns To retract an opinion or take a less belligerent stand; to restrain oneself, to hold or pull back; to repress one's feelings of pride, righteousness, or pretension. In use since the 14th century, this expression alludes to the snail's habit of pulling in its tentacles when disturbed.

go to Canossa See HUMILIATION.

knuckle under To submit or yield, to give in, to acknowledge defeat. The origin of this expression has been linked to the obsolete *knuckle* 'knee joint'; hence *knuckle under*, meaning to 'bend the knee before, to bow down to.'

> They must all knuckle under to
> him. (Mary E. Braddon, *Mount Royal*, 1882)

A similar expression with the same meaning is *to knock under*, an abbreviated form of the obsolete *to knock under board* or *under the table*. Rapping against the underside of a table with the knuckles was apparently once a sign of submission or defeat as illustrated by the following citation:

> He that flinches his glass, and to
> drink is not able,
> Let him quarrel no more, but
> knock under the table.
> (*Gentleman's Journal*, March, 1691)

pass under the yoke To make a humiliating submission; to be humbly forced to acknowledge one's defeat. In ancient Rome vanquished enemies were forced to pass under an arch formed by two spears placed upright in the ground, with a third resting on them. This was a symbol of the even older practice of placing a yoke on the neck of a captive.

The expression is little heard today, although *yoke* is often used figuratively for 'servitude, restraint, or humiliation.'

> Jugurtha grants the Romans life and liberty but upon condition that they should pass under the yoke. (John Ozell, tr., *Aubert de Vertot's History of the Revolutions*, 1720)

raise the white flag To surrender, to indicate one's willingness to make peace; to ask for a truce, to declare an end to hostilities. A white flag, also called the flag of truce, has been the symbol of submission for centuries, perhaps because of its associations with cowardice, or with innocence and goodness.

strike sail To acknowledge defeat; to surrender; to eat humble pie; to defer or pay respect to. It was long a naval custom for a defeated ship to *strike* 'lower' its sails or flag as a sign of surrender or submission. Also, friendly ships, upon meeting each other at sea, often lowered their topsails to half-mast as a salute and sign of respect.

In the following quotation from Shakespeare's *Henry VI, Part III*, Queen Margaret of England is responding to a request by King Lewis of France that she join him at the royal dinner table.

> No, mighty King of France. Now Margaret
> Must strike her sail and learn a while to serve
> Where kings command. (III,iii)

throw in one's hand To give up, to drop out of the proceedings, to cease work on a project. This expression is derived from card games in which a player who is dealt poor cards or who realizes at some point during the game that winning is impossible has the option of turning in his *hand* 'cards' and dropping out of the game.

throw in the sponge To admit defeat, to give up, to surrender, to say uncle. In boxing, a manager has the option of ending a fight if he determines that his contestant has no chance of winning, and is suffering unnecessary physical abuse. The manager signals his desire to stop the bout by throwing his fighter's sponge or towel into the air. This slang Americanism and the variant *throw in the towel* are used figuratively of any surrender or acknowledgment of defeat.

SUBMISSIVENESS (See also **DEFERENCE, OBSEQUIOUSNESS, SUBMISSION.**)

give one's head for the washing To submit to insult or other ill treatment without resistance; to give in tamely or without a fight. This obsolete expression and its variants *give one's head for the polling* and *give one's beard for the washing* date from the 16th century.

> For my part it shall ne'er be said,
> I for the washing gave my head,
> Nor did I turn my back for fear.
> (Samuel Butler, *Hudibras* I,iii, 1663)

kiss the rod To accept punishment submissively, to submit meekly to chastisement. This expression, which dates from at least 1586, is an allusion to the rod (stick or switch) as an instrument of punishment. Thus, "to kiss the rod," figuratively speaking, is to embrace one's punishment without protest.

> Come, I'll be a good child, and kiss the rod. (James Shirley, *The Witty Fair One*, 1628)

like a lamb Meekly, gently, humbly, innocently, harmlessly, naïvely; from *lamb* as a gullible person, one easily deceived or cheated. This expression alludes to the docile, unassuming, placid nature of a young sheep. These characteristics have been associated with the lamb for thousands of years and have been cited in countless works of literature. *Like a lamb* is perhaps best known for its symbolic use in the Bible:

> He is brought as a lamb to the slaughter. (Isaiah 53:7)

> Behold the Lamb of God [Jesus Christ], which taketh away the sin of the world. (John 1:29)

live under the cat's foot To be subjected to the whims of another person, especially a woman; to be henpecked. To live under someone's foot is to be dominated and manipulated. In this picturesque expression, the oppressor is the "cat"—a nagging, overbearing woman.

patient as Griselda See PATIENCE.

take lying down To yield without resisting or fighting back; to give up the fight. A prone position is the most vulnerable and defenseless position one can assume. This expression is used figuratively in referring to a weak or cowardly person who fails to defend himself when subjected to verbal attack.

turn the other cheek To refuse to retaliate in kind even when sorely provoked; to answer an affront or attack with meekness and humility.

> The language was certainly provocative, and nothing but the consciousness of a good cause enabled Lord Salisbury to turn the cheek to the smiter. As it was, he made a conciliatory answer. (J. A. Williamson, *A Short History of British Expansion,* 1930)

This expression, of Biblical origin, literally means to allow or even invite another slap in the face. In His Sermon on the Mount, Jesus admonishes the multitudes:

> Ye have heard that it hath been said, An eye for an eye, and a tooth for a tooth: But I say unto you, That ye resist not evil: but whosoever shall smite thee on thy right cheek, turn to him the other also. (Matthew 5:38–39)

See **an eye for an eye,** RETALIATION.

Uncle Tom A Black person who assumes a submissive or obsequious attitude toward Whites, or one who seeks the favor of Whites. This term alludes to Uncle Tom, the Black hero of Harriet Beecher Stowe's *Uncle Tom's Cabin* (1851). While the expression is often used disparagingly by Blacks for those of their race who deem themselves inferior to Whites, *Uncle Tom* may also describe an Afro-American who voluntarily assumes the offensive stereotype.

> The South, that languorous land where Uncle Toms groaned Biblically underneath the lash. (Stephen Vincent Benét, *John Brown's Body,* 1927)

SUBORDINATION

bench warmer A substitute or replacement; a second- or third-stringer; an idler or observer, as opposed to a participant. The term comes from sports, where it applies to those players not proficient enough to make the first team and who consequently spend most of a game sitting on the bench. The expression has also been used for hobos who while away the time on park benches.

on a back burner See ABEYANCE.

play second fiddle To play a subordinate role, to serve in a secondary capacity; to be of inferior rank or status, to be second best or second rate. Violinists, as well as other musicians in orchestras and bands, are generally categorized into classes of first, second, and third. First is comprised of the best musicians who play the lead parts; second and third consist of musicians of lesser ability who play subordinate parts.

> She had inherited from her mother an extreme objection to playing, in any orchestra whatever, the second fiddle. (James Payn, *A Grape from a Thorn*)

take a back seat To occupy an inferior or subordinate position; to be put aside in favor of someone or something more important. The expression probably derives from the practice of preferential seating at public functions, where the front seats are always reserved for VIP's and other persons of note, while less socially significant persons have to take the seats to the rear and consequently enjoy a less advantageous view of the proceedings. The phrase appeared in its figurative sense as early as 1859 in *Harper's Magazine.*

SUBSISTENCE (See also **POVERTY**.)

boil the pot To make a bare subsistence living. This self-evident expression appeared in William Combe's *The Tour of Doctor Syntax in Search of the Picturesque* (1812):

No fav'ring patrons have I got,
But just enough to boil the pot.

See also **potboiler, LETTERS.**

keep body and soul together To survive economically; to make enough money to take care of basic needs and thus stay alive, death being viewed as the separation of soul and body. This picturesque expression dates from the mid-18th century.

By never letting him see you swallow half enough to keep body and soul together. (Jane Collier, *The Art of Tormenting,* 1753)

keep one's head above water To barely manage to keep out of debt; to remain financially solvent, however slightly. The allusion is to a swimmer too tired to go on who treads water to keep from going under altogether. The expression has been in figurative use since the early 18th century.

Farmer Dobson, were I to marry him, has promised to keep our heads above water. (Alfred, Lord Tennyson, *The Promise of May,* 1882)

keep the wolf from the door To ward off starvation; to prevent want and necessity from becoming all-consuming; to struggle to provide the basic necessities. The rapacious wolf has long been a symbol of a devouring force, such as poverty, which deprives an individual of the basic necessities. Recorded use of this expression dates from the middle of the 15th century.

Endowe hym now, with noble sapience
By whiche he may the wolf werre frome the gate.
(John Hardyng, *Chronicle,* 1457)

make both ends meet To live within one's means, to pay one's expenses, to stay in the black financially. A longer version of the phrase is *to make the two ends of the year meet,* i.e., to live within one's means from January to December. The expressions carry the connotation of struggle and mere subsistence living. The French equivalent expressions are *joindre les deux bouts* and *joindre les deux bouts de l'an.* Use of the phrase dates from the latter half of the 17th century.

Her mother has to contrive to make both ends meet. (*The Graphic,* August, 1884)

make buckle and tongue meet To make both ends meet; to earn enough money or produce enough food to survive; to get by, to manage. This puzzling colloquial Americanism was in print by the mid-19th century. The image is confusing. It may derive from either belts or shoes, but neither possibility casts much light on its relevance to financial survival.

All they cared for was "to make buckle and tongue meet" by raising stock, . . . and a little corn for bread. (*Fisher's River,* 1859)

An even earlier British equivalent is *hold* or *bring buckle and thong together.*

My benefice doth bring me in no more
But what will hold bare buckle and thong together.
(*Weakest Goeth to the Wall,* 1600)

tighten one's belt To implement austere measures during a time of financial uncertainty; to endure hunger with fortitude. This expression alludes to the weight loss and subsequent reduction in waist size of an underfed person. The phrase enjoys common use in the United States and Great Britain.

A travelling troupe who quoted Corneille while tightening their belts. (*Observer,* April, 1927)

SUCCESS   (See also VICTORY.)

bring down the house To elicit a vigorous and lengthy ovation from an audience; to be a smash or great success; sometimes *bring down the gallery.* The image created by this expression, in which *house* means 'theater' or 'playhouse,' is one of such loud, sustained applause as to bring about the collapse of the building. The phrase was in use as early as 1754.

have the last laugh To prove ultimately successful after an apparent defeat; to avenge. The idea of having the last laugh is fairly literal, i.e., though others may laugh now, the butt of their humor will laugh later when, in the final analysis, he is victorious. This phrase was popularized in the 1937 song "They All Laughed," by George and Ira Gershwin:

They all laughed at us and how!
But Ho, Ho, Ho!
Who's got the last laugh now?

Related expressions are *he who laughs last laughs best,* and *he laughs best that laughs last.* The latter appeared in *The Mistake* (1706) by Sir John Vanbrugh.

hit the jackpot See GOOD LUCK.

land on one's feet To achieve success despite predictable loss; to extricate oneself from a potentially dangerous situation; to escape failure narrowly. This popular expression usually appears in a context implying that the one who "lands on his feet" does so through undeserved luck; he repeatedly gets himself into scrapes but somehow survives. It is apparently based on the notion that one plummeting downward is unlikely to land safely, let alone feet first.

pan out To succeed; to yield results, especially favorable ones; to occur. This expression alludes to panning for gold, a method of prospecting in which a shallow pan is used to scoop a small amount of gravel and sand from a stream. Any gold present settles to the bottom of the pan as the gravel and sand are washed away. *Pan out,* then, originally indicated a successful prospecting venture. As the California gold rush that spawned this expression began to subside, *pan out* became more figurative, and has remained in widespread usage since the late 19th century.

Socialism . . . may pan out as a new kind of religion. (Sinclair Lewis, *Our Mr. Wrenn,* 1914)

pay dirt Any desired result or goal, especially one related to wealth or success; a fortunate discovery. Literally, *pay dirt* is a mining term that refers to an area of land that contains enough valuable metals or other resources to merit excavation. After its introduction in the 1870s, *pay dirt* soon became more figurative, commonly being applied to any success.

I didn't hit pay dirt until near the bottom of the second box of discarded telephone directories. (John Evans, *Halo in Blood,* 1946)

In recent years, *pay dirt* has been used frequently to describe the end zone (goal area) of a football field.

ring the bell To succeed, to make a hit; to be the best. The bell of this expression may be that attached to the strength-testing machine at carnivals which rings when a player is successful. Or it may be the bell in target shooting that rings when the bull's-eye is hit.

strike oil To have good luck or success, especially financial; to discover a source of potential personal aggrandizement; to strike it rich; to hit pay dirt. This expression alludes to oil as an entity which inevitably leads to wealth and success, a concept strengthened in recent years by the increasing prominence of Middle East oil barons. Though still used literally to describe the locating of underground oil, *strike oil* is commonly applied figuratively in contexts directly or indirectly related to money or other personal good fortune.

> He has certainly "struck oil" in the Costa Rica and Honduras loans. (*Punch*, March 6, 1875)

turn up trumps To turn out successfully, to come out better than expected, to turn out well or fine; to be lucky, to land on one's feet.

> Instances . . . of short courtships and speedy marriages, which have turned up trumps—I beg your pardon—which have turned out well, after all. (Wilkie Collins, *No Name*, 1862)

The allusion is to drawing or playing a winning trump card. See **trump card**, **PLOY**.

with flying colors Victoriously, triumphantly, successfully; handily, easily; superbly, in extraordinary fashion. This phrase, usually in expressions such as *come off with flying colors* and *come out of it with flying colors,* alludes to a triumphant fleet of ships sailing into home port with their colors (i.e., flags) proudly displayed on the mastheads. Used figuratively, *with flying colors* often implies that one has not only survived a potentially precarious predicament but has been victorious to boot.

SUFFERING   (See **ADVERSITY**.)

SUPERFLUOUSNESS   (See also **ABUNDANCE**, **EXCESSIVENESS**.)

after meat, mustard Too late; no longer of any use. The original expression was the French *c'est de la moutarde après dîner,* which first appeared in English as 'like mustard after dinner' (John Adams, *Adams-Warren Correspondence,* 1807), before evolving into the more common *after meat, mustard.* This phrase expresses the uselessness of offering something after the need for it has already passed, as does the similar Latin expression *post bellum, auxilium* 'after the war, aid.'

third wheel An extra, unnecessary, or unwanted person, especially one whose presence serves no useful purpose; a person who interferes with or prevents the successful completion of a project, task, or other matter. The concept is undoubtedly similar to the sentiments expressed in the familiar adage, "Two's company, but three's a crowd." Although the derivation of this expression is not certain, it probably alludes to the uselessness of a third wheel on a vehicle which normally has two. Today one frequently hears *fifth wheel,* most probably because most vehicles now have four.

SUPERIORITY   (See **EXCELLENCE**.)

SUPERSTITION   (See also **GOOD LUCK**.)

beware the ides of March A warning of impending danger, rarely heard today. This expression alludes to the words of the soothsayer who warned Julius Caesar to "Beware the ides of March." Caesar ignored the advice, only to be killed on that very day, the 15th of March. According to the ancient Roman calendar, the ides falls on the 15th day of March, May, July, and October, and on the 13th day of the other months.

keep one's fingers crossed To hope for good luck or success; literally to hook one finger over another. The expression, which dates from the first half of this century, may be connected with the old superstition that making the sign of the cross kept bad luck away.

> We'll . . . duck when we hear a mortar, and keep our fingers crossed. (*Penguin New Writing,* 1945)

old wives' tale A foolish or nonsensical story; a traditional but inaccurate concept or superstition. This expression is derived from the fanciful yarns often related by elderly women.

> These are the sort of old wives' tales which he sings and recites to

us. (Benjamin Jowett, *The Dialogues of Plato,* 1875)

Today the expression usually describes a superstitious notion still adhered to by many people even though it has been discredited by modern science.

put the whammy on See **THWARTING.**

right foot foremost See **get off on the right foot, BEGINNINGS.**

three on a match Any practice which reputedly brings ill luck, but most often the specific and literal practice of lighting three cigarettes with one match. The superstition supposedly arose among soldiers in wartime who believed that the glow from a match kept alive long enough to light three cigarettes would give the enemy time for careful aim at them as targets, thus quite possibly bringing about their death.

SURPRISE

bolt from the blue A sudden and entirely unexpected or unforeseen occurrence; a complete surprise; also, the adverbial phrases *out of the blue* and *out of a clear blue sky* 'unexpectedly, suddenly; without warning or notice.' The allusion is to suddenness and surprise similar to that which would be experienced if a bolt of lightning were unexpectedly to appear in a cloudless sky. Although *bolt from the blue* was in use as early as 1837, *out of the blue* did not appear until 1919.

bug-eyed Astonished, surprised; aghast with wonder or awe; literally, to have protruding eyes as do certain species of bugs. Though this precise adjective form did not appear until the 1920s, conceptually equivalent expressions date from considerably earlier.

Wouldn't their eyes bug out, to see 'em handled like that? (Mark Twain, *Life on the Mississippi,* 1883)

knock for a loop See **CONFUSION.**

Scarborough warning Little or no forewarning, no previous notice; a total shock. This expression may allude to the 1557 siege of Scarborough castle, which took its inhabitants completely off guard. Another possible origin concerns a harsh law enacted in Scarborough which allowed the punishment of robbery suspects prior to a trial. In any event, the expression, used frequently in Great Britain until the mid-1800s, is virtually never heard today.

The true man for giving Scarborough warning—first knock you down, then bid you stand. (Sir Walter Scott, *Redgauntlet,* 1824)

taken aback Surprised or stunned into immobility. This was originally a nautical term describing a square-rigged ship whose sails are blown against the mast, thus preventing further forward movement. An early figurative usage employs the term *all aback:*

On this subject I am literally as the sailors say all aback. (Edward Winslow, *Winslow Papers,* 1783)

SURRENDER (See **SUBMISSION, SUBMISSIVENESS.**)

SUSPICIOUSNESS (See also **SKEPTICISM.**)

flea in the ear See **IRRITATION.**

nigger in the woodpile Something suspicious, such as an undisclosed fact, hidden element, or ulterior motive. This expression sprang up during the era of slavery in the United States, most specifically in regard to the Underground Railroad, a system whereby abolitionists aided runaway slaves, often concealing them through any expedient—one of which was a woodpile. The phrase first appeared in print in 1852; though the expression has from long figurative use lost its direct association with Blacks, the offensiveness still carried by the word *nigger* inhibits the phrase's use in contemporary speech and writing and may well signal its demise from the language.

> Like a great many others ignorant of facts, he finds "a nigger in the wood pile" when there is neither wood pile nor nigger.
> (*Congressional Record*, February, 1897)

smell a rat To instinctively sense evil, treachery, or wrongdoing; to be suspicious. A cat has a keen sense of smell which enables it to detect an unseen rat. The phrase is quite common in the United States and Great Britain.

> I asked her so many questions, that, though a woman ignorant enough, she began to smell a rat. (William R. Chetwood, *Voyages of W.O.G. Vaughan*, 1736)

something rotten in Denmark An expression used to describe a suspected problem which cannot be pinpointed; something of a questionable or suspicious nature; anything that disconcerts and instills anxiety. In Shakespeare's *Hamlet*, Marcellus is uneasy because the ghost of Hamlet's father had appeared to him. He sees this as a portent and conjectures to Horatio:

> Something is rotten in the state of Denmark. (I,iv)

SWINDLING (See also TRICKERY.)

fleece To swindle, defraud, or con a person out of a sum of money; to cheat someone, take him for a ride or to the cleaners. This expression stems from *fleece* 'to pluck or shear wool from a sheep.' In its figurative sense, *fleece* implies that a victim, usually a gullible person, is led willingly and unknowingly into giving up some of his possessions.

> To divide what they fleeced from these poor drudges. (Thomas Carlyle, *On Heroes, Hero-Worship, and the Heroic in History*, 1840)

fly a kite To raise money through misrepresentation, such as by the sale of bogus bonds, specious stocks, or spurious securities; to write a rubber check, i.e., one for an amount which exceeds available funds. In this expression, *kite*, a Wall Street term for worthless bonds, stocks, or securities, may stem from *kite*, the falcon-like bird with a forked tail (implying dishonesty) and a toothless bill (implying worthlessness). It is more likely, however, that *kite* refers to the paper "toy" that soars in the wind, the implication being that these worthless papers (bonds, etc.) are good only for constructing kites.

gazump To cheat or swindle; to defraud.

> Grafters speak a language comprised of every possible type of slang . . . These include 'gezumph' which means to cheat or overcharge. (P. Allingham, *Cheapjack*, 1934)

This British term (also written *gezumph* or *gazoomph*) is a descendant of *gazamph*, an obscure word for dishonest auctioneering. Nowadays, the term usually describes an unethical increase in the price of real estate after the original asking price has been agreed.

palm off To dispose of fraudulently; to deceive someone into accepting a worthless item, plan, or other matter about which bogus claims have been made. This expression alludes to magicians and other sleight-of-hand artists who are able to trick a viewer into believing that an object concealed in the palm of their hand is actually somewhere else.

> Have you not tried to palm off a yesterday's pun? (Charles Lamb, *Elia*, 1822)

pig in a poke A worthless, uncertain, or misrepresented bargain; a risk or chance; some item purchased or accepted on blind, and possibly misplaced, trust. This expression recalls the county fairs which were once common in England and elsewhere. If a customer bought a suckling pig at one of these fairs, he would usually take it home in a poke, a small sack. Since some pigs were sold at bargain prices sight unseen in a sealed bag, an occasional unscrupulous purveyor substituted a cat for the pig, hoping to deceive the buyer of "a pig in a poke." A cautious customer, however, would open the sack before buying its contents, thus "letting the cat out of the bag." This expression often appears in the context of *to buy a pig in a poke.* The French equivalent, *achêter un chat en poche* 'to buy a cat in a poke,' refers directly to the deceptive practice described above. See also **let the cat out of the bag, EXPOSURE.**

take to the cleaners To defraud someone of all his money; to wipe out; often used passively in the phrase *to be taken to the cleaners.* This rather recent American slang expression is thought to be a modernized version of the earlier slang phrase *cleaned out,* which is still in current use today. Its meaning is similar to that of *taken to the cleaners,* but it lacks the latter's usual connotation of having been duped or swindled.

T

TALENT   (See **ABILITY**.)

TALKATIVENESS

beat one's gums   To talk excessively but ineffectually; to speak volubly but to no purpose; to ramble on idly. Articulatory power lies in tongue, teeth, and palate. Toothless gums mean feebleness and ineffectiveness. The phrase was particularly popular during World War II.

chew the fat   To talk or chat; to shoot the breeze; to have a long-winded conversation. This slang expression has been in print since the last quarter of the 19th century. Today it continues to be a popular phrase for indulging in idle chatter. Chewing on fat provides relatively little sustenance for the amount of mastication involved.

chew the rag   To talk or chat; to discuss a matter, usually in a complaining or argumentative way; to harp on an old grievance. Although *chew the rag* is used interchangeably with *chew the fat*, the former was previously used for complaining or arguing. The insignificancy of such conversation is expressed in the following line from *Scribner's Magazine* (1909):

> How better is conversational impotence characterized than by "chewing the rag"?

flannelmouth   See **FLATTERY**.

flap one's chops   To drivel inanely, to blather; to talk idly; also *flap one's jowls* or *jaw* or *lip*. This phrase is obviously derived from the facial movements of the perpetual chatterbox.

> Well, you weren't just flapping your lip that time. (Peter DeVries, in *The New Yorker*, May, 1951)

flibbertigibbet   A gossip; a mindless and frivolously talkative person; a mischievous and, at times, malicious prattler. This expression, in use since the 16th century, may be either an onomatopoeic representation of meaningless chatter and drivel or a corruption of "flapper of the jibs," where *jib* is slang for 'lip.'

> Good Mrs. Flibber de Jibb, with the French fly-flap of your coxcomb. (Richard Brome, *The Sparagus Garden*, 1635)

People named *Flibbertigibbet* have appeared several times in literature, most notably as a fiend or devil in Shakespeare's *King Lear,* and as a grotesque, ill-mannered, mischievous imp in Sir Walter Scott's *Kenilworth* (1821).

> This is the foul fiend Flibbertigibbet; He begins at curfew, and walks till the first cock. (Shakespeare, *King Lear,* III,iv)

the gift of gab   Fluency or glibness of speech; volubility or talkativeness, often with connotations of shallowness and lack of substance; also *the gift of the gab.* The original expression was apparently *the gift of the gob, gob* being a northern dialectal and slang term for mouth, possibly from the Gaelic and Irish *gob* 'beak, mouth.'

jaw-me-dead   An extremely loquacious person; one who engages in interminable senseless chatter. *Jaw* in this phrase means 'a long conversation, incessant chatter.' *Jaw-me-dead* is an epithet, hyperbolically describing the effect of one who bends someone's ear.

shoot the breeze   To chat, talk aimlessly, or gab; to gossip; to exaggerate. Since a breeze is a mild wind, and *shoot* is 'to send forth,' to *shoot the breeze* implies that a person's babbling is of trivial importance, serving only to create a minor current in the air.

> We were sitting outdoors, enjoying ourselves and shooting the breeze.

(Billy Rose, in a syndicated
newspaper column, 1950)

Two variations are *bat the breeze* and
fan the breeze.

shoot the bull To engage in idle, trivial, or aimless conversation; to gossip; to
boast, flatter, or exaggerate; to lie. In
this expression, *bull* may be derived
from the Middle Latin *bulla* 'game,
jest,' or it may be a shortened, less offensive version of *bullshit* 'nonsense, lies.'
Thus *to shoot the bull* implies that
though many words are being spoken,
nothing of much consequence is being
said.

> You could see he really felt pretty
> lousy about flunking me. So I shot
> the bull for a while. (J. D. Salinger,
> *Catcher in the Rye,* 1951)

talk a blue streak To speak rapidly,
continuously, and at great length; to be
voluble or garrulous. Though most commonly used in reference to speech or
the flow of words, *blue streak* can also
denote rapidity of anything. The term
probably stems from the blinding speed
and vividness of a lightning flash.

> Interspersing his vehement
> comments with a "blue streak" of
> oaths. (*The Knickerbocker,* 1847)

verbal diarrhea Excessive talkativeness; the unleashing of a word hoard; an
overly pompous or verbose discourse.
This obvious analogy has older and
more reputable antecedents than
might be supposed:

> He . . . was troubled with a
> diarrhea of words. (Horace Walpole,
> *Memoirs of George III,* 1797)

TEMPERANCE

on the wagon Abstaining from alcoholic beverages; said of a teetotaler or
nephalist. This expression is a truncated
version of the earlier and more explicit
on the water-wagon.

> But, R-e-m-o-r-s-e!
> The water-wagon is the place for
> me;

> It is no time for mirth and laughter,
> The cold, gray dawn of the
> morning after!
> (George Ade, *Remorse,* 1902)

Antithetically, *off the wagon* implies
the resumption of alcoholic indulgence
after a period of abstinence.

> Like the bartenders, they fell off
> the wagon. (A. J. Liebling, "Yea,
> Verily," in *The New Yorker,*
> September 27, 1952)

teetotal To abstain totally from alcoholic beverages; as an adjective, advocating total abstinence from intoxicating drink. This word is formed by a
reduplication of the initial sound of
total. It was purportedly coined by
Richard Turner (1790–1846) in a
speech delivered in England in September, 1833, advocating total abstinence from liquor. Accounts differ as to
whether *teetotal* was intentional as
Turner claimed, or the result of a
speech defect which caused Turner to
stutter, "N-n-nothing but t-t-t-total abstinence will do." At any rate, John
Livesey, a member of the audience
and founder of the Total Abstinence
Society, credits the word to Turner
in his *Autobiography* (1867), and
Turner's gravestone epitaph reads in
part: "Richard Turner, author of the
word Teetotal as applied to abstinence
from all intoxicating liquors." Furthermore, a full-page advertisement
in the April, 1836, issue of *Preston's
Temperance Advocate* also credits
"Dicky Turner" as the originator of
teetotal.

Rev. Joel Jewell, secretary of a temperance society in Lansing, New York,
claimed that members of his organization coined the word in 1827 when they
handed out pledge cards upon which
were printed "O.P." (Old Pledge—partial abstinence) or "T." (Total abstinence), encouraging people to sign the
latter by crying out "T—total! T—
total!"

Although both England and the

United States claim credit for the word, it is possible that *teetotal* developed independently in the two countries. It has since enjoyed extensive and frequent use.

> Much stress has been laid by the teetotal advocates on the paramount influence of parental intemperance on the procreation of a mentally deficient progeny. (Thomas Allbutt, *A System of Medicine,* 1899)

One who abstains from alcoholic consumption is often called a *teetotaler.*

TEMPORIZING (See also **ABEYANCE.**)

filibuster The use of irregular or obstructive tactics, such as long speeches or trivial objections, by a minority legislator to prevent or hinder the passage or consideration of legislation generally favored by the majority; the use of such tactics to force the passage of unpopular legislation; to waste time for the purpose of obstruction. The filibuster, long a staple of U.S. Congressional politics, derives from the French *filibustier* 'pirate' and the British *flibuster* 'rover, traveler.' These French pirates terrorized the Spanish West Indies in the 17th century. The name *filibusters* was later applied to illegal bands of Americans and Texans who, in the 1850s, entered Central America to foment revolution. Soon the term was applied to anyone who took part in illegal or irregular warfare or other obstructionist activity against a government. The transition to its current meaning was then but a short jump.

> A filibuster was indulged in which lasted . . . for nine continuous calendar days. (*Congressional Record,* February 11, 1890)

hold at bay To fend off one's literal or figurative assailant by taking the offense, thereby bringing about a standstill as both parties are poised and ready to attack. This expression is said to derive from the modern French *être aux bois* 'to be at close quarters with the barking dogs.' Originally a hunting phrase dating from the 16th century, *hold* or *keep at* (*a*) *bay* refers to a situation in which a hunted animal, unable to flee further, turns to defend itself at close quarters. Figurative use, also dating from the 1500s, is now heard more frequently than the literal.

> By riding . . . keep death as it were at a bay. (Francis Fuller, *Medicina Gymnastica,* 1711)

play for time To employ dilatory tactics to stave off defeat; to postpone making a decision, to drag out negotiations. This expression probably derives from those sports in which one team monopolizes control in the remaining minutes of a game in order to prevent a last minute turnaround and victory by the opposing team.

stonewall To obstruct or block legislation; to delay or impede an activity. This term was applied to the Civil War General Thomas J. Jackson, in honor of his steadfastness at the Battle of Bull Run. The expression is also a cricket term for an exclusively defensive or delaying strategy. Its meaning was subsequently extended to include stubborn blocking and delaying tactics on a government level.

> Obstruction did not merely consist in stonewalling Government business. (*Contemporary Review,* November, 1916)

As a result of its use in the Watergate hearings, *stonewall* took on the more specific meaning of the obstruction of or the resistance to government inquiry or investigation, as through vagueness and noncooperation.

TERMINATION (See also **CESSATION, COMPLETION, CULMINATION, THWARTING.**)

bitter end A difficult or disagreeable conclusion; the last or ultimate extremity; death; often in the phrase *to the* *bitter end.* According to Captain John Smith's *A Sea Grammar* (1627):

> A bitter is but the turn of a cable about the bits, and wear it out by little and little. And the bitters end is that part of the cable doth stay within board.

William Henry Smyth in *The Sailor's Word-book* (1867) elaborates further:

> A ship is "brought up to a bitter" when the cable is allowed to run out to that stop. . . . When a chain or rope is paid out to the bitter-end, no more remains to be let go.

A variation of the phrase *bitter end* appears in the Bible (Proverbs 5:4) and some conjecture this usage, rather than the nautical, to be its origin.

> But her end is bitter as wormwood.

The phrase gave rise to the term *bitter-ender* 'a diehard,' in use since 1850.

curtains The end, usually a disastrous or unfortunate one; most often, death itself. This slang term, of obvious theatrical derivation, is often used to indicate the end of some illegitimate enterprise, and as such is similar to expressions such as *the jig is up.*

> It looked like curtains for Ezra then and there. But just that moment he saw a chance of salvation. (Jesse Lilienthal, *Horse Crazy,* 1941)

[one's] days are numbered See ILL HEALTH.

in the homestretch In the final stages; nearing the completion of a project, ordeal, activity, or other matter; the denouement. In racing terminology, the homestretch is the last leg of a race, i.e., the straight part of a racecourse from the last turn to the finish line. Figurative use of this Americanism was recorded as early as the mid-19th century. It usually suggests some degree of relief because in the homestretch, the end is in sight.

> Already we see the slave states . . . on the homestretch to become free.

(*Congressional Globe,* March 12, 1864)

the jig is up This is it, it's all over, this is the end of the line; usually used in reference to being caught or discovered in some wrongdoing. This slang or dialectal expression, which dates from the late 1700s, derives from the obsolete 'prank, joke, trick' meaning of *jig.*

lower the boom See PUNISHMENT.

nip in the bud To terminate a project, plan, or other matter in its early stages; to prevent or stop something before it has had a chance to develop. A bud is an undeveloped part of a plant which, if nipped by frost, pests, or a zealous gardener, does not grow to fruition; hence the expression.

> Dost thou approach to censure our delights, and nip them in the bud? (Sir Aston Cokaine, *Masque,* 1639)

quit cold turkey To stop abruptly and completely the habitual use of alcohol, tobacco, or drugs without substituting nonaddicting alternatives; to terminate any habit suddenly. Although both the origin of this phrase and the rationale for *turkey* are uncertain, *quit cold turkey* clearly implies an abrupt cessation as opposed to a gradual tapering off as a means of ridding oneself of an unwanted behavior or addiction. One theory as to the origin of the phrase holds that when a drug addict stops taking drugs, among the (often severe) withdrawal symptoms is horripilation of the skin (goose bumps) accompanied by a cold, blanched complexion. The similarity of appearance to the skin of a turkey prepared for cooking is obvious. Variations are *stop cold turkey* and *go cold turkey.*

Cold turkey itself is sometimes used to describe any action or performance undertaken in impromptu fashion, without "warming up," so to speak. In this usage, however, the phrase is now usually truncated to the simpler *cold.*

ring down the curtain To terminate or bring to an end. In the theater, the person responsible for raising or lowering the stage curtain once received his cue from the stage manager who would ring a bell at the appropriate moment.

> The curtain had to be rung down before the play was ended. (*Times,* August 31, 1887)

While still used in the theater, *ring down the curtain on* is applied figuratively in other contexts as well. A variation is the shortened *ring down.*

> The functionary whose business it is to "ring down" had satisfied himself that nobody wanted any more of it. (*Daily News,* October 2, 1882)

stem the tide To stop, terminate, end; to squash, quell, check; to block or stifle; to nip in the bud. The most plausible conjecture is that *stem* in this expression is derived from the Icelandic *stemma* 'to stop the flow of'; attempts to relate it to the stem of an ocean-going vessel defy logic. *Tide* implies a flow of events.

> Aristophanes evidently saw the tide that was strongly in favour of the new candidate for scenic supremacy, and he vainly tried to stem it by the barrier of his ridicule. (Fred Paley, *The Tragedies of Aeschylus,* 1855)

TEST (See also CRITERION.)

baptism of fire See INITIATION.

go through fire and water See DESIRE.

have one's work cut out See DIFFICULTY.

ordeal by fire A severe test of character; a very distressing situation. In ancient Britain, an ordeal was a type of trial in which divine intervention was considered the only proof of a suspect's innocence. These ordeals took many brutal forms, ranging from having one's arm immersed in boiling water to being bound and tossed into an icy river. In both cases, an unscathed survivor was proclaimed innocent. The harshest ordeals, however, involved fire. The accused was forced either to grasp a red-hot iron in his hand or to walk barefooted through sizzling rocks and embers. Again, a suspect who emerged uninjured was considered guiltless. Although these cruel trials were abolished shortly after the Norman conquest of Britain, the expression has retained its meaning of an exceedingly agonizing experience undergone to test one's worth.

put through one's facings To require another to exhibit his skill for purposes of scrutiny; to make a person perform to the utmost of his capabilities. Literal facings are military maneuvers.

> Grace, not at all unwillingly, was put through her facings. (Anthony Trollope, *The Last Chronicle of Barset,* 1867)

The expression usually carries connotations of being badgered or harassed, as in the following bit of doggerel by F. Egerton.

> We were scarcely wed a week
> When she put me through my facings.
> And walloped me—and worse;
> She said I did not want a wife,
> I ought to have had a nurse.

put through one's paces To require another to display the full range of his abilities; to test another's resources to the utmost. *Paces* here refers to the training steps or gaits of horses. The equestrian phrase was first extended to persons called upon to perform at their maximum potential, and subsequently to inanimate objects as well.

> The captain affirmed that the ship would show us in time all her paces. (Ralph Waldo Emerson, *English Traits,* 1856)

> The test pilots . . . put the new planes through their paces. (H. H. Arnold and I. C. Eaker, cited in *Webster's Third*)

take the measure of To judge the character of, to size up, to ascertain the good and bad points. *Measure* in this expression refers literally to the dimensions of a body, information necessary to a tailor who needs exact "measurements" to fit someone for clothes. Figuratively the term refers not to size, but to character.

> Our hostess . . . bustled off . . . to take the measure of the new-comer. (Sir A. Conan Doyle, *Micah Clarke,* 1889)

Even further removed from the literal use is the application of this expression to organizations or institutions.

> The people have taken the measure of this whole labor movement. (*Nations,* January 5, 1893)

THOROUGHNESS (See also **INCLUSIVENESS, TOTALITY.**)

bell, book, and candle Thoroughly, completely; formally, with all the trappings. The phrase derives from the Roman Catholic ritual of excommunication, no longer practised, consisting of: 1) formal declaration of a person as anathema, after which the book containing prescribed readings was closed; 2) extinguishment of a candle, symbolic of the person's expulsion from the community of believers into which he had been received when a candle was lighted at his baptism; and 3) the tolling of a bell, to signalize his spiritual death.

go over with a fine-tooth comb To examine thoroughly, to observe every detail or aspect of a thing; to be on the lookout for some problem, defect, or irregularity in order to improve or perfect. This expression derives from the act of brushing with a comb having narrow, closely set teeth, such as the type used in looking for fleas on a cat or dog. Figurative use of the expression, heard by the late 19th century, remains current.

> We've gone through the remains of the helicopter with a fine-tooth comb, but there wasn't much left. (A. Firth, *Tall, Balding, Thirty-Five,* 1966)

hook, line, and sinker Entirely, completely; without reservations. The allusion is to a fish so hungry that it swallows not only the bait but the fishhook, the lead weight (sinker), and some of the fishing line as well. The expression appeared as early as 1838 in T. W. Barnes' *Memoir of T. Weed.* It most often describes the naïveté or gullibility of an accepting, unquestioning attitude, and implies that a person has been easily duped.

leave no stone unturned To spare no effort; to exhaust every expedient to accomplish one's aim or goal. This expression was the advice purportedly given by the Oracle of Delphi to Polycrates the Theban when he asked where he could find the treasure believed to have been hidden by Mardonius, a Persian general whom he had defeated at the Battle of Plataea (477 B.C.). Upon following this advice, Polycrates located the treasure beneath the stone floor of Mardonius' tent.

> We shall not be negligent; no stone will be left unturned. (Edmund Burke, *Correspondence,* 1791)

lock, stock, and barrel Completely, entirely; the whole thing. The allusion is to the three main components of a gun which together comprise essentially the entire weapon. The phrase was used in *Lawrie Todd* by John Galt in 1830.

neck and crop Entirely, completely, altogether; bodily. Though there is disagreement as to whether the *crop* of the expression is *crop* 'craw, gullet' or *crop* 'rounded head or top,' it matters little. The concept is clear, no matter the direction in which the neck is extended to indicate entirety. Common in the 19th century, the phrase is less so today.

> Chuck them neck and crop . . . down a dark staircase. (Michael Scott, *Tom Cringle's Log,* 1833)

root and branch Utterly, completely, without exception or qualification; inside and outside; lock, stock, and barrel. This expression was popularized by the

London Petition of 1640 which advocated the abolition of episcopal government.

> That the said government, with all its dependencies, roots, and branches, be abolished. (*Petition* in John Rushworth's *Historical Collections*, 1640)

When writing this petition, the "root-and-branch men," advocates of the all-out, total abolition of Episcopacy, probably had in mind the following Biblical quotation from Malachi 4:1:

> And the day that cometh shall burn them up, saith the Lord of hosts, that it shall leave them neither root nor branch.

Root and branch is most commonly heard in the expression *destroy root and branch.*

to the hilt Completely, fully, entirely, thoroughly, to the maximum extent or degree; also *up to the hilt.* When a sword or dagger is thrust into an object up to its hilt or handle, the blade is completely covered and can go in no farther. The phrase dates from the late 17th century.

to the teeth Entirely, fully, completely; often in the phrase *armed to the teeth.* Conjecture that the phrase dates from the days when pirates roamed the Spanish Main carrying a pistol or sword in each hand and a knife between their teeth appears dubious because of a 1380 *OED* citation.

touch all bases To include either in action or in speech all important facets of a matter; to leave no stone unturned, to be thorough. This American slang expression comes from baseball where a player is required to touch each base successively in order to score a run.

THOUGHT

brainstorm A sudden and powerful thought; a good idea. The concept of forcefulness contained in the *storm* element seems to be losing ground to that of disorder and chaos, so that *brainstorm* is now most often used ironically to mean a whimsical or ill-considered notion, a stupid idea.

brown study Absorption in thought; a pensive mood; absent-mindedness. This phrase dates from the early 16th century; the *brown* of the expression apparently stemmed from *brown* 'gloomy.' Citations indicate that the phrase varies in meaning: it may be used for serious thought; for apparent pensiveness masking actual absent-mindedness; or for simple idle day-dreaming. John Crowe Ransom uses the phrase poignantly in "Bells for John Whiteside's Daughter":

> There was such speed in her little body,
> And such lightness in her footfall,
> It is no wonder that her brown study
> Astonishes us all.

a horseback opinion A guess, an off-hand impression, a hasty opinion or judgment delivered without "stopping to think," as though from horseback. Use of this U.S. colloquialism dates from the late 19th century.

> I am not here as a judicial authority or oracle. I can only give horseback opinion. (*Congressional Record,* April 23, 1879)

on the carpet Under consideration or up for discussion. This expression, in use since 1726, comes from the earlier *on* or *upon the tapis* (since 1690), a partial translation of the French *sur le tapis* 'on the tablecloth.' The tablecloth in question is the one covering the council table around which the members meet to discuss items of business.

put on one's thinking cap To think about or consider; to ponder; to reflect or concentrate. Although "thinking caps" have been mentioned in children's literature and various legends for hundreds of years, the most likely allusion is to the official headgear which a British magistrate would wear when considering the disposition of a case and when passing sentence. In its figurative use, *put on one's thinking cap* clearly implies that the matter at hand merits serious thought.

> It is satisfactory to know that the Post Office Department has its thinking cap on. (*Daily Chronicle,* January, 1903)

sleep on it To contemplate and reflect upon an important proposal, plan, or other matter without making a hasty decision; to consider something over-night before making up one's mind. This expression, in popular use for centuries, implies that some decisions, particularly portentous ones, merit at least one night of conscious and, while sleeping, subconscious thought.

> His Grace . . . said that he would sleep and dream upon the matter, and give me an answer [in] the morning. (*State Papers of Henry VIII,* 1519)

THWARTING (See also **IMPEDI-MENT, RUINATION.**)

clip [someone's] wings To cripple someone's efforts to reach a goal; to incapacitate; to undermine, directly or indirectly, another's ability to achieve his aspirations. Figurative use of this phrase alludes to the idea that a bird cannot fly with clipped wings. The phrase has been current since its early use in the late 16th century.

> Away to prison with him! I'll clip his wings. (Christopher Marlowe, *The Massacre at Paris,* 1590)

cook [someone's] goose To destroy someone's chances totally and irrevocably; to do someone in or ruin it for someone; to put the kibosh on someone's hopes or plans. The popular and amusing but implausible story offered as the source of this phrase has to do with King Eric of Sweden and his soldiers, who were not taken seriously

when they arrived to capture a town. The townspeople ridiculed the King by hanging out a goose for the soldiers to shoot at. Upon realizing the real threat posed by the King, the people sent someone to negotiate a settlement with him. When asked his intentions, the King replied, "to cook your goose."

The *OED* cites a mid-19th-century street ballad as the earliest printed use of the phrase:

> If they come here we'll cook their goose
> The Pope and Cardinal Wiseman.

This doggerel expressed England's opposition to Pope Pius's attempt to reassert the power of the Catholic Church in England through the appointment of the English Cardinal Nicholas Wiseman.

cramp [someone's] style To inhibit another's freedom of expression or action; to make someone feel ill-at-ease and self-conscious; to have a dampening effect on another's spirits. The person who "cramps another's style" usually does so by his mere presence or the attitudes he embodies, rather than by explicit word or overt action. Impersonal forces such as rules or procedures can also cramp a person's style.

lay by the heels To limit or thwart a person's power or influence; to negate the credibility of a once influential person; to imprison or otherwise confine a person. This expression alludes to stocks, the once common instruments of punishment which were made of a framework with holes for securing the ankles (and sometimes the wrists). An offender locked in the stocks was frequently subjected to public derision, abuse, and humiliation as part of the punishment. Thus, to *lay by the heels* is to shackle someone, either literally or figuratively, thereby reducing or eliminating his influence.

put a spoke in [someone's] wheel To interfere, obstruct, or impede the progress of; to frustrate or thwart. This expression, dating from the 16th century, is said to derive from the practice of thrusting a pin or spoke into a hole on a solid wheel to serve as a break and slow down the vehicle. Current confusion over this expression arises because many kinds of wheels are now made with spokes and it is difficult to conceive of a spoke preventing a wheel from turning.

> Capitalists . . . were trying to put a spoke in the wheel of Socialism. (*Manchester Examiner,* July 1885)

put the kibosh on To render ineffective or nonfunctional; to squelch or quash; to put an end to, to dispose of; to put out of countenance. The origin of this expression is obscure. It has been conjectured that *kibosh* comes from the Irish *cie bais* 'cap of death.' The *OED,* however, does not support this hypothesis, but suggests that the phrase has Yiddish or Anglo-Hebraic origins.

> The directive puts the kibosh on one of the few potentially valuable efforts that the United States has been making in the field of psychological warfare. (R. H. Rovere, cited in *Webster's Third*)

Application of this expression is not limited to ideas and activities, but extends to persons as well, as evidenced by the following citation from C. Roberts' *Adrift in America* (1891):

> It was attending one of these affairs which finally put the "kibosh" on me.

put the whammy on To jinx or hex; to give the evil eye, to mesmerize; to render speechless, to incapacitate; to overpower, ruin, or destroy. The whammy is a gesture or object whose magical properties cast a curse on its victim. As a term it was probably derived onomatopoeically from the sound made by the gesture of "whamming" the fist into the palm. Its popularity stems from the well-known "Li'l Abner" comic strip by Al Capp in which Eagle Eye Feegle's

one-eye stare was dubbed "the whammy." Two eyes made it a *double whammy.*

> So what's put the whammy on the National Science Foundation bill? (H. Alexander, *The Bulletin* [Philadelphia], September, 1949)

spike [someone's] gun To thwart someone's possibilities for success; to hamper or prevent someone from reaching a goal. This expression is derived from the practice of driving a spike into the vent of a gun, thus rendering it inoperable. The expression maintains contemporary use.

steal [someone's] thunder To reduce or negate the effect of an argument, performance, remark, etc., by anticipating it; to thwart, frustrate, or forestall; to use as one's own the ideas, inventions, or techniques of another. This expression is credited to John Dennis (1657–1734), a playwright who developed a new technique for producing stage thunder and used it in his ill-fated and short-lived opus, *Appius and Virginia.* Some time later, upon hearing his "thunder" used in a performance of *Macbeth,* Dennis cried out, "Damn them! . . . They will not let my play run, but they steal my thunder!"

> Harry Truman is no man to let Congress steal his political thunder. (*Time,* May, 1950)

take the teeth out of To render harmless or ineffective; to deprive of strength or power. Teeth are basic for nourishment, attack, or defense. Figuratively the word *teeth* refers to any effective means of accomplishment or compulsion, as in the following *Webster's Third* citation:

> . . . reluctant to pass legislation with *teeth* regarding this issue. (T. L. Reller)

An Aesop's fable also cited as a possible source of this expression tells of a lion in love with a maiden who told him to pull his teeth and trim his claws, after which he was easily overpowered. *Take the teeth out of* is currently used almost exclusively of legislation.

take the wind out of [someone's] sails
To destroy a person's self-confidence by effectively invalidating his argument, stand, or convictions; to frustrate or thwart; to put a pin in someone's balloon. The expression is an expansion of the earlier nautical phrase *to take the wind of* 'to sail windward of another ship so as to intercept the wind.'

A young upstart of a rival, Llanelly . . . which has taken a great deal of the wind out of the sails of its older neighbor. (*Harper's Magazine,* February, 1883)

throw a monkey wrench into the works
To interfere with the smooth operation of things, to upset plans or impede their progress; sometimes to sabotage or undermine deliberately; also, especially British, *to throw a spanner into the works.* The allusion is probably to the chaotic effect such a literal act of sabotage would have on machinery. The American expression dates from at least 1920.

It would throw another big monkey wrench into the already wobbly Japanese economy. (*The Christian Science Monitor,* January, 1947)

throw cold water on To discourage, to have a damping effect upon; to disparage or put down; to put the kibosh on. *Cold* connotes the antithesis of all that is vital, enthusiastic, and passionate. Thus, *to throw cold water* on one's ambitions, ideas, or projects is to have a deadening effect, to be unsupportive in attitude or action.

TIME (See also DURATION, FREQUENCY, OPPORTUNENESS, TIMELINESS.)

before one had nails on one's toes Before one was born; long ago, in the distant past. This expression refers to the fact that a baby's toenails develop prenatally. Thus, an event or other matter that occurred before a person's toe-

nails developed occurred before he was born. In its most common usage, the expression cites a younger person's age as the basis for denigrating his status, experience, ideals, or philosophies.

There's Ulysses and old Nestor, whose wit was moldy ere your grandsires had nails on their toes. (Shakespeare, *Troilus and Cressida,* II,i)

between dog and wolf Neither day nor night; dusk. The dog is a domesticated animal, and therefore associated with all that is civilized and ordered, such as the day. On the other hand, the wild and mysterious wolf is associated with the night, from the image of a wolf baying at the moon. Although they are of the same family, dogs and wolves are as different as day and night. And between dog and wolf, or day and night, is dusk.

blind man's holiday Dusk; neither day nor night. This phrase, used as early as 1599, is said to refer to the time just before candles are lighted when it is too dark to work or read—a fitting time to rest, or "take a holiday." However, this explanation does not account for the use of *blind man* in the phrase. Perhaps dusk is a holiday for a blind man because it offers him a brief respite from his aloneness. He has company because everyone is in the same state of semidarkness until the candles are lit. In fact, being accustomed to the darkness, a blind man can enjoy an advantage. The phrase is rarely heard today.

D-day A deadline, the last hour, the moment of truth; a date established for any significant event, originally for a secret military operation. During World War II, the Allied invasion of Normandy was set for June 5, 1944. To avoid referring to the date, for security reasons, the code word D-day was adopted. Hostile weather conditions, however, forced the postponement of this famous D-day until the next day. The term is currently used in a similar way, especially in the academic world where students often refer to the due date for the submission of work as D-day.

graveyard shift A work shift usually from twelve midnight until eight in the morning; any late-night shift; also the *graveyard watch.* Factories running 24 hours a day employ three shifts—day, swing, and midnight or graveyard. The expression gained currency during World War II when so many factories were operating around-the-clock. The phrase, American slang and dating from the early part of this century, is an allusion to the late hour of the shift, which works in the dead of night when it is quiet and still as a graveyard.

> A month later he and his fellows went on "graveyard" shift. (*The Saturday Evening Post,* November, 1908)

zero hour Deadline; an anticipated stressful or critical period of time; the precise time established for the commencement of a military operation. This phrase originated and was widely used during World War I. It was for the most part replaced by the analogous term *H-hour* during World War II. As currently used, the expression often carries an implication of dread.

TIMELINESS (See also **OPPORTUNENESS.**)

at the eleventh hour At the last possible moment; very late. This expression is found in the parable of the vineyard (Matthew 20:1–16), in which the laborers who did not begin work until the eleventh hour of the day received the same wages as those who had worked all day.

> An 11th-hour attempt . . . to block State Bond Commission approval of $2.8 million for the two new buildings at Western Connecticut State College . . . failed Thursday. (*The Hartford Courant,* March, 1979)

high time Almost too late; the most fitting time. Since the 13th century, *high* has been used to mean 'well advanced,' or 'fully come' (*OED*). Some speculate that there is a connection between this meaning and the time during the day when the sun is highest in the sky. It is a peak time, like the highest point which is also a turning point on a curve.

> It was . . . high time to make a contrary law. (William Lambarde, *Eirenarcha,* 1581)

This expression is almost always heard as part of an exhortation to act immediately.

in the nick of time At the proper or crucial moment; just in time. During the Middle Ages, it was common practice to record payments, debts, etc., by making a *nick* 'a notch or cut' in a stick in order to indicate credits or debits. Since a landowner risked substantial fines or seizure of his property if payments (such as taxes) were not made on time, it was in his best interest to arrive at the appointed place of collection before such penalties would be imposed. But human nature being what it is, a debtor often made payment at the last possible moment, giving rise to the now obsolete *in the nick* 'the precise moment when something requires to be done.' The addition of *of time* is a redundancy that has persisted for centuries.

> If he had not gone at the very nick of time, the ship could not have failed of being very quickly blown up. (Archibald Lovell, *Thevenot's Travels Into the Levant,* 1687)

under the wire Barely meeting time requirements; just at the deadline. The expression comes from horse racing, the wire being the tape stretching across the track. The nose of the winning horse strains forward "under the wire," breaking it for victory as he crosses the finishing line. The expression's figurative use most often refers to temporal rather than spatial proximity.

TIMIDITY (See COWARDICE, FEAR.)

TIPPLING (See also DRUNKENNESS, FOOD and DRINK.)

belt the grape To imbibe heavily; to get drunk; to get a buzz on. *Belt,* an obsolete slang verb meaning to swallow, was popular in the mid-19th century. As part of the U.S. slang phrase *belt the grape,* it again gained currency in the 1930s. *Grape* usually refers to wine but can be used loosely to mean any alcoholic beverage.

> Jack takes to belting the old grape right freely to get his zing back. (Damon Runyon, *Guys and Dolls,* 1931)

bend the elbow To drink liquor excessively and habitually; to tipple, to booze. Variants include *to crook* or *tip* or *lift the elbow,* the last apparently the oldest, since it appears in an *OED* citation dated 1823.

down the hatch A popular toast, usually said before tossing off a drink in one gulp. *Hatch,* a slang term for throat, is a figurative extension of the nautical *hatch* 'covered deck opening on a ship.'

have one for the worms To take an alcoholic drink; to have one for the road. The former belief that alcohol killed worms in the stomach furnished yet another convenient excuse for having a drink.

smash the teapot To fall off the wagon, to resume drinking alcoholic beverages after a period of abstinence. The teapot of this British expression is no doubt a punning reference to that of a teetotaler.

splice the main brace To indulge in alcoholic beverages; to celebrate an occasion with potent whiskey. The main brace of a ship is the rope which controls the main sail. In the British navy, the sailor who performed the difficult task of splicing the main brace was often awarded an extra ration of rum; hence the expression's current figurative use.

> I can tell him enough Navy yarns to fill a book—providing the main brace is spliced occasionally. (J. H. Jennings, in *Life,* November, 1940)

tap the admiral To open a cask of liquor, usually secretly; to open a bottle, to pop the cork; hence simply to drink, to hit the bottle, to have a nip—all usually on the sly. This phrase reputedly derived from an incident in which a group of sailors surreptitiously broached a keg of liquor, only to discover that it contained the corpse of an admiral, apparently placed in the brew for purposes of preservation while being transported back to England.

wet one's whistle To drink, usually a small quantity of hard liquor; to imbibe a bit, to take a nip. *Whistle* is here used jocularly for the mouth or throat, which must be kept moist in order to speak, sing, or whistle. *Wet whistle* appears with this meaning as early as the 14th century, in Chaucer and in the Towneley mysteries. The expression using *wet* as a verb does not appear until the 1500s.

> Lets . . . drink the other cup to wet our whistles, and so sing away all sad thoughts. (Isaak Walton, *The Compleat Angler,* 1653)

TOTALITY (See also INCLUSIVENESS, THOROUGHNESS.)

ins and outs All the details of a subject, occurrence, etc.; all there is to know about something, including nuances and subtle particulars. Some say *ins* originally referred to the party in government, and *outs* to the opposition. However, the meaning of *ins and outs* suggests wholeness and entirety because of the conjunction of opposites, regardless of what each opposite signifies. A somewhat literal application of this phrase is in reference to the windings and turnings in a road, and by extension, of less concrete things, such as a plan or course of action.

love me, love my dog A proverbial way of saying "If you love me, you must accept my faults along with my good qualities." *Dog* stands for an unpleasant or undesirable but intrinsic part of a person's character, one that cannot be ignored or avoided. John Heywood used this expression in his *Proverbs* (1546). It is also said to have been a popular 12th-century Latin proverb from the writings of Saint Bernard: *Qui me amat, amet et canem meum.*

thread and thrum A whole, a totality; anything taken in its entirety, particularly when such is seen as embracing both positive and negative elements; the good and the bad, the wheat and the chaff, the virtues and the vices. *Thread and thrum* represents the entire length of warp yarn, including the tuft which fastens it to the loom and which remains so attached when the web is cut off. In Shakespeare's *Midsummer Night's Dream,* Bottom as Pyramus discovers the blood-stained mantle of his beloved Thisbe and presumes her dead, whereupon he asks the Fates to make the destruction complete:

O Fates! come, come,
Cut thread and thrum,
Quail, crush, conclude, and quell!
(V,i)

The above use also plays on the notion that the Fates determine man's life by spinning, measuring, and cutting its thread at whim. See also **threads and thrums,** MIXTURE.

the whole ball of wax Any entity taken as a totality; any matter or concern together with its ramifications, implications, and consequences; its components, particulars, and details, etc. No satisfactory explanation or origin for this very common expression has yet been found.

TRANQUILLITY (See PEACE.)

TRICKERY (See also PLOY, SWINDLING.)

hocus-pocus See MAGIC.

pull a fast one To trick by doing or saying something clever and unexpected; to gain the upper hand by a sudden show of skill; to swindle or defraud. Perhaps this originally U.S. slang expression first applied to a deft movement, such as in a game of football or some other sport, which caused control of the ball to change hands.

Brick pulled a fast one in the St. Mary's game. (J. Sayre, *Rackety Rax,* 1932)

However, this expression and the analogous *put one over on* or *put over a fast one* now apply to any remark or action which gives a person unfair advantage.

The thought that a girl capable of thinking up a fast one like that should be madly throwing herself away on Blair Eggleston . . . was infinitely saddening. (P. G. Wodehouse, *Hot Water,* 1932)

pull [someone's] leg To harmlessly mislead a person; to bamboozle or trick in a jocular manner; to tease or kid. This expression may have derived from the "trippers-up," a former group of English criminals who tripped and subsequently robbed their victims. The expression's current reference is to a scheme in which the victim is purposely but humorously hoodwinked.

I suspected that he was pulling my leg, but a glance at him convinced me otherwise. (F. Scott Fitzgerald, *The Great Gatsby,* 1925)

pull the wool over [someone's] eyes To deceive or delude, to hoodwink or bamboozle.

He said his only purpose was to "cite substantial evidence that will show just who is trying to pull the wool over the eyes of the American people." (*St. Paul Pioneer Press*, June, 1949)

Attempts to account for the use of *wool* in this expression are unconvincing. This popular Americanism dates from the 19th century.

rope in To draw into some scheme or enterprise by deception; to take in, to ensnare or hook. This expression had its origins in the American West when roundups were commonplace and cowboys spent their time roping or lassoing cattle in order to brand them.

He will probably rope the victim into his favorite charity, the Margaret MacMillan Memorial Fund. (*Time*, February, 1950)

skulduggery See CRIMINALITY.

take for a ride See DEATH.

thimblerig To cleverly manipulate data in order to deceive or confuse; to pull a fast one; to cheat or swindle. Thimblerigging was a swindling game popular in the 19th century at race courses and fairs. The game involved three thimbles, one of which had a pea hidden under it. The victim of this swindle would bet on which thimble was hiding the pea. Reference to the trick appeared in print by the early 1800s. Soon after, the term was used figuratively for any deceitful or underhanded manipulation.

Don't let us have any juggling and thimblerigging with virtue and vice. (William Makepeace Thackeray, *Catherine*, 1839)

throw dust in [someone's] eyes To mislead or deceive, to dupe; to confuse or bewilder, to prevent someone from seeing the reality of a situation; to throw someone off guard, to render someone temporarily unfit to act. The most popular explanation for this expression is that it derives from the Muhammadan practice of casting dust into the air to confound religious enemies. Apparently Muhammad used this common military expedient on a number of occasions. The following quotation from the Koran alludes to the practice.

Neither didst thou, O Mahomet, cast dust into their eyes, but it was God who confounded them.

The figurative use of *throw dust in [someone's] eyes* appeared in print as early as the 1600s.

TRIVIALITY (See INSIGNIFICANCE.)

TYRANNY (See DOMINATION.)

U

UNCERTAINTY (See CONFUSION.)

UNCONVENTIONALITY (See also ECCENTRICITY.)

march to the beat of a different drummer See INDEPENDENCE.

offbeat Unusual, unconventional, nonconformist, odd, weird. The current meaning of the term is a figurative extension of its use in music to denote the unaccented beat of a measure. In traditional music, the downbeat is accented and the upbeat is unaccented. Black musicians deviated from this norm by playing syncopated music, i.e., music which stressed traditionally unaccented beats. Syncopated or offbeat music was thus considered unusual and unconventional. The term *offbeat* itself eventually acquired these senses, along with their usual extended ones of 'strange, bizarre, weird.'

> The off-beat death . . . in a[n] off-Broadway hotel room. (*The Daily News* [New York], September, 1957)

off the wall Strange, far-out, way-out, weird; insane, crazy, out of one's mind.

> Deputy Inspector Martin Duffy said Mrs. Morea was "very, very distraught—really incoherent, off the wall." (*The New York Times,* July, 1972)

The exact origin of this U.S. slang expression is unknown, but it may be an allusion to the padded walls of mental institutions, designed to protect overly distraught inmates from hurting themselves. Of recent coinage, the phrase enjoys great popularity in the United States; like its synonymous slang terms, *off the wall* describes ideas, beliefs, schemes, etc., as well as persons and their behavior.

UNFAIRNESS (See UNSCRUPULOUSNESS.)

UNNATURALNESS

against the grain In opposition to one's basic temperament, against one's will. In this expression *grain* refers to the direction of the fibers in wood. Planing across the natural direction of the fibers is difficult. By analogy, the grain has come to mean the human disposition or will, as exemplified in the following:

> . . . and that your minds,
> Pre-occupied with what you rather must do
> Than what you should made you against the grain
> To voice him consul.
> (Shakespeare, *Coriolanus,* II,iii)

A second explanation is that the phrase came from the French *contre le gré* 'against the will,' partially translated into English as *against the gré,* and so used by Samuel Pepys in his *Diary.*

fish out of water A person not in his regular environment; one working in a job unrelated to his chosen profession; someone who is restless, fidgety, or discontented because of his surroundings. A fish taken out of water begins flopping about in a desperate attempt to return to its natural habitat. Eventually, the lack of its regular environment kills the fish. Thus, a person who is restless or uncomfortable because of strange surroundings is often likened to a fish out of water.

a square peg in a round hole A person whose job is completely unsuited for him; a person who attempts a project or undertaking which is incompatible with his skills and background; also, *a round peg in a square hole.* This self-explanatory expression retains frequent use today.

Was there ever a more glaring case of square peg in round hole and round peg in square? (*Westminster Gazette,* December, 1901)

UNOBTRUSIVENESS

low-key Laid-back, subdued, toned-down, understated, purposefully low-profile. Music played in a low key is softer and more muted than that played in a higher one. Use of the term dates from the late 19th or early 20th century.

With the UDA building its barricades, how long can the "low key" phase last. (*The Guardian,* July, 1972)

a low profile Inconspicuous behavior or policy; an unobtrusive or restrained existence away from the limelight; often in the phrase *to keep a low profile* 'to stay out of the public eye.' *Profile* in this case symbolizes one's public image, and *low* has the sense of not highly visible, nonprotruding—as in low relief.

The Nixon doctrine of "low profile" involvement, in other words a maximum of aid and a minimum of US troops. (*The Guardian,* August, 1970)

wallflower A woman who does not join in the festivities at a dance or ball, either by choice or because she does not have a partner; by stereotypic implication, a shy or homely woman. In the world of plants, the wallflower *(Cheiranthus cheiri)* is a yellow or orange flower that grows on old walls and buildings. According to a legend recounted by the English poet Robert Herrick (1591–1674), a woman who had long been kept in captivity tried to reach her lover by climbing down a steep wall, but slipped and died. Herrick continues:

Love, in pity of the deed,
And her loving luckless speed,
Turned her to this plant we call
Now the "flower of the wall."

Thus, a girl or woman who sits along a wall at a dance is sometimes called a "wallflower," likening her to the blossom of the same name.

[He] dances quadrilles with every wallflower in the room. (*New Monthly Magazine,* 1840)

UNRESTRAINT

as well be hanged for a sheep as a lamb Once involved in a matter, one might as well commit oneself entirely and go the whole hog.

ball the jack See SPEEDING.

catch-as-catch-can Anything goes, no holds barred; everything is up for grabs, and any and all means for getting it are permitted; hence also, unplanned, unsystematic, hit-or-miss. The expression derives from a style of wrestling in which no restraints are placed on permissible holds. Antecedents of the phrase appeared in print as early as the 16th century:

Catch that catch may. (John Heywood, *Proverbs,* 1562)

The expression may carry connotations of opportunism and unethical expediency, or simply of haphazardness and disorganization.

do it up brown To spare no pains or expense in an endeavor or undertaking; to go all out. According to the *OED, to do brown* 'to do thoroughly' may derive from roasting, since meat is brown when thoroughly cooked. Current use of this expression plays on an extended meaning of *thorough*—not just complete but more than complete, or all out, without scrimping or cutting corners.

go for broke To go all out, to do or die, to give one's all. This recent U.S. slang expression refers to the gambler's practice of betting all his money on one throw of the dice, thus risking instant impoverishment.

The enemy is "going all out— . . . he is going for broke." (*The Guardian*, February, 1968)

go whole hog To engage in an activity completely and unreservedly. The most plausible origin for this expression stems from the British slang term *hog* 'shilling'; thus, to go whole hog was to spend the whole shilling at once. Another explanation relates the phrase to the Muslim injunction against eating one unspecified part of the pig. The term gained popularity in the United States during Andrew Jackson's presidential campaign in 1828 and gave rise to the noun *whole-hogger* 'a die-hard political enthusiast.'

let her rip To allow or cause something such as an engine to go as fast as it can; to move ahead quickly, often violently or recklessly; to "open her up." This expression is of uncertain origin, but it is likely that *rip* is adapted from its verbal sense of 'to open up.' One source suggests that the expression should be credited to a steamboat captain who, feeling protected by his newly acquired insurance, may have pushed his vessel's engines to the limit saying, "Let her rip (i.e., it doesn't matter if the engines explode), I'm insured!" Although it has further been suggested that *rip* may have been derived as a bit of cryptic humor from the gravestone epitaph, "R.I.P." [rest in peace], this theory, like the other, seems somewhat implausible.

Why in the name of hell's eternal flints don't the engineer pitch in more pine knots and crack on more steam? Let her rip. (*New Orleans Picayune*, August, 1846)

no holds barred Without restrictions; anything goes. Although the precise origin of this expression is unknown, it would seem to come from the wrestling use of *hold* 'grasp or grip.' Consequently, a match in which no holds were barred (disallowed) would permit any and all of the numerous varieties of wrestling locks. The phrase appeared as early as 1952 in the *Economist*.

over shoes, over boots This phrase expresses reckless abandon in continuing a course of action already entered upon. The *OED* defines *over shoes* literally and figuratively as 'deeply immersed or sunk [in something],' and since boots are usually higher than shoes, *over boots* can only mean even more deeply involved in or committed to a certain course of action.

pull out all the stops To use every resource at one's command; to avail oneself of any and all means at one's disposal to achieve a desired end. *Stops* in this expression refers to the stop knobs on an organ console by means of which the player controls the sets of pipes.

shoot one's bolt To make an all-out effort; to do all that one possibly can; to pull no punches; to shoot the works. This expression is derived from a 13th-century adage later stated by John Heywood in *Proverbs* (1546), and by William Shakespeare in *Henry V* (III,vii): "A fool's bolt is soon shot." A bolt is the missile shot from a crossbow, which, once fired, must be cranked up to produce the tension required for the next shot. Since this cranking takes time, the crossbowman was virtually defenseless during the operation. Therefore, a bolt was shot only after careful deliberation and at considerable risk. Although applied in various contexts, the expression is most popular among sports reporters.

The home players had shot their bolt, and in thirty minutes the Birmingham team added two goals. (*Daily Express*, February 28, 1901)

shoot one's wad In gambling, to bet all of one's money on the outcome of a single race, game, throw of the dice, etc.; in any endeavor, to make a final, all-out effort or a last-ditch, no-holds-barred attempt. Since a wad is a roll of money or a finite quantity of some valuable resource, to *shoot one's wad* is to expend it all at one time in hopes of success, usually with the implication that a fairly substantial risk of failure or defeat is involved.

shoot the works To make an intense effort, utilizing all available resources; to go the limit; to gamble or spend all of one's money; to tell all one knows about a given matter. This expression was probably first used by gamblers to describe a person's betting all the money he had on a single throw of the dice. Though now used in many contexts, *shoot the works* still implies an endeavor in which no effort or expense is spared, and one which involves a certain degree of risk.

> It is not my intention to shoot the whole works, but merely to examine a few specimens [of slang] and guess at their meaning. (*American Speech*, 1941)

the sky's the limit A statement meaning that, in essence, there are no limits, often implying extravagance, lavishness, opulence, etc. This frequently used expression alludes to the concept of *sky* as a limitless, virtually infinite entity, and is derived from an earlier adage, "No limits but the sky," which appeared in Miguel de Cervantes' *Don Quixote, Part I* (1605). A related variation is the phrase *to the sky* or *skies*.

UNSCRUPULOUSNESS

hit below the belt To use unfair means; to go against the rules. The Marquis of Queensberry rules of prize fighting, adopted in 1867, prohibit boxers from hitting their opponents below the waist belt. A derivative, commonly used term is *low blow*.

low blow An unfair or unscrupulous attack, a cheap shot. This term probably derives from *hit below the belt;* in prize fighting, a violation of the Marquis of Queensberry rules. The word is almost always used figuratively, meaning to take unfair advantage, to strike where one is most vulnerable, to hit someone when he is down.

URGENCY

all hands and the cook A state of emergency which of necessity becomes everyone's top priority. This early American cowboy expression described the precarious state of affairs in which the herds were wild and all available persons were needed to bring the situation under control. Under normal circumstances, cowboys tended herds and cooks fed the cowhands; however, an emergency required that everyone chip in, temporarily ignoring differences of rank or task.

D-day See TIME.

sands are running out Time is passing; the remaining time is getting short; life is waning. The allusion is to the sands of an hourglass which have long been a symbol of the time allotted for an individual's life.

> I saw, my time, how it did run, as sand out of the glass. (Lord Henry Haward, *Tottel's Miscellany*, 1557)

when push comes to shove See EXACERBATION.

when the chips are down When the situation is crucial or urgent; when action must be taken; in the clutch. This expression appears to derive from poker; the chips are "down" when they are "in," i.e., when everyone has anted up and must play his hand.

zero hour See TIME.

USELESSNESS (See EXTRANEOUSNESS, FUTILITY.)

V

VACILLATION   (See also **RECANTA-TION**.)

back and fill   To vacillate, tergiversate; to blow hot and cold, to be wishy-washy. *Back and fill* is a nautical phrase describing a method of maneuvering a sailboat in which the sails are trimmed so that the wind strikes them first on the forward and then on the after side, so as to reduce forward movement. The figurative U.S. informal use of the phrase plays on the idea of the alternating forward and backward motion as opposed to a significant movement in any one direction. It is used to describe any lack of commitment to a particular point of view.

blow hot and cold   To accept first, then reject; to seesaw, shilly-shally. This phrase stems from Aesop's fable of a traveler who was entertained by a satyr. The traveler blew his fingers to warm them, and then with the same breath, blew his broth to cool it. Apparently the satyr was appalled to meet one who could blow both hot and cold, and said:

> If you have gotten a trick of blow-ing hot and cold out of the same mouth, I've e'en done with ye. (R. Lestrange, *Fables of Aesop*, 1694)

As commonly used, *blow hot and cold* smacks less of hypocrisy than *back and fill*; it seems more natural and less manipulative.

Box and Cox   Alternately sharing the same position, serving the same function or occupying the same space. *Box and Cox*, an 1847 farce by J. M. Morton, features two men—John Box and James Cox—who occupied the same apartment without being aware of each other's existence. One worked the day shift and the other worked at night. The *OED's* earliest citation for the phrase is from 1881.

Representing mind and body as play-ing a perpetual game of Box and Cox. (C. E. Raven, *Creator Spirit*, 1927)

The French Community . . . shares, Box-and-Coxwise, the Luxembourg Palace with the French Senate. (*Spectator*, August 14, 1959)

fall between two stools   To be indeci-sive, to vacillate; to fail because of the inability to make a choice or decision. This expression implies that if someone cannot decide which of two stools to sit upon, he is likely to fall between them.

> The unphilosophical attempt to sit upon two stools. (Joseph C. Neal, *Charcoal Sketches*, 1837)

The French equivalent, *être assis entre deux chaises*, means literally 'to be seated between two chairs.'

hold with the hare and run with the hounds   To straddle the fence; to play both ends against the middle; to get the best of both worlds. This hunting phrase is stronger than *back and fill* or *blow hot and cold*, implying an inability to commit oneself to one point of view, and an attempt to cover up by espous-ing both sides at once.

in dock, out nettle   Inconstancy, vacil-lation, changeability, instability. This obsolete expression was originally part of a charm repeated while rubbing leaves of the herb dock into nettle stings in order to counteract any ill effects: "Nettle in, dock out, Dock in, nettle out, Nettle in, dock out, Dock rub nettle out." An early figurative use of the expression is found in Nicholas Udall's *Ralph Roister Doister* (1553):

> I can not skill of such changeable mettle,
> There is nothing with them but in dock out nettle.

Jekyll and Hyde   One whose nature is contradictory—sometimes good and benevolent, other times evil and malevolent; a split personality; anything marked by the opposition of antagonistic forces. This popular phrase comes from Robert Louis Stevenson's *The Case of Dr. Jekyll and Mr. Hyde* (1886). In this story, Jekyll appears as a kind, respectable character, Hyde as an ugly, despicable figure; however, both personalities belong to one man. The following quotation from the *Times Literary Supplement* (July 2, 1931) shows a current use of this phrase.

> Turner was a case of Jekyll and Hyde in real life and oscillated continuously between the Victorian respectability of Bloomsbury . . . and the Rabelaisian society of the London Docks.

mugwump See **INDEPENDENCE**.

on the fence Undecided, especially in regard to political issues. This expression alludes to the dilemma of a person atop a wall who must decide which is the safer side to descend. In contemporary usage, this American slang phrase usually describes a politician who waits to see how an issue fares before committing his support in either direction.

> Now all would-but-dare-not-be-politicians who insist in sitting on the fence, will be amerced a penalty for the same. (*Annals of Cleveland*, 1830)

a reed shaken by the wind A spineless, wishy-washy person whose opinions shift with the prevailing political or conventional winds; a tergiversator. As currently used, the image stands on its own; the phrase bears no relationship to the New Testament context in which it was spoken by Jesus regarding John the Baptist.

> "What went ye out into the wilderness to see? A reed shaken with the wind?" (Matthew 11:7)

shilly-shally To vacillate between two ways of thinking or acting; to dally with trifles to avoid making a decision. The original phrase was *shall I, shall I,* which was altered to *shill I, shall I.* The

present form of *shilly-shally* was used as early as the 1700s. It is an innocuous phrase which, like *blow hot and cold,* suggests no hypocrisy or manipulative behavior.

> To shilly-shally on the matter, to act in one way today and in a different way tomorrow. (F. W. Farrar, *Life and Work of St. Paul,* 1879)

weathercock A person of wavering principles; an indecisive person; a trend follower. In the 9th century, a papal decree ordered each church to place the likeness of a cock atop its steeple in allusion to St. Peter's triple denial of Jesus before the cock crowed twice. After a time, these cocks were mounted on pivots so that they pointed to the direction from which the wind was blowing. Thus, *weathercock* acquired the sense of something being directed by the fancy of the prevailing wind. The term, used figuratively since the time of Chaucer, still carries its meaning of one of vacillating principles.

> He was . . . a terrible weathercock in the matter of opinion. (Robert Brough, *Marston Lynch,* 1870)

The expression's figurative meaning has been extended to include a person who quickly adopts the latest styles and fads, perhaps as an analogy between the ever-changing directions of the fashion world.

VALIDITY

hold water To be valid, sound, and defensible; to show no inconsistency or deficiency when put to the test. As early as the beginning of the 17th century, this expression was used figuratively of arguments, statements, etc., although both *hold* and *water* can be taken literally to describe a vessel or other receptacle's soundness in retaining a liquid.

> Let them produce a more rational account of any other opinion, that will hold water . . . better than this mine doth. (John French, *The York-shire Spaw,* 1652)

a leg to stand on Viable proof or justification; something on which to base one's claims or attitudes. A leg provides support and helps to maintain balance. Figuratively this expression is most often heard in the negative *not have a leg to stand on,* referring to one who fails to support his attitudes or behavior. It is frequently used in legal contexts where an inability to provide proof or justification is pronounced. The still current expression dates from the 16th century.

> She hasn't a leg to stand on in the case. He's divorcing her, she's not divorcing him. (M. Spark, *Bachelors,* 1960)

VALUE (See **WORTHINESS, WORTHLESSNESS.**)

VEHICLES

Black Maria A van for conveying prisoners. This U.S. colloquial term reputedly derives from a Black woman named Maria Lee who ran a lodging house for sailors in Boston. Apparently she was a prodigious woman whom the police called on when they needed extra strength to handle rambunctious prisoners. Eventually her name became associated with the van which rounded up prisoners and carried them to jail or court.

> A new Black Maria, . . . a new wagon for the conveyance of prisoners to and from the courts of justice. (*Boston Evening Traveller,* September 25, 1847)

bone-shaker A facetious name for early model bicycles; later applied to similarly unsteady automobiles such as the early model Fords. Since the first bicycles lacked rubber tires and other modern cushioning conveniences and few roads were paved, their ride was something less than smooth and comfortable. The term was in use as early as 1874.

bucket of bolts An irreverent American slang term for an old run-down car that rattles and shakes noisily when moving, producing a sound similar to the rattling of a bucketful of bolts or screws.

meatwagon An ambulance. This slang expression alludes to the damaged human flesh transported to hospitals in these emergency vehicles.

> We'll need a couple of meatwagons. The minister and two other people were killed and . . . there're a lot of injured. (E. McBain, *Hail, Hail, the Gang's All Here,* 1971)

This expression often includes both paddy wagons and hearses.

paddy wagon A patrol wagon; an enclosed truck or van used by the police to transport prisoners; a Black Maria. *Paddy,* a corruption of the common Irish name Patrick, was once used as a nickname for anyone of Irish descent. Since many police officers in major cities at the turn of the century were Irish, their patrol wagons came to be known as *paddy wagons* by association. Although the ethnic implications were gradually lost after the 1920s, the expression has remained in widespread use.

> Police who attempted to enforce city segregation rules met with a torrent of jeers, and several tennis players who sat down on the courts had to be carried to paddy wagons. (*Aurora* [Illinois] *Beacon News,* November 7, 1948)

panda car A police car. This British colloquialism undoubtedly alludes to the appearance of English police cars: small, white vehicles with a broad horizontal blue stripe along the middle.

rattletrap A rickety old car that rattles and clatters and shakes while in motion; a dangerously dilapidated vehicle.

VEXATION (See also **ANGRINESS, FURY, IRRITATION.**)

cross [someone's] bows To annoy, displease, or offend; to overstep one's bounds and behave inappropriately toward another person. This expression has nautical origins. When one ship passes in front of another, crossing her path, the first is said to "cross the bows" of the second. Such a move is considered dangerous and a breach of the rules of the road. Both the nautical and figurative meanings are in use today.

drive up the wall To plague or badger someone to the breaking point; to drive someone "crazy" by repeated harassment. This slang expression brings to mind the picture of someone literally climbing the wall of an enclosing space to escape the source of annoyance. One so driven is said *to climb the wall*.

get [someone's] back up To anger or provoke. The reference is to the way a cat arches its back when angered or threatened. This expression appeared as early as 1728 in *The Provok'd Husband* by Sir John Vanbrugh and Colley Cibber.

get [someone's] dander up To arouse someone's anger or temper. There are two theories as to the origin of the phrase. One hypothesis suggests that *dander* derives from *dandruff* 'the scurf of the scalp.' Another theory is based on the meaning of *dander* as ferment used in making molasses in the West Indies. By extension *ferment* means 'agitation or tumult.' Thus, to get someone's dander up is to provoke and agitate him. This expression dates at least from 1831, when it appeared in the *American Comic Annual* by H. J. Finn.

get [someone's] Dutch up To arouse someone's ire, to madden; also *get [someone's] Irish* or *Indian up*. Although the exact origins of these expressions are unknown, they would seem to be references to the reputed hotheaded nature of the nationalities in question. Barrere and Leland's *Dictionary of Slang, Jargon and Cant* (1888) offers the following:

Irish, Indian, Dutch (American), all of these words are used to signify anger or arousing temper. But to

say that one has his "Indian up," implies a great degree of vindictiveness, while Dutch wrath is stubborn but yielding to reason.

get [someone's] goat To annoy or irritate; to antagonize or frustrate a person. The expression is synonymous with the French *prendre la chèvre,* literally 'to take the goat.' The phrase, in general use since World War I, implies the prodding of someone to anger or irritability.

"You certainly got my goat" she said in the quaint American fashion, "telling me little No-no was too fat." (H. L. Wilson, *Ruggles of Red Gap,* 1915)

get [someone's] hackles up To irritate or annoy; to anger, often with pugilistic potential. This expression stems from the sport of cock-fighting; hackles are the long, shiny feathers on the neck of certain birds such as gamecocks. When confronted by its opponent, a gamecock reacts with a show of strength, causing its hackles to become erect. Through the years, this expression and the related *get [someone's] dander up* (where *dander* may be a corruption of *dandruff,* thus implying hair) have been applied to dogs and cats. When these animals are threatened, the hair on their neck involuntarily stands on end. Eventually, the figurative use to describe a person became common.

As my hackles were now fairly up, I crept and ran as well as I could after my wounded game. (Clive Phillipps-Wolley, *Sport in the Crimea and Caucasus,* 1881)

get [someone's] monkey up To anger or provoke. The reference is to the irritable and irascible temperament of monkeys. Used as early as 1863 in *Tyneside Songs,* the expression is originally British and has never been common in the United States.

ruffle feathers To anger, irritate, annoy; to disturb, upset, agitate. When a bird is threatened or challenged, the feathers on its back and neck become ruffled, that is, erect, in a show of strength and apparent anger. This expression is applied figuratively to describe a manifestation of a person's anger.

> The dean ruffled his plumage, and said with asperity . . . (Frederic Farrar, *Julian Home*, 1859)

VICTIMIZATION (See also DOMI-NATION, MANIPULATION.)

ambulance chaser An overly aggressive lawyer who solicits clients in unethical or at best unprofessional ways. The term derives from those who actually made it a practice to arrive at the scene of a disaster in order to capitalize on its potential for their personal gain.

> In New York City there is a style of lawyers known to the profession as "ambulance chasers," because they are on hand wherever there is a railway wreck, or a street-car collision, or a gasoline explosion with . . . their offers of professional service. (*Congressional Record,* July 24, 1897)

Aunt Sally A victim or scapegoat; also, an object of derision or abuse. This British colloquial phrase is derived from the carnival game called "Aunt Sally," in which the figure of a woman's head with a pipe in its mouth is set up, the object being to knock it down by throwing missiles at it. As an object set up to be knocked down, an "Aunt Sally" is an object for attack. It is a trial balloon on the abstract level when used to refer to a proposition or hypothesis submitted for criticism.

babe in the woods See INEXPERIENCE.

carry the can To be the fall guy, to get the short end of the stick; often *to carry the can back* 'to do the dirty work.' The *can* of this British slang expression is said to be that containing dynamite used in blasting operations.

cat's paw A person tricked into doing another's dirty work; dupe or gull; lackey or flunky; often used in the phrase *to be made a cat's paw of.* The term is derived from a fable in which a monkey persuades a cat to use its paw to obtain roasted chestnuts from a fire. The expression, used since the 17th century, appeared in an 1883 issue of *American:*

> Making themselves mere catspaws to secure chestnuts for those publishers.

daughter of the horseleech Anyone, especially a woman, who is overly demanding, clinging, and critical; an exigent harpy. This expression is based on a Biblical reference:

> The horseleach hath two daughters, crying, Give, give. (Proverbs 30:15)

The horseleech is a large, bloodsucking parasite with a forked tongue. It was sometimes used as a medicinal leech in the medieval practice of bloodletting, i.e., removing blood from a diseased person or animal in the belief that this would effect a cure. Because of its size and voracious appetite, the horseleech was thought to be insatiable. Since each fork of its tongue is called a daughter, the expression *daughter of the horseleech* is appropriate in describing someone who acts like a leech, sponging off other people. The word *horseleech* was once used to describe a veterinarian.

fall guy A loser or victim; a scapegoat. The source of this American expression can be found in the early days of professional wrestling near the turn of the century, when contests were often fixed. One participant, the "fall guy," would agree to feign defeat, providing the other wrestler guaranteed him gentle treatment. In modern usage, the term refers to a person who is duped into taking the blame for another's crime or wrongdoing.

flesh-peddler A person who procures customers for sexual entertainment; a pimp. The phrase originally referred to the agent of an aspiring actor or actress who "peddled" his client's physical and mental attributes to the show business bigwigs. The term's disparaging slang meaning is usually used in reference to leaders of prostitution rings or other sexually based enterprises.

frame-up A scheme in which fabricated evidence causes an innocent person to be accused or convicted of a misdeed; also, *put-up job*. Just as a person must fit wood around a painting or photograph to frame it, evidence must be constructed or "framed" to implicate an innocent person in a crime. The expression remains in common usage.

> He had seen honest men framed, and guilty men let off for political reasons. (Mulford, *Cassidy's Protégé,* 1926)

get the short end of the stick To get the worst part of a transaction; to be put at a disadvantage in a bargain or contest; to be taken advantage of and made the fall guy. The precise origin of the phrase has not been found, but it has been conjectured to be vulgar in nature. Another possibility is that the phrase derives from the custom whereby opponents break a stick to determine advantageous starting positions, order, prerogatives, etc., much the way a coin is often tossed today. This concept is preserved in the superstition surrounding the breaking of a wishbone—the person with the longer portion being the one whose wish will be fulfilled. Another possibility is that the expression refers to the practice of drawing straws or sticks to determine which person among several will be given an unsavory task. The one drawing the short straw or stick is the "winner."

give the shaft To victimize, to take unfair advantage of; to deceive, trick, or cheat; to treat in an abusive, harsh manner; to give someone a raw deal. This relatively new American slang expression is used figuratively and is thought to have an obscene, taboo derivation.

gold digger A woman who becomes romantically involved with a man, usually rich, middle-aged, and not terribly attractive, solely for his money and the lavish gifts he bestows on her in return for her sexual favors.

> "Jerry" Lamar is one of a band of pretty little salamanders known to Broadway as "gold diggers," because they "dig" for the gold of their gentlemen friends and spend it being good to their mothers and their pet dogs. (B. Mantle, in *Best Plays of 1919–20,* 1920)

This U.S. slang term dates from the early part of this century.

guinea pig One who is manipulated by another; a scapegoat or patsy; a human being or animal used in scientific or medical experimentation. This expression is derived from the popular laboratory rodent of the same name.

> In some of my experiments I used other athletes as guinea pigs. (R. Bannister, *First Four Minutes,* 1955)

In Great Britain *guinea pig* is also used to describe a person in a high business position who exercises little or no authority. It is the practice there for certain distinguished individuals to allow their names to be listed among the directors of a company, thus adding prestige to the firm. The expression may have originated from the token annual fee, a guinea (a pound plus a shilling), paid to such people.

henpecked To be nagged at constantly or completely dominated by one's wife. Chickens instinctively develop a pecking order—a hierarchy in which the stronger birds assert their authority and dominance over the weaker ones. Once a chicken has established its position at the top of the pecking order, it may peck at the others with no fear of reprisal. Thus, this expression likens the pecking of a dominant hen to the eternal yammering of a harpy.

An obedient henpecked husband. (Washington Irving, *Sketch Book,* 1820)

holding the bag Bearing the sole responsibility or blame; tricked, duped, made the scapegoat or fall guy; often *left holding the bag.* The British equivalent is *holding the baby.* For both versions the idea is that what was to have been shared responsibility ends up as the task of a single person. Frequently the implication is that one has been deserted or double-crossed. One explanation claims the victim is given a bag to hold or watch, thus distracting his attention from the party about to desert. Another theory suggests that the victim has been given a bag of money or goods according to some prearranged scheme, but finds himself flimflammed, with only an empty bag, after his fellows have made off. The former seems more plausible for that meaning related to responsibility; the latter, for that related to trickery.

looking for a dog to kick Seeking someone to blame, looking for a scapegoat or whipping boy. This expression, apparently first used by American cowboys, is based on the psychological premise that people often tend to vent their frustrations on objects, animals, or persons whose status is inferior to their own.

lounge lizard A ladies' man; a man who searches for a wealthy woman to support him; a gigolo; also, *parlor snake.* This expression originated during the 1920s, when certain posh clubs hired handsome young men to dance with and otherwise entertain older women. The term subsequently evolved its connotation of an idle man who seeks a rich patroness in plush hotels, cafes, and other wealthy establishments.

Formal recognition of those firmly attached appendages of Society, the lounge-lizards. (*Punch,* November, 1926)

The term is sometimes used today to describe a man who, as a fixture of the singles' bars, tries to seduce any woman he meets.

man of straw A (often imaginery) person, object, or abstract entity set up for the purpose of being knocked down; a front, a diversionary tactic, a red herring; a nonentity, an ineffectual person, a cipher; also, now rarely, an impoverished person, an indigent. The common denominator of these various meanings of the term is the sense of *straw* as a thing of little worth, substance, or solidity, a sense current in the language since the time of Chaucer. Apparently the original "man of straw" was a man of little substance or means in the monetary sense, i.e., poor. Such were wont to sell their services as witnesses, willing to act as perjurers to obtain money. Supposedly the sign of their availability was a straw in their shoe. Thus, "man of straw" or the equally common *straw man* came to mean one who let himself be used for others' purposes. It is this latter sense which survives today, though the "man of straw" so exploited may be imaginary or fictitious. The phrase first appeared in print in the late 16th century. Thomas DeQuincey used it in its current sense in 1840 (*Works*).

> It is always Socrates and Crito, or Socrates and Phraedrus, . . . in fact, Socrates and some man of straw or good-humoured nine-pin set up to be bowled down as a matter of course.

pigeon An innocent, naïve, or gullible person; a dupe; the victim of a swindle. The pigeon is a bird easily captured in a snare or trap which would be avoided by most other birds.

> I was instantly looked up to as an impending pigeon . . . and every preparation was made for the plucking. (*The Sporting Magazine,* 1794)

scapegoat A victim; a butt or Aunt Sally; one who bears the blame for the misdeeds of others. This word is of Biblical origin. On the Day of Atonement two goats were chosen by lot, one to be sent alive into the wilderness carrying the sins of the people upon its back, the other to be offered as a pure sacrifice to the Lord. According to the *OED*, the term was apparently invented by William Tyndale in his 1530 translation of the Bible.

> And Aaron cast lots over the two goats; one lot for the Lord, and another for a scapegoat. (Leviticus 16:8)

The modern scapegoat combines the roles of the two Biblical goats. He is blamed for the wrongdoings or folly of another person or group, and is sacrificed in a figurative sense. The fate of a scapegoat is usually to be treated as an outsider, the object of ridicule or cruel indifference.

sponge on To live off another's earnings; to accept hospitality but not return it; to borrow money and not pay it back; to leech or mooch; also, *sponge off*. This expression alludes to the absorptive properties of sponges. The phrase maintains widespread use today.

> It was an easy matter to abandon his own income, as he was able to sponge on that of another person. (Anthony Trollope, *The Warden*, 1855)

A person who leads such a parasitic life is called a *sponge* or a *sponger*.

suck the hind teat To get a raw deal; to get the short end of the stick; to be at a disadvantage. This expression is derived from the supposition that the rearmost nipple of a domestic animal supplies less nourishment to offspring than the other nipples. Thus, the animal that draws from the hind teat will be the weakest of the litter.

take the rap See PUNISHMENT.

throw to the wolves To sacrifice ruthlessly another person to protect oneself or one's interests; to make someone a scapegoat to divert criticism from one-

self. One who is being pursued by a wolf might throw food or other objects to divert the animal's attention, and thereby escape unnoticed. In this expression the "wolf" represents any opposition or threat and the "bait" is a person—friend, colleague, subordinate—who becomes an unwitting victim.

wear the cap and bells See HUMOROUSNESS.

whipping-boy A scapegoat; one who takes the blame for the wrongdoings of another. The origin of this term is the 17th-century British custom of transferring the punishment merited by a young prince or royal personage to another youth called a "whipping-boy." The two boys were playmates and were educated together. William Murray is reputed to have been the first whipping-boy, receiving floggings for the son of King James I. Eventually the custom was abolished, but the term remained in figurative use.

VICTORY (See also SUCCESS.)

bear away the bell To be the winner; to carry off the palm; to be preeminent. The old custom of presenting a golden or silver bell to the winner of a race or other contest is the source of *bear away the bell*. It can be used interchangeably with *bear the bell* (EXCELLENCE) when the emphasis is on the sense of being best, rather than first or victorious. *Lose the bell*, the opposite of *bear away the bell*, means to 'be soundly defeated.'

bear the palm To be the best; to win, to come out on top. The allusion is to the practice at the Roman Games of presenting a victorious gladiator or winner of one of the games with a palm branch as a symbol of victory. George Chapman used the phrase in his famous translation of Homer's *Iliad* (1611).

bring home the bacon To succeed, to win the prize; to earn the money, to be the breadwinner. Country fairs often had contests in which a greased pig was awarded to whoever could catch it. The phrase probably stems from the custom.

carry the day To win out in a struggle or competition, usually one of some duration, such as a political campaign or legislative tug of war. The phrase *carry it* 'to win the battle, bear the palm' appeared earlier than *carry the day*, which too was used first in this more literal fighting sense. The expression implies a series of skirmishes of undecided outcome, a seesawing of ascendancy before a definitive result is ascertained.

Garrison finish A spectacular victory against all odds, a finish in any kind of race or contest in which the winner comes from behind at the last possible moment. This expression, in use since 1892, takes its name from Snapper Garrison, a 19th-century American jockey who was known for winning in this manner. Although first applied only to horse racing, the term now denotes an impressive come-from-behind victory in any sport.

get the whetstone To be proclaimed the paramount liar; to receive a prize for telling the greatest falsehood. This expression is derived from medieval lying contests in which the greatest liar was awarded a whetstone to hang around his neck. Thomas Lupton discusses the lying sessions in *Too Good to Be True* (1580):

Lying with us is so loved and allowed, that there are many times gamings and prizes therefore purposely, to encourage one to outlie the other. And what shall he gain that gets the victory in lying? He shall have a silver whetstone for his labour.

Apparently the whetstone, a rock used to sharpen tools, emerged as the prize for this unusual competition because of its figurative association with sharpness.

By the reading of witty arts (which be as the whetstones of wit).

(Robert Recorde, *The Pathway of Knowledge*, 1551)

Although *get the whetstone* is now an obsolete expression, *whetstone* retains its figurative sense despite its infrequent use in literature since the early 1800s.

Let them read Shakespeare's sonnets, taking thence a whetstone for their dull intelligence. (Percy Shelley, *Epipsychidian*, 1821)

take the cake See OUTDOING.

whitewash To prevent the opponents from scoring any points. The idea of "no score" in this informal Americanism is conveyed by the image of a *whitewashed* 'clean, having no marks' scoreboard.

Gene Costello pitched a three-hitter in whitewashing Beaumont with only two men getting as far as third base. (*Daily Ardmoreite*, May 5, 1948)

VIGILANCE (See ALERTNESS.)

VIGOROUSNESS (See INTENSITY.)

VIRTUOUSNESS

like Caesar's wife Of absolutely impeccable conduct; totally beyond reproach; without even the implication of impropriety. The phrase derives from an episode in the life of Julius Caesar as recounted in Plutarch's *Lives*. The Roman nobleman Publius Clodius was on public trial for having had an affair with Pompeia, wife of Caesar. The latter testified that he knew nothing to substantiate the charges, and Publius Clodius was consequently acquitted. Caesar nevertheless divorced his wife Pompeia as a result of the scandal. When asked why he had done so when he had maintained her innocence, Caesar is reputed to have said, "I thought my wife ought not even to be under suspicion." The more often heard version is the phrase *Caesar's wife must be above suspicion*.

odor of sanctity The appearance of holiness or saintliness; an air of respectability; a virtuous, dignified exterior. This expression grew out of a belief popular in the Middle Ages that the dead bodies of saintly persons exuded a sweet smell. The pleasant odor was interpreted as a sign of the dead person's sanctity or holiness.

> There was also a sensation of aromatic odour, as of a dead body embalmed, for when the celestial angels are present, what is cadaverous then excites a sensation as of what is aromatic.
> (Cookworthy, tr., *Swedenborg's Heaven and Hell*, 1756)

Today the phrase is usually used ironically to imply a disparity between appearance—such as that of an extravagant funeral—and a contrasting reality, such as the deceased's private life. Here *sanctity* is closer to *sanctimoniousness*.

sprout wings See CHARITABLENESS.

VISAGE

beetle-browed Having prominent, shaggy eyebrows; scowling, sullen. Although the exact origin of this expression is unknown, it has been suggested that the reference is to the short-tufted antennae, analogous to eyebrows, protruding at right angles from the head of some types of beetles. The phrase appeared in William Langland's *Piers Plowman* in 1362.

bug-eyed See SURPRISE.

fish eye A blank or quizzical gaze; a hostile stare. The vacuity of piscine eyes is clearly the source of this phrase. The following illustration is cited in *Webster's Third:*

> I saw you guys giving me the fish eye . . . so I ran.

gag-tooth A projecting tooth; a bucktooth. *Gag-toothed* dates from the 16th century and is rarely heard today. The current word for such a condition is *bucktoothed.*

> If she be gag-toothed tell her some merry jest to make her laugh.
> (John Lyly, *Euphues, the Anatomy of Wit,* 1579)

grin like a Cheshire cat To grin broadly and mysteriously; to be constantly smiling widely for no apparent reason. The phrase usually carries connotations of smugness or vacuousness. The expression, which dates from the late 18th century, gained currency because of the perpetually grinning cat in Lewis Carroll's *Alice's Adventures in Wonderland* (1865). The phrase appeared in response to Alice's question as to why the Duchess' cat grinned so broadly and inscrutably:

> "It's a Cheshire cat," said the Duchess, "and that's why."

like an owl in an ivy bush With a vacant, dumb look; with an empty stare, such as some people have when drunk. This expression plays on the fact that the ivy bush is the favorite haunt of the owl, known for its wisdom and solemnity; it is also the favorite plant of Bacchus, the god of wine. Rarely heard today, this expression dates from the early 17th century.

> "Pr'y thee, how did the fool look?"
> "Look! Egad, he look'd for all the world like an owl in an ivy bush."
> (Jonathan Swift, *Polite Conversation,* 1738)

poker face An expressionless face; a visage which does not reveal one's thoughts or emotions; a dead pan. In poker, it is essential that a player not tip his hand by showing emotion in his face, lest the other players bet accordingly and thus limit his winnings or increase his losses. Though still applicable to the card game, *poker face* is also used figuratively in many varied contexts.

> He glanced around the circle and found poker faces, but there was a light in Baldy's eyes that warmed him. (Clarence Mulford, *Rustler's Valley,* 1924)

widow's peak A V-shaped hairline in the middle of the forehead. It was once customary for a widow to wear a black hat which had a "peak," a triangular piece of material that extended down on the forehead, as if pointing at the nose. A similar looking hairline came to be known as a "widow's peak" by association.

She had on her forehead what is sometimes denominated a "widow's peak"—that is to say, her hair grew down to a point in the middle.
(Henry Wadsworth Longfellow, *Kavanagh, A Tale,* 1849)

A related expression, *widow's lock,* describes a lock or tuft of hair that grows apart from the rest of the hair on the head. The term alludes to an ancient superstitious belief that a woman with such a stray shock of hair would be widowed soon after marriage.

VITALITY

full of beans Lively, energetic; full of vim, vigor, and vitality. Popular since the mid-1800s, this expression was originally stable slang. It was used in reference to spirited, bean-fed horses.

live wire A spry, energetic person. This expression, derived from the jumping and sparking of a fallen power line, enjoys common usage in the United States.

He was, if anyone was, the live wire of the Senior Common Room.
(J. C. Masterman, *To Teach Senators Wisdom,* 1952)

rough-and-ready Exhibiting vigor and vitality which, though unrefined and perhaps indelicate, is appropriate for dealing with a given situation; crudely efficient; rough in manner, but prompt and effective in action. Though it has been suggested that this phrase may allude to Colonel Rough, a soldier under the Duke of Wellington at Waterloo, supporting evidence for this allegation is sketchy at best. It is more likely that *rough-and-ready* arose as a description of one's manner or style, its implications being obvious.

The rough-and-ready style which belongs to a people of sailors, foresters, farmers and mechanics.
(Ralph Waldo Emerson, *The Conduct of Life,* 1860)

"Old Rough and Ready" was a nickname given to General Zachary Taylor (1784–1850) for his conduct during the Seminole and the Mexican Wars in the early 1800s. Supporters of Taylor's campaign and presidency (1849–50) were known as the "Rough and Ready Boys."

VULNERABILITY (See also DAN-GER, DISADVANTAGE, INDEBTEDNESS, PRECARIOUSNESS, PREDICAMENT, RISK.)

Achilles heel Any particularly vulnerable area; a weakness; a soft spot. This expression comes to us from Homer's *Iliad,* a Greek epic poem depicting the events of the Trojan war. Achilles was its hero. Legend has it that at his birth Achilles' mother, Thetis, immersed him in the river Styx in order to make him invulnerable. In doing so, she held him by one heel, which was therefore never touched by the water. Later, as a great warrior in the Trojan war, Achilles went unharmed by his enemies until Paris, whom Apollo had told the secret of Achilles' heel, mortally wounded him by shooting an arrow into his heel. The first recorded use of the term was in 1810 in Coleridge's *The Friend:*

Ireland, that vulnerable heel of the British Achilles!

The sinew connecting the back of the heel to the calf of the leg is called the Achilles tendon.

between two fires Under attack from both sides at once; caught in a precarious or dangerous situation with no way out. A soldier who was exposed to gunfire from two or more sides was said to be "between two fires." This literal usage appeared as early as 1885.

He was about to find himself placed between two fires—viz. the Mahdi and the reinforced garrison of Metammeh. (*Times,* February 20, 1885)

On the figurative level current today, *fire* refers to any danger which threatens from all sides simultaneously.

between wind and water In a vulnerable, precarious position; exposed or unprotected, defenseless. Literally, the phrase refers to that part of the ship's side which is alternately exposed and submerged, marking the fluctuation of the water line. Such an area is particularly vulnerable to attack and corrosion. Figuratively, the phrase refers to any vulnerable state or dangerous situation. The literal use appears as early as 1588, the figurative as early as 1652.

Now they have crackt me betwixt wind and water a'most past cure. Stay, let me feel my self. (Arthur Wilson, *Inconstant Ladie,* 1652)

Both levels of meaning remain in use today.

caught bending Taken by surprise; at a disadvantage; in a vulnerable position. A child bending over is not on his guard and is particularly well-positioned for a kicking or spanking. A 1903 song by George Robey included the line:

My word! I catch you bending!

caught flat-footed Caught unprepared, unready, by surprise, not "on one's toes." This phrase probably derives from baseball or football, and dates from the early 1920s. It refers to someone's being caught (thrown out or tackled) while standing still or flat-footed. A person in such a position reacts less quickly than one "on his toes."

caught with one's pants down Taken completely off guard or entirely by surprise; found in a compromising or embarrassing position; hence, also unquestionably guilty; caught in the act, in flagrante delicto. General acceptance of this inelegant expression has been attributed to its appearance in a 1946 issue of *The Saturday Evening Post.*

chink in one's armor A weakness or vulnerability; an area in which one's defenses are inadequate or ineffective; a personality flaw. The phrase alludes to the armor worn by knights. A *chink* 'crack, cleft, or narrow opening' could cost a knight his life. Figuratively, a *chink in one's armor* refers to a personal rather than physical vulnerability. Some modern psychologists have adopted the word *armor* to mean 'character or personality,' emphasizing those aspects of one's character which are formed in defense and serve self-protective functions.

clay pigeon A person or thing in a vulnerable position; an easy mark; one who can be easily taken advantage of; an easy job or task, a cinch. This American slang expression is an extension of the term *clay pigeon* as used in trapshooting, where it represents a disklike object of baked clay thrown into the air as a target. It has been in literal usage since 1888.

fair game A legitimate object of attack or ridicule; an easy target of derision. The term originated with wildlife laws limiting the hunting of certain animals to a specific time or season of the year, during which the hunted animals are "fair game." In its figurative sense, this phrase refers to a person or thing whose manner or appearance makes him a likely victim of mockery.

In that character it becomes fair game for ridicule. (Jeremy Bentham, *Chrestomathia,* 1816)

gone coon One who is in bad straits; a person who is on the brink of disaster, whose goose is cooked; a lost soul, a "goner." A "coon" (raccoon) who cannot escape from a hunter is a "gone coon." A ludicrous fable probably fabricated to explain this expression tells of a raccoon which, trapped in a tree at gunpoint by Davey Crockett, said to the great marksman, "I know I'm a gone coon." The Democratic party was aware of the fable when they applied the label *coon* to the Whigs during the presidential contest of 1840.

live in a glass house To be in a vulnerable position, to be open to attack; to live a public life, to be in the public eye. The expression plays on two well-known properties of glass—its transparency and its brittleness. The phrase is apparently a truncated version of the old proverb *people who live in glass houses shouldn't throw stones,* dating from the early 17th century.

> In the glass house world of commercial publishing, . . . Peter Mayer is something of a superstar. (*Saturday Review,* February, 1979)

on the ropes On the verge of ruin or collapse; at the mercy of whatever forces threaten to overcome one. The metaphor is from the boxing ring. When a prize fighter is on the ropes, he is in a weakened and very vulnerable position. His opponent is in control, and will probably soon be able to "finish him off."

open season A time when persons or ideas in disfavor are subject to attack from all sides. The expression, of American origin, comes from hunting and refers to those periods during which various types of game are legitimate quarry.

out on a limb In a vulnerable, compromising, or risky position; at a disadvantage. This expression refers to the predicament of a person in a tree who, having climbed out onto one of the branches (limbs), faces the prospect of injury if the limb should not be strong enough to support him. The figurative implications are that a person has espoused an unconventional idea or cause which, if it fails, may precipitate his downfall, resulting in a loss of influence, prestige, and credibility.

> No one is willing to go out on any limb. No one is willing to say yes or no to a proposition. He must always

go to someone higher. (John Steinbeck, *Russian Journal,* 1948)

over a barrel In an embarrassing or uncomfortable position or situation; with one's back against the wall, helpless, in someone else's power. This chiefly U.S. slang expression dates from at least 1939. According to the *OED* the allusion is to the helpless condition of a person who, after having been saved from drowning, is placed over a barrel in order to clear the water out of his lungs.

sitting duck An easy mark or target, a ripe victim; a person or thing in an open or vulnerable position. The allusion is to the comparative ease of shooting a duck resting on the water as opposed to one in flight.

stick one's neck out To expose oneself to danger or criticism; to take a chance, to risk failure; to invite trouble. This early 20th-century American expression plays with the idea that sticking one's neck out is equivalent to asking to have one's head chopped off. Thus vulnerability, usually nonphysical, is also implicit in the figurative uses of this expression.

> We've stuck our necks out—we're looking for trouble, see? (H. Hastings, *Seagulls Over Sorrento,* 1950)

turn turtle To be utterly helpless or defenseless. When turned on their backs, turtles are completely powerless and without defense. *Turn turtle* also means 'to overturn, upset, capsize.'

up a tree Cornered, trapped, caught; at another's mercy, in another's power. The expression is said to come from coon hunting; once a raccoon is treed by the hounds, he's a gone coon.

> I had her in my power—up a tree, as the Americans say. (William Makepiece Thackeray, *Major Gahagan,* 1839)

where the shoe pinches The sore spot or vulnerable area; the true source of trouble or distress. This expression purportedly derived from Plutarch's biography of Paulus Aemilius. Questioned as to why he divorced his fair, faithful, and fertile wife, Aemilius removed his shoe and replied, "Is it not handsome? Is it not new? Yet none knows where it pinches, save he that wears it." This expression, equivalents of which exist in most European languages, appeared in English literature as early as the time of Chaucer.

Subtle enemies, that know . . .
where the shoe pincheth us most.
(Gabriel Harvey, *Letterbook*, 1580)

W

WEALTH   (See **AFFLUENCE**.)

WEATHER

dog days   The most oppressively hot, uncomfortable, and unhealthy time of the year; the height of summer, usually calculated to be from about July 3 to August 11. These are supposedly the days when Sirius, the Dog Star, rises at the same time as the sun. The name *dog days* (Latin *dies caniculares*) derives from the ancient belief that the customary sultriness and unwholesomeness of this season were due to the influence of the Dog Star. The origin of the name has also long been associated with the popular superstition that during this particular time of the year dogs were most apt to go mad. The term has been in use since the early 16th century.

gully washer   A very heavy rainstorm, a downpour. This American colloquialism, particularly common in the Texas-Oklahoma area, was obviously coined because of the swirling rush of water through gullies during such storms. An especially violent gully washer is sometimes jocularly called a *gully whomper.* The expression has been figuratively extended to include a great onrush or outpouring of anything.

> The drouth of senatorial candidates in Johnston county will be broken with a "gulley washer" here this week. (*The Capital-Democrat* [Tishomingo, Okla.], June, 1948)

halcyon days   See **PEACE**.

Hulda is making her bed   An expression denoting a snowfall. In ancient German mythology Hulda is the goddess of marriage and fertility. Although this expression is of unknown origin, it is reasonable to conjecture that Hulda had a feather bed which she prepared for the delights of newlyweds and from which some plumes periodically escaped to fall to the earth as snow.

Indian summer   A brief respite in the late autumn of North America, characterized by hazy, balmy weather. This expression is thought to have originated in New England, where the Indians took advantage of the unseasonably warm spell to make their final winter preparations. The term is used frequently in the northern United States and Canada, where this short reappearance of summer regularly occurs each fall.

> Meanwhile the Indian summer continued warm and dusty on the trodden earth of the farmyard. (J. Rae, *Custard Boys,* 1960)

Like other terms denoting time of year or day, *Indian summer* is often analogously applied to one's life, indicating a period of renewed vigor or health amidst a stage of general decline.

> The works of his Indian Summer when, in the last five years of his life, inspiration came to him once more. (N. Del Mar, *Richard Strauss,* 1962)

Mother Carey is plucking her chickens   Sailors' slang for falling snow. In this expression, Mother Carey is derived from the Latin *mater cara* 'mother dear,' apparently a reference to the Virgin Mary. *Mother Carey's chickens* is a sailor's appellation for stormy petrels, friendly birds which warn sea voyagers of upcoming inclement weather. Thus, the expression likens fluffy, falling snow to small tufts of white feathers.

Queen's weather   Ideal weather conditions; magnificent weather occurring on a day set aside for a festival, picnic, or other outdoor activity. This expression originated from the disproportionate number of fine days which coincided with Queen Victoria's public appearances.

> Although the wind is rather high, Queen's weather prevails.
> (*Johannesburg Star,* April, 1899)

rain cats and dogs To pour, to come down in torrents, to teem. This common but puzzling expression has appeared in the writing of such varied authors as Swift, Shelley, and Thackeray. The most repeated explanation relates it to the storm god Odin, often pictured with cat and dog who according to Norse mythology influenced the weather. More plausible but equally undefinitive is the theory suggesting a derivation from an obsolete French word *catadoupe* 'waterfall,' itself related to an actual waterfall of the Nile in Ethiopia.

rain pitchforks To rain hard and piercingly; to rain straight downwards, so that the rainfall appears discernible as separate streaks of water. This primarily U.S. colloquial expression, probably coined by New England farmers, sees infrequent usage today, perhaps because the implement conveying the image is no longer part of most people's immediate experience.

> I'll be even with you, if it rains pitchforks—tines downwards.
> (David Humphreys, *The Yankey in England,* 1815)

three-dog night A bitterly cold night. This expression is derived from the Eskimos, who purportedly measure the cold by determining how many dogs are necessary to keep them warm during the night. Thus, a night which requires the warmth of three dogs is a frigid night indeed. Even though the temperatures in the temperate climate of the United States do not plunge nearly as low as they do in polar regions, the expression has nonetheless become a popular American colloquialism for the coldest winter nights.

weather-breeder A day of unseasonably or otherwise exceptionally magnificent weather, formerly thought to be a harbinger of an approaching storm; a daylong respite in a period of inclement weather. This expression originated in England, where the weather is predominately dank and overcast. It can thus be assumed that, since such fine days were almost invariably followed by foul weather, the English folk saw a weather-breeder as a bad omen.

> Look at a very fair day, as that which may prove a weather-breeder, and usher in a storm.
> (John Arrowsmith, *A Chain of Principles,* 1659)

WHOLENESS (See TOTALITY.)

WICKEDNESS

show one's horns To reveal one's evil intentions; to expose one's malicious, venomous, or insidious nature. This expression alludes to the horns commonly portrayed on the forehead of Satan, an attribute which also gave rise to one of the devil's nicknames, Old Hornie.

show the cloven hoof To reveal a treacherous nature or evil intentions. The allusion is to the cloven hoof of Satan, long representative of evil. Although the simple term *hoof* was in use in this figurative sense as early as 1638, the phrase did not appear until much later.

> [It] had caused him to show the cloven hoof too soon. (James Payn, *The Luck of the Darrells,* 1885)

son of Belial A thoroughly evil and despicable person; the embodiment of wickedness; the devil. This expression originated in the Old Testament (I Samuel 2:12):

> Now the sons of Eli were sons of Belial; they knew not the Lord.

Belial, apparently derived from the Hebrew *b'li ya'al* 'without use,' became the equivalent of Satan in later Jewish writings. Belial was also employed as a name for one of the fallen angels in John Milton's *Paradise Lost* (1667). The expression maintains its theological application for the personification of evil.

A scoffer, a debauched person, and, in brief, a man of Belial. (Sir Walter Scott, *The Monastery,* 1822)

WORTHINESS

great pith and moment Import, significance, weight. This expression comes from Hamlet's most well-known ("To be or not to be") soliloquy:

And enterprises of great pith and moment
With this regard their currents turn awry
And lose the name of action. (III,i)

nothing to sneeze at Not a thing to be ignored or rejected as a trifle; not a person to be treated with derision or contempt; worthy of serious consideration; also *not to be sneezed at.* Now used exclusively in the negative, *to sneeze at* 'to regard as of little value' was common in the 1800s, though precisely how "sneezing at" came to be equated with an estimation of worth is not clear. The expression is most often found with reference to sums of money, as illustrated by the following passage from Lockhart's *Memoirs of Sir Walter Scott:*

As I am situated, £300 or £400 is not to be sneezed at.

pay one's dues To prove oneself worthy by fulfilling obligations; to start at the bottom, gain experience, and work one's way up. As early as the 1600s, *dues* referred to a fee for membership in an organization. In the United States, during the 1900s, *dues* gained currency as a figurative slang term for nonfinancial obligations; *pay one's dues* means to earn rights or recognition with hard work and perseverance. The expression is current especially among jazz musicians in referring to the years of anonymity and financial hardship devoted to learning and developing an individual style.

Duke, Thad, Mel and myself, we've paid considerable amounts of dues

in trying to get this-thing off the ground. (*Down Beat,* April 17, 1969)

worth one's salt To be worthy or deserving of one's wages or pay; to be efficient and hard-working; often used negatively in the phrase *not to be worth one's salt.* The *salt* of this expression is said to have come from the old Roman practice of paying soldiers their wages in salt, then a rare and precious commodity. When money for the purchase of salt was substituted for the salt itself, it was known as *salārium* 'salt money,' the predecessor of the English *salary,* from Latin *sal* 'salt.' *Worth one's salt* has been in common usage since the early 19th century.

worth the whistle Worthy, deserving; acceptable, commendable; of value and importance. This expression, implying that a person is worth the effort of whistling for him, is derived from a proverb cited by John Heywood in *Dialogue Containing the Number in Effect of All the Proverbs in the English Tongue* (1546):

It is a poor dog that is not worth the whistling.

Shakespeare uses the phrase in *King Lear* when Goneril implies that at one time she was held in high regard by Albany, but that now she is being treated more poorly and with less respect than one would accord a common cur:

I have been worth the whistle.
(IV,ii)

The expression is often used in the negative *not worth a whistle,* frequently to describe a person whose friendship is considered worthless.

WORTHLESSNESS (See also **INSIGNIFICANCE.**)

bottom of the barrel The dregs; the lowest of the low; the end of the line; financial or moral bankruptcy; often *bottom of the pickle barrel.* Although the exact origin of this expression is unknown, it apparently refers to the barrels formerly used in grocery stores to keep pickles. By the time the last of the pickles were sold, they were often not fit to eat. The phrase is said to have been popularized by baseball announcer Red Barber in his broadcasts of the Brooklyn Dodger games from 1945–55. A variation is *reach the bottom of the barrel. Scape the bottom of the barrel* means to 'try to find something of use or value after the main resources have been exhausted,' and to 'make do as best one can with what is available.'

catchpenny Worthless, cheap, gimmicky, as an article designed to trap the dollars of unwary buyers. Though originally and still often applied to publications, the story that the term originated from a deliberately misleading headline used by the British printer Catnach in 1824 regarding a sensational murder case is belied by Oliver Goldsmith's 1759 reference to:

one of those catchpenny subscription works.

kickshaw Trivial, insignificant, worthless; gaudy but useless; garish but without value. This expression, derived from the French *quelque chose* 'something, anything,' originally referred to nonsense or buffoonery. In Shakespeare's *Twelfth Night*, for example, when Sir Andrew Aguecheek states, "I delight in masques and revels sometimes altogether," Sir Toby Belch asks:

Are thou good at these kickshaws, knight? (I,iii)

The term, occasionally used in reference to small tidbits of food or hors d'oeuvres, usually describes something of a trivial nature.

He sang . . . no kickshaw ditties. (Charles Dickens, *The Mystery of Edwin Drood*, 1870)

not worth a continental Completely worthless or valueless; good for nothing, useless. A continental was a piece of the paper currency issued by the Continental Congress during the American Revolution. Its value depreciated so drastically that it was virtually worthless by the end of the war. Use of this U.S. colloquialism dates from the 19th century.

The next day he is all played out and not worth a continental. (G. W. Peck, *Sunshine*, 1882)

not worth a damn Worth nothing, of no value or use; also *not worth a tinker's damn* and *not worth a twopenny damn.* A damn is nothing more than a mild curse word, in common use for centuries.

A wrong . . . system, not worth a damn. (George Gordon, Lord Byron, *Diary*, 1817)

It is most probable that a *tinker's damn* has nothing to do with the tinker's tool called a *dam* (a piece of dough used to keep solder from spilling over), as has been frequently theorized; but that it rather refers to the reputation of these itinerant jacks-of-all-trades for their propensity toward cursing. The exact origin of *a twopenny damn,* generally attributed to the Duke of Wellington, is not known. It may, however, be connected with *a tinker's damn* since twopence was apparently once the going rate for a tinker's labor.

not worth a straw Worthless, valueless, insignificant, useless; also *not worth a rush.* Although both expressions date from about the 15th century, *not worth a rush* has been replaced in current usage by *not worth a straw,* most likely a variant or derivative of the former. The allusion may be to the former practice of strewing rushes, or straws on the floor as a kind of carpeting for visitors. Apparently fresh rushes were put down only for the more distinguished guests, while visitors of lower social status used those already trod upon by their superiors or none at all.

Friends' applauses are not worth a rush. (W. Pope, in *Flatman's Poems,* 1674)

Z

ZEALOUSNESS

barnburner A radical, zealot, or extremist; historically, a member of the radical faction of the Democratic party in New York State (1840–50) so eager for political reform that he would through excess of zeal destroy what he wished to preserve. The term, which dates from 1841, comes from the older phrase, *burn a barn to kill the rats,* in use since 1807.

> This school of Democrats was termed Barnburners, in allusion to the story of an old Dutchman, who relieved himself of rats by burning down his barns which they infested, —just like exterminating all banks and corporations, to root out the abuses connected therewith. (*New York Tribune,* 1848)

eager beaver A ball of fire, an especially industrious or zealous person; an excessively aggressive or ambitious person, a go-getter. This American expression, dating from the mid-1900s, is a reference to the beaver's reputation for being particularly hardworking and diligent. Earlier similar phrases include *work like a beaver* 'work very hard or industriously,' which dates from the early 18th century; and *industrious* or *busy as a beaver* 'very busy,' in use since the early 19th century.

gung ho Wholeheartedly enthusiastic; eager, zealous, patriotic, loyal. *Gung ho* is a corruption of the Chinese *kung ho* 'work together' (*kung* 'work' + *ho* 'together'). The unit of United States Marines that served under General Evans F. Carlson in World War II adopted the expression as its slogan. The phrase appeared in its original form, *kung-hou,* as early as 1942.

> In those days he was very gung ho

for National Socialism and the pan-Germanic grandeur it was going to produce. (R. M. Stern, *Kessler Legacy,* 1967)

hellbent Recklessly dogged or stubbornly determined; resolute, persistent; going at breakneck speed. The term, of American origin, dates from at least 1835. It has spawned the expanded forms *hellbent for leather, hellbent for election,* and *hellbent for breakfast. Hell* or *hellbent for leather,* thought to be originally British but popular on both sides of the Atlantic, has only the second sense of *hellbent,* i.e., going at tremendous speed. The reference is to riding on horseback, *leather* referring to the leather of the saddle. The expression is found in Rudyard Kipling's *The Story of the Gadsbys,* published in 1888. *Hellbent for election* is said to have originated in the Maine gubernatorial race of 1840. *Hellbent for breakfast,* dating from at least 1931, is another expanded form of *hellbent;* it is used in the second sense only—going at great speed.

whirling dervish A person who vociferously expounds his opinions and beliefs; a zealot. A dervish is an Islamic priest or monk who, during religious ceremonies and prayers, frequently enters a type of ecstatic rapture marked by wild dancing, violent movements, and loud singing or chanting. Thus, these holy men came to be known as *whirling dervishes* or *howling dervishes.*

> And now, their guttural chorus audible long before they arrived in sight, came the howling dervishes. (Amelia B. Edwards, *A Thousand Miles Up the Nile,* 1877)

The expression is applied in non-Islamic contexts by extension.

Index

A

A1 or A one, EXCELLENCE
a pair of heels, ESCAPE
abiit ad plures, DEATH
above-board, CANDIDNESS
above the salt, STATUS
abracadabra, MAGIC
Abraham's bosom, PARADISE
according to Cocker, PROPRI-
ETY
according to Gunter, PROPRI-
ETY
according to Hoyle, PROPRI-
ETY
AC/DC, SEXUAL ORIENTA-
TION
ace in the hole, ADVANTAGE
ace in the hole, PLOY
ace up one's sleeve, PLOY
Achilles heel, VULNERABIL-
ITY
acid test, CRITERION
across-the-board, INCLUSIVE-
NESS
act the goat, MISCHIEF
add fuel to the fire, EXACER-
BATION
add fuel to the fire, AUGMEN-
TATION
add insult to injury, EXACER-
BATION
after meat, mustard, SUPER-
FLUOUSNESS
after you, my dear Al-
phonse, DEFERENCE
against the grain, UNNATU-
RALNESS
against the gré, UNNATURAL-
NESS
air one's lungs, PROFANITY
albatross around the neck,
BURDEN
Alibi Ike, EVASIVENESS
alea jacta est, DECISIVENESS
all aback, SURPRISE
all adrift, CONFUSION
all along the line, INCLUSIVE-
NESS
all down the line, INCLUSIVE-
NESS
all hands and the cook, UR-
GENCY
all horns and rattles, BELLIG-
ERENCE

all is fish that comes to his
net, ABILITY
all mops and brooms, DRUNK-
ENNESS
*all my eye and Betty Mar-
tin,* EXCLAMATIONS
all one's geese are swans, EX-
AGGERATION
all quiet on the Potomac,
PEACE
all quiet on the Western
Front, PEACE
*all shipshape and Bristol
fashion,* NEATNESS
all systems go, READINESS
all talk and no action, INEF-
FECTUALITY
all talk and no cider, INEF-
FECTUALITY
all the fat is in the fire, IR-
REVOCABLENESS
all thumbs, AWKWARDNESS
all wet, ERRONEOUSNESS
all wool and a yard wide,
GENUINENESS
ambulance chaser, VICTIMI-
ZATION
amen corner, APPROVAL
anise and cummin, INSIGNIFI-
CANCE
Annie Oakley, EPONYMS
another cup of tea, PREFER-
ENCE
another lie nailed to the
counter, EXPOSURE
answer the bell, COMPE-
TENCE
ant's pants, EXCELLENCE
A-number one, EXCELLENCE
anvil chorus, PROTEST
any port in a storm, EXPEDI-
ENCE
A-OK, READINESS
apple of discord, DISSENSION
apple of one's eye, FAVORIT-
ISM
apple-pie order, NEATNESS
apple-polish, OBSEQUIOUS-
NESS
apple-polisher, OBSEQUIOUS-
NESS
applesauce, NONSENSE
apples and oranges, DIS-
SIMILARITY
apply for Chiltern Hun-
dreds, RETIREMENT

apron strings, DEPENDENCE
Argus-eyed, ALERTNESS
an arm and a leg, COST
armchair critic, FAULTFIND-
ING
armchair general, FAULT-
FINDING
armchair politician, FAULT-
FINDING
armchair strategist, FAULT-
FINDING
armed to the teeth, THOR-
OUGHNESS
around the mahogany,
FRIENDSHIP
as a pig loves marjoram, IM-
PROBABILITY
as bold as Beauchamp, BRAV-
ERY
ask for the moon, FUTILITY
asleep at the switch, CARE-
LESSNESS
*as much chance as a snowball
in hell,* IMPROBABILITY
asphalt jungle, LOCALITY
*as quarrelsome as Kilkenny
cats,* COMBAT
ass in a lion's skin, PRETENSE
ass kisser, OBSEQUIOUSNESS
as the crow flies, DIRECTION
as well be hanged for a sheep
as a lamb, UNRESTRAINT
at a pace of two-forty, SPEED-
ING
at a rate of two-forty, SPEED-
ING
at a snail's pace, PACE
at daggers drawn or draw-
ing, BELLIGERENCE
at full blast, INTENSITY
Athanasian wench, PROMIS-
CUOUSNESS
at loggerheads, DISSENSION
at loose ends, CONFUSION
at sea, CONFUSION
at sixes and sevens, DISORDER
at the drop of a hat, INSTAN-
TANEOUSNESS
at the eleventh hour, TIMELI-
NESS
at the end of one's rope or
tether, DESPERATION
at the first blush, INEXPERI-
ENCE
Aunt Sally, VICTIMIZATION
axle grease, MONEY
ax to grind, GRIEVANCE

B

babe in the woods, INEXPERI-ENCE
back and edge, INTENSITY
back and fill, VACILLATION
backdoor man, INFIDELITY
back number, OBSOLES-CENCE
back-seat driver, FAULTFIND-ING
backstairs influence, MANIPU-LATION
back the wrong horse, ER-RONEOUSNESS
back to square one, FAILURE
back to the drawing board, FAILURE
back to the salt mines, OVER-WORK
bad-ball hitter, ERRONEOUS-NESS
bad break, ERRONEOUSNESS
badger game, EXTORTION
badgerworker, EXTORTION
bag, INDIVIDUALITY
bag and baggage, INCLUSIVE-NESS
bag of tricks, PLOY
baker's dozen, EXCESSIVE-NESS
bald as a coot, PHYSICAL AP-PEARANCE
balderdash, NONSENSE
ball and chain, BURDEN
ballocks, DISORDER
ball the jack, SPEEDING
ball up, DISORDER
banana oil, NONSENSE
band-aid treatment, FLIMSI-NESS
bang on, PRECISION
bang one's head against a stone wall, FUTILITY
bang one's head against the wall, FUTILITY
bang on target, PRECISION
bang to rights, CERTAINTY
bank-walker, PROMISCUOUS-NESS
baptism of blood, INITIATION
baptism of fire, INITIATION
baptism of water, INITIATION
barfly, DRUNKENNESS
barhopper, DRUNKENNESS
bark at the moon, FUTILITY

Barkis is willin', READINESS
bark to the tree, DEPEN-DENCE
bark up the wrong tree, ER-RONEOUSNESS
Barmecide feast, ILLUSION
barmy on the crumpet, EC-CENTRICITY
barnburner, ZEALOUSNESS
barnstorm, POLITICKING
Baron Munchhausen, MEN-DACITY
barrack, INSULT
barrelhouse, ESTABLISH-MENTS
bathroom talk, PROFANITY
bat on a sticky wicket, DIF-FICULTY
batten down the hatches, PREPARATION
bat the breeze, TALKATIVE-NESS
battle royal, COMBAT
batty, ECCENTRICITY
bay at the moon, FUTILITY
bay window, CORPULENCE
BBC English, DICTION
bear away the bell, VICTORY
bear coals, SELF-DISPARAGE-MENT
beard the lion in his den, CONFRONTATION
bear leader, GUIDANCE
bearish, IDEALISM
bear the bell, EXCELLENCE
bear the palm, VICTORY
beat a dead horse, FUTILITY
beat all hollow, OUTDOING
beat around the bush, EVA-SIVENESS
beat around the bush, CAN-DIDNESS
beat Banagher, OUTDOING
beat into shape, GUIDANCE
beat one's gums, TALKATIVE-NESS
beat one's head against the wall, FUTILITY
beat the air, FUTILITY
beat the Dutch, OUTDOING
beat the rap, PUNISHMENT
beat the tar out of, COMBAT
beat to the punch, ADVAN-TAGE
bed of down, INDOLENCE
bed of flowers, INDOLENCE
bed of roses, INDOLENCE

be driven round the bend, ECCENTRICITY
bedroom community, LOCAL-ITY
bedswerver, INFIDELITY
bed with a shovel, DRUNKEN-NESS
bed with one's boots on, DRUNKENNESS
beefcake, PRURIENCE
beef up, AUGMENTATION
bee in one's bonnet, OBSES-SION
beer and skittles, REVELRY
beer belly, CORPULENCE
bees in the brain, OBSESSION
bees in the head, OBSESSION
bee's knees, EXCELLENCE
beetle-browed, VISAGE
before one had nails on one's toes, TIME
before you can say "Jack Robinson," INSTANTANE-OUSNESS
before you can say "knife," INSTANTANEOUSNESS
beggar on horseback, AFFLU-ENCE
beggar's bush, POVERTY
behind the eightball, DISAD-VANTAGE
behind the power curve, PRECARIOUSNESS
bell, book, and candle, THOROUGHNESS
bell the cat, CONFRONTA-TION
belly-god, GOURMANDISM
belly-timber, FOOD AND DRINK
belly up, DEATH
below the salt, STATUS
belt the grape, TIPPLING
be made a cat's paw of, VIC-TIMIZATION
bench mark, CRITERION
bench warmer, SUBORDINA-TION
bend the elbow, TIPPLING
bent out of shape, ANGRINESS
be on a short fuse, FURY
be on a sticky wicket, DIF-FICULTY
beside oneself, IRRATIONAL-ITY
beside the cushion, IRRELE-VANCE

beside the mark, IRRELE-VANCE

best bib and tucker, CLOTH-ING

best side outward, PROPRI-ETY

be taken to the cleaners, SWINDLING

bet one's bottom dollar, CER-TAINTY

bet one's life, CERTAINTY

between a rock and a hard place, PREDICAMENT

between dog and wolf, IN-DETERMINATENESS

between hawk and buzzard, INDETERMINATENESS

between hawk and buzzard, PREDICAMENT

between hay and grass, IN-DETERMINATENESS

between Scylla and Charyb-dis, PREDICAMENT

between the devil and the deep blue sea, PREDICA-MENT

between two fires, VULNERA-BILITY

between wind and water, VULNERABILITY

bet your boots, CERTAINTY

beware of Greeks bearing gifts, PRETENSE

beware the ides of March, SU-PERSTITION

beyond the moon, ILLUSION

beyond the pale, IMPRO-PRIETY

the Big Apple, LOCALITY

big brass, PERSONAGE

big bug, PERSONAGE

big cheese, PERSONAGE

big eyes, DESIRE

big gun, PERSONAGE

big jump, DEATH

big shoes to fill, SIMILARITY

big shot, PERSONAGE

big wheel, PERSONAGE

bigwig, PERSONAGE

billingsgate, PROFANITY

bite off more than one can chew, OVEREXTENSION

bite one's thumb at, INSULT

bite [someone's] head off, FURY

bite [someone's] nose off, FURY

bite the bridle, IMPATIENCE

bite the bullet, ENDURANCE

bite the dust, DEATH

bite the hand that feeds you, INGRATITUDE

bitter end, TERMINATION

bitter-ender, TERMINATION

black and white, SIMPLIFICA-TION

blackball, REJECTION

black books, DISFAVOR

blacklist, REJECTION

Black Maria, VEHICLES

the black ox has trod on [someone's] foot, ADVER-SITY

black sheep, DISFAVOR

black-silk barge, CORPU-LENCE

blank check, FREEDOM

blankety-blank, PROFANITY

blarney, FLATTERY

bleed, EXTORTION

bleeding heart, SENTIMEN-TALITY

bless the mark, EXCLAMA-TIONS

bless the world with one's heels, DEATH

blimp, POMPOSITY

the blind leading the blind, FUTILITY

blind man's holiday, TIME

blockbuster, EFFECTIVENESS

blockhead, IGNORANCE

blood and thunder, SENSA-TIONALISM

blood money, BRIBERY

blood, sweat, and tears, EX-ERTION

a bloody sweat, ANXIETY

blow a fuse, FURY

blow a gasket, FURY

blowed-in-the-glass, EXCEL-LENCE

blow hot and cold, VACILLA-TION

blow lunch, ILL HEALTH

blow off steam, FURY

blow one's lid, FURY

blow one's own trumpet, BOASTING

blow one's stack, FURY

blow one's top, FURY

blow the coals, AUGMENTA-TION

blow the gab, EXPOSURE

blow the gaff, EXPOSURE

blow the whistle, EXPOSURE

blow up a storm, INTENSITY

blue around the gills, DRUNKENNESS

blueblood, STATUS

blueblood, SCHOLARLINESS

blue-eyed boy, FAVORITISM

blue-eyed girl, FAVORITISM

blue gown, PROMISCUOUS-NESS

bluenose, PRUDISHNESS

blue-pencil, CRITICISM

blue peter, DEPARTURE

blue ribbon, EXCELLENCE

bluestocking, SCHOLARLI-NESS

blurb, COMMENDATION

board the gravy train, AF-FLUENCE

bobby, AFFIRMATION

Bob's your uncle, AFFIRMA-TION

bogtrotter, OAFISHNESS

boiling the pot, LETTERS

boil the pot, SUBSISTENCE

bold Beauchamp, BRAVERY

bollixed up, DISORDER

bollocks, DISORDER

bolt from the blue, SURPRISE

bolt upright, DIRECTION

bombast, LANGUAGE

bone of contention, DISSEN-SION

bone orchard, BURIAL

bone-shaker, VEHICLES

bone to pick, DISSENSION

bookworm, SCHOLARLINESS

boondoggle, IDLENESS

bootleg, CRIMINALITY

bootlegger, CRIMINALITY

bootlick, OBSEQUIOUSNESS

boots and saddle, PREPARA-TION

born in the purple, STATUS

born to the purple, STATUS

born with a caul on one's head, GOOD LUCK

born with a silver spoon in one's mouth, STATUS

born within the sound of Bow bells, STATUS

borscht belt, LOCALITY

borscht circuit, LOCALITY

bottleneck, IMPEDIMENT

bottom line, OUTCOME

bottom of the bag, PLOY

bottom of the barrel, WORTH-
LESSNESS
bottom of the pickle barrel,
WORTHLESSNESS
Box and Cox, VACILLATION
brainstorm, THOUGHT
brainwashing, MANIPULA-
TION
brand-new, AGE
bran-new, AGE
the brass, PERSONAGE
brass hat, PERSONAGE
bread and circuses, DECA-
DENCE
breadbasket, NICKNAMES
break a butterfly on a
wheel, EXCESSIVENESS
break for tall timber, DEPAR-
TURE
break the ice, INITIATION
break [someone's] bubble,
DISILLUSIONMENT
bridle, HAUGHTINESS
bridle back, HAUGHTINESS
bridle up, HAUGHTINESS
bring buckle and thong to-
gether, SUBSISTENCE
bring down the gallery, SUC-
CESS
bring down the house, SUC-
CESS
bring home the bacon, VIC-
TORY
broach [someone's] claret,
COMBAT
broad in the beam, CORPU-
LENCE
Bronx cheer, INSULT
brothel-creepers, CLOTHING
browbeat, DOMINATION
brown-bagger, STATUS
brown-nose, OBSEQUIOUS-
NESS
brown study, THOUGHT
bucket of bolts, VEHICLES
buckle down, EXERTION
buckle (oneself) to, EXER-
TION
the buck stops here, IRRE-
SPONSIBILITY
bucktoothed, VISAGE
bug, CURIOSITY
bug-eyed, SURPRISE
bull, NONSENSE
bullish, IDEALISM
bumf, LANGUAGE
bum rap, PUNISHMENT

the bum's rush, EXPULSION
buncombe, NONSENSE
bunk, NONSENSE
bunkin, OAFISHNESS
bunkum, NONSENSE
burn a barn to kill the rats,
ZEALOUSNESS
burn one's boats, DECISIVE-
NESS
burn one's bridges, DECISIVE-
NESS
burn one's fingers, KNOWL-
EDGE
burn one's ships, DECISIVE-
NESS
burn rubber, SPEEDING
burn the breeze, SPEEDING
burn the candle at both
ends, OVEREXTENSION
burn the earth, SPEEDING
burn the midnight oil, OVER-
WORK
burn the road, SPEEDING
burn the wind, SPEEDING
burn up the road, SPEEDING
burst [someone's] bubble,
DISILLUSIONMENT
bury one's head in the sand,
EVASIVENESS
bury the ax, PEACE
bury the hatchet, PEACE
bury the tomahawk, PEACE
bush telegraph or jungle telegraph, COMMUNICATION
busman's holiday, RESPITE
busy as a beaver, ZEALOUS-
NESS
but - and - ben, ESTABLISH-
MENTS
butter-and-egg man, OAFISH-
NESS
butterball, CORPULENCE
butterflies, ANXIETY
butter one's bread on both
sides, IMPROVIDENCE
button of the cap, FAVORIT-
ISM
button one's lip, SECRECY
button up, SECRECY
button up one's face, SE-
CRECY
button up one's lip, SECRECY
buy a pig in a poke, SWIN-
DLING
buy it, DEATH
buy the box, DEATH
buy the farm, DEATH

by a long chalk, EXTENT
by a long shot, EXTENT
by a long sight, EXTENT
by and large, PERSPECTIVE
by a nose, EXTENT
by ear, INTUITION
by hook or by crook, EXPEDI-
ENCE
by rote, KNOWLEDGE
by the board, IRRETRIEVA-
BILITY
by the seat of one's pants, IN-
TUITION
by the skin of one's teeth,
PRECARIOUSNESS

C

cabbages and kings, MIXTURE
cackling geese, EXPOSURE
Caesar's wife must be above
suspicion, VIRTUOUSNESS
[one's] cake is dough, FAIL-
URE
cakes and ale, REVELRY
call a spade a spade, CANDID-
NESS
call off the dogs, CESSATION
call one's shots, COMMUNICA-
TION
call on the carpet, REPRI-
MAND
call the shots, COMMUNICA-
TION
calm before the storm, PEACE
camp or campy, AFFECTA-
TION
camp it up, AFFECTATION
camp up, AFFECTATION
candle-holder, ASSISTANCE
candy man, AFFLUENCE
can of worms, COMPLICA-
TION
can't cut the mustard, COM-
PETENCE
cap in hand, DEFERENCE
card up one's sleeve, PLOY
carry a message to Garcia,
SELF-RELIANCE
carry a rope in one's
pocket, GOOD LUCK
carry big guns, PERSONAGE
carry coals, SELF-DISPARAGE-
MENT

carry coals to Newcastle, INAPPROPRIATENESS
carry fire in one hand and water in the other, HYPOCRISY
carry it, VICTORY
carry it hollow, OUTDOING
carry owls to Athens, INAPPROPRIATENESS
carry the ball, CONTROL
carry the can, VICTIMIZATION
carry the can back, VICTIMIZATION
carry the day, VICTORY
carte blanche, FREEDOM
cash in one's chips, DEATH
cash on the barrelhead, PAYMENT
cast a bone between, DISSENSION
cast a sheep's eye, LUST
cast beyond the moon, ILLUSION
cast in [someone's] teeth, REPRIMAND
castles in Spain, ILLUSION
castles in the air, ILLUSION
castle of cards, FLIMSINESS
cast one's bread upon the waters, CHARITABLENESS
cast pearls before swine, IMPRUDENCE
cast stones against the wind, FUTILITY
catcall, INSULT
catch someone napping, ADVANTAGE
catch-22, PREDICAMENT
catch-as-catch-can, UNRESTRAINT
catch a tartar, REVERSAL
catch a weasel asleep, ADVANTAGE
catch napping, ADVANTAGE
catchpenny, WORTHLESSNESS
cat ice, DANGER
a cat may look at a king, FAIRNESS
cat's meow, EXCELLENCE
cat's paw, VICTIMIZATION
cat that swallowed the canary, COMPLACENCY
cat's cuff links, EXCELLENCE
cat's eyebrows, EXCELLENCE
cat's galoshes, EXCELLENCE
cat's pajamas, EXCELLENCE

cat's roller skates, EXCELLENCE
cat's tonsils, EXCELLENCE
cat's whiskers, EXCELLENCE
caught bending, VULNERABILITY
caught dead to rights, CERTAINTY
caught flat-footed, VULNERABILITY
caught with one's hand in the cookie jar, GUILT
caught with one's pants down, VULNERABILITY
caviar to the general, INAPPROPRIATENESS
centerfold, PRURIENCE
chalk from cheese, DIFFERENTIATION
chalk it up, ATTRIBUTION
champ at the bit, IMPATIENCE
change one's tune, RECANTATION
chapter and verse, AUTHORITATIVENESS
charley horse, ILL HEALTH
cheat the worms, RECOVERY
cheek by cheek, PROXIMITY
cheek by jowl, PROXIMITY
cheese, PERSONAGE
cheese and kisses, MARRIAGE
cheesecake, PRURIENCE
cheeseparing, MISERLINESS
chestnut, ANECDOTE
chew it finer, SIMPLIFICATION
chew out, REPRIMAND
chew the fat, TALKATIVENESS
chew the rag, TALKATIVENESS
chicken feed, MONEY
chicken guts, NICKNAMES
chickens come home to roost, RETRIBUTION
chief cook and bottle washer, PERSONAGE
chief itch and rub, PERSONAGE
Chinaman's chance, IMPROBABILITY
chink in one's armor, VULNERABILITY
chip in, COOPERATION
chip off the old block, SIMILARITY

chip of the old block, SIMILARITY
chip of the same block, SIMILARITY
a chip on one's shoulder, BELLIGERENCE
choke-pear, IMPEDIMENT
chop logic, NIT-PICKING
chowhound, GOURMANDISM
circular file, DISORDER
clam's garters, EXCELLENCE
claptrap, LANGUAGE
clay pigeon, VULNERABILITY
clean as a whistle, NEATNESS
cleaned out, SWINDLING
clean house, REFORMATION
cleanse the Augean stables, REFORMATION
a clean slate, BEGINNINGS
clean up one's act, REFORMATION
clear as a whistle, NEATNESS
clear sailing, EFFORTLESSNESS
cliff-hanger, ANXIETY
climb aboard the bandwagon, SIMILARITY
climb Parnassus, LETTERS
climb the wall, VEXATION
climb walls, DESPERATION
clip [someone's] wings, THWARTING
clodhopper, OAFISHNESS
close as a clam, MISERLINESS
close as the bark to the tree, FRIENDSHIP
close shave, PRECARIOUSNESS
close to the bone, SENSITIVITY
clotheshorse, STYLISHNESS
clutch, MISERLINESS
clutch-fist, MISERLINESS
the coast is clear, FREEDOM
cobbler should stick to his last, PROPRIETY
cock, NONSENSE
cock-a-hoop, ELATION
cock and bull story, NONSENSE
cock a snook, INSULT
cocked, DRUNKENNESS
cock of the walk, POMPOSITY
codfish aristocracy, STATUS
codfish gentility, STATUS
cold feet, COWARDICE
colly-west, COMBAT

colors, BRAVERY
colors, EXPOSURE
come a cropper, DOWNFALL
come hell or high water, PER-
SEVERANCE
come home by Weeping
Cross, GRIEVING
come in pudding-time, OP-
PORTUNENESS
come off with flying colors,
SUCCESS
come on like gangbusters,
POWER
come out flat-footed, CANDID-
NESS
come out in the wash, OUT-
COME
*come out in one's true col-
ors,* EXPOSURE
*come out of it with flying
colors,* SUCCESS
come out smelling like a
rose, EXONERATION
come to bat for, ASSISTANCE
come to grips with, CON-
FRONTATION
come up for air, RESPITE
coming or going, CONFUSION
commuting town, LOCALITY
concrete jungle, LOCALITY
confound, EXACERBATION
confusion worse con-
founded, EXACERBATION
cooking with electricity, EF-
FICIENCY
cooking with gas, EFFI-
CIENCY
cook [someone's] goose,
THWARTING
cooking with radar, EFFI-
CIENCY
cool as a cucumber, COMPO-
SURE
the cooler, ESTABLISHMENTS
cooling card, IMPEDIMENT
cool it, COMPOSURE
cool one's heels, IMPATIENCE
cool your jets, COMPOSURE
a coon's age, DURATION
coop-happy, IRRATIONALITY
copybook, SIMPLIFICATION
copycat, SIMILARITY
cordon bleu, EXCELLENCE
cork-brained, IGNORANCE
corker, EFFECTIVENESS
corner the market, CONTROL
corporate gadfly, IRRITATION·

costardmonger, OCCUPATION
coster, OCCUPATION
costermonger, OCCUPATION
cottage industry, SELF-RELI-
ANCE
country bumpkin, OAFISH-
NESS
count to ten, COMPOSURE
court holy water, FLATTERY
cover all bases, CAUTIOUS-
NESS
cover one's tracks, CONCEAL-
MENT
crabs, EPONYMS
crack'd in the ring, IMPER-
FECTION
cracker-barrel, SIMPLIFICA-
TION
cracker-barrel philosophy,
SIMPLIFICATION
crack the whip, DOMINATION
cradlesnatch, LOVE
cramp [someone's] style,
THWARTING
craps, EPONYMS
crestfallen, DEJECTION
cricket, PROPRIETY
crocodile tears, HYPOCRISY
crook the elbow, TIPPLING
cross as two sticks, ANGRI-
NESS
cross [someone's] bows, VEX-
ATION
cross [someone's] palm, BRIB-
ERY
cross over, DEATH
cross the Great Divide,
DEATH
cross the Rubicon, DECISIVE-
NESS
cross to bear, BURDEN
crown of thorns, ADVERSITY
crow over, BOASTING
a crow to pluck, DISSENSION
crow to pull, DISSENSION
cry barley, SUBMISSION
cry for the moon, FUTILITY
crying towel, SELF-PITY
cry in one's beer, SELF-PITY
cry on [someone's] shoul-
der, SELF-PITY
cry over spilt milk, IRREVO-
CABLENESS
cry peccavi, GUILT
cry stinking fish, SELF-DIS-
PARAGEMENT
cry uncle, SUBMISSION

cry wolf, MENDACITY
cuckold, INFIDELITY
[one's] cup of tea, PREFER-
ENCE
cup of tea, PREFERENCE
cupped, DRUNKENNESS
curate's egg, AMALGAMATION
curry favor, OBSEQUIOUSNESS
curry Favel, OBSEQUIOUS-
NESS
curtain lectures, REPRIMAND
curtains, TERMINATION
cushion, ERRONEOUSNESS
Custer's last stand, DOWN-
FALL
cut, ADVERSITY
cut a caper, REVELRY
cut a dido, MISCHIEF
cut and dried, SIMPLIFICA-
TION
cut and run, DEPARTURE
cut a swath, OSTENTATIOUS-
NESS
cut corners, EXPEDIENCY
cut it close, PRECARIOUSNESS
cut monkeyshines, MISCHIEF
cut no ice, INEFFECTUALITY
cut off one's nose to spite
one's face, EXACERBATION
cut off with a shilling, REJEC-
TION
cut off without a shilling, RE-
JECTION
the cut of one's jib, INDIVIDU-
ALITY
cut one's eyeteeth, KNOWL-
EDGE
cut shines, MISCHIEF
cut one's stick, DEPARTURE
cut out of whole cloth, MEN-
DACITY
cutpurse, CRIMINALITY
cut [someone's] comb, HU-
MILIATION
cut the coat according to the
cloth, ADAPTATION
cut the Gordian knot, SOLU-
TION
cut the ground from under,
RUINATION
cut the knot, SOLUTION
cut the mustard, COMPE-
TENCE
cut the muster, COMPETENCE
cutting corners, EXPEDIENCE
cut to the quick, SENSITIVITY
cut up, MISCHIEF

cut up monkey shines, MIS-
CHIEF

D

daffadowndilly, STYLISHNESS
daffydowndilly, STYLISH-
NESS
**Dame Partington and her
mop,** CONSERVATISM
damn with faint praise, CRITI-
CISM
Damocles' sword, DANGER
damp squib, FAILURE
dance attendance, on, OB-
SEQUIOUSNESS
dance in the rope, DEATH
dance on air, DEATH
dance on nothing, DEATH
dance on the razor's edge,
RISK
dance the antic hay, REV-
ELRY
dance the Tyburn jig, DEATH
dandiprat, PHYSICAL STAT-
URE
Darby and Joan, MARRIAGE
daring to do, BRAVERY
dark horse, IMPROBABILITY
daughter of the horseleech,
VICTIMIZATION
Davy Jones's locker, BURIAL
[one's] days are numbered,
ILL HEALTH
days of wine and roses, DECA-
DENCE
D-day, TIME
dead as a doornail, DEATH
dead as Chelsea, ABANDON-
MENT
dead men's shoes, DESIRE
dead to rights, CERTAINTY
deaf as a doornail, DEATH
deaf as an adder, OBSTINACY
Dear John letter, REJECTION
*death joins us to the great
majority,* DEATH
debt to nature, DEATH
debunk, EXPOSURE
deep-six, DISPOSAL
derring-do, BRAVERY
destroy root and branch,
THOROUGHNESS
deus ex machina, RESCUE

devil's advocate, ARGUMEN-
TATION
devil's luck, GOOD LUCK
the devil's own luck, GOOD
LUCK
**the Devil take the hind-
most,** COMPETITION
the devil to pay, PUNISH-
MENT
*devil to pay and no pitch
hot,* PUNISHMENT
diamond in the rough, IM-
PERFECTION
dicey, PRECARIOUSNESS
dickens, PROFANITY
dickens take you, PROFANITY
Dick Tracy, RETORT
Dick Turpin, CRIMINALITY
dido, MISCHIEF
**die for want of lobster
sauce,** EXCESSIVENESS
die-hard, PERSEVERANCE
die in harness, DEATH
die in the last ditch, DESPER-
ATION
die in the saddle, DEATH
the die is cast, IRREVOCABLE-
NESS
die is cast, DECISIVENESS
die like Roland, HUNGER
die with one's boots on,
DEATH
different cup of tea, PREFER-
ENCE
dig one's own grave, SELF-
DISPARAGEMENT
dig up the hatchet, ax, or
tomahawk, COMBAT
dime novel, SENSATIONALISM
dine with Duke Humphrey,
HUNGER
ding-a-ling, FATUOUSNESS
dingbat, FATUOUSNESS
dip into the blue, PROFANITY
dirty word, LANGUAGE
do a guy, ESCAPE
do a 180° turn, RECANTATION
do a moonlight flit, DEPAR-
TURE
do an end run, EVASIVENESS
do a slow burn, FURY
do brown, UNRESTRAINT
doesn't cut the mustard,
COMPETENCE
dog days, WEATHER
dog-eared, SHABBINESS

dog in the manger, RESENT-
MENT
do it up brown, UNRE-
STRAINT
dolce far niente, INDOLENCE
doleful dumps, DEJECTION
dollars to doughnuts, CER-
TAINTY
domino theory, CONSE-
QUENCES
donnybrook, COMBAT
Donnybrook Fair, COMBAT
don't give up the ship, PERSE-
VERANCE
*don't judge a book by its
cover,* CRITERION
**don't let anyone sell you a
wooden nutmeg,** ADVICE
**don't look a gift horse in the
mouth,** INGRATITUDE
*don't put all your eggs in one
basket,* CAUTIOUSNESS
**don't take any wooden nick-
els,** ADVICE
*don't shout until you're out of
the woods,* RECOVERY
dormitory, LOCALITY
dormitory town, LOCALITY
**dot one's i's and cross one's
t's,** PRECISION
double dome, SCHOLARLI-
NESS
double Dutch, GIBBERISH
double whammy, THWART-
ING
doubting Thomas, SKEPTI-
CISM
doughboy, NICKNAMES
*do unto others as you would
have them do unto you,*
RECIPROCITY
dove, PEACE
dove, BELLIGERENCE
down-at-the-heel, POVERTY
down-at-the-heel, AFFLU-
ENCE
down in the dumps, DEJEC-
TION
down in the mouth, DEJEC-
TION
down the drain, IRRETRIEVA-
BILITY
down the hatch, TIPPLING
down the tube, IRRETRIEVA-
BILITY
down to bedrock, FUNDA-
MENTALS

do you know Dr. Wright of Norwich?, IMPROPRIETY

drag over the coals, REPRIMAND

draw a bead on, FOCUS

draw a red herring across the trail, PLOY

drawing card, ENTICEMENT

draw in one's horns, SUBMISSION

draw the longbow, EXAGGERATION

dressed to kill, STYLISHNESS

dressed to the nines, STYLISHNESS

dressed up to the nines, STYLISHNESS

dressing down, REPRIMAND

drink like a fish, DRUNKENNESS

drive one's pigs to market, SLEEP

drive pigs, SLEEP

drive up the wall, VEXATION

a drop in the bucket, INSIGNIFICANCE

drop in the ocean, INSIGNIFICANCE

drop like a hot potato, DIFFICULTY

drug in the market, EXCESSIVENESS

drug on the market, EXCESSIVENESS

drunk as a fiddler, DRUNKENNESS

drunk as a lord, DRUNKENNESS

dry as a whistle, NEATNESS

dry-as-dust, BOREDOM

dry up and blow away, EXPULSION

duck-fit, FURY

duck soup, EFFORTLESSNESS

dumb as a doornail, DEATH

dumps, DEJECTION

dun, SOLICITATION

dunce, IGNORANCE

dunderhead, IGNORANCE

duppy, BURIAL

Dutch, GIBBERISH

Dutch courage, BRAVERY

the Dutch have taken Holland, RETORT

Dutch lunch, party or *supper,* COOPERATION

Dutch treat, COOPERATION

dyed - in - the - wool, CONSTANCY

E

eager beaver, ZEALOUSNESS

early days, IMPETUOUSNESS

earmarked, ALLOCATION

earn one's wings, COMPETENCE

ear to the ground, ALERTNESS

eat boiled crow, HUMILIATION

eat crow, HUMILIATION

eat high off the hog, AFFLUENCE

eat humble pie, HUMILIATION

eat one's hat, CERTAINTY

eat one's heart, SELF-PITY

eat one's heart out, SELF-PITY

eat one's words, RECANTATION

eat out of house and home, GOURMANDISM

eat salt with [*someone*], FRIENDSHIP

eat snakes, RECOVERY

eat [someone's] salt, FRIENDSHIP

eavesdropper, CURIOSITY

eel by the tail, DIFFICULTY

eel's ankles, EXCELLENCE

egghead, SCHOLARLINESS

eggs is eggs, CERTAINTY

eighty-six, ABSENCE

elbow grease, EXERTION

elephant's instep, EXCELLENCE

empty my trash, LUST

end run, EVASIVENESS

end sweep, EVASIVENESS

end up in smoke, FAILURE

English, OSTENTATIOUSNESS

enough [something] to choke Caligula's horse, EXCESSIVENESS

enough to make a cat speak, EXCELLENCE

escape the bear and fall to the lion, EXACERBATION

even break, FAIRNESS

every dog has his day, FAIRNESS

every man Jack, INCLUSIVENESS

everything but the kitchen sink, INCLUSIVENESS

everything but the kitchen stove, INCLUSIVENESS

everything tastes of porridge, DISILLUSIONMENT

every tub must stand on its own bottom, SELF-RELIANCE

every tub on its own black bottom, SELF-RELIANCE

ex cathedra, AUTHORITATIVENESS

an eye for an eye, RETALIATION

F

face made of a fiddle, GOOD HEALTH

face the music, CONFRONTATION

fair game, VULNERABILITY

fair-haired boy, FAVORITISM

fair-haired girl, FAVORITISM

fair shake, FAIRNESS

fair-weather friend, EXPEDIENCE

fall between two stools, VACILLATION

fall guy, VICTIMIZATION

false as Cressida, INFIDELITY

fan the breeze, TALKATIVENESS

fan the fires, AUGMENTATION

far and away, CERTAINTY

a far cry, DISSIMILARITY

far cry from, DISSIMILARITY

fare-you-well, EXCELLENCE

far from the mark, ERRONEOUSNESS

fashion plate, STYLISHNESS

fast buck, MONEY

faster than greased lightning, PACE

Fata Morgana, ENTICEMENT

fat cat, PERSONAGE

the fat's in the fire, IRREVOCABLENESS

fatten the kitty, AUGMENTATION

fatten the pot, AUGMENTATION

fear no colors, BRAVERY
feather in one's cap, ACCOMPLISHMENT
feather one's nest, EXPLOITATION
feed the fishes, DEATH
feed the fishes, ILL HEALTH
feel a draft, PERCEPTIVENESS
feel as if a cat has kittened in one's mouth, DRUNKENNESS
feel in one's bones, INTUITION
feel one's oats, ELATION
feel the draught, FINANCE
feel the pinch, FINANCE
feet of clay, IMPERFECTION
fetch over the coals, REPRIMAND
fiddle-de-dee, NONSENSE
fiddle-faddle, NONSENSE
fiddlesticks, NONSENSE
field day, OPPORTUNENESS
fifth columnist, BETRAYAL
fifth wheel, SUPERFLUOUSNESS
fight fire with fire, RETALIATION
fight like Kilkenny cats, COMBAT
fig of Spain, INSULT
file 13, DISPOSAL
filibuster, TEMPORIZING
filthy lucre, MONEY
fimble-famble, EVASIVENESS
find bones in, CANDIDNESS
fine as a fiddle, GOOD HEALTH
a fine Italian hand, INDIVIDUALITY
finger, EXPOSURE
finger in the pie, MEDDLESOMENESS
fingerman, EXPOSURE
fine kettle of fish, DISORDER
fire, EXPULSION
firebrand, PROVOCATION
fire bug, NICKNAMES
fire-new, AGE
fire one's pistol in the air, EVASIVENESS
firewater, FOOD AND DRINK
first-of-May, INEXPERIENCE
fish eye, VISAGE
fishing expedition, INVESTIGATION

fish in troubled waters, EXPLOITATION
fish or cut bait, DECISIVENESS
fish out of water, UNNATURALNESS
fish story, EXAGGERATION
fishy about the gills, DRUNKENNESS
fit as a fiddle, GOOD HEALTH
fit to be tied, ANGRINESS
five-finger, CRIMINALITY
five-finger discount, CRIMINALITY
fix [someone's] little red wagon, RETALIATION
fix [someone's] wagon, RETALIATION
flannelmouth, FLATTERY
flap one's chops, TALKATIVENESS
flap one's jaw, TALKATIVENESS
flap one's jowls, TALKATIVENESS
flap one's lip, TALKATIVENESS
flash in the pan, FAILURE
flat as a pancake, PHYSICAL APPEARANCE
flatfoot, OCCUPATION
flat-footed, CANDIDNESS
flay alive, REPRIMAND
flea bag, ESTABLISHMENTS
flea in the ear, IRRITATION
fleece, SWINDLING
flesh-peddler, VICTIMIZATION
fleshpot, ESTABLISHMENT
flesh-tailor, OCCUPATION
flibbertigibbet, TALKATIVENESS
flip, IRRATIONALITY
flip one's lid, IRRATIONALITY
flip out, IRRATIONALITY
flog a dead horse, FUTILITY
flourish like a green bay tree, PROSPERING
flourish of trumpets, OSTENTATIOUSNESS
flubadub, RUINATION
flubdub, RUINATION
flub the dub, RUINATION
fly a kite, SWINDLING
fly by night, CRIMINALITY
fly-by-night, CRIMINALITY
fly by night, IRRESPONSIBILITY

fly in amber, INSIGNIFICANCE
flying, DRUNKENNESS
fly in the face of, REBELLION
fly in the face of danger, REBELLION
fly in the face of providence, REBELLION
fly in the ointment, IMPEDIMENT
fly off the handle, FURY
fly on the wall, CURIOSITY
fly the coop, ESCAPE
fly trap, NICKNAMES
follow in the footsteps, SIMILARITY
follow one's nose, INTUITION
follow suit, SIMILARITY
food for fishes, DEATH
food for worms, DEATH
food for worms, RECOVERY
fool's paradise, ILLUSION
foot-in-mouth disease, IMPROPRIETY
a foot in the door, BEGINNINGS
footpad, CRIMINALITY
foot the bill, PAYMENT
for a song, COST
forbidden fruit, DESIRE
force [someone's] hand, COERCION
for Christ's sake, EXCLAMATIONS
for crying out loud, EXCLAMATIONS
fork the fingers, INSULT
forlorn hope, DESPERATION
fort, CONTROL
for love or money, COST
forty winks, SLEEP
foul ball, DISFAVOR
four-eyes, NICKNAMES
four-flusher, PRETENSE
the Four Hundred, STATUS
fox's sleep, PRETENSE
frame-up, VICTIMIZATION
Frankenstein monster, REVERSAL
freak out, IRRATIONALITY
free-lance, OCCUPATION
free-lancer, OCCUPATION
French walk, EXPULSION
Freudian slip, EXPOSURE
a frog in one's throat, ILL HEALTH
from Dan to Beersheba, INCLUSIVENESS

from hand to mouth, PRECARIOUSNESS
from Missouri, SKEPTICISM
from pillar to post, DIRECTION
from post to pillar, DIRECTION
from scratch, BEGINNINGS
from soup to nuts, INCLUSIVENESS
from stem to stern, INCLUSIVENESS
from the hip, IMPETUOUSNESS
from the horse's mouth, AUTHORITATIVENESS
from the teeth outward, MENDACITY
fry in one's own grease, CONSEQUENCES
fry the fat out of, EXTORTION
fruit salad, NICKNAMES
full as a bull, DRUNKENNESS
full as an egg, DRUNKENNESS
full as a tick, DRUNKENNESS
full-bagged, AFFLUENCE
full blast, INTENSITY
full of beans, FATUOUSNESS
full of beans, VITALITY
full tilt, INTENSITY
funny as a barrel of monkeys, HUMOROUSNESS
funny-peculiar or funny ha-ha, DIFFERENTIATION
fuss and feathers, OSTENTATIOUSNESS
fussy as a hen with one chick, ANXIETY

G

gadfly, IRRITATION
gadfly mind, IRRITATION
gag-tooth, VISAGE
gall and wormwood, RESENTMENT
gallery gods, STATUS
game is not worth the candle, WORTHLESSNESS
gandy dancer, OCCUPATION
Garrison finish, VICTORY
gate crasher, IMPROPRIETY
gatemouth, MEDDLESOMENESS
gazump, SWINDLING

gazoomph, SWINDLING
gear oneself up, PREPARATION
gear up, AUGMENTATION
geneva courage, BRAVERY
gentleman of the four outs, STATUS
German goiter, CORPULENCE
Geronimo, EXCLAMATION
get a bang out of, ENJOYMENT
get a charge out of, ENJOYMENT
get a kick out of, ENJOYMENT
get a line on, INFORMATION
get a move on, STARTING
get a rise out of, PROVOCATION
get a wiggle on, STARTING
get burnt, KNOWLEDGE
get cold feet, COWARDICE
get cracking, STARTING
get down off one's high horse, HAUGHTINESS
get down to brass tacks, FUNDAMENTALS
get down to the nitty-gritty, FUNDAMENTALS
get hold of the right end of the stick, CORRECTNESS
get hold of the wrong end of the stick, FALLACIOUSNESS
get in Dutch, DISFAVOR
get in gear, PREPARATION
get in [someone's] hair, IRRITATION
get it in the neck, PUNISHMENT
get it together, REFORMATION
get off on the right foot, BEGINNINGS
get off on the wrong foot, BEGINNINGS
get off scot-free, EXONERATION
get off [someone's] back, HARASSMENT
get off [someone's] case, HARASSMENT
get one's act together, REFORMATION
get one's ashes hauled, LUST
get one's foot in the door, BEGINNINGS
get oneself in gear, PREPARATION

get one's feet wet, INITIATION
get one's lumps, ADVERSITY
get one's signals crossed, COMMUNICATION
get one's teeth into, EXERTION
get one's wires crossed, COMMUNICATION
get on the bandwagon, SIMILARITY
get on the stick, STARTING
get on tick, PAYMENT
get psyched up, PREPARATION
get out from under, RECOVERY
get [someone] off the hook, RESCUE
get [someone's] back up, VEXATION
get [someone's] dander up, VEXATION
get [someone's] Dutch up, VEXATION
get [someone's] goat, VEXATION
get [someone's] hackles up, VEXATION
get [someone's] Indian up, VEXATION
get [someone's] Irish up, VEXATION
get [someone's] monkey up, VEXATION
get the ball rolling, INITIATION
get the drop on, ADVANTAGE
get the gate, REJECTION
get the hook, REJECTION
get the lead out of one's pants, IDLENESS
get the nod, APPROVAL
get the sack, EXPULSION
get the short end of the stick, VICTIMIZATION
get the show on the road, STARTING
get the stick, REPRIMAND
get the weather gage of, ADVANTAGE
get the whetstone, VICTORY
get the wind up, ANXIETY
get the wrong end of the stick, FALLACIOUSNESS
get to first base, BEGINNINGS

get under [someone's] skin, IRRITATION

get up on the wrong side of the bed, ILL TEMPER

get up steam, PREPARATION

get wind of, INFORMATION

gezumph, SWINDLING

the ghost walks, PAYMENT

ghostwrite, OCCUPATION

ghost writer, OCCUPATION

the gift of gab, TALKATIVE-NESS

gift of the gab, TALKATIVE-NESS

gift of the gob, TALKATIVE-NESS

gild refined gold, EXCESSIVE-NESS

gild the lily, EXCESSIVENESS

gild the pill, CONCEALMENT

gingerbread, EXCESSIVENESS

ginger group, PROVOCATION

gippy tummy, ILL HEALTH

gird up one's loins, PREPARA-TION

give a basket, REJECTION

give a leg up, ASSISTANCE

give a wide berth to, FREE-DOM

give enough rope, FREEDOM

give her the bells and let her fly, RESIGNATION

give leg bail, ESCAPE

give one's beard for the washing, SUBMISSIVENESS

give one's eyeteeth, DESIRE

give one's head for the polling, SUBMISSIVENESS

give one's head for the washing, SUBMISSIVENESS

give one's right arm, DESIRE

give pap with a hatchet, HY-POCRISY

give short shrift, CARELESS-NESS

give [someone] a dose of [his] own medicine, RE-TALIATION

give [someone] a run for [his] money, COMPETITION

give [someone] a taste of [his] own medicine, RETALIA-TION

give [someone] Jesse, REPRI-MAND

give [someone] running shoes, EXPULSION

give [someone] the length of one's tongue, REPRIMAND

give the air, REJECTION

give the bag, REJECTION

give the bird, INSULT

give the brush-off, INSULT

give the cold shoulder, RE-JECTION

give the fico, INSULT

give the fig, INSULT

give the gate, REJECTION

give the gate, INSULT

give the gleek, RIDICULE

give the goose, INSULT

give the guy, ESCAPE

give the hook, REJECTION

give the mitten, REJECTION

give the raspberry, INSULT

give the run-around, EVA-SIVENESS

give the sack, INSULT

give the shaft, VICTIMIZA-TION

give the slip, ESCAPE

give the wall, DEFERENCE

give the wind, REJECTION

give up the ghost, DEATH

glad clothes, CLOTHING

glad rags, CLOTHING

glads, CLOTHING

the glass of fashion and the mold of form, STYLISHNESS

glory hole, SANCTUARY

glove-money, BRIBERY

glove-silver, BRIBERY

gnu's shoes, EXCELLENCE

go around Robin Hood's barn, DIRECTION

go bananas, IRRATIONALITY

gobbledegook, LANGUAGE

go belly up, DEATH

go between the bark and the tree, MEDDLESOMENESS

go between the moon and the milkman, IRRESPONSIBIL-ITY

go by beggar's bush, POV-ERTY

go by the board, IRRETRIEVA-BILITY

go-by-ground, PHYSICAL STATURE

go by the marrow-bone stage, LOCOMOTION

go cold turkey, TERMINATION

gods, STATUS

God's acre, BURIAL

God save the mark, EXCLA-MATIONS

go Dutch, COOPERATION

go fly a kite, EXPULSION

go for broke, UNRESTRAINT

go gathering orange blos-soms, QUEST

go great guns, PROSPERING

go haywire, DISORDER

go home by beggar's bush, POVERTY

go in one ear and out the other, INEFFECTUALITY

go in search of the golden fleece, QUEST

go in with good cards, AD-VANTAGE

go jump in the lake, EXPUL-SION

goldbrick, IDLENESS

gold digger, VICTIMIZATION

go like hot cakes, PACE

gone coon, VULNERABILITY

gone to the bad for the shadow of an ass, NIT-PICK-ING

gong [someone], REJECTION

good Samaritan, ASSISTANCE

Goody Two Shoes, PRUDISH-NESS

go off at half-cock, IMPETU-OUSNESS

go off half-cocked, IMPETU-OUSNESS

go off the deep end, IRRA-TIONALITY

go on a tear, REVELRY

go on tick, PAYMENT

goose egg, FAILURE

the goose hangs high, OPPOR-TUNENESS

the goose honks high, OPPOR-TUNENESS

go overboard, EXCESSIVE-NESS

go over like a lead balloon, FAILURE

go over to the majority, DEATH

go over with a fine-tooth comb, THOROUGHNESS

go peddle your papers, EX-PULSION

go play in traffic, EXPULSION

the gorge rises at it, REPUL-SION

go round the bend, ECCEN-TRICITY

go the way of all flesh, DEATH

go through fire and water, DESIRE

go through-stitch, COMPLE-TION

go to bat for, ASSISTANCE

go to Canossa, HUMILIATION

go to heaven in a wheelbar-row, PUNISHMENT

go to heaven in a wheelbar-row, DEGENERATION

go to hell in a handbasket, DEGENERATION

go to Jericho, EXPULSION

go to pot, DEGENERATION

go to rack, DEGENERATION

go to rack and ruin, DEGEN-ERATION

go to ruin, DEGENERATION

go to the dickens, PROFANITY

go to the dogs, DEGENERA-TION

go to the world, MARRIAGE

go to town, PROSPERING

go two-forty, SPEEDING

go up in smoke, FAILURE

go west, DEATH

go whole hog, UNRESTRAINT

go woolgathering, INDO-LENCE

grace-widow, NICKNAMES

grandstand, OSTENTATIOUS-NESS

grandstand finish, OSTENTA-TIOUSNESS

grandstand play, OSTENTA-TIOUSNESS

grapevine, COMMUNICATION

grant the gate, REJECTION

grasp at straws, DESPERA-TION

grass roots, STATUS

grass widow, NICKNAME

graveyard shift, TIME

graveyard watch, TIME

gravy boat, AFFLUENCE

gravy train, AFFLUENCE

grease, CONSEQUENCES

grease [someone's] palm, BRIBERY

grease the hand or *fist,* BRIB-ERY

grease the wheels, BRIBERY

great, EFFICIENCY

great cry and little wool, INEFFECTUALITY

great pith and moment, WOR-THINESS

the great unwashed, STATUS

Greek, GIBBERISH

green around the gills, DRUNKENNESS

green-eyed, RESENTMENT

the green-eyed monster, RE-SENTMENT

green fingers, ABILITY

greenhorn, INEXPERIENCE

green thumb, ABILITY

green with envy, RESENT-MENT

gremlin, MISCHIEF

grin like a Cheshire cat, VIS-AGE

grist for the mill, EXPLOITA-TION

grit one's teeth, PREPARA-TION

grit your teeth, ENDURANCE

groovy, EFFICIENCY

group grope, PROMISCUOUS-NESS

grubstake, FINANCE

Grub Street, LETTERS

grumble in the gizzard, GRIEVANCE

guardhouse lawyer, MED-DLESOMENESS

guinea pig, VICTIMIZATION

gully washer, WEATHER

gully whomper, WEATHER

gumshoe, OCCUPATION

gum up the works, RUINA-TION

gung ho, ZEALOUSNESS

to guy, ESCAPE

H

hack, LETTERS

hackney, LETTERS

hairdown, CANDIDNESS

a hair in the butter, DIF-FICULTY

a hair of the dog that bit you, FOOD AND DRINK

halcyon days, PEACE

half-baked, FLIMSINESS

half-cocked, IMPETUOUSNESS

half-cocked, DRUNKENNESS

half in the bag, DRUNKEN-NESS

half seas over, DRUNKENNESS

hallmark, GENUINENESS

ham, OSTENTATIOUSNESS

hamfat man, OSTENTATIOUS-NESS

hammer and tongs, INTEN-SITY

hammer out, SOLUTION

hancho, PERSONAGE

hand and glove, CONSPIRACY

hand in glove, CONSPIRACY

hand in one's checks, DEATH

handle with kid gloves, CAU-TIOUSNESS

handle with gloves off, CAU-TIOUSNESS

handle without gloves, CAU-TIOUSNESS

hand on the torch, GUIDANCE

hand over hand, PACE

hand over fist, PACE

hands down, EFFORTLESS-NESS

handwriting on the wall, OMEN

hang by a thread, PRECARI-OUSNESS

hang by the eyelids, PRECARIOUSNESS

hanging fire, ABEYANCE

hang loose, CANDIDNESS

hang on [someone's] sleeve, DEPENDENCE

hang out one's shingle, BE-GINNINGS

hang up one's hatchet, RE-TIREMENT

hanky-panky, MISCHIEF

happy as a clam at high tide, ELATION

happy hunting ground, PAR-ADISE

happy warrior, PERSEVER-ANCE

hard-and-fast, CONSTANCY

hard-hat, CONSERVATISM

a hard nut to crack, DIF-FICULTY

hard row to hoe, DIFFICULTY

hard up, POVERTY

harebrained, IRRATIONALITY

hark back, REPETITION

harp on, REPETITION

harp on one string, REPETI-TION

harp on the same string, REP-
ETITION
haste makes waste, IMPA-
TIENCE
hatchet job, CRIMINALITY
hatchet man, CRIMINALITY
hatchet work, CRIMINALITY
hats off, COMMENDATION
hat trick, ACCOMPLISHMENT
haul over the coals, REPRI-
MAND
have a bee in one's bonnet,
OBSESSION
have a bone to pick, GRIEV-
ANCE
have a gadfly, IRRITATION
have a jag on, DRUNKENNESS
have a moonflaw in the
brain, ECCENTRICITY
have an ox on the tongue,
BRIBERY
have a package on, DRUNK-
ENNESS
have a run for one's money,
COMPETITION
have a screw loose, ECCEN-
TRICITY
have a short fuse, FURY
have a tile loose, ECCENTRIC-
ITY
have a worm in one's
tongue, ILL TEMPER
have bats in one's belfry, EC-
CENTRICITY
*have butterflies in one's
stomach,* ANXIETY
have by the short hairs, DOMI-
NATION
*have by the short and curl-
ies,* DOMINATION
have by the tail, DOMINATION
have cold feet, COWARDICE
have eyes for, DESIRE
have kittens, FRENZIEDNESS
have it hollow, OUTDOING
have lead in one's pants,
IDLENESS
have one foot in the grave,
ILL HEALTH
have one for the worms, TIP-
PLING
have one's eyeteeth, KNOWL-
EDGE
have one's foot on [some-
one's] neck, DOMINATION
*have one's head in chan-
cery,* PREDICAMENT

have one's heart in one's
mouth, FEAR
have one's nose in the air, RE-
JECTION
have one's work cut out, DIF-
FICULTY
have other fish to fry, INDIF-
FERENCE
have some marbles missing,
IRRATIONALITY
*have [someone] around one's
little finger,* MANIPULA-
TION
*have someone dead to
rights,* CERTAINTY
have [someone's] number,
PERCEPTIVENESS
have [someone's] number on
it, DESTINY
have something on the ball,
ALERTNESS
have something up one's
sleeve, PLOY
have the ball at one's feet,
ADVANTAGE
have the last laugh, SUCCESS
have the sun in one's eyes,
DRUNKENNESS
*have the words stick in one's
throat,* IMPEDIMENT
have the world on a string,
ELATION
have the world in a string,
ELATION
have two left feet, AWK-
WARDNESS
have two strikes against
one, DISADVANTAGE
have two strings to one's
bow, CAUTIOUSNESS
have windmills in one's
head, FATUOUSNESS
*having both feet planted
on the ground,* DRUNKEN-
NESS
hawk, BELLIGERENCE
haymaker, EFFECTIVENESS
hayseed, OAFISHNESS
head hancho, PERSONAGE
head over ears, INTENSITY
head over heels, INTENSITY
headshrinker, OCCUPATION
heads will roll, PUNISH-
MENT
heap coals of fire on [some-
one's] head, RETALIATION

heap Pelion upon Ossa, EX-
ACERBATION
heart of hearts, SINCERITY
heart of oak, BRAVERY
hearts and flowers, SENTI-
MENTALITY
heartthrob, LOVE
Heath Robinson, CONTRAP-
TION
the heat's on, HARASSMENT
heavy threads, CLOTHING
hedge one's bets, CAUTIOUS-
NESS
heelkicking, REVELRY
heels over head, INTENSITY
*he laughs best that laughs
last,* SUCCESS
hellbent, ZEALOUSNESS
hellbent for breakfast, ZEAL-
OUSNESS
hellbent for election, ZEAL-
OUSNESS
hellbent for leather, ZEAL-
OUSNESS
hell on wheels, BOISTEROUS-
NESS
helter-skelter, DISORDER
hem and haw, EVASIVENESS
henpecked, VICTIMIZATION
here lies the rub, IMPEDI-
MENT
her nibs, PERSONAGE
he that lieth with dogs riseth
with fleas, CONSEQUENCES
*he who laughs last laughs
best,* SUCCESS
H-hour, TIME
Hic jacets, BURIAL
hide one's light under a
bushel, SELF-DISPARAGE-
MENT
higgledy-piggledy, DISORDER
high, DRUNKENNESS
highball, SPEEDING
highbrow, SCHOLARLINESS
Highbrowsville, SCHOLARLI-
NESS
high Dutch, GIBBERISH
higher than Gilderoy's kite,
EXTENT
high-hat, HAUGHTINESS
high jinks, REVELRY
high-kilted, PROMISCUOUS-
NESS
high-muck-a-muck, PERSON-
AGE

high-road to Needham, DE-
GENERATION
high-strung, ANXIETY
high time, TIMELINESS
highwaters, CLOTHING
highway robbery, COST
his nibs, PERSONAGE
hit below the belt, UN-
SCRUPULOUSNESS
hitch one's wagon to a star,
IDEALISM
hit list, DISFAVOR
hit on all four, EFFICIENCY
hit on all six, EFFICIENCY
*hit one's head against a stone
wall,* FUTILITY
*hit one's head against the
wall,* FUTILITY
hit the ceiling, FURY
hit the deck, EXCLAMATIONS
hit the hay, SLEEP
hit the jackpot, GOOD LUCK
hit the nail on the head, PRE-
CISION
hit the roof, FURY
hit the sack, SLEEP
hit the sauce, DRUNKENNESS
hit the sidewalks, QUEST
hit the skids, DEGENERATION
hit the white, CORRECTNESS
hob and nob, FRIENDSHIP
hobby horse, OBSESSION
hobnob, FRIENDSHIP
Hobson's choice, PREDICA-
MENT
hocus-pocus, MAGIC
hodgepodge, MIXTURE
hoe one's own row, SELF-
RELIANCE
hoist the blue peter, DEPAR-
TURE
hoist with one's own pe-
tard, REVERSAL
hokey-pokey, MISCHIEF
hold a candle to, COMPARA-
BILITY
hold an eel by the tail, DIF-
FICULTY
hold at bay, TEMPORIZING
hold a wolf by the ears, PRE-
DICAMENT
*hold buckle and thong to-
gether,* SUBSISTENCE
holding the baby, VICTIMI-
ZATION
holding the bag, VICTIMIZA-
TION

hold one's ground, PERSE-
VERANCE
hold one's heart in one's
hand, LOVE
hold on to your shirttail,
COMPOSURE
hold out the olive branch,
PEACE
hold the fort, CONTROL
hold the line, CONTROL
hold the purse strings, CON-
TROL
hold water, VALIDITY
hold with the hare and run
with the hounds, VACILLA-
TION
hold your horses, COMPO-
SURE
hole in the water, DEATH
Holy Christ, EXCLAMATIONS
holy cow, EXCLAMATIONS
holy mackerel, EXCLAMA-
TIONS
Homer sometimes nods, IM-
PERFECTION
honcho, PERSONAGE
honky-tonk, ESTABLISH-
MENTS
hooked, DEPENDENCE
hook, line, and sinker,
THOROUGHNESS
hop-o'-my-thumb, PHYSICAL
STATURE
hopping mad, ANGRINESS
hornets' nest, PROVOCATION
horn-mad, BELLIGERENCE
horn-thumb, CRIMINALITY
horny, LUST
a horseback opinion,
THOUGHT
a horse of a different color
DISSIMILARITY
a horse of another color, DIS-
SIMILARITY
a horse of the same color, DIS-
SIMILARITY
hotchpot, MIXTURE
hotchpotch, MIXTURE
hot-dog, OSTENTATIOUSNESS
hot dogger, OSTENTATIOUS-
NESS
hot-dog it, OSTENTATIOUS-
NESS
hotfoot, SPEEDING
hotfoot it, SPEEDING
hot potato, DIFFICULTY
hot to trot, LUST

hot under the collar, ANGRI-
NESS
housecleaning, REFORMA-
TION
house of cards, FLIMSINESS
howling dervishes, ZEALOUS-
NESS
huckleberry above one's persimmon, COMPARABILITY
hue and cry, PROTEST
hugger-mugger, SECRECY
Hulda is making her bed,
WEATHER
*hung higher than Gilderoy's
kite,* EXTENT
hunky-dory, EXCELLENCE
hurrah's nest, DISORDER
hurra's nest, DISORDER
hype, EXAGGERATION
hyped-up, EXAGGERATION

I

*if my aunt had been a man
she'd have been my
uncle,* RETALIATION
in a brace of shakes, INSTAN-
TANEOUSNESS
in a flap, FRENZIEDNESS
in a holding pattern, ABEY-
ANCE
in a jam, PREDICAMENT
in a jiffy, INSTANTANEOUS-
NESS
in a nutshell, ESSENCE
in a pickle, PREDICAMENT
in a pig's eye, IMPROBABIL-
ITY
in a pig's whisper, INSTAN-
TANEOUSNESS
in a rut, STAGNATION
in a scrape, PREDICAMENT
in a snit, ANGRINESS
in bed with one's boots on,
DRUNKENNESS
in black and white, AU-
THORITATIVENESS
in cahoots, CONSPIRACY
in Carey Street, POVERTY
in chancery, PREDICAMENT
in clover, AFFLUENCE
in cold storage, ABEYANCE
in deep water, PREDICAMENT
independent as a hog on
ice, INDEPENDENCE

keep one jump ahead, AD-
VANTAGE
keep one's chin up, PERSE-
VERANCE
keep one's ear to the
ground, ALERTNESS
keep one's end up, COOPERA-
TION
keep one's eyes peeled,
ALERTNESS
keep one's eyes skinned,
ALERTNESS
keep one's fingers crossed, SU-
PERSTITION
keep one's ground, PERSE-
VERANCE
keep one's hand in, ABILITY
keep one's head above
water, SUBSISTENCE
keep one's nose clean, PRO-
PRIETY
keep one's nose to the
grindstone, PERSEVER-
ANCE
keep one's pecker up, PERSE-
VERANCE
keep one's powder dry, COM-
POSURE
keep one's weather eye
open, ALERTNESS
*keep something under one's
hat,* SECRECY
keep the ball rolling, INITIA-
TION
keep the wolf from the
door, SUBSISTENCE
keep your breath to cool your
porridge, ADVICE
keep your eye on the ball,
ALERTNESS
keep your shirt on, COMPO-
SURE
kettle of fish, DISORDER
kewpie doll, AFFECTATION
key-cold, CALLOUSNESS
keyed up, ANXIETY
kick, DEATH
kick against the pricks, RE-
BELLION
kick in, COOPERATION
kick in, DEATH
kick off, DEATH
kick over the traces, REBEL-
LION
kickshaw, WORTHLESSNESS
kick the bucket, DEATH
kick-up, REVELRY

kick up one's heels, REVELRY
kick upstairs, EXPULSION
Kilkenny cats, COMBAT
kill the fatted calf, REVELRY
kingdom come, PARADISE
kingpin, PERSONAGE
the King's English, DICTION
a king's ransom, MONEY
kink, SEXUAL ORIENTATION
kinky, SEXUAL ORIENTATION
kiss of death, DESTINY
kiss the rod, SUBMISSIVENESS
kitchen cabinet, ADVICE
kitty, AUGMENTATION
knee-high to a grasshopper,
PHYSICAL STATURE
knobstick wedding, COER-
CION
knock for a loop, CONFUSION
knock for six, RUINATION
knock galley-west, COMBAT
knock into a cocked hat, RUI-
NATION
*knock one's head against a
stone wall,* FUTILITY
*knock one's head against the
wall,* FUTILITY
knock out of the box, EXPUL-
SION
knock the spots out of, OUT-
DOING
knock the tar out of, COMBAT
knock under, SUBMISSION
knock under board, SUBMIS-
SION
knock under the table, SUB-
MISSION
know a hawk from a hand-
saw, PECEPTIVENESS
know chalk from cheese,
PERCEPTIVENESS
*know how many beans make
five,* KNOWLEDGE
know one's beans, KNOWL-
EDGE
know one's business, KNOWL-
EDGE
know one's onions, KNOWL-
EDGE
know one's stuff, KNOWL-
EDGE
know the ropes, KNOWLEDGE
know what's o'clock,
SHREWDNESS
know which side one's bread
is buttered on, EXPEDI-
ENCE

know which way the wind
blows, SHREWDNESS
knuckle under, SUBMISSION

L

laced mutton, PROMISCUOUS-
NESS
la-di-da, AFFECTATION
lame duck, INEFFECTUALITY
Lamourette's kiss, AGREE-
MENT
landmark decision, CRITE-
RION
land-office business, PROS-
PERING
land of milk and honey, PAR-
ADISE
land on one's feet, SUCCESS
lardy-dardy, AFFECTATION
large shoes to fill, SIMILARITY
a lash of scorpions, REPRI-
MAND
last-ditch, DESPERATION
last hurrah, CULMINATION
last one in is a rotten egg,
COMPETITION
last straw, CULMINATION
laugh in one's beard, RIDI-
CULE
laugh in one's cape, RIDI-
CULE
laugh in one's sleeve, RIDI-
CULE
laugh like a drain, HUMOR-
OUSNESS
laugh on the other side of
one's face or mouth, RET-
RIBUTION
*laugh on the wrong side of
one's face,* RETRIBUTION
*laugh on the wrong side of
one's mouth,* RETRIBUTION
laurels, COMPLACENCY
lay an egg, FAILURE
lay by the heels, THWARTING
lay it on, FLATTERY
lay it on the line, RISK
lay it on thick, FLATTERY
lay it on with a shovel, FLAT-
TERY
lay it on with a trowel, FLAT-
TERY
lay out in lavender, REPRI-
MAND

393 □ *loose ends*

lay someone out, REPRIMAND
lazy man's load, OVEREXTEN-
SION
lead a cat and dog life, COM-
BAT
lead a dog's life, ADVERSITY
lead balloon, FAILURE
lead by the nose, DOMI-
NATION
leading light, PERSONAGE
lead-pipe cinch, CERTAINTY
lead up the garden path, EN-
TICEMENT
leap in the dark, DEATH
leave no stone unturned,
THOROUGHNESS
leave the door open, DECI-
SIVENESS
the Left, REBELLION
left field, ERRONEOUSNESS
left high and dry, ABANDON-
MENT
left holding the bag, VICTIMI-
ZATION
left in the lurch, ABANDON-
MENT
left-wing, REBELLION
left-wing, CONSERVATISM
left-winger, CONSERVATISM
left-wingers, REBELLION
a leg to stand on, VALIDITY
lemon, FAILURE
leopard's stripes, EXCEL-
LENCE
let George do it, IRRESPONSI-
BILITY
let her go, Gallagher!, START-
ING
let her rip, UNRESTRAINT
let it all hang out, CANDID-
NESS
let one's hair down, CANDID-
NESS
let sleeping dogs lie, PLACA-
TION
let the cat out of the bag, EX-
POSURE
let the dead bury the dead,
IRREVOCABLENESS
a lick and a promise, CARE-
LESSNESS
lick into shape, GUIDANCE
lick one's chops, ENJOYMENT
lick [someone's] boots, OB-
SEQUIOUSNESS
lick [someone's] shoes, OB-
SEQUIOUSNESS

lickspittle, OBSEQUIOUSNESS
a lick with the rough side of
the tongue, REPRIMAND
lie in one's beard, MEN-
DACITY
lie in one's teeth, MENDACITY
lie in one's throat, MEN-
DACITY
lie through one's teeth, MEN-
DACITY
*life is not all beer and skit-
tles*, REVELRY
*lift oneself up by one's own
bootstraps*, SELF-RELIANCE
lift the elbow, TIPPLING
light-finger, CRIMINALITY
like a bat out of hell, PACE
like a bear with a sore
head, ILL TEMPER
like a cat in a strange garret, ANXIETY
like a cat on hot bricks, ANXI-
ETY
like a cat on a hot tin roof,
ANXIETY
like a chicken with its head
cut off, FRENZIEDNESS
like a dog's breakfast, SHAB-
BINESS
like a dog's dinner, STYLISH-
NESS
like a dog with two tails, ELA-
TION
like a house afire, PACE
like a lamb, SUBMISSIVENESS
like an owl in an ivy bush,
VISAGE
like a trooper, PROFANITY
like Caesar's wife, VIRTUOUS-
NESS
like it or lump it, RESIGNA-
TION
like water off a duck's back,
EFFORTLESSNESS
lily-livered, COWARDICE
lime-juicer, NICKNAMES
limey, NICKNAMES
line one's nest, EXPLOITA-
TION
line one's pockets, GRAFT
lion's share, ALLOCATION
a little bird, INTUITION
little Lord Fauntleroy, INEX-
PERIENCE
little pitchers have long
ears, SECRECY

a little pot is soon hot, ANGRI-
NESS
live high off the hog, AFFLU-
ENCE
live in a glass house, VULNER-
ABILITY
live in cotton wool, INEX-
PERIENCE
live like fighting cocks, GOUR-
MANDISM
live under the cat's foot, SUB-
MISSIVENESS
live wire, VITALITY
L.L. Whisky, FOOD AND
DRINK
loaded, DRUNKENNESS
loaded dice, DISADVANTAGE
loaded for bear, READINESS
loaves and fishes, MONEY
locker-room talk, PROFANITY
lock horns, COMBAT
lock, stock, and barrel,
THOROUGHNESS
logrolling, RECIPROCITY
lone wolf, INDEPENDENCE
long haul, DURATION
long in the tooth, AGE
long row to hoe, DIFFICULTY
look as if butter wouldn't
melt in one's mouth, PRE-
TENSE
look at cross-eyed, PROVOCA-
TION
look babies in the eyes, LOVE
look beneath the surface,
PERCEPTIVENESS
look daggers, BELLIGERENCE
look down one's nose,
HAUGHTINESS
*looking as if [he] just stepped
out of a bandbox*, STYLISH-
NESS
looking for a dog to kick, VIC-
TIMIZATION
look like the cat that swallowed the canary, COMPLA-
CENCY
look through a millstone,
PERCEPTIVENESS
look through blue glasses,
PREJUDICE
look through rose-colored
glasses, IDEALISM
look to one's laurels, CAU-
TIOUSNESS
loose ends, COMPLETION
loose ends, CONFUSION

loose screw, ECCENTRICITY
loosen up, CANDIDNESS
lose one's bearings, CONFU-SION
lose one's breakfast (lunch, dinner, supper), ILL HEALTH
lose one's head, IRRATIONAL-ITY
lose one's marbles, IRRATION-ALITY
lose one's shirt, FAILURE
lose one's tongue, SILENCE
lose the bell, VICTORY
lose the thread, DISCON-TINUITY
lost in the wash, IRRETRIEVA-BILITY
a lot on one's plate, OVER-WORK
lotus-eater, INDOLENCE
lounge lizard, VICTIMIZA-TION
love-brat, EUPHEMISMS
love-child, EUPHEMISMS
love me, love my dog, TOTAL-ITY
love-tooth in the head, LOVE
low blow, UNSCRUPULOUS-NESS
low-brow, SCHOLARLINESS
low-down, INFORMATION
lower the boom, PUNISH-MENT
low-key, UNOBTRUSIVENESS
low man on the totem pole, STATUS
a low profile, UNOBTRUSIVE-NESS
lully prigger, CRIMINALITY
a lump in the throat, IMPEDI-MENT
lump it, RESIGNATION

M

macaroni, STYLISHNESS
mad as a hatter, IRRATIONAL-ITY
mad as a March hare, IRRA-TIONALITY
mad as an otter, IRRATIONAL-ITY
mad as a wet hen, ANGRINESS
mad as hops, ANGRINESS
mad money, MONEY

maggots in the brain, OBSES-SION
maggots in the head, OBSES-SION
magic carpet, MAGIC
the mahogany, FRIENDSHIP
make a beeline, PACE
make a boner, ERRONEOUS-NESS
make a hash of, DISORDER
make a hole in the water, DEATH
make a hole in someone's coat, FAULTFINDING
make a mountain out of a molehill, EXAGGERATION
make bones about, CANDID-NESS
make both ends meet, SUB-SISTENCE
make bricks without straw, FUTILITY
make buckle and tongue meet, SUBSISTENCE
make chalk of one and cheese of the other, FAVORITISM
make cock-a-hoop, ELATION
make dainty, AFFECTATION
make ducks and drakes of, IMPROVIDENCE
make fair weather, OBSEQUI-OUSNESS
make fish of one and flesh of another, FAVORITISM
make fish of one and fowl of another, FAVORITISM
make hamburger of, RUINA-TION
make hay while the sun shines, EXPLOITATION
make head or tail of, DIF-FERENTIATION
make horns at, INSULT
make it hot for, HARASSMENT
make it too hot for, HARASS-MENT
make mincemeat of, RUINA-TION
make no bones about, CAN-DIDNESS
make [someone's] beard, DOMINATION
make [someone's] beard without a razor, DOMI-NATION
make [someone] see stars, COMBAT

make the feathers fly, COM-BAT
make the fur fly, COMBAT
make the hair stand on end, FEAR
make the mouth water, DE-SIRE
make the two ends of the year meet, SUBSISTENCE
make time with, PROMISCU-OUSNESS
make tracks, DEPARTURE
make waves, PROVOCATION
malapropism, LANGUAGE
man for all seasons, CON-STANCY
manna from heaven, GOOD LUCK
a man of my kidney, SIMILARITY
man of straw, VICTIMIZATION
many irons in the fire, OVER-EXTENSION
marble orchard, BURIAL
march to the beat of a different drummer, INDEPEN-DENCE
mare's-nest, DISORDER
marry over the broomstick, MARRIAGE
masher, PROMISCUOUSNESS
maverick, INDEPENDENCE
meal ticket, DEPENDENCE
mealy, INEFFECTUALITY
mealy-mouthed, INEFFECTU-ALITY
measure swords, COMBAT
meat-and-potatoes, FUNDA-MENTALS
meatwagon, VEHICLES
Meddlesome Matty, MED-DLESOMENESS
meet one's Waterloo, DOWN-FALL
megillah, ANECDOTE
melting pot, AMALGAMATION
mend one's fences, POLITICK-ING
merry-andrew, HUMOROUS-NESS
method in one's madness, PRETENSE
Mexican stand-off, CESSA-TION
Mickey Finn, FOOD AND DRINK
Mickey Mouse, INSIGNIFI-CANCE

Mickey Mouse around, EVA-SIVENESS
the Midas touch, ABILITY
middle-brow, SCHOLARLINESS
midnight oil, OVERWORK
milk, EXPLOITATION
milk-and-water, INEFFECTUALITY
milksop, INEFFECTUALITY
milk the bull, FUTILITY
milk the ram, FUTILITY
the mills of God grind slowly, RETRIBUTION
a millstone around the neck, BURDEN
mind one's p's and q's, PROPRIETY
mishmash, MIXTURE
mishmosh, MIXTURE
mishmush, MIXTURE
missing link, ABSENCE
a miss is as good as a mile, FAILURE
miss the boat, FAILURE
miss the bus, FAILURE
miss the cushion, ERRONEOUSNESS
miss the mark, IRRELEVANCE
mite, CHARITABLENESS
Molotov cocktail, EPONYMS
Monday-morning quarterback, FAULTFINDING
moneybags, AFFLUENCE
money talks, POWER
money to burn, AFFLUENCE
monkey about, MISCHIEF
monkey around, MISCHIEF
monkey around with, MISCHIEF
monkey business, MISCHIEF
monkey jacket, CLOTHING
a monkey on one's back, BURDEN
monkey's allowance, MONEY
monkeyshines, MISCHIEF
monkey's money, MONEY
monkey suit, CLOTHING
Montezuma's revenge, ILL HEALTH
a month of Sundays, DURATION
moonflaw, ECCENTRICITY
moonlighting, OVERWORK
moonlight flit, DEPARTURE
moonshine, FOOD AND DRINK
moonshine, NOURISHMENT

mops and brooms, DRUNKENNESS
more cry than wool, INEFFECTUALITY
the most unkindest cut of all, ADVERSITY
mote in the eye, IMPERFECTION
Mother Carey is plucking her chickens, WEATHER
mother of pearl, MARRIAGE
mountain dew, FOOD AND DRINK
mountain oysters, FOOD AND DRINK
mount the high horse, HAUGHTINESS
the mouse that has but one hole is quickly taken, CAUTIOUSNESS
mow [someone] down, EFFECTIVENESS
Mrs. Grundy, PRUDISHNESS
Mrs. Malaprop, LANGUAGE
mud, DISFAVOR
mud-slinging, SLANDER
mud-throwing, SLANDER
Mudville, DEJECTION
mugwump, INDEPENDENCE
mumbo jumbo, GIBBERISH
mum's the word, SECRECY
murder will out, EXPOSURE
music to the ears, ENJOYMENT
mustard, COMPETENCE
muster, COMPETENCE
my cup runneth over, ABUNDANCE
my eye, EXCLAMATIONS
my foot, EXCLAMATIONS
my garbage can is overflowing, LUST
my kingdom for a horse!, DESIRE
my little finger told me that, OMEN
my old dutch, MARRIAGE
my Venus turns out a whelp, REVERSAL

N

nail one's colors to the mast, PERSEVERANCE
naked truth, CANDIDNESS

namby-pamby, INEFFECTUALITY
name in lights, FAME
[one's] name is mud, DISFAVOR
a name to conjure with, PERSONAGE
narrow at the equator, HUNGER
nature of the beast, ESSENCE
near to the bone, SENSITIVITY
neat as a bandbox, STYLISHNESS
neck and crop, THOROUGHNESS
neck and crop, DOWNFALL
neck and neck, EQUIVALENCE
neck of the woods, LOCALITY
necktie frolic, DEATH
necktie party, DEATH
necktie sociable, DEATH
necktie social, DEATH
neither fish nor flesh nor good red herring, INDETERMINATENESS
neither hide nor hair, ABSENCE
neither rhyme nor reason, SENSE
nest egg, MONEY
the never-never plan, PAYMENT
the New Left, REBELLION
a new wrinkle, ADVANCEMENT
nice going, EFFICIENCY
nice kettle of fish, DISORDER
nickel and dime to death, PAYMENT
nickel nurser, MISERLINESS
nigger in the woodpile, SUSPICIOUSNESS
nightcap, FOOD AND DRINK
a night on the tiles, REVELRY
niminy-piminy, AFFECTATION
nine days' wonder, OBSOLESCENCE
nine tailors make a man, RIDICULE
nine tellers mark a man, RIDICULE
nip and chuck, EQUIVALENCE
nip and tack, EQUIVALENCE
nip and tuck, EQUIVALENCE

nip in the bud, TERMINATION
nit-pick, NIT-PICKING
nitty-gritty, FUNDAMENTALS
nix, ABSENCE
no dice, REFUSAL
no eyes, DESIRE
a nod is as good as a wink to a blind horse, FUTILITY
no flies on [someone], ALERTNESS
no great shakes, INSIGNIFICANCE
no holds barred, UNRESTRAINT
no joy in Mudville, DEJECTION
no man's land, DISORDER
the noose is hanging, READINESS
nose of wax, MANIPULATION
Nosey Parker, MEDDLESOMENESS
no soap, REFUSAL
no strings attached, FREEDOM
no sweat, EFFORTLESSNESS
not a shot in the locker, MONEY
not be worth one's salt, WORTHINESS
not by a long chalk or *shot,* EXTENT
not cricket, PROPRIETY
not dry behind the ears, INEXPERIENCE
not for love or money, COST
not give a continental hoot, INDIFFERENCE
not give a damn, INDIFFERENCE
not give a fig, INDIFFERENCE
not give a hoot, INDIFFERENCE
not give a rap, INDIFFERENCE
not have a leg to stand on, VALUE
not have all one's buttons, FATUOUSNESS
nothing like leather, PREJUDICE
nothing to sneeze at, WORTHINESS
not know A from a windmill, IGNORANCE
not know B from a battledore, IGNORANCE

not to know beans, KNOWLEDGE
not know B from a broomstick, IGNORANCE
not know B from a buffalo's foot, IGNORANCE
not know B from a bull's foot, IGNORANCE
not know if one is afoot or on horseback, CONFUSION
not know if one is coming or going, CONFUSION
not know one's ass from one's elbow, IGNORANCE
not know shit from shinola, IGNORANCE
not know which end is up, IGNORANCE
not make head nor tail of, DIFFERENTIATION
not see the forest for the trees, PERSPECTIVE
not see the wood(s) for the trees, PERSPECTIVE
not to be sneezed at, WORTHINESS
not worth a continental, WORTHLESSNESS
not worth a damn, WORTHLESSNESS
not worth a rush, WORTHLESSNESS
not worth a straw, WORTHLESSNESS
not worth a tinker's damn, WORTHLESSNESS
not worth a twopenny damn, WORTHLESSNESS
not worth a whistle, WORTHINESS
not worth powder and shot, WORTHLESSNESS
not worth the candle, WORTHLESSNESS
not worth the paper it's printed on, WORTHLESSNESS
nourish a snake in one's bosom, DANGER
number, DESTINY
[one's] number is up, DEATH
number the streaks of the tulip, PERSPECTIVE
nuts and bolts, FUNDAMENTALS
nutshell, ESSENCE

O

Occam's razor, PRECISION
odor of sanctity, VIRTUOUSNESS
off base, ERRONEOUSNESS
offbeat, UNCONVENTIONALITY
off one's feed, ILL HEALTH
off one's rocker, ECCENTRICITY
off one's trolley, ECCENTRICITY
off the cuff, SPONTANEITY
off the top of one's head, SPONTANEITY
off the track, DISCONTINUITY
off the wagon, TEMPERANCE
off the wall, UNCONVENTIONALITY
of the first water, EXCELLENCE
oil of angels, BRIBERY
oil [someone's] palm, BRIBERY
O.K., AFFIRMATION
okey-dokey, AFFIRMATION
old hat, OBSOLESCENCE
the Old Lady of Threadneedle Street, NICKNAMES
the old one-two, EFFECTIVENESS
old salt, NICKNAMES
the old stamping ground, LOCALITY
old wives' tale, SUPERSTITION
oll korrect, AFFIRMATION
on a back burner, ABEYANCE
on a cloud, ELATION
on an even keel, COMPOSURE
on a shoestring, FINANCE
on a string, DEPENDENCE
once in a blue moon, FREQUENCY
on cloud nine, ELATION
one-armed bandit, NICKNAMES
on Easy Street, AFFLUENCE
one fell swoop, INSTANTANEOUSNESS
one for the Gipper, EXHORTATION
one hand washes the other, RECIPROCITY

one-horse town, INSIGNIFI-CANCE
one-night stand, PROMISCU-OUSNESS
one over the eight, DRUNKEN-NESS
one-track mind, OBSESSION
the one who pays the piper calls the tune, CONTROL
on ice, ABEYANCE
on one's beam-ends, POV-ERTY
on one's high horse, HAUGH-TINESS
on one's last legs, ILL HEALTH
on one's toes, ALERTNESS
on one's uppers, POVERTY
on pins and needles, ANXIETY
on [someone's] coattails, DE-PENDENCE
on tenterhooks, ANXIETY
on the anxious seat, ANXIETY
on the ball, ALERTNESS
on the beach, IDLENESS
on the beam, CORRECTNESS
on the blink, ILL HEALTH
on the button, PRECISION
on the cards, DESTINY
on the carpet, REPRIMAND
on the carpet, THOUGHT
on the cuff, PAYMENT
on the double, INSTANTANE-OUSNESS
on the fence, VACILLATION
on the fritz, ILL HEALTH
on the high-road to Need-ham, DEGENERATION
on the hip, DISADVANTAGE
on the hook, DEPENDENCE
on the horns of dilemma, PREDICAMENT
on the lam, ESCAPE
on the line, RISK
on the money, PRECISION
on the nail, PAYMENT
on the nod, PAYMENT
on the nose, PRECISION
on the q.t., SECRECY
on the quiet, SECRECY
on the qui vive, ALERTNESS
on the rack, ANXIETY
on the razor's edge, RISK
on the rocks, INDEBTEDNESS
on the ropes, VULNERABILITY
on the sauce, DRUNKENNESS
on the shelf, ABEYANCE
on the skids, DEGENERATION

on the spot, PREDICAMENT
on the spur of the moment, SPONTANEITY
on the tapis, THOUGHT
on the tip of one's tongue, RECOLLECTION
on the wagon, TEMPERANCE
on the warpath, BELLIGER-ENCE
on the water-wagon, TEM-PERANCE
on thin ice, PRECARIOUSNESS
open a can of worms, COM-PLICATION
open season, VULNERABILITY
open sesame, SOLUTION
ordeal by fire, TEST
out at elbows, POVERTY
out-at-the-heel, POVERTY
out-Herod Herod, OUTDOING
out in left field, ERRONEOUS-NESS
out in space, FATUOUSNESS
out of a bandbox, STYLISH-NESS
out of a clear blue sky, SUR-PRISE
out of all scotch and notch, EXTENT
out of countenance, ANGRI-NESS
out of joint, DISORDER
out of sorts, ILL TEMPER
out of the blue, SURPRISE
out of the frying pan into the fire, EXACERBATION
out of the red, INDEBTEDNESS
out of the straw, ILL HEALTH
out of the swim, INVOLVE-MENT
out of the woods, RECOVERY
out of whole cloth, MEN-DACITY
out on a limb, VULNERABIL-ITY
out the window, IRRETRIEV-ABILITY
out to lunch, IGNORANCE
over a barrel, VULNERABILITY
over head and ears, INTEN-SITY
over one's head, PREDICA-MENT
over shoes, over boots, UNRE-STRAINT
overshoot the mark, EXCES-SIVENESS

over the eight, DRUNKENNESS
over the hill, AGE
over the long haul, PERSPEC-TIVE
over the mahogany, FRIEND-SHIP

P

package deal, AGREEMENT
paddle one's own canoe, SELF-RELIANCE
paddy wagon, VEHICLES
painted cat, PROMISCUOUS-NESS
painted with the same brush, SIMILARITY
paint the lily, EXCESSIVENESS
paint the town red, REVELRY
palm off, SWINDLING
panda car, VEHICLES
Pandora's box, COMPLICA-TION
panhandle, SOLICITATION
panic button, DESPERATION
pan out, SUCCESS
paper over the cracks, EX-PEDIENCE
paper tiger, INEFFECTUALITY
parlor snake, VICTIMIZATION
part and parcel, ESSENCE
pass in one's checks, DEATH
pass muster, COMPETENCE
pass over to the majority, DEATH
pass the buck, IRRESPONSI-BILITY
pass the hat, SOLICITATION
pass the Rubicon, DECISIVE-NESS
pass under the yoke, SUBMIS-SION
patient as Griselda, PA-TIENCE
Paul Pry, MEDDLESOMENESS
pave the way, PREPARATION
pay dirt, SUCCESS
pay one's debt to nature, DEATH
pay one's dues, WORTHINESS
pay the fiddler, CONSE-QUENCES
pay the piper, CONSE-QUENCES

pay through the nose, COST
pay too dearly for one's whistle, COST
pay with the roll of the drum, IRRESPONSIBILITY
p.d.q., INSTANTANEOUSNESS
pea in the shoe, IRRITATION
peanut gallery, INSIGNIFICANCE
pebble on the beach, INSIGNIFICANCE
pecking order, STATUS
Peck's bad boy, MISCHIEF
peeled garlic, PHYSICAL APPEARANCE
peeping Tom, SEXUAL ORIENTATION
peg out, DEATH
a peg too low, DEJECTION
pell-mell, IMPETUOUSNESS
pencil pusher, OCCUPATION
penny-ante, INSIGNIFICANCE
penny dreadful, SENSATIONALISM
penny pincher, MISERLINESS
penny wise and pound foolish, IMPROVIDENCE
persimmon above one's huckleberry, COMPARABILITY
peter out, CESSATION
Philadelphia lawyer, SHREWDNESS
pick-a-back, LOCOMOTION
pick a hole in someone's coat, FAULTFINDING
pick holes in, FAULTFINDING
pickled, DRUNKENNESS
pickpocket, CRIMINALITY
pick up the pieces, BEGINNINGS
pick up the slack, COOPERATION
pick up the threads, BEGINNINGS
a piece of cake, EFFORTLESSNESS
a piece of the action, INVOLVEMENT
a piece of the pie, ALLOCATION
pie-eyed, DRUNKENNESS
pie in the sky, ILLUSION
pigeon, VICTIMIZATION
piggyback, LOCOMOTION
pig in a poke, SWINDLING
pigs in clover, IMPROPRIETY

pig's wings, EXCELLENCE
piker, MISERLINESS
pilgarlic, PHYSICAL APPEARANCE
pillar to post, DIRECTION
pillars to the temple, EUPHEMISMS
pinch-hit, ASSISTANCE
pinch-hitter, ASSISTANCE
pinch pennies, MISERLINESS
pinchpenny, MISERLINESS
pink slip, EXPULSION
pink-slip, EXPULSION
pin money, MONEY
pins and needles, ANXIETY
pin [someone's] ears back, REPRIMAND
pin-up, PROMISCUOUSNESS
pipe down, SILENCE
pipe dream, ILLUSION
pissing-while, DURATION
piss on ice, AFFLUENCE
pitchers have ears, SECRECY
the pits, DEJECTION
pit stop, RESPITE
a place in the sun, FAME
place on the bed of Procrustes, CRITERION
a plague on both your houses, INSULT
plain as a packstaff, OBVIOUSNESS
plain as a pikestaff, OBVIOUSNESS
plain as the nose on your face, OBVIOUSNESS
plain sailing, EFFORTLESSNESS
plates and dishes, MARRIAGE
play a good knife and fork, GOURMANDISM
play a straight bat, ABILITY
play ball, COOPERATION
play both ends against the middle, MANIPULATION
play cat and mouse with, HARASSMENT
play close to one's vest, CAUTIOUSNESS
play ducks and drakes with, IMPROVIDENCE
play fast and loose, MANIPULATION
play for time, TEMPORIZING
play in Peoria, CRITERION
play is not worth the candle, WORTHLESSNESS

play it by ear, INTUITION
play possum, PRETENSE
play second fiddle, SUBORDINATION
play the ape, SIMILARITY
play the devil, MISCHIEF
play the dickens, PROFANITY
play the field, EXPLOITATION
play the giddy goat, MISCHIEF
play the goat, MISCHIEF
play the papers, FINANCE
play the ponies, FINANCE
play to the gallery, OSTENTATIOUSNESS
play to the grandstand, OSTENTATIOUSNESS
play with a stacked deck, DISADVANTAGE
play with fire, RISK
play with loaded dice, DISADVANTAGE
pleased as Punch, ELATION
plow the sands, FUTILITY
plug-ugly, CRIMINALITY
Podunk, INSIGNIFICANCE
point-blank, CANDIDNESS
point of no return, IRREVOCABLENESS
poker face, VISAGE
policy of pin pricks, PROVOCATION
polish the apple, OBSEQUIOUSNESS
politics makes strange bedfellows, EXPEDIENCE
Pollyanna, IDEALISM
pooh bah, POMPOSITY
pooper-scooper, EUPHEMISMS
poor as a churchmouse, POVERTY
poor as Job, POVERTY
poor as Job's cat, POVERTY
poor as Job's turkey, POVERTY
the pope's mustard maker, POMPOSITY
pop [someone's] bubble, DISILLUSIONMENT
pork barrel, GRAFT
pork chops, NICKNAMES
porter and skittles, REVELRY
portmanteau word, LANGUAGE
posh, OSTENTATIOUSNESS
pot-belly, CORPULENCE

potboiler, LETTERS

the pot calling the kettle black, FAULTFINDING

potluck, MIXTURE

pot shot, CRITICISM

pot-valor, BRAVERY

pound of flesh, RETALIATION

pound the asphalt, QUEST

pound the pavement, QUEST

pound the sidewalks, QUEST

pour oil on troubled waters, PLACATION

the powers that be, POWER

powwow, COMMUNICATION

praise from Sir Hubert, COMMENDATION

praise the Lord, and pass the ammunition, PERSEVERANCE

pretty kettle of fish, DISORDER

prick [someone's] balloon, DISILLUSIONMENT

prime the pump, FINANCE

the primrose path, DECADENCE

primrose path, DECADENCE

Procrustean bed, CRITERION

the proof of the pudding is in the eating, CRITERION

proud below the navel, LUST

prunes and prisms, AFFECTATION

pub-crawl, REVELRY

pudding-time, OPPORTUNENESS

pull a boner, ERRONEOUSNESS

pull a fast one, TRICKERY

pull caps, COMBAT

pull for tall timber, DEPARTURE

pull oneself up by one's own boot straps, SELF-RELIANCE

pull one's socks up, STARTING

pull one's weight, COOPERATION

pull out all the stops, UNRESTRAINT

pull out of a hat, SOLUTION

pull out of the fire, RESCUE

pull punches, EVASIVENESS

pull rank, POWER

pull [someone's] chestnuts out of the fire, MANIPULATION

pull [someone's] leg, TRICKERY

pull strings, MANIPULATION

pull the rug out from under, RUINATION

pull the wool over [someone's] eyes, TRICKERY

pull up stakes, DEPARTURE

pull wires, MANIPULATION

punch-drunk, FATUOUSNESS

punchy, FATUOUSNESS

purple patches, EXCELLENCE

purse strings, CONTROL

push the panic button, DESPERATION

push under the carpet, CONCEALMENT

push up daisies, DEATH

put a cat among the pigeons, PROVOCATION

put a match in a tinder box, PROVOCATION

put a pin in [someone's] balloon, DISILLUSIONMENT

put a rope to the eye of a needle, FUTILITY

put a spoke in [someone's] wheel, THWARTING

put in gear, PREPARATION

put in one's oar, MEDDLESOMENESS

put it on the line, RISK

put new wine in old bottles, IMPRUDENCE

put one over on, TRICKERY

put one's best foot forward, PROPRIETY

put one's foot down, DECISIVENESS

put one's foot in it, IMPROPRIETY

put one's foot in one's mouth, IMPROPRIETY

put one's hand to the plow, STARTING

put one's head in the lion's (wolf's) mouth, RISK

put one's oar in another's boat, MEDDLESOMENESS

put one's shoulder to the wheel, EXERTION

put on one's thinking cap, THOUGHT

put on ice, ABEYANCE

put on the dog, AFFECTATION

put on the map, FAME

put on the spot, PREDICAMENT

put out to pasture, RETIREMENT

put over a fast one, TRICKERY

put [someone] in the hole, INDEBTEDNESS

put [someone's] nose out of joint, HUMILIATION

put teeth into, EFFECTIVENESS

put the acid on, SOLICITATION

put the bee on, EXTORTION

put the bite on, EXTORTION

put the cart before the horse, FALLACIOUSNESS

put the finger on, EXPOSURE

put the kibosh on, THWARTING

put the screws to, COERCION

put the skids under, DEGENERATION

put the squeeze on, COERCION

put the teeth on edge, REPULSION

put the whammy on, THWARTING

put the wind up, ANXIETY

put through one's facings, TEST

put through one's paces, TEST

putting on one's eyes, NICKNAMES

put to bed with a shovel, DRUNKENNESS

put up a smoke screen, CONCEALMENT

put-up job, VICTIMIZATION

put your money where your mouth is, DECISIVENESS

Q

quake in one's boots, FEAR

Quaker guns, PRETENSE

quantum leap, ADVANCEMENT

Queen Anne is dead, RETORT

Queen's English, DICTION

Queen's weather, WEATHER
queer in the attic, ECCEN-TRICITY
quench one's thirst at any dirty puddle, PROMISCU-OUSNESS
quick as a wink, PACE
quick on the draw, ALERT-NESS
quidnunc, MEDDLESOME-NESS
quit cold turkey, TERMINA-TION
quote-unquote, RIDICULE

R

rack and ruin, DEGENERA-TION
ragtag and bobtail, STATUS
rain cats and dogs, WEATHER
rain check, ABEYANCE
rain pitchforks, WEATHER
raise an eyebrow, FAULT-FINDING
raise Cain, BOISTEROUSNESS
raise oneself up by one's own bootstraps, SELF-RELIANCE
raise the ante, AUGMENTA-TION
raise the Devil, BOISTEROUS-NESS
raise the dickens, PROFANITY
raise the white flag, SUBMIS-SION
rake over the coals, REPRI-MAND
the rank and file, STATUS
rare as hen's teeth, ABSENCE
rare kettle of fish, DISORDER
raring to go, READINESS
raspberry, INSULT
rat, BETRAYAL
rat race, FRENZIEDNESS
rattletrap, VEHICLES
reach the botton of the bar-rel, WORTHLESSNESS
read between the lines, PER-CEPTIVENESS
read the riot act, REPRIMAND
the real McCoy, GENUINE-NESS
reap the whirlwind, CONSE-QUENCES
Received Pronunciation, DIC-TION

reck one's own rede, ADVICE
reckon without one's host, IMPRUDENCE
red-carpet treatment, FAVOR-ITISM
red-eye, FOOD AND DRINK
red-flag term, LANGUAGE
red-handed, GUILT
red herring, PLOY
red-letter day, REVELRY
red-light district, LOCALITY
red neck, CONSERVATISM
red tape, COMPLICATION
a reed shaken by the wind, VACILLATION
regular brick, CONSTANCY
resting on one's laurels, COM-PLACENCY
rest on one's laurels, RESPITE
rest on one's oars, RESPITE
return one's breakfast (lunch, dinner, supper), ILL HEALTH
return to one's muttons, REP-ETITION
rhyme or reason, SENSE
ride a hobbyhorse, OBSES-SION
ride for a fall, RISK
ride herd on, DOMINATION
ride in on someone's coat-tails, DEPENDENCE
ride on a rail, PUNISHMENT
ride out of town on a rail, PUNISHMENT
ride roughshod over, DOMI-NATION
ride shanks' horse, LOCOMO-TION
ride shanks' mare, LOCOMO-TION
ride shanks' nag, LOCOMO-TION
ride shanks' pony, LOCOMO-TION
ride shotgun, PROTECTION
ride the gravy train, AFFLU-ENCE
ride the high horse, HAUGH-TINESS
ride Walker's bus, LOCOMO-TION
a rift in the lute, IMPERFEC-TION
right and left, INCLUSIVENESS
right as a trivet, GOOD HEALTH

right as ninepence, GOOD HEALTH
right as rain, CORRECTNESS
right down the line, INCLU-SIVENESS
right end of the stick, COR-RECTNESS
right foot foremost, BEGIN-NINGS
the right hand doesn't know what the left is doing, DIS-ORDER
right off the bat, INSTAN-TANEOUSNESS
right off the reel, INSTAN-TANEOUSNESS
right on, EFFICIENCY
right on the button, PRECI-SION
right on the money, PRECI-SION
right-wing, CONSERVATISM
right-winger, CONSERVATISM
ring a bell, RECOLLECTION
ring down, TERMINATION
ring down the curtain on, TERMINATION
ringer, PRETENSE
ringleader, PROVOCATION
ring the bell, SUCCESS
ring the changes, REPETITION
ring up the curtain on, INITI-ATION
rip and tuck, EQUIVALENCE
roast, RIDICULE
roast snow in a furnace, FU-TILITY
Robin Hood's bargain, DI-RECTION
Robin Hood's mile, DIREC-TION
rob Peter to pay Paul, EX-PEDIENCE
rob the cradle, LOVE
rock the boat, PROVOCATION
a Roland for an Oliver, RE-TALIATION
roll a big wheel, PERSONAGE
a rolling stone gathers no moss, IMPRUDENCE
roll in the hay, LUST
roll of the drum, IRRESPONSI-BILITY
roll out the red carpet, FA-VORITISM
roll with the punches, EN-DURANCE
room to swing a cat, EXTENT

root and branch, THOROUGH-
NESS
rope in, TRICKERY
rope of sand, FLIMSINESS
Rosetta stone, SOLUTION
rotgut, FOOD AND DRINK
Rotten Apple, LOCALITY
roué, PROMISCUOUSNESS
rough-and-ready, VITALITY
rough corners, IMPERFEC-
TION
rough edges, IMPERFECTION
rough-hewn, OAFISHNESS
round as Giotto's O, EXCEL-
LENCE
*rounder than the O of
Giotto*, EXCELLENCE
round peg in a square hole,
UNNATURALNESS
round the bend, ECCENTRIC-
ITY
rubber check, MONEY
rubberneck, CURIOSITY
rubber-stamp, APPROVAL
Rube Goldberg, CONTRAP-
TION
rub it in, EXACERBATION
rub salt in a wound, EXACER-
BATION
rub shoulders, FRIENDSHIP
rub [someone's] nose in it,
HUMILIATION
ruffle feathers, VEXATION
rule of thumb, CRITERION
rule the roast, DOMINATION
rule the roost, DOMINATION
run a tight ship, CONTROL
run interference, PROTEC-
TION
run into the ground, EXCES-
SIVENESS
run-of-the-mill, STATUS
run rings around, OUTDOING
the runs, ILL HEALTH
run that by me again, REPETI-
TION
run the gamut, INCLUSIVE-
NESS
run the gauntlet, ADVERSITY
Russian roulette, RISK

S

sack artist, SLEEP
sack drill, SLEEP
sack duty, SLEEP

sack out, SLEEP
sack time, SLEEP
sacred cow, FAVORITISM
sail against the wind, INDE-
PENDENCE
sail before the wind, PROS-
PERING
sail close to the wind, IMPRO-
PRIETY
sail near to the wind, IMPRO-
PRIETY
sail under false colors, PRE-
TENSE
salad days, AGE
salt, NICKNAMES
salt away, FINANCE
salt mines, OVERWORK
salt of the earth, STATUS
salty dog, NICKNAMES
Samaritan, ASSISTANCE
Sam Hill, EUPHEMISMS
sanctum sanctorum, SANCTU-
ARY
sands are running out, UR-
GENCY
San Quentin quail, ENTICE-
MENT
sardine's whiskers, EXCEL-
LENCE
Saturday night special, NICK-
NAMES
sauce, DRUNKENNESS
saved by the bell, RESCUE
sawbones, OCCUPATION
saw wood, SLEEP
say uncle, SUBMISSION
scab, BETRAYAL
scapegoat, VICTIMIZATION
Scarborough warning, SUR-
PRISE
scarce as hen's teeth, AB-
SENCE
scattergood, IMPROVIDENCE
scofflaw, CRIMINALITY
scot and lot, EXONERATION
scrambled eggs, NICKNAMES
*scrape the bottom of the
barrel*, WORTHLESSNESS
scratch, BEGINNINGS
scratch, COMPETENCE
scratch for oneself, SELF-
RELIANCE
*scratch my back, I'll scratch
yours*, RECIPROCITY
the screaming meemies, ANX-
IETY
screw oneself up to concert
pitch, PREPARATION

scuttlebutt, INFORMATION
the seamy side, DEGENERA-
TION
second wind, RECOVERY
see a dog about a man, EU-
PHEMISMS
see a man about a dog, EU-
PHEMISMS
see a man about a horse, EU-
PHEMISMS
see a wolf, SILENCE
seek a knot in a bulrush, NIT-
PICKING
see the elephant, REVELRY
seize the day, EXPLOITATION
sell down the river, BE-
TRAYAL
sell like hot cakes, QUICKNESS
selling card, ENTICEMENT
*sell the bearskin before one
has caught the bear*, IDE-
ALISM
send a sow to Minerva, IM-
PRUDENCE
send owls to Athens, INAP-
PROPRIATENESS
send the helve after the
hatchet, IMPROVIDENCE
send to Coventry, PUNISH-
MENT
send to the showers, EXPUL-
SION
send up the river, PUNISH-
MENT
serpent's tongue, ILL TEMPER
*serve a sop of the same
sauce*, RETALIATION
*serve a taste of the same
sauce*, RETALIATION
serve the same sauce, RETALI-
ATION
serve two masters, OVEREX-
TENSION
set cock a hoop, ELATION
set one's cap for, QUEST
set one's teeth, PREPARATION
set on six and seven, DIS-
ORDER
set the teeth on edge, REPUL-
SION
set the Thames on fire, FAME
set the world on fire, FAME
settle [someone's] hash, DOM-
INATION
shack up, PROMISCUOUSNESS
a shadow of one's former
self, PHYSICAL APPEAR-
ANCE

shadow of oneself, PHYSICAL APPEARANCE

shaggy dog story, ANECDOTE

shake a leg, STARTING

shakedown, EXTORTION

shakedown, INVESTIGATION

shake in one's boots, FEAR

shake in one's shoes, FEAR

shake like an aspen leaf, FEAR

shake the dust from one's feet, DEPARTURE

shank it, LOCOMOTION

shape up or ship out, DECISIVENESS

shilling shockers, SENSATIONALISM

shilly-shally, VACILLATION

shine up the apple, OBSEQUIOUSNESS

shipshape, NEATNESS

shiver me timbers, EXCLAMATIONS

the shoe is on the other foot, REVERSAL

shoe one's horse, GRAFT

shoe one's mule, GRAFT

shoe the goose, FUTILITY

shoo-in, CERTAINTY

shoot from the hip, IMPETUOUSNESS

shoot one's bolt, UNRESTRAINT

shoot one's breakfast (lunch, dinner, supper), ILL HEALTH

shoot one's cookies, ILL HEALTH

shoot one's cuffs, OSTENTATIOUSNESS

shoot one's linen, OSTENTATIOUSNESS

shoot one's wad, UNRESTRAINT

shoot the breeze, TALKATIVENESS

shoot the bull, TALKATIVENESS

shoot the cat, ILL HEALTH

shoot the works, UNRESTRAINT

short and curlies, DOMINATION

short hairs, DOMINATION

short of the mark, ERRONEOUSNESS

short one's linen, OSTENTATIOUSNESS

short shrift, CARELESSNESS

shotgun marriage, COERCION

shotgun wedding, COERCION

a shot in the arm, RECOVERY

a shot in the dark, INTUITION

a shot in the locker, MONEY

show a clean pair of heels, ESCAPE

show a fair pair of heels, ESCAPE

showdown, CONFRONTATION

show one's colors, EXPOSURE

show one's hand, EXPOSURE

show one's horns, WICKEDNESS

show one's true colors, EXPOSURE

show-stealer, OUTDOING

show the cloven hoof, WICKEDNESS

show the cold shoulder, REJECTION

show the white feather, COWARDICE

shrink, OCCUPATION

shut-eye, SLEEP

sick as a cat, ILL HEALTH

side-track, DISCONTINUITY

sign off, COMPLETION

silk-stocking district, LOCALITY

Simon Legree, DOMINATION

simon-pure, GENUINENESS

sing a different tune, RECANTATION

sing another song, RECANTATION

sing in agony, EXPOSURE

sing in tribulation, EXPOSURE

sink one's teeth into, EXERTION

sit on one's hands, IDLENESS

sit tight, PATIENCE

sitting duck, VULNERABILITY

sitting duck, EFFORTLESSNESS

sitting in the catbird seat, ADVANTAGE

sitting pretty, ADVANTAGE

sit upon hot cockles, IMPATIENCE

sixty-four-dollar question, ESSENCE

sixty-four-thousand-dollar question, ESSENCE

skate on thin ice, PRECARIOUSNESS

skeleton at the feast, IMPEDIMENT

skeleton in the closet, SECRECY

skeleton in the cupboard, SECRECY

skid row, LOCALITY

skids, DEGENERATION

skin a flint, MISERLINESS

skin alive, REPRIMAND

skin an eel by the tail, FALLACIOUSNESS

skin flick, PRURIENCE

skinflint, MISERLINESS

skin the bear at once, CANDIDNESS

skulduggery, CRIMINALITY

the sky's the limit, UNRESTRAINT

slap-bang, CARELESSNESS

slapdash, CARELESSNESS

slaphappy, FATUOUSNESS

a slap in the face, INSULT

slap of the tongue, REPRIMAND

slapstick, HUMOROUSNESS

a sledge-hammer argument, EFFECTIVENESS

sleep like a top, SLEEP

sleep on it, THOUGHT

sleep with one eye open, PRETENSE

sleeveless errand, FUTILITY

sleeveless reason, FUTILITY

sleeveless words, FUTILITY

slings and arrows, CRITICISM

slip of the pen, EXPOSURE

slip of the tongue, EXPOSURE

slip one's trolley, ECCENTRICITY

slip [someone] a Mickey [Finn], FOOD AND DRINK

slough of despond, DEJECTION

slow as cold molasses, PACE

slow as molasses going uphill in January, PACE

slow as molasses in January, PACE

slow burn, FURY

sly as old boots, SHREWDNESS

sly-boots, SHREWDNESS

small potatoes, INSIGNIFICANCE

smart as a whip, SHREWD-
NESS
smashed, DRUNKENNESS
smash the teapot, TIPPLING
smell a rat, SUSPICIOUSNESS
smell of the inkhorn, LAN-
GUAGE
smoke screen, CONCEALMENT
smooth ruffled feathers, PLA-
CATION
snake in the grass, DANGER
sneaky pete, FOOD AND
DRINK
a snowball's chance in hell,
IMPROBABILITY
*a snowflake's chance in
hell,* IMPROBABILITY
snowed under, OVERWORK
snow job, MENDACITY
snug as a bug in a rug, COM-
PLACENCY
soapboxer, EXHORTATION
soapbox orator, EXHORTA-
TION
soapy Sam, EXHORTATION
sob story, SENTIMENTALITY
sock away, FINANCE
sodbuster, OAFISHNESS
soft fire makes sweet malt,
IMPATIENCE
soft-soap, FLATTERY
something rotten in Den-
mark, SUSPICIOUSNESS
song, COST
song and dance, EXAGGERA-
TION
son of a bitch, EUPHEMISMS
son of a gun, EUPHEMISMS
son of Belial, WICKEDNESS
son of thunder, EXHORTA-
TION
a sop to Cerberus, BRIBERY
sorehead, ILL TEMPER
sound as a bell, GOOD
HEALTH
sounding board, CRITERION
soup-and-fish, CLOTHING
soused, DRUNKENNESS
sour grapes, RESENTMENT
sow dragon's teeth, PROVO-
CATION
so what else is new?, RETORT
sow one's wild oats, EXCES-
SIVENESS
sow the wind and reap the
whirlwind, CONSE-
QUENCES

sow wild oats, PROMISCUOUS-
NESS
spacey, DRUNKENNESS
spare at the spigot and spill at
the bung, IMPROVIDENCE
spare tire, CORPULENCE
speak by the card, CANDID-
NESS
speak daggers, BELLIGER-
ENCE
speak-easy, ESTABLISHMENTS
speak for Buncombe, NON-
SENSE
speak-softly shop, ESTAB-
LISHMENTS
spend money like a drunken
sailor, IMPROVIDENCE
spick and span, NEATNESS
spick and span new, NEAT-
NESS
spiff one's biscuits, ILL
HEALTH
spike [someone's] gun,
THWARTING
spill one's guts, EXPOSURE
spill the beans, EXPOSURE
spin a yarn, EXAGGERATION
spinoff, OUTCOME
spit and image, SIMILARITY
spit and polish, NEATNESS
spitten image, SIMILARITY
spitting image, SIMILARITY
splice the main brace, TIP-
PLING
split hairs, NIT-PICKING
sponge, VICTIMIZATION
sponge off, VICTIMIZATION
sponge on, VICTIMIZATION
sponger, VICTIMIZATION
spot on, PRECISION
spread oneself thin, OVEREX-
TENSION
springes to catch wood-
cocks, PLOY
spring up like mushrooms,
ABUNDANCE
sprout wings, CHARITABLE-
NESS
square off, CONFRONTATION
a square peg in a round
hole, UNNATURALNESS
square the circle, FUTILITY
stable push, INFORMATION
stacked deck, DISADVANTAGE
stack up against, COMPARA-
BILITY
stalemate, CESSATION

stalking horse, PLOY
stand in one's own light,
SELF-DISPARAGEMENT
stand one's ground, PERSE-
VERANCE
stand on one's own bottom,
SELF-RELIANCE
stand the gaff, ENDURANCE
stand to one's gun(s), PERSE-
VERANCE
starkers, PROMISCUOUSNESS
stark naked, PROMISCUOUS-
NESS
starko, PROMISCUOUSNESS
start naked, PROMISCUOUS-
NESS
start the ball rolling, INITIA-
TION
steal a march on, ADVANTAGE
steal [someone's] thunder,
THWARTING
steal the show, OUTDOING
stem the tide, TERMINATION
step off, DEATH
step off the carpet, DEATH
step on it, STARTING
step on the gas, STARTING
step on toes, IMPROPRIETY
stew in one's own juice,
CONSEQUENCES
stick in the craw, REPULSION
stick in the crop, REPULSION
stick in the gullet, REPUL-
SION
stick in the throat, REPUL-
SION
stick one's neck out, VULNER-
ABILITY
stick one's spoon in the
wall, BEGINNINGS
stick to one's guns, PERSE-
VERANCE
stick to one's last, PROPRIETY
stickybeak, MEDDLESOME-
NESS
sticky-finger, CRIMINALITY
sticky wicket, DIFFICULTY
stir-crazy, IRRATIONALITY
stir one's stumps, STARTING
stir up a hornets' nest, PROV-
OCATION
a stone's throw, PROXIMITY
stonewall, TEMPORIZING
stool pigeon or stoolie, BE-
TRAYAL
stop cold turkey, TERMINA-
TION

stop-watch critic, CRITICISM
storm and strife, MARRIAGE
storm in a teacup, EXCESSIVE-
NESS
stormy petrel, OMEN
straight, SEXUAL ORIENTA-
TION
*straight from the horse's
mouth,* AUTHORITATIVE-
NESS
straight from the shoulder,
CANDIDNESS
strain at a gnat and swallow a
camel, HYPOCRISY
strain at the leash, IMPA-
TIENCE
straw boss, PERSONAGE
straw man, VICTIMIZATION
the straw that broke the
camel's back, CULMINA-
TION
straw vote, INFORMATION
stretch one's legs according to
the coverlet, ADAPTATION
*stretch on the bed of Pro-
crustes,* CRITERION
strike a bargain, AGREEMENT
strike for tall timber, DEPAR-
TURE
strike hands, AGREEMENT
strike oil, SUCCESS
strike sail, SUBMISSION
strike while the iron is hot,
EXPLOITATION
struggle and strife, MAR-
RIAGE
stumble at a straw, PERSPEC-
TIVE
sub rosa, SECRECY
suck the hind teat, VICTIMI-
ZATION
sugar and honey, MONEY
sugar daddy, AFFLUENCE
Sunday best, CLOTHING
Sunday clothes, CLOTHING
Sunday - go - to - meeting
clothes, CLOTHING
Sunday - go - to - meetings,
CLOTHING
sun in one's eyes, DRUNKEN-
NESS
sup with Sir Thomas
Gresham, HUNGER
sure as eggs is eggs, CER-
TAINTY
sure as shooting, CERTAINTY

swallow the anchor, RETIRE-
MENT
swan song, CULMINATION
swap horses in midstream,
IMPRUDENCE
swear like a trooper, PROFAN-
ITY
sweat blood, ANXIETY
sweep under the carpet, CON-
CEALMENT
sweeten the kitty, AUGMEN-
TATION
sweeten the pot, AUGMENTA-
TION
sweet Fanny Adams, AB-
SENCE
sweet F.A., ABSENCE
switch hitter, SEXUAL ORIEN-
TATION
sword of Damocles, DANGER

T

table, DISCONTINUITY
the tables are turned, REVER-
SAL
tabula rasa, BEGINNINGS
tag and rag, STATUS
take a back seat, SUBORDINA-
TION
take a bath, FAILURE
take a deep breath, ENDUR-
ANCE
take a gander, CURIOSITY
take a message to Garcia,
SELF-RELIANCE
take a page out of [someone's]
book, SIMILARITY
take a rise out of, PROVOCA-
TION
take a shine to, LOVE
take a sight, INSULT
take down a notch, HUMILIA-
TION
take down a peg, HUMILIA-
TION
take eggs for money, SELF-
DISPARAGEMENT
take for a ride, DEATH
take in on the lam, ESCAPE
take in tow, GUIDANCE
take in water, ERRONEOUS-
NESS
take it on the chin, ENDUR-
ANCE

take lying down, SUBMISSIVE-
NESS
taken aback, SURPRISE
take one's hat off to, COM-
MENDATION
take soundings, INVESTIGA-
TION
take the ball before the
bound, ALERTNESS
take the bark off, PUNISH-
MENT
take the bear by the tooth,
RISK
take the bit between one's
teeth, REBELLION
take the bit in one's teeth, RE-
BELLION
take the bull by the horns,
CONFRONTATION
take the cake, OUTDOING
take the measure of, TEST
take the nap, PUNISHMENT
take the plunge, DECISIVE-
NESS
take the rap, PUNISHMENT
take the teeth out of,
THWARTING
take the wall, DEFERENCE
take the wind out of [some-
one's] sails, THWARTING
take time by the forelock, EX-
PLOITATION
take to the cleaners, SWIN-
DLING
take to the hustings, POLI-
TICKING
take to the stump, POLITICK-
ING
take to the tall timber, DE-
PARTURE
take under one's wing, GUID-
ANCE
take up the gauntlet, COMPE-
TITION
take up the hatchet, COMBAT
tale of a tub, PLOY
talk a blue streak, TALKA-
TIVENESS
talk for Buncombe, NON-
SENSE
talk out of both sides of one's
mouth, HYPOCRISY
talk the bark off a tree, PRO-
FANITY
talk through one's hat, EXAG-
GERATION

talk through the back of one's neck, EXAGGERATION

talk to like a Dutch uncle, REPRIMAND

talk turkey, CANDIDNESS

tan [someone's] hide, COMBAT

tap the admiral, TIPPLING

tar and feather, PUNISHMENT

tarred with the same brush, SIMILARITY

teach a bird to fly, IMPRUDENCE

teach a fish to swim, IMPRUDENCE

teach one's grandmother to suck eggs, IMPRUDENCE

tear-jerker, SENTIMENTALITY

tear one's hair out, DESPERATION

tear up the pea patch, REVELRY

teetotal, TEMPERANCE

teetotaler, TEMPERANCE

tell it to Sweeney, SKEPTICISM

tell it to the marines, SKEPTICISM

tell tales out of school, EXPOSURE

tell where to get off, REPRIMAND

tempest in a teacup, EXCESSIVENESS

tempest in a teapot, EXCESSIVENESS

tenderfoot, INEXPERIENCE

tenderloin, LOCALITY

that's music to my ears, ENJOYMENT

that's the ticket, AFFIRMATION

that's the way the ball bounces, RESIGNATION

that's the way the cookie crumbles, RESIGNATION

that's water over the dam, IRREVOCABLENESS

that's water under the bridge, IRREVOCABLENESS

there's the rub, IMPEDIMENT

thick as thieves, FRIENDSHIP

thicket and thin wood, CONSTANCY

thimblerig, TRICKERY

the third degree, INVESTIGATION

third wheel, SUPERFLUOUSNESS

a thorn in the flesh, IRRITATION

thorn in the side, IRRITATION

thread and thrum, TOTALITY

threads and thrums, MIXTURE

three-dog night, WEATHER

three on a match, SUPERSTITION

three sheets in the wind, DRUNKENNESS

three sheets to the wind, DRUNKENNESS

through the mill, ADVERSITY

through the wringer, ADVERSITY

through thick and thin, CONSTANCY

throw a curve or a curve ball, PLOY

throw a monkey wrench into the works, THWARTING

throw a spanner into the works, THWARTING

throw a tub to the whale, PLOY

throw cold water on, THWARTING

throw down the gauntlet, COMPETITION

throw dust in [someone's] eyes, TRICKERY

throw for a loop, CONFUSION

throw in one's hand, SUBMISSION

throw in someone's face, REPRIMAND

throw in the sponge, SUBMISSION

throw in the towel, SUBMISSION

throw one's hat into the ring, COMPETITION

throw one's weight around, POWER

throw out the baby with the bath water, EXCESSIVENESS

throw straws against the wind, FUTILITY

throw the book at, PUNISHMENT

throw the helve after the hatchet, IMPROVIDENCE

throw to the wolves, VICTIMIZATION

thumb one's nose, INSULT

thumbs down, REFUSAL

thumbs up, APPROVAL

tickled pink, ELATION

tickled to death, ELATION

tickle one's fancy, ENJOYMENT

tie a bag on, DRUNKENNESS

tied to [someone's] apron strings, DEPENDENCE

tie one on, DRUNKENNESS

tie up the loose ends, COMPLETION

tiger's milk, FOOD AND DRINK

tiger's spots, EXCELLENCE

tight as the bark on a tree, MISERLINESS

tight ship, CONTROL

tighten one's belt, SUBSISTENCE

tightwad, MISERLINESS

till the cows come home, DURATION

tilt at windmills, ILLUSION

Tinker to Evers to Chance, COOPERATION

tip one's hand, EXPOSURE

tip the elbow, TIPPLING

tit for tat, RETALIATION

toad-eater, OBSEQUIOUSNESS

to a fare-thee-well, EXCELLENCE

to a T, PRECISION

to beat the band, INTENSITY

toe the line, COMPETENCE

toe the mark, COMPETENCE

toffee-nosed, HAUGHTINESS

Tom, Dick, and Harry, INCLUSIVENESS

Tommy Atkins, NICKNAMES

tommyrot, NONSENSE

tongue-banging, REPRIMAND

tongue in cheek, RIDICULE

tongue-lashing, REPRIMAND

too big for one's boots, POMPOSITY

too big for one's britches, POMPOSITY

too far north, SHREWDNESS

too many irons in the fire, OVEREXTENSION

tooth and nail, INTENSITY

toot one's own horn, BOASTING

top banana, PERSONAGE

top billing, STATUS

top dog, PERSONAGE

top-drawer, EXCELLENCE

top-shelf, EXCELLENCE

top-shelfer, EXCELLENCE

topside, turnaway, DISORDER

topside-turvy, DISORDER

topsy-turvy, DISORDER

torpedo juice, FOOD AND DRINK

toss one's cookies, ILL HEALTH

to the bitter end, TERMINATION

to the hilt, THOROUGHNESS

to the manner born, STATUS

to the nines, STYLISHNESS

to the quick, SENSITIVITY

to the skies, UNRESTRAINT

to the sky, UNRESTRAINT

to the teeth, THOROUGHNESS

touch all bases, THOROUGHNESS

touch-and-go, PRECARIOUSNESS

touch bottom, DEJECTION

touché, RETORT

touchstone, CRITERION

tough act to follow, EXCELLENCE

a tough nut to crack, DIFFICULTY

trade off the orchard for an apple, PERSPECTIVE

trail one's coat, BELLIGERENCE

trap, NICKNAMES

tread on eggs, CAUTIOUSNESS

treading water, ABEYANCE

trial balloon, CRITERION

trigger-happy, IMPETUOUSNESS

trim one's sails, ADAPTATION

trip the light fantastic, REVELRY

Trojan horse, PLOY

the trots, ILL HEALTH

trouble and strife, MARRIAGE

true-blue, CONSTANCY

trump card, PLOY

tub-thumper, EXHORTATION

tuft-hunter, OBSEQUIOUSNESS

tun-bellied, CORPULENCE

the tune the old cow died of, ADVICE

turkey on one's back, BURDEN

turn a hair, COMPOSURE .

turncoat, BETRAYAL

turn one's face to the wall, DEATH

turn one's geese to swans, EXAGGERATION

turn one's toes up to the daisies, DEATH

turn on the faucet, DEJECTION

turn on the waterworks, DEJECTION

turn over a new leaf, REFORMATION

turn [someone] around one's little finger, MANIPULATION

turn tables, REVERSAL

turn the heat on, HARASSMENT

turn the other cheek, SUBMISSIVENESS

turn the tables on, REVERSAL

turn the tide, REVERSAL

turn turtle, VULNERABILITY

turn up one's nose at, REJECTION

turn up trumps, SUCCESS

Tweedledum and Tweedledee, SIMILARITY

twenty-three skidoo, EXPULSION

twiddle one's thumbs, IDLENESS

twist [someone] around one's little finger, MANIPULATION

twist [someone's] arm, COERCION

two strikes against one, DISADVANTAGE

U

ubble-gubble, GIBBERISH

ugly duckling, REVERSAL

unbury the hatchet, ax, or tomahawk, COMBAT

Uncle Sam, NICKNAMES

Uncle Tom, SUBMISSIVENESS

underdog, DISADVANTAGE

under one's belt, KNOWLEDGE

under one's hat, SECRECY

under [someone's] thumb, MANIPULATION

under the counter, CONCEALMENT

under the daisies, DEATH

under the rose, SECRECY

under the table, DRUNKENNESS

under the table, CONCEALMENT

under the weather, ILL HEALTH

under the wire, TIMELINESS

up a storm, INTENSITY

up a tree, VULNERABILITY

up for grabs, COMPETITION

up one's alley, PREFERENCE

up one's street, PREFERENCE

upon the tapis, THOUGHT

upper crust, STATUS

up Salt Creek, PREDICAMENT

up Salt River, PREDICAMENT

up shit creek without a paddle, PREDICAMENT

upset the applecart, RUINATION

upstage, OUTDOING

up the ante, AUGMENTATION

up the creek, PREDICAMENT

up the spout, IRRETRIEVABILITY

up to scratch, COMPETENCE

up to snuff, COMPETENCE

up to the gills, DRUNKENNESS

up to the hilt, THOROUGHNESS

up to the mark, TEST

up to the nines, STYLISHNESS

V

verbal diarrhea, TALKATIVENESS

Vermont charity, MISERLINESS

the very spit, image, SIMILARITY

V.I.P., PERSONAGE

a voice in the wilderness, PROTEST

W

wait for dead men's shoes, DESIRE

walk a tightrope, CAUTIOUS-
NESS
walk in the footsteps,
SIMILARITY
walk on eggs, CAUTIOUSNESS
walk Spanish, EXPULSION
walk the carpet, REPRIMAND
walk the chalk, COMPETENCE
walk the plank, EXPULSION
wallflower, UNOBTRUSIVE-
NESS
walls have ears, SECRECY
warm the cockles of the
heart, ENJOYMENT
warts and all, CANDIDNESS
wash a brick, FUTILITY
washed out, FAILURE
wash one's dirty linen in
public, EXPOSURE
water-cooler talk, INFORMA-
TION
waterworks, DEJECTION
Waterloo, DOWNFALL
wave the bloody shirt, PROV-
OCATION
wave the red flag, LANGUAGE
way to go, EFFICIENCY
weak sister, COWARDICE
wear one's heart on one's
sleeve, LOVE
wear the bull's feather, IN-
FIDELITY
wear the cap and bells, HU-
MOROUSNESS
wear the horns, INFIDELITY
wear the pants, DOMINATION
wear the willow, GRIEVING
*wearing sackcloth and
ashes,* GRIEVING
weather-breeder, WEATHER
weathercock, VACILLATION
weep millstones, CALLOUS-
NESS
well-heeled, AFFLUENCE
wet, ERRONEOUSNESS
wetback, CRIMINALITY
wet behind the ears, INEX-
PERIENCE
wet blanket, IMPEDIMENT
wet blanket, ERRONEOUS-
NESS
wet one's whistle, TIPPLING
wet whistle, TIPPLING
*what possible rhyme or rea-
son?,* SENSE
what the Sam Hill (etc.), EU-
PHEMISMS

when push comes to shove,
EXACERBATION
when the cat's away the mice
will play, MISCHIEF
when the chips are down, UR-
GENCY
when two Fridays come to-
gether, FREQUENCY
where the shoe pinches, VUL-
NERABILITY
whip a dead horse, FUTILITY
whip into shape, GUIDANCE
whipping-boy, VICTIMIZA-
TION
whip the cat, ILL HEALTH
whirling dervish, ZEALOUS-
NESS
whistle [someone] down the
wind, REJECTION
whistle-stop, LOCALITY
white elephant, BURDEN
white elephant sales, BUR-
DEN
a white lie, MENDACITY
white feather, COWARDICE
white-haired boy, FAVORIT-
ISM
white-haired girl, FAVORIT-
ISM
white-livered, COWARDICE
white paper, INFORMATION
whitewash, CONCEALMENT
whitewash, VICTORY
the whole ball of wax, TO-
TALITY
whole boodle, INCLUSIVE-
NESS
whole-hogger, UNRESTRAINT
whole kit and biling, INCLU-
SIVENESS
whole kit and boodle, INCLU-
SIVENESS
the whole kit and caboodle,
INCLUSIVENESS
who the Sam Hill (etc.), EU-
PHEMISMS
the whole shooting match,
INCLUSIVENESS
wide of the mark, ERRONE-
OUSNESS
a wide place in the road, LO-
CALITY
widow's lock, VISAGE
widow's mite, CHARITABLE-
NESS
widow's peak, VISAGE
wigs on the green, COMBAT

wild as a March hare, IRRA-
TIONALITY
wild-goose chase, FUTILITY
willing to give one's ears, DE-
SIRE
windfall, GOOD LUCK
window dressing, MEN-
DACITY
*wind [someone] around one's
little finger,* MANIPULA-
TION
wine and roses, DECADENCE
win hands down, EFFORT-
LESSNESS
wing it, SPONTANEITY
win one's spurs, COMPE-
TENCE
wipe the slate clean, BEGIN-
NINGS
wish for the moon, FUTILITY
wishy-washy, INEFFECTUAL-
ITY
with a grain of salt, SKEPTI-
CISM
with a high hand, DOMI-
NATION
with all one's might, INTEN-
SITY
with bells on, ELATION
with bloody hand, GUILT
with egg on one's face, HU-
MILIATION
wither on the vine, FAILURE
with flying colors, SUCCESS
within an ace, PROXIMITY
with might and main, INTEN-
SITY
*with one's feet under the
mahogany,* FRIENDSHIP
with one's tail between one's
legs, HUMILIATION
with red hand, GUILT
without rhyme or reason,
SENSE
without turning a hair, COM-
POSURE
wolf in a lamb's skin, PRE-
TENSE
wolf in sheep's clothing, PRE-
TENSE
wooden nickels, ADVICE
woolgathering, INDOLENCE
work both sides of the
street, EXPLOITATION
work like a beaver, ZEALOUS-
NESS
work the oracle, MANIPULA-
TION

work up to the collar, EXER-
TION
worry and strife, MARRIAGE
worth one's salt, WORTHI-
NESS
worth the whistle, WORTHI-
NESS
wrangle for an ass's shadow,
NIT-PICKING
write in the dust, INEFFECTU-
ALITY
write off, COMPLETION
write on sand, INEFFECTUAL-
ITY

write on the wind, INEFFEC-
TUALITY
write on water, INEFFECTU-
ALITY
writing on the wall, OMEN

Y

yarn, EXAGGERATION
yellow-bellied, COWARDICE
yellow belly, COWARDICE

yellow journalism, SENSA-
TIONALISM
yen, DESIRE
*you can't add apples and
oranges,* DISSIMILARITY
young **Turk,** REBELLION

Z

zero hour, TIME
zero in on, FOCUS